Administrative Law

BUREAUCRACY IN A DEMOCRACY

SIXTH EDITION

Daniel E. Hall, J.D., Ed.D.
Miami University

PEARSON

Boston Columbus Indianapolis New York San Francisco Upper Saddle River
Amsterdam Cape Town Dubai London Madrid Milan Munich Paris Montréal Toronto
Delhi Mexico City São Paulo Sydney Hong Kong Seoul Singapore Taipei Tokyo

Dedication

To Aryana

Editorial Director: Vernon Anthony
Acquisitions Editor: Gary Bauer
Editorial Assistant: Kevin Cecil
Director of Marketing: David Gesell
Marketing Manager: Mary Salzman
Senior Marketing Coordinator: Alicia Wozniak
Marketing Assistant: Les Roberts
Senior Managing Editor: JoEllen Gohr
Project Manager: Linda Cupp
Procurement Specialist: Deidra M. Skahill

Art Director: Jayne Conte
Cover Designer: Suzanne Duda
Cover Art: © Orhan Cam/Shutterstock
Full-Service Project Management: PreMediaGlobal
Full Service Project Manager: Murugesh Namasivayam
Composition: PreMediaGlobal
Printer/Binder: Edwards Brothers
Cover Printer: Lehigh-Phoenix Color
Text Font: Times New Roman

Credits and acknowledgments borrowed from other sources and reproduced, with permission, in this textbook appear on the appropriate page within the text.

Library of Congress Cataloging-in-Publication Data
Hall, Daniel (Daniel E.)
  Administrative law: bureaucracy in a democracy / Daniel E. Hall, J.D., Ed.D., Miami University. — Sixth Edition.
  pages cm Includes bibliographical references and index.
  ISBN-13: 978-0-13-349387-0 (alk. paper)
  ISBN-10: 0-13-349387-3 (alk. paper)
  1. Administrative law—United States. I. Title.
  KF5402.H35 2015
  342.73'06—dc23

                                      2013039062

10 9 8 7 6 5 4 3 2 1

ISBN 10: 0-13-349387-3
ISBN 13: 978-0-13-349387-0

Brief Contents

Contents

CHAPTER 11   Accountability through Liability   337

Preface

INTRODUCTION

The administrative state, both federal and state, continues to expand. Presidents who are committed to small, limited government have had little impact on the size of the United States bureaucracy. Now, under the leadership of President Barack Obama, the United States is embarking on the largest federal policy program since President Franklin D. Roosevelt championed the creation of Social Security in 1935, health care reform. Add to this the growth in the federal government resulting from the War on Terror, the increased regulatory activity of the federal government in response to the nation's banking, financial, and accounting industries crises, and the federal government's stimulus activities to reenergize the economy, and the result is a growing federal government, in size and policy reach.

The continued growth of agencies and the authorities they possess often stress existing notions of the role of government, federalism, accountability, democracy, and governmental structure. These realities are the best evidence of the need for the study of administrative law and for a book that challenges students to think about the administrative state in logical, critical, and analytical ways. It is imperative for professionals in the field to understand the authorities that administrative agencies possess, how agencies are kept accountable, and the existing, and potential, constitutional and other constraints on agency authority that exist. It is my hope that this text does this.

The challenge is to remember what the framers feared and to remain steadfast in preserving what they designed, even in the wake of social, economic, and technological change. This text is devoted to the idea that government is to remain accountable, and that tyranny can be averted by having an informed and engaged population and through a thoughtfully built administrative enterprise. The simple division of power into federal and state and into three branches is no longer realistic, but the principle is the right one, and with some molding it can continue to be an effective structural constraint on agency authority. The reader will learn in this text that most constitutional rules and doctrines that apply to administrative law are intended to keep government accountable.

This text has three objectives:

1. Examine administrative law in the context of accountability and the prevention of governmental abuse of power
2. Assist students in critical thinking and case analysis by including case excerpts
3. Provide students with practical knowledge of administrative agencies and the laws that govern their behavior

ORGANIZATION OF TOPICS

Chapter 1 introduces the student to administrative agencies and administrative law. A discussion of the size of the American bureaucracy and how it affects the daily lives of those living in the United States is intended to pique the reader's interest.

Chapter 2 sets the tone for the remainder of the book. It discusses the concept of free government, how the framers of the Constitution intended to protect freedom, and the contemporary challenges administrative law faces today.

Chapter 3 examines agency discretion and provides many practical examples of discretionary agency authority. The idea of abuse of discretion is a segue to Chapter 4's discussion of due process and fairness.

Chapter 4 explores due process and equal protection in the administrative context. Practical problems are discussed, as is the conceptual aspect of protecting against governmental abuses.

Chapter 5 discusses legislative delegations of authority to agencies.

Chapter 6 continues this discussion by examining the delegation of rulemaking power. Delegations to private parties are included, as privatization is becoming increasingly popular. Delegations of criminal law authority are also discussed because there appears to be an increase in the penal authority of many agencies.

Chapter 7 is concerned with agency investigations and data collection. Fourth Amendment search-and-seizure and Fifth Amendment self-incrimination issues are discussed in detail. Drug and AIDS testing are given special attention.

Chapter 8 is devoted to agency adjudications. The right to participate, adjudicatory procedures, administrative law judges' selection and bias, and other concepts are covered. This leads into the discussion of judicial review found in Chapter 9.

Chapter 9 looks at judicial review of agency action. Limiting doctrines, such as exhaustion and primary jurisdiction, are discussed. Standards of review, scope of review, and sources of common law review are also part of this chapter.

Chapter 10, entitled "Accountability Through Accessibility," addresses open government. The federal Freedom of Information Act, Privacy Act, Open Meetings Act, Federal Advisory Committee Act, and Trade Secrets Act are detailed.

Chapter 11 looks at a form of judicial review different from that in Chapter 9. This chapter is concerned with the civil liability of governments and government officials in the performance of their duties. This chapter examines both federal and state common law remedies and immunities.

Finally, the appendix on researching administrative law issues that appeared in previous editions was updated and can be found at the following resource site: www.pearsonhighered.com/careersresources.

TEXT FEATURES

The writing style and language of this book are intended for the undergraduate student in law, justice, or political science or the graduate student in nonlaw fields. When used, legalese is explained.

As mentioned, I have included **case excerpts** throughout the text. Cases were selected on the basis of the following criteria: importance and impact, currency, clarity of writing, and ability to be edited successfully. The book has been written so that the text can stand alone. The cases are used to illustrate or more fully develop ideas that are discussed in the text.

To keep the cases to an appropriate length, considerable text has been excised from most of them. The guiding principle in the editing process was to reduce the size of each case without jeopardizing its legal and educative integrity. Some internal citations have been retained, others removed. In some instances, especially a long string of citations, the removal of a citation is denoted with an ellipsis. In others, the citations have been removed without notation.

Each chapter opens with a set of **learning objectives** that are sequentially designed around Bloom's taxonomy.

Many **illustrations**, **graphs**, and **figures** are used to assist students in conceptualizing the subjects discussed. These include conceptual mapping diagrams as well as data charts.

Sidebars on topics related to the discussion in the text have been included to increase student interest in the subject.

Legal terms appear in boldface in the text and are defined in the margins.

At the close of each chapter, a legal Web site is featured in **Lawlinks**. In addition, a list of Web sites can be found in the researching administrative law issues supplement found in the Instructor Resource Center.

Review questions and **review problems** can be found at the close of each chapter. Review questions are designed to test the reader's retention of the content of the chapter. The review problems are designed to test the reader's ability to apply the concepts of the chapter to a set of facts or to engage in critical analysis.

Appendices include excerpts from the federal Constitution, the Administrative Procedure Act, selected presidential executive orders, and an appendix describing how to perform administrative law research.

NEW TO THIS EDITION

It is difficult for me to believe that this text is in its sixth edition, representing 20 years of publication. I am honored that so many instructors continue to rely on this text to assist their students in learning this subject. It has changed over time, in part due to the comments and suggestions of reviewers, adopters, and students. Please, share your content suggestions and please don't hesitate to point out typographical and other errors with me at the e-mail address provided.

I don't believe in fixing things that are not broken. Accordingly, as true in prior revisions, the basic architecture of this book has not been changed. While the architecture and pedagogy remain the same, valuable changes were made. These include:

- Since the last edition of this text national health care reform has begun implementation and the constitutional challenges to the law have been heard and decided by the Supreme Court. These developments are included in this edition.
- Of course, the law has been updated through 2013 and indeed, the Supreme Court of the United States issued several decisions concerning standing, Chevron, liability of public officials and private parties when acting as government agents, DNA testing of arrestees and job applicants, and reviewability of final orders.
- Several of the longer cases were shortened, a couple of cases were removed, and new case excerpts were added including *Milner v. Navy* (FOIA), *Clapper v. Amnesty* (standing), and *Sackett v. EPA* (final order under APA).
- New sidebars on President Obama's attempts to increase transparency, the history of civil service, and the importance of the Federal Circuit in administrative law appear, as does a recent executive order by President Obama.
- To manage page length, the appendix on researching administrative law issues has been moved to the online supplments.

- The reviewers made outstanding suggestions that I incorporated, nearly in toto. These included excellent content additions and legal elaborations, better placement of cases and figures, typographical errors and corrections, and harmonizing discrepancies between previous editions. Specifically revisions and additions to the sections on federal employees and the Pendleton Act, right to counsel at administrative hearings, subpoena powers of agencies, FOIA, and review of administrative rules by Congress under the Congressional Review Act were a consequence of the review process.

A note about style and what doesn't appear in these pages is necessary. Many factors influence the choice of cases, including how amendable the case is to being reduced in size and still achieve the intended learning objective, age, effectiveness and clarity of writing, how closely the subject matches the discussion in the text, and whether the case teaches tangential but important material. In the process of editing the cases I have taken some liberties. For example, to ease reading flow I have removed most, but not all, internal references and citations. I have done that without using ellipses or other indicators, lest the flow of reading is too interrupted. A few citations and internal references have been left, sometimes because they reinforce a case that has been learned and other times because they expose the reader to the style of judicial writing.

I hope this text assists you in teaching or learning this subject. Your comments or questions are welcomed. Please direct these to either Pearson editors or me.

Daniel E. Hall

Please share your comments with me at hallslaw@yahoo.com.

INSTRUCTOR SUPPLEMENTS

MyTest and *TestBank* represent new standards in testing material. Whether you use a basic test bank document or generate questions electronically through MyTest, every question is linked to the text's learning objective, page number, and level of difficulty. This allows for quick reference in the text and an easy way to check the difficulty level and variety of your questions. MyTest can be accessed at www.PearsonMyTest.com.

PowerPoint Presentations Our presentations offer clear, straightforward outlines and notes to use for class lectures or study materials. Photos, illustrations, charts, and tables from the book are included in the presentations when applicable.

Other supplements are:
- Instructor's Manual with Test Bank
- Test Item File for ingestion into an LMS, including Blackboard and WebCT.

To access supplementary materials online, instructors need to request an instructor access code. Go to **www.pearsonhighered.com/irc,** where you can register for an instructor access code. Within 48 hours after registering, you will receive a confirming email, including an instructor access code. Once you have received your code, go to the site and log on for full instructions on downloading the materials you wish to use.

ALTERNATE VERSIONS

eBooks This text is also available in multiple eBook formats including Adobe Reader and CourseSmart. *CourseSmart* is an exciting new choice for students looking to save money. As an alternative to purchasing the printed textbook, students can purchase an electronic version of the same content. With a *CourseSmart* eTextbook, students can search the text, make notes online, print out reading assignments that incorporate lecture notes, and bookmark important passages for later review. For more information, or to purchase access to the *CourseSmart* eTextbook, visit **www.coursesmart.com**.

ACKNOWLEDGMENTS

Gary Becker, attorney and part-time instructor at Miami University, reviewed and edited Chapter 11 on civil liability. An experienced litigator in this area of law, his contributions are very much appreciated. Brian Craig of Global University updated the researching administrative law issues found online in the Instructor Resource Center, originally written by Professor Deborah Howard of the University of Evansville, with additional online sources and Internet research tips. His assistance is much appreciated. The reviewers for this edition made valuable suggestions. To them, I extend many thanks:

As always, I extend appreciation to Executive Editor Gary Bauer and the Pearson staff who are courteous, professional and understanding of authors who don't always make deadlines. Many thanks to Susan Gilbert, copyeditor and Murugesh Namasivayam, Project Manager, PreMediaGlobal, for their guidance, support, and attention to detail that has made this book a better read. I also send a special shout out to Linda Cupp of Pearson for all her help and patience.

ABOUT THE AUTHOR

Daniel E. Hall, a native of Indiana, earned his bachelor's degree at Indiana University, Juris Doctor at Washburn University, and Doctor of Education (higher education curriculum and instruction) at the University of Central Florida. Before joining the academy full time, he practiced law in both the United States and the Federated States of Micronesia (FSM), where he clerked for the Supreme Court of the FSM and served as Assistant Attorney General of the FSM. He also clerked for Gene E. Brooks, Chief Judge, United States District Court for the Southern District of Indiana and interned for Congressman Frank McCloskey and Robert Katzmann, J.D., Ph.D., at the Brookings Institution. Subsequent to leaving law practice he has been on the faculties of the Department of Criminal Justice and Legal Studies at the University of Central Florida and the Department of Criminal Justice at the University of Toledo, where he was chair and associate professor. He has also taught as adjunct instructor at the University of Evansville, College of Micronesia, and Barry University School of Law.

Daniel was Campus Dean of Miami Hamilton from 2003–2010 where he was, and continues to be, professor of political science, chair and professor of justice and community studies, and affiliate professor of black world studies. He is also visiting professor of law at Sun Yat-sen University School of Law in Guangzhou, China. Daniel is the author or co-author of 21 textbooks (first and subsequent editions) and more than a dozen journal articles on public law and related subjects. Daniel's greatest joy is being father to Grace and Eva, ages 12 and 8 at the time of publication, who, in spite of continuous efforts by their father, have not yet acquired an appreciation for the constitutional aspects of the modern administrative state. For more information on the author go to www.danielhall.org/. He may be reached at hallslaw@yahoo.com.

chapter **one**

INTRODUCTION

LEARNING OBJECTIVES

After completing this chapter, you should be able to

- Define what administrative law is and isn't.

- Identify and distinguish the sources of administrative law in the United States.

- Describe the nature and complexity of the administrative state at the federal, state, and local levels.

- Distinguish agencies using the models presented in the chapter.

- Identify the most significant factors that have contributed to the growth of the administrative state in the United States.

- Extrapolate from the presented material several examples of how agencies impact your daily life.

A government big enough to give you everything you want is a government big enough to take away from you everything you have.

PRESIDENT GERALD FORD (1974)

From "Address to a Joint Session of the Congress"
by Gerald R. Ford, August 12, 1974.

1.1 ADMINISTRATIVE LAW DEFINED

In elementary and high schools throughout the United States students are taught that legislatures create laws, executive officials enforce laws, and judges adjudicate disputes. Specifically students are taught that the Constitution of the United States creates a Congress to create law, the President to enforce laws, and federal courts to adjudicate disputes and that state constitutions establish similar structures for state governments. While this is true, it is an incomplete picture of government. Federal, state, and local administrative agencies have become important vehicles for the implementation of governmental policies and objectives, provision of services, the creation of law, the enforcement of law, and the adjudication of disputes.

Because the number of agencies in the United States has grown significantly in recent years, as has the authority of these agencies, a body of law has developed to control and regulate their behavior and function. This body of law is known as *administrative law*.

Administrative law defines the powers, limitations, and procedures of administrative agencies. Of particular concern are the rights of individuals when dealing with administrative agencies. This text examines all these issues. This text does not, however, delve into the substantive laws of administrative agencies. For example, the constitutional and statutory procedures that must be used when determining a claim for welfare benefits are examined, but the standards used to decide whether a person is eligible for those benefits are not.

Substantive law cannot be completely ignored, however. Although the substantive laws that agencies enforce and administer are not discussed here, other substantive laws that affect agencies are examined. For example, substantive due process is discussed. Also, because it is important to accountability and to those who work in agencies, Chapter 11 discusses the liability of the governments and their agents when performing governmental functions.

LEGAL TERM

Administrative Law

A body of law that defines the powers, limitations, and procedures of administrative agencies.

1.2 SOURCES OF ADMINISTRATIVE LAW

1.2(a) Constitution

The Constitution of the United States and the Constitutions of the states are a significant source of law in the administrative context. The principles of separation of powers and federalism embodied in the Constitution are important to the structuring of agencies and, to some extent, in limiting the authority of agencies. Article I of the Constitution establishes many the powers of the national government, specifically the power of Congress to regulate interstate commerce and other matters. The concepts of due process of law and equal protection of laws, found in the Fifth and Fourteenth Amendments, are vital limitations on the power of agencies. You will learn more about these and other constitutional principles as you read further.

1.2(b) Enabling Laws

A statute that establishes an agency and sets forth the responsibilities and authority of that agency is an *enabling statute*. Congress enacts enabling laws at the federal level and state legislatures do so at the state level. A group of statutes may combine to constitute an agency's enabling laws. Other legislation aimed at all or a group of agencies may also direct an agency to do something or behave in a certain manner.

1.2(c) Administrative Procedure Act

Concern about the growing power of the "administrative state," led to the enactment of the *Administrative Procedure Act* (APA) in 1946. The APA is the basic law governing the procedures that agencies must use in the performance of their functions. Although comprehensive in coverage, the APA is not the first law of agency governance: The primary law is always an agency's enabling legislation. Often, enabling statutes contain different or more detailed provisions than the APA. The enabling legislation is controlling in such cases, assuming constitutionality. The federal APA applies only to federal agencies.

In addition to the federal APA, the National Conference on Uniform State Laws and the American Bar Association approved a uniform state APA in 1946. That proposed uniform law was amended twice, first in 1961 and again in 1981. A total of 30 states (and the District of Columbia) have adopted the model state APA, and the remaining 20 states have enacted another form of administrative procedure statute.[2]

There are references to the federal APA throughout this book. For the reader's convenience, pertinent provisions of the federal APA are reprinted in Appendix B. It is suggested that the student read the entire APA, because familiarity with it is important to a working understanding of administrative law. Remember that the federal APA applies only to federal agencies. The appropriate state version of the federal APA, as well as other state statutes and administrative regulations, must be consulted when dealing with state agencies.

1.2(d) Executive Orders, Proclamations, and Signing Statements

Although not a lawmaker (this is a power delegated to Congress), the president (and his executive counterparts in the states) may issue executive orders. A lawfully issued executive order (EO) has the effect of a statute. Executive orders have two sources of authority. The first is Article II of the Constitution. Article II establishes the presidency. Although its framing of the presidency is broad with few specific delegations of authority, it is generally recognized that presidents possess considerably authority that is inherent to the broad delegations that exist.

The exercise of these authorities often involve making decisions of broad application that look and smell like law. For example, the president is the chief executive of the government. While Congress creates and defines many of the powers of government agencies, it cannot regulate every detail of their operations, leaving it to the president and the agencies themselves to fill in the gaps. For example, President Barack Obama, as did President George W. Bush before him, declared December 24, 2012, a holiday for federal employees. Presidents may use any power delegated by Article II to issue executive orders. Executive Order 13228, issued in the wake of the terrorist attacks on the United States of September 11, 2001, is an example. This executive order established the Office of Homeland Security as well as a Homeland Security Council. One month later, President Bush issued a "military order," under his authority as commander-in-chief of the

LEGAL TERM

Administrative Procedure Act
A comprehensive statute governing the procedures that agencies must follow when performing their functions. The federal APA was enacted in 1946.

military, establishing special rules for the arrest, detention, and military trial of accused international terrorists. You may review all three of these orders in Appendix C.

Presidential authority is greatest, however, when authorized by Congress. In many instances, Congress will enact a general program or establish a broad policy and then delegate the authority to regulate further to the president. In such a case, the executive order is the presidential mechanism to establish additional law. With few exceptions, if there is a conflict between an executive order and a statute, the statute prevails. That is because Congress is the primary policymaker of the United States. There are exceptions, however. If the Constitution delegates a specific authority to the president, such as regarding foreign affairs matters, then the president's executive order may be a higher form of law than a contrary statute.

Executive orders were not numbered until 1907. According to the American Presidency Project at the University of California Santa Barbara, nearly 14,000 executive orders had been issued by presidents by July 2013.[3] Executive orders may be proposed by any administrative agency, or they may originate in the White House. Before a proposed order is presented to the president, it is reviewed by the Office of Management and Budget and the Attorney General. After being executed, an EO is published in the *Federal Register*. See Appendix C for examples of executive orders.

Presidents also issue presidential proclamations. Like EO, they have the force of law, assuming presidential power exists. Proclamations are often ceremonial, proclaiming the Nation's gratitude for a person's service to humanity, for example. But they are also used to declare a legal state of affairs and to enforce the law. President Barack Obama, for example, issued a proclamation in 2013 withdrawing trade preference status of Bangledesh because of workers' conditions in that Nation. This authority had been delegated to the president by statute.[4]

Presidents also influence law through presidential signing statements. These statements normally occur when a president signs a bill into law. Through a signing statement, a president expresses an opinion about the law. Often a president will indicate what the White House's interpretation of the bill is and how administrative officers are to execute the law. In some cases, presidents have expressed an unwillingness to enforce a portion of the law because it is believed it to be unconstitutional. For example, even though he signed the law, President Barack Obama issued a statement to the National Defense Authorization Act of 2012 challenging the law's directions in regards to the transfer of terrorist suspects into military custody and the indefinite detention of suspects. President Obama wrote, of some of the provisions, that

> Section 1028 modifies but fundamentally maintains unwarranted restrictions on the executive branch's authority to transfer detainees to a foreign country. This hinders the executive's ability to carry out its military, national security, and foreign relations activities and like section 1027, would, under certain circumstances, violate constitutional separation of powers principles. The executive branch must have the flexibility to act swiftly in conducting negotiations with foreign countries regarding the circumstances of detainee transfers. In the event that the statutory restrictions in sections 1027 and 1028 operate in a manner that violates constitutional separation of powers principles, my Administration will interpret them to avoid the constitutional conflict.
>
> Section 1029 requires that the Attorney General consult with the Director of National Intelligence and Secretary of Defense prior to filing criminal charges against or seeking an indictment of certain individuals.

I sign this based on the understanding that apart from detainees held by the military outside of the United States under the 2001 Authorization for Use of Military Force, the provision applies only to those individuals who have been determined to be covered persons under section 1022 before the Justice Department files charges or seeks an indictment. Notwithstanding that limitation, this provision represents an intrusion into the functions and prerogatives of the Department of Justice and offends the longstanding legal tradition that decisions regarding criminal prosecutions should be vested with the Attorney General free from outside interference. Moreover, section 1029 could impede flexibility and hinder exigent operational judgments in a manner that damages our security. My Administration will interpret and implement section 1029 in a manner that preserves the operational flexibility of our counterterrorism and law enforcement professionals, limits delays in the investigative process, ensures that critical executive branch functions are not inhibited, and preserves the integrity and independence of the Department of Justice.

Other provisions in this bill above could interfere with my constitutional foreign affairs powers. . . . Like [other sections of this law], should any application of these provisions conflict with my constitutional authorities, I will treat the provisions as non-binding.[5]

"Statement by the President on H.R. 1540", The White House, Barack Obama.

1.3 ADMINISTRATIVE AGENCIES

Administrative agencies, as referred to in this text, come in many forms and sizes (see Figure 1-1). This is due, in large part, to the fact that agencies are created to confront an array of problems. In addition, agencies exist at all levels of government. The primary focus of this book is federal administrative agencies although many of the principles discussed herein apply to all agencies.

Administrative agencies have many names, including, *departments, commissions, bureaus, councils, groups, services, divisions,* and *agencies.* Agencies often also have subunits bearing these names. For example, the Kansas Division of Motor Vehicles is a subunit of the Kansas Department of Revenue. Just because agencies are known by various names, agency heads hold various titles, including secretary, director, and commissioner. Some are appointed by the applicable executive (president, governor, mayor, city or county manager, and others) and others are elected. In some cases, as discussed later in this book, some agencies are independent after appointment and some are headed by a collegial group, not a single leader.

Not all governmental entities are agencies. Courts and legislatures are not agencies. They are constitutionally created branches of government. Therefore, the principles discussed in this text do not apply to those bodies.

Not all agencies are of great concern to the study of administrative law. The study of administrative law focuses on agencies whose actions affect the rights of individuals, also known as *civil rights.* Agencies such as the U.S. Department of State rarely engage in decision making that affects civil liberties; accordingly, they are not the focus of this book. In contrast, the National Labor Relations Board is an agency that significantly affects civil liberties and, therefore, is of greater interest to the student of administrative law.

To address perceived voter access and other election problems, President Barack Obama created a Presidential Commission on Election Administration in 2013. The Commission was charged to "identify best practices and otherwise

THE GOVERNMENT OF THE UNITED STATES

THE CONSTITUTION

LEGISLATIVE BRANCH

THE CONGRESS

SENATE   HOUSE

ARCHITECT OF THE CAPITOL
UNITED STATES BOTANIC GARDEN
GOVERNMENT ACCOUNTABILITY OFFICE
GOVERNMENT PRINTING OFFICE
LIBRARY OF CONGRESS
CONGRESSIONAL BUDGET OFFICE

EXECUTIVE BRANCH

THE PRESIDENT

THE VICE PRESIDENT

EXECUTIVE OFFICE OF THE PRESIDENT

WHITE HOUSE OFFICE
OFFICE OF THE VICE PRESIDENT
COUNCIL OF ECONOMIC ADVISERS
COUNCIL ON ENVIRONMENTAL QUALITY
NATIONAL SECURITY COUNCIL
OFFICE OF ADMINISTRATION

OFFICE OF MANAGEMENT AND BUDGET
OFFICE OF NATIONAL DRUG CONTROL POLICY
OFFICE OF POLICY DEVELOPMENT
OFFICE OF SCIENCE AND TECHNOLOGY POLICY
OFFICE OF THE UNITED STATES
TRADE REPRESENTATIVE

JUDICIAL BRANCH

THE SUPREME COURT OF THE UNITED STATES

UNITED STATES COURTS OF APPEALS
UNITED STATES DISTRICT COURTS
TERRITORIAL COURTS
UNITED STATES COURT OF INTERNATIONAL TRADE
UNITED STATES COURT OF FEDERAL CLAIMS
UNITED STATES COURT OF APPEALS FOR THE
ARMED FORCES
UNITED STATES TAX COURT
UNITED STATES COURT OF APPEALS FOR VETERANS CLAIMS
ADMINISTRATIVE OFFICE OF THE
UNITED STATES COURTS
FEDERAL JUDICIAL CENTER
UNITED STATES SENTENCING COMMISSION

DEPARTMENT OF AGRICULTURE

DEPARTMENT OF COMMERCE

DEPARTMENT OF DEFENSE

DEPARTMENT OF EDUCATION

DEPARTMENT OF ENERGY

DEPARTMENT OF HEALTH AND HUMAN SERVICES

DEPARTMENT OF HOMELAND SECURITY

DEPARTMENT OF HOUSING AND URBAN DEVELOPMENT

DEPARTMENT OF THE INTERIOR

DEPARTMENT OF JUSTICE

DEPARTMENT OF LABOR

DEPARTMENT OF STATE

DEPARTMENT OF TRANSPORTATION

DEPARTMENT OF THE TREASURY

DEPARTMENT OF VETERANS AFFAIRS

INDEPENDENT ESTABLISHMENTS AND GOVERNMENT CORPORATIONS

AFRICAN DEVELOPMENT FOUNDATION
BROADCASTING BOARD OF GOVERNORS
CENTRAL INTELLIGENCE AGENCY
COMMODITY FUTURES TRADING COMMISSION
CONSUMER PRODUCT SAFETY COMMISSION
CORPORATION FOR NATIONAL AND COMMUNITY SERVICE
DEFENSE NUCLEAR FACILITIES SAFETY BOARD
ENVIRONMENTAL PROTECTION AGENCY
EQUAL EMPLOYMENT OPPORTUNITY COMMISSION
EXPORT-IMPORT BANK OF THE UNITED STATES
FARM CREDIT ADMINISTRATION
FEDERAL COMMUNICATIONS COMMISSION
FEDERAL DEPOSIT INSURANCE CORPORATION
FEDERAL ELECTION COMMISSION

FEDERAL HOUSING FINANCE BOARD
FEDERAL LABOR RELATIONS AUTHORITY
FEDERAL MARITIME COMMISSION
FEDERAL MEDIATION AND CONCILIATION SERVICE
FEDERAL MINE SAFETY AND HEALTH REVIEW COMMISSION
FEDERAL RESERVE SYSTEM
FEDERAL RETIREMENT THRIFT INVESTMENT BOARD
FEDERAL TRADE COMMISSION
GENERAL SERVICES ADMINISTRATION
INTER-AMERICAN FOUNDATION
MERIT SYSTEMS PROTECTION BOARD
NATIONAL AERONAUTICS AND SPACE ADMINISTRATION
NATIONAL ARCHIVES AND RECORDS ADMINISTRATION
NATIONAL CAPITAL PLANNING COMMISSION

NATIONAL CREDIT UNION ADMINISTRATION
NATIONAL FOUNDATION ON THE ARTS AND THE HUMANITIES
NATIONAL LABOR RELATIONS BOARD
NATIONAL MEDIATION BOARD
NATIONAL RAILROAD PASSENGER CORPORATION (AMTRAK)
NATIONAL SCIENCE FOUNDATION
NATIONAL TRANSPORTATION SAFETY BOARD
NUCLEAR REGULATORY COMMISSION
OCCUPATIONAL SAFETY AND HEALTH REVIEW COMMISSION
OFFICE OF THE DIRECTOR OF NATIONAL INTELLIGENCE
OFFICE OF GOVERNMENT ETHICS
OFFICE OF PERSONNEL MANAGEMENT
OFFICE OF SPECIAL COUNSEL
OVERSEAS PRIVATE INVESTMENT CORPORATION

PEACE CORPS
PENSION BENEFIT GUARANTY CORPORATION
POSTAL REGULATORY COMMISSION
NATIONAL RAILROAD RETIREMENT BOARD
SECURITIES AND EXCHANGE COMMISSION
SELECTIVE SERVICE SYSTEM
SMALL BUSINESS ADMINISTRATION
SOCIAL SECURITY ADMINISTRATION
TENNESSEE VALLEY AUTHORITY
TRADE AND DEVELOPMENT AGENCY
UNITED STATES AGENCY FOR INTERNATIONAL DEVELOPMENT
UNITED STATES COMMISSION ON CIVIL RIGHTS
UNITED STATES INTERNATIONAL TRADE COMMISSION
UNITED STATES POSTAL SERVICE

FIGURE 1-1   The government of the United States.

SIDEBAR   *Special Agencies*

In some circumstances, a committee, study group, or task force is created to meet a particular short-term need. This type of agency may be created by Congress or the president. For example, Congress established the Office of Drug Control Policy within the Executive Office of the President. See 21 U.S.C. § 1501. This office is headed by a director, who has become popularly known as the "Drug Czar."

President George W. Bush established the Foreign Terrorist Tracking Taskforce following the attacks of September 11, 2001. This group was charged with coordinating governmental programs in an effort to prevent the entry of foreign terrorists into the United States and to locate, deport, and prosecute foreign terrorists who were already present in the United States.

make recommendations to promote the efficient administration of elections in order to ensure that all eligible voters have the opportunity to cast their ballots without undue delay, and to improve the experience of voters facing other obstacles in casting their ballots, such as members of the military, overseas voters, voters with disabilities, and voters with limited English proficiency."[6]

1.3(a) The Need for Agencies

In the United States, government operations are split among three branches: legislative, executive, and judicial. There is no constitutional provision establishing administrative agencies. Agencies are created by one of the three branches of government—usually Congress. After creation, most administrative agencies fall under the aegis of the executive branch.

Some scholars have referred to administrative agencies as the *fourth branch of government*. Agencies do not actually constitute a fourth branch of government, however, because they remain accountable to the other branches and because the Constitution of the United States establishes only three branches. You will learn more about the exact legal status of agencies in Chapter 2. Understand, though, that agencies are important, often exercising some of the functions of all three branches of government—something that the branches themselves are prohibited from doing.

Why do we have agencies? There are at least two responses to that question. First, the job of government has become too large for Congress, the Courts, and the executive branch to handle. Congress simply does not have time to make all the laws, nor the president to enforce all the laws, nor the Courts to adjudicate all the cases.

Second, agency expertise is needed. Every year Congress must deal with a large and diverse number of issues. Discrimination, environmental concerns, military and national security matters, and funding for science and art are but a few of the issues Congress must address. Congress is too small and too busy to be expert in all the areas it regulates. Agencies, however, specialize, and they possess technical knowledge and expertise in their respective specialties. Agencies can hire whomever they need to complete their tasks; they benefit from continuous involvement with the same policy area. Because of agency expertise, many believe agencies are in a better, more informed, position to make many decisions. Others assert that continued exposure to the same problems, and issues can make an agency indifferent, uncaring, and biased.

LEGAL TERMS

Social Welfare Agencies
Administrative agencies responsible for promoting the general welfare of the people. Such agencies' missions often include providing services or cash distributions to persons who qualify for assistance.

Regulatory Agencies
Administrative agencies responsible for proscribing or requiring certain behavior, determining compliance with the law, and prosecuting (and occasionally punishing) those who violate the law.

Public Service Agencies
Administrative agencies that provide special, nonredistributive services such as research.

Licensing
Granting permission to engage in or practice certain professions, occupations, or trades. Administrative agencies may be delegated the responsibility to license selected professions, occupations, or trades. This usually involves setting standards and administering tests for license applicants. The power to license also usually includes the power to discipline and oversee those licensed.

Ratemaking
The authority to set the rates that may be charged by members of certain industries, such as utilities. This authority is often delegated to an administrative agency.

Executive Agency
An administrative agency whose head answers to the president and may be disciplined or terminated at the president's will.

Independent Agency
An administrative agency that is to some degree independent of the president. Various degrees of independence exist; a common arrangement is to limit the presidential power of removal of the agency head(s) to good cause.

1.3(b) Types of Agencies

Nearly all administrative agencies can be characterized as *social welfare*, *regulatory*, or *public service*. Social welfare agencies are responsible for promoting the general welfare of the people. This mission often includes providing services or cash distributions to persons who qualify for assistance. The Department of Health and Human Resources, the Department of Veterans Affairs, and the Department of Housing and Urban Development are examples of federal social welfare agencies. The Department of Health and Human Resources provides retirement benefits to the elderly, disability benefits to those unable to work, welfare benefits to the financially poor, and Medicare benefits to a number of groups. The Department of Veterans Affairs provides medical and other benefits to the nation's veterans. The Department of Agriculture administers the food stamp program, which provides vouchers to low-income persons for the purchase of food. The Department of Housing and Urban Development administers a program intended to get low-income families into decent housing.

Regulatory agencies are responsible for proscribing or requiring certain behavior, determining compliance with the law, and prosecuting (and occasionally punishing) those who violate the law. For example, state departments of motor vehicles may establish the regulations concerning vehicle licensing, monitor compliance with the licensing rules, and punish those who operate motor vehicles without proper licensing.

Regulatory agencies possess a wide range of authority. Many control *licensing*. For example, the Federal Communications Commission determines who may hold a license to broadcast communications. At the state level, agencies license a number of professions, trades, and occupations. Doctors, lawyers, plumbers, electricians, and real estate brokers are a few examples.

Regulatory agencies also set rates for certain industries. For instance, the Federal Energy Regulatory Commission, another federal agency, is responsible for *ratemaking* for energy matters of a national scale. States have agencies to approve rate changes for utilities, such as gas and electric companies. Finally, regulatory agencies are often given the authority to regulate business practices. For example, the Occupational Safety and Health Administration sets standards for safety in the workplace.

The third type of agency is the public service agency. A public service agency is not involved with the redistribution of money, nor does it regulate. Instead, it provides services to the public. The National Science Foundation, for example, promotes research and provides information to the public.

An agency may also be characterized as either an *executive agency* or an *independent agency*. Executive agencies are organs of the executive branch. The highest officer in such an agency is the *secretary*. This person is nominated by the president of the United States and must be confirmed by the Senate of the United States. This person sits on the president's cabinet and may be fired at the will of the president.

Other agencies are referred to as *independent* because the president exerts less control over them. These agencies are often headed by a group of individuals, often referred to as a *board* or *commission*. Although the heads of independent agencies may undergo the same selection process (nomination and confirmation) as executive agency heads, they are not members of the cabinet and may not be fired at the president's will. Congress typically requires cause—usually not political—before a board member of an independent agency may be fired. This political independence allows an agency head to make decisions that may be unpopular

TABLE 1-1 Executive v. Independent Agencies	
Executive	**Independent**
Appointed by president or other executive, sometimes with congressional approval. New appointees with every change of administration.	Appointed by president or other executive, sometimes with Senate confirmation. Appointments are often for staggered terms, extending beyond the terms of presidents.
Reports to president or other executive officer.	Doesn't report to president or executive officers. Members are independent, except for removal in cases of malfeasance, etc.
Serves at will of supervisor or may be removed with senatorial consent by supervisor.	Can be removed only in specific cases, e.g., malfeasance. Presidential removal with senatorial consent or impeachment by Congress possible.
Single head of agency common.	Collegial boards most common.
Partisan appointments common.	Bipartisan membership commonly required.
Examples: Department of State, Department of Justice, Department of Homeland Security, Department of Defense, Department of Energy, Department of Education, Department of Interior	Examples: Board of Governors of the Federal Reserve System, National Labor Relations Board, Postal Regulatory Commission, Federal Energy Regulatory Commission

with the president, but correct in the agency's determination, without fear of losing his or her job. In spite of this limitation on executive authority, independent agencies are, in theory, part of the executive branch. Table 1-1 delineates the differences between executive and independent agencies.

1.3(c) The History and Size of the Bureaucracy

Administrative agencies have existed since the birth of the nation. The Departments of War, Foreign Affairs, Treasury, Post Office, and Patents were established by the first Congress. These agencies provided needed services, such as mail delivery and protection from foreign enemies. Their "regulation" of Americans was minimal. Later, in 1887, Congress created the Interstate Commerce Commission, the first federal agency with significant authority to regulate people and business operations directly although it was later abolished.[7]

The boom era for federal administrative agencies was during the Great Depression and World War II. President Franklin D. Roosevelt initiated the creation of many new agencies as part of his New Deal efforts to revive the economy and to correct other social problems the nation was experiencing. Congress supported the president's efforts through legislation creating new agencies and programs such as the Tennessee Valley Authority, Works Progress Administration, Agricultural Adjustment Act, Civilian Conservation Corps, and Social Security. The authority and number of administrative agencies continued to expand in the following decades, particularly during the 1970s.

Several factors have contributed to the growth in government, and, specifically, the growth in the administrative state. First, the increasing interdependence of people is a significant factor. Today, nearly everyone provides highly

Franklin D. Roosevelt Presidential Library & Museum

specialized services. We depend on others for our food, health care, technology, and other needs. This change, along with our increasing population, is driving people together, but often in impersonal ways. This interdependence without social connectedness (also known as social distance) not only causes greater conflict, but also leaves society without the social infrastructure to informally resolve disputes. The need for more law and government is a consequence. In order for people to be comfortable with their food, medicine, and other products, assurances of safety and quality are needed. As corporate information gathering increases (what happens to the personal information you provide when you register a purchase, complete an application for credit, or provide personal information at the cash register?), regulation to protect privacy has increased in importance.

A second factor is the growing expectation of the public for its government to regulate in new ways. So-called social engineering is an example. Today, government is used to addressing social issues in new ways. The regulation of race, gender, age, disability, and sexual orientation discrimination is an example.

A third factor is the expectation that government will provide more services and benefits than in the early years of the Republic. The framers of the U.S. Constitution did not live in a world where government provided recreation, educational tutoring, unemployment assistance, welfare, Medicare, Medicaid, and Social Security benefits. The President Obama initiative to expand access to health care and to reform the health care system is a contemporary example of services and regulation that the framers of the United States Republic didn't foresee.

It was the perceived need for government to address the complex economic ills of the nation (as opposed to trusting the free market to right itself), the desire to increase government services as a catalyst to economic development, and the desire to provide benefits to individuals suffering from the Great Depression that caused the growth of the administrative state (all the administrative agencies and their respective authorities when taken together) during the New Deal administration.

A fourth factor is the increasing mobility of people. Travel and increasingly frequent relocation itself creates regulatory needs. Beyond this, as people become less familiar with one another, informal social control becomes less effective, increasing the need for law. The result of these, and undoubtedly other, factors precipitated an unprecedented growth in the administrative state, both at the state and federal levels, beginning with the New Deal era.

The government of the United States as it exists today is diagrammed in Figure 1-1. To illustrate the size of the federal bureaucracy, the organizational structure of two of the agencies found in Figure 1-1 can be found in Figures 1-2 and 1-3. Be aware that many programs and subagencies of these departments are quite large and have subdivisions of their own. As you can see, the number of federal agencies is quite large. To get a complete picture of the size of the administrative state, though, all state and local agencies would have to be included.

To illustrate the growth of the federal government, consider the number of people employed by the government. In 1800, 3,000 people were employed by the federal government. There were approximately 5,084,000 people in the United States at that time; thus, federal employees constituted about .0005 of the total population. By 1995, the number of employees had increased to nearly three million, a number representing more than 1 percent of the total population. Scholar Paul Light points out that one must consider not only direct employees, but also indirect or "shadow" employees in the calculation. Indirect employees include people who work for quasi-governmental agencies, independent agencies, and private industries that serve the government, as well as people who are not in government service but are paid under government contracts or grants. If you include these

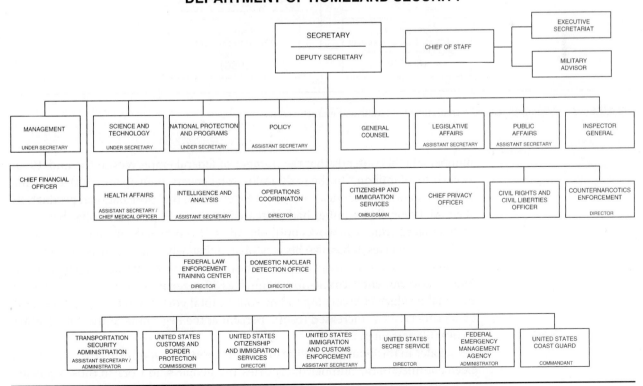

FIGURE 1-2   Organizational chart: Department of Homeland Security.

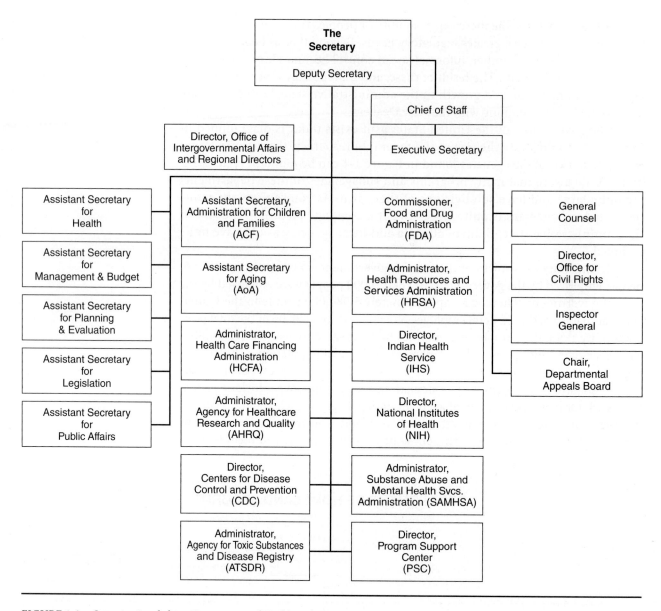

FIGURE 1-3   Organizational chart: Department of Health and Human Services.

numbers, Light contends that the number of federal employees in the mid-1990s swelled to 17 million.[8] In the early 1900s, total government spending (federal and local) for goods and services was about 8 percent of the gross national product. By the mid-1990s, that number had increased to about 19 percent.[9] It has been estimated that an American works until May of each year before earning more than he or she pays in taxes. It has also been estimated that, when all the costs of regulation are included, the real tax-clearance date is July 1. Some estimates report that the federal government accounts for as much as 30 percent of the nation's total gross national product.[10] According to one source, total government spending, federal, state, and local has increased from 7 percent at the beginning of the 20th century to over 40 percent in 2010.[11]

Later in this book you will read that the growth in administrative law has not been confined to the number of agencies and people who work in those agencies. The number of laws created and enforced by agencies has seen significant growth as well.

SIDEBAR   *Health Care Reform and Bureaucracy*

On March 23, 2010, President Barack Obama signed the Patient Protection and Affordable Care Act (PPACA) into law. Seven days later he signed a second health care reform bill, the Health Care and Education Reconciliation Act, into law as well. The PPACA is the largest social service reform in the United States since the creation of the social security system in the 1930s, dealing with a policy area that represents somewhere between 15 percent and 20 percent of the U.S. gross national product. The legislation is huge—the bill is more than 2,400 pages in length. The Obama administration claims that the law will expand coverage to tens of millions of people who were previously uninsured and the Congressional Budget Office estimates that the national deficit will be reduced by over $100 billion in the first ten years and $1.2 trillion in years eleven to twenty.

The laws, referred to here as PPACA or health care reform, include expanding Medicaid eligibility, incentives for employers to provide insurance to employees, the creation of health exchanges where the uninsured can secure coverage with subsidies for low-income individuals and families, additional exchanges created for small businesses, insurance provided regardless of pre-existing conditions, mandatory insurance coverage for individuals, longer periods that pharmaceutical companies can market drugs before generics may be marketed, support for medical research, and various taxes and fees on high-income individuals, tanning parlors, and medical and pharmaceutical companies. Hundreds of other provisions of the law regulate all dimensions of health care.

Implementation of this massive, diverse, and complex policy area is no small task. Although estimates vary, most agree that when done, more than 100 new agencies, boards, commissions, offices, and other entities will be created to implement the bill. Although the precise number is unknown now, there is little doubt that tens of thousands of new federal employees will be required.

Although many agencies will be involved (e.g., Internal Revenue Service, Department of Labor), the United States Department of Health and Human Services (HHS) is primarily responsible for implementation and oversight of the PPACA. HHS has announced the creation of several new agencies, boards, and offices to fulfill its mandate, including an Office of Consumer Information and Insurance Oversight, Office of Insurance Programs, Office of Consumer Information and Insurance Oversight, Office of Health Insurance Exchanges, Office of Consumer Support, Independent Payment Advisory Board, Innovation Center, and Patient-Centered Outcomes Research Institute.

New agencies with congressional mandates and new delegations to existing agencies will also mean new regulations. Indeed, the Internal Revenue Service, Department of Labor, and HHS have already promulgated their first set of regulations.

1.3(d) The Impact of Agencies on Daily Life

The large number of agencies and agency officials is the result, and possibly the cause, of, in some situations, a large amount of services and regulation. Consider the extent to which administrative law is present in just a few hours of your morning. You sleep in a bed that was manufactured in accordance with federal guidelines. The bed, like most consumer products, was shipped in interstate commerce. The Federal Department of Transportation, therefore, regulated the bed shipment, whether by air (Federal Aviation Administration), rail (Federal Railroad Administration), or highway (Federal Highway Administration and National Highway Traffic Safety Administration). In addition, if shipped by truck, state traffic and motor vehicle regulations also had to be followed and managed by the carrier.

You arise to an alarm that is likely powered by electricity, a product regulated by your local public service commission and, in some cases, provided by your local government. After you leave your bed, you may eat breakfast and dress for work. The Consumer Product Safety Commission, Food and Drug Administration, and Department of Agriculture are three federal agencies charged with ensuring that the clothes you wear, the products you use (e.g., your toaster and coffee maker), and the food you purchase are safe. Again, state and local agencies play a significant role as well. The food you purchase in a grocery or in your local bistro, for example, must comply with local health codes. One study estimated that a hamburger purchased in a local restaurant is governed by more than 41,000 federal and state regulations![12] Freshly showered (with water that has satisfied federal and state water standards and, in most cases, provided by local government), you leave your home (the construction of which should have been in compliance with local construction standards and permitting requirements and upon which you have paid local taxes) and get into your new automobile. Of course, the design and manufacture of your new SUV was regulated by the federal government, and you paid taxes, registered the vehicle, and obtained a driver's license with state and local authorities. Your drive to work is regulated as well. Your driver's license was issued by a state administrative agency and the rules of the road were created by your state legislature, county or city government, or possibly an agency.

At work, you are subject to federal and local laws concerning discrimination in the workplace. Agencies exist to deal with this issue as well, such as the federal Equal Employment Opportunity Commission. Your safety and that of your coworkers is regulated by the Federal Occupational Safety and Health Administration, as well as by local officials. Under federal law, you are entitled, with certain exceptions, to receive overtime pay and a minimum wage. Other federal laws concern employer-provided health insurance and retirement benefits. You may also have a right to form a union at work. The National Labor Relations Board is charged with enforcing this right.

All this regulation is not free. Your earnings are taxed by federal and local governments. At the federal level, the Internal Revenue Service is responsible for collecting a portion of your earnings; state and local agencies will collect income taxes as well. Your employer must also pay taxes. In addition, both you and your employer must spend time and money complying with regulations. The Small Business Administration, for example, estimated that small business owners spend nearly a billion hours per year completing government forms![13]

These are only a few examples of how a person's life is regulated by state and federal laws. As you can see, the amount of regulation of daily life is high. Little activity today has no connection to the administrative state, and, therefore, administrative law. As will be discussed later in this book, administrative agencies are responsible for more lawmaking than are our elected representatives. They are also responsible for the enforcement of the laws created by our lawmakers, and as you will see, they also enforce the laws they create.

1.4 CONCLUSION

Administrative regulation is omnipresent in American life. The high level of regulation is likely the result of many factors, such as technological complexity, increases in population, and an increased interdependence of the members of the American family. As a field of law, administrative law is concerned with defining the duties and powers of administrative agencies. More important, administrative law also defines the limits of agency powers. Most agency structure and authority are defined by statute or executive order. Limitations on agency authority can be found in statutes, executive orders, and, most prominently, the Constitution.

REVIEW **QUESTIONS**

1. What does the acronym APA stand for?

2. Does the APA define the substantive or procedural aspects of administrative law?

3. Do the requirements of the federal APA apply to state and local agencies?

4. Distinguish between social welfare, regulatory, and public service agencies.

5. Identify and discuss three sources of administrative law.

6. Identify three ways that are not mentioned in this book in which you are regulated by administrative agencies.

CRITICAL THINKING AND **APPLICATIONS PROBLEMS**

1. State Legislature has enacted a law that prohibits the hunting of deer in the State. In addition to this prohibition, the statute creates a new state agency, the Bureau of Deer Preservation (BDP), which is to oversee enforcement of the law, including adjudicating and fining violators. Is the BDP a social welfare or a regulatory agency? Explain your answer.

2. Two years later, State Legislature amends the law in response to public opinion, directing the BDP to establish a system of deer hunting during specified periods of time, whereby each would-be hunter must apply and pay for a hunting license. In addition, the agency is directed to set the maximum kills allowed per hunter each year, after considering the deer population and other factors. As before, the BDP is delegated the responsibility to enforce the law.

   The revenues derived from this system are to be distributed to "qualified indigent persons" to purchase food. In the alternative, "qualified indigent persons" may request a waiver of the licensing fee and kill limit so that they may hunt deer to be used as food. Is the BDP a social welfare or a regulatory agency? Explain your answer.

3. Identify two factors discussed in the chapter that have contributed to the growth of the administrative state. For each factor, discuss whether you expect the factor to continue to fuel growth. Explain your answers fully.

ENDNOTES

1. 5 U.S.C. § 551 *et seq.*
2. Bernard Schwartz, *Administrative Law* 32–33 (3d ed. 1991).
3. Search for executive orders at *www.presidency.ucsb.edu*
4. Presidential Proclamation 8997 (June 27, 2013).
5. Statement on Signing the National Defense Authorization Act of Fiscal Year 2012, December 31, 2011.
6. E.O. 13639 (March 28,2013).
7. Jerry L. Mashaw, Richard A. Merrill, & Peter M. Shane, *Administrative Law: The American Public Law System* (1998).
8. Mashaw, note 3, at 6; Inter-University Consortium for Political and Social Research, Study 00003 (Ann Arbor, 1992).
9. Mashaw, *supra* note 3, at 7.
10. Craig E. Richardson & Geoff C. Ziebart, *Strangled by Red Tape* 2 (1995), citing another source.
11. See http://www.usgovernmentspending.com/.
12. See Joe Teague, *Administrative Law for Paralegals* 2 (1994).
13. *Strangled by Red Tape*, p. 5.

chapter **two**

BUREAUCRACY AND DEMOCRACY

LEARNING OBJECTIVES

After completing this chapter, you should be able to

- Identify and describe the major structural characteristics of the U.S. government and provisions of the Constitution of the United States that are intended to divide governmental authority and, hence, reduce abuses of authority.

- List and describe the structural controls of administrative agencies that exist in the U.S. government.

- Fully explain why agencies pose a challenge to the separation of powers control model. You should also be able to identify and describe this problem as it appears in a real-life setting.

- Brief a case using the format suggested in the chapter.

- Become familiar with the basic architecture and style of judicial opinions.

[Agencies] have become a veritable fourth branch of government, which has deranged our three-branch legal theories much as the concept of a fourth dimension unsettles our three-dimensional thinking.

JUSTICE ROBERT JACKSON[1]

Robert Jackson, FTC v. Ruberoid Co. - 343 U.S. 470 (1952), U.S Supreme Court.

2.1 DEMOCRACY AND ACCOUNTABILITY

2.1(a) Democracy Defined

An underlying assumption of this text is that "democracy" in the administrative context is desirable. So, what exactly is democracy? It may surprise you to learn that the United States does not employ a purely democratic form of government. The framers of the U.S. Constitution intentionally chose not to create a democracy. Instead, they established a republic.[2] A well-known story is told of Benjamin Franklin. After he exited Independence Hall, the site where the Constitution had been debated and drafted, he was asked by a woman, "Well, Dr. Franklin, do we have a republic or a monarchy?" In reply, he stated, "We have given you a republic—if you can keep it." Democracy, as found in ancient Greece, is a form of direct popular government. The people vote on and, accordingly, directly decide all important issues. A republic, in contrast, is a form of government, as originated in ancient Rome, in which the people elect representatives who make the laws for the people. To most of the framers, indirect lawmaking through representatives was preferable to direct popular lawmaking because they believed that representatives would be less likely to succumb to momentary passions and trends and were more likely to be better educated on the issues than the public at large.

Democratic and republican forms of government share an important feature: The authority to govern rests in the hands of the governed, not in the hands of the governors. The two differ in how that authority is exercised. In a democracy, it is exercised through direct popular vote. In a republic, the people's sovereignty is exercised through their elected representatives. In a republic, accountability of those who govern is checked by periodic elections. Today, the United States can best be characterized as a democratic republic because most laws are made through elected representatives but popular referenda are also used to make law in many jurisdictions. In addition, many jurisdictions provide for direct recall of elected representatives by the people and there is a growing movement of deliberative democracy, a form of democracy where people are involved in the discussions and development of public policy at multiple stages of the law and policy making processes. In deliberative democracy, the role of the people transcends voting and law and governmental decision making is viewed as a community, not solely a legislative, process.[3] Today, the term *democracy*, as it is commonly used, refers to more than the source of lawmaking. It has also become synonymous with the notion that the authorities of government should be limited by fundamental civil liberties and that government officers are accountable for their actions.

In the context of administrative law, this author assumes that keeping administrative officers, who are not elected and who rarely engage citizens in decision-making, accountable is a generally accepted ideal. Congress and the president are accountable through the ballot box. Federal judges are less accountable—as intended by the framers of the Constitution—although they are selected through a democratic process (nomination by the president and confirmation by the Senate), and they may be removed through impeachment (by the House of Representatives) and conviction (by the Senate). Agency officials, however, come to office through an appointment process and, in some instances, they are not directly accountable to the people who appointed them, e.g. president and Congress, after appointed. Furthermore, the authority of the president (or Congress) to remove some administrative officials is limited. Accordingly, much of administrative law is concerned with how to keep the bureaucracy accountable in our democratic republic. As you proceed through this book and your course, consider how the subject you are discussing relates to keeping agencies from becoming too independent, arbitrary, and a threat to freedom. Because the word *democracy* has become a popular way of referring to accountability in government, it is so used in this text.

In 1781, the "Articles of Confederation and Perpetual Union" was adopted as the first written Constitution of the United States. The Articles of Confederation established a government comprised of strong, sovereign states in a "firm league of friendship." Within a few years of its adoption, the loose confederation established by the Articles of Confederation threatened the integrity and survival of the young nation. Hence, an attitude cautiously favoring a stronger national government developed. There remained, however, a fear of centralized power. The framers of the new Constitution, which was drafted in 1787 and became effective in 1789, believed that greater power was needed at the national level to protect the nation and to provide for its general welfare. They also subscribed to the belief that power corrupts and absolute power corrupts absolutely.[4] The resulting Constitution was the framers' attempt to balance the need for the government to have the authority to be effective while protecting individuals from the evils of excessive power. Two structural elements found in the Constitution that are intended to keep any single group or person in government from becoming too powerful are federalism and separation of powers.

2.1(b) Federalism

LEGAL TERMS

Federalism
The division of governmental power between the federal government and state governments.

The Constitution of the United States establishes a federal form of government by recognizing two forms of government: the federal (national) government and the governments of the states.[5] This horizontal division of authority is known as *federalism*. The powers of the federal government are spelled out in the Constitution, but the powers of the states are not. This concerned many people at the time the Constitution was ratified. Fearing that the governments of the states would be subsumed by the federal government, the Tenth Amendment to the Constitution was ratified two years later as part of the original Bill of Rights. The Tenth Amendment reads:

> The powers not delegated to the United States by the Constitution, nor prohibited by it to the States, are reserved to the States respectively, or to the people.

On the surface, the Tenth Amendment appears to establish two discrete zones of authority and one zone of rights. Beginning with the latter, the amendment protects individuals from both state and federal authority in some circumstances. This is also accomplished by the many rights explicitly protected by the Constitution and its amendments. As to the relationship of the states to the federal government, the Constitution is not clear. Two primary theories about the relationship of federal and state authority have been asserted to define the federal–state relationship. The first, which was advocated by James Madison, is *dual federalism*. James Madison said of the relationship between the federal and state governments:

Dual Federalism
A federal system of government where both the federal and state governments are sovereign with different, and occasionally concurrent, jurisdictions.

> The powers delegated by the proposed Constitution to the federal government are few and defined. Those which are to remain in the State governments are numerous and indefinite. The former will be exercised principally on external objects, such as war, peace, negotiation, and foreign commerce; with which last the power of taxation will, for the most part, be connected. The powers reserved to the several States will extend to all the objects which, in the ordinary course of affairs, concern the lives, liberties, and properties of the people, and the internal order, improvement, and prosperity of the State.[6]

From "Alleged Danger From the Powers of the Union to the State Governments Considered" in THE FEDERALIST 45, 313–314, January 26, 1788.

Models of federalism

Model/Theory	State/Federal Relationship	Tenth Amendment	Supreme Court Orientation (examples of periods when dominant)
Dual	Co-sovereigns with federal government limited to enumerated authorities and states possessing all else.	Independent source of state authority. Federal government limited by rights of people and specific authorities of states. Specific federal authorities are construed narrowly.	Taney, pre–New Deal: Burger, Rehnquist, Roberts courts
Hierarchical	Federal government is supreme and state governments have residual authority.	A truism. States have residual authority not held by federal government. Federal authority is expansive.	Marshall Court, post–Civil War, New Deal courts
Cooperative	A relational model more than a structural one, different from the dual and heirarchical models.		

FIGURE 2-1   Summary comparison of dual and hierarchical federalism.

So, to dual federalists, the authority of the federal government is not only limited to those powers specifically listed in the Constitution, but the delegations are narrowly construed, thereby limiting expansions of federal authority. The president, for example, under Article II is commander-in-chief of the military, and under Article I Congress may coin money; regulate interstate, foreign, and Indian commerce; make bankruptcy rules; and declare war. The states possess all other authority, limited by the rights held by the people. The general authority of the states to regulate for the health and welfare of the people is known as the ***police power***. The police power includes the authority to declare crimes, provide for police and fire protection, prosecute criminals, regulate health matters, and regulate most professions. The states also possess the authority to regulate the land and property within their boundaries.

The second theory, advanced by Madison's contemporary, Alexander Hamilton, is ***hierarchical federalism***. This approach positions the federal government as supreme, with the states possessing only the residual powers not claimed by the federal government. As the authority of the federal government expands or contracts, the authority of the states changes in the opposite direction. See Figure 2-1 for a summary comparison of dual and hierarchical federalism.

Because of social, economic, technological, and political change, the jurisdiction of the federal government has expanded considerably since 1789. Several provisions of the Constitution have facilitated this expansion of federal power. Article I, section 8, clause 8 lists many powers of Congress.

LEGAL TERMS

Police Power
The authority of government to regulate for the public welfare. In the United States, the police power generally is held by state governments.

Hierarchical Federalism
A federal system that recognizes both federal and state governments, but where state authority is limited to those authorities not exercised by the federal government or reserved to the people.

SIDEBAR   *Briefing a Case*

Courts often issue judicial opinions or orders after hearing a case. These opinions are published in reports. For example, the opinions of the U.S. Supreme Court are found in the *United States Reports*, and U.S. Courts of Appeals decisions are published in the *Federal Reporter*. These opinions are published to inform the public about judicial interpretations of the law. An opinion normally recites the facts of a case, legal issues raised, applicable law, and court's decision and analysis.

continued

Brief the cases (judicial opinions) that appear in this book. Through the process of briefing, you will increase your understanding of the case while making notes to be used later. There is no one right method for briefing a case, but the author suggests the following. First, read the case. Take no notes at this time; simply get a feel for the case. Second, read the case again and answer the following questions: (1) What are the important and relevant facts of the case? (2) What issue is the court addressing? Said another way, what is the legal problem? (3) What law is the court applying? (4) What is the court's decision, analysis, and rationale? Record your answers.

LEGAL TERMS

Necessary and Proper Clause
Provision found in Article I, § 8, cl. 18 of the federal Constitution. Provides that Congress may enact all laws necessary and proper to carry out Congress's other enumerated powers.

Clause 18 of Article I, section 8 contains the ***necessary and proper clause***. This clause provides that Congress shall have the power to "make all Laws which shall be necessary and proper for carrying into execution" all of its other powers. This Clause recognizes that Congress possesses implied powers. Remember that while the framers of the Constitution intended to create a stronger national government than existed under the Articles of Confederation, most of them also feared the centralization of power. Among them were men like Alexander Hamilton, who favored a stronger national government and advocated for an expansive interpretation of the congressional authority. Thomas Jefferson, on the other hand, was one of many framers who favored a more limited national government and wanted to be clear in Congress's limitations.

A compromise was reached between the two schools of thought. Congress would be limited to the enumerated powers in Article I and to only those unenumerated powers that arise naturally from its enumerated powers. They provided for the extension of enumerated powers as powers *necessary and proper* to execute their expressly granted powers. The earliest example of this was the famous case *McCulloch v. Maryland* in 1819.[7] In *McCulloch,* the Supreme Court upheld Congress's authority to create a national bank even though there is no specific delegation of authority to do this in the Constitution. The Court held that the creation of a national bank was necessary and proper to execute Congress's authority to tax, borrow money, to declare war, and to raise and support armies and navies, all powers enumerated in Article I.

The idea of extending congressional authority beyond the actual language of the Constitution can also be found in the post–Civil War amendments. The Thirteenth Amendment, which forbids slavery, the Fourteenth Amendment, which provides for privileges and immunities, due process, equal protection, and other matters, and the Fifteenth Amendment, which extended the vote to men of all races, all end with a clause providing that "Congress shall have power to enforce this article by appropriate legislation." Most of the authority possessed by federal agencies that enforce civil rights, such as the Equal Employment Opportunity Commission, Department of Education's Office for Civil Rights, and Department of Housing and Urban Development's Office of Fair Housing and Equal Opportunity, springs from these amendments.

Supremacy Clause
Provision found in Article VI of the federal Constitution. Provides that properly enacted federal laws are superior to all state and local laws.

The ***supremacy clause*** is another factor in the growth of federal power. The Supremacy Clause of Article VI provides that federal law shall be the supreme law of the land. Thus, if the federal government has the power to regulate a subject, then all contrary state laws are void and state officials have an obligation to respect and often enforce the federal law. Returning to *McCulloch*, the case ended up in the courts because of a disagreement between the federal government and a state. Maryland, which taxed all businesses in the state, attempted to collect a tax from the national bank. The United States refused to pay it and Maryland sued.

In addition, finding that Congress had the implied authority to create the bank under the Necessary and Proper Clause it held that the Supremacy Clause forbid Maryland from taxing or otherwise interfering with the national bank.

Another provision that has contributed to the growth of federal power is the *commerce clause* of Article I, section 8, clause 3. Under this clause, Congress has the authority to regulate commerce between the states, with foreign nations, and with Indian tribes. The Commerce Clause is frequently invoked by Congress to establish federal jurisdiction.

If read strictly, it would seem to include all commercial activity in the 21st century because few products do not travel in *interstate* commerce. Even fewer are products manufactured using items not manufactured in another state. For most of the 20th century, the Supreme Court's dominant philosophy favored hierarchical federalism, and it appeared that the federal government could regulate any subject, even if not commercial, if some connection to interstate commerce could be established. A good illustration of the breadth of federal power under the Commerce Clause is the 1942 case *Wickard v. Filburn*[8] where a farmer's production of wheat for personal consumption was penalized for exceeding a federal statute that established limits on wheat production. The Court upheld the law under the theory that personal production of wheat substantially impacted wheat prices by keeping growers from purchasing from others in the market. Therefore, the growing of wheat amounted to interstate commerce even though the product never directly entered the channels of commerce.

However, late in the 1990s and early in the new century, the Supreme Court began to shift back to a dual federalism approach, drawing a line over which the federal government could not cross. In 1992, the Supreme Court issued a decision in *City of New York v. United States*.[9] This case involved a federal statute that both provided incentives to the states to provide for the disposal of radioactive waste produced within their borders and, in some instances, required them to so regulate. The Court stated:

> Some truths are so basic that, like the air around us, they are easily overlooked. Much of the Constitution is concerned with setting forth the form of our government, and the courts have traditionally invalidated measures deviating from that form. The result may appear "formalistic" in a given case to partisans of the measure at issue, because such measures are typically the product of the era's perceived necessity. But the Constitution protects us from our own best intentions: It divides power among sovereigns and among branches of government precisely so that we may resist the temptation to concentrate power in one location as an expedient solution to the crisis of the day. The shortage of disposal sites for radioactive waste is a pressing national problem, but a judiciary that licensed extraconstitutional government with each issue of comparable gravity would, in the long run, be far worse.
>
> States are not mere political subdivisions of the United States. State governments are neither regional offices nor administrative agencies of the federal government. The positions occupied by state officials appear nowhere on the federal government's most detailed organizational chart. The Constitution instead "leaves to the several States a residuary and inviolable sovereignty," reserved explicitly to the states by the Tenth Amendment.
>
> Whatever the outer limits of that sovereignty may be, one thing is clear: The federal government may not compel the states to enact or administer a federal regulatory program.[10]

The Court reviewed another federalism case three years later in *United States v. Lopez*.[11] This law made it a crime to possess a gun in or around schools.

LEGAL TERM

Commerce Clause
Provision found in Article I, § 8, cl. 3 of the federal Constitution. States that Congress has the power to regulate interstate commerce, commerce with foreign nations, and commerce with Indian tribes.

The federal Gun-Free School Zone Act was challenged in the *Lopez* case as exceeding the scope of Congress's power under the Commerce Clause. The government contended that it had jurisdiction because gun violence affects interstate commerce. The United States claimed, for example, that gun violence reduced the interest of citizens to travel to "unsafe" areas. The Court rejected this jurisdictional claim, finding that the law had no connection to interstate commerce. This, the Court held, was a policy area the states may regulate but not the federal government.

The Court heard yet another federalism case in 1997. In *Printz v. United States*,[12] a federal statute, the Brady Handgun Violence Protection Act (BHVPA), was invalidated for the same reason as the Gun-Free School Zone Act. The BHVPA required the federal government to establish a system for conducting background checks on gun buyers. In addition, it commanded local police agencies to conduct these checks until the federal system became operational. Again, the Supreme Court held the line between state and federal sovereignty, holding that local officials can't be co-opted by the federal government. Additionally, the Court found the scheme in violation of the separation of powers because it delegated an executive function to officials who do not report to, or through a chain to, the president. The Court addressed the issue again in two 2000 cases, *United States v. Jones* and *United States v. Morrison*.[13]

In *Jones,* the Supreme Court invalidated the extension of federal jurisdiction to the bombing of a home in Indiana. Federal statute made it a crime to commit arson on any building used in interstate commerce or on a building where activities occur that affect interstate commerce. The United States asserted jurisdiction over the arson because the mortgage for the home, the homeowners' insurance, and the natural gas used to heat the home were all purchased from companies outside of Indiana. The Supreme Court rejected these as establishing federal jurisdiction, holding that if it "were we to adopt the Government's expansive interpretation of [the federal arson statute], hardly a building in the land would fall outside the federal statute's domain." The Court reached a similar conclusion in *Morrison.*

United States v. Morrison

529 U.S. 598 (2000)

In these cases we consider the constitutionality of 42 U.S.C. § 13981, which provides a federal civil remedy for the victims of gender-motivated violence. The United States Court of Appeals for the Fourth Circuit, sitting en banc, struck down § 13981 because it concluded that Congress lacked constitutional authority to enact the section's civil remedy. Believing that these cases are controlled by our decisions in *United States v. Lopez*, 514 U.S. 549 (1995), *United States v. Harris*, 106 U.S. 629 (1883), and the *In re Civil Rights Cases*, 109 U.S. 3 (1883), we affirm.

Petitioner Christy Brzonkala enrolled at Virginia Polytechnic Institute (Virginia Tech) in the fall of 1994. In September of that year, Brzonkala met respondents Antonio Morrison and James Crawford, who were both students at Virginia Tech and members of its varsity football team.

Brzonkala alleges that, within 30 minutes of meeting Morrison and Crawford, they assaulted and repeatedly raped her. After the attack, Morrison allegedly told Brzonkala, "You better not have any . . . diseases." In the months following the rape, Morrison also allegedly announced in the dormitory's dining room that he "like[d] to get girls drunk and. . . ." The omitted portions, quoted verbatim in the briefs on file with this Court, consist of boasting, debased remarks about what Morrison would do to women, and vulgar remarks that cannot fail to shock and offend.

Brzonkala alleges that this attack caused her to become severely emotionally disturbed and depressed. She sought assistance from a university psychiatrist, who prescribed antidepressant medication. Shortly after the rape Brzonkala stopped attending classes and withdrew from the university. . . .

In December 1995, Brzonkala sued Morrison, Crawford, and Virginia Tech in the United States District Court for the Western District of Virginia. Her complaint alleged that Morrison's and Crawford's attack violated § 13981 and that Virginia Tech's handling of her complaint violated Title IX of the Education Amendments of 1972, 86 Stat. 373–375, 20 U.S.C. §§ 1681–1688. Morrison and Crawford moved to dismiss this complaint on the grounds that it failed to state a claim and that § 13981's civil remedy is unconstitutional. The United States intervened to defend § 13981's constitutionality. . . .

Section 13981 was part of the Violence Against Women Act of 1994, § 40302, 108 Stat. 1941–1942. It states that "[a]ll persons within the United States shall have the right to be free from crimes of violence motivated by gender." 42 U.S.C. § 13981(b). To enforce that right, subsection (c) declares:

> A person (including a person who acts under color of any statute, ordinance, regulation, custom, or usage of any State) who commits a crime of violence motivated by gender and thus deprives another of the right declared in subsection (b) of this section shall be liable to the party injured, in an action for the recovery of compensatory and punitive damages, injunctive and declaratory relief, and such other relief as a court may deem appropriate.

* * * *

Every law enacted by Congress must be based on one or more of its powers enumerated in the Constitution. "The powers of the legislature are defined and limited; and that those limits may not be mistaken or forgotten, the constitution is written."*Marbury v. Madison*, 1 Cranch 137, 176 (1803) (Marshall, C.J.). Congress explicitly identified the sources of federal authority on which it relied in enacting § 13981. It said that a "federal civil rights cause of action" is established "[p]ursuant to the affirmative power of Congress . . . under section 5 of the Fourteenth Amendment to the Constitution, as well as under section 8 of Article I of the Constitution." 42 U.S.C. § 13981(a). We address Congress' authority to enact this remedy under each of these constitutional provisions in turn.

[The Court discussed *Lopez* and its other cases concerning the economic or commercial aspect of the Commerce Clause.] With these principles underlying our Commerce Clause jurisprudence as reference points, the proper resolution of the present cases is clear. Gender-motivated crimes of violence are not, in any sense of the phrase, economic activity. While we need not adopt a categorical rule against aggregating the effects of any noneconomic activity in order to decide these cases, thus far in our Nation's history our cases have upheld Commerce Clause regulation of intrastate activity only where that activity is economic in nature.

We accordingly reject the argument that Congress may regulate noneconomic, violent criminal conduct based solely on that conduct's aggregate effect on interstate commerce. The Constitution requires a distinction between what is truly national and what is truly local. *Lopez*, 514 U.S., at 568 (citing *Jones & Laughlin Steel*, 301 U.S., at 30). In recognizing this fact we preserve one of the few principles that has been consistent since the Clause was adopted. The regulation and punishment of intrastate violence that is not directed at the instrumentalities, channels, or goods involved in interstate commerce has always been the province of the States. . . .

Because we conclude that the Commerce Clause does not provide Congress with authority to enact § 13981, we address petitioners' alternative argument that the section's civil remedy should be upheld as an exercise of Congress' remedial power under § 5 of the Fourteenth Amendment. As noted above, Congress expressly invoked the Fourteenth Amendment as a source of authority to enact § 13981. [The Court concluded by also rejecting Brzonkala's Fourteenth Amendment claim. Accordingly, the provisions of the statute establishing a federal civil cause of action were stricken.]

In yet another decision favoring state authority, the Supreme Court struck down a federal rule making it a crime for a physician to assist a terminally ill patient in committing suicide when Oregon had authorized the practice in *Gonzales v. Oregon.*

Gonzales v. Oregon

546 U.S. 243 (2006)

Justice Kennedy delivered the opinion of the Court.

The question before us is whether the Controlled Substances Act allows the United States Attorney General to prohibit doctors from prescribing regulated drugs for use in physician-assisted suicide, notwithstanding a state law permitting the procedure. As the Court has observed, "Americans are engaged in an earnest and profound debate about the morality, legality, and practicality of physician-assisted suicide." *Washington v. Glucksberg,* 521 US. 702, 735 (1997). The dispute before us is in part a product of this political and moral debate, but its resolution requires an inquiry familiar to the courts: interpreting a federal statute to determine whether executive action is authorized by, or otherwise consistent with, the enactment.

In 1994, Oregon became the first State to legalize assisted suicide when voters approved a ballot measure enacting the Oregon Death With Dignity Act (ODWDA). ODWDA, which survived a 1997 ballot measure seeking its repeal, exempts from civil or criminal liability state-licensed physicians who, in compliance with the specific safeguards in ODWDA, dispense or prescribe a lethal dose of drugs upon the request of a terminally ill patient.

The drugs Oregon physicians prescribe under ODWDA are regulated under a federal statute, the Controlled Substances Act (CSA or Act). The CSA allows these particular drugs to be available only by a written prescription from a registered physician. In the ordinary course the same drugs are prescribed in smaller doses for pain alleviation.

A November 9, 2001, Interpretive Rule issued by the Attorney General addresses the implementation and enforcement of the CSA with respect to ODWDA. It determines that using controlled substances to assist suicide is not a legitimate medical practice and that dispensing or prescribing them for this purpose is unlawful under the CSA. The Interpretive Rule's validity under the CSA is the issue before us. . . .

In deciding whether the CSA can be read as prohibiting physician-assisted suicide, we look to the statute's text and design. The statute and our case law amply support the conclusion that Congress regulates medical practice insofar as it bars doctors from using their prescription-writing powers as a means to engage in illicit drug dealing and trafficking as conventionally understood. Beyond this, however, the statute manifests no intent to regulate the practice of medicine generally. The silence is understandable given the structure and limitations of federalism, which allow the States " 'great latitude under their police powers to legislate as to the protection of the lives, limbs, health, comfort, and quiet of all persons.' " *Medtronic, Inc. v. Lohr,* 518 US 470, 475 (1996) (quoting *Metropolitan Life Ins. Co. v. Massachusetts,* 471 US 724, 756 [1985]).

The structure and operation of the CSA presume and rely upon a functioning medical profession regulated under the States' police powers. The Attorney General can register a physician to dispense controlled substances "if the applicant is authorized to dispense . . . controlled substances under the laws of the State in which he practices." When considering whether to revoke a physician's registration, the Attorney General looks not just to violations of federal drug laws; but he "shall" also consider "[t]he recommendation of the appropriate state licensing board or professional disciplinary authority" and the registrant's compliance with state and local drug laws. The very definition of a "practitioner" eligible to prescribe includes physicians "licensed, registered, or otherwise permitted, by the United States or the jurisdiction in which he practices" to dispense controlled substances. §802(21). Further cautioning against the conclusion that the CSA effectively displaces the States' general regulation of medical practice is the Act's pre-emption provision, which indicates that, absent a positive conflict, none of the Act's provisions should be "construed as indicating an intent on the part of the Congress to occupy the field in which that provision operates . . . to the exclusion of any State law on the same subject matter which would otherwise be within the authority of the State."

Oregon's regime is an example of the state regulation of medical practice that the CSA presupposes. Rather than simply decriminalizing assisted suicide, ODWDA limits its exercise to the attending physicians of terminally ill patients, physicians who must be licensed by Oregon's Board of Medical Examiners. The statute gives attending physicians a central role, requiring them to provide prognoses and prescriptions, give information about palliative alternatives and counseling, and ensure patients are competent and acting voluntarily. Any eligible patient must also get a second opinion from another registered physician, and the statute's safeguards require physicians to keep and submit to inspection detailed records of their actions.

Even though regulation of health and safety is "primarily, and historically, a matter of local concern," *Hillsborough County v. Automated Medical Laboratories, Inc.*, 471 U.S. 707, 719 (1985), there is no question that the Federal Government can set uniform national standards in these areas. See Raich. . . . In connection to the CSA, however, we find only one area in which Congress set general, uniform standards of medical practice. Title I of the Comprehensive Drug Abuse Prevention and Control Act of 1970, of which the CSA was Title II, provides that

> "[The Secretary], after consultation with the Attorney General and with national organizations representative of persons with knowledge and experience in the treatment of narcotic addicts, shall determine the appropriate methods of professional practice in the medical treatment of the narcotic addiction of various classes of narcotic addicts, and shall report thereon from time to time to the Congress."
>
> "United States Code", 42 USC § 290bb–2a -
> Medical treatment of narcotics addiction; report to Congress

This provision strengthens the understanding of the CSA as a statute combating recreational drug abuse, and also indicates that when Congress wants to regulate medical practice in the given scheme, it does so by explicit language in the statute.

In the face of the CSA's silence on the practice of medicine generally, and its recognition of state regulation of the medical profession, it is difficult to defend the Attorney General's declaration that the statute impliedly criminalizes physician-assisted suicide. . . .

Although the Court did not foreclose the possibility of federal regulation in *Gonzales v. Oregon*, it made it clear that in respect for federalism principles, congressional intent to regulate a historic state area is not to be lightly inferred.

In spite of these limitations, the jurisdiction of the federal government continues to deepen and broaden. A case involving the late Ernest Hemingway, author of many great books including *For Whom the Bell Tolls* and *The Old Man and the Sea*, and cats is an example. Hemingway's home in Key West, Florida is today a museum operated by his descendants. In addition to housing Hemingway's typewriter and other artifacts, the property is alive with cats, polydactyl, or six- and seven-toed, cats. Story has it that the cats are descendants of Snowball, a polydactyl cat owned by Hemingway. In 2003 a volunteer at the Museum complained about the treatment of the cats after one wandered beyond the walls of the museum. This is when the federal government stepped in. The United States Department of Agriculture

(USDA) is responsible for administering the Animal Welfare Act, a law intended to protect the welfare of animals used in circuses and traveling exhibitions. The USDA asserted jurisdiction over the situation because the cats were used in advertising, cat memorabilia was sold, and the use of the cats met the definition of being an exhibit under the law. USDA inspectors investigated and concluded that the museum must obtain an exhibition license and that the cats needed protection, even though by all accounts the cats lived a pampered life. Indeed an investigator from the People for the Ethical Treatment of Animals (PETA) who was hired by the USDA wrote "[w]hat I found was a bunch of fat, happy and relaxed cats. God save the cats."[14] The USDA demanded that the museum erect a higher fence, install electric wire, or in the alternative, hire a night watchperson to ensure the cats don't leave the property. The inspectors also demanded that the museum provide the cats with separate cages for sleeping and elevated resting surfaces. The museum resisted the exercise of federal authority. The USDA won at the trial level and again before the Eleventh Circuit Court of Appeals, subjecting the cats to federal authority.

907 Whitehead Street, Inc., d.b.a. Ernest Hemingway Home and Museum v. Secretary of the U.S. Department of Agriculture 11th Circuit Court of Appeals (2012)

* * *

[The museum first argued that the USDA Secretary misinterpreted the Animal Welfare Act to give the USDA authority over intrastate, fixed-site exhibitions.]

The Secretary's reasonable and consistent interpretation of "exhibitor" as articulated in Good is entitled to Chevron deference. . . .

But when "the statute is silent or ambiguous with respect to the specific issue," and an administrating agency has interpreted the statute, courts are bound to show deference to the agency's reasonable interpretation, so long as it is not "arbitrary, capricious, or manifestly contrary to the statute." The statute is ambiguous on the question whether "distribution" includes the display of animals by a fixed-site commercial enterprise. And, given Congress's intent to regulate zoos, which are notably stationary and which could potentially exhibit animals that are neither purchased nor transported in commerce, we cannot see how the Secretary's interpretation of "exhibitor" is unreasonable. The Museum makes no attempt to explain why that interpretation is not entitled to Chevron deference.

Based on this reasonable interpretation to which we accord deference, the district court correctly found that the Museum qualifies as an animal exhibitor under the AWA. . . .

We must now address whether the regulation of the Museum and its Hemingway cats exceeds Congress's authority under its power "[t]o regulate Commerce among the several States." U.S. Const. Art. I, § 8, cl. 3. The Commerce Clause authorizes Congress to regulate "the channels of interstate commerce, persons or things in interstate commerce, and those activities that substantially affect interstate commerce." This case involves only the final object of Congress's commerce jurisdiction because the Hemingway cats themselves are neither channels of interstate commerce nor things in interstate commerce.

We conclude that the Museum's exhibition of the cats substantially affects interstate commerce. The Museum argues that its activities are of a purely local nature because the Hemingway cats spend their entire lives at the Museum—the cats are never purchased, never sold, and never travel beyond 907 Whitehead Street. But the local character of an activity does not necessarily exempt it from federal regulation. "[W]hen a general regulatory statute bears a substantial relation to commerce, the de minimis character of individual instances arising under that statute is of no consequence." *Gonzales v. Raich*, see also *Wickard v. Filburn*, . . . And it is well-settled that, when local businesses solicit out-of-state tourists, they engage in activity affecting interstate commerce. The Museum invites and receives thousands of admission-paying visitors from beyond Florida, many of whom are drawn by the Museum's reputation for and purposeful marketing of the Hemingway cats. The exhibition of the Hemingway cats is integral to the Museum's commercial purpose, and thus, their exhibition affects interstate commerce. For these reasons, Congress has the power to regulate the Museum and the exhibition of the Hemingway cats via the AWA.

Notwithstanding our holding, we appreciate the Museum's somewhat unique situation, and we sympathize with its frustration. Nevertheless, it is not the court's role to evaluate the wisdom of federal regulations implemented according to the powers constitutionally vested in Congress. Therefore, we affirm the judgment of the district court in favor of the USDA.

907 Whitehead Street, Inc., d.b.a. Ernest Hemingway Home and
Museum v. Secretary of the U.S. Department of Agriculture, 11th Circuit Court
of Appeals 2012),United States District Court for the Southern District of Florida.

The limits of federal regulatory authority were again tested by the Patient Protection and Affordable Care Act of 2010 (PPACA) and its companion statute, the Health Care and Education Reconciliation Act of 2010. This legislation is commonly known as Obamacare because it was a vital part of President Barack Obama's policy agenda. PPACA, a bill of more than 2,400 pages, represented the largest social welfare and regulatory change since the creation of Social Security in the 1930s.

The laws include an expansion of health coverage to millions of previously uninsured people through an enlargement of Medicaid and other programs, incentives for employers to provide insurance for their employees, the creation of "health exchanges" where the uninsured can obtain coverage, subsidies for people who can't afford insurance, providing insurance regardless of pre-existing conditions, mandatory insurance coverage for the individual (commonly referred to as the *individual mandate*), longer periods before generic drugs may be introduced into the market, financial support for medical research, and various taxes and fees on high-income individuals, tanning parlors, and medical and pharmaceutical companies.

Enforcement and execution of this initiative is a huge undertaking. Most analysts agree that more than 100 new agencies, boards, commissions, offices, and other entities will be created and thousands of new federal and state employees will be hired to implement the law.

Many agencies will be involved (e.g., Internal Revenue Service, Department of Labor) but it is the U.S. Department of Health and Human Services (HHS) that will bear primary responsibility for implementation and oversight of the PPACA. By 2013, HHS had planned to create several new agencies, offices, and boards, including an Office of Consumer Information and Insurance Oversight, Office of Insurance Programs, Office of Oversight, Office of Health Insurance Exchanges, Office of Consumer Support, Independent Payment Advisory Board, Innovation Center, and Patient-Centered Outcomes Research Institute. New rules are also needed. Indeed, the Internal Revenue Service, Department of Labor, and HHS have already promulgated their first sets of regulations.

No initiative so large can go unchallenged, politically and legally. Those opposed to the law promised its repeal if President Obama lost his bid for reelection. But he won a second term and it is unlikely the law will be repealed. The first legal challenges to the law were filed the day President Obama signed the law and they came from the states. Eventually a total of 26 states would join in a lawsuit seeking to enjoin the United States from enforcing several provisions of the law, including Congress's assertion of jurisdiction. Several private parties filed separate actions also challenging congressional authority and the individual mandate. The cases made their way to the Supreme Court where they were consolidated and given over five hours of oral arguments, an unusually long period in the recent history of the Court.[15] The Court issued its decision in a case entitled *National Federation of Independent Business v. Sebelius.*

National Federation of Independent Business v. Sebelius

567 U.S. (2012)

Today we resolve constitutional challenges to two provisions of the Patient Protection and Affordable Care Act of 2010: the individual mandate, which requires individuals to purchase a health insurance policy providing a minimum level of coverage; and the Medicaid expansion, which gives funds to the States on the condition that they provide specified health care to all citizens whose income falls below a certain threshold. We do not consider whether the Act embodies sound policies. That judgment is entrusted to the Nation's elected leaders. We ask only whether Congress has the power under the Constitution to enact the challenged provisions. . . .

In our federal system, the National Government possesses only limited powers; the States and the people retain the remainder. Nearly two centuries ago, Chief Justice Marshall observed that "the question respecting the extent of the powers actually granted" to the Federal Government "is perpetually arising, and will probably continue to arise, as long as our system shall exist." *McCulloch v. Maryland*, 4 Wheat. 316, 405 (1819). In this case we must again determine whether the Constitution grants Congress powers it now asserts, but which many States and individuals believe it does not possess. Resolving this controversy requires us to examine both the limits of the Government's power, and our own limited role in policing those boundaries.

The Federal Government "is acknowledged by all to be one of enumerated powers." That is, rather than granting general authority to perform all the conceivable functions of government, the Constitution lists, or enumerates, the Federal Government's powers. Congress may, for example, "coin Money," "establish Post Offices," and "raise and support Armies." Art.I, §8, cls.5, 7, 12. The enumeration of powers is also a limitation of powers, because "[t]he enumeration presupposes something not enumerated." *Gibbons v. Ogden*, 9 Wheat. 1, 195 (1824). The Constitution's express conferral of some powers makes clear that it does not grant others. And the Federal Government "can exercise only the powers granted to it." *McCulloch*, supra, at 405.

Today, the restrictions on government power foremost in many Americans' minds are likely to be affirmative prohibitions, such as contained in the Bill of Rights. These affirmative prohibitions come into play, however, only where the Government possesses authority to act in the first place. If no enumerated power authorizes Congress to pass a certain law, that law may not be enacted, even if it would not violate any of the express prohibitions in the Bill of Rights or elsewhere in the Constitution. . . .

The same does not apply to the States, because the Constitution is not the source of their power. The Constitution may restrict state governments—as it does, for example, by forbidding them to deny any person the equal protection of the laws. But where such prohibitions do not apply, state governments do not need constitutional authorization to act. The States thus can and do perform many of the vital functions of modern government—punishing street crime, running public schools, and zoning property for development, to name but a few—even though the

Constitution's text does not authorize any government to do so. Our cases refer to this general power of governing, possessed by the States but not by the Federal Government, as the "police power." . . .

This case concerns two powers that the Constitution does grant the Federal Government, but which must be read carefully to avoid creating a general federal authority akin to the police power. The Constitution authorizes Congress to "regulate Commerce with foreign Nations, and among the several States, and with the Indian Tribes." Art.I, §8, cl.3. Our precedents read that to mean that Congress may regulate "the channels of interstate commerce," "persons or things in interstate commerce," and "those activities that substantially affect interstate commerce." The power over activities that substantially affect interstate commerce can be expansive. That power has been held to authorize federal regulation of such seemingly local matters as a farmer's decision to grow wheat for himself and his livestock, and a loan shark's extortionate collections from a neighborhood butcher shop.

Congress may also "lay and collect Taxes, Duties, Imposts and Excises, to pay the Debts and provide for the common Defence and general Welfare of the United States." U.S. Const., Art.I, §8, cl.1. Put simply, Congress may tax and spend. This grant gives the Federal Government considerable influence even in areas where it cannot directly regulate. The Federal Government may enact a tax on an activity that it cannot authorize, forbid, or otherwise control. And in exercising its spending power, Congress may offer funds to the States, and may condition those offers on compliance with specified conditions.

The reach of the Federal Government's enumerated powers is broader still because the Constitution authorizes Congress to "make all Laws which shall be necessary and proper for carrying into Execution the foregoing Powers." Art.I, §8, cl.18. . . .

Our permissive reading of these powers is explained in part by a general reticence to invalidate the acts of the Nation's elected leaders. "Proper respect for a co-ordinate branch of the government" requires that we strike down an Act of Congress only if "the lack of constitutional authority to pass [the] act in question is clearly demonstrated." . . .

Our deference in matters of policy cannot, however, become abdication in matters of law. "The powers of the legislature are defined and limited; and that those limits may not be mistaken, or forgotten, the constitution is written." *Marbury v. Madison* . . ..

The individual mandate requires most Americans to maintain "minimum essential" health insurance coverage. The mandate does not apply to some individuals, such as prisoners and undocumented aliens. §5000A(d). Many individuals will receive the required coverage through their employer, or from a government program such as Medicaid or Medicare. But for individuals who are not exempt and do not receive health insurance through a third party, the means of satisfying the requirement is to purchase insurance from a private company.

Beginning in 2014, those who do not comply with the mandate must make a "[s]hared responsibility payment" to the Federal Government. That payment, which the Act describes as a "penalty," is calculated as a percentage of household income, subject to a floor based on a specified dollar amount and a ceiling based on the average annual premium the individual would have to pay for qualifying private health insurance. In 2016, for example, the penalty will be 2.5 percent of an individual's household income, but no less than $695 and no more than the average yearly premium for insurance that covers 60 percent of the cost of 10 specified services (e.g., prescription drugs and hospitalization). The Act provides that the penalty will be paid to the Internal Revenue Service with an individual's taxes, and "shall be assessed and collected in the same manner" as tax penalties, such as the penalty for claiming too large an income tax refund. The Act, however, bars the IRS from using several of its normal enforcement tools, such as criminal prosecutions and levies. And some individuals who are subject to the mandate are nonetheless exempt from the penalty—for example, those with income below a certain threshold and members of Indian tribes. . . .

continued

[Florida and other states challenged Congress' authority under Article I enact the provision. The federal trial court agreed, determined that the individual mandate could not be severed from the remainder of the Act, and therefore invalidated the law. The Court of Appeals for the Eleventh Circuit affirmed the trial court's conclusion that Congress exceeded its authority but reversed on the severance issue. Several other courts heard challenges to the mandate and their decisions varied.]

The Government advances two theories for the proposition that Congress had constitutional authority to enact the individual mandate. First, the Government argues that Congress had the power to enact the mandate under the Commerce Clause. . . .Second, the Government argues that if the commerce power does not support the mandate, we should nonetheless uphold it as an exercise of Congress's power to tax. . . .

The Government's first argument is that the individual mandate is a valid exercise of Congress's power under the Commerce Clause and the Necessary and Proper Clause. According to the Government, the health care market is characterized by a significant cost-shifting problem. Everyone will eventually need health care at a time and to an extent they cannot predict, but if they do not have insurance, they often will not be able to pay for it. Because state and federal laws nonetheless require hospitals to provide a certain degree of care to individuals without regard to their ability to pay, hospitals end up receiving compensation for only a portion of the services they provide. To recoup the losses, hospitals pass on the cost to insurers through higher rates, and insurers, in turn, pass on the cost to policy holders in the form of higher premiums. Congress estimated that the cost of uncompensated care raises family health insurance premiums, on average, by over $1,000 per year. . . .

The individual mandate was Congress's solution to these problems. By requiring that individuals purchase health insurance, the mandate prevents cost-shifting by those who would otherwise go without it. In addition, the mandate forces into the insurance risk pool more healthy individuals, whose premiums on average will be higher than their health care expenses. This allows insurers to subsidize the costs of covering the unhealthy individuals the reforms require them to accept. The Government claims that Congress has power under the Commerce and Necessary and Proper Clauses to enact this solution. . . .

As expansive as our cases construing the scope of the commerce power have been, they all have one thing in common: They uniformly describe the power as reaching "activity." . . .

The individual mandate, however, does not regulate existing commercial activity. It instead compels individuals to become active in commerce by purchasing a product, on the ground that their failure to do so affects interstate commerce. Construing the Commerce Clause to permit Congress to regulate individuals precisely because they are doing nothing would open a new and potentially vast domain to congressional authority. Every day individuals do not do an infinite number of things. In some cases they decide not to do something; in others they simply fail to do it. Allowing Congress to justify federal regulation by pointing to the effect of inaction on commerce would bring countless decisions individuals could potentially make within the scope of federal regulation, and—under the Government's theory—empower Congress to make those decisions for them.

Wickard has long been regarded as "perhaps the most far reaching example of Commerce Clause authority over intrastate activity," *Lopez*, 514 U.S., at 560, but the Government's theory in this case would go much further. Under *Wickard* it is within Congress's power to regulate the market for wheat by supporting its price. But price can be supported by increasing demand as well as by decreasing supply. The aggregated decisions of some consumers not to purchase wheat have a substantial effect on the price of wheat, just as decisions not to purchase health insurance have on the price of insurance. Congress can therefore command that those not buying wheat do so, just as it argues here that it may command that those not buying health insurance do so. The farmer in *Wickard* was at least actively engaged in the production of wheat, and the Government could regulate that activity because of its effect on commerce. The Government's theory here would effectively override that limitation, by establishing that individuals may be regulated under the Commerce Clause whenever enough of them are not doing something the Government would have them do. . . .

Indeed, the Government's logic would justify a mandatory purchase to solve almost any problem. To consider a different example in the health care market, many Americans do not eat a balanced diet. That group makes up a larger percentage of the total population than those without health insurance. The failure of that group to have a healthy diet increases health care costs, to a greater extent than the failure of the uninsured to purchase insurance. Those increased costs are borne in part by other Americans who must pay more, just as the uninsured shift costs to the insured. Congress addressed the insurance problem by ordering everyone to buy insurance. Under the Government's theory, Congress could address the diet problem by ordering everyone to buy vegetables.

People, for reasons of their own, often fail to do things that would be good for them or good for society. Those failures—joined with the similar failures of others— can readily have a substantial effect on interstate commerce. Under the Government's logic, that authorizes Congress to use its commerce power to compel citizens to act as the Government would have them act.

That is not the country the Framers of our Constitution envisioned. James Madison explained that the Commerce Clause was "an addition which few oppose and from which no apprehensions are entertained." *The Federalist* No.45, at 293. While Congress's authority under the Commerce Clause has of course expanded with the growth of the national economy, our cases have "always recognized that the power to regulate commerce, though broad indeed, has limits." The Government's theory would erode those limits, permitting Congress to reach beyond the natural extent of its authority, "everywhere extending the sphere of its activity and drawing all power into its impetuous vortex." *The Federalist* No.48, at 309 (J. Madison). Congress already enjoys vast power to regulate much of what we do. Accepting the Government's theory would give Congress the same license to regulate what we do not do, fundamentally changing the relation between the citizen and the Federal Government.

The proposition that Congress may dictate the conduct of an individual today because of prophesied future activity finds no support in our precedent. We have said that Congress can anticipate the effects on commerce of an economic activity. But we have never permitted Congress to anticipate that activity itself in order to regulate individuals not currently engaged in commerce. Each one of our cases . . . involved preexisting economic activity.

Everyone will likely participate in the markets for food, clothing, transportation, shelter, or energy; that does not authorize Congress to direct them to purchase particular products in those or other markets today. The Commerce Clause is not a general license to regulate individuals from cradle to grave, simply because they will predictably engage in particular transactions. Any police power to regulate individuals as such, as opposed to their activities, remains vested in the States. . . .

Just as the individual mandate cannot be sustained as a law regulating the substantial effects of the failure to purchase health insurance, neither can it be upheld as a "necessary and proper" component of the insurance reforms. The commerce power thus does not authorize the mandate. . . .

The Government's tax power argument asks us to view the statute differently than we did in considering its commerce power theory. In making its Commerce Clause argument, the Government defended the mandate as a regulation requiring individuals to purchase health insurance. The Government does not claim that the taxing power allows Congress to issue such a command. Instead, the Government asks us to read the mandate not as ordering individuals to buy insurance, but rather as imposing a tax on those who do not buy that product. . . .

continued

> Congress's authority under the taxing power is limited to requiring an individual to pay money into the Federal Treasury, no more. If a tax is properly paid, the Government has no power to compel or punish individuals subject to it. We do not make light of the severe burden that taxation—especially taxation motivated by a regulatory purpose—can impose. But imposition of a tax nonetheless leaves an individual with a lawful choice to do or not do a certain act, so long as he is willing to pay a tax levied on that choice.
>
> The Affordable Care Act's requirement that certain individuals pay a financial penalty for not obtaining health insurance may reasonably be characterized as a tax. Because the Constitution permits such a tax, it is not our role to forbid it, or to pass upon its wisdom or fairness.

National Federation of Independent Business v. Sebelius (2012),
648 F. 3d 1235,Supreme Court of United States.

Not only has the jurisdiction of the federal government increased, but so has its ability to coerce the states into adopting policies or laws in areas over which the federal government has no jurisdiction. The federal government does this by attaching conditions to subsidies and other appropriations awarded to the states. For example, when the federal government wanted to impose a nationwide 55-mile-an-hour speed limit, it accomplished this by threatening to withhold funding from states that did not adopt the 55-mile-an-hour limit.

Although this tactic is denounced by states' rights advocates as encroaching upon the sovereignty of the states, it is also proof of the powers held by the states. States' rights advocates contend that the federal government is not providing incentives but is engaging in economic coercion because the states have become dependent upon the federal government for revenues.

In addition to exclusively held powers, there are areas in which both governments may regulate; said another way, they have *concurrent jurisdiction* over such matters. The lines of power between the federal and state governments are not always clear. See Figure 2-2 for examples of state, federal, and concurrently held powers.

Exclusive Federal Powers	Exclusive State Powers	Concurrent Powers
Post Office	General Health and Welfare	Taxation
Foreign Diplomacy	Police and Fire Protection	Chartering Banks
Making Treaties	Licensing Most Professions	Constructing Roads
Regulating Naturalization	Providing Education	Borrowing Money
Regulating Immigration and Emigration		Punishing Crime
Regulating Bankruptcy		

Powers Denied to Both

Ex Post Facto Laws
Bills of Attainder
Other Encroachments of Civil Rights Protected by the Constitution

FIGURE 2-2   Examples of federal, state, and concurrent powers.

If concurrent jurisdiction exists over a subject, then both the federal government and the states may regulate. However, if a state law is in conflict with federal law, it fails because Article VI declares that "This Constitution, and the laws of the United States which shall be made in pursuance thereof; and all treaties made, or which shall be made, under the authority of the United States, shall be the supreme law of the land; and the judges in every state shall be bound thereby, anything in the Constitution or laws of any State to the contrary notwithstanding." Further, there are circumstances where the federal government is said to have excluded state regulation of the subject. This is known as the ***preemption doctrine***. If preempted, states are forbidden from regulating. There are three instances where preemption exists:

1. When Congress expressly preempts the states from regulating.
2. When a state law is inconsistent with federal law.
3. When Congress has enacted a comprehensive scheme of regulation over a subject.

Of course, federal authority must exist. Congress cannot declare jurisdiction where none exists. The inverse of preemption can also occur. That is, Congress can endorse state regulation of a subject where concurrent jurisdiction exists.

An example of direct preemption can be found in the 2008 Supreme Court case *Rowe v. New Hampshire Motor Transport Association*. In the late 1970s and early 1980s, the United States adopted a policy of deregulation of the airline and motor carrier industries. Congress's rationale for the deregulation was that better prices and improved service would result from a free market approach in both industries. To prevent the states from undermining the effort by regulating the industries themselves, the statutes that deregulated the industries provided that "no State . . . shall enact or enforce any law . . . relating to rates, routes, or services of any air carrier." In 2003, Maine enacted a statute intended to regulate the sales of, and to prevent teen use of, tobacco products. Although the intention of the law was not to regulate the trucking industry generally, its provisions that regulated the transport and delivery of tobacco products were held, by unanimous vote, to be preempted by the plain language of the federal statute. This is true even if the state possesses the authority, as it claimed, to prohibit all shipments and sale of tobacco products within its border.

The Supreme Court handed down three other preemption cases in 2008. In *Riegel v. Medtronic, Inc.*, 552 U.S. 312 (2008), a federal law governing medical devices that preempted state tort law actions for injuries resulting from the medical devices was upheld. In *Altria Group v. Good*, 555 U.S. 70 (2008) the Supreme Court held that the federal government's extensive regulation of tobacco, including an express preemption of state labeling and warning requirements about smoking and health, didn't preempt a state law tort claim for fraudulent advertising by a tobacco company. The television personality Judge Alex was a party to the third case, *Preston v. Ferrer*.

LEGAL TERM
Preemption Doctrine
Pursuant to the Supremacy Clause, some subjects may be exclusively federal even though concurrent jurisdiction initially existed because of their national character. Preemption may occur expressly or implicitly through comprehensive federal regulation of the subject.

Preston v. Ferrer

552 U.S. 346 (2008)

[T]he Federal Arbitration Act (FAA or Act), 9 U.S.C. §1 *et seq.* (2000 ed. and Supp. V), establishes a national policy favoring arbitration when the parties contract for that mode of dispute resolution. The Act, which rests on Congress's authority under the Commerce Clause, supplies not simply a procedural framework applicable in federal courts; it also calls for the application, in state as well as federal courts, of federal substantive law regarding arbitration. More recently, in *Buckeye Check Cashing, Inc*

continued

v. Cardegna, 546 U.S. 440 (2006), the Court clarified that, when parties agree to arbitrate all disputes arising under their contract, questions concerning the validity of the entire contract are to be resolved by the arbitrator in the first instance, not by a federal or state court.

The instant petition presents the following question: Does the FAA override not only state statutes that refer certain state-law controversies initially to a judicial forum, but also state statutes that refer certain disputes initially to an administrative agency? We hold today that, when parties agree to arbitrate all questions arising under a contract, state laws lodging primary jurisdiction in another forum, whether judicial or administrative, are superseded by the FAA.

This case concerns a contract between respondent Alex E. Ferrer, a former Florida trial court judge who currently appears as "Judge Alex" on a *Fox* television network program, and petitioner Arnold M. Preston, a California attorney who renders services to persons in the entertainment industry. Seeking fees allegedly due under the contract, Preston invoked the parties' agreement to arbitrate "any dispute . . . relating to the terms of [the contract] or the breach, validity, or legality thereof . . . in accordance with the rules [of the American Arbitration Association]."

Preston's demand for arbitration, made in June 2005, was countered a month later by Ferrer's petition to the California Labor Commissioner charging that the contract was invalid and unenforceable under the California Talent Agencies Act (TAA), Cal. Lab. Code Ann. §1700 *et seq.* (West 2003 and Supp. 2008). Ferrer asserted that Preston acted as a talent agent without the license required by the TAA, and that Preston's unlicensed status rendered the entire contract void. . . .

An easily stated question underlies this controversy. Ferrer claims that Preston was a talent agent who operated without a license in violation of the TAA. Accordingly, he urges, the contract between the parties, purportedly for "personal management," is void and Preston is entitled to no compensation for any services he rendered. Preston, on the other hand, maintains that he acted as a personal manager, not as a talent agent; hence, his contract with Ferrer is not governed by the TAA and is both lawful and fully binding on the parties. . .

Section 2 [of FAA] "declare[s] a national policy favoring arbitration" of claims that parties contract to settle in that manner. *Southland Corp.*, 465 U.S., at 10. That national policy, we held in *Southland*, "appli[es] in state as well as federal courts" and "foreclose[s] state legislative attempts to undercut the enforceability of arbitration agreements.". The FAA's displacement of conflicting state law is "now well-established,". . .

Ferrer attempts to distinguish *Buckeye* by arguing that the TAA merely requires exhaustion of administrative remedies before the parties proceed to arbitration. We reject that argument. . . .

Ferrer contends that the TAA is nevertheless compatible with the FAA because §1700.44(a) merely postpones arbitration until after the Labor Commissioner has exercised her primary jurisdiction. . . .

A prime objective of an agreement to arbitrate is to achieve "streamlined proceedings and expeditious results." That objective would be frustrated even if Preston could compel arbitration in lieu of *de novo* Superior Court review. Requiring initial reference of the parties' dispute to the Labor Commissioner would, at the least, hinder speedy resolution of the controversy. . . .

When parties agree to arbitrate all questions arising under a contract, the FAA supersedes state laws lodging primary jurisdiction in another forum, whether judicial or administrative. . . .

Preston v Ferrer, 552 U.S. 346 (2008),
Supreme Court of United States.

In some circumstances, laws that favor local businesses against interstate businesses are invalid, as are laws that otherwise burden interstate commerce. So, a law that prohibits out-of-state businesses from selling toys in the state, while permitting local companies to sell toys, is unconstitutional. These are commonly known as *dormant commerce clause* cases. The Dormant Commerce Clause limits the authority of states to discriminate against interstate businesses even if Congress has not spoken to the subject. Regulations that are not facially discriminatory against out-of-state businesses but overly burden them are also invalid. For example, a law that required trucks to have specific mud flaps was invalidated even though the rule applied to both intrastate and interstate trucks because it made a common mudflap, that was legal in nearly every state, illegal in *Bibb v. Navajo Freight Lines, Inc.*, 359 U.S. 520 (1959). The safety gain to the state was minimal, but the cost to interstate commerce was high. However, reasonable regulation that does not overly burden interstate commerce is permitted. This was the case in *American Trucking Associations, Inc. v. Michigan Public Service Comm'n.*

LEGAL TERM
Dormant Commerce Clause
The rule that a state may not excessively burden interstate commerce even if Congress has not regulated the subject.

American Trucking Associations, Inc. v. Michigan Public Service Comm'n

545 U.S. 440 (2005)

[Under federal law, the states' authority to charge a registration fee on trucks licensed in other states that travel in interstate commerce was limited to $10. Michigan charged the $10 fee. In addition, Michigan established a separate $100 fee for all state-licensed intrastate carriers and another $100 fee for all truck carriers that make intrastate trips. The purpose of the fee was to support road maintenance and traffic enforcement. All trucks that made intrastate trips were required to pay the fee. This is the fee that was at issue in this case. To maximize profits, some interstate carriers who have delivered a load or who are passing through a state with less than a full load stop and "top off" with another load and deliver it elsewhere, often within the same state, during the haul. The plaintiffs allege that because these top-off intrastate deliveries are a smaller part of their business than for purely intrastate carriers, and because both pay the same fee, the fee is disproportionately high and burdensome to interstate trucking companies.]

Justice Breyer delivered the opinion of the Court.

In this case, we consider whether a flat $100 fee that Michigan charges trucks engaging in intrastate commercial hauling violates the dormant Commerce Clause. We hold that it does not.

A subsection of Michigan's Motor Carrier Act imposes upon each motor carrier "for the administration of this act, an annual fee of $100.00 for each self-propelled motor vehicle operated by or on behalf of the motor carrier." The provision assesses the fee upon, and only upon, vehicles that engage in intrastate commercial operations—that is, on trucks that undertake point-to-point hauls between Michigan cities. Petitioners, USF Holland, Inc., a trucking company with trucks that engage in both interstate and intrastate hauling, and the American Trucking Associations, Inc. (ATA), asked the Michigan courts to invalidate the provision. Both petitioners told those courts that trucks that carry *both* interstate *and* intrastate loads engage in intrastate business less than trucks that confine their operations to the Great Lakes State. Hence, because Michigan's fee is flat, it discriminates against interstate carriers and imposes an unconstitutional burden upon interstate trade. . . .

continued

Our Constitution "was framed upon the theory that the peoples of the several states must sink or swim together." Thus, this Court has consistently held that the Constitution's express grant to Congress of the power to "regulate Commerce . . . among the several States," Art. I, §8, cl. 3, contains "a further, negative command, known as the dormant Commerce Clause," *Oklahoma Tax Comm'n v. Jefferson Lines, Inc.*, 514 U.S. 175, 179 (1995), that "create[s] an area of trade free from interference by the States," *Boston Stock Exchange v. State Tax Comm'n*, 429 U.S. 318, 328 (1977) (internal quotation marks omitted). This negative command prevents a State from "jeopardizing the welfare of the Nation as a whole" by "plac[ing] burdens on the flow of commerce across its borders that commerce wholly within those borders would not bear."

Thus, we have found unconstitutional state regulations that unjustifiably discriminate on their face against out-of-state entities or that impose burdens on interstate trade that are "clearly excessive in relation to the putative local benefits." We have held that States may not impose taxes that facially discriminate against interstate business and offer commercial advantage to local enterprises, that improperly apportion state assessments on transactions with out-of-state components, or that have the "inevitable effect [of] threaten[ing] the free movement of commerce by placing a financial barrier around the State."

Applying these principles and precedents, we find nothing in §478.2(1) that offends the Commerce Clause. To begin with, Michigan imposes the flat $100 fee only upon intrastate transactions—that is, upon activities taking place exclusively within the State's borders. Section 478.2(1) does not facially discriminate against interstate or out-of-state activities or enterprises. The statute applies evenhandedly to all carriers that make domestic journeys. It does not reflect an effort to tax activity that takes place, in whole or in part, outside the State. Nothing in our case law suggests that such a neutral, locally focused fee or tax is inconsistent with the dormant Commerce Clause. . . .

The record, moreover, shows no special circumstance suggesting that Michigan's fee operates in practice as anything other than an unobjectionable exercise of the State's police power. To the contrary, as the Michigan Court of Appeals pointed out, the record contains little, if any, evidence that the $100 fee imposes any significant practical burden upon interstate trade. . . .

The present fee, as we have said, taxes purely local activity; it does not tax an interstate truck's entry into the State nor does it tax transactions spanning multiple States. See 255 Mich. App., at 592–594, 662 N. W. 2d, at 789. We lack convincing evidence showing that the tax deters, or for that matter discriminates against, interstate activities. See *supra*, at 5. Nor is the tax one that, on its face, would seem to call for an assessment measured per mile rather than per truck. See *supra*, at 6. Consequently, we lack any reason to infer that Michigan's lump-sum levy erects, as in *Scheiner*, an impermissible discriminatory road block.

Petitioners add that Michigan's fee fails the "internal consistency" test—a test that we have typically used where taxation of interstate transactions are at issue. Generally speaking, that test asks, "What would happen if all States did the same?" See, e.g., *Goldberg v. Sweet*, 488 U.S. 252, 261 (1989); *Jefferson Lines, supra*, at 185 (test looks to the structure of the tax to see whether its identical application by every State "would place interstate commerce at a disadvantage as compared with commerce intrastate"). We must concede that here, as petitioners argue, if all States did the same, an interstate truck would have to pay fees totaling several hundred dollars, or even several thousand dollars, were it to "top off" its business by carrying local loads in many (or even all) other States. But it would have to do so only because it engages in *local* business in all those States. An interstate firm with local outlets normally expects to pay local fees that are uniformly assessed upon all those who engage in local business, interstate and domestic firms alike. . . . A motor carrier is not special in this respect.

> In sum, petitioners have failed to show that Michigan's fee, which does not seek to tax a share of interstate transactions, which focuses upon local activity, and which is assessed evenhandedly, either burdens or discriminates against interstate commerce, or violates the Commerce Clause in any other relevant way. See *Complete Auto Transit, Inc. v. Brady*, 430 U.S. 274, 279 (1977) (noting that a tax will be sustained where it is applied to an activity with a "substantial nexus" to the taxing State; where, if applied to interstate activity, it is "fairly apportioned"; where it does not discriminate; and where it is "fairly related to the services provided").
>
> For these reasons, the judgment of the Michigan Court of Appeals is affirmed [and the fee is upheld].
>
> It is so ordered.

American Trucking Associations, Inc. v. Michigan Public Service Comm'n,
545 U.S. 440 (2005), Supreme Court of United States.

The extent to which the state is exercising its police power is also a factor. For example, in *United Haulers Association, Inc., et al. v. Oneida-Herkimer Solid Waste Management Authority, et al. (2007)*, the Supreme Court validated a state's authority to create a waste-processing facility, to require trash collection companies to use the facility, and to charge a fee for use against a claim that it discriminated against out-of-state facilities. The plaintiff collection companies pointed out that it was less expensive for them to use out-of-state processing companies. The law creating the facilities was formed in response to an environmental crisis, caused by corruption, price gouging, and collusion by private waste companies. That the law treated all waste companies, both local and out-of-state, equally was important to the court. Also, the court referred to the state's historic jurisdiction over the subject matter.

> We should be particularly hesitant to interfere with the Counties' efforts under the guise of the Commerce Clause because "[w]aste disposal is both typically and traditionally a local government function." 261 F. 3d, at 264 (case below) (Calabresi, J., concurring); see *USA Recycling, Inc. v. Town of Babylon*, 66 F. 3d 1272, 1275 (CA2 1995) ("For ninety years, it has been settled law that garbage collection and disposal is a core function of local government in the United States"); M. Melosi, Garbage in the Cities: Refuse, Reform, and the Environment, 1880–1980, pp. 153–155 (1981). Congress itself has recognized local government's vital role in waste management, making clear that "collection and disposal of solid wastes should continue to be primarily the function of State, regional, and local agencies." Resource Conservation and Recovery Act of 1976, 90 Stat. 2797, 42 U. S. C. §6901(a)(4). The policy of the State of New York favors "displac[ing] competition with regulation or monopoly control" in this area. N. Y. Pub. Auth. Law Ann. §2049-tt(3). We may or may not agree with that approach, but nothing in the Commerce Clause vests the responsibility for that policy judgment with the Federal Judiciary.

The Court upheld state authority in another dormant commerce clause case one year after United Haulers in *Department of Revenue of Kentucky v. Davis, 553 U.S. 328 (2008)*. This case involved an effort by Kentucky (and many other states) to promote its own government bonds over the bonds of other states. To do this, it taxed bonds from other states but made Kentucky-issued bonds tax exempt. The Court recognized that states have greater authority when acting as market participants (as opposed to a market regulator attempting to favor in-state businesses), that Kentucky had a legitimate interest in promoting its own bonds, that there is a long history of this practice, and that this practice is protected by the Tenth Amendment as a traditional state function.

The authority of the states to directly govern the federal government, and vice versa, has also been the subject of several Supreme Court cases but is beyond the scope of this book.[16]

Because the federal government and state governments often regulate different areas, each must establish its own agencies to administer and enforce its own laws and policies. Accordingly, there are a multitude of agencies, each with its own particular rules and procedures. In addition to federal and state agencies, many local governments have their own agencies.

Finally, note that although the dual and hierarchical federalism models provide a framework for understanding the authority relationship, the federal government and state governments often cooperate in the administration of many programs. This form of partnership is commonly known as *cooperative federalism*. Cooperative federalism, as a descriptor, is not a structural or legal model. It is, instead, a relational model. Examples of cooperative federalism can be found in periods where dual and hierarchical federalism are dominant.

2.1(c) Separation of Powers

A horizontal division of power, known as *separation of powers*, also exists. The doctrine of separation of powers divides the powers of a government into three branches: executive, legislative, and judicial.

At the national level, the executive branch consists of the president of the United States, the president's subordinates, and agencies. At the state level, it is comprised of the state governor and his or her subordinates, and state agencies. The executive branch of government is responsible for administering and enforcing the laws of government.

The legislative branch is represented by the Congress of the United States at the national level and the various state legislatures at the state level. The legislative branch is responsible for the creation of law. A written law enacted by a legislative body is called a *statute*.

The judicial branch is represented at the federal level by the various federal courts, with the Supreme Court of the United States as the highest court. Each state also has its own court system. The judicial branch is responsible for administering justice, resolving disputes, and interpreting the law. The second responsibility, dispute resolution, has many dimensions. Courts hear private lawsuits (individuals bringing suit against individuals, corporate bodies, or governments), such as contract, property, and tort (harm caused by negligent and intentional conduct), criminal cases (government charges individuals), administrative cases (government takes noncriminal action against an individual or corporate body), and cases where one government sues another government. Through these various forms of action courts not only provide an outlet for citizen-to-citizen disputes but also serve the very important function of maintaining the balance of governmental powers and the preservation of individual liberties.

Unlike the two "political" branches of government, federal courts are countermajoritarian bodies. That is, whereas the president and Congress are popularly elected (the president through the electoral college) and, therefore, responsive to the will of the majority, courts are not. The framers intended for courts to be free

LEGAL TERMS

Cooperative Federalism
An intergovernmental model that describes a relationship between the federal government and state governments that is characterized by close, collaborative relations and a common objective, and a lessened focus on legal jurisdictional boundaries.

Separation of Powers
The division of governmental power into three branches: executive, legislative, and judicial.

Statute
A written law of a legislative body.

from political pressure, conventional wisdom, and the waves of popular opinion. To make this system work, the framers gave federal judges appointed under Article III of the Constitution lifetime tenure and a guarantee of no reduction in salary.

SIDEBAR   *Organization of Statutes and Regulations*

In most jurisdictions, statutes are organized and published by subject matter. Such compilations are commonly known as codes. For example, all laws enacted by a legislature dealing with the procedure to be used in civil cases might be found in a code of civil procedure. The regulations created by federal administrative agencies are compiled in the Code of Federal Regulations.

Normally, one governmental branch may not exercise the responsibilities of another even if the two branches agree that one is to delegate a particular function to the other. This maintains a balance of power. The branches also "check" one another. That is, rarely does the Constitution establish a procedure whereby a branch may exercise its authority without being reviewed or authorized by another branch. For example, Congress is responsible for the creation of law. However, laws must be presented to the president for signature. Then, if the president vetoes a law, Congress may override the veto with a two-thirds majority vote. As another example, the president nominates cabinet members, ambassadors, and other officials. In most instances, however, Congress must confirm these presidential nominations before an appointment is final.

The framers of the Constitution of the United States embodied these principles in the Constitution. The purpose of the doctrines of federalism and the separation of powers is to prevent the centralization of power in one person or group. This checks-and-balances system protects civil liberties (see Figure 2-3).

The concept of separation of powers is important in administrative law because agencies have the unique characteristic of exercising legislative, executive, and judicial functions. That is, agencies perform the duties of all three branches of government. This authority is granted or *delegated* by Congress to agencies, which are usually executive branch entities. Because of the expertise agencies can bring to rulemaking, Congress often delegates to agencies the authority to create rules more detailed than those Congress has created. In such instances, Congress will establish the basic policy and then call upon the agency to "fill in the gaps." In such instances, Congress is delegating a portion of its own authority to make law. Congress often also delegates the authority to hear cases. In such instances, Congress is delegating judicial power. As you can imagine, delegations of its own authorities and those of the judiciary raise constitutional separations of powers issues.

	Governmental Entity	Separation of Powers		
		Executive	**Legislative**	**Judicial**
Federalism	United States	President	Congress	Federal Courts
	States	Governors	Legislatures	State Courts

FIGURE 2-3   The Constitution's system of checks and balances.

2.2 CONTROLLING THE BUREAUCRACY

Generally, the Constitution does not address federal agencies. It creates the three branches of government and all three branches of government are involved with agencies. All three also play a role in checking agency behavior.

2.2(a) Bureaucracy Defined

The term *bureaucracy* is loaded. That is, many people have preconceived notions about the meaning of the term, and often those ideas are not positive. Max Weber, commonly referred to as the Father of Sociology, used the term to describe a rational management system. To Weber, who lived from 1864 to 1920, *bureaucracy* described a system in which leadership positions were not inherited or obtained through wealth, as had been the case around most of the world before and during his lifetime. Other characteristics of a bureaucracy, to Weber, included a division of labor; creation of specialists within offices; a set of rational, objective, and purposeful rules to be enforced; seniority- and merit-based promotion; a hierarchy of officials within the system; and a strict system of control and discipline of public officials. There are disadvantages to bureaucracies. For example, specialization of individual employees leads to excessive empowerment and less oversight, less mobility between jobs, a decrease in flexibility in the workplace, and excessive "red tape."

In this text, *bureaucracy* is used to describe the management systems of the United States, the states, and local governments. These include the executive leaders, executive agencies, and other agencies of all of these forms of government, including a few private agencies that provide public services.

2.2(b) Presidential Control

Under the system of separation of powers, Congress creates, defines, and funds agencies. The president, in contrast, is the national government's chief executive officer. As such, the president is the highest officer responsible for enforcing and administering the law. At this juncture, it is important to note that the executive's authority is almost always greater in foreign affairs than in domestic matters. All recent presidents have complained that their control over domestic agency matters is too limited. President Carter, for example, complained that as the result of a territorial dispute between two administrative agencies (Department of the Interior and General Services Administration), he could not get a mouse out of his office.[17]

It may seem odd that a president, the chief executive of government under Article II of the Constitution, is unable to control the government. There are several reasons for this. First, there has been a movement to detach the bureaucracy from the political branches of government. Refer Figure 1-1. You will see many independent agencies listed. These are agencies that Congress has imbued with some autonomy. The purpose of this independence is to keep agencies free from politics. Some scholars argue that this independence also frees agencies from public accountability. You will learn more about the structure of these agencies later. A second barrier to effective presidential control of agencies is size. Agencies are simply too numerous and too large for the White House to micromanage. A third limiting factor is the system of checks and balances. It is Congress that creates agencies, defines their powers, and sets their budgets.

In spite of these limitations, presidents exercise some control over agencies. First, the president is the direct head of executive agencies. As such, the president has considerable authority in the operation of these agencies. Second, the president can recommend to Congress agency reorganizations and amendments to enabling laws. President George W. Bush did this following the attacks of September 11, 2001. Dissatisfied with the performance of the Immigration and Naturalization Service and the lack of interagency cooperation in terrorism matters, he proposed the creation of the Department of Homeland Security (see Figure 1-2). This new agency now comprises the Immigration and Naturalization Service, the Federal Emergency Management Agency, and other federal agencies that were previously part of other departments or were stand-alone units. Third, the president has some authority to establish policy. This is done through executive orders. Recent presidents have asserted greater executive control over agency behavior, particularly rulemaking, by conducting policy oversight. President Nixon began a trend of using what is today the Office of Management and Budget (an executive agency) to conduct agency oversight. Each successive president has expanded White House involvement and oversight.[18]

Fourth, the president plays a role in the appointment of agency heads. Executive agency heads, such as the Attorney General and the Secretary of Commerce, fall directly into the presidential chain of command. However, as was mentioned earlier, Congress has created a number of independent agencies over which the president's authority is limited. For example, the enabling legislation may state that the agency is to work independent of presidential and congressional control. Congress also often limits the role of the president into the appointment and removal of the heads of such agencies.

Article II, section 2, clause 2 of the Constitution is applicable to this area of the law. It states, in part:

> [The president shall have the power to] nominate, and by and with the Advice and Consent of the Senate, shall appoint Ambassadors, other public Ministers and Consuls, Judges of the Supreme Court, and all other Officers of the United States, whose Appointments are not herein otherwise provided for, and which shall be established by Law: but the Congress may by Law vest the Appointment of such inferior Officers, as they think proper, in the President alone, in the Courts of Law, or in the Heads of Departments.

This provision is clear about the role of the president and Congress in appointing federal officials. Officers are to be nominated by the president and confirmed by the Senate. Because the latter half of the provision refers to "inferior officers," this initial requirement is interpreted as referring to "superior officers." Agency heads, such as department secretaries, are superior officers. Congress decides how inferior officers are to be appointed. Congress may delegate this responsibility to the president, to a department head, or to a court. Congress did this with the independent counsel.

The independent counsel is a federal prosecutor charged with investigating and prosecuting government officials. You may recall that it was independent counsel Kenneth Starr who investigated President Clinton and many officials in the Clinton administration. Pursuant to statute, the appointment of the independent counsel is made by a special panel of federal judges. This process was challenged as violative of the separation of powers by improperly involving judges in executive matters. In *Morrison v. Olson*,[19] the Supreme Court rejected this attack, holding that such an appointment is constitutional under Article II, section 2, clause 2.

As you have seen, the Constitution is specific about the powers of the president and Congress in the appointment of agency officials. Removal of federal officers is different. Clearly, Congress may remove federal officers pursuant to the impeachment and removal provisions of Article II, section 4, and Article I, sections 2 and 3. The Constitution is silent about the authority of the president to remove federal officers. Regardless, presidents have long maintained that they possess the authority to fire officers of the executive branch. In recent decades, Congress has found it desirable to limit the authority of the president in this regard. The primary reason Congress limits the presidential removal power is to improve the efficiency and quality of agency decisions by reducing the degree to which the agency head is influenced by politics. The constitutionality of limiting presidential control over the tenure of agency officers has been the subject of several Supreme Court decisions.

In *Myers v. United States,* the Supreme Court invalidated a statute that required Senate approval to fire postmasters. The Court stated that "article 2 grants to the President the executive power of the government—i.e., the general administrative control of those executing the laws, including the power of appointment and removal of executive officers—a conclusion confirmed by his obligation to take care that the laws be faithfully executed. . . ."[20] *Myers* appears to stand for the proposition that Congress may not interject itself into an executive function. The Court reaffirmed this in the 1986 case of *Bowsher v. Synar.*[21] In *Bowsher,* Congress gave itself the authority to remove the comptroller general. The Court concluded that the comptroller was an executive official; accordingly, it held that Congress could not control the removal of the comptroller. Some scholars interpreted *Myers* to mean that Congress may not limit the presidential removal power in any way. Later cases would prove otherwise.

In 1935, the Supreme Court issued a decision in *Humphrey's Executor v. United States.*[22] This case involved an appointment to the Federal Trade Commission (FTC), an independent agency. Removal of FTC commissioners by the president was limited by statute to good cause, including inefficiency, neglect of duty, and malfeasance of office. President Roosevelt removed Humphrey from his post without establishing good cause, and Humphrey's estate (Humphrey died between the time of his termination and the filing of the civil action) filed suit to collect unpaid wages. The Court held that the nature of the position in dispute is critical. *Myers,* for example, involved a "purely executive" official. The Court found postmasters to be purely executive because they do not make policy (a legislative function), nor do they perform judicial functions. Instead, postmasters administer programs—an executive function. An FTC commissioner, in contrast, is different. The FTC, for example, hears disputes like a court. It also assists Congress in lawmaking. Thus, the Court held that Congress could make reasonable attempts to limit the authority of the president over FTC commissioners.

As mentioned earlier, the constitutionality of the independent counsel statute was challenged in *Morrison v. Olson.* In addition to the challenge to the appointment provision discussed earlier, the appellant asserted that the independent counsel law violated Article II by limiting the authority of the president to control an executive function (investigation and prosecution of crimes) and to fire a purely executive official (the independent counsel). Of course, limiting presidential authority is the purpose of such a law. The Supreme Court upheld the statute for the following four reasons:

1. Unlike *Myers* and *Bowsher,* Congress did not attempt to control this function. The appointment of the independent counsel lies with a special panel of judges and with the attorney general.
2. An executive officer, the attorney general, has the authority to terminate the independent counsel.

3. The president's ability to discharge his constitutionally assigned duties was not impaired by the law.
4. The independent counsel's appointment is temporary; the counsel does not make policy decisions, nor does the counsel possess much administrative authority.

It appears that *Morrison* has shifted the focus from whether an official is performing executive functions to whether Congress has improperly delegated an executive function to itself and whether the ability of the president to perform constitutional functions has been impaired.[23]

In 2010, the Supreme Court issued the following decision where it reaffirmed the president's role as the head of government. Although the president may, in certain circumstances, have the power of appointment and removal limited (e.g., for cause), the president must have some control to ensure agency accountability to the executive. In this case, the Court invalidated a structure that limited the president's authority over a board that had limited authority over another agency, the so-called dual for-cause limitation on executive authority. The law (commonly known as Sarbanes-Oxley) was enacted in 2002 in response to a number of scandals that involved accounting firms and practices, including Enron. The purpose of the law is to improve accounting and accountability in public corporations.

Free Enterprise Fund v. Public Corporation Accounting Oversight Board

561 U.S. ____(2010)

Our Constitution divides the "powers of the new Federal Government into three defined categories, Legislative, Executive, and Judicial." Article II vests "[t]he executive Power . . . in a President of the United States of America," who must "take Care that the Laws be faithfully executed." Art. II, §1, cl. 1; *id.,* §3. In light of "[t]he impossibility that one man should be able to perform all the great business of the State," the Constitution provides for executive officers to "assist the supreme Magistrate in discharging the duties of his trust."

Since 1789, the Constitution has been understood to empower the President to keep these officers accountable—by removing them from office, if necessary. See generally *Myers v. United States*, 272 U.S. 52 (1926). This Court has determined, however, that this authority is not without limit. In *Humphrey's Executor v. United States*, 295 U.S. 602 (1935), we held that Congress can, under certain circumstances, create independent agencies run by principal officers appointed by the President, whom the President may not remove at will but only for good cause. Likewise, in *United States v. Perkins,* 116 U.S. 483 (1886), and *Morrison v. Olson*, 487 U.S. 654 (1988), the Court sustained similar restrictions on the power of principal executive officers—themselves responsible to the President—to remove their own inferiors. The parties do not ask us to reexamine any of these precedents, and we do not do so.

We are asked, however, to consider a new situation not yet encountered by the Court. The question is whether these separate layers of protection may be combined. May the President be restricted in his ability to remove a principal officer, who is in turn restricted in his ability to remove an inferior officer even though that inferior officer determines the policy and enforces the laws of the United States?

We hold that such multilevel protection from removal is contrary to Article II's vesting of the executive power in the President. The President cannot "take Care that the Laws be faithfully executed" if he cannot oversee the faithfulness of the

continued

officers who execute them. Here the President cannot remove an officer who enjoys more than one level of good-cause protection even if the President determines that the officer is neglecting his duties or discharging them improperly. That judgment is instead committed to another officer, who may or may not agree with the President's determination, and whom the President cannot remove simply because that officer disagrees with him. This contravenes the President's "constitutional obligation to ensure the faithful execution of the laws."....

Congress created the Board as a private "nonprofit corporation," and Board members and employees are not considered Government "officer[s] or employee[s]" for statutory purposes. The Board can thus recruit its members and employees from the private sector by paying salaries far above the standard Government pay scale....

Unlike [private] organizations, however, the Board is a Government-created, Government-appointed entity, with expansive powers to govern an entire industry. Every accounting firm—both foreign and domestic—that participates in auditing public companies under the securities laws must register with the Board, pay it an annual fee, and comply with its rules and oversight....

The Board promulgates auditing and ethics standards, performs routine inspections of all accounting firms, demands documents and testimony, and initiates formal investigations and disciplinary proceedings. The willful violation of any Board rule is treated as a willful violation of the Securities Exchange Act of 1934—a federal crime punishable by up to 20 years' imprisonment or $25 million in fines ($5 million for a natural person). And the Board itself can issue severe sanctions in its disciplinary proceedings, up to and including the permanent revocation of a firm's registration, a permanent ban on a person's associating with any registered firm, and money penalties of $15 million ($750,000 for a natural person). Despite the provisions specifying that Board members are not Government officials for statutory purposes, the parties agree that the Board is "part of the Government" for constitutional purpose....

The Act places the Board under the SEC's oversight, particularly with respect to the issuance of rules or the imposition of sanctions (both of which are subject to Commission approval and alteration). But the individual members of the Board—like the officers and directors of the self-regulatory organizations—are substantially insulated from the Commission's control. The Commission cannot remove Board members at will, but only "for good cause shown," "in accordance with" certain procedures....

As explained, we have previously upheld limited restrictions on the President's removal power. In those cases, however, only one level of protected tenure separated the President from an officer exercising executive power. It was the President—or a subordinate he could remove at will—who decided whether the officer's conduct merited removal under the good-cause standard.

The Act before us does something quite different. It not only protects Board members from removal except for good cause, but withdraws from the President any decision on whether that good cause exists. That decision is vested instead in other tenured officers—the Commissioners—none of whom is subject to the President's direct control. The result is a Board that is not accountable to the President, and a President who is not responsible for the Board.

The added layer of tenure protection makes a difference. Without a layer of insulation between the Commission and the Board, the Commission could remove a Board member at any time, and, therefore, would be fully responsible for what the Board does. The President could then hold the Commission to account for its supervision of the Board, to the same extent that he may hold the Commission to account for everything else it does.

A second level of tenure protection changes the nature of the President's review. Now the Commission cannot remove a Board member at will. The President, therefore, cannot hold the Commission fully accountable for the Board's conduct, to the same extent that he may hold the Commission accountable for everything else that it does. The Commissioners are not responsible for the Board's actions. They are only responsible for their own determination of whether the Act's rigorous good-cause standard is met. And even if the President disagrees with their determination, he is powerless to intervene—unless that determination is so unreasonable as to constitute "inefficiency, neglect of duty, or malfeasance in office."

This novel structure does not merely add to the Board's independence, but transforms it. Neither the President, nor anyone directly responsible to him, nor even an officer whose conduct he may review only for good cause, has full control over the Board. The President is stripped of the power our precedents have preserved, and his ability to execute the laws—by holding his subordinates accountable for their conduct—is impaired.

That arrangement is contrary to Article II's vesting of the executive power in the President. Without the ability to oversee the Board, or to attribute the Board's failings to those whom he *can* oversee, the President is no longer the judge of the Board's conduct. He is not the one who decides whether Board members are abusing their offices or neglecting their duties. He can neither ensure that the laws are faithfully executed, nor be held responsible for a Board member's breach of faith. This violates the basic principle that the President "cannot delegate ultimate responsibility or the active obligation to supervise that goes with it," because Article II "makes a single President responsible for the actions of the Executive Branch."

The diffusion of power carries with it a diffusion of accountability. . . .

The people do not vote for the "Officers of the United States." Art. II, §2, cl. 2. They instead look to the President to guide the "assistants or deputies . . . subject to his superintendence." Without a clear and effective chain of command, the public cannot "determine on whom the blame or the punishment of a pernicious measure, or series of pernicious measures ought really to fall." . . .

Free Enterprise Fund v. Public Corporation Accounting Oversight Board, 561 U.S. ____(2010), Supreme Court of United States.

Finally, note that most federal employees are not "officers" of the United States. Congress enacted a civil service system providing for competitive merit appointment of employees in the Pendleton Civil Service Reform Act of 1883 (***Pendleton Act***).[24] Further most nonprobationary employees cannot be fired without good cause. When the civil service system was challenged as violating the appointments clause of Article II, the Court distinguished between "employees" and "officers" and held that the former need not be appointed in a manner consistent with Article II.[25]

LEGAL TERM
Pendleton Act
Federal statute that creates civil service system.

SIDEBAR *Assassination and Civil Service*

James Garfield, America's twentieth president, only served 200 days before Charles Guiteau shot him with a revolver on July 2, 1881. Several people were with him at the moment he was shot, including his sons and Robert Todd Lincoln, son of Abraham Lincoln. He died on September 19, largely due to the unsterile medical procedures that were common in his day.

Guiteau was apprehended, convicted, and hanged. He confessed to shooting the president because he didn't receive an appointment to a federal position and he blamed the president. Outrage over the assassination led to a national consensus that the spoils system (to the victor goes the spoils), or the system of patronage in appointing federal officers, needed to be changed. Ironically Garfield, and presidents before him, advocated for reducing their authority to hand out appointments to political allies in favor of a more objective, merit system. The Pendleton

continued

Civil Service Reform Act of 1883 was the product of the nation's anger and sorrow. Chester A. Arthur, Garfield's Vice President who ascended to be president, signed the bill into law. The law created a system of merit hiring and for cause dismissal for some federal employees. Initially the reach of the law was limited to a small number of federal employees. Today, nearly all federal employees are hired, work, and are disciplined under the civil service system. The system is not without its critics. Some people contend that it creates employees who are too independent, particularly of executive oversight.

The power to recommend an agency's budget to Congress is another source of presidential power. Although Congress must ultimately approve a budget, the president's recommendation is important. Therefore, agencies want to remain in the president's good favor. In the mid-1990s, Congress enlarged the president's authority over the budget when it passed the Line Item Veto Act. This law delegated to the president the power to strike individual expenditures from the congressionally enacted budget. This law was challenged as violating the separation of powers in *Clinton v. City of New York*.

Clinton v. City of New York

524 U.S. 417 (1998)

[Congress enacted the Line Item Veto Act in 1996, and it became effective on January 1, 1997.] The Act gives the President the power to "cancel in whole" three types of provisions that have been signed into law: "(1) any dollar amount of discretionary budget authority; (2) any item of new direct spending; or (3) any limited tax benefit."

The President exercised his authority to cancel one provision in the Balanced Budget Act of 1997 and two provisions in the Taxpayer Relief Act of 1997. Appellees, claiming that they had been injured by two of those cancellations, filed these cases in the District Court...

In both legal and practical effect, the President has amended two Acts of Congress by repealing a portion of each. "[R]epeal of statutes, no less than enactment, must conform with Art. I." *INS v. Chadha*, 462 U.S. 919, 954 (1983). There is no provision in the Constitution that authorizes the President to enact, to amend, or to repeal statutes. Both Article I and Article II assign responsibilities to the President that directly relate to the lawmaking process, but neither addresses the issue presented by these cases. The President "shall from time to time give to the Congress Information on the State of the Union, and recommend to their Consideration such Measures as he shall judge necessary and expedient. . . ." Art. II, § 3. Thus, he may initiate and influence legislative proposals. Moreover, after a bill has passed both Houses of Congress, but "before it become[s] a Law," it must be presented to the President. If he approves it, "he shall sign it, but if not he shall return it, with his Objections to that House in which it shall have originated, who shall enter the Objections at large on their Journal, and proceed to reconsider it." Art. I, § 7, cl. 2. His "return" of a bill, which is usually described as a "veto," is subject to being overridden by a two-thirds vote in each House.

"Every Bill which shall have passed the House of Representatives and the Senate, shall, before it become[s] a Law," be presented to the President of the United States; if he approve[s] he shall sign it, but if not he shall return it, with his Objections to that House in which it shall have originated, who shall enter the Objections at large on their Journal, and proceed to reconsider it. "If after such Reconsideration two thirds of that House shall agree to pass the Bill, it shall be sent, together with the Objections, to the other House, by which it shall likewise be reconsidered, and if approved by two thirds of that House, it shall become a Law. But in all such Cases the Votes of both Houses shall be determined by Yeas and Nays, and the Names of the Persons voting for and against the Bill shall be entered on the Journal of each House respectively. If any Bill shall not be returned by the President within ten Days (Sundays excepted) after it shall have been presented to him, the Same shall be a Law, in like Manner as if he had signed it, unless the Congress by their Adjournment prevent its Return, in which Case it shall not be a Law."

There are important differences between the President's "return" of a bill pursuant to Article I, § 7, and the exercise of the President's cancellation authority pursuant to the Line Item Veto Act. The constitutional return takes place *before* the bill becomes law; the statutory cancellation occurs *after* the bill becomes law. The constitutional return is of the entire bill; the statutory cancellation is of only a part. Although the Constitution expressly authorizes the President to play a role in the process of enacting statutes, it is silent on the subject of unilateral Presidential action that either repeals or amends parts of duly enacted statutes.

There are powerful reasons for construing constitutional silence on this profoundly important issue as equivalent to an express prohibition. The procedures governing the enactment of statutes set forth in the text of Article I were the product of the great debates and compromises that produced the Constitution itself. Familiar historical materials provide abundant support for the conclusion that the power to enact statutes may only "be exercised in accord with a single, finely wrought and exhaustively considered, procedure." *Chadha*, 462 U.S., at 951 [103 S. Ct., at 2784]. Our first President understood the text of the Presentment Clause as requiring that he either "approve all the parts of a Bill, or reject it in toto." What has emerged in these cases from the President's exercise of his statutory cancellation powers, however, are truncated versions of two bills that passed both Houses of Congress. They are not the product of the "finely wrought" procedure that the Framers designed.

[For these reasons, the Court invalidated the Line Item Veto Act.]

Clinton v. City of New York, 524 U.S. 417 (1998), Supreme Courts of United states.

2.2(c) Congressional Control

In many respects, of the three constitutional branches of government, Congress possesses the greatest ability to control the federal bureaucracy. First, it is Congress that creates, disbands, and reorganizes agencies. Second, Congress establishes the budget. An agency that is not in favor with Congress can suffer at budget time. Third, Congress sets the policy objectives of agencies, as well as the rules that govern agencies' operations. Fourth, Congress engages in oversight of agencies through its committees. Agency officials are commonly required to testify before Congress concerning agency behavior.

Fifth, Congress can reverse or amend agency-created rules and administrative decisions. At one time, Congress used single-house *legislative vetoes* to check agency decisions. A legislative veto is a process whereby Congress reviews an agency decision. For convenience, and to increase the number of decisions it could review, Congress has on thousands of occasions delegated the review authority to one of its Houses. It did this in the Immigration and Naturalization Act, which provided that deportation decisions by the Immigration and Naturalization Service (INS) could be reversed by either the House of Representatives or the Senate. In 1982 the House of Representatives reversed an INS decision to permit an alien to remain in the United States. This decision was appealed to the Supreme Court in

LEGAL TERM

Legislative Vetoes

A mechanism used by Congress to invalidate agency action that falls short of the constitutional method of making law (bicameral action with presentment to the president).

INS v. Chadha.[26] For many of the same reasons it found the ***line-item veto*** unconstitutional in the *Clinton* case, the Court invalidated the single-house legislative veto. Specifically, the Court held that Congress could not bypass the bicameralism requirement (both the House and Senate must pass laws), nor could it remove the president from the process of making laws. Congress enacted the Congressional Review Act in response to *Chadha*, a statute that delays the enactment of new rules to give Congress time to review them and with either presidential approval or by overriding a presidential veto, invalidate (disapprove) them. You will learn more about the Congressional Review Act in a later chapter.

The Court's strict adherence to the doctrine of separation of powers has been criticized for leaving agencies without adequate oversight, increasing their independence from the democratic government, and decreasing their accountability. This is ironic because the purpose of separating powers is to prevent the centralization of power and abuse of citizens by government.

Sixth, as you have seen, the Senate must approve the appointment of agency officers. Seventh, Congress controls the appointment of inferior officers by designating who is responsible for making the nomination. These are a few examples of the power Congress has over the federal bureaucracy.

Even though Congress may technically have the power to control agencies, it often does not. Political reasons abound for this. For example, even if a majority of both Houses agree that an agency should be checked, it is difficult to get a majority in both Houses to agree on what specific action should be taken. Congress often also delegates the tough decisions to an agency. Bureaucrats do not run for reelection, and most are protected by the selective service system. There are many other political, practical, and legal reasons Congress does not exercise the full extent of its authority over agencies. Because Congress does not engage in much oversight, a great deal of that responsibility falls to the courts.

Some scholars believe that greater control over agencies by the executive and legislative branches is needed. Other scholars believe that there are benefits to agency independence. For example, Steven Croley, a law professor at the University of Michigan, argues that administrative law "liberates" both Congress and agencies from interest group politics and thereby permits agencies to pursue the general public interest to a greater degree than Congress may. [27]

INS v. Chadha

462 U.S. 919 (1983)

We granted certiorari [to review] a challenge to the constitutionality of the provision in § 244(c)(2) of the Immigration and Nationality Act . . . authorizing one House of Congress, by resolution, to invalidate the decision of the Executive Branch, pursuant to authority delegated by Congress to the Attorney General of the United States, to allow a particular deportable alien to remain in the United States.

Chadha is an East Indian who was born in Kenya and holds a British passport. He was lawfully admitted to the United States in 1966 on a nonimmigrant student visa. His visa expired on June 30, 1972. On October 11, 1973, the District Director of the Immigration and Naturalization Service ordered Chadha to show cause why he should not be deported for having "remained in the United States for a longer time than permitted." . . . [A] deportation hearing was held before an immigration judge on January 11, 1974. Chadha conceded that he was deportable for overstaying his visa and the hearing was adjourned to enable him to file an application for suspension of deportation under [federal law]. . . . [T]he immigration judge, on June 25, 1974, ordered that Chadha's deportation be suspended. The immigration judge found that Chadha met the requirements of [the federal statute by establishing that] he had resided continuously in the United States for over seven years, was of good moral character, and would suffer "extreme hardship" if deported. . . .

We turn now to the question whether action of one House of Congress under § 244(c)(2) violates strictures of the Constitution. We begin, of course, with the presumption that the challenged statute is valid. Its wisdom is not the concern of the courts; if a challenged action does not violate the Constitution, it must be sustained. . . .

THE PRESENTMENT CLAUSES

The records of the Constitutional Convention reveal that the requirement that all legislation be presented to the president before becoming law was uniformly accepted by the framers. Presentment to the president and the presidential veto were considered so imperative that the draftsmen took special pains to assure that these requirements could not be circumvented. During the final debate on Art. I, § 7, cl. 2, James Madison expressed concern that it might easily be evaded by the simple expedient of calling a proposed law a "resolution" or "vote" rather than a "bill." As a consequence, Art. I, § 7, cl. 3, was added.

The decision to provide the president with a limited and qualified power to nullify proposed legislation by veto was based on the profound conviction of the framers that the powers conferred on Congress were the powers to be most carefully circumscribed. It is beyond doubt that lawmaking was a power to be shared by both houses and the president. In *The Federalist No. 73* (H. Lodge ed. 1888), Hamilton focused on the president's role in making laws:

If even no propensity had ever discovered itself in the legislative body to invade the rights of the Executive, the rules of just reasoning and theoretic propriety would of themselves teach us that the one ought not to be left to the mercy of the other, but ought to possess a constitutional and effectual power of self-defence.

* * *

BICAMERALISM

The bicameral requirement of Art. I, §§ 1, 7 was of scarcely less concern to the framers than was the Presidential veto, and indeed the two concepts are interdependent. By providing that no law could take effect without the concurrence of the prescribed majority of the Members of both Houses, the Framers reemphasized their belief, already remarked upon in connection with the Presentment Clauses, that legislation should not be enacted unless it has been carefully and fully considered by the Nation's elected officials. In the Constitutional Convention debates on the need for a bicameral legislature, James Wilson, later to become a Justice of this Court, commented:

Despotism comes on mankind in different shapes. Sometimes in an Executive, sometimes in a military, one. Is there danger of a Legislative despotism? Theory & practice both proclaim it. If the Legislative authority be not restrained, there can be neither liberty nor stability; and it can only be restrained by dividing it within itself, into distinct and independent branches. In a single house there is no check, but the inadequate one, of the virtue & good sense of those who compose it. . . .

Hamilton argued that a Congress comprised of a single House was antithetical to the very purposes of the Constitution. Were the Nation to adopt a Constitution providing for only one legislative organ, he warned:

> [w]e shall finally accumulate, in a single body, all the most important prerogatives of sovereignty, and thus entail upon our posterity one of the most execrable forms of government that human infatuation ever contrived. Thus we should create in reality that very tyranny which the adversaries of the new Constitution either are, or affect to be, solicitous to avert. *The Federalist,* No. 22, p. 135

We see, therefore, that the Framers were acutely conscious that the bicameral requirement and the Presentment Clauses would serve essential constitutional functions. The President's participation in the legislative process was to protect the Executive Branch from Congress and to protect the whole people from improvident laws. The division of the Congress into two distinctive bodies assures that the legislative power would be exercised only after opportunity for full study and debate in separate settings. The President's unilateral veto power, in turn, was limited by the power of two thirds of both Houses of Congress to overrule a veto thereby precluding final arbitrary action of one person. . . . It emerges clearly that the prescription for legislative action in Art. I, §§ 1, 7 represents the framers' decision that the legislative power of the Federal government be exercised in accord with a single, finely wrought and exhaustively considered, procedure. . . .

The Constitution sought to divide the delegated powers of the new federal government into three defined categories, legislative, executive and judicial, to assure, as nearly as possible, that each branch of government would confine itself to its assigned responsibility. The hydraulic pressure inherent within each of the separate branches to exceed the outer limits of its power, even to accomplish desirable objectives, must be resisted. Although not "hermetically" sealed from one another . . . the powers delegated to the three branches are functionally identifiable?

We hold that the Congressional veto provision in § 244(c)(2) is severable from the Act and that it is unconstitutional.

[Justice Powell concurred with the majority, but differed in reasoning. He concluded that "when Congress finds that a particular person does not satisfy the statutory criteria for permanent residence in this country it has assumed a judicial function in violation of the separation of powers." Justice White dissented, arguing that the legislative veto is an appropriate method of keeping nonelected officials accountable to elected officials.]

Ins v. Chadha, 462 U.S. 919 (1983), Supreme Court of United States.

2.2(d) Judicial Control

Courts also play a role in controlling agencies. As the final arbiters of the law, courts interpret Congress's mandate and jurisdictional delegations to agencies; courts also review agency adjudications and rules. You will learn more about the role of the judiciary in administrative law in later chapters.

Lawlinks.   Jurist is a Web site designed for law professors, yet it has information that may be of interest to anyone studying the law. The site has links to law schools, law school admissions information, video lectures on law topics, current events, academic articles and research, and Web law courses, including several administrative law courses offered by professors across the nation. Go to *www.jurist.law .pitt.edu/index.htm.*

2.3 CONCLUSION

The need for a large administrative state was not anticipated by the framers of the Constitution; accordingly, they did not account for it in the constitutional scheme. The large, complex agencies that are typical in the 21st century give rise to unique constitutional questions. The most significant concern is how to keep agencies that exercise the functions of all three constitutional branches accountable to the American people. This arrangement looks much like what the framers of the Constitution feared. Tyranny by bureaucracy is one reason to control agencies, but there are other reasons as well. For example, the American bureaucracy is expensive to maintain. Most recent presidents have had the desire to control agencies, but they have often discovered that they lack the authority to do so. Congress often has the authority but lacks the desire. As you will see later, this has left much of the responsibility for controlling agencies to the courts. As you proceed through this text, think about the democratic republic issue. Are agencies accountable? Do they pose a threat to the republic? Where are the faults in the existing law? How would you restructure the system or reform the law to correct the problems you have identified?

REVIEW **QUESTIONS**

1. What is a benefit of having an agency independent of the executive branch?
2. What are the disadvantages of having agencies independent of the executive branch?
3. Define federalism.
4. Define separation of powers.
5. Identify two ways in which the president has authority over executive agencies.
6. Identify two ways in which Congress has authority over executive agencies.
7. Give two examples of exclusive federal powers.
8. Give two examples of exclusive state powers.
9. Give one example of a policy area over which the federal government and state governments share jurisdiction.
10. Why does the contemporary administrative state challenge the historical separation of powers model?
11. Distinguish hierarchical from dual federalism.

CRITICAL THINKING AND **APPLICATIONS PROBLEMS**

Answer questions 1 and 2 using the following scenario. Congress creates a statute, the Biotechnology Review Act. Three sections of this law read:

Section One: The Biotechnology Review Board (BRB)

The BRB shall consist of seven commissioners. The term of appointment for each commissioner shall be seven years. Each commissioner shall be nominated by the president and confirmed by the Senate. The commissioners may be removed by the president with the concurrence of the Senate in cases of malfeasance, incompetence, or neglect of office.

Section Two: Jurisdiction and Mandate

The BRB shall conduct research into biotechnological issues, including genetic engineering, as they concern the health and safety of food products. The jurisdiction of the BRB over these matters is exclusive. The BRB shall have the authority to: (1) issue cease-and-desist orders to producers of biologically altered foods that pose a threat to the health and safety of the public; (2) hear claims and issue damage awards to individuals who have been harmed by biologically altered foods; and (3) promulgate regulations necessary to carry out numbers 1 and 2 above.

Section Three: Congressional Oversight

All regulations promulgated by the BRB shall be presented to the clerk of the House of Representatives. The House may amend or repeal any rule promulgated by the BRB.

1. Is the appointment and removal provision constitutional? Explain your answer.
2. Is the congressional oversight provision constitutional? Explain your answer.
3. Do you believe the independent counsel law violates the separation of powers? Explain your answer.

ENDNOTES

1. *Federal Trade Comm'n v. Ruberoid*, 343 U.S. 470, 487 (1951).

2. See, for example, *The Federalist* Nos. 10, 14 (James Madison).

3. For more on deliberative democracy, see Matt Leighninger's *The Next Form of Democracy: How Expert Rule Is Giving Way to Shared Governance — and Why Politics Will Never Be the Same* (Vanderbilt University Press 2006) and Gastil, J. and Levine, P., *The Deliberative Democracy Handbook* (John Wiley and Sons 1995).

4. For a brief account of the Articles of Confederation and the development of the Constitution of 1789, *see* Daniel E. Hall and John Feldmeier, *Constitutional Values: Governmental Powers and Individual Freedoms*, Ch. 1 (Pearson Prentice Hall 2009).

5. Native American tribal governments also possess a degree of sovereignty. A discussion of tribal governments is outside the scope of this text.

6. *The Federalist* No. 45 (James Madison).

7. 17 U.S. (4 Wheat.) 316 (1819).

8. 317 U.S. 111 (1942).

9. 505 U.S. 144 (1992).

10. *Id.* at 187.

11. 514 U.S. 549 (1995).

12. 521 U.S. 98 (1997).

13. *U.S. v. Jones*, 529 U.S. 848 and *U.S. v. Morrison*, 529 U.S. 598

14. Alvarez, L. "Cats at Hemingway Museum Draw Tourists, and Legal A Battle," *The New York Times*, December 22, 2012, http://www.nytimes.com/2012/12/23/us/cats-at-hemingway-museum-draw-a-legal-battle.html?_r=1&.

15. Debra Cassens Weiss, "Five Plus Hours of Oral Argument On Health Care Law Isn't That Long, Historically Speaking," *ABA Journal*, News, November 15, 2011 found at http://www.abajournal.com/news/article/five-plus_hours_of_oral_arguments_on_health_care_law_isnt_that_long_histori/

16. For more on this subject, see Daniel E. Hall & John P. Feldmeier, *Constitutional Values: Governmental Power and Individual Freedoms in American Politics* (Prentice Hall, 2008).

17. Steven Cann, (2nd ed. 1998). p. 22

18. Matthew J. Matule, *Congress, the Courts, and Regulatory Oversight after Meyer v. Bush: Should the Executive Office of the President Be Shielded from Congressional Sunshine?* 18 Vermont L. R. 834 (1994).

19. 487 U.S. 654 (1988).

20. *Myers v. U.S.,* 272, U.S. 52 (1926).

21. 478 U.S. 714 (1986). See also *Buckley v. Valeo*, 424 U.S. 1 (1976).

22. 295 U.S. 602 (1935).

23. The federal independent counsel law sunset in 1999. Unless it is renewed, it will be the sole responsibility of the attorney general to order investigations previously delegated to the independent counsel.

24. Subsequent laws, such as the Hatch Acts (which prohibit all federal employees except the President, Vice President, and a few other high ranking officers from engaging in politics) and the Civil Service Reform Act of 1978, have elaborated or modified the original Pendleton Act.

25. *Buckley v. Valeo*, 424 U.S. 1 (1976).

26. 462 U.S. 919 (1983).

27. Steven P. Croley, 28 Flordia St. Univ. L. R. 7 (2000) "Public Interested Regulation."

chapter **three**

AGENCY
DISCRETION

LEARNING OBJECTIVES

After completing this chapter, you should be able to

- Identify three different forms of commonly exercised discretion by agency officials.

- Define advisory opinions and declaratory orders and explain how they are used in practice.

- Explain why informal processes have been characterized as the lifeblood of the administrative process.

- Explain why too little discretion and too much discretion in government officials both present the possibility of abuse of authority. You should also be able to apply this understanding to real-life scenarios.

- Demonstrate comfort and familiarity with the style and format of judicial opinions.

- Brief a judicial opinion with little outside assistance. You should be successful in identifying the relevant facts. You should also be successful in identifying the legal issue and analyzing the court's rationale in at least 33 percent of your briefs.

Informal administrative procedures are the lifeblood

of the administrative process.[1]

Adapted from Chapter III - Informal Methods of Adjudication
in ATTORNEY GENERAL REPORT, 1941.

3.1 INTRODUCTION

A great majority of agency actions are informal. It is the exception, not the rule, in both rulemaking and adjudication, that formal procedures must be used. As you have learned, the Administrative Procedures Act (APA) and other laws govern both rulemaking and adjudication. Agencies also perform many functions that fall outside the rulemaking and adjudication models. These acts are governed by the rules concerning informal procedures. However, because these actions constitute the bulk of administrative work, informal procedures are the "lifeblood of the administrative process."

Generally, informal actions are not governed by statute. Accordingly, agencies exercise significant discretion when performing these functions. An agency has *discretion* when it has the authority to choose between two or more options. Too much discretion can lead to arbitrariness. For this reason, discretion should not be too broad. However, too little discretion leads to inflexible public administration, which may be equally unjust. The challenge is to find a satisfactory middle ground. Regrettably, agencies are often given too much discretion and are not adequately checked.

3.2 DETRIMENTS AND BENEFITS OF DISCRETION

Unquestionably, excessive and unchecked discretion can lead to arbitrary decision making. The framers were concerned about this. That is why they protected civil rights through the federal Constitution, state constitutions, and statutory law. These rights act as limits on the discretion of lawmakers and law enforcers. To be sure, Americans are suspicious, if not fearful, of discretion.

Nevertheless, discretion has its benefits. In his book *The Death of Common Sense: How Law Is Suffocating America,*[2] Philip Howard posits that discretion is an inherent and necessary element of public administration. Discretion is, according to Howard, needed to ensure humanity in governance. He suggests that in an effort to achieve fairness, we have excessively limited the discretion of public officials in some policy areas.

In addition to questioning whether discretion should be eliminated, Howard questions whether discretion can be successfully substituted with detailed rules. In some cases, limiting discretion has achieved its objectives. For example, police departments have been successful in reducing deaths resulting from high-speed police chases and the use of deadly force by establishing policies regulating chases and the use of deadly force.[3] In other cases, however, controlling discretion has proven difficult. Sometimes the cure is worse than the symptom; that is, the control may have unintended and counterproductive consequences. For example, Howard points out that today there are so many workplace safety rules that inspectors have to pick and choose the rules to enforce. Yet the purpose of creating so many rules was to limit the authority of the inspectors. One study estimated that 80 percent of the thousands of rules promulgated by the Occupational Safety and Health Administration's (OSHA) rules go unenforced.[4] So, too few rules and too many rules both leave inspectors with significant discretion. See Figure 3-1 for an illustration of the relationship between discretion and the number of rules an agency must enforce.

This would not be true if an agency had the resources and the will to enforce all its rules. However, this arrangement has its problems as well. First, it is costly. Taxpayers may want to spend the money necessary to strictly enforce every safety rule in a nuclear power plant, but not to enforce local building codes that apply to the construction of household swimming pools. Also, as Howard points out,

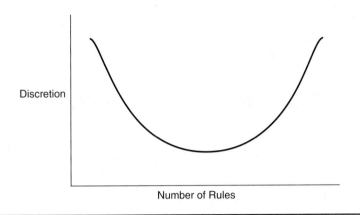

FIGURE 3-1   The relationship of discretion to number of rules.

rulemakers cannot foresee every possibility. Hence, the strict enforcement of rules can lead to unfairness by: (1) enforcing rules when the objective of the rule is not satisfied, and (2) not acting when needed because the drafters of the rules did not foresee the problem. Discretion, Howard asserts, is necessary to achieve fairness.

Howard also points out that rules by themselves even if respected and enforced, cannot solve every problem. For example, OSHA is charged with regulating workplace safety. Pursuant to this delegation, OSHA has promulgated thousands of rules. Howard, citing another source, states that "OSHA's false premise . . . is its fixation with physical conditions and paperwork. Five out of six accidents are caused by human error. . . . [T]rying to make everything 'idiot-proof' is itself dangerous: Workers don't have to think, and bosses get tied down with nit-picking regulations."[5] Howard concludes that discretion is not something to be totally eliminated. It is, with some limits, necessary to address the myriad of problems that confront public administrators. The relationship of fairness to discretion is illustrated in Figure 3-2.

At the other extreme is the rare case where not only is discretion satisfactorily controlled, but there are also positive unintended consequences. Fearing that prosecutorial discretion over plea bargaining was leading to unfair results, several jurisdictions have limited the authority of prosecutors to bargain with criminal defendants. Alaska, for example, abolished plea bargaining in the 1970s. Opponents of the change argued that this would significantly increase the number of jury trials and subsequently break down Alaska's court system. As it turned out, the increase was less dramatic. Jury trials increased from 6.7 percent to 9.6 percent of criminal cases. The unexpected, but welcomed, consequence was that cases

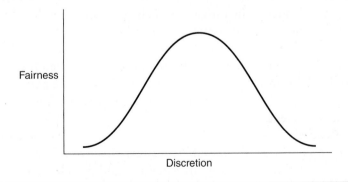

FIGURE 3-2   The relationship of fairness to discretion.

were being processed more quickly than when plea bargaining was in effect. Note, however, that some observers believed that discretion was not eliminated; rather, it was shifted from prosecutors to judges.[6]

3.3 LIMITS ON AGENCY DISCRETION

There are instances where Congress has created significant limitations on the discretion of agency officials and others where officials possess considerable discretion. As you can imagine, it is much easier for a court to review an allegation that an agency has not complied with a rule than it is to review an allegation that an agency has abused its discretion. In particular, agency decisions not to act are rarely successfully challenged. It is when an agency acts that it is most at risk of reversal or of civil liability.

Often when agencies act informally, there are few or no procedures to protect individuals. Discretion may be either unfettered or hampered by only minimal constraints. Therefore, questions of fairness are common in this area, and due process is often at issue. Judicial review of discretionary decisions, however, is limited. You will learn more about the judicial review of agency decisions in a later chapter.

Be aware, however, that the law (as enforced by the judiciary) is not the only limitation on agency discretion. Political accountability is also a limitation. Angering Congress, the president, or the public can have detrimental consequences for an agency. What follows are several examples of agency discretion.

3.4 EXAMPLES OF AGENCY DISCRETION

3.4(a) Prosecutorial Discretion

As you learned earlier, as a part of the executive branch, agencies perform law enforcement functions. Generally, the Department of Justice, through its offices of U.S. attorneys, is responsible for enforcing criminal statutes even when the subject matter of a criminal prohibition falls within the jurisdiction of another agency. Agencies, however, prosecute the administrative aspects of such violations. While performing such functions, they exercise the same discretion that federal prosecutors do when enforcing criminal laws. Prosecutorial discretion includes deciding whom to investigate and prosecute; whether to settle a case before, during, or after a prosecution; and related decisions.

Why must agencies decide whom to investigate? Because agencies do not have the resources to investigate every person and business for compliance with the law. Therefore, agencies investigate selected cases. Many factors affect the decision whether to conduct an investigation, such as the likelihood of discovering a violation, the expense and inconvenience of conducting a particular investigation, and the expense and inconvenience of enforcing the law if a violation is discovered during the investigation. Generally, administrators are granted the discretion to decide who should be investigated for a violation. Therefore, a party subject to an investigation may not object by claiming selective prosecution, with a few exceptions noted in a moment.

In the *General Motors* case, a party filed a complaint pursuant to an agency's rules. The complaint was dismissed. The alternative would have been for the agency to conduct a more lengthy investigation and possibly take further corrective action. The dismissal was upheld on the ground that the agency properly exercised its discretion to proceed no further.

General Motors v. Federal Energy Regulatory Commission

613 F.2d 939 (D.C. Cir. 1979)

Petitioner General Motors Corporation (GM) seeks to set aside an order of the Federal Energy Regulatory Commission (Commission), which dismissed without a hearing GM's complaint against a natural gas curtailment plan filed with the Commission by the Natural Gas Pipeline Company of America (Pipeline). GM contends that the Commission abused its discretion in dismissing its complaint. We hold that it did not, and we accordingly deny the petition to set aside the Commission's order.

Pipeline operates a natural gas pipeline system extending from the southwestern United States to the Chicago metropolitan area. It makes interstate sales of natural gas to municipalities, utility companies, and several industrial users. Among its customers are two Illinois natural gas distributors doing business as the Northern Illinois Gas Company (NI-Gas). . . . GM, which operates three industrial plants in Illinois, purchases natural gas from NI-Gas. . . .

In January 1973 the Commission adopted Order No. 467 in which it described its policies on the priorities of deliveries to be observed by interstate pipelines during periods of curtailment. . . .

In April 1976 GM filed a complaint with the Commission pursuant to Rule 1.6 of the Commission's Rules of Practice. Citing the Commission's Order No. 467 Series, GM alleged that Pipeline's curtailment plan is unjust, unreasonable, and discriminatory. . . .

In our judgment, GM's contentions misconceive the Commission's authority to conduct an investigation and misapprehend the import of its past policy statements. . . . In general, an administrative agency's decision to conduct or not to conduct an investigation is committed to the agency's discretion. . . . If an agency considers all the relevant factors so that a court can satisfy itself that the agency has actually exercised its discretion, an agency's decision to refrain from investigation is unreviewable. . . .

GM does not contend that the Commission ignored any factor relevant to its decision making, and our own inspection of the record indicates that the Commission confronted the salient features of the GM complaint. For example, it considered GM's charges concerning curtailments at GM's Illinois plants and found that those curtailments were not attributable to any element of the curtailment plan. It also examined GM's charges of declining gas supply and found that these charges did not show the presence of an immediate and direct injury to GM, which would warrant the relief GM requested. . . . We are fully satisfied that the Commission actually exercised its discretion to refrain from an investigation of the Pipeline plan. We, therefore, find that the Commission's orders dismissing the GM complaint are not subject to review in this court.

General Motors v. Federal Energy Regulatory Commission, 613 F.2d 939 (D.C. Cir. 1979), United States Court of Appeals, District of Columbia Circuit.

Agencies also exercise discretion to decide who shall be prosecuted. As previously mentioned, agencies do not possess the resources to prosecute every discovered violator. Factors in such a decision include the likelihood of victory at trial, the seriousness of the violation, the expense of prosecution, the deterrent effect of such a prosecution, and the need to resolve presented legal or factual issues.

Although the discretion as to whom to prosecute is broad, it is still limited. For example, a decision to investigate or prosecute based on race or gender would be unconstitutional.[7] Said another way, prosecutorial discretion is limited by the Constitution. A prosecutor may not employ unconstitutional criteria, such as race, gender, or religious affiliation, when making a decision on whether to prosecute.

Because agencies have huge caseloads, negotiation and settlement of cases are common agency practices. This avoids the time and expense of trial and pretrial procedures. Settlement may occur before a case has been filed, while a case is pending, or later (to avoid appeal). The APA requires that agencies give respondents in complaint cases the opportunity to settle "when time, the nature of the proceeding, and the public interest permit."[8] Though agencies must consider settlement proposals, there is little limitation on the agency's authority to accept or reject proposals. When contemplating settlement, an agency must consider the public interest as well as how consumers, regulated parties, and others will be affected. Many agencies have established rules governing settlement.

3.4(b) Rulemaking and Policy Discretion

As you learned previously, agencies are often empowered by Congress to promulgate regulations to further their mandate. An agency that is delegated rulemaking authority has the discretion to promulgate what rules it finds necessary, and a party cannot claim that a better rule should have been promulgated. Of course, if a regulation exceeds an agency's statutory mandate or is unconstitutional, it will fail. As a general rule, the courts are to defer to an agency's interpretation of its congressional mandates. Said another way, if Congress is not clear on a subject within an agency's jurisdiction, the agency's decision is to be respected by a reviewing court unless that decision is unreasonable. Similarly, an agency decision concerning policy is within an agency's discretion and is valid unless it is ***ultra vires*** or unconstitutional. Disagreement with an agency's policy decision is no more a proper basis for a lawsuit than is dissatisfaction with a policy decision by Congress. Indeed, courts generally defer to agencies in the interpretation of the statutes that govern them. This is known as the *Chevron Doctrine*. The *Chevron Doctrine* is discussed later in this chapter and more thoroughly in Chapter 9.

In 1999, Elián Gonzalez, a six-year-old boy, arrived in the United States. He was the only survivor of a raft carrying 12 Cubans, including Elián's mother, who were attempting to come to the United States. In the months that followed, the Immigration and Naturalization Service became embroiled in a battle between the boy's father, who wanted Elián to be returned to Cuba, and other members of the family living in Florida, who wanted the boy to remain with them. Litigation ensued in both state and federal courts, and various theories were advanced by both parties.

LEGAL TERM
Ultra Vires
Acting outside the scope or legal limits. An agency that exceeds its statutory mandate acts *ultra vires*.

Gonzalez v. Reno

---

212 F.3d 1338 (11th Cir. 2000)

This case, at first sight, seems to be about little more than a child and his father. But, for this Court, the case is mainly about the separation of powers under our constitutional system of government: a statute enacted by Congress, the permissible scope of executive discretion under that statute, and the limits on judicial review of the exercise of that executive discretion.

Elian Gonzalez ("Plaintiff"), a six-year-old Cuban child, arrived in the United States alone. His father in Cuba demanded that Plaintiff be returned to Cuba. Plaintiff, however, asked to stay in the United States; and asylum applications were submitted on his behalf. The Immigration and Naturalization Service ("INS")—after, among other things, consulting with Plaintiff's father and considering Plaintiff's age—decided that Plaintiff's asylum applications were legally void and refused to consider their merit. Plaintiff then filed this suit in federal district court, seeking on several grounds to compel the INS to consider and to determine the merit of his asylum applications. The district court dismissed Plaintiff's suit. . . .

In December 1993, Plaintiff was born in Cuba to Juan Miguel Gonzalez and Elizabeth Gonzalez. When Plaintiff was about three years old, Juan Miguel and Elizabeth separated. Elizabeth retained custody of Plaintiff after the separation. Juan Miguel, however, continued to have regular and significant contact with his son. Plaintiff, in fact, attended school in the district where his father lived and often stayed at Juan Miguel's home.

In November 1999, Elizabeth decided to leave Cuba and to take her son to the United States. In the pre-dawn hours of 22 November, Plaintiff and Elizabeth, along with twelve other Cuban nationals, left Cuba aboard a small boat. The next day, the boat capsized in strong winds and rough seas off the coast of Florida. Eleven of the passengers, including Elizabeth, died. Plaintiff, clinging to an inner tube, endured and survived.

Two days later, Plaintiff was rescued at sea by Florida fishermen and was taken to a hospital in Miami for medical treatment. While Plaintiff was receiving medical treatment, the INS was contacted by Plaintiff's great-uncle: Miami resident Lazaro Gonzalez. INS officials decided, upon Plaintiff's release from the hospital, not to remove Plaintiff immediately to Cuba. Instead, the INS deferred Plaintiff's immigration inspection and paroled Plaintiff into Lazaro's custody and care.

Soon thereafter, Lazaro filed an application for asylum on Plaintiff's behalf with the INS. . . . The applications [three applications for asylum were filed] stated that Plaintiff "is afraid to return to Cuba." The applications claimed that Plaintiff had a well-founded fear of persecution because many members of Plaintiff's family had been persecuted by the Castro government in Cuba. . . . The applications also alleged that, if Plaintiff were returned to Cuba, he would be used as a propaganda tool for the Castro government and would be subjected to involuntary indoctrination in the tenets of communism.

Plaintiff's father, however, apparently did not agree that Plaintiff should remain in the United States. Soon after Plaintiff was rescued at sea, Juan Miguel sent to Cuban officials a letter, asking for Plaintiff's return to Cuba. The Cuban government forwarded this letter to the INS.

Because of the conflicting requests about whether Plaintiff should remain in the United States, INS officials interviewed both Juan Miguel and Lazaro. An INS official, on 13 December, met with Juan Miguel at his home in Cuba. At that meeting, Juan Miguel made this comment:

> [Plaintiff], at the age of six, cannot make a decision on his own. . . . I'm very grateful that he received immediate medical assistance, but he should be returned to me and my family. . . . As for him to get asylum, I am not allowing him to stay or claim any type of petition; he should be returned immediately to me. . . .

On 31 December, an INS official again met with Juan Miguel in Cuba to investigate further Lazaro's claim that Juan Miguel's request had been coerced. At that meeting, Juan Miguel repeated that he desired Plaintiff's return to Cuba. Juan Miguel also reasserted that he was under no undue influence from any individual or government. The INS official—taking Juan Miguel's demeanor into account—determined that Juan Miguel, in fact, genuinely desired his son's return to Cuba.

[Plaintiffs claimed that the INS abused its discretion by not adjudicating the asylum claim.] The INS Commissioner, on 5 January 2000, rejected Plaintiff's asylum applications as legally void. The Commissioner—concluding that six-year-old children lack the capacity to file personally for asylum against the wishes of their parents—determined that Plaintiff could not file his own asylum applications. Instead, according to the Commissioner, Plaintiff needed an adult representative to file for

(continued)

asylum on his behalf. The Commissioner—citing the custom that parents generally speak for their children and finding that no circumstance in this case warranted a departure from that custom—concluded that the asylum applications submitted by Plaintiff and Lazaro were legally void and required no further consideration. . .

Our consideration of Plaintiff's statutory claim must begin with an examination of the scope of the statute itself. . . . "First, always, is the question whether Congress has directly spoken to the precise question at issue. If the intent of Congress is clear, that is the end of the matter; for the court, as well as the agency, must give effect to the unambiguously expressed intent of Congress.". . . We turn, therefore, to the plain language of the statute.

Section 1158 provides, in pertinent part:

> *Any alien* who is physically present in the United States or who arrives in the United States (whether or not at a designated port of arrival and including an alien who is brought to the United States after having been interdicted in international or United States waters), irrespective of such alien's status, *may apply for asylum* in accordance with this section or, where applicable, section 1225(b) of this title.

[This statute] is neither vague nor ambiguous. The statute means exactly what it says: "[a]ny alien . . . may apply for asylum.". . . The important legal question in this case, therefore, is not whether Plaintiff may apply for asylum; that a six-year-old is eligible to apply for asylum is clear. The ultimate inquiry, instead, is whether a six-year-old child has applied for asylum within the meaning of the statute when he, or a non-parental relative on his behalf, signs and submits a purported application against the express wishes of the child's parent.

About this question, more important than what Congress said in section 1158 is what Congress left unsaid. In reading statutes, we consider not only the words Congress used, but the spaces between those words. Section 1158 is silent on the precise question at issue in this case. Although section 1158 gives "[a]ny alien" the right to "apply for asylum," the statute does not command how an alien applies for asylum. The statute includes no definition of the term "apply." The statute does not set out procedures for the proper filing of an asylum application. Furthermore, the statute does not identify the necessary contents of a valid asylum application. In short, although the statute requires the existence of some application procedure so that aliens may apply for asylum, section 1158 says nothing about the particulars of that procedure. See 8 U.S.C. § 1158.

Because the statute is silent on the issue, Congress has left a gap in the statutory scheme. From that gap springs executive discretion. As a matter of law, it is not for the courts, but for the executive agency charged with enforcing the statute (here, the INS), to choose how to fill such gaps. . . . Moreover, the authority of the executive branch to fill gaps is especially great in the context of immigration policy. . . . Our proper review of the exercise by the executive branch of its discretion to fill gaps, therefore, must be very limited. . . .

The INS, in its discretion, decided to require six-year-old children—who arrive unaccompanied in the United States from Cuba—to act in immigration matters only through (absent special circumstances) their parents in Cuba. The INS could have shaped its policy in a different fashion, perhaps allowing relatives (for example, those within the fourth degree of relationship) in the United States to act for such children. But it did not, and we cannot. That choice was the sole prerogative of the executive branch. According to the principles set out in Chevron, we can only disturb that choice if it is unreasonable. . . .

That the courts owe some deference to executive policy does not mean that the executive branch has unbridled discretion in creating and in implementing policy. Executive agencies must comply with the procedural requirements imposed by statute. . . . Agencies must respect their own procedural rules and regulations . . . and the policy selected by the agency must be a reasonable one in the light of the statutory scheme. . . . To this end, the courts retain the authority to check agency policymaking for procedural compliance and for arbitrariness. But the courts cannot properly reexamine the wisdom of an agency-promulgated policy. . . .

We accept that the INS policy at issue here comes within the range of reasonable choices. First, we cannot say that the foundation of the policy—the INS determination that six-year-old children necessarily lack sufficient capacity to assert, on their own, an asylum claim—is unreasonable. . . . Because six-year-old children must have some means of applying for asylum, see 8 U.S.C. § 1158(a)(1), and because the INS has decided that the children cannot apply personally, the next element of the INS policy—that a six-year-old child must be represented by some adult in applying for asylum—necessarily is reasonable.

The INS determination that ordinarily a parent (even one outside of this country)—and, more important, only a parent—can act for his six-year-old child (who is in this country) in immigration matters also comes within the range of reasonable choices. In making that determination, INS officials seem to have taken account of the relevant, competing policy interests: the interest of a child in asserting a non-frivolous asylum claim; the interest of a parent in raising his child as he sees fit; and the interest of the public in the prompt but fair disposition of asylum claims. The INS policy—by presuming that the parent is the sole, appropriate representative for a child—gives paramount consideration to the primary role of parents in the upbringing of their children. But we cannot conclude that the policy's stress on the parent-child relationship is unreasonable.

We are not untroubled by the degree of obedience that the INS policy appears to give to the wishes of parents, especially parents who are outside this country's jurisdiction. Because Congress has decided that "[a]ny alien" (including six-year-old children) may apply for asylum, 8 U.S.C. § 1158(a)(1), Congress has charged the INS—when it promulgates policy and fills gaps in the statutory scheme—with facilitation, not hindrance, of that legislative goal. . . . We recognize that, in some instances, the INS policy of deferring to parents—especially those residing outside of this country—might hinder some six-year-olds with non-frivolous asylum claims and prevent them from invoking their statutory right to seek asylum. But, considering the well-established principles of judicial deference to executive agencies, we cannot disturb the INS policy in this case just because it might be imperfect. . . . And we cannot invalidate the policy—one with international-relations implications—selected by the INS merely because we personally might have chosen another. . . . Because we cannot say that this element of the INS policy—that, ordinarily, a parent, and only a parent, can act for a six-year-old child in immigration matters—is unreasonable, we defer to the INS policy.

The final aspect of the INS policy also worries us some. According to the INS policy, that a parent lives in a communist-totalitarian state is no special circumstance,

Elian Gonzalez with Cuban President Castro in 2005.

(continued)

sufficient in and of itself, to justify the consideration of a six-year-old child's asylum claim (presented by a relative in this country) against the wishes of the non-resident parent. We acknowledge, as a widely-accepted truth, that Cuba does violate human rights and fundamental freedoms and does not guarantee the rule of law to people living in Cuba. . . .

Nonetheless, we cannot properly conclude that the INS policy is totally unreasonable in this respect. The INS policy does take some account of the possibility of government coercion: where special circumstances—such as definite coercion directed at an individual parent—exist, a non-parental representative may be necessary to speak for the child. In addition and more important, in no context is the executive branch entitled to more deference than in the context of foreign affairs.

CONCLUSION

As policymakers, it is the duty of the Congress and the executive branch to exercise political will. Although courts should not be unquestioning, we should respect the other branches' policymaking powers. The judicial power is a limited power. It is the duty of the judicial branch not to exercise political will, but only to render judicial judgment under the law.

When the INS was confronted with Plaintiff's purported asylum applications, the immigration law of the United States provided the INS with no clear answer. The INS accordingly developed a policy to deal with the extraordinary circumstances of asylum applications filed on behalf of a six-year-old child, by the child himself and a non-parental relative, against the express wishes of the child's parents (or sole parent). The INS then applied this new policy to Plaintiff's purported asylum applications and rejected them as nullities. Because the preexisting law compelled no particular policy, the INS was entitled to make a policy decision. The policy decision that the INS made was within the outside border of reasonable choices. And the INS did not abuse its discretion or act arbitrarily in applying the policy and rejecting Plaintiff's purported asylum applications. The Court neither approves nor disapproves the INS's decision to reject the asylum applications filed on Plaintiff's behalf, but the INS decision did not contradict 8 U.S.C. § 1158.

The judgment of the district court is AFFIRMED.

Gonzalez v. Reno, 212 F.3d 1338 (11th Cir. 2000),
United States Court of Appeals for the Eleventh Circuit.

As you learned in the *Gonzalez* case the Supreme Court's decision *Chevron v. Natural Resources Defense Council*, one of the most important decisions in administrative law, was the decisive law of the case.

In those instances when an agency official is interpreting his agency's own rule, as opposed to a statute, the Supreme Court held in *Auer v. Robbins*, 519 U.S. 452 (1997), that the agency's interpretation is to be set aside only if clearly erroneous. This is a very high standard that requires courts to significantly defer to agency interpretations. It will mean that in some circumstances, a court will uphold and apply an agency's interpretation even though the court may disagree with it. In 2006, the Court summarized the rules of judicial deference to agency interpretations of statutes and rules in *Gonzales v. Oregon*, 546 U.S. 243:

Executive actors often must interpret the enactments Congress has charged them with enforcing and implementing. The parties before us are in sharp disagreement both as to the degree of deference we must accord the Interpretive Rule's substantive conclusions and whether the Rule is authorized by the statutory text at all. Although balancing the necessary respect for an agency's knowledge, expertise, and constitutional office with the courts' role as interpreter of laws can be a delicate matter, familiar principles guide us. An administrative rule may receive substantial deference if it interprets the issuing agency's own ambiguous regulation. *Auer v. Robbins,* 519 U.S. 452, 461–463 (1997). An interpretation of an ambiguous statute may also receive substantial deference. *Chevron U.S. A. Inc. v. Natural Resources Defense Council, Inc.,* 467 U.S. 837, 842–845 (1984). Deference in accordance with *Chevron,* however, is warranted only "when it appears that Congress delegated authority to the agency generally to make rules carrying the force of law, and that the agency interpretation claiming deference was promulgated in the exercise of that authority." *United States v. Mead Corp.,* 533 U.S. 218, 226–227 (2001). Otherwise, the interpretation is "entitled to respect" only to the extent it has the "power to persuade." *Skidmore v. Swift & Co.,* 323 U.S. 134, 140 (1944).

So, the first question to be answered is whether Congress intended to invest the agency official with the authority to make the rule. That delegation may be ambiguous, but it must exist before the higher *Chevron* standard applies. If it does not, then a reviewing court is more likely to set aside the agency's interpretation of the rule. The difference between *Chevron* deference and *Skidmore* deference is real. In *Gonzales,* just cited, the difference impacted the outcome. The Court found that the agency was entitled to only *Skidmore* deference, and when that standard was applied to the facts, the agency was found to have exceeded its authority. The decision would likely have been different if a greater deferential standard had been applied.

Chevron deference is extended to agencies when they interpret statutes through their own rules. When agencies interpret statutes through other actions, such as opinion letters, operations and policy manuals, and enforcement guidelines, their interpretations receive less deference by reviewing courts. Instead of *Chevron* deference they are entitled "respect" to the extent they "persuasive."[9]

3.4(c) Claims and Applications Decisions

An important function performed by many administrative agencies is the processing of claims and applications. Agencies establish practices and policies to govern the processing of these claims. Each agency has the discretion to decide its processing method.

Most claims for benefits, such as unemployment, Social Security, and disability, are initially made informally by agency officials with first appeals often to the employees' supervisors. After this level, a dissatisfied claimant may have a hearing before an administrative law judge (ALJ).

Agency officials must exercise discretion when deciding such claims. However, this discretion is limited by due process (what steps must be taken) and equal protection (not discriminating between individuals because of race, gender, religion, or other improper reason) concerns. See Chapter 4 for a discussion of due process and equal protection. Agencies must also make determinations on applications for licenses. Again, a person may have a protected interest in a license. If so, due process must be satisfied. Additionally, the APA contains a provision establishing the process for license determinations. See Chapter 4 for further discussion of the APA's procedural requirements in license application, , suspension, and revocation.

3.4(d) Protective Action

Some statutes authorize agencies to act to protect the health, safety, and economic well-being of individuals or the public at large. Recalls, seizures of goods or other items, suspensions of licenses, cease-and-desist orders, and actions for

SIDEBAR   *Protection of the Public*

The Consumer Product Safety Commission (CPSC) is a federal administrative agency that has been charged with protecting the public from dangerous products. The CPSC has the authority to file federal court actions seeking seizure orders, inspection warrants, and civil penalties. Violation of some consumer protection laws may lead to criminal prosecution. The CPSC may require a manufacturer to recall or correct a dangerous product. To enforce its mandate, the CPSC conducts product safety research and testing, which includes an accounting of product-related deaths and injuries. The CPSC reported that 3,607 deaths in 1989 were product related. Hospital emergency rooms treated 12,617,095 people as a result of product-related accidents in the same year.

Source: Annual Report to Congress of the Consumer Product Safety Commission (1991).

Annual Report to Congress of the Consumer Product Safety Commission (1991).

civil penalties are all forms of protective action. For example, the Food and Drug Administration may seize or recall contaminated food, drugs, or cosmetics; a state licensing board may suspend a physician's right to practice medicine; and an attorney general's office may issue a cease-and-desist order to a company that engages in deceptive consumer practices.

The decision whether to take action falls within the discretion of agency officials. Of course, some conditions must exist before action may be taken. For example, a state medical licensing board must have some measure of reasonably reliable evidence that a physician is incompetent before issuing a suspension. Summary protective action that is factually supported is not per se violative of due process although due process does require that an immediate postaction hearing be conducted.

The *Brock* case involved a statute that authorizes the secretary of the Department of Labor to reinstate a terminated employee prior to a full evidentiary hearing on the propriety of the discharge. The Court held that the prehearing order of reinstatement was valid because the statute adequately provided for a postreinstatement hearing. (Due process is discussed in more detail in Chapter 4.)

Brock v. Roadway Express, Inc.

481 U.S. 254 (1987)

Section 405 of the Surface Transportation Assistance Act of 1982, 96 Stat. 2157, 49 U.S.C. App. § 2305, protects employees in the commercial motor transportation industry from being discharged in retaliation for refusing to operate a motor vehicle that does not comply with applicable state and federal safety regulations or for filing complaints alleging such noncompliance. The statute provides for an initial investigation of an employee's discharge by the Secretary of Labor and, upon a finding of reasonable cause to believe that the employee was discharged in violation of the Act, requires the Secretary to issue an order directing the employer to reinstate the employee. The employer may then request an evidentiary hearing and a final decision from the Secretary, but this request does not operate to stay the preliminary order of reinstatement. The issue presented in this appeal is whether the failure of § 405 to provide for an evidentiary hearing before temporary reinstatement deprives the employer of procedural due process under the Fifth Amendment.

Appellee Roadway Express, Inc. (Roadway), is a large interstate trucking company engaged primarily in cargo transportation; it is subject to the requirements of [§ 405]. On November 22, 1983, Roadway discharged one of its drivers, Jerry Hufstetler, alleging that he had disabled several lights on his assigned truck in order to obtain extra pay while waiting for repairs. Hufstetler filed a grievance, contending that he had not been discharged for an "act of dishonesty" as defined in the governing collective-bargaining agreement, but rather had been discharged in retaliation for having previously complained of safety violations. The grievance was submitted to arbitration, which ultimately resulted in a ruling on January 30, 1984, that Hufstetler had been properly discharged.

On February 7, 1984, Hufstetler filed a complaint with the Department of Labor alleging that his discharge had violated § 405. The Occupational Safety and Health Administration notified Roadway of the complaint and began an investigation. . . .

Determining the adequacy of predeprivation procedures requires consideration of the government's interest in imposing the temporary deprivation, the private interests of those affected by the deprivation, the risk of erroneous deprivations through the challenged procedures, and the probable value of additional or substitute procedural safeguards. . . .

The property right of which Roadway asserts it has been deprived without due process derives from the collective-bargaining agreement between Roadway and its employees' union. It is the right to discharge an employee for cause. . . .

We begin by accepting as substantial the Government's interests in promoting highway safety and protecting employees from retaliatory discharge. . . .

We also agree with the District Court that Roadway's interest in controlling the makeup of its workforce is substantial. . . . In assessing the competing interest, however, the District Court failed to consider another private interest affected by the Secretary's decision: Hufstetler's interest in not being discharged for having complained about the allegedly unsafe condition of Roadway's trucks. This Court has previously acknowledged the "severity of depriving a person of the means of livelihood." . . .

Reviewing this legislative balancing of interests, we conclude that the employer is sufficiently protected by procedures that do not include an evidentiary hearing before the discharged employee is temporarily reinstated. So long as the prereinstatement procedures establish a reliable "initial check against mistaken decisions," . . . and complete and expeditious review is available, then the preliminary reinstatement provision of § 405 fairly balances the competing interests of the Government, the employer, and the employee, and a prior evidentiary hearing is not otherwise constitutionally required.

Brock v. Roadway Express, Inc., 481 U.S. 252 (1987), U.S. Supreme Court.

3.4(e) Tests and Inspections Generally

Agencies often establish testing and inspection requirements. The authority to test and inspect is extensive. Streams may be tested for contaminants; vehicles for emissions; food or drugs for contaminants; persons for driving skills; and lawyers for competence. Because of the scientific, objective nature of testing, the risk of unfairness is minimal. One may challenge the validity or reliability of the testing procedures, but the decision as to where and whether to conduct a test, and when a test is performed, is within agency discretion. Again, whether an agency has the right to conduct a test or inspection is an issue different from the exercise of that discretion. The authority to conduct a test or inspection may be limited by statute or constitution. Similarly, a statute may require an agency to conduct a test in some circumstances. The decision, however, is normally entrusted to the agency's discretion. In regard to constitutional limitations, a pressing contemporary problem is whether the Fourth Amendment to the U.S. Constitution and similar state constitutional provisions limit the right of agencies to conduct alcohol, drug, and AIDS testing. See Chapter 7 for a discussion of this topic.

3.4(f) Advisory Opinions and Declaratory Orders

Laws can be ambiguous and vague. How a statute or regulation will be applied to particular facts may be unknown or unclear. This is problematic to those who desire to comply with the law but do not know exactly what the law is. To remedy this problem, some agencies issue *advisory opinions*. Upon a request from a person regulated, an agency may issue a statement—an *advisory opinion*—expressing its interpretation of a law or explaining its policy, practices, or procedures. For example, if a taxpayer is not sure if a particular deduction is valid, he or she may request an advisory opinion from the taxing authority.

Advisory opinions are a good tool for assuring compliance with the law. It is often easier to comply with requirements before engaging in a practice than it is to cease the practice later. Further, the use of advisory opinions assists small businesses that do not have the resources to research and master the applicable regulations. Obtaining an advisory opinion is less time consuming and expensive than conducting an investigation and prosecution to gain compliance at a later date. Also, the opinion process is appealing to those regulated as being a fair method of discovering their rights and obligations. If someone is willing to contact the government to ensure compliance with the law, fairness dictates that the government inform the person of his or her responsibilities under the law.

Many agencies have established procedures governing the issuance of advisory opinions. In some circumstances, an agency may wish to promulgate a regulation to respond to a recurring problem. In others, a fact-specific advisory opinion may be issued.

Through regulations, an agency will prescribe its own internal procedures for issuing advisory opinions, such as who in the agency has the authority to issue such opinions. This can be a troubling issue. Agencies do not want to leave important legal or policy decisions to field officers; however, requiring the agency head or upper-level agency officials to be involved with every opinion is impractical. The Internal Revenue Service (IRS) has dealt with this problem by creating two forms of advisory opinions: private letter rulings, which can be relied on only by the requesting party; and formal rulings, which are for the public at large. Private letter rulings may be issued by agents in the field, but formal rulings must be cleared by officials higher in the IRS administration.

The question of whether an advisory opinion is binding is often not easy to answer. Clearly, if an agency has adopted a rule stating that its advisory opinions are binding, they are. Otherwise, agencies and reviewing courts will consider the nature and extent of—and harm resulting from—a person's reliance, the public interest, the position and authority of the official who issued the opinion, and the effect on the agency of binding it to the opinion. See § 9.8 for a discussion of estoppel, which concerns binding the government by the representations of its agents.

A similar tool is the *declaratory order*. The APA provides that an agency, "in its sound discretion, may issue a declaratory order to terminate a controversy or remove uncertainty."[10] The declaratory order is the administrative equivalent of the judicial declaratory judgment. Its purpose is to resolve questions of law that have arisen but have not yet been contested.

LEGAL TERM

Advisory Opinion
Opinion issued by an agency, upon request, that offers the agency's interpretation of law or asserts the agency's policy, practices, or procedures.

Declaratory Order
Administrative equivalent of a judicial declaratory judgment. An agency may issue a declaratory order to terminate a controversy or remove uncertainty. Such orders have the same effect as orders resulting from adjudications.

Declaratory orders have the same effect as orders issued after adjudications. They differ from adjudications, however, because they may be issued before a controversy arises, which is why they are similar to advisory opinions. The APA limits the issuance of declaratory orders to situations in which a formal adjudication is required. Therefore, in most situations a declaratory order is not issued.

Declaratory orders are subject to judicial review. The APA commits the decision on whether to grant a declaratory order to the agency's "sound discretion." Therefore, courts may review agency refusals to issue declaratory orders, as well as the issuance of such orders, for abuses of discretion.[11]

3.4(g) Mediation and Arbitration

Some administrative agencies are charged with the responsibility of conducting *mediation* and *arbitration*. *Mediation*, also known as *conciliation*, is the process of intervening in a dispute with the intent of assisting the parties to reach a resolution. *Arbitration* is a process whereby the parties submit their respective positions and arguments to a third party for decision. Mediators act as go-betweens and arbitrators act as decision makers.

Mediation is usually voluntary although some statutes require it. Arbitration is also usually voluntary although some statutes also require it. Arbitration is sometimes binding on the parties.

An administrative agency that conducts mediation is the Federal Mediation and Conciliation Service (FMCS). The FMCS acts as mediator in labor disputes that affect interstate commerce. It has no authority to compel arbitration, but its enabling statute allows it to conduct arbitrations upon agreement of the parties. In addition, the statute provides that the FMCS shall encourage parties to engage in arbitration to resolve their disputes.[12]

3.4(h) Other Action

Not all situations in which agencies exercise discretion can be mentioned in this text. Agency officials daily make decisions that are trusted to their sound discretion. As administrators, agencies manage public projects, lands, and other property. Decisions concerning purchases, leases, sales, employee concerns, and the like must be made.

Agencies must also deal with the media; agency officials must make decisions concerning the release of information and the issuance of statements. (Chapter 10 discusses the mandatory release of information by the government.) Publicity may be used to inform the public, to warn the public of danger, or to sanction offenders against the law.

3.5 CONCLUSION

Most agency action is informal. Most informal action is discretionary and subject to little judicial review. The debate over the degree of discretion that should be afforded by public officials will continue indefinitely. This is healthy in a free republic. However, meaningful standards, fueled by empirical research and public debate, defining when and how much discretion is needed, are essential. The APA, the common law, and the Constitution have laid the framework from which Congress, the courts, and the president must build upon to keep agencies accountable.

LEGAL TERMS

Mediation
Process of having a neutral third party intervene in a dispute in an attempt to assist the parties in reaching a resolution.

Arbitration
Process of having the parties to a dispute present their evidence and arguments to a neutral third party for decision. The decision of an arbitrator may be binding.

REVIEW **QUESTIONS**

1. What is meant by the statement that "informal administrative procedures are the lifeblood of the administrative process"?
2. What is the primary reason why agencies must select cases to investigate and prosecute rather than investigating and prosecuting all possible violations?
3. What is an advisory opinion?
4. What is a declaratory order?
5. Describe the relationship between discretion and fairness.
6. Describe the relationship between discretion and the number of rules that an agency official must enforce.
7. Briefly describe the deference that is afforded in an agency's interpretation of (1) its own rule, and (2) a statute, applying the *Chevron* and *Skidmore* decisions.

CRITICAL THINKING AND **APPLICATIONS PROBLEMS**

1. Identify three reasons why Howard believes discretion is necessary in public administration. What are the opposing arguments? What evidence is needed to prove these arguments?
2. Name, describe, and give an example of two forms of agency discretion discussed in this text.

ENDNOTES

1. Final Report of the Attorney General's Committee on Administrative Procedure 35 (1941).
2. Warner Books, 1994. See also Philip K. Howard, *The Lost Art of Drawing the Line: How Fairness Went Too Far* (Random House, 2001).
3. Samuel Walker, *Taming the System: The Control of Discretion in Criminal Justice, 1950–1990,* at 32 (New York: Oxford University Press, 1993).
4. *Id.* at 32.
5. Howard, *The Death of Common Sense, supra* note 2, at 15. For more on how Howard believes the U.S. legal system is disabling the U.S. economy, see his TED Talk entitled *Four Ways to Fix a Broken Legal System,* http://www.ted.com/talks/philip_howard.html and read his book *Life Without Lawyers: Liberating Americans From Too Much Law* (W.W. Norton 2010).
6. Walker, *supra* note 3, at 95. For additional information on discretion in policing, see Kenneth Culp Davis, *Police Discretion* (St. Paul MN: West, 1975).
7. *Newman v. United States,* 382 F.2d 479 (D.C. Cir. 1967).
8. APA § 554(c).
9. See *United States v. Mead,* 533 U.S. 218 (2001), *Christensen v. Harris County,* 529 U.S. 576 (2000), and *Skidmore v. Swift and Co.,* 323 U.S. 134 (1944).
10. *Id.* § 554(d).
11. Schwartz, *Administrative Law* § 3.21, at 159 (3d ed. 1989).
12. 29 U.S.C. § 172.

chapter **four**

THE REQUIREMENT OF FAIRNESS

LEARNING OBJECTIVES

After completing this chapter, you should be able to

- Identify the various forms of rights secured by the Due Process and Equal Protection Clauses.

- Describe due process cost-benefit analysis.

- Apply due process cost-benefit analysis to factual scenarios where the government is seeking to deprive a person of a protected interest, reaching a conclusion about the minimal process that must be followed.

- Describe the three review standards for due process and equal protection cases.

- Apply the correct due process and equal protection review standard to factual scenarios.

- Brief a judicial opinion with little outside assistance. You should be successful in identifying the relevant facts. You should also be successful in identifying the legal issue and analyzing the Court's rationale in at least 33 percent of your briefs.

The history of liberty has largely been the history of procedural safeguards.

JUSTICE FRANKFURTER[1]

Quote by Felix Frankfurter from "McNabb v. United States, 318 U.S. 332," 1943.

4.1 DUE PROCESS IN GENERAL

In the chapters that follow, you will learn that agency officials act as lawmakers, law enforcers, and judges. Agency officials, therefore, possess a considerable amount of diverse authority. As you learned in the last chapter, much of that authority is discretionary. Agency officials do not have carte blanche authority, however, over the people and businesses they regulate. Many rules limit their discretion. Many of these rules come from legislative bodies and agencies themselves, but the fundamental law requiring fairness is the Constitution. This chapter explores two constitutional fairness protections: due process[2] and equal protection.

The Fifth Amendment to the Constitution of the United States provides that "no person shall be deprived of life, liberty, or property without due process of law." The Fifth Amendment applies to actions of the federal government. The Fourteenth Amendment, one of three post–Civil War Amendments, contains another due process clause that applies specifically to the states. Section One of the Fourteenth Amendment reads:

> All persons born or naturalized in the United States and subject to the jurisdiction thereof, are citizens of the United States and of the State wherein they reside. No State shall make or enforce any law, which shall abridge the privileges or immunities of citizens of the United States; nor shall any State deprive any person of life, liberty, or property, without due process of law; nor deny to any person within its jurisdiction the equal protection of the laws.

In addition to due process, the Amendment protects privileges or immunities and equal protection. You will learn more about equal protection later. For reasons beyond the scope of this text, the Privileges or Immunities Clause has been interpreted by the Supreme Court into near oblivion. The Court has held that the Fourteenth Amendment's Privileges or Immunities Clauses didn't add to the rights found in Article IV's Privileges or Immunities Clause, that the purpose of the Fourteenth Amendment's Clause is to extend the rights secured by Article IV to African Americans, and that the Clauses were not intended to protect the rights found in the original Bill of Rights.[3]

Intended to prohibit states from discriminating against residents of other states, today the Privileges and Immunities Clause protects the right to travel within the states and to take up residence and citizenship in another state. The Clause also prohibits discriminatory practices by states when regulating work. A state law that favors the hiring of its own citizens by its resident employers violates the Privileges or Immunities Clause. However, such rules are legitimate if a state can show cause for a differentiation. States are permitted, for example, to establish independent rates of competence to enter the professions (law, medicine, etc.) so long as they treat every person, regardless of residency, the same in the process to prove competency. The Clauses protect a few other rights, such as the right to engage in business in other states, to have the full benefit of federal law, to have the full benefit of state law, and to purchase and lease property.

Where the Privileges or Immunities Clauses fail in protecting individual rights, the Due Process Clauses are robust. Due process is a broad concept that is intended to protect people from arbitrary government conduct. The Due Process Clauses mandate that state and federal government treat all persons with a minimum amount of fairness when taking life, liberty, or property from them. Due process has two aspects: procedural and substantive.

Procedural due process describes the minimum steps that must be taken by a government before it can deprive a person of life, liberty, or property. It is not

LEGAL TERM
Procedural Due Process
The minimum procedural steps a government must take before depriving a person of life, liberty, or property. Generally, due process includes the right to notice and a fair hearing.

concerned with the substance of an agency's action; rather, its concern is the process by which the government pursues its objective. Whether a person is entitled to notice or a hearing are questions of procedural due process.

Substantive due process is concerned not with the procedures used to make a rule or adjudicate an individual case, but with the substance of a rule or adjudication. It is possible for constitutional procedures to be used to implement a rule but for the rule itself to violate the Constitution. Substantive due process protects people from arbitrary laws.

For example, assume a law provides that businesses that serve food may not schedule female employees to work after dark. Suppose also that a restaurant nevertheless scheduled female employees for after-dark hours. If the violating restaurant were provided with notice of a hearing and an opportunity to present its case at that hearing, procedural due process would have been satisfied. However, the substance of the law could be questioned on both substantive due process (both liberty and property interests are implicated by restricting a person's right to move about and earn a living) and equal protection (treating people differently because of sex) grounds.

At one time, the federal Courts of the United States were active in reviewing legislation and rules under a substantive due process analysis. Little or no deference was given to rulemakers. A law would not be upheld unless a Court determined that its goal was lawful and the means to achieve the goal were reasonable. However, today reviewing Courts give legislatures and agencies deference when reviewing most laws. That is, so long as a statute or rule is rationally related to a lawful governmental objective, it is upheld. *Most* laws, when reviewed under the *rational relationship test,* are upheld. The Supreme Court has employed the rational relationship test to determine if laws and executive action are legitimate under the due process clauses for a very long time.[4]

Courts are more active, however, whenever a fundamental right or suspect class is being regulated. Examples of fundamental rights include most of those found in the Bill of Rights and elsewhere in the Constitution, including speech and expression, religious choice and practice, association, freedom of travel and relocation, the right to vote, and freedom of the press. Suspect classes are groups that have historically been discriminated against. Race and national origin are examples of suspect classes.

Whenever the government regulates a fundamental right or groups people around a suspect class, the regulation must pass a more difficult test than that of rational relationship. The law must survive *strict scrutiny*. For a regulation of this sort to be valid, it must be narrowly tailed to further a compelling governmental interest. The strict scrutiny test is referred to as an end-means review, the government's ends must be compelling and achieved through very targeted means. *Most* laws subjected to strict scrutiny fail.

An example of a compelling interest that justified racial classification is found in the 2003 case *Grutter v. Bollinger*,[5] where the Supreme Court upheld an admission policy of the University of Michigan Law School that took race into consideration. The Supreme Court issued a decision in a companion case to Grutter that stands as an example of a racial classification that didn't survive strict scrutiny. In *Gratz v. Bollinger*, the Court struck down the University of Michigan's undergraduate admissions policy because its assignment of points for race was deemed by the Court as quota like and not narrowly tailored to achieve the University's diversity objective. You will read more about these decisions later in this section.

In recent years, another more middle-ground test has begun to develop. This test requires that a regulation bear a *substantial relationship* to an important

Substantive Due Process
Requirement that laws be related to the purpose intended or that the government has some substantial reason for the regulation. Today, most laws are upheld as long as they bear a rational relationship to their objective. If a law encroaches upon civil liberties or classifies individuals, using certain criteria, it is held to a higher standard.

	Least demanding for government to satisfy		Most demanding for government to satisfy
	←		→
Test	**Rational Relationship**	**Substantial Relationship**	**Strict Scrutiny**
Defined	Law or action valid if it bears a rational relationship to a lawful governmental objective	Law or action valid if it is substantially related to a lawful government objective	Law or action valid only if it furthers a compelling governmental interest and reasonable alternatives don't exist
When Applied	Default test	Applied in limited cases, such as classifications based upon sex or "legitimacy of birth"	Applied when fundamental right is impinged or when law or act classifies by race, ethnicity, religion, etc.

TABLE 4-1   Due Process and Equal Protection Standards of Review

governmental interest to be valid. The Supreme Court has applied this test to laws that distinguish by gender. The prohibition of women working at night mentioned earlier could be scrutinized under this test.

Although it is impossible to quantify any of these tests, the substantial relationship test requires more than the rational relationship test and less than the strict scrutiny test. A law subjected to the substantial relationship test is more likely to fail than if held only to the rational relationship standard and more likely to be upheld than if subjected to strict scrutiny (see Table 4-1).

In administrative law, due process affects more than just rulemaking. Administrative officials make decisions daily that affect the lives of many people. These decisions are often not easily characterized as either rulemaking or adjudication. Regardless, such actions may have to comply with the fairness requirements imposed by the Due Process Clauses.

To determine if agency action (governmental action) must satisfy due process, two questions must be asked and answered. First, is state action being taken? Because this text is concerned with the actions of administrative agencies, there is usually no question that state action is at issue. Second, does the action deprive a person of life, liberty, or property? If both these questions are answered in the affirmative, then a decision as to what process is due must be made. Generally, a cost-benefit analysis is used to make this decision. Let's begin by examining what is protected by due process.

4.2 PROTECTED INTERESTS

The three interests protected by the Due Process Clauses are life, liberty, and property. This section examines each individually.

4.2(a) Life

Agencies rarely perform acts that threaten life although a few exceptions exist. Life may be threatened by the termination of gas or electric service in winter.

The Supreme Court has also recognized that terminating a needy mother's welfare benefits may be life-threatening. If life is threatened by agency action, due process must be afforded to the threatened person.

4.2(b) Liberty

Liberty interests are also protected by the Due Process Clauses. Liberty encompasses a multitude of personal freedoms. The right to move about as one pleases, without governmental interference, is an example. This is not particularly relevant to administrative law, because agencies do not normally restrain or incarcerate people. However, a few exceptions can be found. For example, state parole boards must provide due process before revoking the parole of a convict. Similarly, a probationer is entitled to a hearing before probation is revoked.[6] Also, the Immigration and Customs Enforcement has the authority to detain illegal aliens.

Liberty interests are not only physical in nature; more metaphysical rights are also protected. For example, a person's interest in his or her good name and reputation is a protected liberty interest. Thus, agencies must consider due process concerns before publicly accusing an individual of something that is humiliating, stigmatizing, or damaging to the reputation.

4.2(c) Property

A person may have a property interest in tangible or intangible property. Automobiles, houses, money, and jewelry are examples of tangible property. Obviously, if an agency attempts to take a person's tangible property (by forfeiture or condemnation proceedings, for instance), the agency must afford due process.

Entitlements.   Less obvious are the many intangible property interests people hold, such as an interest in receiving government benefits or entitlements. For example, does a person have a property interest in the receipt of welfare benefits?

At one time, due process did not reach such matters. If a person did not have an express constitutional right to something, then the government could take or withhold it almost at will. Government entitlements (such as welfare) were viewed as privileges or gratuities. Because benefits and grants were "gifts" from the government, they could be revoked at will. Not until a right was encroached upon did the government have to comply with due process. However, the rights-versus-privileges viewpoint is no longer used to analyze such issues.

The Supreme Court of the United States examined the rights-versus-privileges doctrine in *Goldberg v. Kelly*, wherein the Court stated that "[i]t may be realistic today to regard welfare entitlements as more like 'property' than a 'gratuity'. Much of the existing wealth in this country takes the form of rights that do not fall within traditional common-law concepts of property."[7] The Court stated that a person has a protected property interest in a benefit if he or she has a "legitimate claim or expectation to that benefit." In short, the Court rejected the rights-versus-privileges analysis. The question now is whether a person has an *entitlement*, that is, a legitimate expectation of receiving a benefit.

Governmental Employment.   It is possible, therefore, for a person to have no right to a benefit from the government but to have a protected interest in that benefit once the benefit is created. For example, there is no right to governmental employment. Once employed by the government, however, a nonprobationary employee has a property interest, under the Due Process Clause, in his or her employment.

As the *Sindermann* case shows, an employee must have a legitimate claim of entitlement to employment in order to be protected by due process. Unilateral claims of expected employment do not create a property interest under the Due Process Clause.[8] An employee's claim can be based on a contract (express or implied), a statute, or another law. You must refer to the law of the applicable jurisdiction when determining whether a sufficient entitlement exists. For example, teachers may reach tenure (and have a legitimate claim to continued employment) after different periods of time in different states.

Perry v. Sindermann

408 U.S. 593 (1972)

From 1959 to 1969 the respondent, Robert Sindermann, was a teacher in the state college system of the State of Texas. After teaching for two years at the University of Texas and for four years at San Antonio Junior College, he became a professor of Government and Social Science at Odessa Junior College in 1965. He was employed at the college for four successive years, under a series of one-year contracts. He was successful enough to be appointed, for a time, the cochairman of his department.

During the 1968–69 academic year, however, controversy arose between the respondent and the college administration. The respondent was elected president of the Texas Junior College Teachers Association. In this capacity, he left his teaching duties on several occasions to testify before committees of the Texas Legislature, and he became involved in public disagreements with the policies of the college's Board of Regents. . . .

Finally, in May 1969, the respondent's one-year employment contract terminated and the Board of Regents voted not to offer him a new contract for the next academic year. . . .

We have held today in *Board of Regents v. Roth*, 408 U.S. 564, 92 S. Ct. 2701, that the Constitution does not require opportunity for a hearing before the non-renewal of a nontenured teacher's contract, unless he can show that the decision not to rehire him somehow deprived him of an interest in "liberty" or that he had a "property" interest in continued employment, despite the lack of tenure or formal contract. . . .

[The plaintiff] alleged that this interest though not secured by a formal contractual tenure provision, was secured by a no less binding understanding fostered by the college administration. In particular, the respondent alleged that the college had a *de facto* tenure program, and that he had tenure under that program. He claimed that he and others legitimately relied upon an unusual provision that had been in the college's official Faculty Guide for many years:

> *Teacher Tenure:* Odessa College has no tenure system. The Administration of the College wishes the faculty member to feel that he has permanent tenure as long as his teaching services are satisfactory and as long as he displays a cooperative attitude toward his co-workers and his superiors, and as long as he is happy in his work.

Moreover, the respondent claimed legitimate reliance upon guidelines promulgated by the Coordinating Board of the Texas College and University System that provided that a person, like himself, who had been employed as a teacher in the state college and university system for seven years or more has some form of job tenure. Thus, the respondent offered to prove that a teacher with his long period of service at this particular State College had no less a "property" interest in continued employment than a formally tenured teacher at other colleges, and had no less a procedural due process right to a statement of reasons and a hearing before college officials upon their decision not to retain him. . . .

In this case, the respondent has alleged the existence of rules and understandings, promulgated and fostered by state officials, that may justify his legitimate claim of entitlement to continued employment absent "sufficient cause [for termination]."

[*Author's comment:* Note that the Court decided that Sindermann had a property interest, and, therefore, was entitled to due process before his employment could be terminated. It didn't decide whether he was entitled to continued employment.]

Perry v. Sindermann, 408 U.S. 593 (1972), U.S. Supreme Court.

Government employees may also have a protected interest in the benefits of employment. Insurance, vacation time, rewards, and other benefits may be protected by due process if an employee has an entitlement.

Also in the employment context, governmental agencies cannot encroach upon an employee's political rights, such as the right to political affiliation under the First Amendment, by requiring or prohibiting membership in a particular party or group, unless membership or neutrality is necessary to the performance of the job. However, the Supreme Court has held, in some circumstances, that the Constitution does not protect individuals when they are acting as government employees. The *Garcetti* case is an example in the First Amendment free speech context.

Garcetti v. Ceballos

547 U.S. 410 (2006)

Justice Kennedy delivered the opinion of the Court.

It is well settled that "a State cannot condition public employment on a basis that infringes the employee's constitutionally protected interest in freedom of expression." *Connick v. Myers*, 461 U.S. 138, 142 (1983). The question presented by the instant case is whether the First Amendment protects a government employee from discipline based on speech made pursuant to the employee's official duties.

Respondent Richard Ceballos has been employed since 1989 as a deputy district attorney for the Los Angeles County District Attorney's Office. During the period relevant to this case, Ceballos was a calendar deputy in the office's Pomona branch, and in this capacity he exercised certain supervisory responsibilities over other lawyers. In February 2000, a defense attorney contacted Ceballos about a pending criminal case. The defense attorney said there were inaccuracies in an affidavit used to obtain a critical search warrant. The attorney informed Ceballos that he had filed a motion to traverse, or challenge, the warrant, but he also wanted Ceballos to review the case. According to Ceballos, it was not unusual for defense attorneys to ask calendar deputies to investigate aspects of pending cases.

After examining the affidavit and visiting the location it described, Ceballos determined the affidavit contained serious misrepresentations. The affidavit called a long driveway what Ceballos thought should have been referred to as a separate roadway. Ceballos also questioned the affidavit's statement that tire tracks led from a stripped-down truck to the premises covered by the warrant. His doubts arose from his conclusion that the roadway's composition in some places made it difficult or impossible to leave visible tire tracks.

(continued)

Ceballos spoke on the telephone to the warrant affiant, a deputy sheriff from the Los Angeles County Sheriff's Department, but he did not receive a satisfactory explanation for the perceived inaccuracies. He relayed his findings to his supervisors, petitioners Carol Najera and Frank Sundstedt, and followed up by preparing a disposition memorandum. The memo explained Ceballos' concerns and recommended dismissal of the case. On March 2, 2000, Ceballos submitted the memo to Sundstedt for his review. A few days later, Ceballos presented Sundstedt with another memo, this one describing a second telephone conversation between Ceballos and the warrant affiant.

Based on Ceballos' statements, a meeting was held to discuss the affidavit. Attendees included Ceballos, Sundstedt, and Najera, as well as the warrant affiant and other employees from the sheriff's department. The meeting allegedly became heated, with one lieutenant sharply criticizing Ceballos for his handling of the case.

Despite Ceballos' concerns, Sundstedt decided to proceed with the prosecution, pending disposition of the defense motion to traverse. The trial court held a hearing on the motion. Ceballos was called by the defense and recounted his observations about the affidavit, but the trial court rejected the challenge to the warrant.

Ceballos claims that in the aftermath of these events he was subjected to a series of retaliatory employment actions. The actions included reassignment from his calendar deputy position to a trial deputy position, transfer to another courthouse, and denial of a promotion. Ceballos initiated an employment grievance, but the grievance was denied based on a finding that he had not suffered any retaliation. Unsatisfied, Ceballos sued in the United States District Court for the Central District of California, asserting, as relevant here, a claim under Rev. Stat. §1979, 42 U. S. C. §1983. He alleged petitioners violated the First and Fourteenth Amendments by retaliating against him based on his memo of March 2.

Petitioners responded that no retaliatory actions were taken against Ceballos and that all the actions of which he complained were explained by legitimate reasons such as staffing needs. They further contended that, in any event, Ceballos' memo was not protected speech under the First Amendment. Petitioners moved for summary judgment, and the District Court granted their motion. Noting that Ceballos wrote his memo pursuant to his employment duties, the Court concluded he was not entitled to First Amendment protection for the memo's contents. It held in the alternative that even if Ceballos' speech was constitutionally protected, petitioners had qualified immunity because the rights Ceballos asserted were not clearly established.

The Court of Appeals for the Ninth Circuit reversed, holding that "Ceballos' allegations of wrongdoing in the memorandum constitute protected speech under the First Amendment." In reaching its conclusion the Court looked to the First Amendment analysis set forth in *Pickering v. Board of Ed. of Township High School Dist. 205, Will Cty.*, 391 U.S. 563 (1968), and *Connick*, 461 U.S. 138. Connick instructs Courts to begin by considering whether the expressions in question were made by the speaker "as a citizen upon matters of public concern." The Court of Appeals determined that Ceballos' memo, which recited what he thought to be governmental misconduct, was "inherently a matter of public concern." The court did not, however, consider whether the speech was made in Ceballos' capacity as a citizen. Rather, it relied on Circuit precedent rejecting the idea that "a public employee's speech is deprived of First Amendment protection whenever those views are expressed, to government workers or others, pursuant to an employment responsibility." Having concluded that Ceballos' memo satisfied the public-concern requirement, the Court of Appeals proceeded to balance Ceballos' interest in his speech against his supervisors' interest in responding to it. The court struck the balance in Ceballos' favor, noting that petitioners "failed even to suggest disruption or inefficiency in the workings of the

District Attorney's Office" as a result of the memo. The court further concluded that Ceballos' First Amendment rights were clearly established and that petitioners' actions were not objectively reasonable. . . .

We granted certiorari, 543 U.S. 1186 (2005), and we now reverse.

As the Court's decisions have noted, for many years "the unchallenged dogma was that a public employee had no right to object to conditions placed upon the terms of employment—including those which restricted the exercise of constitutional rights." That dogma has been qualified in important respects. The Court has made clear that public employees do not surrender all their First Amendment rights by reason of their employment. Rather, the First Amendment protects a public employee's right, in certain circumstances, to speak as a citizen addressing matters of public concern. *Pickering* provides a useful starting point in explaining the Court's doctrine. There the relevant speech was a teacher's letter to a local newspaper addressing issues including the funding policies of his school board. "The problem in any case," the Court stated, "is to arrive at a balance between the interests of the teacher, as a citizen, in commenting upon matters of public concern and the interest of the State, as an employer, in promoting the efficiency of the public services it performs through its employees." *Id.*, at 568. The Court found the teacher's speech "neither [was] shown nor can be presumed to have in any way either impeded the teacher's proper performance of his daily duties in the classroom or to have interfered with the regular operation of the schools generally." Thus, the Court concluded that "the interest of the school administration in limiting teachers' opportunities to contribute to public debate is not significantly greater than its interest in limiting a similar contribution by any member of the general public."

Pickering and the cases decided in its wake identify two inquiries to guide interpretation of the constitutional protections accorded to public employee speech. The first requires determining whether the employee spoke as a citizen on a matter of public concern. If the answer is no, the employee has no First Amendment cause of action based on his or her employer's reaction to the speech. If the answer is yes, then the possibility of a First Amendment claim arises. The question becomes whether the relevant government entity had an adequate justification for treating the employee differently from any other member of the general public. See *Pickering*, 391 U.S., at 568. This consideration reflects the importance of the relationship between the speaker's expressions and employment. A government entity has broader discretion to restrict speech when it acts in its role as employer, but the restrictions it imposes must be directed at speech that has some potential to affect the entity's operations.

To be sure, conducting these inquiries sometimes has proved difficult. This is the necessary product of "the enormous variety of fact situations in which critical statements by teachers and other public employees may be thought by their superiors . . . to furnish grounds for dismissal." The Court's overarching objectives, though, are evident.

When a citizen enters government service, the citizen by necessity must accept certain limitations on his or her freedom. See, e.g., *Waters v. Churchill*, 511 U.S. 661, 671 (1994) (plurality opinion) ("[T]he government as employer indeed has far broader powers than does the government as sovereign"). Government employers, like private employers, need a significant degree of control over their employees' words and actions; without it, there would be little chance for the efficient provision of public services. ("[G]overnment offices could not function if every employment decision became a constitutional matter"). Public employees, moreover, often occupy trusted positions in society. When they speak out, they can express views that contravene governmental policies or impair the proper performance of governmental functions.

(continued)

At the same time, the Court has recognized that a citizen who works for the government is nonetheless a citizen. The First Amendment limits the ability of a public employer to leverage the employment relationship to restrict, incidentally or intentionally, the liberties employees enjoy in their capacities as private citizens. See *Perry v. Sindermann*, 408 U.S. 593, 597 (1972). So long as employees are speaking as citizens about matters of public concern, they must face only those speech restrictions that are necessary for their employers to operate efficiently and effectively. See, e.g., *Connick* ("Our responsibility is to ensure that citizens are not deprived of fundamental rights by virtue of working for the government").

The Court's employee-speech jurisprudence protects, of course, the constitutional rights of public employees. Yet the First Amendment interests at stake extend beyond the individual speaker. The Court has acknowledged the importance of promoting the public's interest in receiving the well-informed views of government employees engaging in civic discussion. . . . The Court's decisions, then, have sought both to promote the individual and societal interests that are served when employees speak as citizens on matters of public concern and to respect the needs of government employers attempting to perform their important public functions. See, e.g., *Rankin*, 483 U.S., at 384 (recognizing "the dual role of the public employer as a provider of public services and as a government entity operating under the constraints of the First Amendment"). Underlying our cases has been the premise that while the First Amendment invests public employees with certain rights, it does not empower them to "constitutionalize the employee grievance." . . .

With these principles in mind we turn to the instant case. Respondent Ceballos believed the affidavit used to obtain a search warrant contained serious misrepresentations. He conveyed his opinion and recommendation in a memo to his supervisor. That Ceballos expressed his views inside his office, rather than publicly, is not dispositive. Employees in some cases may receive First Amendment protection for expressions made at work. Many citizens do much of their talking inside their respective workplaces, and it would not serve the goal of treating public employees like "any member of the general public," to hold that all speech within the office is automatically exposed to restriction.

The memo concerned the subject matter of Ceballos' employment, but this, too, is nondispositive. The First Amendment protects some expressions related to the speaker's job. As the Court noted in *Pickering*: "Teachers are, as a class, the members of a community most likely to have informed and definite opinions as to how funds allotted to the operation of the schools should be spent. Accordingly, it is essential that they be able to speak out freely on such questions without fear of retaliatory dismissal." The same is true of many other categories of public employees.

The controlling factor in Ceballos' case is that his expressions were made pursuant to his duties as a calendar deputy. That consideration—the fact that Ceballos spoke as a prosecutor fulfilling a responsibility to advise his supervisor about how best to proceed with a pending case—distinguishes Ceballos' case from those in which the First Amendment provides protection against discipline. We hold that when public employees make statements pursuant to their official duties, the employees are not speaking as citizens for First Amendment purposes, and the Constitution does not insulate their communications from employer discipline.

Ceballos wrote his disposition memo because that is part of what he, as a calendar deputy, was employed to do. It is immaterial whether he experienced some personal gratification from writing the memo; his First Amendment rights do not depend on his job satisfaction. The significant point is that the memo was written pursuant to Ceballos' official duties. Restricting speech that owes its existence to a public employee's professional responsibilities does not infringe any liberties the employee might have enjoyed as a private citizen. It simply reflects the exercise of employer control over what the employer itself has commissioned or created. . . . Ceballos did not act as a citizen when he went about conducting his daily professional activities, such as supervising attorneys, investigating charges, and preparing filings. In the same way he did not speak as a citizen by writing a memo that addressed the proper disposition of a pending criminal case. When he went to work and performed the tasks he was paid to perform, Ceballos acted as a government employee. The fact that his duties sometimes required him to speak or write does not mean his supervisors were prohibited from evaluating his performance.

This result is consistent with our precedents' attention to the potential societal value of employee speech. Refusing to recognize First Amendment claims based on government employees' work product does not prevent them from participating in public debate. The employees retain the prospect of constitutional protection for their contributions to the civic discourse. This prospect of protection, however, does not invest them with a right to perform their jobs however they see fit.

Our holding likewise is supported by the emphasis of our precedents on affording government employers sufficient discretion to manage their operations. Employers have heightened interests in controlling speech made by an employee in his or her professional capacity. Official communications have official consequences, creating a need for substantive consistency and clarity. Supervisors must ensure that their employees' official communications are accurate, demonstrate sound judgment, and promote the employer's mission. Ceballos' memo is illustrative. It demanded the attention of his supervisors and led to a heated meeting with employees from the sheriff's department. If Ceballos' superiors thought his memo was inflammatory or misguided, they had the authority to take proper corrective action. . . .

Proper application of our precedents thus leads to the conclusion that the First Amendment does not prohibit managerial discipline based on an employee's expressions made pursuant to official responsibilities. Because Ceballos' memo falls into this category, his allegation of unconstitutional retaliation must fail.

Two final points warrant mentioning. First, as indicated above, the parties in this case do not dispute that Ceballos wrote his disposition memo pursuant to his employment duties. We thus have no occasion to articulate a comprehensive framework for defining the scope of an employee's duties in cases where there is room for serious debate. We reject, however, the suggestion that employers can restrict employees' rights by creating excessively broad job descriptions. The proper inquiry is a practical one. Formal job descriptions often bear little resemblance to the duties an employee actually is expected to perform, and the listing of a given task in an employee's written job description is neither necessary nor sufficient to demonstrate that conducting the task is within the scope of the employee's professional duties for First Amendment purposes.

Second, Justice Souter suggests today's decision may have important ramifications for academic freedom, at least as a constitutional value. There is some argument that expression related to academic scholarship or classroom instruction implicates additional constitutional interests that are not fully accounted for by this Court's customary employee-speech jurisprudence. We need not, and for that reason do not, decide whether the analysis we conduct today would apply in the same manner to a case involving speech related to scholarship or teaching. . . .

The judgment of the Court of Appeals is reversed, and the case is remanded for proceedings consistent with this opinion.

Garcetti v. Ceballos, 547 U.S. 410 (2006), U.S. Supreme Court.

Recall that due process limits governmental actions, not private actions. Therefore, due process does not protect private-sector employees from employer acts not coerced or required by the government.

Licenses.   To engage in some occupations, one must first obtain a license. If a government chooses to impose a licensure requirement, it must satisfy the Due Process and Equal Protection Clauses when issuing, suspending, revoking, or otherwise acting concerning those licenses. For example, in one case an applicant for admission to a state bar passed the bar exam but was denied admission, without being given the opportunity to be heard because he was determined to be of unfit character. Further, the applicant was not given any information as to why he had been determined unfit. The Supreme Court found that the bar's action violated due process. The Court held that the applicant was entitled to know what evidence the bar was relying on and to be heard on that evidence.[9]

Licensing decisions may not be based on criteria that violate equal protection. For instance, a licensing scheme that favors one race or sex is likely unconstitutional.

A driver's license is also protected if possession of that license is necessary to earn one's livelihood.[10]

Utilities.   When the government provides electricity or gas to the public at large, service cannot be terminated without providing the customer an opportunity to contest the charges or prove that payment was made.

Education.   A person may also have a protected interest in attending a public school, college, university, or other educational program. This is the issue in the *Goss* case.

Goss v. Lopez

419 U.S. 565 (1975)

This appeal by various administrators of the Columbus, Ohio, Public School System (CPSS) challenges the judgment of a three-judge federal court, declaring that appellees—various high school students in the CPSS—were denied due process of law contrary to the command of the Fourteenth Amendment in that they were temporarily suspended from their high schools without a hearing either prior to suspension or within a reasonable time thereafter, and enjoining the administrators to remove all references to such suspensions from the student's records.

Ohio law, Rev. Code Ann. § 3313.64 (1972), provides for free education to all children between the ages of six and 21. Section 3313.66 of the Code empowers the principal of an Ohio public school to suspend a pupil [for] misconduct for up to 10 days or to expel him. In either case, he must notify the student's parents within 24 hours and state the reasons for his action. A pupil who is expelled, or his parents, may appeal the decision to the Board of Education. . . . No similar procedure is provided . . . for a suspended student. . . .

The nine named appellees, each of whom alleged that he or she had been suspended from public high school in Columbus for up to 10 days without a hearing pursuant to § 3313.66, filed an action under 42 U.S.C. § 1983 against the Columbus Board of Education and various administrators of the CPSS. The complaint sought a declaration that § 3313.66 was unconstitutional in that it permitted public school administrators to deprive plaintiffs of their rights to an education without a hearing of any kind, in violation of the procedural due process component of the Fourteenth Amendment. It also sought to enjoin the public school officials from issuing future suspensions pursuant to § 3313.66 and to require them to remove references to the past suspensions from the records of the students in question.

The proof below established that the suspensions arose out of a period of widespread student unrest in the CPSS during February and March 1971. Six of the named plaintiffs, Rudolph Sutton, Tyrone Washington, Susan Cooper, Deborah Fox, Clarence Byars, and Bruce Harris, were students at the Marion-Franklin High School and were each suspended for 10 days on account of disruptive or disobedient conduct committed in the presence of the school administrator who ordered the suspension. One of these, Tyrone Washington, was among a group of students demonstrating in the school auditorium while a class was being conducted there. He was ordered by the school principal to leave, refused to do so, and was suspended. Rudolph Sutton, in the presence of the principal, physically attacked a police officer who was attempting to remove Tyrone Washington from the auditorium. He was immediately suspended. The other four Marion-Franklin students were suspended for similar conduct. None was given a hearing to determine the operative facts underlying the suspension, but each, together with his or her parents, was offered the opportunity to attend a conference, subsequent to the effective date of the suspension, to discuss the student's future.

Two named plaintiffs, Dwight Lopez and Betty Crome, were students at the Central High School and McGuffey Junior High School, respectively. The former was suspended in connection with a disturbance in the lunchroom, which involved some physical damage to school property. Lopez testified that at least 75 other students were suspended from his school on the same day. He also testified below that he was not a party to the destructive conduct but was instead an innocent bystander. Because no one from the school testified with regard to this incident, there is no evidence in the record indicating the official basis for concluding otherwise. Lopez never had a hearing.

Betty Crome was present at a demonstration at a high school other than the one she was attending. There she was arrested together with others, taken to the police station, and released without being formally charged. Before she went to school on the following day, she was notified that she had been suspended for a 10-day period. Because no one from the school testified with respect to this incident, the record does not disclose how the McGuffey Junior High School principal went about making the decision to suspend Crome, nor does it disclose on what information the decision was based. It is clear from the record that no hearing was ever held. . . .

Although Ohio may not be constitutionally obligated to establish and maintain a public school system, it has nevertheless done so and has required its children to attend. Those young people do not "shed their constitutional rights" at the schoolhouse door. . . . The authority possessed by the State to prescribe and enforce standards of conduct in its schools although concededly very broad, must be exercised consistently with constitutional safeguards. Among other things, the State is constrained to recognize a student's legitimate entitlement to a public education as a property interest, which is protected by the Due Process Clause and, which may not be taken away for misconduct without adherence to the minimum procedures required by that Clause.

The Due Process Clause also forbids arbitrary deprivations of liberty. "Where a person's good name, reputation, honor, or integrity is at stake because of what the government is doing to him," the minimal requirements of the Clause must be satisfied. . . . School authorities here suspended appellees from school for periods of up

(continued)

to 10 days based on charges of misconduct. If sustained and recorded, those charges could seriously damage the students' standing with their fellow pupils and their teachers as well as interfere with later opportunities for higher education and employment. It is apparent that the claimed right of the State to determine unilaterally and without process whether that misconduct has occurred immediately collides with the requirements of the Constitution. . . .

A short suspension is, of course, a far milder deprivation than expulsion. But "education is perhaps the most important function of state and local governments," . . . and the total exclusion from the educational process for more than a trivial period, and certainly if the suspension is for 10 days, is a serious event in the life of the suspended child. Neither the property interest in educational benefits temporarily denied nor the liberty interest in reputation, which is also implicated, is so insubstantial that suspensions may constitutionally be imposed by any procedure the school chooses, no matter how arbitrary.

"Once it is determined that due process applies, the question remains what process is due." . . .

The difficulty is that our schools are vast and complex. Some modicum of discipline and order is essential if the educational function is to be performed. Events calling for discipline are frequent occurrences and sometime require immediate, effective action. . . . But it would be a strange disciplinary system in an educational institution if no communication was sought by the disciplinarian with the student in an effort to inform him of his dereliction and to let him tell his side of the story in order to make sure that an injustice is not done. "[F]airness can rarely be obtained by secret, one-sided determination of facts decisive of rights. . . ."

We do not believe that school authorities must be totally free from notice and hearing requirements if their schools are to operate with acceptable efficiency. Students facing temporary suspensions have interests qualifying for protection of the Due Process Clause, and due process requires, in connection with a suspension of 10 days or less, that the student be given oral or written notice of the charges against him and, if he denies them, an explanation of the evidence the authorities have and an opportunity to present his side of the story. The Clause requires at least these rudimentary precautions against unfair or mistaken findings of misconduct and arbitrary exclusion from school.

There need be no delay between the time "notice" is given and the time of the hearing. In the great majority of cases the disciplinarian may informally discuss the alleged misconduct with the student minutes after it has occurred. We hold only that, in being given an opportunity to explain his version of the facts at this discussion, the student first be told what he is accused of doing and what the basis of the accusation is. . . .

We should also make it clear that we have addressed ourselves solely to the short suspension, not exceeding 10 days. Longer suspensions or expulsions for the remainder of the school term, or permanently, may require more formal procedures.

Goss v. Lopez–419 U.S. 565 (1975), U.S. Supreme Court.

4.3 COST-BENEFIT ANALYSIS

Once it is determined that there is state action and that a life, property, or liberty interest is being affected, then due process must be afforded. What does that mean?

Generally, due process requires that the affected person or entity be provided with notice of a possible deprivation and a hearing. The form of the notice and hearing varies, depending on the facts of each case. Due process is a flexible concept, adapting to the facts of each case. Courts employ a cost-benefit analysis when deciding what procedure must be afforded.

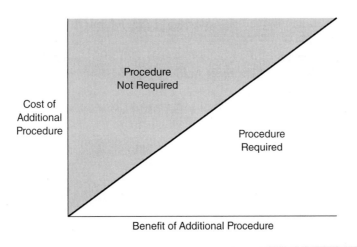

FIGURE 4-1   Due process cost-benefit analysis.

In all instances, due process requires notice and an opportunity to respond. What must be determined is whether a person is entitled to notice before or after some governmental action is taken and the type of response that must be permitted. Will a simple informal presentation to an agency official satisfy due process, or must a full evidentiary-type hearing be conducted? These are not easy questions to answer in all instances.

The interests of the individual in receiving extended procedural protections are weighed against the interests of the government in minimizing the process. The "risk of an erroneous deprivation of interest through the procedures used, and the probable value, if any, of additional or substitute procedural safeguards,"[11] is considered. Said another way, the harm and cost to the government of providing additional process must be weighed against the harm the individual will suffer if not afforded additional process. From this balancing, the determination of what procedures are justified is made. Section 4.5 examines the cost-benefit analysis as it has been applied by the Supreme Court of the United States in specific cases. The graph in Figure 4-1 illustrates the relationship of costs to benefits in this context.

President Obama after signing the PPACA.

4.4 NOTICE

The right to notice is central to due process. The notice aspect of due process has two prongs. First, an interested person is entitled to notice of what the agency is about to do or, in some instances, what it has already done. This may include the basic facts and charges upon which the agency is going to act. For example, a notice to appear before the Bureau of Motor Vehicles for "disciplinary action" is not sufficient; a notice to appear for "potential license revocation for driving while intoxicated on date [X]" is adequate. The APA requires that a person receive notice of the law and facts at issue and the legal authority under which the hearing is being conducted.[12]

The second prong is notice of the date, time, and location of the hearing. This is also required by the APA.[13] Notice of a hearing must be timely. Due process does not specifically require a certain period of time; rather, notice must simply be sufficient to allow a person to prepare for the hearing. A few days' notice is rarely adequate, but a month's notice normally is. However, timeliness differs from case to case. The best notice is personal. Most notices, however, are sent by first-class or registered mail.

In some circumstances, an agency may take summary action, usually to protect the public health and safety. In such instances, due process may not require preaction notice or hearing. When this occurs, though, there must be immediate postaction notice and a hearing. This is discussed more fully in Section 4.5.

4.5 HEARINGS

Hearings take many forms. Courts use the cost-benefit analysis discussed in Section 4.3 when determining exactly what must be done to satisfy due process. Where, when, and what type of hearing is required by the Due Process Clauses before a life, liberty, or property interest may be taken by the government?

4.5(a) Where

First, due process requires that hearings be held in such a place that those interested will not be severely burdened by appearing. The APA permits an agency to conduct its hearings at its office in Washington, D.C., or elsewhere, taking into consideration the convenience of parties. However, the Due Process Clause may mandate that a hearing be conducted near a party's residence if he or she has no money or method of getting to Washington, D.C.

4.5(b) What

Another important question is what type of hearing must be conducted to satisfy due process. The Due Process Clauses do not require trial-type hearings in all cases. In fact, what is required differs depending on the facts of each case. In all cases, the procedure must be fair. In some circumstances, a person may be entitled to an oral hearing before an administrative law judge. In others, an interested party may be limited to submitting a written argument. Even when oral hearings are held, the Due Process Clauses do not require that trial-like procedures be used. In reality, many administrative hearings are informal meetings between agency official and individuals, without attorneys and unbounded by rules of procedure.

Whether a party is entitled to an oral hearing depends largely upon the issues to be considered. If the issues in dispute are factual, then the parties must be given the opportunity to present their side of the story, call witnesses, and cross-examine those who testify conversely to their position. Chief Justice Warren of the U.S. Supreme Court stated that

> [c]ertain principles have remained relatively immutable in our jurisprudence. One of these is that where governmental action seriously injures an individual, and the reasonableness of the action depends on fact findings, the evidence used to prove the Government's case must be

disclosed to the individual so that he has an opportunity to show that it is untrue.[14]

There is no need for an evidentiary hearing, however, when the facts central to the case are test results or other scientific information. This is reflected in the APA, which exempts from the hearing requirements "proceedings in which decisions rest solely on inspections, tests, or elections."[15]

There is also no requirement of an evidentiary hearing if legislative rather than adjudicative facts are found. The distinction is a matter of scope. Legislative facts are broader and less concerned with individual adjudications than are adjudicative facts. For example, the determination of what an industry practice has been is a legislative fact although it may be material to an individual adjudication. What the particular practice of a specific member of that industry has been is an adjudicative fact.

If an issue is purely legal, an agency may limit the party's participation to a written submission arguing the law.

If a matter has a factual element but the outcome is obvious, then due process may not require an oral hearing. For example, there need not be a hearing on the question of whether a person scored enough points on a written driving test to pass.

Agencies make many decisions and take many actions that do not fall squarely within the definitions of *adjudication* or *rulemaking*. These actions may nevertheless be limited by due process concerns. That is, due process may require agencies to confront the person against whom some action is being taken, present the problem, and give the person the opportunity to tell his or her side of the story. An informal meeting will likely satisfy due process. Requiring a public utility to give a customer an opportunity to explain nonpayment before terminating service is an example.

4.5(c) When

When must a hearing be conducted? Must the government provide individuals with a hearing before depriving them of a liberty or property interest, or will a postdeprivation hearing satisfy due process? In most cases, a predeprivation hearing is not required. Providing a fair hearing after a decision has been made satisfies due process, provided an individual is not significantly harmed by that process. The *Goldberg* case illustrates an exception to this basic rule.

Goldberg requires a pretermination hearing when welfare benefits are at issue. The Court in *Goldberg* stressed that the harm to individual welfare recipients that could result from erroneous termination of benefits outweighed any competing governmental interests in protecting the public fisc. On the benefits side, qualified recipients who are wrongly terminated are provided the means to stay healthy and alive. Also, the Court thought such a policy serves a larger objective, in that it fosters the dignity and well-being of the people. On the other side of the equation are several costs to the public. First, there is the cost of the hearing. That includes hearings for those who do not qualify for benefits. Second, and more significant, there is the cost of providing benefits to unqualified applicants during the period of appeal, hearing, and final decision. The Court found that the benefits outweighed the costs, and today welfare recipients have a right to an evidentiary hearing before having their benefits terminated.

Goldberg v. Kelly

397 U.S. 254 (1970)

The question for decision is whether a State that terminates public assistance payments to a particular recipient without affording him the opportunity for an evidentiary hearing prior to termination denies the recipient procedural due process in violation of the Due Process Clause of the Fourteenth Amendment.

This action was brought in the District Court for the Southern District of New York by residents of New York City receiving financial aid under the federally assisted program of Aid to Families with Dependent Children (AFDC) or under New York State's general Home Relief Program. Their complaint alleged that the New York State and New York State officials administering these programs terminated, or were about to terminate, such aid without prior notice and hearing, thereby denying them due process of law. . . .

The constitutional issue to be decided, therefore, is the narrow one [of] whether the Due Process Clause requires that the recipient be afforded an evidentiary hearing *before* the termination of benefits. The District Court held that only a pretermination evidentiary hearing would satisfy the constitutional command. . . .

The extent to which procedural due process must be afforded the recipient is influenced by the extent to which he may be "condemned to suffer grievous loss" . . . and depends upon whether the recipient's interest in avoiding that loss outweighs the governmental interest in summary adjudication. . . .

It is true, of course, that some governmental benefits may be administratively terminated without affording the recipient a pretermination evidentiary hearing. But we agree with the [trial court] that when welfare is discontinued, only a pretermination evidentiary hearing provides the recipient with procedural due process. . . . For qualified recipients, welfare provides the means to obtain essential food, clothing, housing, and medical care. . . . Thus the crucial factor in this context—a factor not present in the case of the blacklisted government contractor, the discharged government employee, the taxpayer denied a tax exemption, or virtually anyone else whose governmental entitlements are ended—is that termination of aid pending resolution of a controversy over eligibility may deprive an *eligible* recipient of the very means by which to live while he waits. Since he lacks independent resources, his situation becomes immediately desperate. His need to concentrate upon finding the means for daily subsistence, in turn, adversely affects his ability to seek redress from the welfare bureaucracy.

Moreover, important governmental interests are promoted by affording recipients a pre-termination evidentiary hearing. From its founding the Nation's basic commitment has been to foster the dignity and well-being of all persons within its borders. We have come to recognize that forces not within the control of the poor contribute to their poverty. This perception, against the background of our traditions, has significantly influenced the development of the contemporary public assistance system. Welfare, by meeting the basic demands of subsistence, can help bring within the reach of the poor the same opportunities that are available to others to participate meaningfully in the life of the community. At the same time, welfare guards against the societal malaise that may flow from a widespread sense of unjustified frustration and insecurity. . . .

Appellant does not challenge the force of these considerations but argues that they are outweighed by countervailing governmental interests in conserving fiscal and administrative resources. These interests, the argument goes, justify the delay of any evidentiary hearing until after discontinuance of the grants. Summary adjudication protects the public fisc by stopping payments promptly upon discovery of reason to believe that a recipient is no longer eligible. . . .

We agree with the District Court, however, that these governmental interests are not overriding in the welfare context. The requirement of a prior hearing doubtless involves some greater expense, and the benefits paid to ineligible recipients pending decision at the hearing probably cannot be recouped since these recipients are likely to be judgment-proof. But the State is not without weapons to minimize these increased costs. Much of the drain on fiscal and administrative resources can be reduced by developing procedures for prompt pre-termination hearings and by skillful use of personnel and facilities. . . . Thus, the interest of the eligible recipient in uninterrupted receipt of public assistance, coupled with the State's interest that his payments not be erroneously terminated, clearly outweighs the State's competing concern to prevent any increase in its fiscal and administrative burdens. . . .

We also agree with the District Court, however, that the pretermination hearing need not take the form of a judicial or quasi-judicial trial. We bear in mind that the statutory "fair hearing" will provide the recipient with a full administrative review. Accordingly, the pretermination hearing has one function only: to produce an initial determination of the validity of the welfare department's grounds for discontinuance of payments in order to protect a recipient against an erroneous termination of his benefits. . . . Thus, a complete record and a comprehensive opinion, which would serve primarily to facilitate judicial review and to guide future decisions, need not be provided at the pretermination stage. . . .

"The fundamental requisite of due process of law is the opportunity to be heard." . . . The hearing must be "at a meaningful time and in a meaningful manner." . . . In the present context these principles require that a recipient have timely and adequate notice detailing the reasons for a proposed termination, and an effective opportunity to defend by confronting any adverse witnesses and by presenting his own arguments and evidence orally. . . .

The city's procedures presently do not permit recipients to appear personally with or without counsel before the official who finally determines continued eligibility. Thus a recipient is not permitted to present evidence to that official orally, or to confront or cross-examine witnesses. These omissions are fatal to the constitutional adequacy of the procedures.

The opportunity to be heard must be tailored to the capacities and circumstances of those who are to be heard. It is not enough that a welfare recipient may present his position to the decision maker in writing or second-hand through his caseworker. Written submissions are an unrealistic option for most recipients, who lack the educational attainment necessary to write effectively and who cannot obtain professional assistance. Moreover, written submissions do not afford the flexibility of oral presentations; they do not permit the recipient to mold his argument to the issues the decision maker appears to regard as important. Particularly where credibility and veracity are at issue, as they must be in many termination proceedings, written submissions are a wholly unsatisfactory basis for decision.

Goldberg v. Kelly, 397 U.S. 254 (1970), U.S. Supreme Court.

Researchers have attempted to determine what the actual costs of the *Goldberg* decision were to governments. One study reported that 80 percent of those who demanded a *Goldberg* hearing were determined to be ineligible for benefits, as initially determined. Another study found that 92 percent of *Goldberg*-type appeals were lost and that the cost in providing benefits to the 92 percent of appellants who lost their appeals was nearly $500,000 in 1971 to the state of Michigan alone. Some costs may be borne by qualified welfare recipients. For example, when funds run low in some states, the total benefits paid to recipients are decreased across the board. Fortunately, it appears that most termination decisions are not appealed; otherwise the costs would be much higher.[16]

Courts examine the following factors when determining if a predetermination or postdetermination hearing must be conducted:

1. The additional harm to the individual that results from not requiring a predetermination hearing
2. The value that requiring additional processes will have to the individual
3. The likelihood of error without additional safeguards
4. The cost and burdens imposed by requiring additional procedures
5. Other public concerns

The *Goldberg* rationale has not been extended to unemployment benefits or to denials of disability benefits. In its 1976 decision in *Mathews v. Eldridge*, the Court reasoned that because the program requires predeprivation notice of findings with an opportunity to respond and because disabled persons will be eligible for other public assistance, such as welfare, the need for a predetermination hearing was not as critical as when welfare benefits are denied. The Court also reasoned that because disability decisions often turn on unbiased medical reports, the value of evidentiary hearings is reduced. Yet the cost of requiring evidentiary predeprivation hearings would be very high.[17] Similarly, although nonprobationary government employees have a protected interest in their positions, no evidentiary presuspension hearing must be conducted. The Court has stated that a brief informal hearing aimed at determining "whether there are reasonable grounds to believe that the charges against the employee are true," followed by a more thorough postsuspension hearing, satisfies due process.[18] The distinction between suspensions and terminations is important in the public employment context. Nonprobationary employees are entitled to full hearings prior to termination. However, as discussed earlier, only an informal hearing is required before suspension, provided the employee is entitled to an evidentiary hearing prior to termination.

Recall that the *Goss* Court determined that a limited presuspension hearing must be afforded to public school students. Again, this is justified because the harm to a student is significant and the cost to the school of conducting the hearing is minimal.

The existence of a civil remedy for a violation of one's due process rights is an important factor in deciding whether a preaction or postaction hearing must be conducted. If no civil or criminal remedy is available to an aggrieved party, the need for additional process is increased. Another factor in the equation is the existence of an independent determination of facts. For example, if a government employee has been charged with a crime that also justifies suspension, there may be no need for a presuspension hearing. That was the issue in the *Homar* case. Similarly, a criminal conviction may justify termination of an employee. In such a case, the government is not required to relitigate the guilt of the employee. However, the employee is entitled to a hearing to establish that the crime is not one that can lead to termination or to establish that he or she was not the person convicted.

Gilbert v. Homar

520 U.S. 924 (1997)

Justice Scalia delivered the opinion of the Court.

This case presents the question whether a State violates the Due Process Clause of the Fourteenth Amendment by failing to provide notice and a hearing before suspending a tenured public employee without pay.

Respondent Richard J. Homar was employed as a police officer at East Stroudsburg University (ESU), a branch of Pennsylvania's State System of Higher Education. On August 26, 1992, when respondent was at the home of a family friend, he was arrested by the Pennsylvania State Police in a drug raid. Later that day, the state police filed a criminal complaint charging respondent with possession of marijuana, possession with intent to deliver, and criminal conspiracy to violate the controlled substance law, which is a felony. The state police notified respondent's supervisor, University Police Chief David Marazas, of the arrest and charges. Chief Marazas in turn informed Gerald Levanowitz, ESU's Director of Human Resources, to whom ESU President James Gilbert had delegated authority to discipline ESU employees. Levanowitz suspended respondent without pay effective immediately. Respondent failed to report to work on the day of his arrest, and learned of his suspension the next day, when he called Chief Marazas to inquire whether he had been suspended. That same day, respondent received a letter from Levanowitz confirming that he had been suspended effective August 26 pending an investigation into the criminal charges filed against him. The letter explained that any action taken by ESU would not necessarily coincide with the disposition of the criminal charges.

Although the criminal charges were dismissed on September 1, respondent's suspension remained in effect while ESU continued with its own investigation. On September 18, Levanowitz and Chief Marazas met with respondent in order to give him an opportunity to tell his side of the story. Respondent was informed at the meeting that the state police had given ESU information that was "very serious in nature," but he was not informed that that included a report of an alleged confession he had made on the day of his arrest; he was consequently unable to respond to damaging statements attributed to him in the police report.

In a letter dated September 23, Levanowitz notified respondent that he was being demoted to the position of groundskeeper effective the next day, and that he would receive backpay from the date the suspension took effect at the rate of pay of a groundskeeper. (Respondent eventually received backpay for the period of his suspension at the rate of pay of a university police officer.) The letter maintained that the demotion was being imposed "as a result of admissions made by yourself to the Pennsylvania State Police on August 26, 1992 that you maintained associations with individuals whom you knew were dealing in large quantities of marijuana and that you obtained marijuana from one of those individuals for your own use. Your actions constitute a clear and flagrant violation of Sections 200 and 200.2 of the [ESU] Police Department Manual." Upon receipt of this letter, the president of respondent's union requested a meeting with President Gilbert. The requested meeting took place on September 24, at which point respondent had received and read the police report containing the alleged confession. After providing respondent with an opportunity to respond to the charges, Gilbert sustained the demotion. Respondent filed this suit under Rev. Stat. § 1979, § 42 U.S.C. 1983, in the United States District Court for the Middle District of Pennsylvania against President Gilbert, Chief Marazas, Levanowitz, and a Vice President of ESU, Curtis English, all in both their individual and official capacities. He contended, inter alia, that petitioners' failure to provide him with notice and an opportunity to be heard before suspending him without pay violated due process. . . .

The protections of the Due Process Clause apply to government deprivation of those perquisites of government employment in which the employee has a constitutionally protected "property" interest. Although we have previously held that public employees who can be discharged only for cause have a constitutionally protected property interest in their tenure and cannot be fired without due process, see *Board of Regents of State Colleges v. Roth* . . . [and] *Perry v. Sindermann* . . . we have not

(continued)

had occasion to decide whether the protections of the Due Process Clause extend to discipline of tenured public employees short of termination. Petitioners, however, do not contest this preliminary point, and so without deciding it we will, like the District Court, "[a]ssum[e] that the suspension infringed a protected property interest," and turn at once to petitioners' contention that respondent received all the process he was due.

In *Cleveland Bd. of Ed. v. Loudermill*, we concluded that a public employee dismissable only for cause was entitled to a very limited hearing prior to his termination, to be followed by a more comprehensive post-termination hearing. Stressing that the pretermination hearing "should be an initial check against mistaken decisions—essentially, a determination of whether there are reasonable grounds to believe that the charges against the employee are true and support the proposed action," we held that pretermination process need only include oral or written notice of the charges, an explanation of the employer's evidence, and an opportunity for the employee to tell his side of the story. In the course of our assessment of the governmental interest in immediate termination of a tenured employee, we observed that "in those situations where the employer perceives a significant hazard in keeping the employee on the job, it can avoid the problem by suspending with pay." Relying on this dictum, which it reads as "strongly suggest[ing] that suspension without pay must be preceded by notice and an opportunity to be heard in all instances," 89 F. 3d, at 1015, and determining on its own that such a rule would be "eminently sensible," the Court of Appeals adopted a categorical prohibition: "[A] governmental employer may not suspend an employee without pay unless that suspension is preceded by some kind of presuspension hearing, providing the employee with notice and an opportunity to be heard." Respondent (as well as most of his amici) makes no attempt to defend this absolute rule, which spans all types of government employment and all types of unpaid suspensions. This is eminently wise since under our precedents such an absolute rule is indefensible.

It is by now well established that " 'due process,' unlike some legal rules, is not a technical conception with a fixed content unrelated to time, place and circumstances." *Cafeteria & Restaurant Workers v. McElroy.* "[D]ue process is flexible and calls for such procedural protections as the particular situation demands." . . . This Court has recognized, on many occasions, that where a State must act quickly, or where it would be impractical to provide predeprivation process, postdeprivation process satisfies the requirements of the Due Process Clause. . . .

To say that when the government employer perceives a hazard in leaving the employee on the job, it "can avoid the problem by suspending with pay" is not to say that that is the only way of avoiding the problem. Whatever implication the phrase "with pay" might have conveyed is far outweighed by the clarity of our precedents, which emphasize the flexibility of due process as contrasted with the sweeping and categorical rule adopted by the Court of Appeals. To determine what process is constitutionally due, we have generally balanced three distinct factors:

> First, the private interest that will be affected by the official action; second, the risk of an erroneous deprivation of such interest through the procedures used, and the probable value, if any, of additional or substitute procedural safeguards; and finally, the Government's interest. . . .

Respondent contends that he has a significant private interest in the uninterrupted receipt of his paycheck. But while our opinions have recognized the severity of depriving someone of the means of his livelihood, they have also emphasized that in determining what process is due, account must be taken of "the length" and "finality of the deprivation." Unlike the employee in *Loudermill*, who faced termination, respondent faced only a temporary suspension without pay. So long as the suspended employee receives a sufficiently prompt post-suspension hearing, the lost income is relatively insubstantial (compared with termination), and fringe benefits such as health and life insurance are often not affected at all. . . . On the other side of the balance, the State has a significant interest in immediately suspending, when felony charges are filed against them, employees who occupy positions of great public trust and high public visibility, such as police officers. Respondent contends that this interest in maintaining public confidence could have been accommodated by suspending him with pay until he had a hearing. We think, however, that the government does not have to give an employee charged with a felony a paid leave at taxpayer expense. If his services to the government are no longer useful once the felony charge has been filed, the Constitution does not require the government to bear the added expense of hiring a replacement while still paying him. ESU's interest in preserving public confidence in its police force is [significant]. . . .

The last factor in the *Mathews* balancing, and the factor most important to resolution of this case, is the risk of erroneous deprivation and the likely value of any additional procedures. Petitioners argue that any pre-suspension hearing would have been worthless because pursuant to an Executive Order of the Governor of Pennsylvania a state employee is automatically to be suspended without pay "[a]s soon as practicable after [being] formally charged with . . . a felony." According to petitioners, supervisors have no discretion under this rule, and the mandatory suspension without pay lasts until the criminal charges are finally resolved. If petitioners' interpretation of this order is correct, there is no need for any presuspension process since there would be nothing to consider at the hearing except the independently verifiable fact of whether an employee had indeed been formally charged with a felony.

We noted in *Loudermill* that the purpose of a pretermination hearing is to determine "whether there are reasonable grounds to believe that the charges against the employee are true and support the proposed action." By parity of reasoning, the purpose of any presuspension hearing would be to assure that there are reasonable grounds to support the suspension without pay. But here that has already been assured by the arrest and the filing of charges.

In *Mallen*, we concluded that an "exparte finding of probable cause," such as a grand jury indictment, provides adequate assurance that the suspension is not unjustified. The same is true when an employee is arrested and then formally charged with a felony. First, as with an indictment, the arrest and formal charges imposed upon respondent "by an independent body demonstrat[e] that the suspension is not arbitrary." Second, like an indictment, the imposition of felony charges "itself is an objective fact that will in most cases raise serious public concern." It is true, as respondent argues, that there is more reason to believe an employee has committed a felony when he is indicted rather than merely arrested and formally charged; but for present purposes arrest and charge give reason enough. They serve to assure that the state employer's decision to suspend the employee is not "baseless or unwarranted," in that an independent third party has determined that there is probable cause to believe the employee committed a serious crime.

[Accordingly, the Court concluded that no pre-suspension hearing was required.]

Gilbert v. Homar, 520 U.S. 924 (1997), U.S. Supreme Court.

Again, a predeprivation hearing is not required in most cases. *Goldberg* is the exception, not the rule. However, even if no predetermination hearing is required, a postdetermination hearing may be required to satisfy due process. The Supreme Court addressed this in the *Ingraham* case.

Ingraham v. Wright

430 U.S. 651 (1977)

This case presents questions concerning the use of corporal punishment in public schools: First, whether the paddling of students as a means of maintaining school discipline constitutes cruel and unusual punishment in violation of the Eighth Amendment, and second, to the extent that paddling is constitutionally permissible, whether the Due Process Clause of the Fourteenth Amendment requires prior notice and an opportunity to be heard. . . .

Petitioner's evidence may be summarized briefly. In the 1970–71 school year many of the 237 schools in Dade County used corporal punishment as a means of maintaining discipline pursuant to Florida legislation and a local School Board regulation. . . . The authorized punishment consisted of paddling the recalcitrant student on the buttocks with a flat wooden paddle measuring less than two feet long, three to four inches wide, and about one-half inch thick. The normal punishment was limited to one to five "licks" or blows with the paddle and resulted in no apparent physical injury to the student.

[The Court concluded that the Eighth Amendment's prohibition of cruel and unusual punishment is inapplicable in the school setting.]

The Fourteenth Amendment prohibits any state deprivation of life, liberty, or property without due process of law. . . . [W]e find that corporal punishment in public schools implicates a constitutionally protected liberty interest, but we hold that the traditional common-law remedies are fully adequate to afford due process. . . .

Because it is rooted in history, the child's liberty interest in avoiding corporal punishment while in the care of public school authorities is subject to historical limitations. Under the common law, an invasion of personal security gave rise to a right to recover damages in a subsequent judicial proceeding. But the right of recovery was qualified by the concept of justification. Thus, there could be no recovery against a teacher who gave only "moderate correction" to a child. . . .

Florida has continued to recognize, and indeed has strengthened by statute, the common-law right of a child not to be subjected to excessive corporal punishment in school. Under Florida law the teacher and principal of the school decide in the first instance whether corporal punishment is reasonably necessary under the circumstances in order to discipline a child who has misbehaved. But they must exercise prudence and restraint[, f]or Florida has preserved the traditional judicial proceedings for determining whether the punishment was justified. If the punishment inflicted is later found to have been excessive—not reasonably believed at the time to be necessary for the child's discipline or training—the school authorities inflicting it may be held liable in damages to the child, and, if malice is shown, they may be subject to criminal penalties. . . .

Petitioners cannot prevail on either of the theories before us in this case. The Eighth Amendment's prohibition against cruel and unusual punishment is inapplicable to school paddlings, and the Fourteenth Amendment's requirement of procedural due process is satisfied by Florida's preservation of common-law constraints and remedies. We, therefore, agree with the Court of Appeals that petitioner's evidence affords no basis for injunctive relief, and that petitioners cannot recover damages on the basis of any Eighth Amendment or procedural due process violation.

Ingraham v. Wright, 430 U.S. 651 (1977), U.S. Supreme Court.

In the governmental employment context, due process applies not only to terminations, but also to reductions in pay and benefits. Because reductions do not harm individuals as much as terminations, postreduction hearings satisfy due process in nearly all cases. The amount of reduction is important, of course, to this inquiry.

Finally, in emergency situations, agencies may take temporary summary action, such as seizing property or suspending a license, without providing a predeprivation notice or hearing. Protection of the public health or safety is the most common justification for summary administrative action. For example, an agency may prevent the sale of dangerous food or drugs without first providing notice and a hearing. The *Dixon* case decided that an agency could properly summarily revoke a driver's license to remove a threat to the public. Of course, the agency must justify any summary action at a hearing conducted as soon as possible after the summary action has taken place.

The Supreme Court of the United States has extended the emergency action theory to protection of the public treasury. It has been applied in tax cases, when the exigency of losing revenues justifies immediate action.[19] Similarly, although public school students must normally receive presuspension hearings, a postsuspension hearing will satisfy due process if immediate suspension is necessary to protect students, faculty, or school property. In another case, the U.S. Supreme Court affirmed the authority of the Food and Drug Administration to seize products with misleading labels without first conducting a hearing.[20]

After summary action occurs a hearing must be conducted immediately. Notice of the action taken, as well as of the time and place of the postaction hearing, must be given either contemporaneously with, or immediately after, the action is taken.

4.5(d) Counsel

The APA provides that all persons compelled to appear before an agency (i.e., witnesses) and all parties are entitled to the assistance of counsel.[21] The Due Process Clauses also mandate that agencies permit the representation of counsel in some administrative hearings. Because the APA mandates allowing counsel at all federal hearings, the Due Process Clauses are most important in the context of state action.

The U.S. Supreme Court recognized the importance of counsel in *Goldberg* and held that a recipient was entitled to have a lawyer present at the pretermination hearing. However, the right to have retained counsel has not been extended to a right to have counsel appointed, as is true in the criminal context.

Even the right to have retained counsel is not extended to all administrative hearings. If the purpose of a hearing is to find facts or discuss complex issues of law, there is likely a right to have counsel present. It has been held that there is no right to counsel at prison disciplinary hearings,[22] some probation revocation hearings,[23] or school suspension guidance conferences. [24] The theories in all three cases are similar: the issues to be examined are not purely factual or legal. Issues of punishment and rehabilitation are considered at such proceedings and legal counsel would be of little assistance with regard to those issues. See Figure 4-1 for a chart of due process analysis.

4.6 EQUAL PROTECTION

In addition to guaranteeing due process, the Fourteenth Amendment also declares that no state shall "deny to any person within its jurisdiction the equal protection of the laws." This is the **Equal Protection Clause**. The Supreme Court has determined that even though this language does not appear in the Fifth Amendment, its

LEGAL TERM
Equal Protection Clause
Part of the Fourteenth Amendment to the U.S. Constitution; provides that no state shall deny a person the equal protection of the laws. The Fifth Amendment to the U.S. Constitution has been interpreted to extend the same limitation to the federal government.

prohibition is implicit in the Fifth Amendment's Due Process Clause and, therefore, is applicable to the federal government as well as to the states. Equal protection is concerned with laws and actions that classify and treat people differently.

Equal protection is important to administrative law in two respects. First, the Equal Protection Clause applies to all laws, both state and federal, regardless of their source. Hence, administrative regulations may be invalidated if they violate equal protection. Second, it is possible for a law to be consistent with equal protection, but an agency's enforcement of that law to be violative of equal protection.

Not all classifications are violative of equal protection. Actually, most classifications are necessary and lawful. Classifying people is inherent in the lawmaking process. For example, a law that requires applicants for a medical license to be graduates of a medical school distinguishes between persons with medical degrees and those without. Such a classification is necessary and proper. In contrast, a law that prohibits persons of certain races from obtaining medical licenses is violative of equal protection.

Dixon v. Love

431 U.S. 105 (1977)

The issue in this case is whether Illinois has provided constitutionally adequate procedures for suspending or revoking the license of a driver who repeatedly has been convicted of traffic offenses. The statute and administrative regulations provide for an initial summary decision based on official records, with a full administrative hearing available only after the suspension or revocation has taken effect.

The case centers on § 6-206 of the Illinois Driver Licensing Law (c. 6 of the Illinois Vehicle Code). The section is entitled "Discretionary authority to suspend or revoke license or permit." It empowers the Secretary of State to act "without preliminary hearing upon a showing by his records or other sufficient evidence" that a driver's conduct falls into any one of 18 enumerated categories. Pursuant to his rulemaking authority under this law, § 6-211(a), the Secretary has adopted administrative regulations that further define the bases and procedures for discretionary suspensions. These regulations generally provide for an initial summary determination based on the individual's driving record. . . .

Appellee Love, a resident of Chicago, is employed as a truck driver. His license was suspended in November 1969, under § 6-206(a)(2), for three convictions within a twelve-month period. He was then convicted of a charge of driving while his license was suspended, and consequently another suspension was imposed in March 1970 pursuant to § 6-303(b). Appellee received no further citation until August 1974, when he was arrested twice for speeding. He was convicted of both charges and then received a third speeding citation in February 1975. On March 27, he was notified by letter that he would lose his driving privileges if convicted of a third offense. On March 31 appellee was convicted of the third speeding charge.

On June 3, appellee received a notice that his license was revoked effective June 6. . . .

It is clear that the Due Process Clause applies to the deprivation of a driver's license by the State. . . .

Moreover, the risk of an erroneous deprivation in the absence of a prior hearing is not great. Under the Secretary's regulations, suspension and revocation decisions are largely automatic. Of course, there is the possibility of clerical error, but written objection will bring a matter of that kind to the Secretary's attention. In this case appellee had the opportunity for a full judicial hearing in connection with each of the traffic convictions on which the Secretary's decision was based. Appellee has not challenged the validity of those convictions or the adequacy of his procedural rights at the time they were determined. Since appellee does not dispute the factual basis for the Secretary's decision, he is really asserting the right to appear in person only to argue that the Secretary should show leniency and depart from his own regulations. Such an appearance might make the licensee feel that he has received more personal attention, but it would not serve to protect any substantial rights. We conclude that requiring additional procedures would be unlikely to have significant value in reducing the number of erroneous deprivations.

Finally, the substantial public interest in administrative efficiency would be impeded by the availability of a predetermination hearing in every case. Giving licensees the choice thus automatically to obtain a delay in the effectiveness of a suspension or revocation would encourage drivers routinely to request full administrative hearings. Far more substantial than the administrative burden, however, is the important public interest in safety on the roads and highways, and in the prompt removal of a safety hazard. . . . [T]he Illinois statute at issue in the instant case is designed to keep off the roads those drivers who are unable or unwilling to respect traffic rules and the safety of others.

We conclude that the public interests present under the circumstances of this case are sufficiently visible and weighty for the State to make its summary initial decision effective without a predecision administrative hearing.

Dixon v. Love, 431 U.S. 105 (1977), U.S. Supreme Court.

4.6(a) The Tests

What law or action violates the Equal Protection Clause? The Supreme Court has developed a three-tiered test to determine if equal protection has been violated. This test is also used to determine if substantive due process has been violated. Hence, the test is used if the government classifies people for purposes of regulation and when the law encroaches upon a constitutional right. The test uses the same three-tiered standards that are applied in due process cases. See Table 4-1.

Most classifications are valid if they bear a fair and rational relationship to a lawful governmental objective. As is true of due process, there are two questions. First, is the objective of the law itself lawful? If so, does the law bear a rational relationship to that objective? If both questions are answered affirmatively, the law does not violate equal protection. As is also true of due process analysis, a law will be upheld if any legitimate government purpose can be found to support it, regardless of whether the government can establish that the legitimate purpose was the actual purpose. An example of a classification that was tested under and failed the rational relationship test is found in *Romer v. Evans*.

Romer v. Evans

517 U.S. 620 (1996)

Justice Kennedy delivered the opinion of the Court.

The enactment challenged in this case is an amendment to the Constitution of the State of Colorado, adopted in a 1992 statewide referendum. . . .

[The Amendment] prohibits all legislative, executive or judicial action at any level of state or local government designed to protect the named class, a class we shall refer to as homosexual persons or gays and lesbians. The amendment reads:

"No Protected Status Based on Homosexual, Lesbian, or Bisexual Orientation. Neither the State of Colorado, through any of its branches or

(continued)

departments, nor any of its agencies, political subdivisions, municipalities or school districts, shall enact, adopt or enforce any statute, regulation, ordinance or policy whereby homosexual, lesbian or bisexual orientation, conduct, practices or relationships shall constitute or otherwise be the basis of or entitle any person or class of persons to have or claim any minority status, quota preferences, protected status or claim of discrimination. This Section of the Constitution shall be in all respects self executing."

The State's principal argument in defense of Amendment 2 is that it puts gays and lesbians in the same position as all other persons. So, the State says, the measure does no more than deny homosexuals special rights. This reading of the amendment's language is implausible. We rely not upon our own interpretation of the amendment but upon the authoritative construction of Colorado's Supreme Court. The state court, deeming it unnecessary to determine the full extent of the amendment's reach, found it invalid even on a modest reading of its implications. The critical discussion of the amendment, set out in *Evans I*, is as follows:

"The immediate objective of Amendment 2 is, at a minimum, to repeal existing statutes, regulations, ordinances, and policies of state and local entities that barred discrimination based on sexual orientation. . . ."

Amendment 2 fails, indeed defies, even this conventional inquiry. First, the amendment has the peculiar property of imposing a broad and undifferentiated disability on a single named group, an exceptional and, as we shall explain, invalid form of legislation. Second, its sheer breadth is so discontinuous with the reasons offered for it that the amendment seems inexplicable by anything but animus toward the class that it affects; it lacks a rational relationship to legitimate state interests.

Taking the first point, even in the ordinary equal protection case calling for the most deferential of standards, we insist on knowing the relation between the classification adopted and the object to be attained. The search for the link between classification and objective gives substance to the Equal Protection Clause; it provides guidance and discipline for the legislature, which is entitled to know what sorts of laws it can pass; and it marks the limits of our own authority. In the ordinary case, a law will be sustained if it can be said to advance a legitimate government interest, even if the law seems unwise or works to the disadvantage of a particular group, or if the rationale for it seems tenuous. . . . By requiring that the classification bear a rational relationship to an independent and legitimate legislative end, we ensure that classifications are not drawn for the purpose of disadvantaging the group burdened by the law. . . .

Amendment 2 confounds this normal process of judicial review. It is at once too narrow and too broad. It identifies persons by a single trait and then denies them protection across the board. The resulting disqualification of a class of persons from the right to seek specific protection from the law is unprecedented in our jurisprudence. The absence of precedent for Amendment 2 is itself instructive; "[d]iscriminations of an unusual character especially suggest careful consideration to determine whether they are obnoxious to the constitutional provision." . . .

A second and related point is that laws of the kind now before us raise the inevitable inference that the disadvantage imposed is born of animosity toward the class of persons affected. "[I]f the constitutional conception of 'equal protection of the laws' means anything, it must at the very least mean that a bare . . . desire to harm a politically unpopular group cannot constitute a *legitimate* governmental interest." Even laws enacted for broad and ambitious purposes often can be explained by reference to legitimate public policies which justify the incidental disadvantages they impose on certain persons. Amendment 2, however, in making a general

> announcement that gays and lesbians shall not have any particular protections from the law, inflicts on them immediate, continuing, and real injuries that outrun and belie any legitimate justifications that may be claimed for it. We conclude that, in addition to the far reaching deficiencies of Amendment 2 that we have noted, the principles it offends, in another sense, are conventional and venerable; a law must bear a rational relationship to a legitimate governmental purpose . . . .
>
> We must conclude that Amendment 2 classifies homosexuals not to further a proper legislative end but to make them unequal to everyone else. This Colorado cannot do. A State cannot so deem a class of persons a stranger to its laws. Amendment 2 violates the Equal Protection Clause, and the judgment of the Supreme Court of Colorado is affirmed.

Romer v. Evans, 517 U.S. 620 (1996), U.S. Supreme Court.

Certain classifications are intrinsically suspect, however, and are subject to the strict scrutiny test. Particular groups are entitled to greater protection because they are particularly vulnerable to unfair discrimination or bear a stigma of inferiority, or because a history of discrimination in the United States disfavors the group. In addition, a classification based on an immutable condition or status may be subjected to strict scrutiny. An *immutable condition* is permanent and outside a person's control. Skin color is an example of an immutable condition, and race and national origin are examples of suspect classes. Alienage is treated as suspect in some cases. However, laws that prohibit aliens from voting or holding public office have been tested under the rational basis standard and held constitutional.

Although the Court has not recognized a new suspect class in decades, the possibility that homosexuality and lesbianism may be constitutionally recognized, either through Equal Protection or as a substantive due process right, is looming. As mentioned in Section 4.1, to survive the strict scrutiny test, a law must be more than rationally related to a lawful objective. The law must be necessary to further a compelling governmental interest. Most laws subjected to the strict scrutiny test fail.

In recent years, yet another test has been developed. This intermediate test requires that a regulation, to be valid, must bear a substantial relationship to an important governmental interest. The exact boundaries of this classification have not been defined, but case law is beginning to discover its limits. The U.S. Supreme Court has refused to protect illegitimate children as a group with strict scrutiny, but has required the government to show more than a mere rational relationship when legislation is aimed at the group. Gender-based classifications are another example of when the intermediate test is applied. Under this test, a state law preferring men as executors of estates was found to violate equal protection.[25] See Table 4-1 for a summary of these tests.

A law may violate equal protection if it is either overtly or covertly discriminatory. Returning to the previous example, assume that a state law prohibits members of a certain race from applying for medical licenses. Such a law is overtly unlawful. Said another way, it is *discriminatory on its face.*

Some laws may not be overtly discriminatory but may be covertly discriminatory. For example, assume that the State Medical Licensing Board conducts a study of the nation's medical schools and limits license applications to graduates from the "best" 30 schools, to improve the quality of medical care in the state. Facially, the law appears legitimate. However, if it can be shown that the student bodies at these schools are almost entirely white and that schools with a more diverse racial and ethnic mix were not included in the state's list, the law may be violative of equal protection—depending, of course, on other relevant evidence.

Proving covert discrimination is not easy. Plaintiffs frequently use statistical evidence to prove that a law that appears legitimate is actually discriminatory. However, proof of discriminatory impact is not adequate; it must be shown that the purpose of the law is discriminatory. Statistics evincing discriminatory impact may be used to indicate discriminatory purpose, but are usually not sufficient in themselves to prove discriminatory purpose. Other evidence, such as the government's awareness of the law's discriminatory impact, must also be shown.

Similarly, a law may be valid as written but violate equal protection because it is administered in a discriminatory manner by an administrative agency. In *FSK Drug Corp. v. Perales*, a plaintiff alleged that a state administrative agency violated the Equal Protection Clause by selectively enforcing a facially lawful state regulation. In such cases, the courts will attempt to fashion a remedy that brings the agency's actions into compliance with the Equal Protection Clause, if possible, rather than invalidate the legislation under which the agency is acting.

Laws that draw classifications that burden the exercise of individual rights may also violate equal protection. This area is similar, and often parallel, to substantive due process. If a fundamental right is being significantly burdened, strict scrutiny is applied. Two essential elements must be proved to be successful with this type of claim.

First, the right burdened by the law must be fundamental. The First Amendment's rights of speech, association, and religion are examples of fundamental rights. The rights to privacy, franchise, travel, and access to the judicial system are other fundamental rights. For example, a state law required divorced parents of minor children, which children are not in their custody but to whom they owe support, to get court approval before remarrying. This statute was held violative of equal protection because the classification unfairly interfered with the right to marry.[26] Laws that classify people by religion also fall into this category. They violate both the First Amendment's Free Exercise Clause and Equal Protection.

Second, the burden must be significant. A classification that only affects, but does not significantly burden, the exercise of a fundamental right is tested by the rational relationship test.

Some jurists believe the Supreme Court is slowly moving away from the three-tiered standards approach to due process and equal protection analysis toward a sliding-scale reasonableness standard. It is not known to what extent due process and equal protection would change if the Court were to adopt a reasonableness test. The factors used today to decide what standard applies, and to decide if that standard has been violated, are essentially the same as would be used when determining if a law is reasonable: the nature of the classification, the nature of the interests or rights burdened by the classification, the government's interest and purpose, and the necessity of the classification to achieving the government's purpose.

FSK Drug Corp. v. Perales

960 F. 2d 6 (2d Cir. 1992)

This appeal raises equal protection challenges to the re-enrollment provisions of New York's Medicaid regulations. . . .

FSK Drug Corporation (the "Company") appeals from the November 4, 1991, judgment of the District Court for the Eastern District of New York (Weinstein, Judge) granting the defendant's motion for summary judgment and dismissing its complaint alleging that the New York State Department of Social Services' (the "Department") denial of its application for re-enrollment as a Medicaid provider pursuant to [New York statutes and regulations] violated the Due Process and Equal Protection Clauses of the United States Constitution. . . .

FSK is a registered pharmacy in Brooklyn, New York, and has been enrolled as a Medicaid provider for over twenty years. Pursuant to [New York law], effective January 5, 1987, the Company was required to submit an application, to re-enroll as a provider. Upon timely submission of the application, the Department conducted an on-site inspection and reviewed the Company's billing records. By letter dated August 3, 1990, the Department informed the Company that its re-enrollment application had been rejected, and, therefore, its status as a Medicaid provider would terminate within 60 days. The letter provided a "summary of factors" supporting the Department's decision. The Department's Appeal Committee reviewed the Company's written appeal, and recommended denial of the re-enrollment application. By letter dated November 16, 1990, the Department informed the Company of the final decision to deny enrollment. . . .

SELECTIVE APPLICATION OF THE RE-ENROLLMENT REQUIREMENT

The Company further contends that the Department selectively enforces its re-enrollment provision by requiring only large pharmacy and physician providers to re-enroll, pursuant to [New York law], while excusing hospital pharmacies and drug store chains from the requirement. . . .

A claim of selective application of a facially lawful state regulation requires a showing that: (1) the person, compared with others similarly situated, was selectively treated, and (2) the selective treatment was motivated by an intention to discriminate on the basis of impermissible considerations, such as race or religion, to punish or inhibit the exercise of constitutional rights, or by a malicious or bad faith intent to injure the person. *Wayte v. United States*, 470 U.S. 598, 608–09. . . . Because the Company does not allege discriminatory treatment based on either an impermissible factor or on its exercise of constitutional rights, we review the record for evidence of malicious or bad faith intent to injure.

The affidavit of Mary A. Brankman, Coordinator for Enrollment and Collections in the Department's Office of Audit and Control, states that all free standing pharmacies, including those that are part of the chains, are required to re-enroll in the Medicaid program. The affidavit states that hospital-based pharmacies are required to re-enroll, as are other categories of providers, including podiatrists, durable medical equipment suppliers, and transportation providers. The Brankman affidavit indicates that in 1990 the Department's Office of Audit and Quality Control received 315 re-enrollment applications for review. The Department approved 128 re-enrollment applications, denied 39, with 167 still pending. . . . Because the record does not contain evidence of bad faith or a malicious intent, we affirm the District Court's grant of summary judgment in favor of the Department.

FSK Drug Corp. v. Perales, 960 F. 2d 6 (2d Cir. 1992),
U.S. Court of Appeals for the Second Circuit.

4.6(b) Affirmative Action and Diversity

A contemporary challenge in equal protection law concerns government programs that advantage historically disadvantaged groups. These policies, commonly known as *affirmative action*, are, in some people's eyes, violative of equal protection. To the supporters of such policies, they are a means by which greater equality can be achieved. The Supreme Court wrestled with this issue in *Regents of University of California v. Bakke*,[27] wherein the Court examined the University of California's "quota" system of holding a certain number of seats in its medical class for racial minorities. The Court held that all racial classification systems are subject to strict scrutiny. After applying this test, the Court concluded that the quota system violated equal protection. However, it also concluded that race may be a factor in admissions decisions. In short, the Court found race to be an appropriate factor to increase diversity when considered in the context of other factors and in comparison with all other applicants. Holding seats for any group, without such context, was excessive.

The Court turned its attention to affirmative action on several occasions between 1978 and 1995 in the context of government programs that favored minority-owned service and materials providers. Those cases[28] raised, but did not answer, the question of what test should be applied to such programs. Then, in 1995, the Supreme Court emphatically stated, in *Adarand Constructors v. Pena*,[29] that all racial classifications are subject to the strict scrutiny test. *Adarand* involved a challenge by a contractor who lost a bid for a highway contract to a minority contractor. The federal government and most state and local governments require large projects and purchases to be "bid"; that is, to make the expenditure, the agency is required to advertise or invite competitors to submit bids for the work or products. Unless special circumstances exist allowing it to do otherwise, the agency is required to accept the lowest bid. The federal government had an affirmative action policy that favored minority contractors and subcontractors. In this case, Adarand Constructors submitted a bid, to construct the guard rail on a new stretch of highway, to the Central Federal Lands Highway Division (CFLHD) of the federal Department of Transportation. Although it was the lowest bidder, the contract was awarded to a company controlled by an individual who was a racial minority. Adarand challenged the decision as violative of equal protection. On appeal, the Supreme Court held that all racial classifications, including the challenged rule, were subject to strict scrutiny. About the test, the Court said "we wish to dispel the notion that strict scrutiny is 'strict in theory, but fatal in fact.'"[30] Said another way, it is possible for a government to demonstrate a compelling interest in support of a racial classification. The purpose of applying strict scrutiny is not to end the examination. Quite the contrary: the purposes are to require Courts to engage in exacting examinations and to "smoke out" illegitimate classifications. In response to *Adarand*, several minority preference programs were redrawn and others were invalidated upon review. However, a narrowly tailored affirmative action program is likely to be upheld on review.

What does it mean to be a narrowly tailored program? The most fundamental principle is that if a race-neutral alternative exists to remedy the problem (e.g., underrepresentation of a particular minority group), that alternative must be used unless totally impracticable. It is also important that race not be exclusively dispositive (rather, that it should be one of many factors in the decision; that individuals who fall outside the favored class not be overly disadvantaged; and that the program be subject to periodic review and amendment as conditions change). For example, a preference may need to decrease as minority numbers increase.

Affirmative action and diversity initiatives in college admissions were again the subject of Supreme Court review in two 2003 cases, *Grutter* and *Gratz*.

Grutter v. Bollinger

539 U.S. 306 (2003)

The Law School ranks among the Nation's top law schools. It receives more than 3,500 applications each year for a class of around 350 students. Seeking to "admit a group of students who individually and collectively are among the most capable," the Law School looks for individuals with "substantial promise for success in law school" and "a strong likelihood of succeeding in the practice of law and contributing in diverse ways to the wellbeing of others." . . . More broadly, the Law School seeks "a mix of students with varying backgrounds and experiences who will respect and learn from each other." In 1992, the dean of the Law School charged a faculty committee with crafting a written admissions policy to implement these goals. In particular, the Law School sought to ensure that its efforts to achieve student body diversity complied with this Court's most recent ruling on the use of race in university admissions. See *Regents of Univ. of Cal. v. Bakke*, 438 U.S. 265 (1978). Upon the unanimous adoption of the committee's report by the Law School faculty, it became the Law School's official admissions policy.

The hallmark of that policy is its focus on academic ability coupled with a flexible assessment of applicants' talents, experiences, and potential "to contribute to the learning of those around them." The policy requires admissions officials to evaluate each applicant based on all the information available in the file, including a personal statement, letters of recommendation, and an essay describing the ways in which the applicant will contribute to the life and diversity of the Law School. In reviewing an applicant's file, admissions officials must consider the applicant's undergraduate grade point average (GPA) and Law School Admissions Test (LSAT) score because they are important (if imperfect) predictors of academic success in law school. The policy stresses that "no applicant should be admitted unless we expect that applicant to do well enough to graduate with no serious academic problems."

The policy makes clear, however, that even the highest possible score does not guarantee admission to the Law School. Nor does a low score automatically disqualify an applicant. Rather, the policy requires admissions officials to look beyond grades and test scores to other criteria that are important to the Law School's educational objectives. So-called "'soft' variables" such as "the enthusiasm of recommenders, the quality of the undergraduate institution, the quality of the applicant's essay, and the areas and difficulty of undergraduate course selection" are all brought to bear in assessing an "applicant's likely contributions to the intellectual and social life of the institution."

The policy aspires to "achieve that diversity which has the potential to enrich everyone's education and thus make a law school class stronger than the sum of its parts." The policy does not restrict the types of diversity contributions eligible for "substantial weight" in the admissions process, but instead recognizes "many possible bases for diversity admissions." The policy does, however, reaffirm the Law School's longstanding commitment to "one particular type of diversity," that is, "racial and ethnic diversity with special reference to the inclusion of students from groups which have been historically discriminated against, like African-Americans, Hispanics and Native Americans, who without this commitment might not be represented in our student body in meaningful numbers." By enrolling a "'critical mass' of [underrepresented] minority students," the Law School seeks to "ensur[e] their ability to make unique contributions to the character of the Law School."

The policy does not define diversity "solely in terms of racial and ethnic status." Nor is the policy "insensitive to the competition among all students for admission to the [L]aw [S]chool." Rather, the policy seeks to guide admissions officers in "producing classes both diverse and academically outstanding, classes made up of students

(continued)

who promise to continue the tradition of outstanding contribution by Michigan Graduates to the legal profession."

Petitioner Barbara Grutter is a white Michigan resident who applied to the Law School in 1996 with a 3.8 grade point average and 161 LSAT score. The Law School initially placed petitioner on a waiting list, but subsequently rejected her application. . . . [The Court discussed the evidence received at trial, including statistical evidence indicating that if race had not been considered in the admission decision, the Law School's minority population would have been only one-third as large.]

The Equal Protection Clause provides that no State shall "deny to any person within its jurisdiction the equal protection of the laws." U.S. Const., Amdt. 14, § 2. Because the Fourteenth Amendment "protect[s] *persons*, not *groups*," all "governmental action based on race—a *group* classification long recognized as in most circumstances irrelevant and, therefore, prohibited—should be subjected to detailed judicial inquiry to ensure that the *personal* right to equal protection of the laws has not been infringed." *Adarand Constructors, Inc. v. Peña*, 515 U.S. 200, 277 (1995) (emphasis in original; internal quotation marks and citation omitted). We are a "free people whose institutions are founded upon the doctrine of equality." It follows from that principle that "government may treat people differently because of their race only for the most compelling reasons." *Adarand Constructors, Inc. v. Peña*, 515 U.S., at 227. . . .

With these principles in mind, we turn to the question whether the Law School's use of race is justified by a compelling state interest. Before this Court, as they have throughout this litigation, respondents assert only one justification for their use of race in the admissions process: obtaining "the educational benefits that flow from a diverse student body." . . .

The Law School's educational judgment that such diversity is essential to its educational mission is one to which we defer. The Law School's assessment that diversity will, in fact, yield educational benefits is substantiated by respondents and their *amici*. Our scrutiny of the interest asserted by the Law School is no less strict for taking into account complex educational judgments in an area that lies primarily within the expertise of the university. Our holding today is in keeping with our tradition of giving a degree of deference to a university's academic decisions, within constitutionally prescribed limits. . . .

We have long recognized that, given the important purpose of public education and the expansive freedoms of speech and thought associated with the university environment, universities occupy a special niche in our constitutional tradition. . . .

As part of its goal of "assembling a class that is both exceptionally academically qualified and broadly diverse," the Law School seeks to "enroll a 'critical mass' of minority students." The Law School's interest is not simply "to assure within its student body some specified percentage of a particular group merely because of its race or ethnic origin." *Bakke*, 438 U.S., at 307 (opinion of Powell, J.). That would amount to outright racial balancing, which is patently unconstitutional. "Racial balance [is] not to be achieved for its own sake"; *Richmond v. J.A. Croson Co.*, 488 U.S., at 507. Rather, the Law School's concept of critical mass is defined by reference to the educational benefits that diversity is designed to produce.

These benefits are substantial. As the District Court emphasized, the Law School's admissions policy promotes "cross-racial understanding," helps to break down racial stereotypes, and "enables [students] to better understand persons of different races." These benefits are "important and laudable," because "classroom discussion is livelier, more spirited, and simply more enlightening and interesting" when the students have "the greatest possible variety of backgrounds." . . .

The Law School's claim of a compelling interest is further bolstered by its *amici*, who point to the educational benefits that flow from student body diversity.

In addition to the expert studies and reports entered into evidence at trial, numerous studies show that student body diversity promotes learning outcomes, and "better prepares students for an increasingly diverse workforce and society, and better prepares them as professionals." . . . These benefits are not theoretical but real, as major American businesses have made clear that the skills needed in today's increasingly global marketplace can only be developed through exposure to widely diverse people, cultures, ideas, and viewpoints. . . .

We have repeatedly acknowledged the overriding importance of preparing students for work and citizenship, describing education as pivotal to "sustaining our political and cultural heritage" with a fundamental role in maintaining the fabric of society. This Court has long recognized that "education . . . is the very foundation of good citizenship." . . .

In order to cultivate a set of leaders with legitimacy in the eyes of the citizenry, it is necessary that the path to leadership be visibly open to talented and qualified individuals of every race and ethnicity. All members of our heterogeneous society must have confidence in the openness and integrity of the educational institutions that provide this training. As we have recognized, law schools "cannot be effective in isolation from the individuals and institutions with which the law interacts." . . .

Even in the limited circumstance when drawing racial distinctions is permissible to further a compelling state interest, government is still "constrained in how it may pursue that end: [T]he means chosen to accomplish the [government's] asserted purpose must be specifically and narrowly framed to accomplish that purpose." . . .

To be narrowly tailored, a race-conscious admissions program cannot use a quota system—it cannot "insulat[e] each category of applicants with certain desired qualifications from competition with all other applicants." Instead, a university may consider race or ethnicity only as a " 'plus' in a particular applicant's file," without "insulat[ing] the individual from comparison with all other candidates for the available seats." In other words, an admissions program must be "flexible enough to consider all pertinent elements of diversity in light of the particular qualifications of each applicant, and to place them on the same footing for consideration, although not necessarily according them the same weight." . . .

We are satisfied that the Law School's admissions program, like the Harvard plan described by Justice Powell, does not operate as a quota. . . .

That a race-conscious admissions program does not operate as a quota does not, by itself, satisfy the requirement of individualized consideration. When using race as a "plus" factor in university admissions, a university's admissions program must remain flexible enough to ensure that each applicant is evaluated as an individual and not in a way that makes an applicant's race or ethnicity the defining feature of his or her application. The importance of this individualized consideration in the context of a race-conscious admissions program is paramount. . . .

Here, the Law School engages in a highly individualized, holistic review of each applicant's file, giving serious consideration to all the ways an applicant might contribute to a diverse educational environment. The Law School affords this individualized consideration to applicants of all races. There is no policy, either *de jure* or *de facto*, of automatic acceptance or rejection based on any single "soft" variable. Unlike the program at issue in *Gratz v. Bollinger, ante*, the Law School awards no mechanical, predetermined diversity "bonuses" based on race or ethnicity. . . .

The Law School does not, however, limit in any way the broad range of qualities and experiences that may be considered valuable contributions to student body diversity. To the contrary, the 1992 policy makes clear "[t]here are many possible bases for diversity admissions," and provides examples of admittees who have lived or traveled widely abroad, are fluent in several languages, have overcome personal adversity and family hardship, have exceptional records of extensive community service, and have had successful careers in other fields. The Law School seriously

(continued)

considers each "applicant's promise of making a notable contribution to the class by way of a particular strength, attainment, or characteristic— e.g., an unusual intellectual achievement, employment experience, nonacademic performance, or personal background." All applicants have the opportunity to highlight their own potential diversity contributions through the submission of a personal statement, letters of recommendation, and an essay describing the ways in which the applicant will contribute to the life and diversity of the Law School. . . .

We agree with the Court of Appeals that the Law School sufficiently considered workable race-neutral alternatives. The District Court took the Law School to task for failing to consider race-neutral alternatives such as "using a lottery system" or "decreasing the emphasis for all applicants on undergraduate GPA and LSAT scores." App. to Pet. for Cert. 251a. But these alternatives would require a dramatic sacrifice of diversity, the academic quality of all admitted students, or both.

The Law School's current admissions program considers race as one factor among many, in an effort to assemble a student body that is diverse in ways broader than race. Because a lottery would make that kind of nuanced judgment impossible, it would effectively sacrifice all other educational values, not to mention every other kind of diversity. So too with the suggestion that the Law School simply lower admissions standards for all students, a drastic remedy that would require the Law School to become a much different institution and sacrifice a vital component of its educational mission. The United States advocates "percentage plans," recently adopted by public undergraduate institutions in Texas, Florida, and California to guarantee admission to all students above a certain class-rank threshold in every high school in the State. The United States does not, however, explain how such plans could work for graduate and professional schools. Moreover, even assuming such plans are race-neutral, they may preclude the university from conducting the individualized assessments necessary to assemble a student body that is not just racially diverse, but diverse along all the qualities valued by the university. We are satisfied that the Law School adequately considered race-neutral alternatives currently capable of producing a critical mass without forcing the Law School to abandon the academic selectivity that is the cornerstone of its educational mission.

[The Court then concluded that nonminorities are not unduly harmed by the policy and that it accepted the university's statement that it would terminate the program as soon as practicable. The Court stated that it assumed that such programs will be unnecessary in 25 years.]

Gratz v. Bollinger

539 U.S. 244 (2003)

Petitioners Gratz and Hamacher, both of whom are Michigan residents and Caucasian, applied for admission to the University of Michigan's (University) College of Literature, Science, and the Arts (LSA) in 1995 and 1997, respectively. Although the LSA considered Gratz to be well qualified and Hamacher to be within the qualified range, both were denied early admission and were ultimately denied admission. In order to promote consistency in the review of the many applications received, the University's Office of Undergraduate Admissions (OUA) uses written guidelines for each academic year. The guidelines have changed a number of times during the period relevant to this litigation. The OUA considers a number of factors in making admissions decisions, including high school grades, standardized test scores, high school quality, curriculum strength, geography, alumni relationships, leadership, and race. During all relevant periods, the University has considered African-Americans,

Hispanics, and Native Americans to be "underrepresented minorities," and it is undisputed that the University admits virtually every qualified applicant from these groups. The current guidelines use a selection method under which every applicant from an underrepresented racial or ethnic minority group is automatically awarded 20 points of the 100 needed to guarantee admission.

Petitioners filed this class action alleging that the University's use of racial preferences in undergraduate admissions violated the Equal Protection Clause of the Fourteenth Amendment, Title VI of the Civil Rights Act of 1964, and 42 U.S.C. § 1981. . . .

During 1995 and 1996, OUA counselors evaluated applications according to grade point average combined with what were referred to as the "SCUGA" factors. These factors included the quality of an applicant's high school (S), the strength of an applicant's high school curriculum (C), an applicant's unusual circumstances (U), an applicant's geographical residence (G), and an applicant's alumni relationships (A). After these scores were combined to produce an applicant's "GPA 2 " score, the reviewing admissions counselors referenced a set of "Guidelines" tables, which listed GPA 2 ranges on the vertical axis, and American College Test/Scholastic Aptitude Test (ACT/SAT) scores on the horizontal axis. Each table was divided into cells that included one or more courses of action to be taken, including admit, reject, delay for additional information, or postpone for reconsideration.

In both years, applicants with the same GPA 2 score and ACT/SAT score were subject to different admissions outcomes based upon their racial or ethnic status. For example, as a Caucasian in-state applicant, Gratz's GPA 2 score and ACT score placed her within a cell calling for a postponed decision on her application. An in-state or out-of-state minority applicant with Gratz's scores would have fallen within a cell calling for admission. . . .

Beginning with the 1998 academic year, the OUA dispensed with the Guidelines tables and the SCUGA point system in favor of a "selection index," on which an applicant could score a maximum of 150 points. This index was divided linearly into ranges generally calling for admissions dispositions as follows: 100–150 (admit); 95–99 (admit or postpone); 90–94 (postpone or admit); 75–89 (delay or postpone); 74 and below (delay or reject).

Each application received points based on high school grade point average, standardized test scores, academic quality of an applicant's high school, strength or weakness of high school curriculum, in-state residency, alumni relationship, personal essay, and personal achievement or leadership. Of particular significance here, under a "miscellaneous" category, an applicant was entitled to 20 points based upon his or her membership in an underrepresented racial or ethnic minority group. The University explained that the "development of the selection index for admissions in 1998 changed only the mechanics, not the substance of how race and ethnicity were considered in admissions."

In all application years from 1995 to 1998, the guidelines provided that qualified applicants from underrepresented minority groups be admitted as soon as possible in light of the University's belief that such applicants were more likely to enroll if promptly notified of their admission. Also from 1995 through 1998, the University carefully managed its rolling admissions system to permit consideration of certain applications submitted later in the academic year through the use of "protected seats." Specific groups—including athletes, foreign students, ROTC candidates, and underrepresented minorities—were "protected categories" eligible for these seats. . . .

It is by now well established that "all racial classifications reviewable under the Equal Protection Clause must be strictly scrutinized." *Adarand Constructors, Inc. v. Peña*, 515 U.S. 200, 224 (1995). . . .

To withstand our strict scrutiny analysis, respondents must demonstrate that the University's use of race in its current admission program employs "narrowly

(continued)

tailored measures that further compelling governmental interests." *Id.*, at 227. . . . "Racial classifications are simply too pernicious to permit any but the most exact connection between justification and classification." . . .

In *Bakke*, Justice Powell reiterated that "[p]referring members of any one group for no reason other than race or ethnic origin is discrimination for its own sake." 438 U.S., at 307. He then explained, however, that in his view it would be permissible for a university to employ an admissions program in which "race or ethnic background may be deemed a 'plus' in a particular applicant's file." He explained that such a program might allow for "[t]he file of a particular black applicant [to] be examined for his potential contribution to diversity without the factor of race being decisive when compared, for example, with that of an applicant identified as an Italian-American if the latter is thought to exhibit qualities more likely to promote beneficial educational pluralism." Such a system, in Justice Powell's view, would be "flexible enough to consider all pertinent elements of diversity in light of the particular qualifications of each applicant." . . .

Justice Powell's opinion in *Bakke* emphasized the importance of considering each particular applicant as an individual, assessing all of the qualities that individual possesses, and in turn, evaluating that individual's ability to contribute to the unique setting of higher education. The admissions program Justice Powell described, however, did not contemplate that any single characteristic automatically ensured a specific and identifiable contribution to a university's diversity. . . .

The current LSA policy does not provide such individualized consideration. The LSA's policy automatically distributes 20 points to every single applicant from an "underrepresented minority" group, as defined by the University. . . . [T]he LSA's automatic distribution of 20 points has the effect of making "the factor of race . . . decisive" for virtually every minimally qualified underrepresented minority applicant. . . .

Respondents contend that "[t]he volume of applications and the presentation of applicant information make it impractical for [LSA] to use the . . . admissions system" upheld by the Court today in *Grutter*. But the fact that the implementation of a program capable of providing individualized consideration might present administrative challenges does not render constitutional an otherwise problematic system. . . .

We conclude, therefore, that because the University's use of race in its current freshman admissions policy is not narrowly tailored to achieve respondents' asserted compelling interest in diversity, the admissions policy violates the Equal Protection Clause of the Fourteenth Amendment.

Gratz v. Bollinger, 539 U.S. 244 (2003), U.S Supreme Court.

In response to this decision, the University of Michigan redesigned its undergraduate admissions policy. UM literature described the new policy as follows:

The new application, which is being sent out in early September to prospective students and high school counselors, includes several new questions designed to elicit more information about a student's background, personal achievement, and ways in which that student may contribute to the intellectual vibrancy and diversity of the student body.

In addition, the essay questions are designed to provide the richest possible picture of the student's intellect, character, and personal values. A new form also has been developed for high school counselors and teachers to provide the University with more information about each student's academic preparation and background.

The process for reviewing each application has been revised to include more personal, individualized review. . . . The point system previously used in the undergraduate admissions process has been discarded. Instead, each applicant's file will be considered holistically in the context of all the facets of the individual applicant's accomplishments and experiences.

What can be gleaned from this line of cases is that equal protection review of affirmative action and diversity programs is fact-sensitive. The deference Courts have historically given universities to make academic determinations provides colleges and universities with more latitude than most other government agencies enjoy. Still, a few concrete rules can be extracted. First, policies intended solely to increase the number of members of a historically disadvantaged class are likely to fail. Such objectives must be secondary to other legitimate objectives, such as enriching the learning environment. Second, reasonable neutral alternatives must be employed. Third, plans employing race criteria must be very narrowly tailored.

At the time this book went to press the Supreme Court had granted *certiorari* in *Schuette v. Coalition to Defend Affirmative Action*, a case that involved a challenge to a Michigan voter referendum that banned race as a factor in state education, contracting, and employment decisions.

4.6(c) Fifteenth Amendment

The Fourteenth Amendment is not the only constitutional provision that mandates equal protection. The Fifteenth Amendment, also a post–Civil War amendment, provides that the right to vote shall not be "denied or abridged by the United States or by any State on account of race, color, or previous condition of servitude." This amendment was at issue in the Hawaiian case of *Rice v. Cayetano*.

Lawlinks

Information on the federal Courts of the United States can be found at http://www.uscourts.gov/Home.aspx. General information on the Courts, data on cases filed and other judicial business, and connections to the home pages of the federal Courts are all available at this location.

Rice v. Cayetano

528 U.S. 495 (2000)

A citizen of Hawaii comes before us claiming that an explicit, race-based voting qualification has barred him from voting in a statewide election. The Fifteenth Amendment to the Constitution of the United States, binding on the National Government, the States, and their political subdivisions, controls the case.

The Hawaiian Constitution limits the right to vote for nine trustees chosen in a statewide election. The trustees compose the governing authority of a state agency known as the Office of Hawaiian Affairs, or OHA. Haw. Const., Art. XII, § 5. The agency administers programs designed for the benefit of two subclasses of the Hawaiian citizenry. The smaller class comprises those designated as "native Hawaiians," defined by statute, with certain supplementary language later set out in full, as descendants of not less than one-half part of the races inhabiting the Hawaiian Islands prior to 1778. The second, larger class of persons benefited by OHA programs is "Hawaiians," defined to be, with refinements contained in the statute we later quote, those persons who are descendants of people inhabiting the Hawaiian Islands in 1778. The right to vote for trustees is limited to "Hawaiians," the second, larger class of persons, which of course includes the smaller class of "native Hawaiians." Haw. Const., Art XII, § 5.

(continued)

Petitioner Rice, a citizen of Hawaii and thus himself a Hawaiian in a well-accepted sense of the term, does not have the requisite ancestry even for the larger class. He is not, then, a "Hawaiian" in terms of the statute; so he may not vote in the trustee election. The issue presented by this case is whether Rice may be so barred. Rejecting the State's arguments that the classification in question is not racial or that, if it is, it is nevertheless valid for other reasons, we hold Hawaii's denial of petitioner's right to vote to be a clear violation of the Fifteenth Amendment.

[The Court then provided a history of the Hawaiian people and of the islands, including the original population of the islands by native Hawaiians around 750, the era of colonial powers in the islands, the rise of King Kamehameha I in 1810 and his successors, and the eventual cession of the islands to the United States as a territory in 1898 and statehood in 1959.]

In 1978 Hawaii amended its Constitution to establish the Office of Hawaiian Affairs, Haw. Const., Art. XII, § 5, which has as its mission "[t]he betterment of conditions of native Hawaiians . . . [and] Hawaiians," Haw. Rev. Stat. § 10-3 (1993). Members of the 1978 constitutional convention, at which the new amendments were drafted and proposed, set forth the purpose of the proposed agency:

> Members [of the Committee of the Whole] were impressed by the concept of the Office of Hawaiian Affairs which establishes a public trust entity for the benefit of the people of Hawaiian ancestry. Members foresaw that it will provide Hawaiians the right to determine the priorities which will effectuate the betterment of their condition and welfare and promote the protection and preservation of the Hawaiian race, and that it will unite Hawaiians as a people.

Implementing statutes and their later amendments vested OHA with broad authority to administer two categories of funds: a 20 percent share of the revenue from the 1.2 million acres of lands granted to the State pursuant to § 5(b) of the Admission Act, which OHA is to administer "for the betterment of the conditions of native Hawaiians," Haw. Rev. Stat. § 10-13.5, and any state or federal appropriations or private donations that may be made for the benefit of "native Hawaiians" and/or "Hawaiians," Haw. Const., Art. XII, § 6. See generally Haw. Rev. Stat. §§ 10-1 to 10-16. (The 200,000 acres set aside under the Hawaiian Homes Commission Act are administered by a separate agency. See Haw. Rev. Stat. §26-17 (1993).) The Hawaiian Legislature has charged OHA with the mission of "[s]erving as the principal public agency . . . responsible for the performance, development, and coordination of programs and activities relating to native Hawaiians and Hawaiians," "[a]ssessing the policies and practices of other agencies impacting on native Hawaiians and Hawaiians," "conducting advocacy efforts for native Hawaiians and Hawaiians," "[a]pplying for, receiving, and disbursing, grants and donations from all sources for native Hawaiian and Hawaiian programs and services," and "[s]erving as a receptacle for reparations." OHA is overseen by a nine-member board of trustees, the members of which "shall be Hawaiians" and—presenting the precise issue in this case—shall be "elected by qualified voters who are Hawaiians, as provided by law." Haw. Const., Art. XII, § 5; see Haw. Rev. Stat. §§ 13D-1, 13D-3 (b)(1) (1993). The term "Hawaiian" is defined by statute:

> "Hawaiian" means any descendant of the aboriginal peoples inhabiting the Hawaiian Islands which exercised sovereignty and subsisted in the Hawaiian Islands in 1778, and which peoples thereafter have continued to reside in Hawaii. § 10-2.

The statute defines "native Hawaiian" as follows:

> "Native Hawaiian" means any descendant of not less than one-half part

of the races inhabiting the Hawaiian Islands previous to 1778, as defined by the Hawaiian Homes Commission Act, 1920, as amended; provided that the term identically refers to the descendants of such blood quantum of such aboriginal peoples which exercised sovereignty and subsisted in the Hawaiian Islands in 1778 and which peoples thereafter continued to reside in Hawaii.

Petitioner Harold Rice is a citizen of Hawaii and a descendant of pre-annexation residents of the islands. He is not, as we have noted, a descendant of pre-1778 natives, and so he is neither "native Hawaiian" nor "Hawaiian" as defined by the statute. Rice applied in March 1996 to vote in the elections for OHA trustees. To register to vote for the office of trustee he was required to attest: "I am also Hawaiian and desire to register to vote in OHA elections." Rice marked through the words "am also Hawaiian and," then checked the form "yes." The State denied his application.

Rice sued Benjamin Cayetano, the Governor of Hawaii, in the United States District Court for the District of Hawaii. (The Governor was sued in his official capacity, and the Attorney General of Hawaii defends the challenged enactments. We refer to the respondent as "the State.") Rice contested his exclusion from voting in elections for OHA trustees and from voting in a special election relating to native Hawaiian sovereignty, which was held in August 1996. After the District Court rejected the latter challenge, the parties moved for summary judgment on the claim that the Fourteenth and Fifteenth Amendments to the United States Constitution invalidate the law excluding Rice from the OHA trustee elections. [Rice lost at the district court and appellate court levels.]

The purpose and command of the Fifteenth Amendment are set forth in language both explicit and comprehensive. The National Government and the States may not violate a fundamental principle: They may not deny or abridge the right to vote on account of race. Color and previous condition of servitude, too, are forbidden criteria or classifications though it is unnecessary to consider them in the present case.

Enacted in the wake of the Civil War, the immediate concern of the Amendment was to guarantee to the emancipated slaves the right to vote, lest they be denied the civil and political capacity to protect their new freedom. Vital as its objective remains, the Amendment goes beyond it. Consistent with the design of the Constitution, the Amendment is cast in fundamental terms, terms transcending the particular controversy, which was the immediate impetus for its enactment. The Amendment grants protection to all persons, not just members of a particular race.

The design of the Amendment is to reaffirm the equality of races at the most basic level of the democratic process, the exercise of the voting franchise. . . .

Ancestry can be a proxy for race. It is that proxy here. Even if the residents of Hawaii in 1778 had been of more diverse ethnic backgrounds and cultures, it is far from clear that a voting test favoring their descendants would not be a race-based qualification. But that is not this case. For centuries Hawaii was isolated from migration. The inhabitants shared common physical characteristics, and by 1778 they had a common culture. Indeed, the drafters of the statutory definition in question emphasized the "unique culture of the ancient Hawaiians" in explaining their work. ("Modern scholarship also identified such race of people as culturally distinguishable from other Polynesian peoples.") The provisions before us reflect the State's effort to preserve that commonality of people to the present day. In the interpretation of the Reconstruction era civil rights laws we have observed that "racial discrimination" is that which singles out "identifiable classes of persons . . . solely because of their ancestry or ethnic characteristics." *Saint Francis College v. Al-Khazraji*, 481 U.S. 604, 613 (1987). The very object of the statutory definition in question and of its earlier congressional counterpart in the Hawaiian Homes Commission Act is to treat

(continued)

the early Hawaiians as a distinct people, commanding their own recognition and respect. The State, in enacting the legislation before us, has used ancestry as a racial definition and for a racial purpose. . . .

The ancestral inquiry mandated by the State is forbidden by the Fifteenth Amendment for the further reason that the use of racial classifications is corruptive of the whole legal order democratic elections seek to preserve. The law itself may not become the instrument for generating the prejudice and hostility all too often directed against persons whose particular ancestry is disclosed by their ethnic characteristics and cultural traditions. "Distinctions between citizens solely because of their ancestry are by their very nature odious to a free people whose institutions are founded upon the doctrine of equality." . . . .

When the culture and way of life of a people are all but engulfed by a history beyond their control, their sense of loss may extend down through generations; and their dismay may be shared by many members of the larger community. As the State of Hawaii attempts to address these realities, it must, as always, seek the political consensus that begins with a sense of shared purpose. One of the necessary beginning points is this principle: The Constitution of the United States, too, has become the heritage of all the citizens of Hawaii.

In this case the Fifteenth Amendment invalidates the electoral qualification based on ancestry. The judgment of the Court of Appeals for the Ninth Circuit is reversed.

Rice v. Cayetano, 528 U.S. 495 (2000), U.S. Supreme Court.

4.7 CONCLUSION

Due process protects people from arbitrary agency behavior. The Due Process Clauses of the Fifth and Fourteenth Amendments provide a safety net of fairness. Often, however, Congress or an agency itself will provide more process than is required by the Constitution.

Courts use the three-tiered approach to due process and equal protection analysis when reviewing agency action. If a law encroaches upon a person's substantive or procedural rights or classifies people by race, ethnicity, religion, or other protected characteristics, the strict scrutiny test is applied to determine if the action is constitutional. If the government cannot show a compelling and legitimate reason for encroaching upon the right or for its classification, the action is unconstitutional. In a few instances, such as classifications based on gender or illegitimacy, the intermediate test is applied. In all other instances, the rational relationship test is used. Laws tested by the rational relationship test are likely to be found valid.

REVIEW **QUESTIONS**

1. The Constitution of the United States has two Due Process Clauses: one in the _____ Amendment, which applies to the federal government, and another in the _____ Amendment, which applies to the states.

2. Normally, to survive a due process or equal protection violation claim, a law must bear a rational relationship to its purpose. If a fundamental right or suspect class is involved, however, it must pass the _____ test.

3. Generally, due process requires that the government provide _____ and a _____ before depriving a person of life, liberty, or property.

4. Which of the following statements is most true concerning the rights-versus-privileges doctrine in due process analysis?
   a. The doctrine is currently used to determine whether the government has violated the Due Process Clause.
   b. The doctrine has been replaced by the strict scrutiny doctrine.
   c. The doctrine has been replaced by the legal entitlements doctrine.
   d. The doctrine was never used in due process analysis.

5. In which of the following cases is a Court most likely to require a hearing where the parties may call and examine witnesses?

   a. State Motor Vehicle Agency is considering revoking Driver's license after Driver suffers a loss of vision. State law requires that all drivers have at least 20/100 vision with correction. Driver and Agency agree that Driver has 20/100 in his left eye and 20/150 in the right eye. Agency contends that each eye must meet the 20/100 requirement; Driver contends that only one eye must meet the 20/100 requirement.

   b. Sandy, an Australian, has applied for U.S. citizenship based on her marriage to Glen, a U.S. citizen. The Immigration and Naturalization Service questions whether the marriage is lawful or merely a sham to obtain citizenship for Sandy because the two have known each other only two months. Glen and Sandy agree that they have known each other for only two months, but contend that the marriage is valid.

   c. The Kasten Company has been cited for violating air emission standards. Kasten agrees with Agency's findings concerning its plant's emissions, but contends that the law does not prohibit its emissions. Kasten brings an agency appeal.

6. Which of the following is most true?

   a. Due process requires that one be permitted the representation of counsel at all administrative hearings.

   b. Due process requires that one be permitted the representation of counsel at all administrative hearings involving substantial issues of law.

   c. Due process requires that one be permitted the representation of counsel at all administrative hearings involving substantial issues of fact.

   d. Both b and c.

7. T or F The Due Process Clause requires that all notices of agency action be given at least 30 days in advance.

8. T or F In emergency situations, an agency may be justified in depriving a person of property without first providing notice or a hearing.

9. T or F As a general rule, due process does not require that predeprivation hearings be conducted.

10. T or F Cost-benefit analysis is a static concept, leading Courts to require the same procedures in nearly all cases.

CRITICAL THINKING AND **APPLICATIONS PROBLEMS**

1. Jane is hired as a full-time permanent employee by State. She works for State's revenue agency as a clerk-typist. As a permanent employee, she is entitled to life, health, and dental insurance. Pursuant to statute, State provides these automatically and immediately when an employee is hired. The employee then has 30 days within which to waive any particular insurance (and save the employee's share of the premium).

   Because of a clerical error, Jane was never enrolled in State's group health insurance plan, nor was she informed of her option to waive. On February 1, Jane is involved in an automobile accident. Jane's husband contacts Jane's immediate supervisor about the accident. The total medical bills exceed $50,000. State's group medical insurance would cover 80 percent of these bills.

   Because of her injuries, Jane, at the recommendation of her physician, does not return to work until April 1. Upon her arrival, she discovers that she has been terminated. She is given access to her file and discovers that she was placed on "probation" on March 1 for failure to appear for work. The notation in the file states that "if the employee does not return to work within fifteen days she is to be terminated after a hearing is conducted." The file further reflects that a hearing was conducted. Jane's immediate supervisor and a State personnel officer appeared. The file reflects that Jane was "terminated because there is no evidence to justify the employee's failure to appear for duty." Jane was not informed of the hearing. State law provides that

   [e]very employee who fails to report for duty 30 days or longer within one calendar year shall be terminated regardless of the cause of the failure to report.

   Jane sues the state, praying that she be restored to her position and that state be ordered to pay her medical bills. Discuss her claim and prayers for remedies thoroughly.

2. Dr. Ima Dangerous works for a Florida county clinic that provides medical services to those who cannot afford private medical care and who are uninsured. On June 1, Ima was indicted in Georgia for murder. The indictment alleges that he intentionally killed two people who were his patients when he worked in Big Hospital in Atlanta. Ed Minster, the manager of the clinic, learned of the indictment the next day. He immediately suspended Ima without pay and scheduled a hearing for June 21. On June 15, Ima was provided with copies of the following documents that Ed had received from the prosecutor in Georgia: the indictment; copies of affidavits from nurses and physicians indicating that they had seen Ima inject the victims with an unknown substance directly before their deaths; a copy of a psychiatric report in which Ima was

diagnosed as dangerous; and a copy of a letter from the administrator of Big Hospital to Ima reprimanding Ima for having contact with dying patients of other physicians. In the letter, the administrator penned that "several staff members are concerned about your preoccupation with death." Ima was given the opportunity to present his case. At the close of the hearing, a board of physicians and administrators of the clinic voted to terminate Ima's employment. Three months later Ima was tried and acquitted of the charges in Georgia. Ima has sued the Florida county clinic for violating his due process rights in both his suspension and termination. Discuss his claims thoroughly.

3. Do you believe the Supreme Court was correct in not extending the *Goldberg* hearing requirement to disability and unemployment benefits? Consider the facts of *Mathews v. Eldridge*, 424 U.S. 319 (1976). The plaintiff, George Eldridge, had a fifth-grade education. While in the military, he suffered a back injury. Because he could not find less strenuous employment, he returned to a labor job with a railroad after his discharge from the military. Later, he found work as a deliveryman with a soft-drink company. He worked for that company until his injury caused him to lose the use of his legs. He applied for disability benefits. This application was denied twice. Eventually, he was given a hearing at which he prevailed. The entire process took about one year. Then, about one year after the award, he was asked to provide evidence that he was still disabled. He complied, but the agency decided to terminate his benefits. He again appealed within the agency. Simultaneously, he hired an attorney who filed an action in federal Court. The trial judge ordered the agency to continue benefits until it rendered its final decision. Before the judge issued the order, George, his wife, and their family of six children depended on the disability check ($136 a month) to live. To make matters worse, Mrs. Eldridge was suffering from cancer during much of this. She died the same month the Court issued its order. The Social Security Administration had its new hearing and the administrative law judge found George to be totally disabled and awarded back pay and future benefits. Then, about one year later, the agency again asked him to prove his disability. He did so. Again, he received notice that his benefits were to be terminated. George again filed suit in federal Court. He prevailed in the lower courts on the issue of continuation of benefits while the agency was hearing his appeal. The Supreme Court reversed, finding that the risk of erroneous decision was low and that disability benefits were not as essential as welfare benefits. This did not end the case, however. George had his

appeal within the agency. Two years after the denial, the agency conducted another hearing. As was the case in his prior hearing, the administrative law judge found him to be totally disabled, awarding back pay and future benefits. By that time, however, the family home had been foreclosed on by the bank and the family's furniture repossessed. In the end, George and his children moved into a trailer and all slept in the same bed.[31]

4. Federal Agency adopts a rule concerning contracting for construction projects. The rule reads:

Preamble: The following rule is adopted in order to remedy a history of discrimination against certain racial minorities and to stimulate local economic development.

Rule: All contracts for remodeling and new construction of facilities that exceed $10,000 shall be competitively bid. The Request for Proposal shall be published in the local newspaper of general distribution for three business days on two occasions within the same month and bidders shall be given no less than thirty days to submit their bids. The bids shall be opened in a closed session and ranked by the bid price. The lowest bidder shall be awarded the contract, except that the lowest minority or the lowest experienced bidder shall be awarded the contract if his or her bid is no more than 10 percent greater in price than the lowest nonminority or experienced bidder. For purposes of this rule, a minority bidder is any company qualified to conduct the work that is owned by an individual of African American, Hispanic, or Asian ethnicity. An experienced bidder is any company qualified to conduct the work that has completed three or more construction projects for the agency in the three years prior to the date the bids are opened.

Depend Able Construction, Inc., bid on two contracts with Federal Agency. It lost both, one to a minority bidder and the other to an experienced bidder. It has challenged both decisions on equal protection grounds. During discovery, it discovered that 11 percent of the contract awardees in the two years prior to adoption of the rule were minority-owned, as defined by the rule; 13 percent of the population served by the agency are minorities, as defined by the rule (African American, Hispanic, and Asian).

Discuss the following:

a. What standard will a Court apply to the minority preference provision? Do you believe Depend Able Construction, Inc., will prevail? Explain.

b. What standard will a Court apply to the experienced contractor preference provision? Do you believe Depend Able Construction, Inc., will prevail? Explain.

ENDNOTES

1. *McNabb v. United States*, 318 U.S. 332, 347 (1943).
2. Instructors are encouraged to read Dean J. Spader's article, *Teaching Due Process: A Workable Method of Teaching the Ethical and Legal Aspects*, 5 J. of Crim. Just. Educ. 81 (1994), for a suggested method of teaching due process.
3. See the Slaughter-House Cases, 83 U.S. 36 (1873).
4. *McCulloch v. Maryland*, 17 U.S. 316 (1819).
5. *Grutter v. Bollinger*, 539 U.S. 306 (2003).
6. *Morrissey v. Brewer*, 408 U.S. 471 (1972); *Gagnon v. Scarpelli*, 411 U.S. 778 (1973).
7. 397 U.S. 254, n. 8 (1970).
8. *Board of Regents of State Colleges. v. Roth*, 408 U.S. 564 (1972).
9. *Willner v. Committee on Character & Fitness*, 373 U.S. 96 (1963).
10. *Bell v. Burson*, 402 U.S. 535 (1971).
11. *Mathews v. Eldridge*, 424 U.S. 319 (1976).
12. APA § 554(b).
13. *Id.*
14. *Greene v. McElroy*, 360 U.S. 474, 496–97 (1959).
15. APA § 554(a)(3).
16. See Jerry Mashaw, Richard Merrill, & Peter Shane, *Administrative Law: The American Public Law System*, ch. 4 (West, 1998) for a more thorough discussion of this topic.
17. 424 U.S. 319 (1976).
18. *Cleveland Board. of Education. v. Loudermill*, 470 U.S. 532 (1985).
19. *Phillips v. Commissioner of Internal Revenue*, 283 U.S. 589, 598 (1931).
20. *Ewing v. Mytinger & Casselberry, Inc.*, 339 U.S. 594 (1950).
21. APA § 555(b).
22. *Wolff v. McDonnell*, 418 U.S. 539 (1974).
23. *Gagnon v. Scarpelli*, 411 U.S. 778 (1973).
24. *Madera v. Board of Education.*, 386 F. 2d 778 (2d Cir. 1967), *cert. denied*, 390 U.S. 1028 (1968).
25. *Reed v. Reed*, 404 U.S. 71 (1971).
26. *Zablocki v. Redhail*, 434 U.S. 374 (1978).
27. 438 U.S. 265 (1978).
28. See, for example, *Fullilove v. Klutznick*, 448 U.S. 448 (1980); *City of Richmond v. J. A. Croson*, 488 U.S. 469 (1989); *Metro Broad., Inc. v. FCC*, 497 U.S. 547 (1990).
29. 515 U.S. 200 (1995).
30. *Id.* at 223.
31. See Steven J. Cann, *Administrative Law*, 2d ed. 312 (2d ed., Sage, 1998), citing Phillip J. Cooper, *Public Law and Public Administration* (2d ed., Prentice Hall, 1988).

chapter **five**

DELEGATION

OUTLINE

LEARNING OBJECTIVES

After completing this chapter, you should be able to

- Define *delegation* and explain how and why delegations occur in the administrative context.

- Explain the history, citing cases for each point you make, of delegations of legislative authority.

- Explain the state of the delegation doctrine today, as well the legal standard(s) that are applied to delegations of legislative and judicial authorities, citing cases to support your points.

- Explain why delegations of authority to private parties present different legal questions than delegations to governmental actors.

- Brief a judicial opinion with little outside assistance. You should be successful in identifying the relevant facts. You should be successful in identifying the legal issue and analyzing the court's rationale in at least 33 percent of your briefs.

I have always thought, from my earliest youth until now, that the greatest scourge an angry Heaven ever inflicted upon an ungrateful and a sinning people, was an ignorant, a corrupt, or a dependent judiciary.

JOHN MARSHALL[1]

Virginia Constitutional Convention, 1829–1830, Debates 619.

5.1 WHAT IS DELEGATION?

You learned in a previous chapter that Congress creates agencies. This process begins with the identification of a problem or need. Once a problem is identified, Congress may conduct an investigation of it with an eye toward enacting legislation to solve or at least confront the problem. As you already learned, an act through which Congress creates an agency to address a specific problem is known as *enabling legislation*. Through enabling legislation, Congress defines an agency's mandate, how the agency is to satisfy its mandate, how the agency is to be structured (including how its leaders will be appointed), and what authority the agency possesses.

Most authority that Congress defines for an agency is executive authority. Remember, all duties that involve execution of the law and administration of a program are executive in nature. As a general rule, there is no separation-of-powers problem with an agency possessing executive authority because nearly all agencies fall under the executive branch. However, Congress also delegates legislative and judicial responsibilities to agencies. When Congress delegates its authority to make laws to an agency, the agency is receiving *quasi-legislative authority*. Agency-created laws are not known as statutes, as are the laws created by Congress. Instead, they are referred to as *rules* or regulations. When Congress gives an agency the responsibility to hear disputes as a court would, the agency has been delegated *quasi-judicial power*.

As discussed in Chapter 1, Congress delegates these authorities for a variety of reasons. For example, Congress does not have the ability or expertise to fully regulate all subjects. Therefore, it transfers some of its lawmaking authority to agencies that possess the expertise and resources to develop a complete regulatory scheme. Additionally, Congress sometimes delegates limited or quasi-judicial authority to agencies. However, the possession of legislative and judicial powers by executive-branch agencies raises fundamental separation-of-powers questions. That is the subject of this chapter.

Generally, a delegation may violate the Constitution in one (or more) of three ways. First, Congress may delegate too much of its own authority to an agency. Second, Congress cannot delegate to an agency its own essential functions or the essential functions of the judicial branch. While the former violation is about the quantity of a delegation, this type is about the nature of the delegated authorities. For example, the Constitution vests the authority to ratify treaties in the Senate. The Senate may not delegate this authority to one of its committees or to an agency. This is an essential function that it alone must perform. As you will learn later, similar issues are implicated with delegations of judicial authority.

Third, Congress may not make a delegation that gives one branch oversight or control over an agency that is performing the functions of another branch. For example, Congress may give an agency the authority to conduct hearings—a judicial function—but it may not attempt to direct the decisions that the agency makes when performing its delegated judicial duties. These separation-of-powers limitations on congressional authority to delegate are known as the *delegation doctrine* or negatively as the *nondelegation doctrine*.

5.2 DELEGATING LEGISLATIVE AUTHORITY

Article I, section 1, of the Constitution provides that all legislative authority of the United States rests with Congress. There is no mention of agency rulemaking power in the Constitution. Regardless, the Supreme Court has permitted delegations of legislative authority to executive officers since the earliest days of the 1789 Constitution. In the early years, however, the Supreme Court was reluctant to acknowledge that it was legislative authority that was being delegated. The Supreme Court decided a delegation case as early as 1825 in *Wayman v. Southard*.[2] Chief Justice Marshall, writing for the Court, upheld a congressional delegation to the courts to make certain rules of operation. Marshall definitely held that Congress may not delegate its own authority but upheld the rulemaking power under the theory that Congress may legislate generally and then delegate the authority to fill in the details and procedures used to implement Congress's intentions:

> Congress could not delegate this power to the judiciary, or to any other department of the government. The right to liberty and property is a sacred vested right under the constitution and laws of the Union and States. The regulations by which it is to be devested, for the purpose of enforcing the performance of contracts, are of vital importance to the citizen. The power of making such regulations is exclusively vested in the legislative department, by all our constitutions, and by the general spirit and principles of all free government. It is the office of the legislator to prescribe the rule, and of the Judge to apply it; and it is immaterial whether it respects the right in controversy, or the remedy by which it is to be enforced. The mere forms and style of writs, and other process, may, indeed, be regulated by the Courts, but the regulation of the substantive part of the remedy belongs to the legislature. The power to establish Courts, with the jurisdiction defined by the constitution, does not involve, by necessary implication, the authority of delegating any portion or incident of that power to the Courts themselves. That authority is not expressly given; consequently it does not exist.
>
> Congress has not, in fact, delegated this authority to the Court. The several Process Acts passed by Congress, regulate the forms only; they give to the Courts the power to regulate the forms only.
>
> Every Court has, like every other public political body, the power necessary and proper to provide for the orderly conduct of its business. This may be compared to the separate power which each house of Congress has to determine the rules of its proceedings, and to punish contempts. This is altogether different from the general legislative power, which Congress cannot delegate, and never has attempted to delegate, to either house, separately, or to the executive and judicial departments of the government. To construe the power to regulate the forms of process and modes of proceeding, into a power in the Courts to make execution laws, would be to suppose Congress intended to violate the constitution, by delegating their legislative power to the judiciary. . .
>
> It will not be contended that Congress can delegate to the courts or to any other tribunals powers which are strictly and exclusively legislative.
>
> But Congress may certainly delegate to others powers which the legislature may rightfully exercise itself. Without going further for examples, we will take that the legality of which the counsel for the defendants admit. The 17th section of the Judiciary Act and the 7th section of the additional act empower the courts respectively to regulate their practice. It certainly will not be contended that this might not be done by Congress. The courts, for example, may make rules directing the returning of writs and processes, the filing of declarations and other pleadings, and other things of the same description. It will not be contended that these things might not be done by the legislature without the intervention of the courts, yet it is not alleged that the power may not be conferred on the Judicial Department.
>
> The line has not been exactly drawn which separates those important subjects which must be entirely regulated by the legislature itself from those of less interest in which a general provision may be made and power given to those who are to act under such general provisions to fill up the details.[3]

The 1911 case of *United States v. Grimaud* is another example of a delegation of legislative authority—or, as the Court characterized it, a delegation of "power to determine some fact or state of things upon which the law makes or intends to make its own action depend."

United States v. Grimaud

220 U.S. 506 (1911)

By the act of March 3, 1891 . . . the President was authorized, from time to time, to set apart and reserve, in any state or territory, public lands, wholly or in part covered with timber or undergrowth, whether of commercial value or not, as public forest reservations. And by [statute] the purposes of these reservations were declared to be "to improve and protect the forest within the reservation, or for the purpose of securing favorable conditions of water flows, and to furnish a continuous supply of timber for the use and necessities of citizens of the United States. . . . All waters on such reservations may be used for domestic, mining, milling, or irrigation purposes, under the laws of the state wherein such forest reservations are situated. . . ."

The original act provided that the management and regulation of these reserves should be by the Secretary of Interior; but in 1905 that power was conferred upon the Secretary of Agriculture . . . and he may make such rules and regulations and establish such service as will insure the objects of such reservations; namely, to preserve the forests thereon from destruction; and any violation of the provisions of this act or such rules and regulations shall be punished. . . .

Under these acts, the Secretary of Agriculture, on June 12, 1906, promulgated and established certain rules for the purpose of regulating the use and occupancy of the public forest reservations and preserving the forests from destruction, and among those established was the following: "Regulation 45. All person[s] must secure permits before grazing any stock in a forest reserve. . . ."

The defendants were charged with driving and grazing sheep on a reserve, without a permit. . . .

In the nature of things it was impracticable for Congress to provide general regulations for these various and varying details of management. Each reservation had its peculiar and special features; and in authorizing the Secretary of Agriculture to meet these local conditions, Congress was merely conferring administrative functions upon an agent, and not delegating to him legislative power. . . .

"The legislature cannot delegate its power to make a law, but it can make a law to delegate a power to determine some fact or state of things upon which the law makes or intends to make its own action depend. To deny this would be to stop the wheels of government. There are many things upon which wise and useful legislation must depend which cannot be known to the lawmaking power, and must therefore be a subject of inquiry and determination outside of the halls of legislation."

United States v. Grimaud, 220 U.S. 506 (1911), U.S Supreme Court.

The situation changed during the 1930s. The Great Depression led to the creation of many new agencies, each with a broad delegation of authority. Because of the need to confront the serious economic crisis quickly, much of the enabling legislation was hurriedly drafted, poorly written, and involved delegations on a scale the nation had not experienced before. For one brief period, in the mid 1930s, the Supreme Court scrutinized delegations very closely. During this brief period the Court invalidated two delegations in two well-known cases. The first occurred in *Panama Refining Co. v. Ryan*,[4] wherein the National Industrial Recovery Act of 1933 (NIRA) was challenged.

The NIRA authorized the president of the United States to prohibit the transportation of certain oil products in interstate commerce. The Supreme Court found the delegation unlawful because Congress granted too much legislative authority to the president. The Court further stated that the decision whether a product should be allowed in interstate commerce is legislative. It is the president's duty to see that such a prohibition is enforced, not to create the prohibition.

Another delegation was invalidated in *Schechter Poultry Corp. v. United States.*[5] That case challenged the authority of the president of the United States to approve "codes of fair competition" for the poultry industry. The defendant corporation was convicted of violating a code established by an agency (acting on the president's behalf), over the corporation's objection that the delegation to the president was unlawful. The Supreme Court of the United States reversed the conviction because it found no solid policy statement to guide the agency when it created the code. In fact, the Court found that the policy statement issued by Congress had conflicting goals. For example, Congress wanted the code not only to discourage monopolies, but also to encourage cooperative actions among competitors.

Panama Refining Co. v. Ryan

293 U.S. 388 (1935)

Mr. Chief Justice Hughes delivered the opinion of the Court.

On July 11, 1933, the President, by Executive Order No. 6199 (15 USCA § 709 note), prohibited "the transportation in interstate and foreign commerce of petroleum and the products thereof produced or withdrawn from storage in excess of the amount permitted to be produced or withdrawn from storage by any State law or valid regulation or order prescribed thereunder, by any board, commission, officer, or other duly authorized agency of a State." This action was based on section 9(c) of title 1 of the National Industrial Recovery Act of June 16, 1933, 48 Stat. 195, 200, 15 U.S.C. tit. 1, § 709 (c), 15 USCA § 709 (c). That section provides:

Sec. 9.

* * *

(c) The President is authorized to prohibit the transportation in interstate and foreign commerce of petroleum and the products thereof produced or withdrawn from storage in excess of the amount permitted to be produced or withdrawn from storage by any State law or valid regulation or order prescribed thereunder, by any board, commission, officer, or other duly authorized agency of a State. Any violation of any order of the President issued under the provisions of this subsection shall be punishable by fine of not to exceed $1,000, or imprisonment for not to exceed six months, or both.

On July 14, 1933, the President, by Executive Order No. 6204 (15 U.S.C.A. § 709 note), authorized the Secretary of the Interior to exercise all the powers vested in the President "for the purpose of enforcing Section 9(c) of said act and said order" of July 11, 1933, "including full authority to designate and appoint such agents and to set up such boards and agencies as he may see fit, and to promulgate such rules and regulations as he may deem necessary." That order was made under section 10(a) of the National Industrial Recovery Act, 48 Stat. 200, 15 U.S.C. § 710(a), 15 USCA § 710 (a), authorizing the President "to prescribe such rules and regulations as may be necessary to carry out the purposes" of title 1 of the National Industrial Recovery Act and providing that "any violation of any such rule or regulation shall be punishable by fine of not to exceed $500, or imprisonment for not to exceed six months, or both."

On July 15, 1933, the Secretary of the Interior issued regulations to carry out the President's orders of July 11 and 14, 1933. . . .

These regulations were amended by orders of July 25, 1933, and August 21, 1933, prior to the commencement of these suits. Regulation IV provided, in substance, that every producer of petroleum should file a monthly statement under oath, beginning August 15, 1933, with the Division of Investigations of the Department of the Interior giving information with respect to the residence and post office address of the producer, the location of his producing properties and wells, the allowable production as prescribed by state authority, the amount of daily production, all deliveries of petroleum, and declaring that no part of the petroleum or products produced and shipped had been produced or withdrawn from storage in excess of the amount permitted by state authority. Regulation V required every purchaser, shipper (other than a producer), and refiner of petroleum, including processors, similarly to file a monthly statement under oath, giving information as to residence and post office address, the place and date of receipt, the parties from whom and the amount of petroleum received and the amount held in storage, the disposition of the petroleum, particulars as to deliveries, and declaring, to the best of the affiant's information and belief, that none of the petroleum so handled had been produced or withdrawn from storage in excess of that allowed by state authority. Regulation VII provided that all persons embraced within the terms of section 9(c) of the act, 15 USCA § 709(a) and the executive orders and regulations issued thereunder, should keep "available for inspection by the Division of Investigations of the Department of the Interior adequate books and records of all transactions involving the production and transportation of petroleum and the products thereof.". . .

These suits were brought in October, 1933.

In No. 135, the Panama Refining Company, as owner of an oil refining plant in Texas, and its coplaintiff, a producer having oil and gas leases in Texas, sued to restrain the defendants, who were federal officials, from enforcing Regulations IV, V, and VII prescribed by the Secretary of the Interior under section 9(c) of the National Industrial Recovery Act. Plaintiffs attacked the validity of section 9(c) as an unconstitutional delegation to the President of legislative power and as transcending the authority of the Congress under the commerce clause. The regulations, and the attempts to enforce them by coming upon the properties of the plaintiffs, gauging their tanks, digging up pipe lines, and otherwise, were also assailed under the Fourth and Fifth Amendments of the Constitution. . . .

Section 9[c] is assailed upon the ground that it is an unconstitutional delegation of legislative power. The section purports to authorize the President to pass a prohibitory law. The subject to which this authority relates is defined. It is the transportation in interstate and foreign commerce of petroleum and petroleum products, which are produced or withdrawn from storage in excess of the amount permitted by state authority. Assuming for the present purpose, without deciding, that the Congress has power to interdict the transportation of that excess in interstate and foreign commerce, the question whether that transportation shall be prohibited by law is obviously one of legislative policy. Accordingly, we look to the statute to see whether the Congress has declared a policy with respect to that subject; whether the Congress has set up a standard for the President's action; whether the Congress has required any finding by the President in the exercise of the authority to enact the prohibition.

Section 9(c) is brief and unambiguous. It does not attempt to control the production of petroleum and petroleum products within a state. It does not seek to

(continued)

lay down rules for the guidance of state Legislatures or state officers. It leaves to the states and to their constituted authorities the determination of what production shall be permitted. It does not qualify the President's authority by reference to the basis or extent of the state's limitation of production. section 9(c) does not state whether or in what circumstances or under what conditions the President is to prohibit the transportation of the amount of petroleum or petroleum products produced in excess of the state's permission. It establishes no criterion to govern the President's course. It does not require any finding by the President as a condition of his action. The Congress in section 9(c) thus declares no policy as to the transportation of the excess production. So far as this section is concerned, it gives to the President an unlimited authority to determine the policy and to lay down the prohibition, or not to lay it down, as he may see fit. And disobedience to his order is made a crime punishable by fine and imprisonment.

We examine the context to ascertain if it furnishes a declaration of policy or a standard of action, which can be deemed to relate to the subject of section 9(c) and thus to imply what is not there expressed. It is important to note that section 9 (15 U.S.C.A. § 709) is headed "Oil Regulation"—that is, section 9 is the part of the National Industrial Recovery Act which particularly deals with that subject matter. But the other provisions of section 9 afford no ground for implying a limitation of the broad grant of authority in section 9(c). Thus section 9(a) authorizes the President to initiate before the Interstate Commerce Commission "proceedings necessary to prescribe regulations to control the operations of oil pipe lines and to fix reasonable, compensatory rates for the transportation of petroleum and its products by pipe lines," and the Interstate Commerce Commission is to grant preference "to the hearings and determination of such cases." section 9(b) authorizes the President to institute proceedings "to divorce from any holding company any pipeline company controlled by such holding company which Pieline company by unfair practices or by exorbitant rates in the transportation of petroleum or its products tends to create a monopoly." It will be observed that each of these provisions contains restrictive clauses as to their respective subjects. Neither relates to the subject of section 9(c).

We turn to the other provisions of title 1 of the act. The first section (15 USCA § 701) is a "declaration of policy." It declares that a national emergency exists which is "productive of widespread unemployment and disorganization of industry, which burdens interstate and foreign commerce, affects the public welfare, and undermines the standards of living of the American people." It is declared to be the policy of Congress "to remove obstructions to the free flow of interstate and foreign commerce which tend to diminish the amount thereof;" "to provide for the general welfare by promoting the organization of industry for the purpose of cooperative action among trade groups;" "to induce and maintain united action of labor and management under adequate governmental sanctions and supervision;" "to eliminate unfair competitive practices, to promote the fullest possible utilization of the present productive capacity of industries, to avoid undue restriction of production (except as may be temporarily required), to increase the consumption of industrial and agricultural products by increasing purchasing power, to reduce and relieve unemployment, to improve standards of labor, and otherwise to rehabilitate industry and to conserve natural resources.". . .

This general outline of policy contains nothing as to the circumstances or conditions in which transportation of petroleum or petroleum products should be prohibited—nothing as to the policy of prohibiting or not prohibiting the transportation of production exceeding what the states allow. The general policy declared is "to remove obstructions to the free flow of intersate and foreign commerce." As to production, the section lays down no policy of limitation. It favors the fullest possible utilization of the present productive capacity of industries. It speaks, parenthetically, of a possible temporary restriction of production, but of what, or in what circumstances, it gives no suggestion. The section also speaks in general terms of the conservation of natural resources, but it prescribes no policy for the achievement of that end. It is manifest that this broad outline is simply an introduction of the act, leaving the legislative policy as to particular subjects to be declared and defined, if at all, by the subsequent sections.

It is no answer to insist that deleterious consequences follow the transportation of "hot oil"—oil exceeding state allowances. The Congress did not prohibit that transportation. The Congress did not undertake to say that the transportation of "hot oil" was injurious. The Congress did not say that transportation of that oil was "unfair competition." The Congress did not declare in what circumstances that transportation should be forbidden, or require the President to make any determination as to any facts or circumstances. Among the numerous and diverse objectives broadly stated, the President was not required to choose. The President was not required to ascertain and proclaim the conditions prevailing in the industry, which made the prohibition necessary. The Congress left the matter to the President without standard or rule, to be dealt with as he pleased. The effort by ingenious and diligent construction to supply a criterion still permits such a breadth of authorized action as essentially to commit to the President the functions of a Legislature rather than those of an executive or administrative officer executing a declared legislative policy. We find nothing in section 1, which limits or controls the authority conferred by section 9(c)....

"If Congress shall lay down by legislative act an intelligible principle to which the person or body authorized to fix such rates is directed to conform, such legislative action is not a forbidden delegation of legislative power. If it is thought wise to vary the customs duties according to changing conditions of production at home and abroad, it may authorize the Chief Executive to carry out this purpose, with the advisory assistance of a Tariff Commission appointed under congressional authority." The Court sustained the provision upon the authority of *Field v. Clark,* supra, repeating with approval what was there said, that "What the President was required to do was merely in execution of the act of Congress." *Id.,* pages 409–411 of 276 U.S., 48 S. Ct. 348, 352.

Thus, in every case in which the question has been raised, the Court has recognized that there are limits of delegation which there is no constitutional authority to transcend. We think that section 9(c) goes beyond those limits. As to the transportation of oil production in excess of state permission, the Congress has declared no policy, has established no standard, has laid down no rule. There is no requirement, no definition of circumstances and conditions in which the transportation is to be allowed or prohibited.

If section 9(c) were held valid, it would be idle to pretend that anything would be left of limitations upon the power of the Congress to delegate its lawmaking function. The reasoning of the many decisions we have reviewed would be made vacuous and their distinctions nugatory. Instead of performing its lawmaking function, the Congress could at will, and as to such subjects as it chooses, transfer that function to the President or other officer or to an administrative body....

The *Panama Refining* and *Schechter Poultry* cases are often respectively referred to as the "hot oil" and "sick chicken" cases, because the former involved the alleged illegal sale of oil and the latter the sale of sick poultry (and other violations), both in violation of federal law. In addition to the substantive legal problems, the *Schechter* Court found that the statute was also procedurally flawed. The statute did not require that interested persons be given notice, nor did it provide for judicial review of agency decisions. For all these reasons, the law was found unconstitutional.

Panama Refining Co. v. Ryan, 293 U.S. 388 (1935), U.S. Supreme Courts.

SIDEBAR *The Court-Packing Plan*

Within two years of President Franklin D. Roosevelt's inauguration, the Supreme Court had invalidated several pieces of New Deal legislation, and more than 1,600 injunctions against enforcement of New Deal legislation had been issued.[6] Displeased by the Supreme Court decisions in *Schechter*, *Panama Refining*, and other cases, President Roosevelt proposed to Congress that it enlarge the Supreme Court by permitting a new appointment for every justice over the age of 70. At the time of the proposal, six justices were over the age of 70. This would have enlarged the Court to 15. Roosevelt contended that the older justices were out of touch with America's challenges at the time and that adding younger members would make the Court more contemporary. Opponents of the plan asserted that the plan was a transparent attempt by the president to control the judiciary.

There was considerable opposition to the plan throughout the nation. Some people attribute the eventual defeat of the plan to Justice Roberts, who had voted with the majority in the cases that were contrary to the wishes of President Roosevelt. However, Roberts changed his direction beginning with the 1937 case of *West Coast Hotel v. Parrish*.[7] Because the votes on many of the New Deal cases had been close, Roberts's change of position resulted in fewer Supreme Court decisions invalidating New Deal legislation. This, along with other factors, led to the defeat of President Roosevelt's proposal. For this reason, Justice Roberts's actions are referred to as the "switch in time that saved nine."

President Franklin D. Roosevelt discussing the court-packing plan with Senator Joseph T. Robinson.

5.3 THE DELEGATION DOCTRINE TODAY

After the New Deal delegation cases, *Schechter Poultry* and *Panama Refining*, the situation changed again. Since 1935, the delegation doctrine has not been used by the Supreme Court as a constitutional basis to strike down any delegation of legislative power. The Supreme Court continues to recognize the doctrine, but little is required to satisfy its limitations. Pursuant to the doctrine, a delegation of legislative authority is constitutional if Congress establishes the nation's fundamental legislative policy and leaves only the "gap filling" to an agency. Through the years, courts have used different language to express this idea. Some cases speak in terms of "standards;" others refer to an ***intelligible principle***. Regardless, the idea is the same: Congress must provide sufficient ***standards*** to an agency to guide it (and limit its discretion) in the administration of the power it has been delegated. "A congressional delegation of power . . . must be accompanied by discernible standards, so that the delegate's actions may be measured by its fidelity to the legislative will."[8]

What follows are a few examples of delegations that have been upheld since the 1935 cases. In *Arizona v. California*,[9] the U.S. Secretary of Interior was delegated considerable authority over the apportionment of water from the Colorado River through the Boulder Canyon Project Act. This delegation was upheld because the statute ordered the secretary to consider various factors when deciding priority for water use. For example, he was ordered to consider river regulation, flood control, irrigation, domestic water consumption, and power production needs. The Court found that this provided the secretary with sufficient standards from which to work. If Congress had simply left the decision to the secretary's discretion, without listing these factors to be considered, the delegation would have failed.

In *Lichter v. United States*,[10] the Court upheld a delegation to administrative officers to recover "excessive profits" when renegotiating contracts involving war goods. Those who challenged the statute claimed that the phrase "excessive profits" was too vague and broad a delegation. The U.S. Supreme Court disagreed, holding that the phrase provided a sufficient standard to the executive-branch officers and that the delegation was a proper exercise of congressional war powers.

Mistretta v. United States[11] involved a delegation to the U.S. Sentencing Commission. Congress established the commission to research sentencing in the federal courts and to draft a set of sentencing guidelines for use by federal judges. The enabling statute was challenged as an unlawful delegation of a legislative function: namely, determining what punishment should be imposed for criminal behavior.

The delegation was upheld because (1) the commission was mandated to use current sentence averages as a "starting point"; (2) the purposes and goals of sentencing (the policy issues) were determined by Congress; and (3) the commission had to work within statutorily prescribed minimums and limits when setting the guideline range; that is, the guidelines could not be used to sentence an individual to more or less time than Congress had set out by statute. The Court held that Congress had provided the commission with an intelligible principle from which to act.

Two years later, the Supreme Court issued a decision upholding a delegation in *Touby v. United States*. *v. Touby*[12] involved a statute authorizing the Attorney General of the United States to temporarily declare a drug as Schedule I controlled under the Controlled Substances Act. Possession, distribution, or use of controlled substances is criminal under that statute, and, therefore, the U.S. Attorney General was delegated the responsibility of declaring penal law. Congress delegated the responsibility because it normally takes six months to a year to permanently schedule new drugs. Drug dealers took advantage of this time gap by developing new "designer" drugs that were similar in effect to existing drugs but different in chemical composition. Until permanently scheduled, designer drugs could be possessed, distributed, or used lawfully. To resolve this problem, Congress delegated to the Attorney General the authority to temporarily add, remove, and reschedule drugs.

Touby v. United States

500 U.S. 160 (1991)

Petitioners were convicted of manufacturing and conspiring to manufacture "Euphoria," a drug temporarily designated as a schedule I controlled substance pursuant to § 201(h) of the Controlled Substance Act, 98 Stat 2071, 21 USC § 811(h) [21 USCS § 811 (h)]. We consider whether § 201(h) unconstitutionally delegates legislative power to the Attorney General and whether the Attorney General's subdelegation to the Drug Enforcement Administration (DEA) was authorized by statute.

(continued)

In 1970, Congress enacted the Controlled Substances Act (Act), 84 Stat 1242, as amended, 21 U.S.C. § 801 et seq. The Act establishes five categories or "schedules" of controlled substances, the manufacture, possession, and distribution of which the Act regulates or prohibits. Violations involving schedule I substances carry the most severe penalties, as these substances are believed to pose the most serious threat to public safety. Relevant here, § 201(a) of the Act authorizes the Attorney General to add or remove substances, or to move a substance from one schedule to another. § 201(a), 21 USC § 811(a).

When adding a substance to a schedule, the Attorney General must follow specified procedures. First, the Attorney General must request a scientific and medical evaluation from the Secretary of Health and Human Services (HHS), together with a recommendation as to whether the substance should be controlled. A substance cannot be scheduled if the Secretary recommends against it. § 201(b), 21 USC § 811(b).

Second, the Attorney General must consider eight factors with respect to the substance, including its potential for abuse, scientific evidence of its pharmacological effect, its psychic or physiological dependence liability, and whether the substance is an immediate precursor of a substance already controlled. § 201(c), 21 USC § 811(c). Third, the Attorney General must comply with the notice-and-hearing provisions of the Administrative Procedure Act, 5 USC §§ 551–559, which permit comment by interested parties. § 201(a), 21 USC § 811(a). In addition, the Act permits any aggrieved person to challenge the scheduling of a substance by the Attorney General in a court of appeals. § 507, 21 USC § 877.

It takes time to comply with these procedural requirements. From the time when law enforcement officials identify a dangerous new drug, it typically takes 6 to 12 months to add it to one of the schedules. S. Rep. No. 98–225, p. 264 (1984). Drug traffickers were able to take advantage of this time gap by designing drugs that were similar in pharmacological effect to scheduled substances but differing slightly in chemical composition, so that existing schedules did not apply to them. These "designer drugs" were developed and widely marketed long before the government was able to schedule them and initiate prosecutions.

To combat the "designer drug" problem, Congress in 1984 amended the Act to create an expedited procedure by which the Attorney General can schedule a substance on a temporary basis when doing so is "necessary to avoid an imminent hazard to the public safety." § 201(h), 21 USC § 811(h). Temporary scheduling under § 201(h) allows the Attorney General to bypass, for a limited time, several of the requirements for permanent scheduling. The Attorney General need consider only three of the eight factors required for permanent scheduling. § 201(h)(3), 21 USC § 811(3). Rather than comply with the APA notice-and-hearing provisions, the Attorney General need provide only a 30-day notice of the proposed scheduling in the Federal Register. § 201(h)(1), 21 USC § 811(h)(1). Notice also must be transmitted to the Secretary of HHS, but the Secretary's prior approval of a proposed scheduling order is not required. See § 201(h)(4), 21 USC § 811(h)(4). Finally, § 201(h)(6), 21 USC § 811(h)(6), provides that an order to schedule a substance temporarily "is not subject to judicial review."

Because it has fewer procedural requirements, temporary scheduling enables the government to respond more quickly to the threat posed by dangerous new drugs. A temporary scheduling order can be issued 30 days after a new drug is identified, and the order remains valid for one year. During this 1-year period, the Attorney General presumably will initiate the permanent scheduling process, in which case the temporary scheduling order remains valid for an additional six months. § 201(h)(2), 21 U.S.C § 811(h)(2).

The Attorney General promulgated regulations delegating to the DEA his powers under the Act, including the power to schedule controlled substances on a temporary basis. See 28 CFR § 0.100(b) (1990). Pursuant to that delegation, the DEA Administrator issued an order scheduling temporarily 4-methylaminorex, known more commonly as "Euphoria," as a schedule I controlled substance. 52 Fed Reg 38225 (1987). The Administrator subsequently initiated formal rulemaking procedures, following which Euphoria was added permanently to schedule I.

While the temporary scheduling order was in effect, DEA agents, executing a valid search warrant, discovered a fully operational drug laboratory in Daniel and Lyrissa Touby's home. The Toubys were indicted for manufacturing and conspiring to manufacture Euphoria. They moved to dismiss the indictment on the grounds that § 201(h) unconstitutionally delegates legislative power to the Attorney General, and that the Attorney General improperly delegated his temporary scheduling authority to the DEA. The United States District Court for the District of New Jersey denied the motion to dismiss, 710 F Supp 551 (1989); and the Court of Appeals for the Third Circuit affirmed petitioners' subsequent convictions, 909 F2d 759 (1990). We granted certiorari, . . . and now affirm.

II

The Constitution provides that "[a]ll legislative Powers herein granted shall be vested in a Congress of the United States." US Const, Art I, § 1. From this language the Court has derived the nondelegation doctrine: that Congress may not constitutionally delegate its legislative power to another Branch of government. "The nondelegation doctrine is rooted in the principle of separation of powers that underlies our tripartite system of Government." *Mistretta v. United States*.

We have long recognized that the nondelegation doctrine does not prevent Congress from seeking assistance, within proper limits, from its coordinate Branches. Thus, Congress does not violate the Constitution merely because it legislates in broad terms, leaving a certain degree of discretion to executive or judicial actors. So long as Congress "lay[s] down by legislative act an intelligible principle to which the person or body authorized to [act] is directed to conform, such legislative action is not a forbidden delegation of legislative power." *J. W. Hampton, Jr. & Co. v. United States* (1928).

Petitioners wisely concede that Congress has set forth in § 201(h) an "intelligible principle" to constrain the Attorney General's discretion to schedule controlled substances on a temporary basis. We have upheld as providing sufficient guidance statutes authorizing the War Department to recover "excessive profits" earned on military contracts, see *Lichter v. United States* (1948); authorizing the Price Administrator to fix "fair and equitable" commodities prices, see *Yakus v. United States* (1944); and authorizing the Federal Communications Commission to regulate broadcast licensing in the "public interest," see *National Broadcasting Co. v. United States* (1943). In light of these precedents, one cannot plausibly argue that § 201(h)'s "imminent hazard to the public safety" standard is not an intelligible principle.

Petitioners suggest, however, that something more than an "intelligible principle" is required when Congress authorizes another Branch to promulgate regulations that contemplate criminal sanctions. They contend that regulations of this sort pose a heightened risk to individual liberty and that Congress must, therefore, provide more specific guidance. Our cases are not entirely clear as to whether or not more specific guidance is in fact required. We need not resolve the issue today. We conclude that 201(h) passes muster even if greater congressional specificity is required in the criminal context.

Although it features fewer procedural requirements than the permanent scheduling statute, § 201(h) meaningfully constrains the Attorney General's discretion to define criminal conduct. To schedule a drug temporarily, the Attorney General must find that doing so is "necessary to avoid an imminent hazard to the public safety."

(continued)

In making this determination, he is "required to consider" three factors: the drug's "history and current pattern of abuse;" "[t]he scope, duration, and significance of abuse;" and "[w]hat, if any, risk there is to the public health." Included within these factors are three other factors on which the statute places a special emphasis; "actual abuse, diversion from legitimate channels, and clandestine importation, manufacture, or distribution." The Attorney General also must publish 30-day notice of the proposed scheduling in the Federal Register, transmit notice to the Secretary of HHS, and "take into consideration any comments submitted by the Secretary in response." In addition to satisfying the numerous requirements of § 201(h), the Attorney General must satisfy the requirements of § 202(b), 21 USC § 812(b). . . . Thus, apart from the "imminent hazard" determination required by § 201(h), the Attorney General if he wishes to add temporarily a drug to schedule I, must find that it "has a high potential for abuse," that it "has no currently accepted medical use in treatment in the United States," and that "[t]here is a lack of accepted safety for use of the drug . . . under medical supervision." § 202(b)(1), 21 U.S.C. § 812(b)(1).

It is clear that in §§ 201(h) and 202(b) Congress has placed multiple specific restrictions on the Attorney General's discretion to define criminal conduct. These restrictions satisfy the constitutional requirements of the nondelegation doctrine. Petitioners point to two other aspects of the temporary scheduling statute that allegedly render it unconstitutional. They argue first that it concentrates too much power in the Attorney General. Petitioners concede that Congress may legitimately authorize someone in the Executive Branch to schedule drugs temporarily, but argue that it must be someone other than the Attorney General because he wields the power to prosecute crimes. They insist that allowing the Attorney General both to schedule a particular drug and to prosecute those who manufacture that drug violates the principle of separation of powers. Petitioners do not object to the permanent scheduling statute, however because it gives "veto power" to the Secretary of HHS.

This argument has no basis in our separation-of-powers jurisprudence. The principle of separation of powers focuses on the distribution of power among the three coequal Branches, see *Mistretta,* supra, at 382, 102 L. Ed. 2d 714, 109 S. Ct .647; it does not speak to the manner in which authority is parceled out within a single Branch. The Constitution vests all executive power in the President, US Const, Art II, § 1, and it is the President to whom both the Secretary and the Attorney General report. Petitioners' argument that temporary scheduling authority should have been vested in one executive officer rather than another does not implicate separation-of-powers concerns; it merely challenges the wisdom of a legitimate policy judgment made by Congress.

Touby v. United States , 500 U.S. 160 (1991), U.S. Supreme Court.

The Court rejected the defendant's claim that Congress could not delegate this responsibility. The Court found that Congress provided specific standards exceeding the requirements of the intelligible principle test to guide the Attorney General when making scheduling decisions. Specifically, the Attorney General was restricted to acting when it was necessary to "avoid imminent hazard to the public safety." Further, Congress set the following standards, which must be met before the Attorney General may act: The drug must have a high potential for abuse, the drug must have no current accepted medical use, and there must be no accepted safe use under medical supervision.

The Court found that these directives not only satisfied the intelligible principle test, but surpassed it. Whether more than an intelligible principle is required in criminal cases remains to be seen; this question was left unanswered by the Court in *Touby*. In the 2001 Supreme Court case of *Whitman v. American Trucking Associations*, a congressional delegation of rulemaking authority to the EPA was upheld.

Whitman v. American Trucking Associations

531 U.S. 457 (2001)

These cases present the following questions: (1) Whether § 109 (b)(1) of the Clean Air Act (CAA) delegates legislative power to the Administrator of the Environmental Protection Agency (EPA). . . .

Section 109 (a) of the CAA, as added, 84 Stat. 1679, and amended, 42 U.S.C. § 7409 (a), requires the Administrator of the EPA to promulgate NAAQS for each air pollutant for which "air quality criteria" have been issued under § 108, 42 U.S.C. § 7408. Once a NAAQS [national ambient air quality standards] has been promulgated, the Administrator must review the standard (and the criteria on which it is based) "at five-year intervals" and make "such revisions . . . as may be appropriate." CAA § 109 (d)(1), 42 U.S.C. § 7409 (d)(1). These cases arose when, on July 18, 1997, the Administrator revised the NAAQS for particulate matter (PM) and ozone. . .

Section 109 (b)(1) of the CAA instructs the EPA to set "ambient air quality standards the attainment and maintenance of which in the judgment of the Administrator, based on [the] criteria [documents of § 108] and allowing an adequate margin of safety, are requisite to protect the public health." 42 U.S.C. § 7409 (b)(1). The Court of Appeals held that this section as interpreted by the Administrator did not provide an "intelligible principle" to guide the EPA's exercise of authority in setting NAAQS. "[The] EPA," it said, "lack[ed] any determinate criteria for drawing lines. It has failed to state intelligibly how much is too much." The court hence found that the EPA's interpretation (but not the statute itself) violated the nondelegation doctrine. We disagree.

In a delegation challenge, the constitutional question is whether the statute has delegated legislative power to the agency. Article I, § 1, of the Constitution vests "[a]11 legislative Powers herein granted . . . in a Congress of the United States." This text permits no delegation of those powers. . . .

We agree with the Solicitor General that the text of § 109 (b)(1) of the CAA at a minimum requires that "[f]or a discrete set of pollutants and based on published air quality criteria that reflect the latest scientific knowledge, [the] EPA must establish uniform national standards at a level that is requisite to protect public health from the adverse effects of the pollutant in the ambient air." Requisite, in turn, "mean[s] sufficient, but not more than necessary." These limits on the EPA's discretion are strikingly similar to the ones we approved in *Touby v. United States*, 500 U.S. 160 (1991), which permitted the Attorney General to designate a drug as a controlled substance for purposes of criminal drug enforcement if doing so was "'necessary to avoid an imminent hazard to the public safety.'" They also resemble the Occupational Safety and Health Act provision requiring the agency to "'set the standard which most adequately assures, to the extent feasible, on the basis of the best available evidence, that no employee will suffer any impairment of health'"—which the Court upheld in *Industrial Union Dept., AFL-CIO v. American Petroleum Institute*, 448 U.S. 607, 646 (1980), and which even then—*Justice Rehnquist*, who alone in that case thought the statute violated the nondelegation doctrine, would have upheld if, like the statute here, it did not permit economic costs to be considered. The scope of discretion § 109 (b)(1) allows is in fact well within the outer limits of our nondelegation precedents. In the history of the Court we have found the requisite "intelligible principle" lacking in only two statutes, one of which provided literally no guidance for the exercise of discretion, and the other of which conferred authority to regulate the entire economy on the basis of no more precise a standard than stimulating the economy by assuring "fair competition." See *Panama Refining Co. v. Ryan*, 293 U.S. 388 (1935); *A.L.A. Schechter Poultry Corp. v. United States*, 295 U.S. 495 (1935). We have, on the other hand, upheld the validity of § 11 (b)(2) of the public Utility Holding Company Act of 1935, 49 Stat. 821, which gave the Securities

(continued)

and Exchange Commission authority to modify the structure of holding company systems so as to ensure that they are not "unduly or unnecessarily complicate[d]" and do not "unfairly or inequitably distribute voting power among security holders." We have approved the wartime conferral of agency power to fix the prices of commodities at a level that " 'will be generally fair and equitable and will effectuate the [in some respects conflicting] purposes of th[e] Act.' " And we have found an "intelligible principle" in various statutes authorizing regulation in the "public interest." See, e.g., *National Broadcasting Co. v. United States*, 319 U.S. 190, 225–226 (1943) (FCC's power to regulate airwaves); *New York Central Securities Corp. v. United States*, 287 U.S. 12, 24–25 (1932) (ICC's power to approve railroad consolidations). In short, we have "almost never felt qualified to second-guess Congress regarding the permissible degree of policy judgment that can be left to those executing or applying the law."

It is true enough that the degree of agency discretion that is acceptable varies according to the scope of the power congressionally conferred. While Congress need not provide any direction to the EPA regarding the manner in which it is to define "country elevators," which are to be exempt from new-stationary-source regulations governing grain elevators, see § 7411 (i), it must provide substantial guidance on setting air standards that affect the entire national economy. But even in sweeping regulatory schemes we have never demanded, as the Court of Appeals did here, that statutes provide a "determinate criterion" for saying "how much [of the regulated harm] is too much." In *Touby*, for example, we did not require the statute to decree how "imminent" was too imminent, or how "necessary" was necessary enough, or even—most relevant here—how "hazardous" was too hazardous. Similarly, the statute at issue in *Lichter* authorized agencies to recoup "excess profits" paid under wartime government contracts, yet we did not insist that Congress specify how much profit was too much. It is, therefore, not conclusive for delegation purposes that, as respondents argue, ozone and particulate matter are "nonthreshold" pollutants that inflict a continuum of adverse health effects at any airborne concentration greater than zero, and hence require the EPA to make judgments of degree. "[A] certain degree of discretion, and thus of lawmaking, inheres in most executive or judicial action." Section 109 (b)(1) of the CAA, which to repeat we interpret as requiring the EPA to set air quality standards at the level that is "requisite"—that is, not lower or higher than is necessary—to protect the public health with an adequate margin of safety, fits comfortably within the scope of discretion permitted by our precedent.

We, therefore, reverse the judgment of the Court of Appeals. . . .

https://bulk.resource.org/courts.gov/c/US/531/531.US.457.99-1257.html.

As these cases illustrate, the courts have limited Congress's authority to give away its own authority. On the other side, Congress is also prohibited from taking judicial and executive authority. *Bowsher v. Synar*[13] is an example of such congressional overreaching. *Bowsher* involved a challenge to a statute, commonly known as the "Gramm-Rudman Act," that gave the comptroller general of the United States certain responsibilities concerning implementation of the budget. The Supreme Court concluded that the duties were executive in nature. However, the Comptroller General is the head of a legislative agency, the Government Accountability Office (GAO, formerly the General Accounting Office) and as such Congress possessed oversight, including removal, of the Comptroller. This arrangement led the Court to conclude that Congress was inappropriately attempting to control an executive officer, in violation of the separation-of-powers doctrine.

It appears that the delegation doctrine has limited applicability in those zones of authority shared by the president and Congress, most notably, foreign affairs and war. For example, a group of military personnel, family members of military personnel, and members of Congress challenged President George W. Bush's decision to wage war on Iraq in *Doe v. Bush*.[14] The plaintiffs in this case alleged that the authority to declare war belonged exclusively to Congress and that its resolution authorizing the president to make war with Iraq amounted to an unconstitutional delegation. The First Circuit Court of Appeals rejected this position, finding that the warmaking power was vested in both the president and Congress and, furthermore, that the nondelegation doctrine has less applicability in matters of foreign affairs than it does in domestic affairs.

Even though the Supreme Court has been liberal in permitting delegations of legislative authority, the nondelegation doctrine is not entirely ineffective in limiting congressional delegations. Congress is aware of the restriction and, presumably, it limits the amount of lawmaking power it transfers to agencies as a result. In addition, lower courts enforce the doctrine. The Eighth Circuit Court of Appeals used the doctrine to strike down a federal statute in the 1995 case of *South Dakota v. Department of Interior*. The Supreme Court later reversed this case, but on different grounds.[15]

5.4 DELEGATING JUDICIAL AUTHORITY

Article III of the Constitution provides that the judicial power shall be "vested in one Supreme Court and in such inferior courts as the Congress may from time to time ordain and establish." All federal judges who are appointed under Article III have lifetime tenure of office and come to office through presidential nomination and Senate approval. The language of Article III does not indicate that posts for "non–Article III" judges, who do not enjoy a lifetime appointment or do not come to office through the presidential/Senate appointment process, may be created. Regardless, Congress has delegated judicial powers to non–Article III government officials since the first days of the Constitution.

As early as 1792, the Supreme Court decided that federal judges could not be assigned tasks that would be reviewed by nonjudicial officials.[16] In 1932, the Court issued a landmark decision concerning delegations of quasi-judicial authority to non–Article III officials, in *Crowell v. Benson*.[17] Congress had delegated the authority to hear worker's compensation claims under the Longshoremen's and Harbor Workers Compensation Act to an administrative agency. This case involved a claim by an employee against his employer, Benson, for workers' compensation. The agency found in the employee's favor and Benson appealed. Crowell was the agency official who issued the decision.

The Court held that there is a distinction between "public rights" and "private rights." Public rights commonly involve a suit between the government and a citizen, often a corporation, concerning the enforcement of regulations by the government. Private rights are those between individuals. As a general rule, the Court held that Congress may delegate the adjudication of public rights to non–Article III tribunals though the adjudication of private rights was to occur in Article III courts. The Court further found that the dispute over workers' compensation involved a private right. With these holdings, it could reasonably be expected that the Court would invalidate the delegation to the agency—but it did not. Instead, the Court pointed out that the agency was acting like a master, an official commonly used in federal courts to hear and decide facts. So long as the authority to review the legal decisions of the master, and by analogy the agency, was held by an Article III court, the process did not violate the separation of powers. The Court assumed that Article III courts did have the authority to review the agency's decisions, so the delegation was upheld. *Crowell* is important to the jurisprudence in this area because the Court announced the distinction between private and public rights, a line that continues to be drawn.

South Dakota v. Department of Interior

69 F. 3d 878 (8th Cir. 1995)

LOKEN, Circuit Judge

The State of South Dakota and the City of Oacoma, South Dakota, appeal the district court's dismissal of their challenge to the Secretary of the Interior's acquisition of commercial land in trust for the Lower Brule Tribe of Sioux Indians. Concluding that 25 U.S.C. § 465, the statute authorizing acquisition of the land, is an unconstitutional delegation of legislative power, we reverse.

In March 1990, the Tribe submitted an application under 25 U.S.C. § 465, asking the Secretary to acquire ninety-one acres of land in trust for use by the Tribe. The land is located seven miles from the Tribe's reservation and is partially within the City of Oacoma. The Tribe stated that the land would be used to create an industrial park adjacent to an interstate highway, explaining that "[t]his site, Trust status for the land, and tax advantages are critically necessary for the development to occur."

The State of South Dakota and the City of Oacoma protested in writing to the Secretary's Bureau of Indian Affairs ("BIA"). When BIA's Area Director notified the State and the City in March 1991 that the Tribe's application would be approved, they appealed to the Interior Board of Indian Affairs. BIA then disclosed that the Assistant Secretary for Indian Affairs had approved the application in December 1990, without notifying the protestants. The Board dismissed the appeal because it has no jurisdiction to review decisions by the Assistant Secretary.

In July 1992, the State and the City filed this action against the Department of the Interior and certain of its officials seeking judicial review under the Administrative Procedure Act, 5 U.S.C. §§ 701–706. For convenience, we will refer to the defendants collectively as "the Secretary," because he is the Executive Branch official authorized to act under § 465. We will refer to the State and the City collectively as "plaintiffs." Plaintiffs allege that they are aggrieved by the Secretary's acquisition because it deprives them of tax revenues and may place the land beyond their regulatory powers. They contend that the acquisition is invalid because § 465 is an unconstitutional delegation of legislative power. . . .

On appeal, plaintiffs argue that § 465 provides no legislative standards or boundaries governing the Secretary's acquisitions. The Secretary responds that the statutory purpose of "providing land for Indians" sufficiently defines the general policy and boundaries of the delegated power. The Secretary notes that the Supreme Court has not invalidated a federal statute on delegation grounds since *A.L.A. Schechter Poultry Corp. v. United States*, 295 U.S. 495, 542, 55 S. Ct. 837, 848, 79 L. Ed. 1570 (1935), and *Panama Refining Co. v. Ryan*, 293 U.S. 388, 55 S. Ct. 241, 79 L. Ed. 446 (1935). . . . It is appropriate to consider whether § 465 satisfies the nondelegation doctrine as it has evolved since 1935, particularly because no other appellate court has done so.

The nondelegation doctrine is easy to state: "Congress may not constitutionally delegate its legislative power to another branch of Government." . . . It is difficult to apply. A court must inquire whether Congress "has itself established the standards of legal obligation, thus performing its essential legislative function." *Schechter Poultry.* . . . But the court must be mindful that the doctrine does not prevent Congress from obtaining the assistance of its coordinate Branches. Therefore, so long as Congress "lay[s] down by legislative act an intelligible principle" governing the exercise of delegated power, it has not unlawfully delegated its legislative power. . . . A delegation is overbroad "[o]nly if we could say that there is an absence of standards for the guidance of the Administrator's action, so that it would be impossible in a proper proceeding to ascertain whether the will of Congress has been obeyed."

The Supreme Court has recognized that judicial review is a relevant safeguard in considering delegation issues:

> It is "constitutionally sufficient if Congress clearly delineates the general policy, the public agency which is to apply it, and the boundaries of this delegated authority. . . ."

We begin by examining the very broad language of § 465:

> The Secretary of the Interior is hereby authorized, in his discretion, to acquire . . . any interest in lands . . . within or without existing reservations . . . for the purpose of providing land for Indians.
>
> * * *
>
> Title to any lands or rights acquired . . . shall be taken in the name of the United States in trust for the Indian tribe or individual Indian for which the land is acquired, and such lands or rights shall be exempt from State and local taxation.

By its literal terms, the statute permits the Secretary to purchase a factory, an office building, a residential subdivision, or a golf course in trust for an Indian tribe, thereby removing these properties from state and local tax rolls. Indeed, it would permit the Secretary to purchase the Empire State Building in trust for a tribal chieftain as a wedding present. There are no perceptible "boundaries," no "intelligible principles," within the four corners of the statutory language that constrain this delegated authority—except that the acquisition must be "for Indians." It delegates unrestricted power to acquire land from private citizens for the private use and benefit of Indian tribes or individual Indians. . . .

By defining no boundaries to the exercise of this power, the statute leaves the Secretary free to acquire for a multitude of purposes, for example, to expand a reservation, to provide farm land for rural Indians, to provide a factory for unemployed urban Indians, to provide a golf course for tribal recreation, or to provide a lake home for a politically faithful tribal officer. . . .

Despite the government's broad, inherent power to acquire land for public use, the nondelegation doctrine surely requires at a minimum that Congress, not the Executive, articulate and configure the underlying public use that justifies an acquisition. In some cases, the public use underlying each acquisition is obvious, as when Congress authorizes an agency to acquire lands and buildings to house the agency's operations. But when Congress authorizes the Secretary to acquire land in trust "for Indians," it has given the agency no "intelligible principle," no "boundaries" by which the public use underlying a particular acquisition may be defined and judicially reviewed. This legislative vacuum in turn greatly expands the extent of the standardless delegation.

Those who drafted § 465 failed to incorporate the limited purpose reflected in the legislative history. Presumably, they either drafted poorly or ignored the delegation issue. The agency that received this inartful delegation then used the absence of statutory controls to claim unrestricted, unreviewable power. The result is an agency fiefdom whose boundaries were never established by Congress, and whose exercise of unrestrained power is free of judicial review. It is hard to imagine a program more at odds with separation of powers principles.

In his concurring opinion in *Industrial Union Dept., AFL–CIO v. American Petroleum Inst.* . . . Justice (now Chief Justice) Rehnquist summarized the functions of the nondelegation doctrine as articulated in prior Supreme Court cases:

> First, and most abstractly, it ensures to the extent consistent with orderly governmental administration that important choices of social policy are made by

(continued)

Congress, the branch of our Government most responsive to the popular will. Second, the doctrine guarantees that, to the extent Congress finds it necessary to delegate authority, it provides the recipient of that authority with an "intelligible principle" to guide the exercise of the delegated discretion. Third, and derivative of the second, the doctrine ensures that courts charged with reviewing the exercise of delegated discretion will be able to test that exercise against ascertainable standards.

We conclude that § 465 fails all three of these nondelegation criteria and is invalid. Accordingly, the Secretary had no authority to acquire the lands in question in trust for the Tribe. The judgment of the district court is reversed and the case is remanded for further proceedings consistent with this opinion.

South Dakota v. Department of Interior, 69 F. 3d 878 (8th Cir. 1995), U.S. Supreme Court.

SIDEBAR   *Articles I and II Courts*

Article III of the U.S. Constitution establishes the Supreme Court and such lower courts as Congress decides to establish. Supreme Court justices, judges of district courts, and judges of the federal courts of appeals (circuit courts) are all "Article III" judges. They come to office through nomination by the president and confirmation by the Senate. To keep them independent of politics and the will of the political branches, they enjoy lifetime tenure and a guarantee of no reduction in salary. In addition to Article III judges, Congress has created many non–Article III tribunals and officers. This includes U.S. magistrate-judges, U.S. bankruptcy judges, and military judges. Because these positions are creations of Congress, the officials are generally known as *Article I judges*. Although rare, the president occasionally establishes a court. These judges are Article II judges. For an example of when a president has convened an Article II court, *see United States v. Tiede*, 86 F.R.D. 227 (Berlin Ct. 1979).

Today, however, the definition of a private right is one that existed at the common law at the time the Seventh Amendment was adopted. The Seventh Amendment provides: "In Suits at common law, where the value in controversy shall exceed twenty dollars, the right to trial by jury shall be preserved, and no fact tried by a jury, shall be otherwise reexamined in any Court of the United States, than according to the rules of the common law." If a right did not exist at the common law, then Congress may delegate the adjudication of that right to a non–Article III agency.

Interesting delegation issues have also arisen in the context of the use of U.S. magistrates to relieve some of the burden of U.S. district judges. District judges are empowered under Article III of the Constitution of the United States. Article III judges undergo presidential nomination and congressional confirmation; magistrates do not. Article III judges are insulated from political concerns by life tenure; magistrates are not. Article III judges may be removed only by Congress through impeachment; magistrates may be removed by Article III judges.

Magistrate positions came into being through the Federal Magistrates Act and are, therefore, creations not of the Constitution but of Congress. The Federal Magistrates Act delegates certain responsibilities to magistrates and allows Article III judges to delegate additional duties so long as the delegations are consistent with the Constitution and other laws of the United States.

Because magistrates are not Article III judges, only certain responsibilities may be delegated to magistrates. For example, in *Gomez v. United States*,[18] it was determined that without the parties' consent, a magistrate may not be delegated the responsibility of conducting the voir dire (jury selection) in a felony criminal case. The Court held that voir dire is a critical stage in the proceeding, which must be supervised by a constitutionally empowered judge.

However, because the Federal Magistrates Act was drafted to keep magistrates accountable to Article III judges, rather than to Congress or the executive, most delegations to magistrates have been upheld. Under the act, all decisions made by magistrates may be reviewed *de novo* by district judges, the magistrates may be removed by Article III judges, and magistrates may not receive a reduction in pay during their appointment. For these reasons, the Court has upheld most delegations to magistrates.

In a case similar to *Gomez, Peretz v. United States*,[19] the parties to a criminal case consented to having a magistrate conduct the voir dire. On appeal, the defendant objected, claiming that this was an inherently judicial function that must be presided over by an Article III judge (citing *Gomez*). The Supreme Court rejected the argument. The Court stated that the ultimate decision whether to invoke the magistrate's assistance is made by the district court, subject to veto by the parties. The decision whether to empanel the jury, the selection of which a magistrate has supervised, also remains entirely with the district court. Because the entire process takes place under the district court's total control and jurisdiction, there is no danger that use of the magistrate will affect a congressional transfer of jurisdiction to non–Article III tribunals for the purpose of emasculating constitutional courts.

Because there was no separation-of-powers violation, the issue was whether a party could waive the right to have an Article III judge preside. The Court answered this affirmatively.

The Court reaffirmed *Gomez* in *Peretz*; that is, a defendant in a criminal case can demand that an Article III judge preside over the critical stages of the proceedings. The cases in this area teach that magistrates may not conduct trials in civil or criminal cases over the objections of a party. Magistrates may not be delegated the authority to make final determinations in pretrial matters without the consent of the parties. Also, as *Gomez* illustrates, magistrates may not preside over critical stages of a felony criminal proceeding without the consent of the parties.

As with U.S. magistrates, the authority of U.S. bankruptcy judges to hear private claims has been questioned. Bankruptcy judges are not Article III judges because they do not enjoy lifetime tenure and are not appointed by the president with the advice and consent of the Senate. Although bankruptcy involves a public right created by Congress, it is common for questions concerning private rights (e.g., a dispute concerning whether a debt exists or the amount of a debt) to arise in bankruptcy proceedings. Historically, bankruptcy judges heard these claims. This practice was challenged in *Northern Pipeline Construction Co. v. Marathon Pipe Line Co.*[20] Justice Rehnquist, writing for the Court, found the adjudication of private rights by bankruptcy judges—against the objections of one of the parties—unconstitutional. Congress amended the bankruptcy laws following this decision. Pursuant to those amendments, consent of the parties to have the bankruptcy judge hear private claims is required, all private-rights decisions of bankruptcy judges are reviewable by Article III district judges, and the appointment of bankruptcy judges was transferred from the president to Article III judges.

Although the Court seemed protective of Article III authority in *Northern Pipeline*, it was less so in its 1986 decision in *Commodity Futures Trading Commission v. Schor*.[21] By statute, Congress delegated to the Commodity Futures Trading Commission the authority to hear a specific class of public-rights claims. By rule, the agency increased its adjudicatory authority to hear counterclaims, including private-rights claims, arising out of the same facts that are the basis of the original

LEGAL TERM

de novo

Anew; to reconsider. A standard of review that does not require deference to an agency's decision.

complaint. The counterclaimant had the option of filing the claim in federal court or with the agency. The Court listed all the following factors as supporting its decision to uphold the delegation:

1. Congress had created a legitimate, comprehensive scheme to deal with a broad policy area, and the delegation of judicial authority was only a small part of that scheme. If the sole purpose of a delegation is to transfer the authority to hear a common law claim to a non–Article III tribunal, the delegation is unconstitutional.
2. The agency had the authority to hear only a small class of claims. The Court noted that this situation was different from the one in *Northern Pipeline* because that case involved bankruptcy Courts which had very broad jurisdiction over common law claims.
3. The counterclaimant had the right to file in federal court.
4. The agency had to turn to an Article III judge to enforce its orders, and its orders were reviewable by Article III judges under a *de novo* standard.
5. The scheme did not threaten the independence of the judiciary.

Schor has been criticized by both judges and scholars as retreating from the public-rights doctrine by permitting a private right to be heard by a non–Article III judge. Justice Scalia, for example, believes that the definition of public rights should be limited to claims involving the government. All others, Scalia asserts, are private rights and, accordingly, must be adjudicated by Article III judges.

5.5 DELEGATING TO PRIVATE AGENCIES

Increasingly, both federal and state governments are delegating judicial and law-making authority to private organizations, transforming these organizations into quasi-governmental bodies. The Supreme Court has been suspicious of delegating governmental authority to private parties for a long time. Although its decision in *Schechter Poultry*, which you learned about earlier, focused on the delegation of rulemaking power to the President, the Court was concerned about the role trade associations and merchants played in creating the rule President Roosevelt promulgated. The Court penned:

> But would it be seriously contended that Congress could delegate its legislative authority to trade or industrial associations or groups so as to empower them to enact the laws they deem to be wise and beneficent for the rehabilitation and expansion of their trade or industries? Could trade or industrial associations or groups be constituted legislative bodies for that purpose because such associations or groups are familiar with the problems of their enterprises? And, could an effort of that sort be made valid by such a preface of generalities as to permissible aims as we find in section 1 of title I? The answer is obvious. Such a delegation of legislative power is unknown to our law, and is utterly consistent with the constitutional prerogatives and duties of Congress.[22]

In the states, delegations to private parties are becoming increasingly common. Delegations to insurance companies to regulate worker's compensation and licensing programs are examples. *Foley v. Osborne Court Condominium* is a state court decision dealing with the thorny issue of control of condominium owners by a condominium association. In addition to the issue of delegation of essential judicial functions, *Foley* questions whether governmental authority can be delegated to a private agency. It is becoming increasingly common for governments to contract with private agencies to provide government services. Local governments, states, and the federal government have outsourced school administration, toll roads, social services programs, the collection of child support, and corrections, to name only a few. During the 1990s, Indianapolis, Indiana, privatized more than 70 municipal functions, including water treatment, its airport, and information technology. In 1999, San Diego, California, privatized all of its information technology to a contractor for seven years, at a contract cost of $644 million.[23]

The reasons to privatize are many. Governments often privatize because they lack the expertise to perform the necessary function. Motivated by profit, private companies have proven in many instances to be more productive, resulting in lower costs. Some advocate privatization because it reduces the size of government. Finally, privatization makes sense when a transient or emergent need presents itself and a government lacks the resources to respond adequately.

Some commentators have challenged the notion that privatization is more efficient. Others contend that the privatization of public functions threatens the public good. They point out that efficiency was not foremost on the minds of the framers of our nation when they designed our governmental architecture. On the contrary, they were aware that the system they created was inefficient. They were willing to trade inefficiency for liberty.

However, the framers did not foresee the myriad services that governments would provide. To the framers, governmental functions were policing, corrections, roads, armed services, foreign affairs, and, to a limited extent, education. Today, largely as a result of the expansion of government that occurred in the 1930s, federal and local governments directly provide for citizens' health care, Social Security and pensions, disability, and recreation needs. Governments regulate an even broader range of services.

Can a government delegate its authorities or functions to a private agency? Privatization gives rise to many legal issues. Compliance with civil service, regulatory, environmental, and constitutional laws, for example, must be considered. Even though the Supreme Court of the United States faced this question as early as 1936,[24] the jurisprudence in this area is not well developed. The privatization of public functions is popular today, and, accordingly, this issue will likely be the subject of much litigation in the first decades of the 2000s. Although the existing law is sparse, a few principles can be deduced.

First, there are core governmental functions that cannot be delegated to private parties. Trying criminal cases is an example, as is using contempt power, as seen in *Foley*. There is a debate over whether corrections is a core function because an increasing number of states are contracting with private companies to provide jail and prison services.[25] The importance of the issue is evinced by the numbers. By 2001, 12 percent of federal prisoners and nearly 6 percent of state prisoners (a total of approximately 92,000 prisoners) were housed in private prisons. In addition, many local halfway houses and treatment facilities for offenders are privately operated.[26]

Foley v. Osborne Court Condominium

1999 R. I. Super. Lexis 50 (1999)

This matter is before the Superior Court on remand from the Rhode Island Supreme Court. The case originated in the Superior Court when plaintiff, James Foley, owner of two units in the Osborne Court Condominium, sought injunctive relief against the condominium association. Foley sought to enjoin foreclosure and auction of his condominium units....

(continued)

At all times material hereto, plaintiff was the owner of two units of the Osborne Court Condominium. The declaration to create the condominium and the site plan were recorded in 1981 although the subject units were not constructed until 1985. The Osborne Court Condominium Association is comprised of all owners of units in the condominium. In spring 1995, the Management Committee adopted rules and regulations in response to noise, parking, and other problems, which had occurred during the previous summer.

At various times, the plaintiff was cited for violating these rules and regulations. After affording him notice and an opportunity to be heard, plaintiff was fined for these violations. The fines were unpaid, and in September and October 1995, liens were placed on plaintiff's units. In March 1996, while the association was offering to sell the units at public auction, the parties entered into a consent agreement. The plaintiff paid approximately ten thousand dollars ($10,000) to settle the fines assessed against him.

During the spring and summer of 1996, plaintiff was again cited for violating the rules and regulations, and was again fined for the violations, and liens were recorded on his property. The association threatened foreclosure on his units to enforce the liens. The foreclosure was averted by the filing of the within action for injunctive relief. . . .

On February 11, 1999, the Supreme Court ruled that although other constitutional claims had been waived, the plaintiff had adequately briefed and argued his claim of an unconstitutional delegation of power to a private entity in violation of Article 10 of the Rhode Island Constitution (hereinafter Article 10). The Supreme Court remanded the case to the Superior Court with directions to determine whether Title 34, Chapter 36.1 of the Rhode Island General Laws, entitled "Condominium Law" (hereinafter the 1982 Act), represents an unconstitutional delegation of judicial or police power to the condominium association, a private entity. . . .

Article 10, Constitution of Rhode Island provides:

> Section 1. Power vested in court. The judicial power of this state shall be vested in one supreme court, and in such inferior courts as the general assembly may, from time to time, ordain and establish.

The pertinent provisions of the 1982 Act that allegedly violate Article 10 are those, which empower condominium associations with the right to assess fines and use foreclosure proceedings to collect those fines. The Old Act authorizes an association to charge fees for common expenses and provides that unpaid fees become liens on an owner's interest in the unit. The 1982 Act further authorizes an association to impose charges for late payment of assessments and to assess fines for violating the declaration, bylaws, and rules and regulations of the association. The pertinent provisions of the 1982 Act are set forth below. The Section entitled "Powers of unit owners' association," provides that the Condominium Association has the power to:

> (I) Adopt and amend bylaws and rules and regulations; . . .
> (II) Impose charges for late payment of assessments and, after notice and an opportunity to be heard, levy reasonable fines for violations of the declaration, bylaws, and rules and regulations of the association as provided in R.I.G.L.
> Section 34-36.-3.1.16, entitled "Lien for Assessments" provides:

> The association has a lien on a unit for any assessment levied against that unit or fines imposed against its unit owner from the time the assessment or fine becomes due. The association's lien may be foreclosed in accordance with and subject to the provisions of R.I.G.L.

Section 34-36.1-3.20, entitled "Enforcement of Declaration, By-Laws" provides:

(a) An executive board may impose and assess fines against a unit owner as a method of enforcing the association's declaration, bylaws, and rules and regulations. Such fines may include, but are not limited to, daily fines for continued violative conduct in the future. Notice and the opportunity for a hearing must be provided to an alleged violator before a fine is imposed and assessed. All fines shall be a lien on the unit charged.

(b) Daily fines imposed and assessed pursuant to this section shall be no more than one hundred dollars ($100) per day for residential condominiums nor more than five hundred dollars ($500) per day for commercial condominiums.

(c) Fines other than daily fines imposed and assessed pursuant to this section shall be no more than five hundred dollars ($500) for residential condominiums and no more than one thousand dollars ($1000) for commercial condominiums. . . . [The statute continues by granting the power to forfeit and sell the condominiums of owners in default.]

The association is permitted to assess fines for prior violations of the declaration, bylaws, and rules and regulations, not to exceed five hundred dollars for residential and one thousand dollars. . . . for commercial condominiums. The association may assess daily fines for continuing violations, not to exceed one hundred dollars. . . . for residential and five hundred dollars for commercial condominiums. Unpaid fines are liens on the unit, which may be foreclosed upon by the association.

Although other statutes permit debt collection without court intervention, none authorizes private entities to impose fines. . . .

It is the authority to impose fines and to enforce them that distinguishes the 1982 Act from other legislation. The power to impose daily fines further distinguishes the 1982 Act from other statutes. Although the unit owner is afforded an initial hearing before the fine is imposed, the daily fine continues to accrue without requiring that the owner be given additional opportunities to be heard. It is arguable that the association can permit the daily fines to accrue until they reach the amount of the owner's equity in the unit, and then, the association can choose to foreclose on the lien and deprive the owner of his or her interest in the condominium or the proceeds of its sale.

The power to impose daily fines, which continue to accrue until a violation is corrected can be compared to the inherent power of the Court to punish for civil contempt. The Court possesses the power to impose sanctions to induce the contemnor to purge himself of contemptuous conduct. . . .

> The association is authorized to hear disputes concerning allegations that unit owners have violated the declaration, bylaws, or rules and regulations of the condominium. The 1982 Act permits the association to determine those controversies and to issue orders directing violators to pay fines. Finally, the act empowers the association with the ability to enforce its orders by depriving a violator of his property by foreclosure. In this capacity, the association acts as a tribunal exercising judicial power.

* * *

For the foregoing reasons, the Court finds that the 1982 Act represents an unconstitutional delegation of judicial or police power to the condominium association, a private entity.

Foley v. Osborne Court Condominium, 1999 R. I. Super. Lexis 50 (1999), Rhode Island Judiciary.

Second, courts are more protective of their own authority than they are of legislative authority. That is, a delegation of quasi-legislative authority to a private agency is more likely to be permitted than a delegation of quasi-judicial authority.

Third, private agencies that perform governmental functions may be treated as government agencies by the courts. For example, several courts have held that private state athletic organizations are state actors when public schools universally recognize the authority of the organization to govern high school athletics. [27] In another example, a group of private health care centers was considered a state actor because the centers had an exclusive contract to give government-provided medical care.[28]

Fourth, the private agency receiving the delegation must be in a position to serve the public interest. Delegations to parties that have only a financial interest are suspect. After all, one objective of government is to have a public body that is concerned with the public good, regardless of profit. This issue is being debated in the context of privatizing prisons.[29] Legislatures must also be careful not to give a private agency a market advantage over its competitors. To do so may violate due process. This was the case in *Carter v. Carter Coal Co.*, a 1936 Supreme Court case.[30] At issue in *Carter* was the Bituminous Coal Conservation Act. Through this statute, Congress delegated the authority to regulate some aspects of the coal industry to the largest coal-producing companies in the United States. The Court said of this delegation:

> The power conferred upon the majority is, in effect, the power to regulate the affairs of an unwilling minority. This is legislative delegation in its most obnoxious form; for it is not even delegation to an official or an official body, presumptively disinterested, but to private persons whose interests may be and often are adverse to the interests of others in the same business. . . . The difference between producing coal and regulating its production is, of course, fundamental. The former is a private activity; the latter is necessarily a governmental function, since, in the very nature of things, one person may not be entrusted with the power to regulate the business of another, and especially of a competitor. And a statute, which attempts to confer such power undertakes an intolerable and unconstitutional interference with personal liberty and private property. The delegation is so clearly arbitrary, and so clearly a denial of rights safeguarded by the due process clause of the Fifth Amendment, that it is unnecessary to do more than refer to decisions of this court, which foreclose the question.[31]

Finally, all the limitations on delegations to government agencies that you learned earlier in this chapter, such as the nondelegation doctrine, also apply to delegations to private parties. This discussion was concerned exclusively with the delegation of governmental authority to private parties. For a brief discussion of the potential liabilities for private parties that exercise governmental authority, see Chapter 11.

5.6 DELEGATION AND CRIMINAL LAW

Because violations of criminal law can result in serious limitations of liberty (e.g., imprisonment or death), delegations of criminal law authority are subject to special rules. Separation-of-powers problems are not created when Congress delegates the authority to ferret out and prosecute criminal conduct to executive agencies because these responsibilities are inherently executive. Delegations of penal rulemaking authority and penal adjudicatory authority, however, raise constitutional questions. We begin with penal rulemaking authority.

First, delegations of criminal rulemaking and judicial authority to private actors are very likely unconstitutional. Public agencies, in contrast, may be delegated limited penal rulemaking responsibilities. You have already seen a case in which such a delegation was upheld: the *Grimaud* case. In *Grimaud*, Congress delegated the authority to promulgate penal regulations to an agency. The Supreme Court decided that the delegation was valid. Central to the Court's finding was the fact that the agency was not delegated the authority to establish the penalties for violations of the rule. While delegations of the authority to declare acts criminal, within the limitations of an enabling statute, it has drawn the line at deciding what punishments should be imposed for violating criminal law. Congress may not delegate to an agency the authority to set penalties for penal violations, with the possible exception of small fines.

Because the penalties for violating criminal laws include imprisonment and other punishments, some jurists contend that agency authority must be more limited than in administrative cases where less serious punishments are imposed for violations. For example, the question of whether Congress must be more specific, or delegate less discretion, when delegating the authority to create penal rules to an agency, as opposed to nonpenal rules, was addressed by the Supreme Court in *Touby*. The defendant in that case argued that because of the risk to individual liberty created by criminal prohibitions, Congress should provide agencies with more than an intelligible principle when delegating penal rulemaking authority. The Court did not answer this question because it found that the delegation in this specific case greatly exceeded the intelligible principle test in specificity and, therefore, would satisfy a higher standard, if required. The issue was left to a future case for resolution.

Agencies may also act in a quasi-adjudicative role in penal cases although this authority is extremely limited. In some circumstances, certain misdemeanors or infractions have been recharacterized as civil wrongs, and agencies have been given the authority to adjudicate them. Parking and traffic violations are examples. In such cases, the agency's authority must be limited to levying fines. Constitutional rights, privileges, and protections afforded to criminal defendants cannot be circumvented by calling a crime a civil wrong.

With sufficient guidance from Congress, an agency may establish a rule declaring an act criminal, but it may not determine what punishment should be imposed for violation of the rule. In addition, delegations of judicial authority are limited to hearing infractions or similar wrongs and to assessing monetary fines. Any crime that is more serious, or involves a more severe punishment, must be heard by a competent court of law. Although monetary penalties may be imposed by an agency, imprisonment may not. The authority to impose incarceration or other serious penalties is reserved exclusively to the judiciary.

5.7 ARREST AND DETENTION

Although agencies may not order the imprisonment of individuals as punishment, they may arrest and detain persons if that action is justified by extreme circumstances. Generally, public health officials may be given the authority to arrest and detain (*quarantine*) persons who pose a threat to the community. Similarly, persons who pose a threat to themselves or others may be detained for psychiatric evaluation and treatment.

U. S. immigration officers have been delegated the authority to detain illegal aliens under warrants issued not by a court but by the Attorney General. This delegation was upheld despite the fact that a neutral magistrate is not interposed between the government and the alien. The Supreme Court stressed that there was a long-standing history of alien detention without judicial approval and that this tradition justified continuing the practice.[32] Hence, an alien may not be imprisoned by an agency for being present in the United States illegally, but may be arrested and detained pending deportation. The latter is not viewed as punishment; rather, it is a method of enforcing the Immigration and Naturalization Service's mandate to exclude illegal aliens.

5.8 CONCLUSION

Congress is afforded wide latitude in delegating its authority, as long as it provides sufficient standards or establishes an intelligible principle to guide the delegatee in its exercise of authority. Bear in mind that when individual liberties are involved, as opposed to property interests, a delegation must be more precise. Also, the more technical the area to be regulated, the broader the delegation may be, at least concerning delegations of rulemaking powers.

Courts more closely scrutinize delegations of their authority to agencies than they do Congress's delegations of its own powers. Article III, which establishes the federal judiciary, serves to protect the role of an independent judiciary. It also protects the rights of citizens to have their claims heard by judges independent of politics and of the political branches of government. Reaching an understanding of the jurisprudence of delegations of quasi-judicial authority is not easy. Justice O'Connor commented that the Supreme Court's "precedents in this area do not admit of easy synthesis."[33]

Although not absolute since *Schor*, the public-rights doctrine remains viable. If a right did not exist under the common law, as is true of many statutorily created rights, Congress may delegate the adjudication of that right to an administrative agency. Generally, claims involving personal rights must be heard by Article III judges. However, in some circumstances personal rights may be heard by non–Article III officers. Whether the delegation to hear such claims to an agency is constitutional depends on several factors. The degree to which the decisions of such officers are reviewed by Article III judges is important, as is the standard of review. The less deference the reviewing court must give the agency, the more likely it is that the delegation is lawful. The scope of the agency's authority is important. The Supreme Court characterized the personal right in *Schor* as narrow and particular. It distinguished this from bankruptcy jurisdiction, which it found to be too broad. It also appears that if hearing the private-right claim is only part of a legitimate, comprehensive legislative scheme, the Court will tend to find the delegation lawful. In the end, the Court is concerned with whether the independence and integrity of the judiciary are threatened. Finally, although delegations of legislative and judicial authority to private parties are permitted, such delegations are subject to greater limitations than are delegations to government agencies.

Lawlinks

Both the U.S. House of Representatives and the U.S. Senate have Web sites that contain historical information, law, current events, and other information. Go to www.house.gov/ and www.senate.gov/ to visit these sites.

REVIEW **QUESTIONS**

1. What is delegation?
2. Why is the concept of separation of powers important to administrative law?
3. Why does Congress delegate authority?
4. Define the public-rights doctrine.
5. What was the "court-packing plan," and why is it significant to administrative law?

CRITICAL THINKING AND **APPLICATIONS PROBLEMS**

1. Congress enacts the "Interstate Shipment of Geckos Act." In that act, the president (or a designee) is given authority to: establish rules governing the interstate shipment of geckos; establish penalties for violations of the act and rules promulgated by the president; and appoint gecko magistrates who will hear all cases that arise under the act. The magistrates are answerable to the president and no other judicial review is available. When promulgating rules, the president shall take into account the behavior and needs of geckos, all health considerations, and the effect that geckos will have on indigenous flora and fauna. The goal of the act is to prevent the spread of disease and to protect indigenous animals and plants.

   a. Is the delegation of quasi-legislative authority constitutional? Explain your answer.

   b. Is the delegation of quasi-judicial authority constitutional? Explain your answer.

   c. Do you believe that the law of delegation keeps agencies adequately in check? Explain your answer.

2. Tree Huggers, a nonprofit private organization, has existed in the United States for more than 100 years. The organization's mission has remained the same for its entire existence: "to protect and maintain the natural wonder of the state." Since its inception, Tree Huggers has enlisted volunteers to maintain hiking trails, improve roads that provide access to trails, and to act as "watchdogs" for violations in Big Tree Park. When Tree Huggers began its efforts, Big Tree was not a park. Ten years ago, the area was designated a state park. Recently, the state legislature enacted the following statute with the support of Tree Huggers:

Section 1: Park Maintenance and Rulemaking Authority

Tree Huggers, Inc., shall be responsible for the care and maintenance of Big Tree Park. Tree Huggers shall establish a Board of Commissioners to oversee its management of the park. The Board of Commissioners may make rules necessary to the effective enforcement of this provision. In its rule making, the Board shall preserve the natural state of the park to the greatest extent possible while taking into consideration the recreational and aesthetic desires of park users. The board shall not permit any commercial use of the park, specifically, but not limited to, mining and logging. The board may not establish penal rules.

Section 2: Violations of Park Rules: Hearings

Violations of state misdemeanor penal statutes that can be punished with no more than one year of imprisonment and/or a $10,000 fine, and that apply to park and wildlife areas, shall be heard by administrative law judges appointed by the president of Tree Huggers. Such hearings shall be conducted in accordance with state and federal constitutional and statutory laws. Felony violations shall continue to be heard by state trial judges.

Section 3: Appeals

Appeals of final decisions by the administrative law judges provided for in section 2 shall be to the Board of Commissioners established in section 1. The final orders of the Board of Commissioners are final and unreviewable.

4. Is section 1 constitutional? Explain your answer.

5. Is section 2 constitutional? Explain your answer.

6. Is section 3 constitutional? Explain your answer.

ENDNOTES

1. Virginia Constitutional Convention, 1829–1830, Debates 619.
2. *Wayman v. Southard*, 23 U.S. (Wheat) 1 (1825).
3. *Id.*
4. 293 U.S. 388 (1935).
5. 295 U.S. 495 (1934).
6. McNollgast, *The Political Origins of the Administrative Procedure Act*, 15 J.L. Econ. & Orgs. 180, 189 (1999).
7. 300 U.S. 379 (1937).
8. *Eastlake v. Forest City Enters.*, 426 U.S. 668, 675 (1976).
9. 373 U.S. 546 (1963).

10. 334 U.S. 546 (1948).

11. 488 U.S. 361 (1989).

12. 500 U.S. 160 (1991).

13. 478 U.S. 714 (1986).

14. 323 F. 3d 133 (1st Cir. 2003).

15. 519 U.S. 919 (1996).

16. Hayburn's Case, 2 U.S. 408 (1792).

17. 285 U.S. 22 (1932).

18. 490 U.S. 858 (1989).

19. 501 U.S. 923 (1991).

20. 458 U.S. 50 (1982).

21. 478 U.S. 833 (1986). See also *Granfinanciera, S.A. v. Nordberg*, 492 U.S. 33 (1989).

22. Schechter, infra, 538.

23. See Donald Featherstun, D. Whitney Thornton, II, & J. Gregory Correnti, *State and Local Privatization: An Evolving Process*, 30 Pub. Cont. L.J. 643 (2001).

24. *Carter v. Carter Coal Co.*, 298 U.S. 238 (1936).

25. See Laura Suzanne Farris, *Private Jails in Oklahoma: An Unconstitutional Delegation of Legislative Authority*, 33 Tulsa L.J. 959 (1998).

26. See Gillian Metzger, *Privatization as Delegation*, 103 Colum. L. Rev. 1367, 1393 (2003).

27. See *Crane v. Indiana High Sch. Athletic Ass'n*, 975 F. 2d 1315 (7th Cir. 1992) as an example.

28. *Catanzano v. Dowling*, 60 F. 3d 113 (2d Cir. 1995).

29. See Farris, *Private Jails in Oklahoma*, 33 Tulsa L.J. 959 (1998).

30. 298 U.S. 238 (1936).

31. *Id.* at 311.

32. *Abel v. United States*, 362 U.S. 217 (1960).

33. *Schor*, 478 U.S. at 847.

chapter **six**

AGENCY RULEMAKING

LEARNING OBJECTIVES

After completing this chapter, you should be able to

- Distinguish rulemaking from adjudication in fact scenarios.

- Identify the various forms of rulemaking, explain the circumstances in which each is used, and describe the process used to create each type of rule under the APA.

- Brief a judicial opinion with little outside assistance. You should be successful in identifying the relevant facts. You should also be successful in identifying the legal issue and analyzing the Court's rationale in at least 50 percent of your briefs.

It is not wisdom but authority that makes a law.

THOMAS HOBBES

OUTLINE

6.1 IN GENERAL

All agency actions can be classified as executive, quasi-judicial, or quasi-legislative. When an agency acts in its quasi-judicial capacity, its behavior is referred to as *adjudicatory*. When acting in its quasi-legislative capacity, its behavior is referred to as *rulemaking*. The distinction between adjudication and rulemaking is important because the APA imposes different responsibilities on agencies depending on which function is performed. The rules governing adjudications are discussed later.

Rulemaking is the process whereby agencies establish law to implement or perform a statutory duty. For example, in response to one of the recommendations of the 9/11 Commission, Congress enacted with presidential support the REAL ID Act. This legislation prohibits individuals from using state driver's licenses that do not meet minimum security standards as identification to enter federal facilities, board federally regulated aircraft, enter a nuclear facility, and for other uses designated by the Secretary of Homeland Security. The Act required the Department of Homeland Security to create the standards and to implement the Act's requirements, which became effective on May 11, 2008, with state requests for extension allowed.

In response, the Secretary issued the following rules, after a comment period where the Department received more than 21,000 comments to the proposed final rule.

6 CFR SECTION 37

REAL ID DRIVER'S LICENSES AND IDENTIFICATION CARDS

SUBPART A—GENERAL

Section

PART 37—REAL ID DRIVER'S LICENSES AND IDENTIFICATION CARDS

SUBPART A—GENERAL

Section 37.1 Applicability

(a) Subparts A through E of this part apply to States and U.S. territories that choose to issue driver's licenses and identification cards that can be accepted by Federal agencies for official purposes.

(b) Subpart F establishes certain standards for State-issued driver's licenses and identification cards issued by States that participate in REAL ID, but that are not intended to be accepted by federal agencies for official purpose under section 202(d)(11) of the REAL ID Act. . . .

Sec. 37.5 Validity periods and deadlines for REAL ID driver's licenses and identification cards

(a) Driver's licenses and identification cards issued under this part, that are not temporary or limited-term driver's licenses and identification cards, are valid for a period not to exceed eight years. A card may be valid for a shorter period based on other State or Federal requirements.

(b) On or after December 1, 2014, Federal agencies shall not accept a driver's license or identification card for official purposes from individuals born after December 1, 1964, unless such license or card is a REAL

ID-compliant driver's license or identification card issued by a State that has been determined by DHS to be in full compliance as defined under this subpart.

(c) On or after December 1, 2017, Federal agencies shall not accept a driver's license or identification card for official purposes from any individual unless such license or card is a REAL ID-compliant driver's license or identification card issued by a State that has been determined by DHS to be in full compliance as defined under this subpart.

(d) Federal agencies cannot accept for official purpose driver's licenses and identification cards issued under Sec. 37.71 of this rule.

SUBPART B—MINIMUM DOCUMENTATION, VERIFICATION, AND CARD ISSUANCE REQUIREMENTS

Sec. 37.11 Application and documents the applicant must provide.

(a) The State must subject each person applying for a REAL ID driver's license or identification card to a mandatory facial image capture, and shall maintain photographs of individuals even if no card is issued. The photographs must be stored in a format in accordance with Sec. 37.31 as follows:

   (1) If no card is issued, for a minimum period of five years.

   (2) If a card is issued, for a period of at least two years beyond the expiration date of the card.

(b) Declaration. Each applicant must sign a declaration under penalty of perjury that the information presented on the application is true and correct, and the State must retain this declaration. An applicant must sign a new declaration when presenting new source documents to the Department of Motor Vehicles (DMV) on subsequent visits.

(c) Identity.

   (1) To establish identity, the applicant must present at least one of the following source documents:

      (i) Valid, unexpired U.S. passport.

      (ii) Certified copy of a birth certificate filed with a State Office of Vital Statistics or equivalent agency in the individual's State of birth.

      (iii) Consular Report of Birth Abroad (CRBA) issued by the U.S. Department of State, Form FS-240, DS-1350 or FS-545.

      (iv) Valid, unexpired Permanent Resident Card (Form I-551) issued by DHS or INS.

      (v) Unexpired employment authorization document (EAD) issued by DHS, Form I-766 or Form I-688B.

      (vi) Unexpired foreign passport with a valid, unexpired U.S. visa affixed accompanied by the approved I-94 form documenting the applicant's most recent admittance into the United States.

      (vii) Certificate of Naturalization issued by DHS, Form N-550 or Form N-570.

      (viii) Certificate of Citizenship, Form N-560 or Form N-561, issued by DHS.

      (ix) REAL ID driver's license or identification card issued in compliance with the standards established by this part.

      (x) Such other documents as DHS may designate by notice published in the Federal Register.

   (2) Where a State permits an applicant to establish a name other than the name that appears on a source document (for example, through marriage, adoption, Court order, or other mechanism permitted by State law or regulation), the State shall require evidence of the name change through the presentation of documents issued by a court, governmental body or other entity as determined by the State. The State shall maintain copies of the documentation presented pursuant to Sec.

(continued)

37.31, and maintain a record of both the recorded name and the name on the source documents in a manner to be determined by the State and in conformity with Sec. 37.31.

(d) Date of birth. To establish date of birth, an individual must present at least one document included in paragraph (c) of this section.

(e) Social security number (SSN).

    (1) Except as provided in paragraph (e)(3) of this section, individuals presenting the identity documents listed in Sec. 37.11(c)(1) and (2) must present his or her Social Security Administration (SSA) account number card; or, if a Social Security Administration account card is not available, the person may present any of the following documents bearing the applicant's SSN:

        (i) A W-2 form,

        (ii) A SSA-1099 form,

        (iii) A non-SSA-1099 form, or

        (iv) A pay stub with the applicant's name and SSN on it.

    (2) The State DMV must verify the SSN pursuant to Sec. 37.13(b)(2) of this subpart.

    (3) Individuals presenting the identity document listed in Sec. 37.11(c)(1)(vi) must present an SSN or demonstrate non-work authorized status.

(f) Documents demonstrating address of principal residence. To document the address of principal residence, a person must present at least two documents of the State's choice that include the individual's name and principal residence. A street address is required except as provided in Sec. 37.17(f) of this part.

(g) Evidence of lawful status in the United States. A DMV may issue a REAL ID driver's license or identification card only to a person who has presented satisfactory evidence of lawful status.

    (1) If the applicant presents one of the documents listed under paragraphs (c)(1)(i), (c)(1)(ii), (c)(1)(iii), (c)(1)(iv), (c)(1)(vii) or (c)(1)(viii) of this section, the issuing State's verification of the applicant's identity in the manner prescribed in Sec. 37.13 will also provide satisfactory evidence of lawful status.

    (2) If the applicant presents one of the identity documents listed under paragraphs (c)(1)(v) or (c)(1)(vi), or (c)(1)(ix) of this section, the issuing State's verification of the identity document(s) does not provide satisfactory evidence of lawful status. The applicant must also present a second document from Sec. 37.11(g)(1) or documentation issued by DHS or other Federal agencies demonstrating lawful status as determined by USCIS. All documents shall be verified in the manner prescribed in Sec. 37.13.

(h) Exceptions Process. A State DMV may choose to establish a written, defined exceptions process for persons who, for reasons beyond their control, are unable to present all necessary documents and must rely on alternate documents to establish identity or date of birth. Alternative documents to demonstrate lawful status will only be allowed to demonstrate U.S. citizenship.

    (1) Each State establishing an exceptions process must make reasonable efforts to establish the authenticity of alternate documents each time they are presented and indicate that an exceptions process was used in the applicant's record.

    (2) The State shall retain copies or images of the alternate documents accepted pursuant to Sec. 37.31 of this part.

    (3) The State shall conduct a review of the use of the exceptions process, and pursuant to subpart E of this part, prepare and submit a report with a copy of the exceptions process as part of the certification documentation detailed in Sec. 37.55.

(i)   States are not required to comply with these requirements when issuing REAL ID driver's licenses or identification cards in support of Federal, State, or local criminal justice agencies or other programs that require special licensing or identification to safeguard persons or in support of their other official duties. As directed by appropriate officials of these Federal, State, or local agencies, States should take sufficient steps to safeguard the identities of such persons. Driver's licenses and identification cards issued in support of Federal, State, or local criminal justice agencies or programs that require special licensing or identification to safeguard persons or in support of their other official duties shall not be distinguishable from other REAL ID licenses or identification cards issued by the State.

Sec. 37.13 Document verification requirements

(a)   States shall make reasonable efforts to ensure that the applicant does not have more than one driver's license or identification card already issued by that State under a different identity. In States where an individual is permitted to hold both a driver's license and identification card, the State shall ensure that the individual has not been issued identification documents in multiple or different names. States shall also comply with the provisions of Sec. 37.29 before issuing a driver's license or identification card.

(b)   States must verify the documents and information required under Sec. 37.11 with the issuer of the document. States shall use systems for electronic validation of document and identity data as they become available or use alternative methods approved by DHS.

   (1)   States shall verify any document described in Sec. 37.11(c) or (g) and issued by DHS. . . .

   (2)   States must verify SSNs with the Social Security Administration (SSA) or through another method approved by DHS. . . .

   (3)   States must verify birth certificates presented by applicants. . . .

   (4)   States shall verify documents issued by the Department of State. . . .

   (5)   States must verify REAL ID driver's licenses and identification cards with the State of issuance. . . .

Sec. 37.15 Physical security features for the driver's license or identification card

(a)   General. States must include document security features on REAL ID driver's licenses and identification cards designed to deter forgery and counterfeiting, promote an adequate level of confidence in the authenticity of cards, and facilitate detection of fraudulent cards in accordance with this section. . . . [The regulation elaborates this requirement in detail.]

Sec. 37.17 Requirements for the surface of the driver's license or identification card

To be accepted by a Federal agency for official purposes, REAL ID driver's licenses and identification cards must include on the front of the card (unless otherwise specified below) the following information:

(a)   Full legal name. . . .

(b)   Date of birth.

(c)   Gender, as determined by the State.

(d)   Unique Driver's license or identification card number. This cannot be the individual's SSN, and must be unique across driver's license or identification cards within the State.

(e)   Full facial digital photograph. . . .[The regulation elaborates this requirement in detail.]

(f)   Address of principal residence. . . .

(g)   Signature. . . .

(h)   Physical security features, pursuant to Sec. 37.15 of this subpart.

(i)   Machine-readable technology on the back of the card, pursuant to Sec. 37.19 of this subpart.

(continued)

(j) Date of transaction.

(k) Expiration date.

(l) State or territory of issuance.

(m) Printed information. The name, date of birth, gender, card number, issue date, expiration date, and address on the face of the card must be in Latin alpha-numeric characters. The name must contain a field of no less than a total of 39 characters. . . .

(n) The card shall bear a DHS-approved security marking on each driver's license or identification card that is issued reflecting the card's level of compliance as set forth in Sec. 37.51 of this Rule.

Sec. 37.19 Machine readable technology on the driver's license or identification card

* * *

Sec. 37.25 Renewal of REAL ID driver's licenses and identification cards

* * *

Sec. 37.29 Prohibition against holding more than one REAL ID card or more than one driver's license

* * *

SUBPART C—OTHER REQUIREMENTS

Sec. 37.31 Source document retention

* * *

Sec. 37.33 DMV databases

(a) States must maintain a State motor vehicle database that contains, at a minimum—

(1) All data fields printed on driver's licenses and identification cards issued by the State, individual serial numbers of the card, and SSN;

(2) A record of the full legal name and recorded name established under Sec. 37.11(c)(2) as applicable, without truncation;

(3) All additional data fields included in the MRZ but not printed on the driver's license or identification card; and

(4) Motor vehicle driver's histories, including motor vehicle violations, suspensions, and points on driver's licenses.

(b) States must protect the security of personally identifiable information, collected pursuant to the REAL ID Act, in accordance with Sec. 37.41(b)(2) of this part.

SUBPART D—SECURITY AT DMVS AND DRIVER'S LICENSE AND IDENTIFICATION CARD PRODUCTION FACILITIES

Sec. 37.41 Security plan

(a) In General. States must have a security plan that addresses the provisions in paragraph (b) of this section and must submit the security plan as part of its REAL ID certification under Sec. 37.55.

* * *

Sec. 37.43 Physical security of DMV production facilities

(a) States must ensure the physical security of facilities where driver's licenses and identification cards are produced, and the security of document materials and papers from which driver's licenses and identification cards are produced or manufactured.

(b) States must describe the security of DMV facilities as part of their security plan, in accordance with Sec. 37.41.

Sec. 37.45 Background checks for covered employees

(a) Scope. States are required to subject persons who are involved in the manufacture or production of REAL ID driver's licenses and identification cards, or who have the ability to affect the identity information that appears on the driver's license or identification card, or current employees who will be assigned to such positions ("covered employees" or "covered positions"), to a background check. . . .

SUBPART E—PROCEDURES FOR DETERMINING STATE COMPLIANCE

Sec. 37.51 Compliance—general requirements

* * *

SUBPART F—DRIVER'S LICENSES AND IDENTIFICATION CARDS ISSUED UNDER SECTION 202(D)(11) OF THE REAL ID ACT

Sec. 37.71 Driver's licenses and identification cards issued under section 202(d)(11) of the REAL ID Act

* * * *

Issued in Washington, DC, on January 10, 2008. Michael Chertoff, Secretary.

Real Id Driver's Licenses And Identification Cards, Homeland Security, Issued in Washington, DC, on January 10, 2008. Michael Chertoff, Secretary.

SIDEBAR   *Publishing Federal Rules*

Prior to 1935, there was no systematic or uniform method of communication or organizing federal administrative regulations or notices of administrative action. The result was occasional confusion about the status of regulations, actions, and presidential orders. The Federal Register Act of 1935, and subsequent amendments to it, was intended to systemize federal administrative reporting. The primary means of communication under this law is the *Federal Register*. The *Federal Register* is used to publish federal rules, proposed rules, orders, and related documents and announcements. It is published on federal government working days.

The Federal Register Act was amended in 1937 to include The *Code of Federal Regulations* (CFR), a compilation of federal administrative regulations. To ease research, the numbering systems of the CFR and United States Code (USC) are paralleled in most, but not all, chapters. For example, the titles (and topics) of Chapter 1 in both is general provisions, Chapter 3 is president, Chapter 5 is government organization and employees, Chapter 7 is agriculture, and so on. New rules appear first in the *Federal Register* and are later incorporated into the CFR. In addition to print copies, online searchable versions of the CFR and USC are available today. See Figure 6-1 for the first page of a rule concerning blueberries that was promulgated by the Department of Agriculture.

43961

Rules and Regulations

Federal Register

Vol. 65, No. 137

Monday, July 17, 2000

This section of the FEDERAL REGISTER contains regulatory documents having general applicability and legal effect, most of which are keyed to and codified in the Code of Federal Regulations, which is published under 50 titles pursuant to 44 U.S.C. 1510.

The Code of Federal Regulations is sold by the Superintendent of Documents. Prices of new books are listed in the first FEDERAL REGISTER issue of each week.

DEPARTMENT OF AGRICULTURE

Agricultural Marketing Service

7 CFR Part 1218

[FV–99–701–FR]

RIN 0581–AB78

Blueberry Promotion, Research, and Information Order

AGENCY: Agricultural Marketing Service, USDA.

ACTION: Final rule.

SUMMARY: This rule establishes a Blueberry Promotion, Research, and Information Order (Order) under the Commodity Promotion, Research, and Information Act of 1996. Under the Order, cultivated blueberry producers and importers will pay an assessment of $12 per ton, which will be paid to the U.S.A. Blueberry Council (USABC). Producers and importers of less than 2,000 pounds of fresh and processed cultivated blueberries annually will be exempt from the assessment. First handlers will remit the assessments to the USABC. The USABC will use the funds collected to conduct a generic program of promotion, research, consumer information, and industry information to maintain and expand markets for cultivated blueberries. The U.S. Department of Agriculture (USDA or the Department) conducted a referendum among eligible producers and importers of cultivated blueberries to determine whether they favor the implementation of the Order. The Order was approved by a majority of those voting who also represented a majority of the pounds of cultivated blueberries represented in the referendum.

EFFECTIVE DATE: August 16, 2000.

FOR FURTHER INFORMATION CONTACT: Oliver L. Flake, Research and Promotion Branch, Fruit and Vegetable Programs, AMS, USDA, Stop 0244, 1400

Independence Avenue, SW, Room 2535–S, Washington, DC 20250–0244; telephone (202) 720–5976, fax (202) 205–2800, or e-mail at oliver.flake@usda.gov.

SUPPLEMENTARY INFORMATION: This Order is issued pursuant to the Commodity Promotion, Research, and Information Act of 1996 (Act) [7 U.S.C. 7401–7425; Public Law 104–127].

Previous documents in this proceeding: Proposed Rule Number 1 (July 1999 proposed rule) on the Order published in the July 22, 1999, issue of the **Federal Register** [64 FR 39790]; a proposed rule on referendum procedures published in the July 22, 1999, issue of the **Federal Register** [64 FR 39803]; Proposed Rule Number 2 (February 2000 proposed rule) on the Order, which included a Referendum Order, published in the February 15, 2000, issue of the **Federal Register** [65 FR 7657]; a final rule on referendum procedures published in the February 15, 2000, issue of the **Federal Register** [65 FR 7652].

Question and Answer Overview

Why Is a Final Rule Being Published?

In a recent referendum, eligible producers and importers of cultivated blueberries voted in favor of implementing the Order. This final rule, which will become effective in 30 days, completes the implementation process.

What Is the Purpose of the Program?

The purpose of the program is to develop and finance an effective and coordinated program of promotion, research, and information to maintain and expand the markets for fresh and processed cultivated blueberries.

Who Is Covered by This Rule?

Cultivated blueberry producers who grow and importers who import 2,000 pounds or more of cultivated blueberries annually will be subject to this rule and pay an assessment.

What Is the Assessment Rate?

The assessment rate is $12 per ton.

When Will the Assessment Be Due?

Domestic assessments for the 2001 crop year will be due by November 30, 2001. Assessments for the subsequent crop years will be due by November 30 of the crop year. The U.S. Customs Service will collect assessments on

imports at the time of entry into the United States, starting on January 2, 2001.

Will I Have To Pay the Assessment Forever?

Assessments will be due as long as the Order is in effect. However, every five years, USDA will conduct a referendum to determine whether producers and importers of cultivated blueberries want the program to continue. The program will continue if a majority of the voters in the referendum vote for approval and those voters represent a majority of the pounds of cultivated blueberries produced and imported by the voters in the referendum.

Who Will Administer This Order?

The USABC will administer the Order with supervision from USDA. The USABC members will be appointed by the Secretary of Agriculture (Secretary) from nominations received from the blueberry industry.

Who Will Be on the USABC?

The USABC will consist of 13 members: One producer member from each of four producer regions; one producer member from each of the top five cultivated-blueberry-producing states; one importer; one exporter (a foreign producer who ships cultivated blueberries into the United States from the largest foreign cultivated blueberry production area); one first handler; and one public member. Each member will have an alternate. Currently, the top five states (in descending order) are Michigan, New Jersey, Oregon, Georgia, and North Carolina.

When Will USABC Members Be Appointed?

The nomination process for the producer members and alternates will begin soon after the Order becomes effective. The North American Blueberry Council (NABC) will assist USDA in this process for the initial nominations. Future nominations will be managed by the USABC.

It is expected that the producer members and alternates will be appointed by the Secretary in time for the USABC to hold its organizational meeting in Washington, DC, in late 2000. The USABC will nominate persons to serve as the importer, exporter, handler, and public member.

FIGURE 6-1   Example of final rule in *Federal Register*.

Although regulations are subordinate to statutes, they have equal weight when applied, provided they are soundly created. You will learn later in this chapter that there are different types of rules. Some establish procedures, others create rights and obligations. The authority of an agency to make the latter (*substantive rules*) must stem from an enabling statute. Congress may delegate the authority to create substantive rules consistent with its statutes, but an agency may not assume this authority without such permission. In other words, the creation of an agency and an assignment of duties to it do not implicitly create the authority to promulgate rules; the legislative body must specifically authorize the agency to promulgate rules.

In addition to being within the legislative delegation, rules must also be reasonable. As you learned in Chapter 3, a rule must rationally relate to its enabling statute. If a rule does not so relate, it may be invalidated by a reviewing Court. If the rule classifies a suspect class or impinges upon a fundamental right (such as the right to vote), it is tested under the strict scrutiny test.

In some circumstances, a third test is applied, which falls between the rational relationship and strict scrutiny tests. Under this test, the rule must be substantially related to an important governmental objective. This test has been applied to some gender-based classifications, classifications based on illegitimacy, and (in some cases) a classification that encroaches on a nonfundamental constitutionally protected right.[1] Rules tested under the rational relationship test usually are determined to be valid, whereas most rules tested under the strict scrutiny test are not. See Chapter 4 for a more complete discussion of these tests.

6.2 RULEMAKING AND ADJUDICATION DEFINED

Section 551(4) of the APA defines a *rule* as the "whole or a part of an agency statement of general or particular applicability and future effect designed to implement, interpret, or prescribe law or policy or describing the organization, procedure, or practice requirements of an agency." It is sometimes hard to distinguish between rulemaking (a legislative function) and adjudication (a judicial function). The APA attempts to distinguish "decisions" and "orders" from "rules" and "regulations" by stating that if the action is intended to have future effect, it is a rule. In addition, rules "implement, interpret, or prescribe law or policy" or describe the "organization, procedure, or practice requirements" of agencies. Said another way, if an agency establishes a policy that is to be followed from that date forward, or issues a rule explaining how it will perform some function (e.g., claims for unemployment compensation benefits must be filed within 30 days of leaving one's job), it has created a rule.

Justice Holmes defined *adjudication* as a process that "investigates, declares and enforces liabilities as they stand on present or past facts and under laws supposed already to exist. That is the purpose and end. Legislation, on the other hand, looks to the future and changes existing conditions by making a new rule to be applied thereafter to all or some part of those subject to its power."[2] Generally, adjudications involve individual claims, whereas rules are directed at large groups. Adjudication can result in an immediate sanction against an individual; a rule cannot. An adjudication to enforce a rule must be made before a person or company can be sanctioned (see Figure 6-2).

Often, however, the issues are similar. In the previous example, the agency announced that, to be eligible for unemployment benefits, one must file an application within 30 days of leaving the job. Thus, a rule has been announced. If a claimant is denied benefits because she filed her claim 31 days after leaving her job and she appeals that decision, an adjudication has been started.

There is one significant difference between rulemaking and adjudication: due process. Generally, agencies are free to make rules without conducting hearings. This is not true of adjudications. Due process requires the government to provide some form of notice to persons affected, as well as an opportunity to be heard (see Chapter 4).

Rulemaking	Adjudication
1. Is directed at large groups or policy issues.	1. Is directed at specific individuals (or businesses) or disputes.
2. Concerns future conduct.	2. Concerns past conduct.
3. Goal is establishing a rule to deal with future conduct.	3. Goal is the resolution of disputes.
4. Decisions based on facts and policy.	4. Decisions based on adjudicative facts particular to disputes.
5. Sets standards by which a person may be adjudged and sanctioned.	5. Determines compliance or guilt and sanctions violators.

FIGURE 6-2   Rulemaking versus adjudication.

6.3 THE VOLUME OF RULES

Most people likely think of the U.S. Congress and their state and local legislative bodies as the source of most law in this nation. However, this is not true. Today, the bulk of law is made by agencies, not legislative bodies. Congress may enact only a couple hundred laws in a year, whereas the total number of rules promulgated by agencies is in the thousands; it has been estimated that the total number of federal employees writing rules is more than 100,000.[3] By 1989, the *Code of Federal Regulations* was 196 volumes long and contained more than 60 million words—far larger than the United States Code.[4] The growth of rulemaking can also be seen in the total published pages in the CFR and *Federal Register*. The *Federal Register* was first published in 1936, with a total of 2,620 pages. The *Register* experienced its fastest growth in the 1970s. In 1970, the *Register* totaled slightly more than 20,000 pages. Just 10 years later, the total pages published grew to 73,258! Since that time, the total has varied considerably, seeing a low of 44,812 in 1986 and climbing to 71,161 in 1999. One estimate put it at more than 70,000 in 2010, leaving President George W. Bush and President Barack Obama administrations at the same level of output. [Ryan Young, May 28, 2010, Federal Register Hits 30,000 Pages, *OpenMarket.Org, http://www.openmarket.org/2010/05/28/federal-register-hits-30000-pages/*]. The CFR contained approximately 55,000 pages in 1970. By the close of 1998, that number had increased to nearly 135,000 pages. See Figures 6-3 and 6-4.

Many of these regulations affect only a small number of people and businesses. Others regulate more broadly. In aggregate, the total regulations of federal, state, and local agencies greatly affect the lives of all people. You may recall from Chapter 1 that one researcher estimated that the purchase of a hamburger from a local restaurant is governed by more than 40,000 regulations. Accordingly, an understanding of administrative discretion to make rules, the process used to make rules, and the limitations on the rulemaking authority is an essential aspect of administrative law.

6.4 TYPES OF RULES

There are two types of rules: legislative and interpretive. *Legislative rules* can be further divided into those that are *procedural* and those that are *substantive*. As a general proposition, a legislative delegation of authority carries with it an implicit

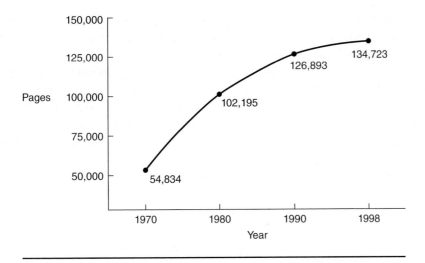

FIGURE 6-3   Total pages of CFR.

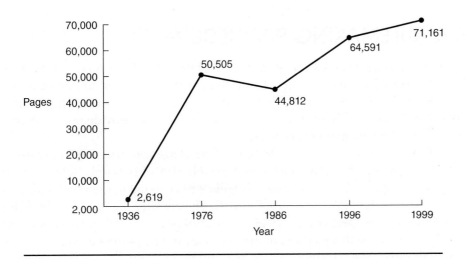

FIGURE 6-4   Total pages of *Federal Register*.

authority to establish procedures necessary to enforce and implement the agency's delegated mandate. Agencies are normally bound by their own procedural rules, as are those who deal with those agencies.

The other form of rule is substantive. These rules affect the rights of individuals and are the functional equivalent of statutes. There is no inherent authority to promulgate substantive rules. Congress must delegate this authority. The Supreme Court has found, however, that the authority may be implicit in the agency's mandate from Congress. That is, the authority may be found in the absence of a statute expressly granting it as long as it is clear that Congress intended for the agency to have the authority to "fill in the gaps."[5] If promulgated properly, such rules have the effect of statutes; they require or prohibit actions and may impose penalties for violations of their mandates. Although a rule must be consistent with the agency's enabling statute, it may declare something that the statute has not. The APA uses the phrase "substantive rules" rather than legislative rules.

A Court may not substitute its judgment for that of a substantive agency rule. That is, a reviewing Court cannot declare that a better standard or procedure must be used. A substantive rule has the force and effect of law.

Interpretive rules do not declare something new; they do not fill in the gaps of legislation. Rather, they represent an agency's interpretation of a statute's meaning. Interpretive rules are used to inform the public of how the agency intends to implement and enforce a statute, based upon its understanding of the statute's meaning and purpose. An agency may issue an interpretive rule even though Congress delegated no authority, expressly or implicitly, to do so.

Whether a rule is interpretive or substantive often depends on whether Congress has given the agency the authority to promulgate rules. If rule-making authority has been granted, the rule is more likely substantive than interpretative.[6]

Unlike substantive rules, interpretive rules do not have the force of statutes. Courts may interpret statutes on their own and are not bound by agency interpretations thereof. However, Courts often give great weight to agency interpretive rules and value agency interpretations because agencies are considered expert and experienced in their respective specialties whereas Courts are not.[7]

6.5 RULEMAKING PROCEDURE

Rulemaking is the administrative equivalent of the legislative process of enacting statutes. Agencies are not subject to stricter constitutional requirements in the rulemaking process than are legislatures in enacting statutes. Because legislatures are not constitutionally required to conduct hearings or provide notice of proposed legislation, neither are agencies.

The process that must be followed by federal agencies when making rules is proscribed by the APA. An appreciation for the APA's historical context aids in understanding why Congress chose to regulate rulemaking in the way it did. You may recall that the APA was enacted in 1946, shortly after the President Franklin D. Roosevelt New Deal era. By 1946, the federal government's jurisdiction was greatly expanded with a plethora of new agencies and employees exercising many new authorities. Many people were deeply concerned about these changes, believing the newly enlarged administrative state threatened liberty by undoing the basic architectural features that were intended to prevent tyranny, federalism and the separation of powers. Other people believed the changes were necessary in the increasingly global and complex world. The APA, born out of this environment, represents a compromise between those perspectives. It empowers agencies to implement their mandates and to make rules and adjudicate cases, but with checks and balances designed around the separation of powers.

Through the APA, Congress established procedures that agencies must follow when adopting rules. Also, many agencies have adopted rules increasing their procedural obligations in an effort to make the process fair. In *NLRB v. Wyman-Gordon Co.*,[8] the U.S. Supreme Court said, "[t]he rulemaking provisions of [the APA] were designed to assure fairness and mature consideration of rules of general application." In most cases, agency failure to comply with these requirements invalidates any rule promulgated under the defective or deficient process.

The APA establishes three procedural forms of rulemaking: formal, informal, and exempted. Federal law also provides for negotiated rulemaking. Each of these forms of rulemaking is discussed in the ensuing sections. Remember that each state has its own rulemaking requirements and they often differ significantly from the federal formal versus informal model.

6.5(a) Formal Rulemaking

Formal rulemaking is the most time-consuming, expensive, and procedurally involved method of rulemaking for agencies. It is not used as often as informal rulemaking because § 553(c) of the APA requires formal rulemaking whenever "rules are required by statute to be made on the record after an opportunity for an agency hearing." Therefore, formal rulemaking is required only when mandated by Congress in a separate statute. The APA alone never mandates formal rulemaking.

A statute must be clear in its command to have rules made "on the record after an opportunity for an agency hearing." If a statute is unclear, or requires only a hearing, Courts are likely to hold that informal rulemaking may be used. This was so in *United States v. Florida East Coast Railroad*,[9] in which Congress's mandate to the Interstate Commerce Commission to have a hearing before setting certain charges was determined not to be a requirement to use formal rulemaking. When formal rulemaking is required, the agency must follow the APA's adjudicatory procedures—that is, a trial-type hearing must be held.

LEGAL TERM
Formal Rulemaking
Rulemaking on the record.

United States v. Florida East Coast Railroad

410 U.S. 224 (1973)

Appellees, two railroad companies, brought this action in the District Court for the Middle District of Florida to set aside the incentive per diem rates established by appellant Interstate Commerce Commission in a rulemaking proceeding. They challenged the order of the Commission on both substantive and procedural grounds. The District Court sustained appellees' position that the Commission had failed to comply with the applicable provisions of the Administrative Procedure Act, 5 U.S.C. § 551 *et seq.*, and, therefore, set aside the order without dealing with the railroads' other contentions. The District Court held [regarding] the language of §1(14)(a) of the Interstate Commerce Act, 5 U.S.C. § 556(d), . . . that the Commission's determination to receive submissions from the appellees only in written form was a violation of that section because the respondents were "prejudiced" by that determination within the meaning of that section. . . .

This case [arose] from the factual background of a chronic freight-car shortage on the Nation's railroads. . . .

The Commission . . . issued in December 1969 an interim report announcing its tentative decision to adopt incentive per diem charges on standard boxcars based on the information supplied by the railroads. Before the enactment of the 1966 amendment to the Interstate Commerce Act, it was generally thought that the Commission's authority to fix per diem payments for freight car use was limited to setting an amount that reflected fair return on investment for the owning railroad, without any regard being had for the desirability of prompt return to the owning line or for the encouragement of additional purchases of freight cars by the railroads as a method of investing capital. The Commission concluded, however, that in view of the 1966 amendment it could impose additional "incentive" per diem charges to spur prompt return of existing cars and to make acquisition of new cars financially attractive to the railroads. . . .

(continued)

> In *United States v. Allegheny-Ludlum Steel Corp.* [citation omitted], we held that the language of § 1(14)(a) of the Interstate Commerce Act authorizing the Commission to act "after hearing" was not the equivalent of a requirement that a rule be made "on the record after an opportunity for an agency hearing" as the latter term is used in § 553(c) of the Administrative Procedure Act. Since the 1966 amendment to § 1(14)(a), under which the Commission was here proceeding, does not by its terms add to the hearing requirement contained in the earlier language, the same result should obtain here unless that amendment contains language that is tantamount to such a requirement. Appellees contend that such language is found in the provisions of the Act requiring that:
>
> > [T]he Commission shall give consideration to the national level of ownership of such type of freight car and to other factors affecting the adequacy of the national freight car supply, and shall, on the basis of such consideration, determine whether compensation should be computed. . . .
>
> While this language is undoubtedly a mandate to the Commission to consider the factors there set forth in reaching any conclusion as to imposition of per diem incentive charges, it adds to the hearing requirements of the section neither expressly nor by implication. We know of no reason to think that an administrative agency in reaching a decision cannot accord consideration to factors such as those set forth in the 1966 amendment by means other than a trial-type hearing or the presentation of oral argument by the affected parties. Congress by that amendment specified necessary components of the ultimate decision, but it did not specify the method by which the Commission should acquire information about those components. . . .
>
> . . . We recognized in *Allegheny-Ludlum* that the actual words "on the record" and "after . . . hearing" used in § 553 were not words of art, and that other statutory language having the same meaning could trigger the provisions of §§ 556 or 557 in rulemaking proceedings. But we adhere to our conclusion, expressed in that case, that the phrase "after hearing" in § 1(14)(a) of the Interstate Commerce Act does not have such an effect.

United States v. Florida East Coast Railroad 410 U.S. 224 (1973),U.S Supreme Court.

Before a hearing is conducted, an agency contemplating a new rule must give notice to the public. This is normally done by publishing the date of the hearing in the *Federal Register*, in what is sometimes referred to as a *notice of proposed rulemaking* (NPR). The APA requires that the notice include "either the terms or substance of the proposed rule or a description of the subjects and issues involved," as well as a reference to the legal authority by which the agency intends to enact the proposed rule. There is no rule requiring an agency to publish the text of the proposed rule although this is sometimes done.

Once the agency has satisfied the notice requirement, it must conduct an evidentiary or trial-type hearing on the date announced in its notice. At this hearing, interested persons must be given an opportunity to present evidence and cross-examine witnesses. A full Court-style hearing need not be conducted to satisfy this requirement. Rules of evidence are relaxed; there is no right to rebuttal; and concerns about disqualification, bias, and related matters are given less scrutiny than in the judicial context. There is no right to have one's case heard by a jury.

Another departure from adjudicatory procedures is found in APA § 556(d). That provision permits an agency to substitute written testimony for oral when conducting formal rulemaking. However, parties are permitted to cross-examine the person who submitted the report. If the person who submitted the information does not appear at the hearing and a party wishes to cross-examine the witness, the information may not be used by the agency in making its decision. One adjudicatory rule that does apply to formal rulemaking concerns ***ex parte communications***. Section 554(d) of the APA prohibits ex parte communications between agency decision makers and interested parties.

Finally, the agency must issue its rule. After a formal adjudication (hearing) is completed, the parties are given an opportunity to submit proposed findings and conclusions. Thereafter, the presiding officer (administrative law judge or other official) issues a tentative decision, which becomes final absent an appeal. Occasionally, an agency head will require that an entire record be certified to it for decision rather than to the presiding officer. In such instances, the presiding officer issues a recommended decision.

The APA requires that the decision include a statement of "findings and conclusions, and the reasons or basis thereof, on all the material issues of fact, law, or discretion presented on the record."[10] Basically, this means that the agency's decision must be in writing and must be reasoned. This is a more stringent requirement than for informal rulemaking, for which the agency must "incorporate in the rules adopted a concise general statement of their basis and purpose."[11] (See § 6.5[b] for further discussion of the findings and conclusions requirement.) In formal rulemaking, however, this process may be omitted. Rather, the agency may require that the record be certified to the agency so that it may issue a tentative decision for public comment. Agencies have a second alternative: They may require that the record be certified to the agency so that one of its responsible employees may issue a recommended decision.[12]

The APA nevertheless provides that all these procedures may be omitted whenever compliance with such procedures would imperatively and unavoidably affect the agency's execution of its functions. Such a decision must be made on the record.

Section 553(d) requires that an agency publish a final rule at least 30 days before the rule becomes effective. This interim period gives those affected by the rule an opportunity to comply before it becomes effective. Also, it provides those who wish to challenge the rule an opportunity to do so before it is enforced. This may be done in a Court or before the agency. Section 553(e) provides that agencies "shall give an interested person the right to petition for the issuance, amendment, or repeal of a rule."

Formal rulemaking has been criticized as being too costly and time-consuming. Proponents of this view point to the Food, Drug, and Cosmetic Act as an example of the problem inherent in formal rulemaking: No formal rulemaking under that act has taken less than two years. One hearing, which generated a transcript of nearly 8,000 pages, dealt with only one question: whether peanut butter should be comprised of 87.5 or 90 percent peanuts.[13] In total, it took 12 years, with a total record exceeding 100,000 pages, for the Food and Drug Administration to determine what percentage of peanut butter should be peanuts.[14] For this reason, many people prefer informal rulemaking.

SIDEBAR *Rivalry, Politics, and Administrative Dysfunction*

Interagency and interjurisdictional cooperation are often factors in the efficacy of administration. Unfortunately interagency rivalry, competition, and jurisdictional disputes are too common. Indeed there is evidence that had federal agencies, such as the Federal Bureau of Investigation and the Central Intelligence Agency, cooperated and shared the information, the attacks of September 11, 2001, on the United States may have been averted.[15] There is also a theory that the internal politics of the FBI thwarted a counterterrorism special agent's investigation of Osama Bin Laden.[16]

(continued)

Another poignant example of interagency rivalry and power concerns the financial crisis of the late 1990s that began in the United States and spread through much of the World.

In 1996, President William J. Clinton nominated and the Senate confirmed Brooksley Born, an attorney, Chairperson of the Commodities Futures Trading Commission (CFTC). The CFTC was created as an independent agency in 1974 to oversee and regulate futures trading. During her tenure as Chairperson of the CFTC Ms. Born became concerned about the absence of regulation of "over-the-counter derivatives (OTC derivatives)," a form of a futures trade. Specifically, the size of the OTC derivatives market and the borrowing to support it had both become enormous and she witnessed a rise in OTC fraud. Because Congress left the OTC derivatives market largely unregulated, Born sought the authority to oversee and regulate the market from Congress. The suggestion was met with considerable opposition not only from banks and financial institutions engaged in the market but also from federal officials of other agencies. Most notable of these individuals was Alan Greenspan, Chairman of the Federal Reserve from 1987 to 2006. The most powerful economist in the United States at the time and a follower of the philosopher Ayn Rand, core to Greenspan's economic philosophy was the belief that smaller government and little or no regulation of business would produce the healthiest economy. Born and the small CFTC were no match for Greenspan and the other powerful people in the government, including Robert Rubin, Secretary of the Treasury, and Lawrence Sommers, Deputy Secretary of the Treasury (who would later succeed Rubin as Secretary), who opposed greater regulation. Not only did she did fail to win regulatory authority, Greenspan and other officials persuaded Congress to enact legislation, that President Clinton signed, prohibiting the CFTC from regulating the OTC derivatives market.

Born warned the nation that the OTC derivatives market would collapse leading to a larger economic crisis, lost the battle with Greenspan, Rubin, and Sommers, left the CFTC in 1999, and subsequently her prediction came true. Greenspan later acknowledged that his free market, no regulation ideology was, at least, partially to blame for the crisis.[17]

6.5(b) Informal Rulemaking

LEGAL TERM

Informal Rulemaking
"Notice and comment" rulemaking.

Under the APA, informal rulemaking exists by default. If a statute does not require formal rulemaking and an exemption does not apply, then *informal rulemaking* may be used.

Three simple requirements are imposed upon an agency using informal rulemaking. First, as for formal rulemaking, the agency must publish a notice of proposed rulemaking, normally in the *Federal Register*. As with formal rulemaking, reference to the legal authority granting the agency the power to enact the rule is required, as is a description of the proposed rule.

Second, the agency must give interested persons the opportunity to participate in the rulemaking process. No trial-type hearing is required of the agency, though. Rather, interested persons have the right to submit to the agency written comments containing data, views, or arguments. Although not required, agencies occasionally permit interested persons to testify orally. The notice of proposed rulemaking will state whether oral testimony will be allowed, as well as the date of the hearing. If the agency decides to have all information and testimony submitted in written form, the notice will recite the address where the information is to be sent and the date by which it must be received.

This process is important to rulemaking. Through public participation, an agency educates itself and is exposed to various thoughts, viewpoints, methods, and alternatives. It is supplied with information that it would otherwise have to pay for or pay to have produced. Also, the agency becomes aware of prevailing public attitudes. All are important and enhance the quality of an agency's decision making.

An agency may receive only a handful or many thousands of comments to a proposed rule. The Food and Drug Administration, for example, received more than 700,000 comments on its proposed rule to regulate tobacco products! Do agencies read these comments? Scholar Cornelius Kerwin concluded that the "amount of attention paid to comments depends on the volume and seriousness of the comments received, but in many instances they dominate the preamble [of the final rule]. There is little question that agencies take public comments seriously."[18]

Finally, APA § 553(c) requires that the agency issue its final rules with a "concise statement of their basis and purpose." This requirement is not as strict as the findings requirement of adjudication and formal rulemaking. However, a rule may be invalidated by a reviewing Court if the purpose for its enactment, or the basis on which it is issued, is so vague that there can be no meaningful judicial review.

This "concise statement" requirement is twofold. First, the agency must articulate the basic rationale underlying its decision. The major policy issues must be identified, as well as the reasons the agency reacted to them as it did. Second, the agency must identify the essential facts on which its decision rests. The statement need not be detailed, but a decision that recites no facts will be overturned.

As with formal rulemaking, an agency must publish a final rule at least 30 days before it becomes effective. Section 553(e) provides interested persons the opportunity to petition for issuance, amendment, or repeal of the rule. Figure 6-5 contrasts the basic legal process for the two types of rulemaking. Even though the APA informal rulemaking process is as simple as just described, in reality, the process is more tedious for agencies. First, there is considerable work, analysis, and consultation that precede the formal and informal rulemaking processes. An agency may be responding to a problem, a lawsuit, political considerations, or other factors that may initiate the pre-APA processes. In some cases, agencies seek public comment before the APA-required public comment period. They may also gather information and conduct impact studies that will later be repeated. Second, even though not required, agencies commonly follow the notice of proposed rulemaking with publication of a proposed rule during the comment period. The development of the proposed rule, as opposed to simply seeking comment to the notice of proposed rulemaking, represents additional work. In addition, through several Executive Orders, agencies must now involve the OMB for compliance with the Paperwork Reduction Act, and in some cases, inter alia, analyze: the impact of the rule on small businesses; the costs of the rule to state, local, and tribal governments; and the proposed rule's environmental impact. These variations on the informal rulemaking model found in the APA are sometimes known as hybrid rulemaking.

6.5(c) Beyond the APA's Requirements: Hybrid Rulemaking

Although formal rulemaking provides for participation by interested persons, it is criticized as being too costly and time-consuming. Informal rulemaking, in contrast, is quicker and less expensive but is criticized for not allowing interested persons enough participation. All recent presidents have also been concerned about

Formal	Informal
1. Required only when a statute clearly commands that a rule be made on the record after an opportunity for an agency hearing.	1. Used when formal rulemaking is not required and no exemption applies.
2. Notice of proposed rulemaking must be published in the *Federal Register.*	2. Notice of proposed rulemaking must be published in the *Federal Register.*
3. A trial-type hearing must be conducted. Interested persons must be permitted to participate, including making arguments, calling witnesses, cross-examining witnesses, and introducing other material evidence.	3. No trial-type hearing is required. Interested persons must be given the opportunity to present their positions in writing.
4. The agency must include with its rules a statement of findings and conclusions, and the reasons or basis thereof, on all the material issues of fact, law, or discretion presented on the record.	4. The agency must incorporate in any rule adopted a concise general statement of the basis and purpose of the rule.

FIGURE 6-5   Comparing formal and informal rulemaking under the APA.

administrative rules running afoul of presidential policy. In an effort to cure such problems, Courts, Congress, and the president have created hybrid procedures. *Hybrid rulemaking* is the addition of a procedural step beyond that required for informal rulemaking. This section discusses just a few of the many hybrids. A common hybrid modification is the requirement that interested persons be permitted to present their comments orally. Another is to require testimony and permit interested persons the opportunity to cross-examine witnesses.

Advance notice of proposed rulemaking may also be added to the informal rulemaking requirements. This occurs earlier than the notice of proposed rulemaking discussed previously in this chapter. An advance notice is used whenever an agency recognizes a problem but does not have sufficient information to draft a proposed rule. The advance notice allows the agency to acquire the information it needs to decide on a course of action. Advance notices are published in the *Federal Register*.

Disclosure of methodology is another variation in the informal rulemaking process. An agency may disclose (usually through the notice of proposed rulemaking) the scientific basis upon which it relied when drafting the proposed rule. This disclosure permits interested persons to examine the technology and science of the agency's position before commenting.

Similarly, an agency may publish a notice of intent to rely, which puts interested persons on notice that it intends to rely on specific data or other science when making its rule. As is true of disclosure of methodology, this provides interested persons an opportunity to examine the data and science before commenting.

Congress may create hybrids by specifying a particular procedure for a particular agency. It has done so on many occasions. Congress has done this, for example, in the Magnuson-Moss Act by requiring oral hearings when the Federal Trade Commission is considering issuing rules governing unfair trade practices. Otherwise, informal procedures are used.[19]

Through the inherent executive power, presidents also mandate hybrid procedures for executive agencies.[20] For example, several successive presidents have issued executive orders requiring agencies to incorporate economic impact analysis into rulemaking. For example, President Carter issued an executive order—Executive Order No. 12,044—requiring agencies to publish statements of economic impact of new rules and to submit major rules to the president for review. The order also required agencies to review existing rules and to repeal those deemed unnecessary or inconsistent with the new policies.

President Reagan issued Executive Order No. 12,291, requiring executive agencies to conduct a Regulatory Impact Analysis (RIA) whereby they assess the costs and benefits of proposed rules that are projected to affect the economy by $100 million or more. The order also requires that any agency demonstrate a net gain to the economy before a proposed rule is enacted. It empowered the Office of Management and Budget, a presidential office, to review all proposed rules for compliance with the cost-benefit and net-gain analysis and to determine if a proposed rule is consistent with the administration's policies. Although not required, many independent agencies have performed such assessments as well. Executive Order No. 12,291 also required that alternatives be considered and that the agency publish an economic justification for its final rule.

Executive Order No. 12,498 goes one step further by requiring the heads of executive departments to attempt to conform regulatory programs to the president's policy objectives. President Clinton also issued several executive orders affecting rulemaking. For example, Executive Order No. 12,866 revoked Executive Orders 12,291 and 12,498. Through this order, President Clinton also directed agencies to use cost-benefit analysis and to assess the risks that the proposed rule posed, and encouraged performance-based regulatory standards. Also significant, the order created a regulatory planning process, with the Office of Information and Regulatory Affairs (OIRA) charged with overseeing agency rulemaking with the stated goal of aligning rules with presidential policy.

Then, President Bush modified Executive Order 12,866 through Executive Order 13,422, which further increased White House involvement in rulemaking and made cost-benefit analysis more significant in the process. Executive Order Nos. 13,132 and 13,083 (the latter was suspended by Executive Order No. 13,875) required agencies to consult the states before enacting rules that affected the states and to more freely grant waivers of federal conditions for federal funding of local programs. Similarly, Executive Order No. 12,372 requires federal agencies to consult with the states if a proposed rule will impact the fiscal affairs of state governments. Although presidents may supplement the rulemaking requirements found in the APA, they may not reduce or lessen them.[21] See Appendix C for examples of executive orders, including Nos. 12,866, 13,132, 13,422, and 13,132.

For many years, the Courts of the United States also directed agencies to take steps beyond the notice-and-comment requirements of the APA. Many Courts found that the APA's notice-and-comment procedure violated the Due Process Clause of the U.S. Constitution. In many cases, Courts ordered agencies to permit oral comment or to conduct trial-type hearings, but this judicial intervention was found to be invalid in all but rare cases in the *Vermont Yankee* case. *Vermont Yankee* prohibits Courts from fashioning variations on the APA's notice-and-comment requirements. This does not mean that hybrids are no longer created, though; the president and Congress continue to enact variations on the APA procedural model for rulemaking and some lower courts continue to order hybrid procedures, fashioning new legal theories to support their decisions.

The consequence of the additional procedures required through a myriad of executive orders and special legislation is that informal rulemaking is much more cumbersome and complex than required by the APA's simple requirements. See Figure 6-6 for a flowchart of the reality of Informal Rulemaking.

Agency Actions　　　　　　　　　　　　　　　　　　　　**OMB Actions**

Prerule Stage

Agencies may include an upcoming rulemaking in the Regulatory Plan, after receiving approval from the agency head or regulatory policy officer,* or in the Unified Agenda. Agencies will continue to do so throughout the rule's lifecycle.

Agencies may solicit public opinion.

Publish an Advanced Notice of Proposed Rulemaking.

Receive petitions for rulemaking.

Hold public meetings.

Agencies may solicit the advice of federal advisory committees.

OMB may send agencies prompt letters.

Agencies may be forced to initiate a rulemaking as a result of a lawsuit.

Review under Paperwork Reduction Act.

Agencies may submit proposals to collect information to OMB.

Revise and resubmit or withdraw.

Disapprove.　　Approve.　　Approve consistent with change.

Agencies may collect information from 10 or more people.

Begin drafting proposed rule after receiving approval from the agency head or regulatory policy officer.*

Analyze potential impact on a variety of entities.

Proposed Rule Stage

Analyze impacts on small businesses or other small entities, under the Regulatory Flexibility Act. Submit analysis to the Small Business Administration Office of Advocacy.

Identify the market failure or other problem the rule would address and assess the significance of that market failure or problem.

OMB may consult with the Small Business Administration Office of Advocacy on rules, which may have impacts on small businesses or other small entities.

Analyze impacts on the quality of the environment under the National Environmental Policy Act.

Analyze costs and benefits to state, local and tribal governments under the Unfunded Mandates Reform Act.

Determine if the rule would require collection of information from ten or more people. If so, prepare and submit proposal to OMB.

Review under Paperwork Reduction Act.

Perform other analysis as necessary or as required by law or executive order.

Revise and resubmit or withdraw.

Disapprove.　　Approve.　　Approve consistent with change.

Determine significance of rule.

If the rule would have an annual effect on the economy of $100 million or more, designate the rule "economically significant." Notify OMB of designation.

If the rule would interfere with the regulatory action of another agency; alter entitlement spending, grants, loans or user fees; or raise new legal or policy issues, designate the rule "significant." Notify OMB of designation.

If the rule would have none of these effects, designate the rule "not significant." Notify OMB of designation.

Approve or change designation. For significant rules, decide whether the agency should prepare a Regulatory Impact Analysis.** Notify the agency.

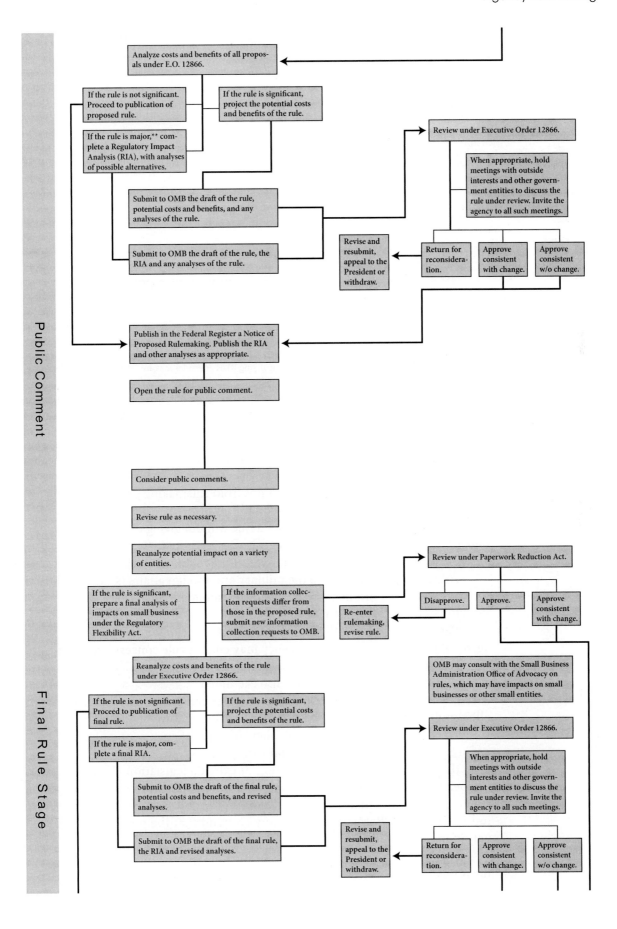

Public Comment

Final Rule Stage

Analyze costs and benefits of all proposals under E.O. 12866.

If the rule is not significant. Proceed to publication of proposed rule.

If the rule is significant, project the potential costs and benefits of the rule.

If the rule is major,** complete a Regulatory Impact Analysis (RIA), with analyses of possible alternatives.

Submit to OMB the draft of the rule, potential costs and benefits, and any analyses of the rule.

Submit to OMB the draft of the rule, the RIA and any analyses of the rule.

Review under Executive Order 12866.

When appropriate, hold meetings with outside interests and other government entities to discuss the rule under review. Invite the agency to all such meetings.

Revise and resubmit, appeal to the President or withdraw.

Return for reconsideration.

Approve consistent with change.

Approve consistent w/o change.

Publish in the Federal Register a Notice of Proposed Rulemaking. Publish the RIA and other analyses as appropriate.

Open the rule for public comment.

Consider public comments.

Revise rule as necessary.

Reanalyze potential impact on a variety of entities.

If the rule is significant, prepare a final analysis of impacts on small business under the Regulatory Flexibility Act.

If the information collection requests differ from those in the proposed rule, submit new information collection requests to OMB.

Review under Paperwork Reduction Act.

Disapprove.

Approve.

Approve consistent with change.

Re-enter rulemaking, revise rule.

OMB may consult with the Small Business Administration Office of Advocacy on rules, which may have impacts on small businesses or other small entities.

Reanalyze costs and benefits of the rule under Executive Order 12866.

If the rule is not significant. Proceed to publication of final rule.

If the rule is significant, project the potential costs and benefits of the rule.

If the rule is major, complete a final RIA.

Review under Executive Order 12866.

When appropriate, hold meetings with outside interests and other government entities to discuss the rule under review. Invite the agency to all such meetings.

Submit to OMB the draft of the final rule, potential costs and benefits, and revised analyses.

Submit to OMB the draft of the final rule, the RIA and revised analyses.

Revise and resubmit, appeal to the President or withdraw.

Return for reconsideration.

Approve consistent with change.

Approve consistent w/o change.

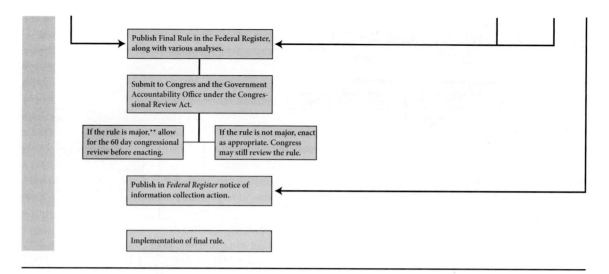

FIGURE 6-6 OMB rulemaking flowchart.

Source: OMB Watch.

*Under E.O. 12866, agencies may only "initiate" a rulemaking with the approval of the agency head or agency regulatory policy officer. The agency head or regulatory policy officer may also halt a rulemaking at any time.

**Rules that are "economically significant" (and, therefore, require an accompanying RIA) and rules that are "significant" but for which OMB requires the preparation of an RIA are collectively known as "major" rules.

From "Notice-and-Comment Rulemaking." This chart was produced by OMB Watch, now named the Center for Effective Government. Reproduced by permission of the Center for Effective Government.

6.5(d) Exempted Rulemaking

The APA contains a number of exemptions from rulemaking procedures. If an exemption applies, an agency need not comply with either formal or informal rulemaking; therefore, the agency may issue a rule without giving interested persons an opportunity to participate. Of course, agencies may permit interested persons to participate in some manner beyond what the APA requires, and this is sometimes done.

All rulemaking relating to the military and foreign affairs is exempted from the procedural requirements of the APA. Presumably, this is largely due to the need for secrecy in such matters.

Personnel matters of the government are also exempted, as are agency management issues. For example, an agency may enact a rule concerning the process for disciplining its own employees, without having to give public notice. Government grant and contract matters are also exempted.

Section 553(b)(3) contains an important exemption: An agency need not allow public participation when developing interpretive rules or procedural rules. This includes statements of "policy, or rules of agency organization, procedure, or practice." Remember that interpretive rules do not state anything new; they are an agency's interpretation of existing legislation. This exemption has been the subject of much criticism. Although interpretive rules and policy statements do not change or add to existing law, they can significantly affect individual rights. Because of this, many contend that the public should be involved in their creation.

Finally, § 553(b)(3)—a catchall provision—permits an agency to bypass the notice-and-comment procedure whenever it is "impracticable, unnecessary, or contrary to the public interest" to use the procedure. An agency relying on this provision must have "good cause" to skip the procedure and must explain its reasons for doing so in its final rule. This decision may be appealed to a Court.

The military, foreign affairs, and agency management exemptions apply to all rulemaking requirements. An agency need not allow public participation or publish notice of its final rules concerning these matters. The other exemptions, however, apply only to public participation. Therefore, in all other instances, an agency must publish its final rule and explain why it did not permit participation of interested persons.

6.5(e) Negotiated Rulemaking

The APA also provides for "negotiated rulemaking."[22] Negotiated rulemaking is not a separate form of rulemaking. It is a congressionally created hybrid. Because public comments in informal rulemaking are not submitted until after an agency proposes a rule, interested parties were often put into antagonistic positions, some favoring the rule and others not. In some instances this leads to an adversarial exchange in which alternatives that may satisfy all the parties are ignored. In addition to not producing the best rule, many people also believe that these problems cause delay in the rulemaking process and push unhappy participants into litigation. To remedy this problem, Congress amended the APA in 1990 to permit agencies to negotiate the development of a proposed rule with specific interested parties. President Clinton took a number of steps to facilitate negotiated rulemaking, including mandating in 1994 that certain agencies use it.[23] The APA requires agencies to consider the following factors when determining whether to use negotiated rulemaking:

1. Is there a need for a rule?
2. Are there a limited number of parties that will be significantly affected by the rule?
3. Can a committee be formed that will adequately represent those with a significant interest? Will these parties negotiate in good faith?
4. Is it reasonably likely that the committee will reach a consensus?
5. Does the agency have, and will it commit, the necessary resources to permit the committee to do its work?
6. Will the process unnecessarily delay the rulemaking process?
7. Is the agency willing to use the rule that is negotiated?

This process may be used when only a small number of parties have an interest in the subject. The agency must first publish a notice of negotiated rulemaking in the *Federal Register*. On the announced date, the interested parties, the agency, and a mediator meet to discuss and develop a proposed rule. The meetings are open to the public. The proposed rule must then undergo the standard notice-and-comment procedure. Many federal agencies have availed themselves of this procedure; the Environmental Protection Agency and the Department of Education are two agencies that have developed final rules through negotiated rulemaking. At least one scholar has concluded, however, that negotiated rulemaking has not been highly successful in reducing the time it takes to develop rules or in preventing litigation.[24]

Vermont Yankee Nuclear Power Corp. v. Natural Resources Defense Council

435 U.S. 519 (1978)

In 1946, Congress enacted the Administrative Procedure Act, which as we have noted elsewhere was not only "a new, basic and comprehensive regulation of procedures in agencies," . . . but was also a legislative enactment, which settled "long-continued and hard-fought contentions, and enacts a formula upon which opposing social and political forces have come to rest." . . . Section 4 of the Act, 5 U.S.C. § 553 (1976 ed.), dealing with rulemaking, requires in subsection (b) that "notice of proposed rulemaking shall be published in the Federal Register . . .," describes the contents of that notice, and goes on to require in subsection (c) that after notice the agency "shall give interested persons an opportunity to participate in the rulemaking through submission of written data, views, or arguments with or without opportunity for oral presentation. After consideration of the relevant matter presented, the agency shall incorporate in the rules adopted a concise general statement of their basis and purpose." Interpreting this provision of the Act in *United States v. Allegheny-Ludlum Steel Corp.*, 406 U.S. 742, 92 S. Ct. 1941, 32 L. Ed. 2d 453 (1972) . . . we held that generally speaking this section of the Act established the maximum procedural requirements, which Congress was willing to have courts impose upon agencies in conducting rulemaking procedures. Agencies are free to grant additional procedural rights in the exercise of their discretion, but reviewing courts are generally not free to impose them if the agencies have not chosen to grant them. This is not to say necessarily that there are no circumstances which would ever justify a court in overturning agency action because of failure to employ procedures beyond those required by statute. But such circumstances, if they exist, are extremely rare.

Even apart from the Administrative Procedure Act this Court has for more than four decades emphasized that the formulation of procedures was basically to be left within the discretion of the agencies to which Congress had confided the responsibility for substantive judgments. . . . [T]his principle [is] "an outgrowth of the congressional determination that administrative agencies and administrators will be familiar with the industries, which they regulate and will be in a better position than federal courts or Congress itself to design procedural rules adapted to the peculiarities of the industry and the tasks of the agency involved." . . .

Respondent NRDC argues that [the Administrative Procedure Act] merely establishes lower procedural bounds and that a court may routinely require more than the minimum when an agency's proposed rule addresses complex or technical factual issues or "Issues of Great Public Import." . . . We have, however, previously shown that our decisions reject that view. . . . We also think the legislative history, even the part which [NRDC] cites, does not bear out its contention. The Senate Report explains what eventually became § 4 thus:

> This subsection states . . . the minimum requirements of public rule-making procedure short of statutory hearing. Under it agencies might in addition confer with industry advisory committees, consult organizations, hold informal hearings, and the like. Considerations of practicality, necessity, and public interest . . . will naturally govern the agency's determination of the extent to which public submission of facts will be either useful to the agency or a protection to the public, [and] should naturally be accorded more elaborate public procedures. S. Rep. No. 752, 79th Cong., 1st Sess., 14–15 (1945).

Vermont Yankee Nuclear Power Corp. v. Natural Resources Defense Council 435 U.S. 519 (1978), U.S Supreme Court.

6.5(f) Advisory Committees

Like negotiated rulemaking, the use of advisory committees is a particular example of hybrid rulemaking. Both Congress and the president have encouraged, and sometimes required, agencies to receive the advice of committees of experts before regulating certain subjects. Because of the significance of these groups, advisory committee meetings are open to the public.

6.6 RATEMAKING

Agencies may be delegated the responsibility of establishing rates for an industry. This function is normally legislative in nature, and therefore, free from due process concerns. However, not every instance of ratemaking is legislative. It is possible for an agency to be engaged in what amounts to an adjudicative function when setting rates.

When an agency sets a rate that applies to an industry that has many producers or providers, it has made a rule of general applicability. For these decisions, legislative-type facts are relied upon. Information about an industry, without particular attention to one member of that industry, is legislative. It is different when there is only one member of an industry and an agency sets its rate. In this latter case, the agency is engaging in decision making that affects an individual business.

If an agency focuses on one particular individual or entity when making a decision—whether that decision is characterized as a rule or an adjudication—it is conducting an adjudication. If there is only one member of an industry, as is often true of gas or electric companies, an examination of that industry is an examination of a single business. Due process applies to adjudicative proceedings; therefore, if there is only one member of an industry, that entity is entitled to due process in ratemaking.

When an agency engages in ratemaking that is legislative in character, it must comply with the APA's rulemaking requirements. When an agency engages in ratemaking that is adjudicative in character, it must not only comply with the APA's adjudication procedures, but also satisfy due process.

6.7 TAXATION AND REVENUES

Tax and revenue-raising rules also deserve special mention. Most revenue-raising law comes from legislative enactment. Taxation by Congress creates no due process concerns because the people have control over who sits in Congress. Congress gets its authority to govern from the governed; further, elected representatives are presumed to keep the citizenry informed and on notice of legislation.

However, the authority to impose a tax may be delegated by Congress to agencies. In such cases, the decision to tax is not being made by elected representatives. Therefore, when administrative bodies engage in revenue-raising rulemaking, due process requires that notice to the public be given and that taxpayers be provided an opportunity to be heard.[25] In a 1907 case addressing this issue, the Supreme Court stated:

> But where the legislature of a state, instead of fixing the tax itself,
> commits to some subordinate body the duty of determining whether,
> in what amount, and upon whom it shall be levied, and of making

its assessment and apportionment, due process of law requires that, at some stage of the proceedings, before the tax becomes irrevocably fixed, the taxpayer shall have an opportunity to be heard, of which he must have notice, either personal, by publication, or by a law fixing the time and place of the hearing.[26]

In addition to due process concerns, the delegation itself must give the agency an "intelligible principle" from which to act, as discussed in Section 5.2.

6.8 CONTROLLING RULEMAKING AUTHORITY

Agency officials possess considerable discretion in rulemaking. At the front end, agency officials decide, in most cases, whether rulemaking is needed at all. During rulemaking, agency officials decide what processes must be followed, what rules govern those processes, and the timing of the various stages of the process. In the end, it is agency officials who review the evidence, find the facts, and draft the final rule. However, this authority is not unchecked. All three constitutionally created governmental branches play a role in controlling the authority of administrative officials in rulemaking.

You have learned many limitations already. To begin with, the rulemaking procedure set forth in the APA is intended to limit the discretion of agency officials by mandating minimum rulemaking procedures. Second, Congress can withhold from, or otherwise limit, the authority of an agency to make rules. As you read earlier, there is no inherent authority to promulgate substantive rules.

The Rulemaking Delegation Congress controls agencies in various ways. Of course the greater authority Congress has is the creation, definition, and funding of agencies. Defining and refining its delegation of rulemaking authority is also an important control. Whether Congress had delegated the authority to regulate tobacco products to the Food and Drug Administration was at issue in *FDA v. Brown & Williamson*.

FDA v. Brown & Williamson

529 U.S. 120529 (2000)

Justice O'Connor delivered the opinion of the Court.

This case involves one of the most troubling public health problems facing our Nation today: the thousands of premature deaths that occur each year because of tobacco use. In 1996, the Food and Drug Administration (FDA), after having expressly disavowed any such authority since its inception, asserted jurisdiction to regulate tobacco products. The FDA concluded that nicotine is a "drug" within the meaning of the Food, Drug, and Cosmetic Act (FDCA or Act), as amended, 21 U.S.C. § 301 *et seq.*, and that cigarettes and smokeless tobacco are "combination products" that deliver nicotine to the body. Pursuant to this authority, it promulgated regulations intended to reduce tobacco consumption among children and adolescents. The agency believed that because most tobacco consumers begin their use before reaching the age of 18, curbing tobacco use by minors could substantially reduce the prevalence of addiction in future generations and thus the incidence of tobacco-related death and disease.

Regardless of how serious the problem an administrative agency seeks to address, however, it may not exercise its authority "in a manner that is inconsistent with the administrative structure that Congress enacted into law." And although agencies are generally entitled to deference in the interpretation of statutes that they administer, a reviewing "court, as well as the agency, must give effect to the unambiguously expressed intent of Congress." *Chevron U.S.A. Inc. v. Natural Resources Defense Council, Inc.*, 467 U.S. 837, 842–843, 104 S. Ct. 2778, 81 L. Ed. 2d 694 (1984). In this case, we believe that Congress has clearly precluded the FDA from asserting jurisdiction to regulate tobacco products. Such authority is inconsistent with the intent that Congress has expressed in the FDCA's overall regulatory scheme and in the tobacco-specific legislation that it has enacted subsequent to the FDCA. In light of this clear intent, the FDA's assertion of jurisdiction is impermissible.

The FDCA grants the FDA, as the designee of the Secretary of Health and Human Services, the authority to regulate, among other items, "drugs" and "devices." The Act defines "drug" to include "articles (other than food) intended to affect the structure or any function of the body." 21 U.S.C. §§ 321(g)(1)(C). It defines "device," in part, as "an instrument, apparatus, implement, machine, contrivance, . . . or other similar or related article, including any component, part, or accessory, which is . . . intended to affect the structure or any function of the body." § 321(h). The Act also grants the FDA the authority to regulate so-called "combination products," which "constitute a combination of a drug, device, or biologic product." § 353(g)(1). The FDA has construed this provision as giving it the discretion to regulate combination products as drugs, as devices, or as both.

On August 11, 1995, the FDA published a proposed rule concerning the sale of cigarettes and smokeless tobacco to children and adolescents. The rule, which included several restrictions on the sale, distribution, and advertisement of tobacco products, was designed to reduce the availability and attractiveness of tobacco products to young people. A public comment period followed, during which the FDA received over 700,000 submissions, more than "at any other time in its history on any other subject."

On August 28, 1996, the FDA issued a final rule entitled "Regulations Restricting the Sale and Distribution of Cigarettes and Smokeless Tobacco to Protect Children and Adolescents." The FDA determined that nicotine is a "drug" and that cigarettes and smokeless tobacco are "drug delivery devices," and, therefore, it had jurisdiction under the FDCA to regulate tobacco products as customarily marketed—that is, without manufacturer claims of therapeutic benefit. First, the FDA found that tobacco products "affect the structure or any function of the body" because nicotine "has significant pharmacological effects." Specifically, nicotine "exerts psychoactive, or mood-altering, effects on the brain" that cause and sustain addiction, having both tranquilizing and stimulation effects, and control weight. Second, the FDA determined that these effects were "intended" under the FDCA because they "are so widely known and foreseeable that [they] may be deemed to have been intended by the manufacturers," consumers use tobacco products "predominantly or nearly exclusively" to obtain these effects. Finally, the agency concluded that cigarettes and smokeless tobacco are "combination products" because, in addition to containing nicotine, they include device components that deliver a controlled amount of nicotine to the body. Having resolved the jurisdictional question, the FDA next explained the policy justifications for its regulations, detailing the deleterious health effects associated with tobacco use. It found that tobacco consumption was "the single leading cause of preventable death in the United States." According to the FDA, "[m]ore that 400,000 people die each year from tobacco-related illnesses, such as cancer, respiratory illnesses, and heart disease." Ibid. The agency also determined that the only way to reduce the amount of tobacco-related illness and mortality was to reduce the level of addiction, a goal that could be accomplished

(continued)

only by preventing children and adolescents from starting to use tobacco. The FDA found that 82% of adult smokers had their first cigarette before the age of 18, and more than half had already become regular smokers by that age. It also found that children were beginning to smoke at a younger age. . . . [The FDA then issued a set of regulations restricting advertising and youth access to tobacco products.]

A threshold issue is the appropriate framework for analyzing the FDA's assertion of authority to regulate tobacco products. Because this case involves an administrative agency's construction of a statute that it administers, our analysis is governed by *Chevron U.S.A. Inc. v. Natural Resources Defense Council, Inc.,* 467 U.S. 837, 104 S. Ct. 2778, 81 L. Ed. 2d 694 (1984). Under *Chevron,* a reviewing court must first ask "whether Congress has directly spoken to the precise question at issue." If Congress has done so, the inquiry is at an end; the court "must give effect to the unambiguously expressed intent of Congress. But if Congress has not specifically addressed the question, a reviewing court must respect the agency's construction of the statute so long as it is permissible. . . .

In determining whether Congress has specifically addressed the question at issue, a reviewing court should not confine itself to examining a particular statutory provision in isolation. The meaning—or ambiguity—of certain words or phrases may only become evident when placed in context. . . . Similarly, the meaning of one statute may be affected by other Acts, particularly where Congress has spoken subsequently and more specifically to the topic at hand. . . . With these principles in mind, we find that Congress has directly spoken to the issue here and precluded the FDA's jurisdiction to regulate tobacco products. . . .

Viewing the FDCA as a whole, it is evident that one of the Act's objectives is to ensure that any product regulated by the FDA is "safe" and "effective" for its intended use. . . .

The FDCA misbranding and device classification provisions, therefore, make evident that were the FDA to regulate cigarettes and smokeless tobacco, the Act would require the agency to ban them. In fact, based on these provisions, the FDA itself has previously taken the position that if tobacco products were within its jurisdiction, "they would have to be removed from the market because it would be impossible to prove they were safe for their intended use." . . .

Congress, however, has foreclosed the removal of tobacco products from the market. A provision of the United States Code currently in force states that "the marketing of tobacco constitutes one of the greatest industries of the United States with ramifying activities, which directly affect interstate and foreign commerce". . . . More importantly, Congress has directly addressed the problem of tobacco and health through legislation on six occasions since 1965. . . . When Congress enacted these statutes, the adverse health consequences of tobacco use were well known, as were nicotine's pharmacological effects. . . . Nonetheless, Congress stopped well short of ordering a ban. Instead, it has generally regulated the labeling and advertisement of tobacco products, expressly providing that it is the policy of Congress that "commerce and the national economy be . . . protected to the maximum extent consistent with" consumers "being adequately informed about any adverse health effects." Congress's decisions to regulate labeling and advertising and to adopt the express policy of protecting "commerce and the national economy . . . to the maximum extent" reveal its intent that tobacco products remain on the market. Indeed, the collective premise of these statutes is that cigarettes and smokeless tobacco will continue to be sold in the United States. A ban of tobacco products by the FDA would, therefore, plainly contradict congressional policy. . . .

FDA v. Brown & Williamson, 529 U.S. 120 (2000), U.S Supreme Court.

By no means do we question the seriousness of the problem that the FDA had sought to address. The agency has amply demonstrated that tobacco use, particularly among children and adolescents, poses perhaps the single most significant threat to public health in the United States. Nonetheless, no matter how "important, conspicuous, and controversial" the issue, and regardless of how likely the public is to hold the Executive Branch politically accountable, an administrative agency's power to regulate in the public interest must always be grounded in a valid grant of authority from Congress. . . . Reading the FDCA as a whole, as well as in conjunction with Congress's subsequent tobacco-specific legislation, it is plain that Congress has not given the FDA the authority that it seeks to exercise here. For these reasons, the FDA's rules are invalid.

Recall also that a congressional delegation of rulemaking authority must be accompanied by an intelligible principle, a requirement aimed at limiting the policy discretion of the receiving agency. Other controls are available to Congress, such as requiring hybrid procedures in special cases. Finally, as the constitutional lawmaker, Congress can repeal or amend all administrative rules.

Congressional Review Act and Legislative Veto   In addition to controlling delegations of rulemaking authority, Congress has often attempted to control rules themselves. The so-called legislative veto is an example. As you learned earlier in this book, Congress has on many occasions empowered one of its houses or a committee to review and invalidate agency rules. However, this practice was found violative of the Presentment Clause of Article I in *INS v. Chadha*,[27] which appears in Chapter 2. The Presentment Clause requires bills to be passed by both houses of Congress and presented to the president for approval or veto. Vetoed laws may still be enacted if two-third of both houses vote to override a presidential veto.

In response to the *Chadha* decision Congress enacted the ***Congressional Review Act (CRA)*** of 1996.[28] This legislation requires agencies to submit newly created major rules to Congress and to the General Accounting Office (GAO) for review. Of course Congress has the authority to change, with presidential support or with a supermajority overriding a veto, any agency rule at any time. No statute can alter this constitutional authority. What the CRA does is to provide a mechanism for Congress to review and disapprove rules before they become effective. And to address the Present Clause problem in *Chadha*, Congress's disapproval of rules occurs through traditional lawmaking procedure. Both houses must disapprove and the resolution is presented to the president.

The CRA distinguishes between major and nonmajor rules. All rules must be submitted to Congress for review but major rules are subject to special review by the GAO. A rule is major if it has resulted in or is likely to result in

(1) an annual effect on the economy of $100 million or more; or
(2) a major increase in costs or prices for consumers, individual industries, federal, state, or local government agencies, or geographic regions; or
(3) significant adverse effects on competition, employment, investment, productivity, or innovation, or on the ability of United States-based enterprises to compete with foreign-based enterprises in domestic and export markets.

LEGAL TERM

Congressional Review Act (CRA) A federal statute that requires agencies to submit newly created rules to Congress for review and possibly disapproval, pursuant to the constitutional lawmaking process, by Congress.

The GAO examines major rules for compliance with rulemaking procedures and reports its findings to Congress. It is not required to do this nonmajor rules.

The APA defines the waiting period, 30 days, before a rule becomes effective. The CRA trumps the APA's 30 day requirement. It delays the effective dates of major rules for 60 days, providing the GAO time to make its report and Congress to conduct its oversight. After its review Congress can do nothing, which enables the rule to become effective, or it may enact a joint resolution disapproving the rule. As required by the Presentment Clause of Article I, such joint resolutions are presented to the President for signature, veto, or no action. If a president vetoes a disapproval, Congress can override the veto with a two-third vote in each house, as is true of any other legislation.

The CRA has not been often used to invalidate rules. Indeed, only one rule was disapproved in the first 14 years of the CRA.[29] The minimal use of the authority can likely be attributed to the presentment procedure. In most cases a president can be expected to veto disapproval legislation of rules promulgated by the president's administration, forcing Congress into the difficult task of securing a two-third vote in each house to override the veto.

Presidential Controls   The president also plays a role in controlling agency rulemaking. Cornelius Kerwin commented in his book on rulemaking that President Nixon was the first of many presidents to take managing agencies seriously.[30] You have already read examples of the many executive orders that are intended to limit the discretion of bureaucrats.

Judicial Controls   The Courts also play a role in checking agency discretion, through judicial review of agency rules. You will learn in a later chapter that agencies are required to issue statements of their findings with their rules. These findings are intended to keep them accountable to the public, Congress, the president, and the Courts. These findings, as you will see, assist a reviewing Court in understanding the reasoning behind an agency's rule. In addition to reviewing the substance of rules, Courts also determine if rules were promulgated correctly. This subject is covered in greater depth in Chapter 9.

Finally, agencies exercise self-control. Many agencies have promulgated rules or developed practices that expand citizen participation, require more impact studies, and in other ways increase the obligations of the agency when it makes rules.

6.9 CONCLUSION

The rulemaking provisions of the APA establish the minimum procedures that agencies must use to develop and promulgate rules. The two forms of rulemaking, informal and formal, are supplemented by presidential, congressional, and self-imposed hybrid procedures. The intention of these additional procedures is to increase public participation, bring more information to the table, increase agency accountability, and facilitate consensus. In short, they are intended to produce better rules—but this has not occurred without a cost. Additional procedures often translate into a more expensive and time-consuming process.

REVIEW **QUESTIONS**

1. If a federal agency wishes to publish a notice of proposed rulemaking, should it publish the notice in the *Federal Register* or the *Code of Federal Regulations*?

2. From where do agencies derive their authority to make rules?

3. Match the following characteristics with either rulemaking (R) or adjudication (A):

   _____ Affects future behavior

   _____ Involves past behavior

   _____ Is directed at large groups

   _____ Normally involves few people

   _____ Decision is based on policy concerns

   _____ Decision is based on specific facts

   _____ May result in individual (or corporate) sanctions

   _____ Establishes standards of conduct on which a person or entity may be sanctioned in the future

4. The primary difference between formal rulemaking and informal rulemaking is that a _____ must be held in formal rulemaking and not in informal rulemaking.

5. Briefly state the three requirements for informal rulemaking under the APA.

State whether each of the following (questions 6–9) would be exempted from the rulemaking procedure requirements of the APA.

6. The Environmental Protection Agency intends to establish the maximum amount of gasoline that may escape from underground gasoline storage containers.

7. The Department of State intends to establish rules concerning passport qualifications.

8. The Interstate Commerce Commission intends to establish rules governing the safe transportation of toxic waste between states.

9. The Interstate Commerce Commission intends to establish rules governing the suspension, termination, and promotion of the officers responsible for overseeing the transportation of toxic waste between states.

10. The administrative equivalent of a congressionally enacted statute is a(n) _____.

11. What is negotiated rulemaking? What factors must an agency take into consideration when determining whether to use negotiated rulemaking?

12. Identify two congressional and two presidential controls of agency rulemaking.

CRITICAL THINKING AND **APPLICATIONS PROBLEMS**

Answer problems 1 and 2 using the following facts:

The Congress of the United States enacts the following statute:

IMPORTATION OF FRUIT

All fruit imported into the United States shall be inspected for dangerousness by the Food and Drug Administration (FDA). Dangerous fruit shall not enter or pass through any port of the United States. The FDA is hereby authorized to promulgate regulations. It shall conduct a hearing before any rule is established.

1. The Food and Drug Administration determines that a definition of *dangerous* is needed. What procedure must the FDA follow when making this decision?

2. The Food and Drug Administration decides to establish a set of guidelines detailing how and when inspections of imported fruit will occur, what fees will

be charged to fruit importers, and what documents must be presented to the agency by fruit importers. What procedure must the FDA follow when making these determinations?

3. You work for a U.S. senator, who asks you to draft a bill providing the Federal Communications Commission (FCC) with the authority to seize cellular telephones that are manufactured, sold, or used in violation of federal law. The senator instructs you to include language permitting the FCC to promulgate the necessary regulations; however, the senator wants the FCC to conduct oral hearings before making rules. Draft a rule, taking into consideration the senator's directives and any constitutional issues you think are implicated.

4. Do you believe that agencies are adequately accountable in rulemaking? Explain your answer.

ENDNOTES

1. *See Craig v. Boren*, 429 U.S. 190 (1976), for an example of when the test was applied to a gender-based classification; *Lalli v. Lalli*, 439 U.S. 259 (1978), for a classification based on illegitimacy; and *Ball v. James*, 451 U.S. 355 (1981), for a case involving a constitutional right.

2. *Prentis v. Atlantic Coast Line Co.*, 211 U.S. 210, 226 (1908).

3. See Cann, *Administrative Law* 19 (Sage, 1998) (citing other authority).

4. Schwartz, *Administrative Law* (3rd ed. 1991).

5. *Chevron v. Natural Resources Defense Council*, 467 U.S. 837 (1984).

6. K. Davis, *Administrative Law* § 5.02 (1972).

7. *Skidmore v. Swift & Co.*, 323 U.S. 134 (1944).

8. 394 U.S. 759, 764 (1969).

9. 410 U.S. 224 (1973).

10. APA § 557(c)(3)(A).

11. *Id.* § 553(c).

12. *Id.* § 557(b).

13. Schwartz, *Administrative Law* (3rd ed. 1991).

14. Mashaw, *Administrative Law* 459 (3rd ed. 1991).

15. See *Frontline: The Interrogator*: PBS (2013) and *Nova: The Spy Factory*: PBS. Both programs can be viewed at no cost at *PBS.org*.

16. See *Frontline: The Man Who Knew*: PBS (2002). The entire program can be viewed at no cost at *PBS.org*.

17. See *Frontline: The Warning*: PBS (2009). The entire program can be viewed at no cost at *PBS.org*. Also Goodman, Peter S., *Taking Hard New Look at a Greenspan Legacy*, October 8, 2008. *New York Times*.

Article Can be found at *http://www.nytimes.com/2008/10/09/business/economy/09greenspan.html?pagewanted=all&_r=0*

18. Cornelius Kerwin, *Rulemaking: How Government Agencies Write Law and Make Policy* (3rd ed. 2003); *Cong. Q.* (1994).

19. 15 U.S.C. § 57(a).

20. *Sierra Club v. Costle*, 657 F.2d 298 (D.C. Cir. 1981), *rev'd on other grounds*, 463 U.S. 680.

21. For additional information on presidential control of rulemaking, *see* Kerwin at 122 *et seq.*; Matthew Matule, *Congress, the Court, and Regulatory Oversight After Myer v. Bush: Should the Executive Office of the President Be Shielded from Congressional Sunshine?* 18 *Vt. L. Rev.* 834 (1994).

22. 5 U.S.C. § 561 *et seq.*

23. Exec. Order No. 12,866 (1994).

24. Cary Coglianese, *Assessing Consensus: The Promise and Performance of Negotiated Rulemaking*, 46 Duke L.J. 1255 (1997).

25. *See Missouri v. Jenkins*, 495 U.S. 33 (1990) (concurring opinion at 66–67); *Londoner v. Denver*, 210 U.S. 373, 385–86 (1907).

26. *Londoner*, 210 U.S. at 385–86.

27. *INS v. Chadha*, 462 U.S. 919 (1983)

28. 5 U.S.C. §§801 et seq.

29. Copeland, Curtis (2010), *Rulemaking Requirements and Authorities in the Dodd-Frank Wall Street Reform and Consumer Protection Act*, Congressional Research Service, p. 27.

30. Kerwin at 122.

chapter **seven**

AGENCY INVESTIGATIONS AND INFORMATION COLLECTION

LEARNING OBJECTIVES

After completing this chapter, you should be able to

- Identify at least three methods discussed in the chapter that agencies use to collect information (or require records to be maintained) from people and businesses under federal law.

- Explain how the Fourth Amendment to the U.S. Constitution limits the authority of agencies to conduct tests and inspections, citing at least two of the major cases discussed in the chapter. You should also be able to explain why the Fourth Amendment is applied differently in the administrative context than in the criminal justice context.

- Apply the law (e.g., APA, Fourth Amendment) that you learned to case scenarios involving agency information collection and inspections.

- Brief a judicial opinion with little outside assistance. You should be successful in identifying the relevant facts. You should also be successful in identifying the legal issue and analyzing the court's rationale in at least 50 percent of your briefs.

Officious examination can be expensive, so much so it eats up men's substance. It can be time consuming, clogging the processes of business. It can become persecution when carried beyond reason.

JUSTICE RUTLEDGE[1]

Justice Rutledge, Oklahoma Press Publ'g Co. v. Walling, 327 U.S. 186, 213 (1946), United States Supreme Court.

7.1 ACQUIRING INFORMATION

Information is the lifeblood of agency decision making. Agencies depend on information when promulgating rules and conducting adjudications, and in all other aspects of performing their mandate. The public benefits from an educated agency; the more informed the agency, the more likely it will be successful in its objectives. Nevertheless, it is a fundamental tenet of American political ideology that individuals should be free from excessive governmental interference in their lives. This chapter examines these two often-competing interests: the administrative agency's interest in obtaining information in order to fulfill its mandate versus the individual's right to be free from excessive governmental interference in personal and business affairs.

7.2 RECORDKEEPING AND REPORTING

One method used by administrative agencies to acquire information is requiring individuals and businesses to produce and maintain records. An agency may require that these records be held subject to review by the agency, or the record producer may be required to provide the records to the agency. The former is known as *recordkeeping* and the latter is known as *reporting*. Most agencies, especially regulatory agencies, possess broad authority to require recordkeeping and reporting. The authority of agencies to require reporting is not limited to instances when violation of a law is suspected. An agency may require individuals or businesses to report information to the agency simply so that the agency can educate itself or monitor compliance with the law.

The costs to individuals and businesses of maintaining records and reporting to the government can be high. According to one source, small businesses commit nearly a billion hours per year to the completion of government forms. This accounts for $100 million in small business expenses.[2] The total costs to all businesses and individuals in the United States must be many times greater. Of course, much of this money is well spent. The Environmental Protection Agency (EPA), for example, estimated that by the late 1990s businesses had spent nearly $523 million to comply with the Clean Air Act. On the other side, the EPA also estimated that the Clean Air Act had saved as much as $41 trillion in health care costs.[3]

The APA does not require particular recordkeeping or reporting, in line with the theory that the APA is intended to be a procedural rather than a substantive statute. The APA does, however, provide that reporting may be required as provided for by other laws.[4] In general, an agency may require the disclosure of information, or that records be kept if the following criteria are met:

1. The agency has jurisdiction over the subject and individual concerned *and*
2. The requirement is reasonable and not overly burdensome *and*
3. The information is not privileged.

The first of these three criteria is easy to meet in most instances. An agency's enabling and controlling statutes define its jurisdiction, and broad interpretations are normal. However, if an agency attempts to regulate a subject area or individual not within its jurisdictional ambit, its actions are void. For example, the Food and Drug Administration may not regulate the disposal of toxic materials, a responsibility delegated to other agencies, such as the EPA.

Agencies may not require recordkeeping or reporting that is unduly burdensome or harmful. For example, if the cost of providing the required information (i.e., locating, tallying, and copying the information) is extremely high, the individual or business may be excused from compliance. In addition, a regulated party may be excused if some harm results from compliance. For instance, a demand for trade secret or patented information would probably be invalid. The damage that could result from this type of information becoming available may be so great as to excuse compliance. The authority of the Federal Trade Commission to require a regulated company to submit reports is discussed in the *Morton Salt* case.

Finally, privileged information is exempt from the compulsory process of agencies. The Fifth Amendment's privilege against self-incrimination is an example of a federal constitutional privilege. State constitutions also contain privileges; common law and statutory privileges apply. Husband–wife, attorney–client, and physician–patient are examples of common law and statutory privileges.

United States v. Morton Salt Co.

338 U.S. 632 (1950)

This is a controversy as to the power of the Federal Trade Commission to require corporations to file reports showing how they have complied with a decree of the Court of Appeals enforcing the Commission's cease and desist order, in addition to those reports required by the decree itself. . . . The decree expressly was "without prejudice to the right of the United States, as provided in Section 5(l) of the Federal Trade Commission Act, to prosecute suits to recover civil penalties for violations of the said modified order to cease and desist hereby affirmed, and without prejudice to the right of the Federal Trade Commission to initiate contempt proceedings for violations of this decree." The reports of compliance were subsequently filed and accepted, and the matter appears to have rested there for slightly more than four years.

On September 2, 1947, the Commission ordered additional and highly particularized reports to show continuing compliance with the decree. This was done without application to the court, was not authorized by any provision of its decree, and is not provided for in § 5 of the statute under which the Commission's original cease and desist order had issued. The new order recited that it was issued on the Commission's own motion pursuant to its published Rule of Practice . . . and the authority granted by subsections (a) and (b) of § 6 of the Trade Commission Act. It ordered these and other parties restrained by the earlier decree to file within 30 days "additional reports showing in detail the manner and form in which they have been, and are now, complying with said modified order to cease and desist and said decree." It demanded of each producer a "complete statement" of the "prices, terms, and conditions of sale of salt, together with books or compilations of freight rates used in calculating delivered prices, price lists and price announcements distributed, published or employed in marketing salt from and after January 1, 1944.". . .

The Court of Appeals found the Commission to be without statutory authority to require additional reports as to compliance. Section 6 of the Federal Trade Commission Act, it thought, could not be invoked in connection with a decree sought and entered pursuant to § 5, which sections the court regarded as insulated from each other and directed to wholly different situations. Section 6, so it was held, authorized requirements only of "special reports" supplemental to "annual reports" and could not be authority for requiring special supplement[s] to a report of compliance required by a court decree in a § 5 case.

The Commission's Organic Act, § 5, comprehensively provides substantive and procedural rules for checking unfair methods of competition. The procedure is complete from complaint and service of process through final order, court review, and enforcement proceedings. . . . It is to be noted, however, that although complete

(continued)

otherwise, this section confers no power to investigate this or any other matter. That power, without which all others would be vain, must be found in other sections of the Act. The Commission, for power to investigate compliance with a § 5 order, has turned to § 6, which authorizes it to require certain reports but is not expressly applicable to § 5 case[s]. . . .

Section 6, on which the Commission relies, among other things and with exceptions not material, adds the power "to investigate from time to time the organization, business, conduct, practices, and management of any corporation engaged in commerce, . . . and its relation to other corporations and to individuals, associations, and partnerships." It also authorizes the Commission "to require, by general or special orders, corporations engaged in commerce . . . to file with the commission in such form as the commission may prescribe, annual or special, or both annual or special, reports or answers in writing to specific questions. . . ." It is argued, however, and the court below agreed, that the "special report" authorized by statute does not embrace the one here asked as to the method of compliance with the decree. We find nothing in the legislative history that would justify so limiting the meaning of special reports, or holding that the report here asked is not such a one. . . . An annual report of a corporation is a recurrent and relatively standardized affair. The special report was used to enable the Commission to elicit any information beyond the ordinary data of a routine annual report. If the report asked here is not a special report, we would be hard put to define one. . . .

We conclude that the authority of the Commission under § 6 to require special reports of corporations includes special reports of the manner in which they are complying with decrees enforcing § 5 cease and desist orders. . . .

United States v. Morton Salt Co, 338 U.S. 632 (1950), United States Supreme Court.

7.2(a) Fifth Amendment Aspects

Recordkeeping and reporting requirements raise important constitutional issues usually involving the Fifth Amendment to the U.S. Constitution. The Fifth Amendment contains the privilege against self-incrimination, which provides that a person cannot be forced to give evidence against himself, whether oral or written. The provision is important to recordkeeping and reporting requirements because a person may be required by an agency to provide information that could prove the person committed a crime. For example, the Internal Revenue Service requires individuals to file tax returns. Federal tax law requires that taxpayers claim all income, whether derived from legal or illegal activity. Hence, a person engaged in prostitution is required to report all income from that enterprise to the Internal Revenue Service. May that information then be used to prosecute the individual for prostitution? No, the privilege against self-incrimination applies to such reporting requirements.

People may not be forced to provide information that could be used to prove their guilt. However, for a claimed privilege to be valid, a person must have a reasonable belief that the information provided could later be used in a criminal prosecution. If the person has a reasonable concern that the information might be used in a criminal prosecution, it does not matter that the information is sought in a civil context. Whether a proceeding is criminal, civil, or administrative, a person may not be compelled to give self-inculpatory evidence.

In the preceding tax example, Congress has avoided the Fifth Amendment problem by providing that information given by taxpayers may not be passed on to law enforcement officials. The privilege is not applicable, therefore, because no reasonable belief that a prosecution will result exists.

There are, however, several limitations on the Fifth Amendment's privilege against self-incrimination in the administrative context. Business entities, such as corporations, may not claim the privilege against self-incrimination; the privilege is reserved for natural persons.

The privilege applies only to compelled information—that is, communications that are testimonial in nature, not previously recorded information. For example, if Stacey voluntarily maintains records and is later required to produce those records, the privilege is inapplicable even if the records are incriminating. Stacey is not being compelled to produce or collect the information contained in the record (which would be testimonial); she has already done that voluntarily. Rather, she is being compelled by the order to take the physical act of providing the records to the agency, which is not a testimonial act.

In addition, the privilege does not apply to information in the possession of a third party. For example, John may not claim the Fifth Amendment privilege for tax information that his accountant possesses concerning him. Once the information is given up to a third party, the government may compel that party to produce the information. Be aware, however, that a common law or statutory privilege against disclosure may apply. For example, if John lives in a state that recognizes the information provided by a client to an accountant as privileged, the agency will not be able to acquire such information, regardless of the inapplicability of the Fifth Amendment.

7.2(b) Immunity

Finally, the privilege against self-incrimination may be overcome with a grant of immunity from the government. Before an agency can offer immunity, it must get the approval of the Attorney General of the United States and determine that the information is necessary to the public interest.[5] There are three types of immunity: transactional, derivative use, and use (see Figure 7-1).

Transactional immunity shields a witness from prosecution of all offenses related to his or her testimony. For example, if a witness testifies about a robbery, the government may not prosecute the witness for that robbery even though the government may have evidence of guilt independent of the witness's testimony. Transactional immunity gives more protection to the citizen than is required by the Constitution; hence, when it is granted, a witness may be ordered to testify.

For a witness to be compelled to testify (or produce information to an agency), ***derivative use immunity*** must be provided. This prohibits the government from using the witness's testimony or any evidence derived from that testimony to prosecute the witness. However, any independently obtained evidence may be used against the individual.

Use immunity prohibits only the government from using witnesses' testimony against them. Statutes that provide for use immunity are unconstitutional because derivative use is the minimum protection required by the Fifth Amendment.

An example of when immunity becomes an issue in administrative law is the collection of taxes for criminal conduct. Under federal law, profits of criminal enterprises are taxable. Thus, taxes must be paid on money obtained from the criminal sale of drugs, from prostitution, from theft, from extortion, and from any other profitable criminal conduct. In some instances, federal and state laws require the purchase of revenue stamps for the sale of drugs, legal or not. Such laws require that the revenue stamps, similar to the stamps that appear on cigarettes, be affixed to the sold goods.

LEGAL TERMS

Transactional Immunity
Full immunity from prosecution for all crimes evinced by the information compelled by the government.

Derivative Use Immunity
An incomplete immunity. The information compelled by the government and evidence derived therefrom may not be used to prove a person's guilt; independent evidence, however, may be used to prove guilt.

Use Immunity
An incomplete immunity. The information provided may not be used to prove a person's guilt; however, independent evidence and evidence derived from the compelled testimony may be used. Use immunity is not constitutionally adequate.

**COMPELLING TESTIMONY AND
THE FIFTH AMENDMENT**

Stan is compelled to testify at an administrative hearing, over his Fifth Amendment claim. He testifies that he "stole stock certificates and Treasury notes from his employer." He testifies further that "the documents are hidden in a closet in my office." The hearing officer provides this information to law enforcement officials, who obtain a search warrant for Stan's office. The documents are discovered in the closet. Stan is charged with theft.

Use immunity:	→	Compelled testimony may not be used to prove guilt. Does not satisfy the Fifth Amendment. Stan's statements at the hearing may not be used, but the documents may be introduced to prove his guilt.
Derivative use immunity:	→	Neither compelled testimony nor evidence resulting therefrom may be used to prove guilt. Satisfies the Fifth Amendment. Stan's statements at the hearing may not be used, nor may the documents because they are derived from his testimony (assuming that the law enforcement officials conducted their investigation following the report from the administrative officer). Suppose, however, they interviewed a co-employee, Iva, during that investigation, and she told the officers that she witnessed the theft and saw Stan store the documents in his office. The documents would then be admissible, as an independent source exists.
Transactional immunity:	→	No criminal prosecution for the crimes testified to may be had. Not only satisfies, but goes beyond, the Fifth Amendment. Stan may not be prosecuted for the theft.

FIGURE 7-1   Compelling testimony.

These laws have been challenged as violative of the Fifth Amendment because disclosure of the criminal acts is required under tax laws. Failure to report such income is punished both civilly and criminally. One such challenge was upheld by the U.S. Supreme Court because tax officials made the information they received available to law enforcement officers. The Court has held that such laws do not violate the Fifth Amendment if disclosure of the information to law enforcement officers is prohibited.[6] Hence, the government can compel a taxpayer to report the income, but it must provide immunity from use of the information for purposes of prosecution. Of course, the offender may be prosecuted if the government obtains independent evidence of the crime. All modern revenue statutes require that illegally earned income be reported and that such information is not to be disclosed.

7.3 INSPECTIONS, TESTS, AND SEARCHES

Administrative agencies frequently conduct inspections and tests. For example, the U.S. Environmental Protection Agency conducts tests at toxic disposal facilities to ensure compliance with federal environmental laws. The U.S. Nuclear Regulatory Commission inspects nuclear facilities for the same purpose. The U.S. Occupational

Safety and Health Administration inspects businesses to ensure that worker safety rules are obeyed. Local health inspectors routinely inspect local restaurants for compliance with health codes. In short, a host of federal and state agencies are responsible for inspecting business premises to protect the health and welfare of employees, customers, and the public. An inspection may be conducted to view records, conditions, and premises. Typically, an inspection is not as expensive for a business or individual as the production and submission of records. However, inspections often represent a greater invasion of privacy than recordkeeping requirements.

As is the case with recordkeeping and reporting requirements, the APA does not specifically authorize inspections. It does provide for inspections "as authorized by law."[7] Tests and inspections are made important by another provision of the APA, which states that no hearing is necessary when adjudicative decisions rest solely on tests, inspections, or elections.[8] Thus, an agency need not conduct a hearing if it relies only on tests, inspections, or elections when making a decision in a case. If any other evidence is relied on, standard notice and hearing requirements must be satisfied.

7.3(a) Fourth Amendment Aspects

Most administrative inspections are not intended to uncover or discover crimes. Rather, their purpose is to discover administrative violations. Whatever the purpose underlying an administrative inspection or test, the Fourth Amendment to the U.S. Constitution must be considered. The Fourth Amendment reads:

> The right of the people to be secure in their persons, houses, papers, and effects, against unreasonable searches and seizures, shall not be violated, and no Warrants shall issue, but upon probable cause, supported by Oath or affirmation, and particularly describing the place to be searched and the persons or things to be seized.

> Amendment 4, United States Constitution.

Although once not true, today the law regards most administrative inspections as "searches" subject to the Fourth Amendment's warrant, probable cause, and reasonableness requirements. However, application of the Fourth Amendment to administrative inspections is different from its application to searches in the criminal context. This is because the Courts have recognized that administrative inspections differ from searches in criminal cases in several respects.

First, administrative searches usually do not have as their purpose the securing of evidence to support a criminal prosecution. If it can be shown that the purpose of an administrative inspection was to obtain evidence in support of a criminal prosecution, a full search has been conducted and the Fourth Amendment applies in the same manner as it would in a criminal case.

Second, it is generally recognized that in today's complex, urbanized society, agencies must be given broad authority to enforce their mandates. With the large number of social problems and issues that agencies must confront, Courts have come to realize that if the requirements of the Fourth Amendment were not relaxed, administrative agencies would be prevented from effectively monitoring compliance with the law.

Third, there is a lower expectation of privacy in business premises, which are normally public operations, than in the home or in one's person.

Although its requirements are usually relaxed in the administrative context, the Fourth Amendment does apply to administrative agency actions that constitute searches. Not all inspections amount to searches. Agency officials commonly enter public places and make observations, but such observations are not considered searches for Fourth Amendment purposes. Accordingly, a health inspection official may inspect the dining room and restrooms of a public restaurant without concern for the Fourth Amendment.

Generally, a Fourth Amendment search has been conducted when an agency official has inspected an area within which the owner, possessor, or occupant has a reasonable expectation of privacy. For example, an inspector may visually observe the dining room of a restaurant. Because the restaurant owner has no reasonable expectation of privacy for such an area, there has been no search and the Fourth Amendment is inapplicable. However, if the inspector demanded entry into the owner's private office in the back of the restaurant or into a closed kitchen area, then a search was conducted.

Once it has been determined that there has been a search, the Fourth Amendment must be satisfied. In the majority of cases, this involves probable cause, a warrant, and reasonableness requirements. The Fourth Amendment requires that a warrant authorizing a search be obtained before the search is conducted. A warrantless search by an administrative officer is unreasonable and void unless some exception to the warrant requirement exists. Many exceptions have been recognized in the criminal law context, but the most important in administrative law is *consent*. A person may agree or consent to a warrantless search, but consent must be given voluntarily.

Although the Fourth Amendment speaks only of "dwellings," it has been interpreted as extending protection to other structures as well, including businesses. However, it has been held that there is a lesser expectation of privacy in businesses than there is in one's home. Two reasons are advanced in support of this conclusion. First, businesses are open to the public. Therefore, it is not a search for an officer to enter a business and make observations that could also be made by any member of the general public. Second, because businesses are public establishments regulated by the government, they generally have a lessened privacy interest. The greater the amount of regulation by the government, the less privacy interest a business possesses.

In criminal cases, a **warrant** may not issue unless probable cause exists to believe that contraband, the fruits or evidence of a crime, or a wanted person will be found in the place to be searched. The Fourth Amendment to the U.S. Constitution provides that warrants be issued only on a showing of probable cause, supported by oath or affirmation. Further, the warrant must particularly describe the place to be searched and the persons or things to be seized.

The standard for obtaining a search warrant is lower in administrative cases than in criminal cases, as shown by the *Camera* case. Administrative search warrants (*inspection warrants*) may be issued without probable cause to believe that at a specific location contraband or the fruits or evidence of a crime will be found, as long as the legislature has established reasonable inspection standards. Also, closely regulated businesses may be inspected without first obtaining a warrant.

Camera and its progeny held that the Fourth Amendment should not be applied in the same manner in administrative law as in the criminal context. These cases stand for the principle that the privacy interest is not as great, nor is the invasion of that interest, in the administrative context. Further, the Courts have recognized that inspections are an important part of effective enforcement of health, housing, sanitation, employment, and related laws and that the purpose of administrative inspections is not to discover and prosecute criminal acts; rather, it is to ensure compliance with health and safety regulations. All these factors contribute to the lowering of the Fourth Amendment standard in administrative cases.

LEGAL TERM

Warrant

A court order directing that a search, seizure, or arrest occur. It is issued on a showing of probable cause, supported by oath and affirmation, particularly describing the place to be searched and/or the persons or things to be seized.

As a result of these differences, the U.S. Supreme Court determined that a warrant may be issued without probable cause to believe that, at a specific location, contraband or the fruits or evidence of a crime will be found. Rather, *area inspections* may be conducted, provided the legislature has established reasonable standards for the conduct of such inspections. It is important to recall that the exceptions discussed here apply to businesses, not private parties or private areas. For example, during an area inspection of an apartment building, inspectors may enter the basement to search for code violations, but they are not permitted to search the building's individual apartments.

Also, administrative warrants would not be valid in a criminal case; criminal warrants must be based on probable cause and limited to particular locations. The Supreme Court has analogized the authority of agencies to acquire information to that of a grand jury, which "does not depend on a case or controversy for power to get evidence but can investigate merely on suspicion that the law is being violated, or even just because it wants assurance that it is not."[9]

Camera v. Municipal Court

387 U.S. 523 (1967)

On November 6, 1963, an inspector of the Division of Housing Inspection of the San Francisco Department of Public Health entered an apartment building to make a routine annual inspection for possible violations of the city's House Code. The building's manager informed the inspector that appellant, lessee of the ground floor, was using the rear of his leasehold as a personal residence. Claiming that the building's occupancy permit did not allow residential use of the ground floor, the inspector confronted appellant and demanded that he permit an inspection of the premises. Appellant refused to allow the inspection because the inspector lacked a search warrant.

The inspector returned on November 8, again without a warrant, and appellant again refused to allow an inspection. A citation was then mailed ordering appellant to appear at the district attorney's office. When appellant failed to appear, two inspectors returned to his apartment on November 22. They informed appellant that he was required by law to permit an inspection under § 503 of the Housing Code. Appellant nevertheless refused the inspectors access to his apartment without a search warrant. Thereafter, a complaint was filed charging him with refusing to permit a lawful inspection in violation of § 507 of the Code. Appellant was arrested on December 2 and released on bail. When his demurrer to the criminal complaint was denied, appellant filed his petition for a writ of prohibition.

Appellant has argued throughout this litigation that § 503 is contrary to the Fourth and Fourteenth Amendments in that it authorizes municipal officials to enter a private dwelling without a search warrant and without probable cause to believe that a violation of the House Code exists therein. Consequently, appellant contends, he may not be prosecuted under § 507 for refusing to permit an inspection unconstitutionally authorized by § 503. . . .

The Fourth Amendment provides that "[t]he right of the people to be secure in their persons, houses, papers, and effects, against unreasonable searches and seizures, shall not be violated, and no Warrants shall issue, but upon probable cause, supported by Oath or affirmation, and particularly describing the place to be searched, and the person or things to be seized." The basic purpose of this Amendment, as recognized in countless decisions of this Court, is to safeguard the privacy and security of individuals against arbitrary invasions by governmental officials. The Fourth Amendment thus gives concrete expression to a right of the people, which "is basic to a free society.". . .

(continued)

In summary, we hold that administrative searches of the kind at issue here are significant intrusions upon the interests protected by the Fourth Amendment, that such searches when authorized and conducted without a warrant procedure lack the traditional safeguards which the Fourth Amendment guarantees to the individual. . . . Because of the nature of municipal programs under consideration, however, these conclusions must be the beginning, not the end, of our inquiry. . . .

The Fourth Amendment provides that, "no Warrants shall issue, but upon probable cause." Borrowing from more typical Fourth Amendment cases, appellant argues not only that code enforcement inspection programs must be circumscribed by a warrant procedure, but also that warrants should issue only when the inspector possesses probable cause to believe that a particular dwelling contains violations of the minimum standards prescribed by the code being enforced. We disagree.

In cases in which the Fourth Amendment requires that a warrant to search be obtained, "probable cause" is the standard by which a particular decision to search is tested against the constitutional mandate of reasonableness. To apply this standard, it is obviously necessary first to focus upon the governmental interest, which allegedly justifies official intrusion upon the constitutionally protected interests of the private citizen. For example, in a criminal investigation, the police may undertake to recover specific stolen or contraband goods. But that public interest would hardly justify a sweeping search of an entire city conducted in the hope that these goods might be found. Consequently, a search for these goods, even with a warrant, is "reasonable" only when there is "probable cause" to believe that they will be uncovered in a particular dwelling.

Unlike the search pursuant to a criminal investigation, the inspection programs at issue here are aimed at securing city-wide compliance with minimum physical standards for private property. The primary governmental interest at stake is to prevent even the unintentional development of conditions, which are hazardous to public health and safety. . . . In determining whether a particular inspection is reasonable—and thus in determining whether there is probable cause to issue a warrant for that inspection—the need for the inspection must be weighed in terms of these reasonable goals of code enforcement.

There is unanimous agreement among those most familiar with this field that the only effective way to seek universal compliance with the minimum standards required by municipal codes is through routine periodic inspections of all structures. It is here that the probable cause debate is focused, for the agency's decision to conduct an area inspection is unavoidably based on its appraisal of conditions in the area as a whole, not on its knowledge of conditions in each particular building. Appellee contends that, if the probable cause standard urged by appellant is adopted, the area inspection will be eliminated as a means of seeking compliance with code standards and the reasonable goals of code enforcement will be dealt a crushing blow. . . . But we think that a number of persuasive factors combine to support the reasonableness of area code-enforcement inspections. First, such programs have a long history of judicial and public acceptance. . . . Second, the public interest demands that all dangerous conditions be prevented or abated. . . . Finally, because the inspections are neither personal in nature nor aimed at the discovery of evidence of crime, they involve a relatively limited invasion of urban citizens' privacy. . . .

Having concluded that the area inspection is a "reasonable" search of private property within the meaning of the Fourth Amendment, it is obvious that "probable cause" to issue a warrant to inspect must exist if reasonable legislative or administrative standards for conducting an area inspection are satisfied with respect to a particular dwelling. Such standards, which will vary with the municipal program being enforced, may be based upon the passage of time, the nature of the building (e.g., a multifamily apartment house), or the condition of the entire area, but they will not necessarily depend upon specific knowledge of the condition of the particular dwelling. . . . The warrant procedure is designed to guarantee that a decision to search private property is justified by a reasonable government interest. But reasonableness is still the ultimate standard. Such an approach neither endangers time-honored doctrines applicable to criminal investigations nor makes a nullity of the probable cause requirement in this area. It merely gives full recognition to the competing public and private interests here at stake and, in so doing, best fulfills the historic purpose behind the constitutional right to be free from unreasonable government invasions of privacy. . . .

In this case, appellant has been charged with a crime for his refusal to permit housing inspectors to enter his leasehold without a warrant. There was no emergency demanding immediate access; in fact, the inspectors made three trips to the building in an attempt to obtain appellant's consent to search. Yet no warrant was obtained and thus appellant was unable to verify either the need for or the appropriate limits of the inspections. . . . It appears from the opinion of the District Court of Appeal that under these circumstances a writ of prohibition will issue to the criminal court. . . .

Camera v. Municipal Court, 387 U.S. 523 (1967), United States Supreme Court.

In administrative cases, the nature of the potential violation, the likelihood that a violation will be found in the area to be searched, and similar facts may be considered. A warrant may issue, therefore, authorizing the inspection of a number of area businesses that are housed in old structures and likely to have health and safety violations even though there is no probable cause to believe that specific violations exist.

7.3(b) Drug, Alcohol, AIDS, and DNA Testing

Mandatory alcohol, drug, and AIDS testing have become increasingly common in recent years. When required by the government, these forms of testing raise a host of constitutional issues. Is a mandatory test a search for purposes of the Fourth Amendment? If so, must an agency have probable cause to conduct the test? Further, must the agency obtain a warrant before conducting the test? Is it a deprivation of liberty under the Due Process Clauses to require a person to submit to a breath, blood, or urinalysis test? Is it cruel and unusual punishment to subject a prison inmate to mandatory testing? These are a few of the constitutional questions raised by mandatory testing laws. The Supreme Court addressed some of these issues in the *Skinner* case.

Skinner involved a regulation promulgated by the Secretary of Transportation of the United States pursuant to a delegation in the Federal Railroad Safety Act, which required railroad employers to conduct drug and alcohol testing of specified employees after a railway accident occurred. The regulations specified which employees were to be tested. Further, the regulations gave railroad employers the option of testing other employees. However, the regulations limited that discretion by specifying which employees could be tested and under what circumstances. For example, a railroad may require an employee to be tested who violates certain rules, such as speeding or failing to stop at a signal. The plaintiffs alleged that the regulation violated the Fourth Amendment because it did not require a finding of probable cause or the issuance of a warrant before subjecting the employees to the testing.

The Supreme Court found that the Fourth Amendment was applicable because the regulation required the testing in some circumstances, and encouraged it in others. Even though the testing was being conducted by a private party rather than the government, the testing was being conducted under the authority of the government, and therefore, the employers were acting as agents or instrumentalities of the United States. Further, the Court found that drug testing, especially blood and urine testing, is invasive of a person's privacy. Therefore, testing constitutes a search under the Fourth Amendment.

The Court held, however, that the regulation was valid because the governmental interest in protecting the employees and the public from a disaster outweighed the privacy interests of the employees. In particular, the Court stated:

> Employees subject to tests discharge duties fraught with such risks of injury to others that even a momentary lapse of attention can have disastrous consequences. Much like persons who have routine access to dangerous nuclear power facilities, employees who are subject to testing under the FRA regulations can cause great human loss before any signs of impairment become noticeable to supervisors or others.[10]

The Court also found that the Fourth Amendment did not impose a probable cause or warrant requirement because of the administrative, rather than criminal, nature of the governmental objectives.

Because the employers' discretion was limited by the regulation, the Court found that imposing a neutral magistrate between the employer and employee would be futile. Under the regulatory scheme, there would be little for a magistrate to review, because the regulation was narrowly drawn. Further, alcohol and drugs in the bloodstream are evanescent evidence—that is, they vanish on their own over time. The evidence may disappear in the time it takes to obtain a warrant, and therefore, a warrant would hinder or totally frustrate the lawful objectives of the government. This is consistent with the destruction-of-evidence exception to the search warrant requirement previously recognized by the Court in criminal cases.[11]

Skinner v. Railway Labor Executive Ass'n

489 U.S. 602 (1989)

The Federal Railroad Safety Act of 1970 authorizes the Secretary of Transportation to "prescribe, as necessary, appropriate rules, regulations, orders, and standards for all areas of railroad safety." Finding that alcohol and drug abuse by railroad employees poses a serious threat to safety, the Federal Railroad Administration (FRA) has promulgated regulations that mandate blood and urine tests of employees who are involved in certain train accidents. The FRA also has adopted regulations that do not require, but do authorize, railroads to administer breath and urine tests to employees who violate certain safety rules. The question presented by this case is whether these regulations violate the Fourth Amendment.

The problem of alcohol use on American railroads is as old as the industry itself, and efforts to deter it by carrier rules began at least a century ago. For many years, railroads have prohibited operating employees from possessing alcohol or being intoxicated while on duty and from consuming alcoholic beverages while subject to being called for duty. More recently, these proscriptions have been expanded to forbid possession or use of certain drugs. These restrictions are embodied in "Rule G," an industry-wide operating rule promulgated by the Association of American Railroads, and are enforced, in various formulations, by virtually every railroad in the country. The customary sanction for Rule G violations is dismissal.

In July 1983, the FRA expressed concern that these industry efforts were not adequate to curb alcohol and drug abuse by railroad employees. The FRA pointed to evidence indicating that on-the-job intoxication was a significant problem in the railroad industry. The FRA also found, after a review of accident investigation reports, that from 1972 to 1983 "the nation's railroads experienced at least 21 significant train accidents involving alcohol or drug use as a probable cause or contributing factor," and that these accidents "resulted in 25 fatalities, 61 nonfatal injuries, and property damage estimated at $19 million (approximately $27 million in 1982 dollars)." The FRA further identified an "additional 17 fatalities to operating employees working on or around rail rolling stock that involved alcohol or drugs as a contributing factor." In light of these problems, the FRA solicited comments from interested parties on various regulatory approaches to the problems of alcohol and drug abuse throughout the Nation's railroad system.

After reviewing further comments from representatives of the railroad industry, labor groups, and the general public, the FRA, in 1985, promulgated regulations addressing the problem of alcohol and drugs on the railroads. The final regulations apply to employees assigned to perform service subject to the Hours of Service Act. The regulations prohibit covered employees from using or possessing alcohol or any controlled substance. The regulations further prohibit those employees from reporting for covered service while under the influence of, or impaired by, alcohol, while having a blood alcohol concentration of .04 or more, or while under the influence of, or impaired by, any controlled substance. The regulations do not restrict, however, a railroad's authority to impose an absolute prohibition on the presence of alcohol or any drug in the body fluids of persons in its employ, and, accordingly, they do not "replace Rule G or render it unenforceable."

To the extent pertinent here, two subparts of the regulations relate to testing. Subpart C, which is entitled "Post-Accident Toxicological Testing," is mandatory. It provides that railroads "shall take all practicable steps to assure that all covered employees of the railroad directly involved . . . provide blood and urine samples for toxicological testing by FRA," upon the occurrence of certain specified events. Toxicological testing is required following a "major train accident," which is defined as any train accident that involves (i) a fatality, (ii) the release of hazardous material accompanied by an evacuation or a reportable injury, or (iii) damage to railroad property of $500,000 or more. The railroad has the further duty of collecting blood and urine samples for testing after an "impact accident," which is defined as a collision that results in a reportable injury, or in damage to railroad property of $50,000 or more. Finally, the railroad is also obligated to test after "[a]ny train incident that involves a fatality to any onduty railroad employee."

Subpart D of the regulations, which is entitled "Authorization to Test for Cause," is permissive. It authorizes railroads to require covered employees to submit to breath or urine tests in certain circumstances not addressed by Subpart C. Breath or urine tests, or both, may be ordered (1) after a reportable accident or incident, where a supervisor has a "reasonable suspicion" that an employee's acts or omissions contributed to the occurrence or severity of the accident or incident; or (2) in the event of certain specific rule violations, including noncompliance with a signal and excessive speeding. A railroad also may require breath tests where a supervisor has a "reasonable suspicion" that an employee is under the influence of alcohol, based upon specific, personal observations concerning the appearance, behavior, speech, or body odors of the employee. Where impairment is suspected, a railroad, in addition, may require urine tests, but only if two supervisors make the appropriate determination, and, where the supervisors suspect impairment due to a substance other than alcohol, at least one of those supervisors must have received specialized training in detecting the signs of drug intoxication.

(continued)

The Fourth Amendment provides that "[t]he right of the people to be secure in their persons, houses, papers, and effects, against unreasonable searches and seizures, shall not be violated. . . ." The Amendment guarantees the privacy, dignity, and security of persons against certain arbitrary and invasive acts by officers of the Government or those acting at their direction. Before we consider whether the tests in question are reasonable under the Fourth Amendment, we must inquire whether the tests are attributable to the Government or its agents, and whether they amount to searches or seizures. We turn to those matters.

Although the Fourth Amendment does not apply to a search or seizure, even an arbitrary one, effected by a private party on his own initiative, the Amendment protects against such intrusions if the private party acted as an instrument or agent of the Government. A railroad that complies with the provisions of Subpart C of the regulations does so by compulsion of sovereign authority, and the lawfulness of its acts is controlled by the Fourth Amendment. Petitioners contend, however, that the Fourth Amendment is not implicated by Subpart D of the regulations, as nothing in Subpart D compels any testing by private railroads.

We are unwilling to conclude, in the context of this facial challenge, that breath and urine tests required by private railroads in reliance on Subpart D will not implicate the Fourth Amendment. Whether a private party should be deemed an agent or instrument of the Government for Fourth Amendment purposes necessarily turns on the degree of the Government's participation in the private party's activities. The fact that the Government has not compelled a private party to perform a search does not, by itself, establish that the search is a private one. Here, specific features of the regulations combine to convince us that the Government did more than adopt a passive position toward the underlying private conduct.

The regulations, including those in Subpart D, pre-empt state laws, rules, or regulations covering the same subject matter, and are intended to supersede "any provision of a collective bargaining agreement, or arbitration award construing such an agreement." They also confer upon the FRA the right to receive certain biological samples and test results procured by railroads pursuant to Subpart D. In addition, a railroad may not divest itself of, or otherwise compromise by contract, the authority conferred by Subpart D. As the FRA explained, such "authority . . . is conferred for the purpose of promoting the public safety, and a railroad may not shackle itself in a way inconsistent with its duty to promote the public safety." Nor is a covered employee free to decline his employer's request to submit to breath or urine tests under the conditions set forth in Subpart D. An employee who refuses to submit to the tests must be withdrawn from covered service.

In light of these provisions, we are unwilling to accept petitioner's submission that tests conducted by private railroads in reliance on Subpart D will be primarily the result of private initiative. The Government has removed all legal barriers to the testing authorized by Subpart D, and indeed has made plain not only its strong preference for testing, but also its desire to share the fruits of such intrusions. In addition, it has mandated that the railroads not bargain away the authority to perform tests granted by Subpart D. These are clear indices of the Government's encouragement, endorsement, and participation, and suffice to implicate the Fourth Amendment.

Our precedents teach that where, as here, the Government seeks to obtain physical evidence from a person, the Fourth Amendment may be relevant at several levels. The initial detention necessary to procure the evidence may be a seizure of the person, if the detention amounts to a meaningful interference with his freedom of movement. Obtaining and examining the evidence may also be a search, if doing so infringes an expectation of privacy that society is prepared to recognize as reasonable.

We have long recognized that a "compelled intrusio[n] into the body for blood to be analyzed for alcohol content" must be deemed a Fourth Amendment search. In light of our society's concern for the security of one's person, it is obvious that this physical intrusion, penetrating beneath the skin, infringes an expectation of privacy that society is prepared to recognize as reasonable. The ensuing chemical analysis of the sample to obtain physiological data is a further invasion of the tested employee's privacy interests. Much the same is true of the breath-testing procedures required under Subpart D of the regulations. Subjecting a person to a breathalyzer test, which generally requires the production of alveolar or "deep lung" breath for chemical analysis, implicates similar concerns about bodily integrity and, like the blood-alcohol test we considered in *Schmerber*, should also be deemed a search.

Unlike the blood-testing procedure at issue in *Schmerber*, the procedures prescribed by the FRA regulations for collecting and testing urine samples do not entail a surgical intrusion into the body. It is not disputed, however, that chemical analysis of urine, like that of blood, can reveal a host of private medical facts about an employee, including whether he or she is epileptic, pregnant, or diabetic. Nor can it be disputed that the process of collecting the sample to be tested, which may in some cases involve visual or aural monitoring of the act of urination, itself implicates privacy interests. As the Court of Appeals for the Fifth Circuit has stated:

> There are few activities in our society more personal or private than the passing of urine. Most people describe it by euphemisms if they talk about it at all. It is a function traditionally performed without public observation; indeed, its performance in public is generally prohibited by law as well as social custom. *National Treasury Employees Union v. Von Raab,* 816 F.2d 170, 175 (1987).

Because it is clear that the collection and testing of urine intrudes upon expectations of privacy that society has long recognized as reasonable, the Federal Courts of Appeals have concluded unanimously, and we agree, that these intrusions must be deemed searches under the Fourth Amendment.

* * *

To hold that the Fourth Amendment is applicable to the drug and alcohol testing prescribed by the FRA regulations is only to begin the inquiry into the standards governing such intrusions. For the Fourth Amendment does not proscribe all searches and seizures, but only those that are unreasonable. What is reasonable, of course, "depends on all of the circumstances surrounding the search or seizure and the nature of the search or seizure itself." Thus, the permissibility of a particular practice "is judged by balancing its intrusion on the individual's Fourth Amendment interests against its promotion of legitimate governmental interests."

In most criminal cases, we strike this balance in favor of the procedures described by the Warrant Clause of the Fourth Amendment. Except in certain well-defined circumstances, a search or seizure in such a case is not reasonable unless it is accomplished pursuant to a judicial warrant issued upon probable cause. We have recognized exceptions to this rule, however, "when 'special needs, beyond the normal need for law enforcement, make the warrant and probable-cause requirement impracticable.'" When faced with such special needs, we have not hesitated to balance the governmental and privacy interests to assess the practicality of the warrant and probable cause requirements in the particular context.

The Government's interest in regulating the conduct of railroad employees to ensure safety, like its supervision of probationers or regulated industries, or its operation of a government office, school, or prison, "likewise presents 'special needs' beyond normal law enforcement that may justify departures from the usual warrant and probable-cause requirements." The hours of service employees covered by the FRA regulations include persons engaged in handling orders concerning train movements, operating crews, and those engaged in the maintenance and repair of signal systems.

(continued)

It is undisputed that these and other covered employees are engaged in safety-sensitive tasks. The FRA so found, and respondents conceded the point at oral argument. As we have recognized, the whole premise of the Hours of Service Act is that "[t]he length of hours of service has direct relation to the efficiency of the human agencies upon which protection [of] life and property necessarily depends." . . .

The question that remains, then, is whether the Government's need to monitor compliance with these restrictions justifies the privacy intrusions at issue absent a warrant or individualized suspicion.

An essential purpose of a warrant requirement is to protect privacy interests by assuring citizens subject to a search or seizure that such intrusions are not the random or arbitrary acts of government agents. A warrant assures the citizen that the intrusion is authorized by law, and that it is narrowly limited in its objectives and scope. A warrant also provides the detached scrutiny of a neutral magistrate, and thus ensures an objective determination [of] whether an intrusion is justified in any given case. In the present context, however, a warrant would do little to further these aims. Both the circumstances justifying toxicological testing and the permissible limits of such intrusions are defined narrowly and specifically in the regulations that authorize them, and doubtless are well known to covered employees. Indeed, in light of the standardized nature of the tests and the minimal discretion vested in those charged with administering the program, there are virtually no facts for a neutral magistrate to evaluate.

We have recognized, moreover, that the Government's interest in dispensing with the warrant requirement is at its strongest when, as here, "the burden of obtaining a warrant is likely to frustrate the governmental purpose behind the search." As the FRA recognized, alcohol and other drugs are eliminated from the bloodstream at a constant rate, and blood and breath samples taken to measure whether these substances were in the bloodstream when a triggering event occurred must be obtained as soon as possible. Although the metabolites of some drugs remain in the urine for longer periods of time and may enable the FRA to estimate whether the employee was impaired by those drugs at the time of a covered accident, incident, or rule violation, the delay necessary may result in the destruction of valuable evidence.

The Government's need to rely on private railroads to set the testing process in motion also indicates that insistence on a warrant requirement would impede the achievement of the Government's objective. Railroad supervisors . . . are not in the business of investigating violations of the criminal laws or enforcing administrative codes, and otherwise have little occasion to become familiar with the intricacies of this Court's Fourth Amendment jurisprudence. "Imposing unwieldy warrant procedures . . . upon supervisors, who would otherwise have no reason to be familiar with such procedures, is simply unreasonable." In sum, imposing a warrant requirement in the present context would add little to the assurances of certainty and regularity already afforded by the regulations, while significantly hindering, and in many cases frustrating, the objectives of the Government's testing program. We do not believe that a warrant is essential to render the intrusions here at issue reasonable under the Fourth Amendment.

Our cases indicate that even a search that may be performed without a warrant must be based, as a general matter, on probable cause to believe that the person to be searched has violated the law. When the balance of interests precludes insistence on a showing of probable cause, we have usually required "some quantum of individualized suspicion" before concluding that a search is reasonable. We made it clear, however, that a showing of individualized suspicion is not a constitutional floor, below which a search must be presumed unreasonable. In limited circumstances, where the privacy interests implicated by the search are minimal, and where an important governmental interest furthered by the intrusion would be placed in jeopardy by a requirement of individualized suspicion, a search may be reasonable despite the absence of such suspicion. We believe this true of the intrusions in question here.

By and large, intrusions on privacy under the FRA regulations are limited. To the extent transportation and like restrictions are necessary to procure the requisite blood, breath, and urine samples for testing, this interference alone is minimal given the employment context in which it takes place. Ordinarily, an employee consents to significant restrictions in his freedom of movement where necessary for his employment, and few are free to come and go as they please during working hours. Any additional interference with a railroad employee's freedom of movement that occurs in the time it takes to procure a blood, breath, or urine sample for testing cannot, by itself, be said to infringe significant privacy interests.

Our decision in *Schmerber v. California,* 382 U.S. 757 . . . (1966), indicates that the same is true of the blood tests required by the FRA regulations. In that case, we held that a State could direct that a blood sample be withdrawn from a motorist suspected of driving while intoxicated, despite his refusal to consent to the intrusion. We noted that the test was performed in a reasonable manner, as the motorist's "blood was taken by a physician in a hospital environment according to accepted medical practices." We said also that the intrusion occasioned by a blood test is not significant, since such "tests are a commonplace in these days of periodic physical examinations and experience with them teaches that the quantity of blood extracted is minimal, and that for most people the procedure involves virtually no risk, trauma, or pain." *Schmerber* thus confirmed "society's judgment that blood tests do not constitute an unduly extensive imposition on an individual's privacy and bodily integrity."

The breath tests authorized by Subpart D of the regulations are even less intrusive than the blood tests prescribed by Subpart C. . . .

A more difficult question is presented by urine tests. Like breath tests, urine tests are not invasive of the body and, under the regulations, may not be used as an occasion for inquiring into private facts unrelated to alcohol or drug use. We recognize, however, that the procedures for collecting the necessary samples, which require employees to perform an excretory function traditionally shielded by great privacy, raise concerns not implicated by blood or breath tests. Although we would not characterize these additional privacy concerns as minimal in most contexts, we note that the regulations endeavor to reduce the intrusiveness of the collection process. The regulations do not require that samples be furnished under the direct observation of a monitor, despite the desirability of such a procedure to ensure the integrity of the sample. The sample is also collected in a medical environment, by personnel unrelated to the railroad employer, and is thus not unlike similar procedures encountered often in the context of a regular physical examination.

More importantly, the expectations of privacy of covered employees are diminished by reason of their participation in an industry that is regulated pervasively to ensure safety, a goal dependent, in substantial part, on the health and fitness of covered employees.

We do not suggest, of course, that the interest in bodily security enjoyed by those employed in a regulated industry must always be considered minimal. Here, however, the covered employees have long been a principal focus of regulatory concern. As the dissenting judge below noted: "The reason is obvious. An idle locomotive, sitting in the roundhouse, is harmless. It becomes lethal when operated negligently by persons who are under the influence of alcohol or drugs." Although some of the privacy interests implicated by the toxicological testing at issue reasonably might be viewed as significant in other contexts, logic and history show that a diminished expectation of privacy attaches to information relating to the physical condition of covered employees and to this reasonable means of procuring such information. We conclude, therefore, that the testing procedures contemplated by

(continued)

Subparts C and D pose only limited threats to the justifiable expectations of privacy of covered employees.

By contrast, the Government interest in testing without a showing of individualized suspicion is compelling. Employees subject to the tests discharge duties fraught with such risks of injury to others that even a momentary lapse of attention can have disastrous consequences. Much like persons who have routine access to dangerous nuclear power facilities, employees who are subject to testing under the FRA regulations can cause great human loss before any signs of impairment become noticeable to supervisors or others. An impaired employee, the FRA found, will seldom display any outward "signs detectable by the lay person or, in many cases, even the physician."...

While no procedure can identify all impaired employees with ease and perfect accuracy, the FRA regulations supply an effective means of deterring employees engaged in safety-sensitive tasks from using controlled substances or alcohol in the first place. The railroad industry's experience with Rule G persuasively shows, and common sense confirms, that the customary dismissal sanction that threatens employees who use drugs or alcohol while on duty cannot serve as an effective deterrent unless violators know that they are likely to be discovered. By ensuring that employees in safety-sensitive positions know they will be tested upon the occurrence of a triggering event, the timing of which no employee can predict with certainty, the regulations significantly increase the deterrent effect of the administrative penalties associated with the prohibited conduct, concomitantly increasing the likelihood that employees will forgo using drugs or alcohol while subject to being called for duty.

The testing procedures contemplated by Subpart C also help railroads obtain invaluable information about the causes of major accidents, and to take appropriate measures to safeguard the general public. Positive test results would point toward drug or alcohol impairment on the part of members of the crew as a possible cause of an accident, and may help to establish whether a particular accident, otherwise not drug related, was made worse by the inability of impaired employees to respond appropriately. Negative test results would likewise furnish invaluable clues, for eliminating drug impairment as a potential cause or contributing factor would help establish the significance of equipment failure, inadequate training, or other potential causes, and suggest a more thorough examination of these alternatives. Tests performed following the rule violations specified in Subpart D likewise can provide valuable information respecting the causes of those transgressions, which the FRA found to involve "the potential for a serious train accident or grave personal injury, or both."

A requirement of particularized suspicion of drug or alcohol use would seriously impede an employer's ability to obtain this information, despite its obvious importance. . . .

* * *

More importantly, the Court of Appeals overlooked the FRA's policy of placing principal reliance on the results of blood tests, which unquestionably can identify very recent drug use, while relying on urine tests as a secondary source of information designed to guard against the possibility that certain drugs will be eliminated from the bloodstream before a blood sample can be obtained. The court also failed to recognize that the FRA regulations are designed not only to discern impairment but also to deter it. Because the record indicates that blood and urine tests, taken together, are highly effective means of ascertaining on-the-job impairment and of deterring the use of drugs by railroad employees, we believe the Court of Appeals erred in concluding that the postaccident testing regulations are not reasonably related to the Government objectives that support them.

We conclude that the compelling Government interests served by the FRA's regulations would be significantly hindered if railroads were required to point to specific facts giving rise to a reasonable suspicion of impairment before testing a given employee. In view of our conclusion that, on the present record, the toxicological testing contemplated by the regulations is not an undue infringement on the justifiable expectations of privacy of covered employees, the Government's compelling interests outweigh privacy concerns.

The possession of unlawful drugs is a criminal offense that the Government may punish, but it is a separate and far more dangerous wrong to perform certain sensitive tasks while under the influence of those substances. Performing those tasks while impaired by alcohol is, of course, equally dangerous, though consumption of alcohol is legal in most other contexts. The Government may take all necessary and reasonable regulatory steps to prevent or deter that hazardous conduct, and since the gravamen of the evil is performing certain functions while concealing the substance in the body, it may be necessary, as in the case before us, to examine the body or its fluids to accomplish the regulatory purpose. The necessity to perform that regulatory function with respect to railroad employees engaged in safety-sensitive tasks, and the reasonableness of the system for doing so, have been established in this case.

Alcohol and drug tests conducted in reliance on the authority of Subpart D cannot be viewed as private action outside the reach of the Fourth Amendment. Because the testing procedures mandated or authorized by Subparts C and D effect searches of the person, they must meet the Fourth Amendment's reasonableness requirement. In light of the limited discretion exercised by the railroad employers under the regulations, the surpassing safety interests served by toxicological tests in this context, and the diminished expectation of privacy that attaches to information pertaining to the fitness of covered employees, we believe that it is reasonable to conduct such tests in the absence of a warrant or reasonable suspicion that any particular employee may be impaired. We hold that the alcohol and drug tests contemplated by Subparts C and D of the FRA's regulations are reasonable within the meaning of the Fourth Amendment.

Skinner v. Railway Labor Executive Ass'n, 489 U.S. 602 (1989), United States Supreme Court

Finally, the regulations minimized privacy invasions. For example, the regulations required that a urine sample be taken in a medical environment by medical professionals rather than by coworkers. Further, the sample was to be given in a private, unwitnessed environment. For these reasons, the Court determined that the testing provided for in the regulation could be conducted without first obtaining a warrant.

For similar reasons, the Eighth Circuit Court of Appeals upheld drug testing of employees of a nuclear power plant who had access to protected areas of the plant.[12] The Eighth Circuit stressed that the privacy interest of employees of a *closely regulated business* was less than that of other employees; the law had an administrative, not penal, objective; the invasion of privacy was minimized (employees produced the sample in private); and because the harm that could result from a nuclear accident is high, the government has a compelling interest in the regulation. Because breath, blood, and urine tests involve an invasion of privacy, the court concluded that conduct of such tests constitutes a search for Fourth Amendment purposes. The court also concluded that such tests were reasonable and did not require probable cause or a warrant before being administered.

In another case, *National Treasury Employees Union v. Von Raab*,[13] a drug-testing requirement of the U.S. Commissioner of Customs was challenged. The commissioner required employees who applied for transfers into positions involving drug interdiction, requiring the use of weapons, or handling classified documents to submit to drug testing. The Supreme Court upheld the rule,[14] finding

LEGAL TERM

Closely Regulated Business

An industry that is subject to significant licensing, reporting, disclosure requirements, inspections, required operating procedures, and other regulations is *closely regulated*. Nuclear power plants, restaurants, firearm sales, and liquor sales are examples of closely regulated businesses.

that the testing had an administrative rather than criminal purpose. Specifically, the commissioner had provided that the information resulting from the testing could not be used in a criminal prosecution unless the employee consented to its use. Again, the Court determined that because of the special nature of the positions, the privacy interests of the individuals were outweighed by the governmental interest in conducting the testing.

Whether a special need exists to test high school athletes for drugs made its way to the Supreme Court in *Vernonia School District v. Acton*. In that case, the Court found that the suspicionless drug testing of student athletes was consistent with the Fourth Amendment.

Vernonia School District v. Acton

515 U.S. 646 (1995)

Petitioner Vernonia School District 47J (District) operates one high school and three grade schools in the logging community of Vernonia, Oregon. As elsewhere in small-town America, school sports play a prominent role in the town's life, and student athletes are admired in their schools and in the community.

Drugs had not been a major problem in Vernonia schools. In the mid-to-late 1980s, however, teachers and administrators observed a sharp increase in drug use. Students began to speak out about their attraction to the drug culture, and to boast that there was nothing the school could do about it. Along with more drugs came more disciplinary problems. Between 1988 and 1989 the number of disciplinary referrals in Vernonia schools rose to more than twice the number reported in the early 1980s, and several students were suspended. Students became increasingly rude during class; outbursts of profane language became common.

Not only were student athletes included among the drug users but, as the District Court found, athletes were the leaders of the drug culture. 796 F. Supp. 1354, 1357 (Ore. 1992). This caused the District's administrators particular concern, since drug use increases the risk of sports-related injury. Expert testimony at the trial confirmed the deleterious effects of drugs on motivation, memory, judgment, reaction, coordination, and performance. The high school football and wrestling coach witnessed a severe sternum injury suffered by a wrestler, and various omissions of safety procedures and misexecutions by football players, all attributable in his belief to the effects of drug use.

Initially, the District responded to the drug problem by offering special classes, speakers, and presentations designed to deter drug use. It even brought in a specially trained dog to detect drugs, but the drug problem persisted. According to the District Court:

> [T]he administration was at its wits end and . . . a large segment of the student body, particularly those involved in interscholastic athletics, was in a state of rebellion. Disciplinary actions had reached "epidemic proportions." . . .

At that point, District officials began considering a drug-testing program. They held a parent "input night" to discuss the proposed Student Athlete Drug Policy (Policy), and the parents in attendance gave their unanimous approval. The school board approved the Policy for implementation in the fall of 1989. Its expressed purpose is to prevent student athletes from using drugs, to protect their health and safety, and to provide drug users with assistance programs. . . .

The Policy applies to all students participating in interscholastic athletics. Students wishing to play sports must sign a form consenting to the testing and must obtain the written consent of their parents. Athletes are tested at the beginning of the season for their sport.

In addition, once each week of the season the names of the athletes are placed in a "pool" from which a student, with the supervision of two adults, blindly draws the names of 10% of the athletes for random testing. Those selected are notified and tested that same day, if possible.

The student to be tested completes a specimen control form, which bears an assigned number. Prescription medications that the student is taking must be identified by providing a copy of the prescription or a doctor's authorization. The student then enters an empty locker room accompanied by an adult monitor of the same sex. Each boy selected produces a sample at a urinal, remaining fully clothed with his back to the monitor, who stands approximately 12 to 15 feet behind the student. Monitors may (though do not always) watch the student while he produces the sample, and they listen for normal sounds of urination. Girls produce samples in an enclosed bathroom stall, so that they can be heard but not observed. After the sample is produced, it is given to the monitor, who checks it for temperature and tampering and then transfers it to a vial.

The samples are sent to an independent laboratory, which routinely tests them for amphetamines, cocaine, and marijuana. . . .

The laboratory's procedures are 99.94% accurate. The District follows strict procedures regarding the chain of custody and access to test results. The laboratory does not know the identity of the students whose samples it tests. . . .

If a sample tests positive, a second test is administered as soon as possible to confirm the result. If the second test is negative, no further action is taken. If the second test is positive, the athlete's parents are notified, and the school principal convenes a meeting with the student and his parents, at which the student is given the option of (1) participating for six weeks in an assistance program that includes weekly urinalysis, or (2) suffering suspension from athletics for the remainder of the current season and the next athletic season. The student is then retested prior to the start of the next athletic season for which he or she is eligible. The Policy states that a second offense results in automatic imposition of option (2); a third offense in suspension for the remainder of the current season and the next two athletic seasons.

In the fall of 1991, respondent James Acton, then a seventh grader, signed up to play football at one of the District's grade schools. He was denied participation, however, because he and his parents refused to sign the testing consent forms. The Actons filed suit, seeking declaratory and injunctive relief from enforcement of the Policy on the grounds that it violated the Fourth and Fourteenth Amendments to the United States Constitution and Article I, § 9, of the Oregon Constitution. . . .

In *Skinner v. Railway Labor Executives' Assn* . . . we held that state-compelled collection and testing of urine, such as that required by the Policy, constitutes a "search" subject to the demands of the Fourth Amendment. . . .

A search unsupported by probable cause can be constitutional, we have said, "when special needs, beyond the normal need for law enforcement, make the warrant and probable-cause requirement impracticable. . . ."

We have found such "special needs" to exist in the public school context. There, the warrant requirement "would unduly interfere with the maintenance of the swift and informal disciplinary procedures [that are] needed," and "strict adherence to the requirement that searches be based upon probable cause" would undercut "the substantial need of teachers and administrators for freedom to maintain order in the schools. . . ."

Central, in our view, to the present case is the fact that the subjects of the Policy are (1) children, who (2) have been committed to the temporary custody of the State as schoolmaster. Traditionally at common law, and still today, unemancipated minors lack some of the most fundamental rights of self-determination—including

(continued)

even the right of liberty in its narrow sense, i.e., the right to come and go at will. They are subject, even as to their physical freedom, to the control of their parents or guardians. . . .

For their own good and that of their classmates, public school children are routinely required to submit to various physical examinations, and to be vaccinated against various diseases. According to the American Academy of Pediatrics, most public schools "provide vision and hearing screening and dental and dermatological checks. . . . Others also mandate scoliosis screening at appropriate grade levels." Committee on School Health, American Academy of Pediatrics, School Health: A Guide for Health Professionals 2 (1987). In the 1991–1992 school year, all 50 States required public school students to be vaccinated against diphtheria, measles, rubella, and polio. . . .

Legitimate privacy expectations are even less with regard to student athletes. School sports are not for the bashful. They require "suiting up" before each practice or event, and showering and changing afterwards. Public school locker rooms, the usual sites for these activities, are not notable for the privacy they afford. The locker rooms in Vernonia are typical: No individual dressing rooms are provided; shower heads are lined up along a wall, unseparated by any sort of partition or curtain; not even all the toilet stalls have doors. As the United States Court of Appeals for the Seventh Circuit has noted, there is "an element of 'communal undress' inherent in athletic participation. . . ."

There is an additional respect in which school athletes have a reduced expectation of privacy. By choosing to "go out for the team," they voluntarily subject themselves to a degree of regulation even higher than that imposed on students generally. . . .

Having considered the scope of the legitimate expectation of privacy at issue here, we turn next to the character of the intrusion that is complained of. We recognized in *Skinner* that collecting the samples for urinalysis intrudes upon "an excretory function traditionally shielded by great privacy." 489 U.S., at 626, 109 S. Ct., at 1418. We noted, however, that the degree of intrusion depends upon the manner in which production of the urine sample is monitored. . . . [Considering the process used by the school district to obtain the urine samples], the privacy interests compromised by the process of obtaining the urine sample are in our view negligible. . . .

Taking into account all the factors we have considered above—the decreased expectation of privacy, the relative unobtrusiveness of the search, and the severity of the need met by the search—we conclude Vernonia's Policy is reasonable and hence constitutional.

We caution against the assumption that suspicionless drug testing will readily pass constitutional muster in other contexts. The most significant element in this case is the first we discussed: that the Policy was undertaken in furtherance of the government's responsibilities, under a public school system, as guardian and tutor of children entrusted to its care. Just as when the government conducts a search in its capacity as employer (a warrantless search of an absent employee's desk to obtain an urgently needed file, for example), the relevant question is whether that intrusion upon privacy is one that a reasonable employer might engage in . . . so also when the government acts as guardian and tutor the relevant question is whether the search is one that a reasonable guardian and tutor might undertake. Given the findings of need made by the District Court, we conclude that in the present case it is.

Vernonia School District v. Acton, 515 U.S. 646 (1995), United States Supreme Court.

The Supreme Court heard another challenge to mandatory drug testing in the 1997 case *Chandler v. Miller*.[15] A Georgia statute requiring candidates for political office to submit to drug tests was at issue. The Court held that Georgia's interest in having drug-free political officials did not rise to the level of a special need. The Court stated:

> Georgia's certification requirement is not well designed to identify candidates who violate antidrug laws. Nor is the scheme a credible means to deter illicit drug users from seeking election to state office. The test date—to be scheduled by the candidate anytime within 30 days prior to qualifying for a place on the ballot—is no secret. As counsel for respondents acknowledged at oral argument, users of illegal drugs, save for those prohibitively addicted, could abstain for a pretest period sufficient to avoid detection. . . . Respondents and the United States as amicus curiae rely most heavily on our decision in *Von Raab*, which sustained a drug-testing program for Customs Service officers. . . . Hardly a decision opening broad vistas for suspicionless searches, *Von Raab* must be read in its unique context. As the Customs Service reported in announcing the testing program: "Customs employees, more than any other Federal workers, are routinely exposed to the vast network of organized crime that is inextricably tied to illegal drug use. . . ." We stressed that "[d]rug interdiction ha[d] become the agency's primary enforcement mission" . . . and that the employees in question would have "access to vast sources of valuable contraband." . . . Furthermore, Customs officers "ha[d] been the targets of bribery by drug smugglers on numerous occasions," and several had succumbed to the temptation. . . . Respondents overlook a telling difference between *Von Raab* and Georgia's candidate drug-testing program. In *Von Raab*, it was "not feasible to subject employees [required to carry firearms or concerned with interdiction of controlled substances] and their work product to the kind of day-to-day scrutiny that is the norm in more traditional office environments." *Id.*, at 674, 109 S. Ct., at 1395. Candidates for public office, in contrast, are subject to relentless scrutiny—by their peers, the public, and the press. Their day-to-day conduct attracts attention notably beyond the norm in ordinary work environments.
>
> What is left, after close review of Georgia's scheme, is the image the State seeks to project. By requiring candidates for public office to submit to drug testing, Georgia displays its commitment to the struggle against drug abuse. The suspicionless tests, according to respondents, signify that candidates, if elected, will be fit to serve their constituents free from the influence of illegal drugs. But Georgia asserts no evidence of a drug problem among the State's elected officials, those officials typically do not perform high-risk, safety-sensitive tasks, and the required certification immediately aids no interdiction effort. The need revealed, in short, is symbolic, not "special," as that term draws meaning from our case law. . . . However well meant, the candidate drug test Georgia has devised diminishes personal privacy for a symbol's sake. The Fourth Amendment shields society against that state action.[16]

AIDS testing has also become a controversial topic in recent years. In *Dunn v. White*,[17] the issue of mandatory AIDS testing was raised by a prison inmate. The inmate, who was being disciplined for refusing to submit to AIDS testing, claimed that the government was violating his Fourth Amendment rights by compelling him to submit to an AIDS test without having probable cause or a warrant. The Tenth Circuit Court of Appeals found that such a test is a search under the Fourth Amendment. However, because prison officials have the responsibility of making placement, segregation, and treatment decisions concerning inmates, and because they must consider the health and safety of all the inmates and employees of the institution, mandatory AIDS testing is reasonable and can be conducted without first obtaining a warrant and without probable cause. Again, the AIDS test was being conducted for administrative purposes, not as part of a criminal investigation.

Another case, however, evinces the limitation on the government's authority to conduct AIDS testing. In *Glover v. Eastern Nebraska Community Office of Retardation*,[18] the issue was whether a multicounty health agency, which provided services to the developmentally disabled, could require its employees to undergo AIDS and hepatitis testing. The agency contended that the policy was implemented to prevent the transmission of those diseases from employees to disabled citizens. The court found that the evidence indicated there was no danger of transmission in some circumstances, such as when staff members tended to the hygienic needs of the disabled citizens, and only minimal in others, such as when patients bit or scratched themselves and the staff. Furthermore, there was no evidence of sexual abuse of the patients by the staff. Therefore, the governmental interest did not outweigh the employees' interests in privacy.

To conduct a blood, urine, or breath test is clearly a search under the Fourth Amendment. If the purpose of such a test is the detection and prosecution of criminal conduct, there must be a showing of probable cause, and in most circumstances a warrant must be issued before the test is conducted.

If the objective is not the detection and prosecution of crime, but is administrative, the standard is different. If a test encroaches on a person's reasonable expectation of privacy, then the test constitutes a search. However, it is likely that the test need satisfy only the Fourth Amendment's reasonableness requirement, not its probable cause and warrant requirements. Therefore, a balancing of the government's interest against the individual's privacy interest must be made. The more invasive the testing procedure, the greater the government's interest must be to satisfy the Fourth Amendment.

In sum, most testing occurs in the commercial setting and does not encroach on civil rights. Agencies have broad testing authority in these situations. The authority of agencies to conduct tests is, however, more limited whenever a constitutional right is implicated.

Deoxyribonucleic acid, commonly referred to as DNA, is a complex compound with two strands that spiral around one another, forming what is known as a double helix. Inside each helix are molecules, called nucleotide bases that connect the two strands of the helix in a twisted fashion. There are four bases, identified by the letters *A*, *T*, *G*, and *C*. The A base of one strand attaches to the T base of its counterpart strand. In the same manner, the G base of one strand connects to the C base of the opposing strand. There are more than three billion base pairs in human DNA with about three million differencing between humans. The resulting code is unique to every person and can be found in nearly all the cells of a person's body: blood, semen, hair, and saliva. DNA testing is reliable and common today. Beyond identity, DNA reveals a host of personal information, such as predispositions to disease, ethnicity, sex, eye and hair color.

Commonly depicted in popular media and often reported by journalists, DNA is a tool used by law enforcement to apprehend and prosecute offenders. But it isn't just law enforcement officers who use DNA testing. In 2009, the University of Akron, a public university, adopted a policy requiring applicants to provide DNA samples for criminal background checks. After considerable opposition by faculty and civil rights groups to the swab for a job policy, the University rescinded the DNA requirement.[19]

In 1994, the Maryland General Assembly created a statewide DNA database and mandated DNA samples from individuals arrested for violent crimes. In 2009, Alonzo Jay King was arrested for assault, swabbed pursuant to the law, and his DNA matched the DNA of an alleged rapist from years before. He was convicted of the rape, but his conviction was reversed by the Court of Appeals of Maryland which found the warrantless, suspicionless DNA collection to be violative of the Fourth Amendment's probable cause and warrant requirements. The Supreme Court of the United States reversed this decision finding that the collection of DNA through a cheek swab was the equivalent of taking fingerprints and photos of convicted persons, practices the Court had previously upheld.[20]

7.3(c) Closely Regulated Businesses

In the area of administrative inspections, one important exception to the warrant requirement of the Fourth Amendment has been recognized. Closely regulated businesses may be inspected without a warrant being obtained first.[21]

The rationale for the exception is that owners and operators of closely regulated businesses have a reduced expectation of privacy. Also, enterprises are usually closely regulated because the government perceives an important interest, such as safety, that warrants special attention. To require the government to obtain a warrant in these extreme circumstances would disable the agency's attempts to protect the public.

For a warrantless inspection to be valid, the following elements must be found:

1. The government must have a substantial interest *and*
2. The warrantless inspection must further the government's substantial interest *and*
3. The statutory scheme that substitutes for the warrant procedure must be reasonable.

If these criteria are met, a warrantless search of a closely regulated business by an administrative agency acting within its mandate is constitutionally sound. The warrantless inspection of a mine was at issue in *Donovan v. Dewey*.

Donovan v. Dewey

452 U.S. 594 (1981)

In this case we consider whether §103(a) of the Federal Mine Safety and Health Act of 1977 . . . which authorizes warrantless inspections of underground and surface mines, violates the Fourth Amendment. . . .

The Federal Mine Safety and Health Act of 1977 . . . requires the Secretary of Labor to develop detailed mandatory health and safety standards to govern the operation of the Nation's mines. . . . [It also] provides that federal mine inspectors are to inspect underground mines at least four times per year and surface mines at least twice a year to insure compliance with these standards, and to make followup inspections to determine whether previously discovered violations have been corrected. This section also grants mine inspectors "a right of entry to, upon, or through any coal or other mine" and states that "no advance notice of an inspection shall be provided to any person." If a mine operator refuses to allow a warrantless inspection conducted pursuant to § 103(a), the Secretary is authorized to institute a civil action

(continued)

to obtain injunctive or other appropriate relief. . . . [The Act also delegated rulemaking authority to the Secretary to regulate violations of the Act. Pursuant to this authority, the Secretary instituted civil fines for mine operators who refused to permit inspections under the Act.]

In July 1978, a federal mine inspector attempted to inspect quarries owned by appellee Waukesha Lime and Stone Co. in order to determine whether all 25 safety and health violations uncovered during a prior inspection had been corrected. After the inspector had been on the site for about an hour, Waukesha's president, appellee Douglas Dewey, refused to allow the inspection to continue unless the inspector first obtained a search warrant. The inspector issued a citation to Waukesha for terminating the inspection, and the Secretary subsequently filed this civil action in the District Court for the Eastern District of Wisconsin seeking to enjoin appellees from refusing to permit warrantless searches of the Waukesha facility. . . .

Our prior cases have established that the Fourth Amendment's prohibition against unreasonable searches applies to administrative inspections of private commercial property. *Marshall v. Barlow's, Inc.* . . . However, unlike searches of private homes, which generally must be conducted pursuant to a warrant in order to be reasonable under the Fourth Amendment, legislative schemes authorizing warrantless administrative searches of commercial property do not necessarily violate the Fourth Amendment. . . .

[I]n *Colonnade Corp. v. United States*, we recognized that because the alcoholic beverage industry had long been "subject to close supervision and inspection," Congress enjoyed "broad power to design such powers of inspection . . . as it deems necessary to meet the evils at hand." . . . Similarly, in *United States v. Biswell*, this Court concluded that the Gun Control Act of 1968, 18 U.S.C. § 921 *et seq.*, provided a sufficiently comprehensive and predictable inspection scheme that the warrantless inspections mandated under the statute did not violate the Fourth Amendment. After describing the strong federal interest in conducting unannounced, warrantless inspections, we noted:

> It is also plain that inspections for compliance with the Gun Control Act pose only limited threats to the dealer's justifiable expectations of privacy. When a dealer chooses to engage in this pervasively regulated business . . ., he does so with the knowledge that his records, firearms, and ammunition will be subject to effective inspection. . . . The dealer is not left to wonder about the purposes of the inspector or the limits of his task. . . .

These decisions make clear that a warrant may not be constitutionally required when Congress has reasonably determined that warrantless searches are necessary to further a regulatory scheme and the federal regulatory presence is sufficiently comprehensive and defined that the owner of commercial property cannot help but be aware that his property will be subject to periodic inspections undertaken for specific purposes.

We re-emphasized this exception to the warrant requirement most recently in *Marshall v. Barlow's, Inc.* In that case, we held that absent consent a warrant was constitutionally required in order to conduct administrative inspections under § 8(a) of the Occupational Safety and Health Act of 1970, 29 U.S.C. § 657(a). That statute imposes health and safety standards on all businesses engaged in or affecting interstate commerce that have employees, 29 U.S.C. § 652(5), and authorizes representatives of the Secretary to conduct inspections to ensure compliance with the Act. . . .

Applying this analysis to the case before us, we conclude that the warrantless inspections required by the Mine Safety and Health Act do not offend the Fourth Amendment. As an initial matter, it is undisputed that there is a substantial federal interest in improving the health and safety conditions in the Nation's underground and surface mines. In enacting the statute, Congress was plainly aware that the mining industry is among the most hazardous in the country and that the poor health and safety record of this industry has significant deleterious effects on interstate commerce. . . .

[When investigating mine safety, a congressional committee stated,] "[I]n [light] of the notorious ease with which many safety or health hazards may be concealed if advance warning of inspection is obtained, a warrant requirement would seriously undercut this Act's objectives." S. Rep. No. 95–181, p. 27 (1977), *U.S. Code Cong. & Admin. News 1977*, pp. 3401, 3427.

We see no reason not to defer to this legislative determination. Here, as in *Biswell*, Congress could properly conclude: "[I]f inspection is to be effective and serve as a credible deterrent, unannounced, even frequent inspections are essential. In this context, the prerequisite of a warrant could easily frustrate inspection." . . .

Because a warrant requirement clearly might impede the "specific enforcement needs" of the Act, *Marshall v. Barlow's, Inc.*, 436 U.S., at 321, 98 S. Ct., at 1825, the only real issue before us is whether the statute's inspection program, in terms of the certainty and regularity of its application, provides a constitutionally adequate substitute for a warrant. We believe that it does. Unlike the statute at issue in *Barlow's*, the Mine Safety and Health Act applies to industrial activity with a notorious history of serious accidents and unhealthful working conditions. The Act is specifically tailored to address those concerns, and the regulation of mines it imposes is sufficiently pervasive and defined that the owner of such a facility cannot help but be aware that he "will be subject to effective inspection." First, the Act requires inspection of all mines and specifically defines the frequency of inspection. Representatives of the Secretary must inspect all surface mines at least twice annually and all underground mines at least four times annually. Similarly, all mining operations that generate explosive gases must be inspected at irregular 5-, 10-, or 15-day intervals. § 813(i). Moreover, the Secretary must conduct followup inspections of mines where violations of the Act have previously been discovered, § 813(a), and must inspect a mine immediately if notified by a miner or a miner's representative that a violation of the Act or an imminently dangerous condition exists. § 813(g). Second, the standards with which a mine operator is required to comply are all specifically set forth in the Act or in Title 30 of the Code of Federal Regulations. Indeed, the Act requires that the Secretary inform mine operators of all standards proposed pursuant to the Act. § 811(e). Thus, rather than leaving the frequency and purpose of inspections to the unchecked discretion of Government officers, the Act establishes a predictable and guided federal regulatory presence. Like the gun dealer in *Biswell*, the operator of a mine "is not left to wonder about the purposes of the inspector or the limits of his task.". . .

Finally, the Act provides a specific mechanism for accommodating any special privacy concerns that a specific mine operator might have. The Act prohibits forcible entries, and instead requires the Secretary, when refused entry onto a mining facility, to file a civil action in federal court to obtain an injunction against future refusals. . . . This proceeding provides an adequate forum for the mineowner to show that a specific search is outside the federal regulatory authority, or to seek from the district court an order accommodating any unusual privacy interests that the mineowner might have. . . .

Under these circumstances, it is difficult to see what additional protection a warrant requirement would provide. The Act itself clearly notifies the operator that inspections will be performed on a regular basis. Moreover, the Act and the regulations issued pursuant to it inform the operator of what health and safety standards must be met in order to be in compliance with the statute. The discretion of Government officials to determine what facilities to search and what violations to search for is thus directly curtailed by the regulatory scheme. In addition, the statute itself embodies a means by which any special Fourth Amendment interests can be accommodated. Accordingly, we conclude that the general program of warrantless inspections authorized by § 103(a) of the Act does not violate the Fourth Amendment.

Donovan v. Dewey, 452 U.S. 594 (1981), United States Supreme Court.

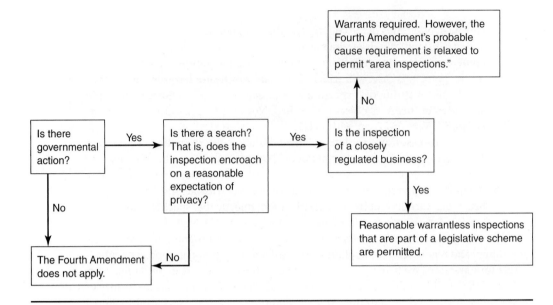

FIGURE 7-2   Administrative inspection and the Fourth Amendment.

Finally, be aware that if an administrative agency performs a criminal law enforcement function or assists a law enforcement agency in the performance of its duties, general principles of criminal law and procedure usually apply. For example, criminal law principles apply if the police contact an agency and request that it conduct an inspection of a business for the purpose of discovering illegal drugs on the premises. Such an inspection would be constitutionally unsound unless probable cause existed to believe that drugs would be found on the premises and a warrant had been obtained to conduct the search. The lesser probable cause standard of administrative inspections would not apply (see Figure 7-2).

7.4 SUBPOENAS

LEGAL TERM

Subpoenas
(also called *summonses* in administrative law) Directives to a person or organization to appear to testify or to appear with specified documents. The latter is a *subpoena duces tecum.*

What is an agency to do if an individual or business refuses to provide required information? Most agencies may issue *subpoenas* to compel production. Without subpoena power, agencies would have no method of enforcing compliance with reporting or other production-of-information requirements. Agencies do not have an inherent power to issue subpoenas, though; Congress must expressly grant that power in the agency's enabling statute.

Some statutes specify who has the authority to issue subpoenas: often the head of the agency. Because it is impractical to have every subpoena issued by a large agency signed by the agency head, the agency head often signs and provides blank subpoenas for use by lower agency officials (see Figure 7-3). In some instances, the authority to sign subpoenas is delegated to subordinates. In the case of Equal Employment Opportunity Commission, any member of the commission (referred to as the board in the law) may issue a subpoena. [22]

In federal court proceedings, subpoenas must be issued by the court clerk at the request of a party. The subpoena may be issued blank, to be filled out later by the requesting party. The requesting party need not show materiality or relevance to obtain a subpoena.

FORM NLRB-32
(12/91)

SUBPOENA

UNITED STATES OF AMERICA
NATIONAL LABOR RELATIONS BOARD

To _____

_____

As requested by :_____

_____

whose address is _____
              (Street)   (City)   (State)   (ZIP)

YOU ARE HEREBY REQUIRED AND DIRECTED TO APPEAR BEFORE _____

_____ of the National Labor Relations Board

at _____

in the City of _____

on the _____ day of _____ 20 _____ at _____ (a.m.) (p.m.) to testify in

_____
(Case Name and Number)

_____

_____

_____

_____

_____

A-137301

Under the seal of the National Labor Relations Board, and authorized by the undersigned Member of the Board, this Subpoena is

Issued at

this   day of   20

Signature of Agency Official

NOTICE TO WITNESS. Witness fees for attendance, subsistence, and mileage under this subpoena are payable by the party at whose request the witness is subpoenaed. A witness appearing at the request of the General Counsel of the National Labor Relations Board shall submit this subpoena with the voucher when claiming reimbursement.

FIGURE 7-3   Subpoena used by the National Labor Relations Board.

The same is not true in administrative proceedings. The APA itself does not confer the power to issue subpoenas; it does provide that agency subpoenas authorized by another statute may be issued at the request of a party. It further states that an agency may require the requesting party to submit a statement showing "general relevance and reasonable scope of the evidence sought."[23] An agency may, if these elements are not proved, deny the request for a subpoena. Even though not required to do so, some federal agencies have adopted the practice of not requiring submission of a statement of relevance and scope of evidence sought.[24]

7.4(a) Enforcement of Subpoenas

If a person or entity refuses to comply with a reporting or disclosure requirement, the agency's next step is to issue a subpoena for the information. What if the subpoena is not respected? Generally, the agency is powerless at this point. It has no authority to punish the violator.

That does not mean that no remedy exists. Agencies may seek to enforce their subpoenas in court. The agency actually files a suit seeking an order of the court requiring the party to comply with the administrative subpoena. If the reviewing court determines that the request is lawful, it issues an order requiring compliance. Refusal to comply with the court order can be punished as contempt of court.

Although a few statutes provide that refusal to comply with an administrative subpoena may be punished with criminal penalties, most do not allow criminal penalties until court enforcement has occurred. This is a good practice because it gives the nondisclosing parties an opportunity to present their objections to an impartial judicial officer before risking penal sanctions.

Some statutes require that an objection to an administrative subpoena be made to the agency directly within a certain period of time. This is the administrative law equivalent of the motion to quash a court subpoena. If a party fails to make a timely objection to the subpoena before the agency, the doctrine of exhaustion of administrative remedies will prevent the party from objecting in court. Objections to subpoenas issued by the Equal Employment Opportunity Commission, for example, must first be made to the Director of the EEOC or to its General Counsel. The Director or General Counsel is then charged with reviewing the objections and making a recommendation to the commission, which makes the final agency decision whether to sustain or rescind the subpoena. If the order is sustained and the employer or other person refuses to comply, then the EEOC must file an enforcement action in a United States district court.[25]

When before a court, at an agency's request to enforce an administrative subpoena, the nondisclosing party is given the opportunity to present objections to the subpoena. Ironically, one of the most obvious defenses—that the agency does not have jurisdiction—may not be raised in federal court. It has been held that the determination of jurisdiction is best made by the agency at the subpoena stage; therefore, reviewing courts are not to entertain objections based on lack of jurisdiction.[26]

A party may raise objections based on violation of a privilege, such as attorney–client or accountant–client privilege. Subpoenas that lack a lawful purpose, are intended as harassment, or unduly burdensome, may also be objectionable. Constitutional challenges, such as those based on the First Amendment's free exercise of religion and association clauses, the Fourth Amendment, and the Fifth Amendment, may also be raised.

It has been determined that administrative subpoenas for information do come within the ambit of the Fourth Amendment. As discussed previously, though, the Fourth Amendment is applied differently in the administrative context than in the criminal. There is no real probable cause requirement for subpoenas, although the Fourth Amendment does require that any subpoenas issued be reasonable. Administrative subpoenas are reasonable if the agency investigation is for a lawful purpose, the information sought is relevant to that purpose, and the request is not unreasonably burdensome, oppressive, or invasive of privilege.

7.5 PARALLEL PROCEEDINGS

Civil and administrative laws often overlap with criminal laws. In some instances, a single statute may have both a criminal and a civil (often administrative) aspect. In such cases, parallel civil and criminal proceedings are possible. Generally, parallel proceedings are constitutionally sound. Courts may, however, suspend an administrative proceeding if necessary to preserve a constitutional or statutory right. For example, discovery is broader in civil cases than in criminal. It would be inappropriate for the government to initiate a civil case parallel to a criminal case in hopes of benefiting from the broader discovery rules. Likewise, the same theory could be used to circumvent protection for prosecution or defense strategy, violate the Fifth Amendment's privilege against self-incrimination, or otherwise prejudice a case.[27]

7.6 PAPERWORK REDUCTION ACT

In 1980, the Paperwork Reduction Act[28] became law. The goals of the law are many:

- To minimize paperwork for individuals, businesses, and the federal government
- To minimize the cost to the federal government of collecting, maintaining, and disseminating information
- To maximize the usefulness of information collected by the federal government
- To make federal law on the collection and dissemination of information uniform
- To reduce fraud and waste
- To assure that privacy and confidentiality are preserved, including the requirements of the Privacy Act

As you can see, the goals of the law are lofty. The Paperwork Reduction Act creates a comprehensive administrative scheme to reduce paperwork and preserve the privacy of individuals and businesses. The Supreme Court commented that the Paperwork Reduction Act was enacted in response to one of the less auspicious aspects of the enormous growth of our federal bureaucracy: its seemingly insatiable appetite for data. Outcries from small businesses, individuals, and state and local governments, which were buried under demands for paperwork, led Congress to institute these controls.[29]

The Office of Information and Regulatory Affairs (OIRA) was established within the Office of Management and Budget (OMB) to oversee the management of the Paperwork Reduction Act. The OIRA is charged with establishing policies and standards for the collection, maintenance, and dissemination of information by federal administrative agencies.

The OMB was also delegated the responsibility of monitoring federal agency compliance with the Privacy Act. In fact, all requests for the collection of information by administrative agencies must be approved by the OMB. In this effort, the OMB enforces Congress's mandate that 10 elements be present before an agency establishes a new reporting requirement. These include a determination that the data are necessary to the functioning of the agency, are within the jurisdiction of the agency, and have practical utility.

The OMB reports that the total paperwork burden has been reduced, as have the hours committed to satisfying information demands since the law came into effect. Therefore, the Paperwork Reduction Act serves as an additional check against overzealous attempts by administrative agencies to collect information.

7.7 CONCLUSION

Agencies need information from individuals and businesses to perform their functions, but too much information collection is costly and a threat to privacy. The Courts have done little to control the information-gathering power of agencies. Thus, Congress enacted the Paperwork Reduction Act, and recent presidents have issued executive orders limiting the discretion of agency officials to require citizens to maintain and report data to the government.

Inspections by agency officials may give rise to privacy concerns. Today, the Courts distinguish searches in the criminal context from administrative inspections. Although all searches and inspections are governed by the Fourth Amendment and must be reasonable, the Fourth Amendment's probable cause requirement is relaxed in the administrative context. If an inspection is authorized by the appropriate legislative body, does not have the enforcement of criminal laws as its purpose, and is reasonable in method, a court can issue an inspection warrant, regardless of probable cause to believe that there has been a code violation. Moreover, if the business to be inspected is closely regulated, no warrant is necessary. Again, the inspection must be authorized by statute or ordinance and be reasonable.

LAWLINKS

The Washburn University School of Law has an award-winning Web site with state, federal, and academic legal materials. Point your browser to http://washlaw .edu/ to access this site.

REVIEW **QUESTIONS**

1. When does an agency possess the authority to require disclosure of records?
2. Define and distinguish derivative use immunity from transactional immunity.
3. Does the Fourth Amendment's warrant requirement apply to administrative inspections?
4. What must be shown to justify a warrantless inspection of a closely regulated business?
5. What is a subpoena?
6. What justifications have been given by the Supreme Court for lowering the Fourth Amendment standard of probable cause in administrative inspection cases?

CRITICAL THINKING AND **APPLICATIONS PROBLEMS**

1. Do you believe that the Fourth Amendment's probable cause requirement should be different in administrative cases than in criminal cases? Explain your answer.
2. Should agencies be given the authority to enforce orders, or should they be forced to resort to judicial enforcement? Explain your answer.
3. Is it a search under the Fourth Amendment to require employees of a nuclear power plant to submit to drug testing?
4. Must an agency obtain a warrant before requiring a commercial airline pilot to submit to a drug test? What about an airline telephone reservations employee? Explain your answers.
5. State Motor Vehicles and Transportation Agency (SMVTA) conducts a study and concludes that most accidents involving passenger buses are caused by bus drivers who are under the influence of alcohol or drugs. As a result, SMVTA promulgates a regulation pursuant to a delegation of rulemaking authority from State Legislature, which reads:

Applicability of Law

This law applies to any organization, whether public or private, that provides passenger transportation in motor vehicles that have the capacity of carrying 10 or more passengers at one time.

Mandatory Drug and Alcohol Testing—Drivers

All employers shall require all employee-drivers to submit to a blood or urine test designed to detect the presence of controlled substances or alcohol immediately after the employee has been involved in an accident while driving one of the employer's transportation vehicles. Such test is to be conducted in a safe and medical environment. Urine testing shall be conducted privately without the presence of witnesses. If a test reveals that a driver is impaired, the employer is to immediately suspend the driver and conduct a hearing on the fitness of the driver to continue work within 48 hours of the suspension.

Mandatory Drug and Alcohol Testing—Nondrivers

All employers shall require all employees to submit to a blood or urine test designed to detect the presence of controlled substances or alcohol if the employer has a reasonable suspicion, based on particularized facts, that an employee is impaired while at work. Such test is to be conducted in a safe and medical environment. Urine testing shall be conducted privately without the presence of witnesses. If a test reveals that the employee is impaired, the employer may either suspend the employee or require the employee to enroll in a certified treatment program. Employees may contest the results of the test at a hearing that is to be conducted within 48 hours of the suspension or referral for treatment.

Mandatory HIV/AIDS Testing—Drivers

All employers shall require their employee-drivers to submit to an HIV/AIDS test once yearly. Such test is to be conducted in a safe and medical environment. If a driver tests positive, the employer is to immediately suspend the driver and conduct a hearing on the fitness of the driver to continue work within 48 hours of the suspension. The driver may contest the results of the test at that hearing.

Discuss this statute, considering all the Fourth Amendment issues you discover.

ENDNOTES

1. *Oklahoma Press Publ'g Co. v. Walling*, 327 U.S. 186, 213 (1946).
2. Craig E. Richardson & *Strangled by Red Tape* 5 (Heritage Foundation, 1995).
3. Paulette L. Stenzel, *Can the ISO 14000 Series Environmental Management Standards Provide a Viable Alternative to Government Regulations?*, 37 Am. Bus. L.J. 237 (2000).
4. APA § 555(c).
5. 18 U.S.C. § 6004.
6. *Marchetti v. United States*, 390 U.S. 39 (1968).
7. APA § 555(c).
8. *Id.* § 554(a)(3).
9. *United States v. Morton Salt Co.*, 338 U.S. 632, 643–44 (1950).
10. *Skinner v. Railway Labor Executive Ass'n*, 489 U.S. 602, 628 (1989).
11. See *Schmerber v. California*, 384 U.S. 757 (1966).
12. *Ruston v. Nebraska Pub. Power Dist.*, 844 F.2d 562 (8th Cir. 1988).
13. 489 U.S. 656 (1989).
14. The Supreme Court upheld the rule in regard to the first two groups of employees—those who engaged in drug interdiction and those who handled classified documents—because it could not glean from the record whether the classification was too broad (specifically, whether it included employees who did not handle classified documents). On remand, the court of appeals remanded to the District Court, which found the classification to be improper.
15. 520 U.S. 305 (1997).
16. *Id.* at 319.
17. 880 F.2d 1188 (10th Cir. 1989), *cert. denied*, 493 U.S. 1059 (1990).
18. 867 F.2d 461 (8th Cir. 1989), *cert. denied*, 493 U.S. 932 (1989).
19. Audrey Williams June, *U. of Akron Rescinds DNA Requirement in Policy on Criminal Background Checks.* Chronicle of Higher Education, December 16, 2009; Audrey Williams June, *U. of Akron Rethinks Hiring Policy that Could Ask for DNA Sample*, Chronicle of Higher Education, November 8, 2009.
20. *Maryland v. King*, 569 U.S. _____ (2013)
21. *New York v. Burger*, 482 U.S. 691 (1987).
22. 42 U.S.C. §2000e-9.
23. APA § 555(d).
24. Schwartz, *Administrative Law* (3rd ed. 1991).
25. Id.
26. *Oklahoma Press Publ'g Co. v. Walling*, 327 U.S. 186 (1946).
27. Modjeska, *Administrative Law, Practice and Procedure* 32–33 (Lawyers Cooperative, 1982).
28. 44 U.S.C. § 3501 *et seq.*
29. *Dole v. Steelworkers*, 494 U.S. 26, 32 (1990).

chapter **eight**

FORMAL ADJUDICATIONS

LEARNING OBJECTIVES

After completing this chapter, you should be able to

- Define and distinguish adjudications from rulemaking under the federal APA.

- Explain when an adjudication is required under the APA, and apply this principle to a set of facts.

- Understand what is required for notice and a hearing to be adequate under the APA, to satisfy due process, and applicable case law.

- Distinguish formal from informal adjudications, including the process differences and when each is required.

- Identify and explain the various forms of discovery used in adjudications.

- Identify the different forms of decisions made in adjudications and the circumstances in which each form is issued.

- Explain how administrative law judges are appointed, the efforts that have been made to ensure their independence, and how the law addresses bias concerns.

- Brief a judicial opinion with little outside assistance. You should be successful in identifying the relevant facts. You should also be successful in identifying the legal issue and analyzing the court's rationale in at least 50 percent of your briefs.

The one who decides must hear.

JUDGE VINSON[1]

Southern Garment Mfrs. Ass'n V. Fleming, 122 F.2d 622, 626 (D. C. Cir.)

8.1 IN GENERAL

In this chapter you will learn more about agency adjudication. This extended treatment of formal adjudications is important because lawyers and legal assistants play an important role in this aspect of administrative procedure.

The APA provides that all proceedings that result in an order are adjudications.[2] *Order* is defined to include all actions, including licensing, that are not rulemaking.[3] As a result, a great number of agency actions are considered adjudications.

A proceeding involving an agency's charge that a person or business has violated a regulation or statute is an adjudication. It is an adjudication when an agency considers issuing, suspending, or revoking a permit or license. Most government employees are entitled to adjudicatory procedures when suspended or fired from government employment. Justice Holmes defined *adjudication* as a process that "investigates, declares and enforces liabilities as they stand on present or past facts and under laws supposed to already exist. That is the purpose and end."[4]

Remember that the procedures used for formal rulemaking are borrowed from formal adjudication. Therefore, many of the procedures should appear familiar to you. This chapter examines the procedures of adjudication but gives only an outline of the basic process. There is no uniform method of adjudication. For example, the process of adjudicating a claim for Social Security benefits is quite different from the process used to adjudicate a license claim to transport hazardous chemicals. Due process and the APA require of all agencies, however, that notice and a fair hearing be provided to interested parties. This discussion begins with the right to notice.

8.2 NOTICE

Adjudications are the administrative equivalent of court trials. Although the procedures and formalities may be more relaxed than in court trials, and may vary significantly from case to case, adversarial parties may present evidence, examine and cross-examine witnesses, and make arguments to a presiding agency official.

For this process to work, all parties must receive notice of an impending adjudication. The APA requires that parties be "timely informed" of the time, place, and nature of the hearing.[5] In addition, the agency is to inform the parties of the "legal authority and jurisdiction under which the hearing is to be held; and the matters of fact and law asserted."[6] These requirements are central to fairness, and the Due Process Clauses, as well as the APA, require such disclosures.

The reason for requiring notice of the time and location of a hearing is obvious. The rule requires "timely" notice and sets no specific date by which a party must have notice of an upcoming hearing. To be timely, notice must be made far enough in advance of a hearing to allow the parties to adequately prepare their cases. A few hours' notice is not likely to be adequate in any circumstance. Neither is only a few days. Whether a longer period is adequate will vary from case to case, and the decision is left to the courts if a party challenges the notice provided.

Statutes often set a specific minimum notice period. Unless it is unreasonable, courts will defer to this legislative judgment. Service of notice may be made by first-class mail; however, personal service is best. (See Figure 8-1.)

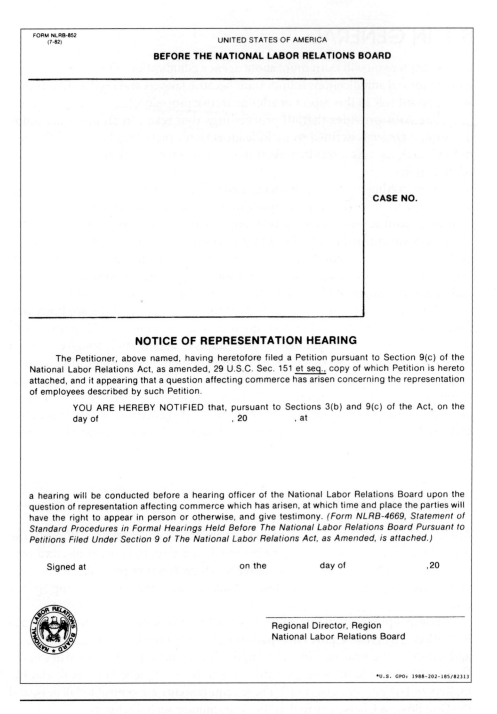

FIGURE 8-1 Notice of hearing used by the National Labor Relations Board. The right to appear can be either in person or otherwise.

The rule goes further than merely requiring notice of the time and location of a hearing. It recognizes that for notice to have value, a party must be informed of the "nature" of the hearing, the legal authority under which the agency believes it is empowered to hold such a hearing, and the issues of fact and law to be considered. Again, the test for determining whether a party has been given adequate notice of the nature of the case or issues to be considered is whether the information provided permitted the party to adequately prepare his or her case. If a notice is couched in "bureaucratic gobbledegook, jargon, double talk, federalese and insurancese, and double speak," it will fail.[7] Notice of both legal and factual issues must be made under the APA. Therefore, a notice that simply states that a party has violated a law is inadequate. The notice must also recite the basic facts that the agency believes constitute the violation.

At a hearing, the agency may try new issues as long as it is reasonable to do so. If a new issue is so unrelated to the issues described in the notice that a party could not have been prepared to address them, a continuance must be granted. Surprise by an agency is violative of due process.

Notices will not be invalidated because of technical defects. The purpose behind notice pleading is to make the parties aware of the issues to be tried at the hearing. As long as the notice contains sufficient information for the parties to prepare their cases, it is adequate. Therefore, a technical defect, such as a misspelled name, does not invalidate a notice. Of course, an incorrect hearing date is not merely technical and likely violates due process.

8.3 PARTIES AND PARTICIPATION

Two important questions that agencies must answer in adjudications is who must be given notice and who may participate in adjudications. There are a number of ways one can participate in an administrative proceeding. Obviously, if one is a named party, participation is required.

8.3(a) Parties in Interest and Intervention

Many APA provisions refer to *parties in interest*. For example, notice must be provided to all parties in interest, and parties in interest are entitled to appear at hearings. In addition, a person who qualifies as a party in interest may seek **intervention**. That is, if a person is not a named party in an administrative proceeding or lawsuit but is a party in interest, he or she may become part of the proceeding. Thus, it must be determined who qualifies to be a party in interest.

LEGAL TERM
Intervention
Process whereby a nonparty to a case becomes a party by claiming that he or she has an interest in the outcome of the case.

The APA does not expressly define the phrase *party in interest*. However, the courts have provided some guidance in this area. First, obvious parties must be allowed to participate. Those who are the subject of an agency action must be provided with notice and given an opportunity to participate in all hearings. A claimant for benefits, a licensee, and an applicant for services are obvious examples of interested parties. The problem is when an agency's action will affect those beyond the circle of obvious parties.

The line between those who are parties in interest and those who are not is not always easy to draw. For example, suppose that the Nuclear Regulatory Commission were to consider changing the safety standards under which nuclear power plants operate. Clearly, all nuclear power plants would be obvious parties. Would the residents of the areas surrounding the plants be parties in interest? What about the entire public?

Generally, the law of party in interest parallels the law on standing. That is, if an individual satisfies the standing requirements for participating in a judicial proceeding, the individual is a party in interest and eligible to participate at the administrative level.

The trend is to open administrative proceedings to participation by a broader range of parties. It is possible in federal administrative proceedings, in some circumstances, for an individual who does not satisfy standing requirements to qualify to participate. A few states have taken the opposite approach; there, some individuals who satisfy standing requirements do not qualify to participate at the administrative level. However, this represents the minority position. For a complete discussion, see Chapter 9 on the standing doctrine. A few important examples are examined there.

As is true for standing, those who will suffer some economic injury or loss pursuant to an agency action, even if that action is directed against another, qualify to intervene. For example, competitors of obvious parties, who will be affected by an agency decision, may be entitled to intervene to protect their interests.

In some instances, individual consumers may intervene on behalf of the consuming public. Although agencies are expected to guard the public's interest, the courts have come to realize that they do not always do so. Therefore, consumer advocacy groups occasionally intervene on behalf of all consumers, as in *Office of Communication v. FCC.*[8] This case involved the renewal of a television station's license without a prior hearing. Various groups representing the viewing audience petitioned the FCC to intervene in the administrative proceeding. The FCC refused to allow the groups to participate, finding that the public was not a party in interest. The circuit court of appeals reversed the FCC and held that the public need not suffer economic injury to be a party in interest. The interest of the viewing public in the content of the station's broadcasts was sufficient to mandate intervention.

An important development in the right to participation was the *Ashbacker Radio* decision issued by the Supreme Court of the United States. The rule established by this case, known as the *Ashbacker doctrine*, mandates that an agency have one consolidated comparative hearing whenever two or more parties are competing for one license. If granting one license (or other authority or benefit) excludes others from receiving the same, then both parties must be permitted to participate in a comparative hearing.

Ashbacker Radio Corp. v. Federal Communications Commission

326 U.S. 327 (1946)

The primary question in this case is whether an applicant for a construction permit under the Federal Communications Act . . . is granted the hearing to which he is entitled by [the Federal Communications Act], where the Commission, having before it two applications which are mutually exclusive, grants one without a hearing and sets the other for hearing.

In March 1944, the Fetzer Broadcasting Company filed with the Commission an application for authority to construct a new broadcasting station at Grand Rapids, Michigan, to operate at 1230 kc with 250 watts power, unlimited time. In May 1944, before the Fetzer application had been acted upon, petitioner filed an application for authority to change the operating frequency of its station WKBZ of Muskegon, Michigan, from 1490 kc with 250 watts power, unlimited time, to 1230 kc. The Commission, after stating that the simultaneous [use] on 1230 kc at Grand Rapids and Muskegon "would result in intolerable interference to both applicants," declared that the two applications were "mutually exclusive." The Commission, upon an examination of the Fetzer application and supporting data, granted it in June 1944, without a hearing. On the same day the Commission designated petitioner's application for hearing. Petitioner thereupon filed a petition for hearing, rehearing and other relief directed against the grant of the Fetzer application. The Commission denied this petition, stating, "The Commission has not denied petitioner's application. It has designated the application for hearing as required by Section 309(a) of the Act. At this hearing, petitioner will have ample opportunity to show that its operation as proposed will better serve the public interest than will the grant of the Fetzer application as authorized June 27, 1944. Such grant does not preclude the Commission at a later date from taking any action which it may find will serve the public interest. . . ." Petitioner filed a notice of appeal from the grant of the Fetzer construction permit in the Court of Appeals for the District of Columbia, asserting that it was a "person aggrieved or whose interests are adversely affected.". . .

Our chief problem is to reconcile two provisions of § 309(a) where the Commission has before it mutually exclusive applications. The first authorizes the Commission "upon examination" of an application for a station license to grant it if the Commission determines that "public interest, convenience, or necessity would be served" by the grant. The second provision of § 309(a) says that if, upon examination of such an application, the Commission does not reach such a decision, "it shall notify the applicant thereof, shall fix and give notice of a time and place for hearing thereon, and shall afford such applicant an opportunity to be heard under such rules and regulations as it may prescribe." It is thus plain that § 309(a) not only gives the Commission authority to grant licenses without a hearing, but also gives applicants a right to a hearing before their applications are denied. We do not think it is enough to say that the power of the Commission to issue a license on a finding of public interest, convenience or necessity supports its grant of one of two mutually exclusive applications without a hearing of the other. For if the grant of one effectively precludes the other, the statutory right to a hearing which Congress has accorded applicants before denials of their applications becomes an empty thing. We think that is the case here.

The Commission in its notice of hearing on petitioner's application stated that the application "will not be granted by the Commission unless the issues listed above are determined in favor of the applicant on the basis of a record duly and properly made by means of a formal hearing." One of the issues listed was the determination of "the extent of any interference which would result from the simultaneous operation" of petitioner's proposed station and Fetzer's station. Since the Commission itself stated that simultaneous operation of the two stations would result in "intolerable interference" to both, it is apparent that petitioner carries a burden which cannot be met. To place that burden on it is in effect to make its hearing a rehearing on the grant of the competitor's license rather than a hearing on the merits of its own application. That may satisfy the strict letter of the law but certainly not its spirit or intent.

The Fetzer application was not conditionally granted pending consideration of petitioner's application. Indeed, a stay of it pending the outcome of this litigation was denied. Of course the Fetzer license, like any other license granted by the Commission, was subject to certain conditions which the Act imposes as a matter of law. We fully recognize that the Commission, as it said, is not precluded "at a later date from taking any action which it may find will serve the public interest." No licensee obtains any vested interest in any frequency. The Commission for specified reasons may revoke any station license pursuant to the procedure prescribed by § 312(a) and may suspend the license of any operator on the grounds and in the manner specified by § 303(m). It may also modify a station license if in its judgment "such action will promote the public interest, convenience, and necessity, or the provisions of this chapter will be more fully complied with." § 312(b). And licenses for broadcasting stations are limited to three years, the renewals being subject to the same considerations and practice which affect the granting of original applications. § 307(d). But in all instances the licensee is given an opportunity to be heard before final action can be taken. What the Commission can do to Fetzer it can do to any licensee. As the Fetzer application has been granted, petitioner, therefore, is presently in the same position as a newcomer who seeks to displace an established broadcaster. By the grant of the Fetzer application petitioner has been placed under a greater burden

(continued)

> than if its hearing had been earlier. Legal theory is one thing. But the practicalities are different. . . .
>
> The public, not some private interest, convenience, or necessity, governs the issuance of licenses under the Act. But we are not concerned here with the merits. This involves only a matter of procedure. Congress has granted applicants a right to a hearing on their applications for station licenses. Whether that is wise policy or whether the procedure adopted by the Commission in this case is preferable is not for us to decide. We only hold that where two bona fide applications are mutually exclusive the grant of one without a hearing to both deprives the loser of the opportunity which Congress chose to give him. . . .
>
> Reversed.

Ashbacker Radio Corp. v. Federal Communications Commission,
326 U.S. 327 (1946), United States Supreme Court.

In summary, the right to participate has been extended beyond obvious parties. Competitors and other parties who may suffer some form of economic harm are allowed to participate. Economic injury is not, however, the only test of intervention. If a person can demonstrate the existence of some other legitimate interest, intervention may be permitted. The public itself may be represented when a general public concern exists. Any agency may set reasonable limitations on the right to participate, taking into consideration the party's interest in the outcome of the case, how adequately the party will be represented by other participants in its absence, and the effect intervention will have on the agency and the proceedings.

All parties in interest must receive notice and must be permitted to participate in the hearing. Those who are not named parties may seek to intervene.

In formal adjudications, all parties are entitled to make opening and closing statements, call witnesses, cross-examine witnesses, and otherwise participate. The joinder of a party, therefore, may add significant time and cost to a hearing.

8.3(b) Other Methods of Participation

Being a party is not the only way one can participate in a hearing. A person may be called as a witness. For many who are interested in a case but do not want to go so far as intervening, having the opportunity to testify may be satisfactory. Such an individual must, however, have information relevant to the proceeding; a mere narrative of opinion is not likely to be permitted.

A person or group may also seek to file an *amicus curiae* brief. Amicus participation is most common at the appellate stage of court proceedings although it sometimes occurs in administrative proceedings. Amicus briefs are an efficient tool because they permit a person or group to express a perspective or opinion without becoming a party. This is time-efficient.

Finally, a note about class-action suits: A *class action* is a lawsuit brought by an individual, group, agency, or other entity on behalf of a larger number of people. The person, persons, or entity responsible for litigating on behalf of the class is known as the *class representative*. All members of the class must have a similar interest in the case. For example, the Equal Employment Opportunity Commission may file a discrimination action against an employer on behalf of all female employees who were denied promotions during the years 1992 to 1994. Class actions are sometimes filed against administrative agencies as well. For example, all persons who were overcharged by a public utility may bring a class action to recover overpayments or enjoin the agency from collecting.

LEGAL TERMS

Amicus Curiae
Latin for "friend of the court"; a person or group that is not a party but is nevertheless allowed to file a brief with the court to express a particular opinion or point of view.

Class Action
Lawsuit brought by one person or a few persons on behalf of many others with similar interests.

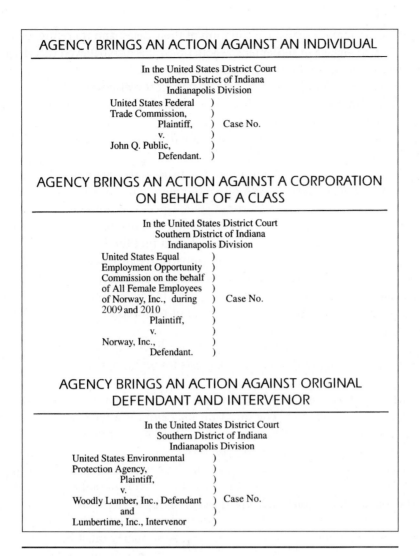

FIGURE 8-2   Sample captions in administrative suits.

Generally, all members of a class must be provided with notice of the filed lawsuit, any proposed settlement, or any impending agency or court hearing. A person who falls into a class may actively participate or may take a passive role, awaiting a settlement or decision after hearing. In either circumstance, all class members are entitled to full and zealous representation. Courts oversee settlements in class-action suits to be sure that the interests of unnamed class members are properly protected and not "sold out" by the class representative or the named class members, who are more likely to be involved with settlement negotiations.

Figure 8-2 shows various captions for agency suits.

8.4 DISCOVERY

Rules of civil procedure of the courts of the United States provide for ***discovery*** after a case has been initiated. Discovery is the pretrial process whereby the parties to a case exchange information and obtain information from nonparties to allow the parties to prepare for trial in an informed manner. Discovery prevents "trial by surprise." In addition, it encourages settlement because the parties learn the facts of the case and each others' legal theories early in the game. With this knowledge,

LEGAL TERM

Discovery
Pretrial process whereby the parties exchange information about the case.

the parties can make a realistic evaluation of their cases, and therefore, be in better positions to engage in settlement negotiations. It is also believed that discovery makes trials more fair, efficient, and smooth-running.

The Federal Rules of Civil Procedure permit the discovery of anything "reasonably calculated to lead to the discovery of admissible evidence."[9] However, exceptions are recognized. A party may seek a protective order whenever discovery is unduly burdensome or encroaches on a privilege, such as the attorney–client or work product privileges.

The rules of discovery in administrative proceedings are much different from those used in courts. First, the APA does not mention discovery except in the context of the Freedom of Information Act (that aspect is examined in Chapter 10). The APA, therefore, does not require agencies to disclose information prior to the hearing. Similarly, it has been determined that the U.S. Constitution does not require prehearing discovery in administrative proceedings.[10] Regardless, many agencies, such as the Federal Trade Commission, have adopted a set of discovery rules. Some are similar to the rules used in the federal courts. In addition, many agencies provide information even if not required to do so. Therefore, it is good practice always to make a request.

There are six primary tools of discovery: interrogatories, depositions, requests for production of documents, requests for admissions, bills of particulars, and subpoenas.

Interrogatories are written questions presented to a party to be answered under oath and in writing. The question may call for a narrative answer (e.g., "Explain what occurred on the night of . . .") or it may require a short, factual answer (e.g., "How many vehicles do you own . . .").

A ***deposition*** is oral testimony, given under oath, not in court. Usually, a certified court reporter takes a deposition—that is, administers the oath to the witness (deponent) and records the deposition either by audio, visual, or stenographic means. Generally, a party may be ordered to appear at a deposition by providing notice of the date, time, and place to appear. A nonparty must be served with a subpoena. All parties must be given notice that a deposition will take place and must be given the opportunity to examine the deponent.

Requests for production of documents may also be made. When so asked, a party must produce all documents named by the requesting party. A party need only produce copies of the documents, not originals.

A ***request for admissions*** is similar to an interrogatory. It is a written statement or statements that must be responded to in writing. However, unlike an interrogatory, the response cannot be narrative. The party responding must either admit that the statement is true, deny the statement, or articulate its objection to the statement.

If a pleading or complaint by an agency does not contain enough information to permit the other parties to prepare for hearing, a motion for more definite statement may be requested. If information in the possession of a nonparty is desired, the presiding judge may issue a subpoena requiring the person to appear for a deposition or to produce the documents or physical evidence desired.

Another discovery device that may be used by those charged by an agency is the ***Jencks Act***.[11] Under this statute, attorneys who are performing prosecutorial functions for the government must disclose prior statements of government witnesses after those witnesses have testified. This statute applies to both criminal and administrative enforcement cases. Because this causes delays in hearings, the government will often provide this information in advance of the hearing.

The Freedom of Information Act (FOIA) may also provide another means of discovery. This federal statute permits citizens access to public documents and information. Although not intended to be a discovery tool, a litigant or someone anticipating litigation can acquire information through the FOIA in most circumstances, as is discussed in more detail in Chapter 10.

Finally, one nondiscovery device should be mentioned: stipulations. A *stipulation* is an agreement between the parties that a particular matter is true. Stipulations expedite trial because they eliminate testimony and other evidence from being presented. For example, the parties to a hearing may agree that a company uses a particular procedure in disposing of toxic materials but may disagree as to whether that procedure is lawful. To save time, the parties can stipulate to the particular disposal procedure used. Once stipulated, the matter is treated as true at hearing, and the parties are bound by the terms of the stipulation agreement.

Stipulation
Binding agreement between the parties concerning a particular matter.

8.5 PREHEARING CONFERENCE

Section 556(c)(6) of the APA states, "employees presiding at hearings may hold conferences for the settlement or simplification of the issues by consent of the parties." The *prehearing conference* is the administrative equivalent of a judicial pretrial conference.

Because of the issues discussed during the conference, it is a good source of discovery for the parties. At the prehearing conference, the parties may discuss and identify the issues, discuss stipulations, review exhibits and other evidence, provide a list of witnesses expected to be called, and consider settlement. Also, the presiding official reviews the format and procedure of the hearing with the attorneys. The presiding officer decides when the prehearing conference is to take place and may conduct the conference days, weeks, or even months before the date of hearing.

8.6 PREHEARING SETTLEMENT AND ALTERNATIVE DISPUTE RESOLUTION

As you learned in the previous chapter, agencies possess considerable discretion in settling cases. This may occur anytime in the life of a case. Little attention is given to settlement in the APA, but §554(b) does require agencies to entertain settlement offers prior to the commencement of adjudicatory hearings if "time, the nature of proceedings, and the public interest permit." Even if permitted, the decision whether to accept such an offer is within the discretion of the appropriate agency officials.

In addition to settlement, the APA encourages agencies to use alternative dispute resolution (ADR) to dispose of cases. ADR is generally regarded as less expensive and less time-consuming than formal adjudication or litigation. Mediation, arbitration, and conciliation are commonly used forms of ADR.

8.7 THE HEARING

Simply because a proceeding qualifies as an adjudication under the APA does not mean that trial-type procedures must be used. As mentioned earlier, the APA mandates trial-type procedures only whenever another statute specifically requires them. Section 554 of the APA, entitled "Adjudications," applies only to those adjudications "required by statute to be determined on the record after opportunity for an agency hearing."

As you previously learned, a congressional mandate for a hearing is not likely to be construed as requiring a trial-type hearing; Congress must clearly state that the right to a trial-type hearing is granted. For example, one federal statute requires the Federal Trade Commission to provide a hearing at which the party "complained of shall have the right to appear . . . and show cause why an order should not be entered."[12] This clearly grants the right to have an evidentiary hearing.

If a full trial-type hearing is not required, an agency may use any other form of hearing within the limits of due process. Remember that in rare circumstances the Due Process Clauses may require that some form of evidentiary hearing be held, regardless of whether such a hearing is required by statute. This chapter is concerned with only formal adjudications or trial-type evidentiary hearings.

Such hearings are similar in many respects to court trials. The parties may make opening and closing statements—they are permitted to call and cross-examine witnesses; and they may introduce other evidence and make objections. An administrative law judge or other officer presides at the hearing. However, as you will learn, some important differences exist between judicial trials and administrative adjudications.

8.7(a) Evidence Admissibility

In federal and state courts, rules of evidence govern whether testimony, exhibits, or other evidence may be admitted. Evidence that is untrustworthy, irrelevant, or unduly prejudicial will be excluded from trial under various rules of evidence. For example, *hearsay* is generally not admissible in federal court (although many exceptions exist). Hearsay is a statement, made out of court by a declarant, that is offered to prove the matter asserted. Suppose that Cynthia is being sued by Kensleen for assault. At trial, Kensleen wishes to introduce testimony by Myoreen that Cynthia stated to Myoreen that Cynthia "punched Kensleen in the nose and she deserved it." This statement was made out of court and is being introduced to prove that the assault occurred. Therefore, it is hearsay and inadmissible.

The rules of evidence attempt to exclude certain forms of evidence because it is believed that lay jurors will give such evidence too much value. Because of this, the rules of evidence are not strictly enforced in bench trials (nonjury trials); it is presumed that judges will not be unduly influenced by such evidence. The same reasoning applies in administrative hearings. There is a presumption that administrative law judges can fairly determine the value and trustworthiness of evidence. Because of this, the Federal Rules of Evidence do not apply in federal administrative hearings.

The APA states, "[a]ny oral or documentary evidence may be received, but the agency as a matter of policy shall provide for the exclusion of irrelevant, immaterial, or unduly repetitious evidence."[13] Thus, agencies must establish policies concerning the exclusion of evidence, but they are not bound by common law or statutory rules of evidence.

A presiding officer of an administrative hearing may admit hearsay or other evidence that would be excluded from a judicial trial unless the agency has a rule of evidence that requires otherwise. Administrative law judges commonly take a liberal approach to evidence and admit nearly all evidence offered, often with the qualification "for what it's worth." This means that the fact finder will consider not only the substance of the evidence when making a decision, but also its weight, reliability, and value.

Prejudicial Error Rule   If an agency wrongfully admits evidence at a hearing, the mistake may not be fatal. Like courts, agency hearings are governed by the distinction between harmless and prejudicial error. Section 706 of the APA provides that on appeal to a court, "due account shall be taken of the rule of prejudicial error." An error is prejudicial if it had an impact on the outcome of the case. Accordingly, harmless errors are not reversible.

LEGAL TERM

Hearsay
Declarant's statement, made out of court, that is offered to prove the truth of the matter asserted.

SIDEBAR   *Two Different Examples of Discovery in Adjudications*

Agencies vary widely in the amount of discovery permitted in formal adjudications. The U.S. Department of Labor has promulgated a set of evidence rules that permit many of the same forms of discovery as permitted by the Federal Rules of Civil Procedure, the rules governing discovery in the federal courts. For example, 29 C.F.R. §18.13 provides that "[p]arties may obtain discovery by one or more of the following methods: Depositions upon oral examination or written questions; written interrogatories; production of documents or other evidence for inspection and other purposes; and requests for admission." Unless the administrative law judge orders otherwise, the frequency or sequence of these methods is not limited. Title 29 C.F.R., §18.14(b), mirrors the Federal Rules of Civil Procedure as well: "It is not ground for objection that information sought will not be admissible at the hearing if the information sought appears reasonably calculated to lead to the discovery of admissible evidence."

An example of the other extreme is the Small Business Administration's discovery rule in "size determination" cases. A *size determination* is the agency decision concerning whether a business qualifies as a "small business." Title 13 C.F.R., §134.310, is simple and direct: "Discovery will not be permitted in appeals from size determinations. . . ."

Legal Residuum Rule   Although agencies are not bound by court rules of evidence and, therefore, may admit incompetent evidence, their decisions should not be based on such evidence alone. Evidence that the courts view as incompetent may be used to support an agency decision, but it cannot be used as the only support for an agency decision. This is known as the ***legal residuum rule***. That is, there must be some minimal competent evidence supporting an agency decision. If there is not, the decision is invalid.

Under the legal residuum rule, most courts generally hold that an agency may not rely solely on hearsay evidence when making a decision. However, exceptions to this rule exist, as shown by the *Richardson* case.

Since *Richardson*, some lower courts have held that hearsay evidence may provide the sole basis for an agency decision in some administrative contexts. Others, however, have continued to apply the rule, reading *Richardson* not as overruling the legal residuum rule but as creating a narrow exception for cases in which a claimant has not exercised the right to subpoena an expert or where the administrative burden of requiring live testimony is significant.

LEGAL TERM

Legal Residuum Rule
Legal doctrine stating that although agency decisions may be based in large part on evidence that would be inadmissible in court, an agency's decision may not be based entirely on such evidence; a minimal "residuum" of competent evidence must support the agency's determination.

Richardson v. Perales

402 U.S. 389 (1971)

In 1966 Pedro Perales, a San Antonio truck driver, then aged 34, height [5 feet 9 inches], weight about 220 pounds, filed a claim for disability insurance benefits under the Social Security Act. . . .

The issue here is whether physicians' written reports of medical examinations they have made of a disability claimant may constitute "substantial evidence" supportive of a finding of nondisability, within the [statutory] standard, when the claimant objects to the admissibility of those reports and when the only live testimony is presented on his side and is contrary to the reports. . . .

(continued)

The hearing took place at the time designated. A supplemental hearing was held March 31. The claimant appeared at the first hearing with his attorney and with Dr. Morales. The attorney formally objected to the introduction of the several reports of Drs. Langston, Bailey, Mattson, and Lampert, and of the hospital records. Various grounds of objection were asserted, including hearsay, absence of an opportunity [to] cross-examine, absence of proof [that] the physicians were licensed to practice in Texas, [and] failure to demonstrate that the hospital records were proved under the Business Records Act. . . . Their objections were overruled and the reports and hospital records were introduced. The reports of Dr. Morales and of Dr. Munslow were then submitted by the claimant's counsel and admitted.

At the two hearings oral testimony was submitted by claimant Perales, by Dr. Morales, by a former fellow employee of the claimant, by a vocational expert, and by Dr. Lewis A. Leavitt, a physician board-certified in physical medicine and rehabilitation. . . .

We may accept the propositions advanced by the claimant, some of them long established, that procedural due process is applicable to the adjudicative administrative proceeding involving "the differing rules of fair play, which through the years, have become associated with differing types of hearings." . . .

The question, then, is as to what procedural due process requires with respect to examining physicians' reports in a Social Security disability claim hearing.

We conclude that a written report by a licensed physician who has examined the claimant and who sets forth in his report his medical findings in his area of competence may be received as evidence in a disability hearing and, despite its hearsay character and an absence of cross-examination, and despite the presence of opposing direct medical testimony and testimony by the claimant himself, may constitute substantial evidence supportive of a finding by the hearing examiner adverse to the claimant, when the claimant has not exercised his right to subpoena the reporting physician and thereby provide himself with the opportunity [to] cross-examine the physician.

We are prompted to this conclusion by a number of factors that, we feel, assure underlying reliability and probative value:

1. The identity of the five reporting physicians is significant. Each report presented here was prepared by a practicing physician who had examined the claimant. A majority (Drs. Langston, Bailey, and Mattson) were called into the case by the state agency. . . . We cannot, and do not, ascribe bias to the work of these independent physicians, or any interest on their part in the outcome of the administrative proceeding beyond the professional curiosity a dedicated medical man possesses.

2. The vast workings of the Social Security system make for reliability and impartiality in the consultant reports. We bear in mind that the agency operates essentially, and is intended so to do, as an adjudicator and not as an advocate or adversary. This is the congressional plan. We do not presume on this record to say that it works unfairly.

3. One familiar with medical reports and the routine of the medical examination, general or specific, will recognize their elements of detail and of value. The particular reports of the physicians who examined claimant Perales were based on personal consultation and personal examination and rested on accepted medical procedures and tests. . . .

4. So far as we can detect, there is no inconsistency whatsoever in the reports of the five specialists. Yet each result was reached by independent examination in the writer's field of specialized training.

5. Although the claimant complains of the lack of opportunity to cross-examine the reporting physicians, he did not take advantage of the opportunity afforded him under 20 C.F.R. §404.926 to request subpoenas for the physicians. . . .

6. Courts have recognized the reliability and probative worth of written medical reports even in formal trials and, while acknowledging their hearsay character, have admitted them as an exception to the hearsay rule. . . .

7. There is an additional and pragmatic factor which, although not controlling, deserves mention. This is what Chief Judge Brown has described as "[t]he sheer magnitude of that administrative burden," and the resulting necessity for written reports without "elaboration through the traditional facility of oral testimony.". . . With over 20,000 claims hearings annually, the cost of providing live medical testimony at those hearings, where need has not been demonstrated by a request for a subpoena, over and above the cost of the examinations, would be a substantial drain on the trust fund and on the energy of physicians already in short supply.

Richardson v. Perales, 402 U.S. 389 (1971), United States Supreme Court.

Privileged and Illegal Evidence Common law, recognizing the importance of the privacy of certain communications, developed privileges prohibiting the government from compelling disclosure of such communications. Husband–wife, parent–child, physician–patient, and attorney–client are but a few of the many privileges in the common law; many are now protected by statute as well.

The APA does not deal with the issue of privileged communication. Nevertheless, it is generally held that well-established privileges may be invoked in administrative proceedings.

Who may invoke a privilege? To answer this question, one must consider who the privilege is intended to protect. The purpose of the husband–wife privilege is to enhance communication between spouses and thereby promote marital harmony. Therefore, true to its purpose, either spouse may invoke the privilege as to his or her statements. Thus, if a wife intends to testify as to what her husband stated, he may object and have her testimony excluded. The same is not true in the physician–patient context. Because the purposes behind that privilege are to protect a patient's privacy, ensure confidence that such communications will remain confidential, and thereby promote better medical care, the patient may object to any evidence the physician might give. The physician, however, cannot claim privilege when the patient testifies.

Other evidence may be excluded from an administrative hearing if it was obtained illegally. In criminal cases, evidence obtained in an unconstitutional manner is inadmissible at trial pursuant to the *exclusionary rule*. Whether the exclusionary rule must be applied in administrative proceedings was the subject of the *Lopez-Mendoza* case. *Lopez-Mendoza* established that courts are to apply a cost-benefit analysis when deciding whether the exclusionary rule should apply to a particular proceeding. Courts have held in nearly all cases that the constitutionally based exclusionary rule is inapplicable in civil proceedings.

Congress may provide, however, that illegally obtained evidence is inadmissible in an administrative proceeding, even when the Constitution does not. For example, it has been determined that the Federal Wiretap Act[14] applies to all criminal, civil, and administrative proceedings. Therefore, any evidence obtained in violation of the act is inadmissible in administrative proceedings even though the Constitution does not require its exclusion. Further, Congress may broaden what is excludable to evidence obtained in violation of the Constitution and laws of the nation.

Finally, some agencies have established exclusionary rules that apply to that agency's proceedings alone. Thus, it is possible that evidence obtained in violation of the Constitution, a statute, or a regulation may be inadmissible because of an exclusionary rule created by any one of the three.

LEGAL TERM
Exclusionary Rule
Doctrine holding that evidence obtained unconstitutionally or illegally is inadmissible in criminal cases. The rule applies in some, but not all, administrative proceedings.

Immigration & Naturalization Service v. Lopez-Mendoza

468 U.S. 1032 (1984)

This litigation requires us to decide whether an admission of unlawful presence in this country made subsequent to an allegedly unlawful arrest must be excluded as evidence in a civil deportation hearing. We hold that the evidentiary rule need not be applied in such a proceeding.

Respondents Adan Lopez-Mendoza and Elias Sandoval-Sanchez, both citizens of Mexico, were summoned to separate deportation proceedings in California and Washington, and both were ordered deported. . . .

A deportation proceeding is a purely civil action to determine eligibility to remain in this country, not to punish an unlawful entry, though entering or remaining unlawfully in this country is itself a crime. . . .

A deportation hearing is held before an immigration judge. The judge's sole power is to order deportation; the judge cannot adjudicate guilt or punish the respondent for any crime related to unlawful entry into or presence in this country. Consistent with the civil nature of the proceeding, various protections that apply in the context of a criminal trial do not apply in a deportation hearing. . . .

The "body" or identity of a defendant or respondent in a criminal or civil proceeding is never itself suppressible as a fruit of an unlawful arrest, even if it is conceded that an unlawful arrest, search, or interrogation occurred. . . .

Respondent Sandoval-Sanchez has a more substantial claim. He objected not to his compelled presence at a deportation proceeding, but to evidence offered at that proceeding. The general rule in a criminal proceeding is that statements and other evidence obtained as a result of an unlawful, warrantless arrest are suppressible if the link between the evidence and the unlawful conduct is not too attenuated. . . . The reach of the exclusionary rule beyond the contest of a criminal prosecution, however, is less clear. . . .

In *United States v. Janis*, 428 U.S. 433, 96 S. Ct. 3021, 49 L. Ed. 2d 1046 (1976), this Court set forth a framework for deciding in what types of proceeding application of the exclusionary rule is appropriate. Imprecise as the exercise may be, the court recognized in *Janis* that there is no choice but to weigh the likely social benefits of excluding unlawfully seized evidence against the likely costs. On the benefit side of the balance "the 'prime purpose' of the [exclusionary] rule, if not the sole one, 'is to deter future unlawful police conduct.'". . . On the cost side there is the loss of often probative evidence and all of the secondary costs that flow from the less accurate or more cumbersome adjudication that therefore occurs. . . .

The likely deterren[t] value of the exclusionary rule in deportation proceedings is difficult to assess. On the one hand, a civil deportation proceeding is a civil complement to a possible criminal prosecution, and to this extent it resembles the civil proceeding under review in *Janis*. The INS does not suggest that the exclusionary rule should not continue to apply in criminal proceedings against an alien who unlawfully enters or remains in this country, and the prospect of losing evidence that might otherwise be used in a criminal prosecution undoubtedly supplies some residual deterrent to unlawful conduct by INS officials. But it is acknowledged that only a very small percentage of arrests of aliens are intended or expected to lead to criminal prosecutions. Thus the arresting officer's primary objective, in practice, will be to use evidence in a civil deportation proceeding. Moreover, here, in contrast to *Janis*, the agency officials who effect[ed] the unlawful arrest are the same officials who subsequently [brought] the deportation action. As recognized in *Janis*, the exclusionary rule is likely to be most effective when applied to such "intrasovereign" violations.

Nevertheless, several other factors significantly reduce the likely deterrent value of the exclusionary rule in a civil deportation proceeding. First, regardless of how the arrest is effected, deportation will still be possible when evidence not derived directly from the arrest is sufficient to support deportation. As the [Board of Immigration Appeals] has recognized, in many deportation proceedings "the sole matters necessary for the Government to establish are the respondent's identity and alienage—at which point the burden shifts to the respondent to prove the time, place and manner of entry. . . ." Since the person and identity of the respondents are not themselves suppressible . . . the INS must prove only alienage, and that will sometimes be possible using evidence gathered independently of, or sufficiently attenuated from, the original arrest. . . .

The second factor is a practical one. In the course of a year the average INS agent arrests almost 500 illegal aliens. Over 97.5% apparently agree to voluntary deportation without a formal hearing. . . . Among the remainder who do request a formal hearing (apparently a dozen or so in all, per officer, per year) very few challenge the circumstances of their arrest. . . . Every INS agent knows, therefore, that it is highly unlikely that any particular arrestee will end up challenging the lawfulness of his arrest in a formal deportation proceeding. . . .

Finally, the deterrent value of the exclusionary rule in deportation proceedings is undermined by the availability of alternative remedies for institutional practices by the INS that might violate Fourth Amendment rights. The INS is a single agency, under central federal control, and engaged in operations of broad scope but highly repetitive character. The possibility of declaratory relief against the agency thus offers a means for challenging the validity of INS practices, when standing requirements for bringing such an action can be met. . . .

Respondents contend that retention of the exclusionary rule is necessary to safeguard the Fourth Amendment rights of ethnic Americans, particularly Hispanic-Americans lawfully in this country. We recognize that respondents raise legitimate and important concerns. But application of the exclusionary rule to civil deportation proceedings can be justified only if the rule is likely to add significant protection to these Fourth Amendment rights. . . . For the reasons we have discussed we conclude that application of the rule in INS civil deportation proceedings, as in the circumstances discussed in *Janis*, "is unlikely to provide significant, much less substantial, additional deterrence." . . .

On the other side of the scale, the social costs of applying the exclusionary rule in deportation proceedings are both unusual and significant. The first cost is one that is unique to continuing violations of the law. Applying the exclusionary rule in proceedings not intended to punish past transgressions but to prevent their continuance or renewal would require the courts to close their eyes to ongoing violations of the law. . . .

Other factors also weigh against applying the exclusionary rule in deportation proceedings. The INS currently operates a deliberately simple deportation hearing system, streamlined to permit the quick resolution of very large numbers of deportation actions, and it is against this backdrop that the costs of the exclusionary rule must be assessed. . . .

At issue here is exclusion of credible evidence gathered in connection with peaceful arrests by INS officers. We hold that evidence derived from such arrests need not be suppressed in an INS civil deportation hearing.

Immigration & Naturalization Service v. Lopez-Mendoza, 468 U.S. 1032 (1984),
United States Supreme Court.

Official Notice   In judicial courts, parties may request (or a court may do it *sua sponte*) that the judge take judicial notice of facts. *Judicial notice* is a method of avoiding the need to prove the well known or obvious. The purpose of judicial notice is to save time. Rule 201(b) of the Federal Rules of Evidence provides that judicial notice may be taken of facts "generally known" or "capable of accurate and ready determination by resort to sources whose accuracy cannot readily be

LEGAL TERM
Sua Sponte
Latin for "on a court's own initiative."

questioned." For example, a court may take judicial notice that the United States was a participant in World War II.

Similar to judicial notice, a presiding officer at an agency adjudication may take **official notice** of facts. Official notice is broader than judicial notice. In the federal courts, judges may take judicial notice of facts that are obvious to the average person. Presiding officers are not so limited. Because officers of agencies are considered experts in their fields, official notice may be taken of any fact that is obvious not only to the average person but also to experts in the field being dealt with. Official notice of facts that an agency has come to know are true through its experience is permitted, as is notice of information in the agency's files. For example, the Environmental Protection Agency may take notice of the level of danger posed by a particular toxin if the agency has conducted a substantial study of the issue.

Notice may be taken only of those facts that are obvious or known to be true to the average person or expert. An expectation, prediction, or strong belief that something is true or will be proven true after the evidence is heard is insufficient to support official notice. Notice may not be taken of facts particular to an individual suit or litigation. The hearing officer may, however, notice a fact that is commonly seen by an agency and is relevant to a particular litigation. For example, notice may not be taken of whether received goods were actually paid for in a case. The agency may, however, take notice of the common business practice of paying for goods in advance of receipt and then give the company the opportunity to prove that the common business practice was not followed in a specific case. Notice may be taken of laws.

Whenever notice is taken of a material fact, the agency must give the parties an opportunity to disprove the truth of the fact noticed.[15] This is a due process fairness requirement. The fact noticed must be material to the adjudication before the right to disprove it exists. Further, the APA requires that any objection to a noticed fact be timely. The party opposing the noticed fact has the burden of disproving it.

An agency may notice a fact before, during, or after the hearing. If before, no problems are presented. If during, a hearing may be postponed until the parties have had an opportunity to refute the noticed fact. Sometimes an agency does not know it will rely on such a fact until the decisional stage of the proceeding; in such instances, the agency may either conduct another hearing on that issue or render its decision with the noticed fact included. If the latter is done, any party objecting to the noticed fact may then seek rehearing or reconsideration based on its objection to the noticed fact.

Whenever official notice is invoked, the parties are deprived of the due process rights to confrontation and cross-examination. Therefore, official notice must be used with caution. When used properly, official notice can greatly expedite a hearing without encroaching on any party's due process rights.

8.7(b) Burdens

When a trial or hearing is conducted, there are questions as to which party bears the burden of proving its contentions and by which standard the evidence and law are to be evaluated. *Burden* refers to the obligation of a party to prove its case. *Standard* refers to the level or degree by which a case must be proven.

Two burdens are recognized by law: production and persuasion. The *burden of production* concerns who in a proceeding has the responsibility to produce evidence or raise an issue. Once the burden of production is met, one party has the burden of persuading the trier of fact that its position is correct. This is the *burden of persuasion*.

Official Notice (also called *administrative notice*)
A presiding officer's declaration that a fact is true without any proof of that fact being offered.

In most instances, the party who carries the burden of production also carries the burden of persuasion. In administrative practice, as in judicial practice, the moving party has the **burden of proof**.[16] Presumably, this means the burden of both production and persuasion.

One exception to the rule that the burdens of production and persuasion fall on the same person (usually the moving party) is in Social Security cases. A claimant for Social Security benefits has only the burden of production—that is, the claimant need only produce evidence of disability. The burden then shifts to the agency to prove that the claimant is not entitled to benefits.

8.7(c) Standards

By what standard must a party prove something true? As in civil judicial trials, the standard of proof is usually **preponderance of the evidence**, which is met when the trier of fact believes that the fact asserted is more likely true than not. In terms of percentages, this means 51 percent or greater. Some litigants have contended that due process requires a higher standard when an agency is engaged in a quasi-prosecutorial function (i.e., when the agency is prosecuting an individual for violating a statute or regulation). This position was rejected by the Supreme Court of the United States in *Steadman*.

When Congress has not specified what standard should be applied, courts sometimes impose a higher standard, such as when civil liberties are threatened. *Woodby* is such a case. Note that the *Woodby* Court imposed the "clear and convincing" standard, which falls between the lower standard of preponderance of the evidence and the higher standard of beyond a reasonable doubt. (See Figure 8-3.)

The government cannot circumvent the protections afforded to individuals in criminal proceedings by transferring such cases to administrative agencies and then imposing criminal-law sanctions. When an administrative proceeding has too many characteristics of a criminal prosecution, the defendant in the proceeding is entitled to all the protections afforded by the criminal courts. For example, a state may transfer jurisdiction over traffic cases to administrative agencies, provide for a lower standard of review, and not apply the privilege against self-incrimination and similar rights in such proceedings if the most severe punishment possible is revocation of a driver's license and a fine. A state could not, however, transfer jurisdiction over assault and battery cases to the same agency under the same circumstances and then allow the agency to incarcerate offenders.

LEGAL TERMS

Burden of Proof
Consists of two aspects: the *burden of production*, which concerns who in a proceeding has the duty to produce evidence or raise an issue; and the *burden of persuasion*, which concerns who in a proceeding has the duty of persuading the trier of fact that its position is correct.

Preponderance of the Evidence
Standard of proof that is met when the trier of fact believes that what is asserted is more likely true than not.

Most Demanding Standard	Beyond a reasonable doubt	A doubt that causes a reasonable and prudent person to question the truth of an allegation is reasonable. Used in criminal cases, rarely in administrative cases.
More Demanding Standard	Clear and convincing evidence	Less demanding than the beyond-a-reasonable-doubt standard, but more than the preponderance standard. Used in administrative cases only when an agency's action encroaches on a legally protected right.
Least Demanding Standard	Preponderance of the evidence	More likely true than not; any probability greater than 50 percent. Standard used in most administrative cases.

FIGURE 8-3   Standards of proof.

8.7(d) Administrative Law Judges

The right to a hearing does not entail a right to have one's case heard by any particular individual, such as the head of an agency. Nor does the right to be heard carry with it the right to be heard by the agency official who will ultimately make the final decision. It is common practice for an agency to have a case heard by one official and decided by another. This is so because some statutes require that final adjudicative decisions be made by agency heads. This is, of course, impossible in every case. Therefore, agency heads delegate the responsibility to other agency officials, often called *administrative hearing officers*, *hearing examiners*, *referees*, *presiding officers*, or *administrative law judges*, to name a few. Today, most are titled administrative law judges, or ALJs, at the federal level. Nearly all hearings must be presided over by the agency head (rare) or an ALJ (common). The APA gives ALJs the authority to administer oaths and affirmations; issue subpoenas authorized by law; make decisions concerning the evidence offered at hearings; take or cause depositions to be taken; control the hearing presided at; hold settlement and other conferences with the consent of the parties; dispose of procedural requests and similar matters; make or recommend the decision, as provided for elsewhere in the APA; and take other actions authorized by the agency that are consistent with the APA.[17]

Steadman v. United States

450 U.S. 91 (1981)

In administrative proceedings, the Securities and Exchange Commission applies a preponderance-of-the-evidence standard of proof in determining whether the antifraud provisions of the federal securities laws have been applied. The question presented is whether such violations must be proved by clear and convincing evidence rather than by a preponderance of the evidence.

I

In June 1971, the Commission initiated a disciplinary proceeding against petitioner and certain of his wholly owned companies. The proceeding against petitioner was brought pursuant to § 9(b) of the Investment Company Act of 1940, and § 203(f) of the Investment Advisers Act of 1940. The Commission alleged that petitioner had violated numerous provisions of the federal securities laws in his management of several mutual funds registered under the Investment Company Act.

After a lengthy evidentiary hearing before an Administrative Law Judge and review by the Commission in which the preponderance-of-the-evidence standard was employed, the Commission held that between December 1965 and June 1972, petitioner had violated antifraud, reporting, conflict of interest, and proxy provisions of the federal securities laws. Accordingly, it entered an order permanently barring petitioner from associating with any investment adviser or affiliating with any registered investment company, and suspending him for one year from associating with any broker or dealer in securities.

Petitioner sought review of the Commission's order in the United States Court of Appeals for the Fifth Circuit on a number of grounds, only one of which is relevant for our purposes. Petitioner challenged the Commission's use of the preponderance-of-the-evidence standard of proof in determining whether he had violated antifraud provisions of the securities laws. He contended that because of the potentially severe sanctions that the Commission was empowered to impose and because of the circumstantial and inferential nature of the evidence that might be used to prove intent to defraud, the Commission was required to weigh the evidence against a clear-and-convincing standard of proof. The Court of Appeals rejected petitioner's argument, holding that in a disciplinary proceeding before the Commission violations of the antifraud provisions of the securities laws may be established by a preponderance of the evidence. . . . Because this was contrary to the position taken by the United States Court of Appeals for the District of Columbia Circuit . . . we granted certiorari. . . . We affirm.

II

Where Congress has not prescribed the degree of proof which must be adduced by the proponent of a rule or order to carry its burden of persuasion in an administrative proceeding, this Court has felt at liberty to prescribe the standard, for "[i]t is the kind of question which has traditionally been left to the judiciary to resolve." . . . However, where Congress has spoken, we have deferred to "the traditional powers of Congress to prescribe rules of evidence and standards of proof in the federal courts" absent countervailing constitutional constraints. . . . For Commission disciplinary proceedings . . . we conclude that Congress has spoken, and has said that the preponderance-of-the-evidence standard should be applied.

Steadman v. United States, 450 U.S. 91 (1981), United States Supreme Court.

Woodby v. Immigration & Naturalization Service

385 U.S. 276 (1966)

The question presented by these cases is what burden of proof the Government must sustain in deportation proceedings. We have concluded that it is incumbent upon the Government in such proceedings to establish the facts supporting deportability by clear, unequivocal, and convincing evidence. . . .

We conclude, therefore, that Congress has not addressed itself to the question of what degree of proof is required in deportation proceedings. It is the kind of question which has traditionally been left to the judiciary to resolve, and its resolution is necessary in the interest of the evenhanded administration of the Immigration and Naturalization Act.

The petitioners urge that the appropriate burden of proof in deportation proceedings should be that which the law imposes in criminal cases—the duty of proving the essential facts beyond a reasonable doubt. The Government, on the other hand, points out that a deportation proceeding is not a criminal case, and that the appropriate burden of proof should consequently be the one generally imposed in civil cases and administrative proceedings—the duty [of] prevailing by a mere preponderance of the evidence.

To be sure, a deportation proceeding is not a criminal prosecution. . . . But it does not syllogistically follow that a person may be banished from this country upon no higher degree of proof than applies in a negligence case. This Court has not closed its eyes to the drastic deprivations that may follow when a resident of this country is compelled by our Government to forsake all the bonds formed here and go to a foreign land where he often has no contemporary identification. . . .

In denaturalization cases the Court has required the Government to establish its allegations by clear, unequivocal, and convincing evidence. The same burden has been imposed in expatriation cases. The standard of proof is no stranger to the civil law.

No less a burden of proof is appropriate in deportation proceedings. The immediate hardship of deportation is often greater than that inflicted by denaturalization,

(continued)

which does not, immediately at least, result in expulsion from our shores. Many resident aliens have lived in this country longer and established stronger family, social, and economic ties here than some who have become naturalized citizens.

We hold that no deportation order may be entered unless it is found by clear, unequivocal, and convincing evidence that the facts alleged as grounds for deportation are true.

Woodby v. Immigration & Naturalization Service, 385 U.S. 276 (1966),
United States Supreme Court.

Independence   A hallmark of the U.S. judicial branch is independence. Article III of the Constitution creates the Supreme Court of the United States and such inferior courts that Congress decides to create. Article III judges are nominated by the president and confirmed by Congress. Once appointed, federal judges serve for life, save retirement and impeachment, and their salaries may not be reduced. The framers of the Constitution structured the federal courts in this manner to give it independence from Congress and the president.

Administrative law judges are not, however, judges under Article III of the Constitution of the United States. Therefore, they are not entitled to the protections afforded federal judges by the Constitution. This is particularly troubling because each ALJ works directly for the agency that is a party to every case the ALJ hears. Congress addressed this concern in the APA by providing for the "quasi-independence" of ALJs from their respective agencies. Although ALJs are "employed" by their respective agencies, their quasi-independence, akin but not identical to that of Article III judges, is ensured by several provisions of the APA and other laws, including the following four.

SIDEBAR   *Administrative Law Judges*

In 2009, there were 1,422 federal ALJs in 30 different agencies. . . .[18] Eighty-five percent of federal ALJs are employed in the Social Security Administration (SSA). In 2011, SSA ALJs presided over more than 550,000 cases with more than $80 billion at stake.[19]

First, ALJs' salaries are to be set by the Civil Service Commission, not by the agencies themselves. Second, ALJs are to be selected from a list of qualified applicants prepared by the Office of Personnel Management (OPM), creating a corps of merit appointed judges. The OPM reviews applications to determine if the minimum qualifications are met, administers a competitive ALJ examination, and in some instances, conducts interviews.[20] Generally, to qualify to sit for the ALJ exam a person must be an attorney with at least seven years of experience as a litigator or in administrative law. OPM provides the agency seeking the ALJ with a list of qualified applicants, from which the agency makes its appointment from among the top three candidates, taking the location of the position, the geographic preferences of the candidates, and military veteran status.

Third, ALJs may be removed for good cause only.[21] ALJs may not be removed by their agencies. If an agency wants one of its ALJs removed, it must file the action and prove good cause before the Merit Systems Protection Board. This shields ALJs from retribution by agencies for unfavorable or unpopular decisions. Fourth, ALJs are to be assigned to cases in rotation, in most instances.[22] This prevents agency officers from appointing ALJs they believe will be sympathetic to the agency's point of view in specific cases. The *Abruzzo* case involved an ALJ's appeal of his dismissal. Read the case both as an example of good cause for termination and in preparation for the next chapter where you will learn about how appeals work in administrative cases. In this case you have an ALJ of SSA appealing his dismissal by an ALJ of MSPB to a united states district court.

Abruzzo v. Social Security Administration

United States Court of Appeals for Federal District (July 16, 2012)

Mr. Douglas W. Abruzzo ("Abruzzo") is a former Administrative Law Judge ("ALJ") with the Social Security Administration ("SSA"). The SSA charged Abruzzo with failure to follow instructions and conduct unbecoming an ALJ, all of which were detailed in twenty-four specifications. Abruzzo appeals the final decision of the Merit Systems Protection Board ("MSPB" or "Board") which sustained each charge and found good cause to remove him from his ALJ position. Because we find the Board's determination is supported by substantial evidence, not an abuse of discretion, and otherwise according to law, we affirm. . . .

Pertaining to charge one, failure to follow instructions, three specifications allege that Abruzzo's supervisors ordered him to stop directly contacting sources for test data and to correct at least three portions of his standard pretrial order that failed to comply with SSA regulations and policy.

Pertaining to charge two, failure to follow a direct order to treat coworkers and the public with courtesy, seven specifications allege that Abruzzo acted offensively and failed to conduct himself with propriety. For example, Abruzzo warned employees of the potential for harm from supervisors, likened the management of the office to "Nazis," and stated that the director would send people to gas chambers. In addition, numerous e-mail messages from Abruzzo, many copied to other SSA employees, contain personal and derogatory comments about superiors, such as claiming the director has "neo-Nazis" attitudes.

Pertaining to charge three, conduct unbecoming an ALJ, specifications five and six dealt with an incident in early-April 2009. Abruzzo was allegedly observed by employees painting with an oily substance what appeared to be the sign of the cross above the office doors of Hearing Office Chief ALJ ("HOCALJ") Barbeito and Director James. The unknown substance soon began to drip onto the office floor, and caused a great disruption because it was uncertain whether it posed a danger. HOCALJ Barbeito was "stunned" and "frighten[ed]," Director James was "terrified," and other staff members were "fearful." HOCALJ Barbeito explained that the staff was "speaking amongst themselves . . . and they were very concerned." Abruzzo explained that he had used "blessed oil" because he believed that HOCALJ Barbeito and Director James "were under the influence of evil at that particular time." Regional Chief ALJ ("RCALJ") Garmon ordered Judge Abruzzo "not to put anymore substance [sic] of any kind" on Federal property. Notwithstanding this order, four days later Abruzzo was again observed painting with an oily substance above his own door while purportedly "speaking in tongues." This behavior further alarmed co-workers and SSA placed additional security officers at the building in response. Eight other specifications were added under this charge, essentially asserting that the same facts alleged under charge two also demonstrated conduct unbecoming an ALJ.

Pertaining to charge four, failure to follow a direct order, three specifications allege that Abruzzo refused to conduct scheduled hearings, claiming that he was too occupied responding to the complaints lodged against him by the SSA. Despite being ordered by HOCALJ Barbeito to conduct the hearing as scheduled, Abruzzo refused. . . .

(continued)

Regarding charge one, Abruzzo did not dispute the factual assertions that he circumvented the chain of command in obtaining data or that he failed to correct his pretrial order. He argued instead that his judicial independence was impinged by such SSA orders. The ALJ determined that the superiors' orders to Abruzzo were lawful, and sustained the charge, finding that it alone established good cause for removal.

Regarding charge two, Abruzzo did not dispute his conduct relating to discourtesy to co-workers and lack of propriety, asserting only that he did not know what standard he was required to meet. The ALJ found that Abruzzo did know and understand generally accepted rules of conduct and that his remarks were discourteous and offensive. The ALJ again sustained the charge.

Regarding charge three, Abruzzo again did not dispute the facts relating to his conduct, including the alleged incidents of April 2009. The ALJ found that

> It is clear Judge Abruzzo's admitted conduct, as outlined above, clearly constitutes conduct unbecoming an administrative law judge.
>
> Judge Abruzzo's actions, whether intended or not, instilled fear and terror into the work place. His actions, for which he alone is responsible, caused interruptions in the operation of the office. Many staff hours, both Hearing and Regional staffs were expended attempting to resolve these incidents. Additional security was even necessary and absolutely no justification exists for Judge Abruzzo's conduct. Judge Abruzzo not only engaged in the conduct on April 3, 2009, but, even after being told not to engage in such conduct, returned to work on April 7, 2009 and proceeded to engage in the same conduct again.

Judge Abruzzo's actions on April 3, and 7, 2009 were very serious and disruptive and standing alone constitute good cause for discipline up to and including removal.

The ALJ found further that several specifications overlapping with the incidents from count two also supported finding conduct unbecoming an ALJ.

Regarding count four, Abruzzo did not dispute his conduct. He challenged HOCALJ Barbeito's authority to make the order, and explained that he would not have had the disposition necessary to conduct a hearing at that time. The ALJ, sustaining the count, stated: "Judge Abruzzo has an irrational perception that he is not subject to any orders or directives from the hearing office chief. . . ."

The ALJ found that the SSA had established, by preponderant evidence, good cause to remove Abruzzo from his position as ALJ. The full Board affirmed each of the four charges in a final order issued August 3, 2011. . . .

The scope of our review in an appeal from a decision of the Board is limited. This court affirms the Board decision unless it is (1) arbitrary, capricious, an abuse of discretion, or otherwise not in accordance with law; (2) obtained without procedures required by law, rule, or regulation having been followed; or (3) unsupported by substantial evidence. Petitioner bears the burden of establishing reversible error on appeal. . . .

Abruzzo admits that the events of April 2009 amounted to conduct unbecoming and ALJ, but argues that removal was excessive. Petitioner Br. Here, the ALJ conducted a very thorough analysis of the factors outlined in *Douglas v. Veterans Administration*, 5 M.S.P.R. 280 (1981), and found the misconduct intentional, frequent, disruptive, and incompatible with his ability to adequately perform his judicial duties. The Board's findings that Abruzzo cannot effectively serve as an ALJ due to his sustained misconduct does not amount to an abuse of discretion. Accordingly, we uphold the Board's penalty of removal.

We have considered all of Abruzzo's remaining contentions on appeal and find them without merit. In light of the foregoing, we *affirm*.

Abruzzo v. Social Security Administration, United States
Court of Appeals for Federal District.

Interest, Bias, and Prejudgment   It is a basic tenet of due process that to have a fair hearing there must be an unbiased and neutral ALJ. Three issues are raised in this context: interest, bias, and prejudgment.

Interest refers to situations in which an ALJ has a personal financial stake in the matter being presided over. This is well illustrated by *Tumey v. Ohio*,[23] a 1927 U.S. Supreme Court case. In *Tumey*, the mayor of a town was responsible for hearing traffic cases. The law also provided that the mayor was to share in the fines levied for traffic offenses. This arrangement was found unconstitutional because the person responsible for determining the guilt of those accused (the mayor) had a personal financial interest in the outcome of each case. Personal interest was also at issue in the *Gibson* case.

An ALJ may also be disqualified from hearing a case because of personal bias. If an ALJ has personal feelings in favor of or against one of the parties, then due process requires ***recusal*** of the ALJ. The bias may be directed at a particular party or a party's lawyer. Prejudice against a party's race, origin, ethnic group, or other characteristic may also mandate disqualification under the Due Process and Equal Protection Clauses.

Deciding a case before all the evidence has been heard (*prejudgment*) also violates due process. Possessing a belief about a case before it has been heard does not require recusal unless the ALJ has a firmly established belief as to what the case outcome should be. As a general proposition, prehearing ideology, philosophy, positions, and beliefs on a subject do not require disqualification. Therefore, an ALJ or administrator who has made public statements concerning a particular subject is not disqualified from presiding over a case that involves those issues.

LEGAL TERM
Recusal
Disqualification of a judge or hearing officer because of interest or bias.

Gibson v. Berryhill

411 U.S. 564 (1973)

Prior to 1965, the laws of Alabama relating to the practice of optometry permitted any person, including a business firm or corporation, to maintain a department in which "eyes are examined or glasses fitted," provided that such department was in the charge of a duly licensed optometrist. This permission was expressly conferred by § 210 of Title 46 of the Alabama Code of 1940, and also inferentially by § 211 of the Code which regulates the advertising practices of optometrists, and which, until 1965, appeared to contemplate the existence of commercial stores with optical departments. In 1965, § 210 was repealed in its entirety by the Alabama Legislature, and § 211 was amended so as to eliminate any direct reference to optical departments maintained by corporations or their business establishments under the direction of employee optometrists.

Soon after these statutory changes, the Alabama Optometric Association, a professional organization whose membership is limited to independent practitioners of optometry *not* employed by others, filed charges against various named optometrists, all of whom were duly licensed under the Alabama law but were the salaried employees of Lee Optical Co. The charges were filed with the Alabama Board of Optometry, the statutory body with authority to issue, suspend, and revoke licenses for the practice of optometry. The gravamen of these charges was that the named optometrists, by accepting employment from Lee Optical, a corporation, had engaged in "unprofessional conduct" within the meaning of § 206 of the Alabama optometry statute and hence were practicing their profession unlawfully. More particularly, the Association charged the named individuals with, among other things, aiding and abetting a corporation in the illegal practice of optometry; practicing optometry

(continued)

under a false name, that is, Lee Optical Co.; unlawfully soliciting the sale of glasses; lending their licenses to Lee Optical Co.; and splitting or dividing fees with Lee Optical. It was apparently the Association's position that, following the repeal of § 210 and the amendment of § 211, the practice of optometry by individuals as employees of business corporations was no longer permissible in Alabama, and that by accepting such employment the named optometrists had violated the ethics of their profession. It was prayed that the Board revoke the licenses of the individuals charged following due notice and a proper hearing.

Two days after these charges were filed by the Association in October 1965, the Board filed a suit of its own in state court against Lee Optical, seeking to enjoin the company from engaging in the "unlawful practice of optometry." The Board's complaint also named 13 optometrists employed by Lee Optical as parties defendant, charging them with aiding and abetting the company in its illegal activities, as well as with other improper conduct very similar to that charged by the Association in its complaint to the Board.

Proceedings on the Association's charges were held in abeyance by the Board while its own state court suit progressed. The individual defendants in that suit were dismissed on grounds that do not adequately appear in the record before us; and, eventually, on March 17, 1971, the state trial court rendered judgment for the Board. . . .

Meanwhile, following its victory in the trial court, the Board reactivated the proceedings pending before it since 1965 against the individual optometrists employed by Lee, noticing them for hearings to be held. . . . Those individuals countered on May 14, 1971, by filing a complaint in the United States District Court naming as defendants the Board of Optometry and its individual members, as well as the Alabama Optometric Association and other individuals. . . . The thrust of the complaint was that the Board was biased and could not provide plaintiffs with a fair and impartial hearing in conformity with due process of law. . . .

The District Court thought the Board to be impermissibly biased for two reasons. First, the Board had filed a complaint in state court alleging that appellant[s had] aided and abetted Lee Optical Co. in the unlawful practice of optometry and also that they had engaged in other forms of "unprofessional conduct" which, if proved, would justify revocation of their licenses. These charges were substantially similar to those pending against appellees before the Board and concerning which the Board had noticed hearings following its successful prosecution of Lee Optical in the state trial court.

Secondly, the District Court determined that the aim of the Board was to revoke the licenses of all optometrists in the State who were employed by business corporations such as Lee Optical, and that these optometrists accounted for nearly half of all the optometrists practicing in Alabama. Because the Board of Optometry was composed solely of optometrists in private practice for their own account, the District Court concluded that success in the Board's efforts would possibly redound to the personal benefit of members of the Board, sufficiently so that in the opinion of the District Court the Board was constitutionally disqualified from hearing the charges filed against the appellees.

The District Court apparently considered neither source of possible bias—prejudgment of the facts or personal interest—sufficient to disqualify the members of the Board. Arguably, the District Court was right on both scores, but we need reach, and we affirm, only the latter ground of possible personal interest.

It is sufficiently clear from our cases that those with substantial pecuniary interest in legal proceedings should not adjudicate disputes. . . .

Affirmed.

Gibson v. Berryhill, 411 U.S. 564 (1973), United States Court of Appeals for Federal District.

Further, previous contact with a case, such as through a prior decision, does not necessarily warrant recusal. If an ALJ was previously involved with investigating the facts of the case or prosecuting the case when employed in a different position, then due process may require recusal, though. This occurred in *American Cyanamid Co. v. FTC*.[24] In *American Cyanamid*, an appeal from a hearing examiner's decision was made to the Federal Trade Commission. The chairman of the commission, who would have presided over the appeal, had previously worked as chief counsel to the Senate subcommittee that investigated the same issues raised in the appeal. Even more, it was determined that he acted in a prosecutorial manner when he investigated companies for the Senate. Therefore, his refusal to disqualify himself was held improper by the reviewing court.

In some cases, an entire agency may be disqualified from presiding over an adjudication because of prejudgment. However, this is rare. A court is unlikely to disqualify an entire agency unless another tribunal is qualified and available to hear the case.

Even if every individual authorized to hear a case has some conflict that would normally lead to disqualification, the *rule of necessity* may provide a method for the case to be heard. This rule was recognized by the U.S. Supreme Court in *United States v. Will*,[25] a lawsuit brought by a group of federal judges concerning a pay issue. The Court acknowledged that all federal judges, including themselves, had a financial interest in the case. However, there would be no one to preside over the case if every federal judge were to be disqualified. For that reason, the Court found that it could hear the case by "necessity." This rule applies to administrative adjudications as well.

Finally, note that a person seeking disqualification of an ALJ must file a timely affidavit of disqualification with the ALJ. The ALJ makes the initial decision on his or her own disqualification. That decision is then appealable to the agency. However, no judicial review is immediately available. That is, if the ALJ is not recused, the case must proceed although the issue can be appealed to a court after the case is concluded.

LEGAL TERM

Rule of Necessity

Judge-made rule that permits one who would not normally be qualified to preside over a case, because of personal interest or bias, to preside when no other qualified individual is available to do so.

Separation and Combination of Functions   As discussed in Chapter 1, agencies hold a special position in American government. Many perform the functions of all three branches of government. This is known as a *combination of functions*. (See Figure 8-4.)

Normally, one unit may not act as investigator, prosecutor, and judge in a case. The unfairness in such an arrangement is apparent. The framers of the Constitution were familiar with the dangers inherent in centralized power; that is why the powers of the U.S. government are divided among three branches.

Executive Functions	Legislative Functions	Judicial Functions
The administration takes claims applications, maintains records, responds to inquiries, studies problems, and investigates violations of law within its jurisdiction.	The administration has been delegated the authority to promulgate regulations.	Within the administration is an Office of Hearings and Appeals, which performs quasi-judicial functions.

FIGURE 8-4   Combination of functions by an administrative agency. The Social Security Administration is an example of an administrative agency that performs executive, legislative, and judicial functions.

Agencies do, however, combine functions. The challenge is to prevent agency abuse of such combinations. One way to prevent abuse is to have a separation of the functions within the agency. This is the approach of the APA. To date, the courts of the United States have not read the Due Process Clauses as mandating agency separation of functions. This position has nevertheless been the subject of much criticism, and Congress has responded by requiring internal separation of functions through the APA.

The APA contains one important separation: that of prosecutorial from adjudicatory functions. This separation is ensured, in part, by the independence granted to ALJs, as discussed earlier in this section. In addition, the APA prohibits those who participate in the investigation or prosecution of a case from participating in the decision, including giving advice to the decision maker.[26] Input from agency officials responsible for investigation or prosecution of a case must come through participation as a witness or counsel, with all interested parties participating. Be aware that this restriction applies only to accusatory and adversarial hearings. Initial licensing, ratemaking, and rulemaking are not included.

Ex parte contacts with all persons, not just agency officials, are prohibited by the APA. *Ex parte* means contact between an individual and the decision maker without the other parties being present. Ex parte contacts are prohibited because it is unfair for one party to have an opportunity to discuss the case with the administrative law judge when other parties cannot. The prohibition of *ex parte* communication applies to decision-makers in adjudications (§554(d)) and formal rulemaking (§556). Some agencies prohibit *ex parte* communications in informal rulemaking as well. Upon review if such a communication is found to be prejudicial, the final rule or decision may be amended, reversed, or found invalid.

The APA contains a few exceptions to these rules. Separation rules do not apply to agency heads. Hence, an agency head may initiate an investigation, oversee a prosecution, and make the final decision. Also, as previously mentioned, initial licensing, ratemaking, and rulemaking are not subject to separation rules.

8.7(e) Counsel and Attorney Fees

As a general proposition, parties have a right to be represented by counsel in administrative adjudications. In most cases today, the right is established by statute or rule. The APA expressly provides for the right to be "accompanied, represented, and advised by counsel" in section 555.

If there is no statute or rule permitting representation, then the Constitution may demand it. The Sixth Amendment's right to counsel is not the source, however, because that provision applies only to criminal proceedings. Instead, the Supreme Court has found the right in the Due Process Clauses. The right does not extend to all administrative hearings.

Generally though, there is a right in adjudications, and in practice more than 80 percent of the parties who appear before administrative law judges are represented.[27] Investigatory hearings are an example of when the right likely does not attach.

Section 555 of the APA enables agencies to permit interested parties to be represented by non-attorneys. The Social Security Administration, for example, permits nonlawyers to represent claimants. Because the federal government has the authority to define who may represent people in its agencies, state laws concerning the practice of law do not apply. Accordingly, it is not a violation of law for a paralegal to represent a Social Security claimant, but it would be for the same paralegal to represent the claimant in state court on another matter.

Generally, the "American rule" concerning attorney fees applies. This means that each party before the agency must pay for his or her attorney regardless of the outcome. However, the APA was amended to reflect the Equal Access to Justice Act in 1980. This provision, now found in §504 of the APA, provides that a prevailing party in a formal agency adjudication or in court may request that the government be ordered to pay attorney fees and other expenses of that party unless the agency's position was "substantially justified" or such an award would be unjust. The statute also requires that the agency be represented at the hearing before fees can be awarded—that is, the agency must act in the role of a party. If the agency is only hearing the claim and does not advance a position or theory, fees may not be awarded.

This provision was enacted to protect small businesses from overzealous agencies. However, individuals have requested fees and costs under it more often than businesses. The most common group to request fees is wrongly denied Social Security claimants. They are also the most successful in having fees awarded.[28] These claimants cannot obtain an award of fees for the agency's adjudications, because the agency is not represented in those hearings. A denied claimant must wait until all administrative hearings have been exhausted and the agency has rendered its final denial. When that has happened, the denied person can appeal to a federal district court. At this hearing the Social Security Administration is a party and, unless its position is substantially justified, the claimant can have the fees and costs associated with the court hearing paid by the agency.

8.7(f) The Decision

The final stage in the adjudicative process is the issuance of a decision. The APA requires that the parties to an adjudication be permitted to submit proposed findings and conclusions before any decision (initial, recommended, or final, as discussed later) is rendered.[29] Once these documents are filed, the decision will be issued.

Institutional Decision   The decisional process is much different in administrative adjudications than in judicial trials. Courts issue personal decisions. The judge, perhaps with the aid of a law clerk, hears the evidence and arguments of counsel, reads the parties' filings, considers the evidence and law, and then issues his or her decision.

Administrative agencies issue institutional decisions. The decision maker in administrative proceedings is the governing body of the agency, be it the agency head, board, or commission. Although such individuals may preside over adjudications, in fact they rarely do. In most instances, the agency official who has been vested with the authority to issue the decision delegates the authority to preside over adjudications to subordinates. Prior to the APA, this situation created problems. Many claimed that agency heads were rubber-stamping decisions made by their subordinates in violation of a direct statutory duty to "hear" the case. As one judge stated, "The one who decides must hear."[30] This led to a series of cases, including the well-known *Morgan* cases, that dealt with the extent to which an agency head could delegate the responsibility to hear an adjudication.[31]

The APA remedied this problem, for the most part. Specifically, the APA provides that hearings are to be presided over by administrative law judges unless an agency head presides. After the hearing is completed, the parties may submit proposed findings and conclusions to the agency.[32]

Final, Initial, and Recommended Decisions   If an agency head presides over a hearing, a final decision can be rendered by that official in a manner similar to a judge's issuing an opinion after conducting a trial. The same is not true when another person presides over the hearing. If an ALJ conducts a hearing, APA §557(b) provides that the ALJ shall issue either an initial or a recommended decision.

The difference between the two decisions is significant. The *initial decision* becomes the final decision, absent an appeal; *recommended decisions* must be certified and transmitted to the agency for action. Unless an agency requires an ALJ to issue a recommended decision, an initial decision will be issued. Hence, most decisions are initial. The APA provides, however, that an agency can require, either by rule covering an entire class of cases or in specific cases, that the record be certified to it for decision.

If a proceeding involves routine or well-settled issues, the agency is likely to permit the ALJ to render an initial decision. However, if a case presents novel issues of law or policy, the agency is more likely to require the ALJ to present a recommended decision. This is sound policy, because agency heads are selected by, and answerable to, the president. They are more familiar with the policy goals and objectives of the administration. In short, agency heads are better suited than ALJs to make decisions concerning law and policy.

Initial decisions become the decision of the agency unless an appeal is taken from the decision by any party. The appeal from an ALJ's initial decision is made to the agency. Some agencies have created an appeals board to act on behalf of the agency. In others, the appeals are to the agency head.

On appeal from an initial decision, the reviewer (whether an appeals board or agency head) need not give any deference to the ALJ's findings or conclusions. The APA states that on "appeal from or review of the initial decision, the agency has all the powers which it would have in making the initial decision, except as it may limit the issues on notice or by rule."[33] This is different from the practice in judicial proceedings, in which appellate courts defer to the factual findings of trial courts unless those findings are clearly erroneous. On review of an initial decision, the agency can defer entirely to, or throw in the wastebasket, an ALJ's findings. This is known as *de novo* review. In practice, some deference is likely to be afforded an ALJ's factual findings, because the ALJ was present during the hearing, heard the arguments of counsel, observed witnesses, and is generally more familiar with the case than the person reviewing the decision.

After this level of appeal, an aggrieved party must seek redress in court. Failure to exhaust administrative appeal remedies may prevent a court from entertaining a claim. (The exhaustion-of-remedies doctrine is discussed more fully in Section 9.5.)

Finally, in formal rulemaking and applications for initial licenses, the APA permits ALJs to certify and transmit the record to the agency, which may then issue a tentative decision or have one of its "responsible employees" issue a recommended decision. The parties may then comment on the tentative decision.[34]

Findings in Formal Adjudications   The APA requires that all "decisions, including initial, recommended, and tentative decisions, are a part of the record and shall include a statement of findings and conclusions, and the reasons or basis therefore, on all the material issues of fact, law, or discretion presented on the record."[35] Agencies were required to make findings even at common law, and the APA codified many of the common law findings requirements.

The APA requires much more than a bare decision; a statement that a claim or license is granted, denied, suspended, revoked, or the like is not adequate and will be remanded by a reviewing court to the agency to make findings. An agency must issue its findings in writing. An ALJ may make an oral decision at the close of the hearing, but it must be followed by a written decision containing the findings and conclusions supporting the decision.

The APA requires that findings and conclusions be rendered on all material issues of fact. *Material* means not only relevant, but also important to the outcome of the case. If a fact is material, an agency must address it by making a finding and conclusion in its decision. Judge Posner stated that the Constitution may also require findings. He characterized findings as a "back-up safeguard, designed to make sure, so far as it is possible to do so, that the hearing which due process requires is a meaningful one."[36]

In addition, the decision must recite the reasons and bases underlying the agency's decision. This fundamental requirement of reasoned opinions forces the agency to tie its findings in with its decision. Thus, the agency must find the facts, reach a conclusion, render a decision, and explain why the facts and conclusions reached led it to the decision it rendered.

There are many reasons for having agencies issue reasoned opinions. First, a reasoned opinion provides some accountability for administrators. Second, it improves the decisional process by requiring agencies to analyze each case. Third, it serves to educate the public about an agency's role, policy, and method of enforcing its mandate. Fourth, an explained decision provides precedent for future agency adjudications. Fifth, a reasoned opinion allows for meaningful judicial review.

If an agency renders a decision without explanation, a reviewing court will be unable to determine if the decision is lawful. In such cases a reviewing court will remand the case to the agency with an order that findings be issued.

SIDEBAR   *Ethics—Lay Representation in Administrative Cases*

In both the states and federal government, laypeople are sometimes permitted to represent others before administrative agencies without committing the unauthorized practice of law. In fact, the Supremacy Clause empowers federal agencies to decide who may act as advocates, regardless of state rules. In *Sperry v. Florida*, 373 U.S. 379 (1963), a layperson who had been authorized to practice patent law by the U.S. Patents Office was sued by the Florida Bar for the unauthorized practice of law. The Supreme Court of the United States held, "Florida may not deny to those failing to meet its own qualifications the right to perform the functions within the scope of the federal authority."

In addition to the Patent Office, many agencies permit nonlawyer representation. According to Orlik, these include, *inter alia*, the Small Business Administration, National Credit Union Administration, Federal Energy Regulatory Commission, Drug Enforcement Administration, Aid to Families with Dependent Children, Food and Drug Administration, Comptroller of the Currency, Citizenship and Immigration Service, and Environmental Protection Agency.

Source: Deborah K. Orlik, *Ethics for the Legal Professional*, 6th ed. (Pearson 2008).

From Ethics for Legal Professional, 6E by Deborah K. Orlik.
Upper Saddle River: Prentice Hall, 2008.

Findings in Informal Adjudications   Recall that this chapter concerns formal adjudications. There is no findings requirement for informal adjudications (hearings). Rather, the APA requires that

[p]rompt notice shall be given of the denial in whole or in part of a written application, petition, or other request of an interested person made in connection with any agency proceeding. Except in affirming

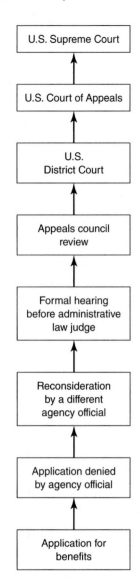

FIGURE 8.5   Example of adjudication process: Social Security cases.

a prior denial or when the denial is self-explanatory, the notice shall be accompanied by a brief statement of the grounds for denial.[37]

This section applies to every claim, application, petition, or other request to an agency by an interested person. Hence, all claims for Social Security disability benefits, as well as applications for broadcasting licenses, are covered. The agencies are not required to issue reasoned opinions; they must issue only a brief statement of the grounds for denial (see Figures 8-5 and 8-6).

The Right to a Jury in Administrative Proceedings   The Seventh Amendment to the Constitution of the United States reads:

> In Suits at common law, where the value in controversy shall exceed twenty dollars, the right of trial by jury shall be preserved, and no fact tried by a jury, shall be otherwise re-examined in any Court of the United States, than according to the rules of the common law.

Under the Seventh Amendment, a person has a right to a jury in common law actions that existed in 1791, the year the Seventh Amendment was ratified. Notice that the right to a jury trial is limited to common law actions; there is no right to a jury trial in equitable cases.

Further, the right extends to statutory actions that are codifications of, or closely resemble, common law actions. Is there, then, a right to a jury trial in administrative proceedings that involve common law claims or claims closely resembling common law claims? The answer is no, for two reasons.

First, the issue of right to a jury trial under the Seventh Amendment is nearly parallel to the issue of exclusive judicial power to hear a case. That is, if the Seventh Amendment requires a jury trial, Article III of the Constitution will also require that a competent judicial court hear the case. Therefore, a delegation of quasi-judicial authority to an agency that implicates a Seventh Amendment issue is likely an invalid delegation, because it has delegated an essential, nondelegatable judicial function.

Second, there is another qualification on the right to a jury trial: The claim must involve a private right, not a public one. If a right is public in nature, there is no right to a jury trial under the Seventh Amendment. Actions against the government are examples of public actions. The Supreme Court has held, however, that the government does not have to be a party to an action for that action to have a public nature.

Congress can assign actions closely analogous to common law actions to administrative tribunals if the private right is part of a public regulatory scheme. The private right must, however, be integrated into the public scheme. Said another way,

Decision Form	Description
Final	Agency heads preside over hearing and render a final decision.
Initial	Common form of ALJ decision. Final unless appealed to the agency.
Recommended	Agency delegates the authority to conduct the hearing to an ALJ or other official but requires that the decision be reviewed by the agency before it becomes final.

FIGURE 8-6   Forms of decision in formal adjudications under APA § 557(b).

having the private right adjudicated in the administrative forum must be necessary and consistent with the regulatory scheme. Congress cannot transform a private right into a public right by assigning its adjudication to an administrative agency. Rather, the private right must be part of a larger regulatory scheme. For example, in *NLRB v. Jones & Laughlin Steel Corp.*,[38] the Supreme Court held that there was no right to a jury trial in a claim under the National Labor Relations Act for back pay even though it appeared analogous to an award for damages at common law.

In *Atlas Roofing Co. v. Occupational Safety & Health Review Comm'n*,[39] the Court examined the jury right issue in the context of the Occupational Safety and Health Act, which empowered the commission to impose civil penalties on employers for maintaining unsafe and unhealthy working conditions. Again, it was asserted that the actions created by the statute were analogous to common law damage actions. The Court disagreed, finding that such administrative regulatory actions did not exist at common law, and, therefore, there was no right to a jury trial. The Court emphasized that its decision does not affect the right to a jury trial in purely private actions, such as those arising under contract or tort law.

The Court found that a private right was implicated in *Granfinanciera, S.A.v. Nordberg*,[40] which involved a bankruptcy proceeding. Generally, bankruptcy actions are equitable in nature and, therefore, there is no right to a jury trial, but in *Granfinanciera* the Court held that the act of a trustee in bankruptcy in recovering fraudulently conveyed property was private in nature, not public. Accordingly, the law that delegated the factual decision making in such cases to bankruptcy judges was invalidated. The Court did not resolve the issue of whether bankruptcy judges, whose positions are statutorily created, may preside over jury trials that arise during bankruptcy proceedings.

The Seventh Amendment right to a jury trial in civil cases has not been incorporated—that is, it does not apply against the states. Therefore, the Constitution does not limit the states' authority to delegate civil adjudicatory authority to administrative tribunals. However, state constitutional provisions providing for juries in civil cases do limit the authority of state legislatures to delegate adjudication of civil cases to administrative tribunals. Forty-six states have constitutional provisions similar to the federal Constitution's Seventh Amendment.[41]

Finally, whenever Congress has created a right to a jury trial, it has done so within the context of claims heard by Article III courts. In cases for which there is no Seventh Amendment right to a jury trial, Congress could require an agency to conduct a jury trial. This is not likely, however, because it is more efficient and less costly to have claims adjudicated by administrative law judges.

8.7(g) Observing an Administrative Hearing

You may want to attend an administrative hearing as an observer. To prepare for such a project, you should select an agency that you find interesting and inquire as to its policies and practices and potential hearing dates. Decide which hearing you want to attend. Request to review the case file or other record before the hearing is conducted. The following form is provided to help you record what transpires at a hearing. You may want to amend the form, by adding or deleting questions, to conform to your particular needs.

ADMINISTRATIVE HEARING RECORD ▮▮▮▮▮▮▮

I. GENERAL INFORMATION

1. What are the date, time, and location of the hearing?
2. Name all parties to the case. Name all counsel appearing.
3. Name the administrative official presiding at the hearing.
4. What is the nature of the dispute? How did the case originate (e.g., through a complaint or claim for benefits)?
5. Upon what authority is the hearing being conducted?
6. Cite and describe the law governing the subject matter of the dispute.
7. Cite and describe the law governing the authority of the presiding officer of the hearing.
8. Cite and describe the law governing the admissibility of evidence and the conduct of the hearing.
9. Briefly describe what occurred at the prehearing stage of the case, including discovery and prehearing conferences.

II. THE HEARING

10. Did the presiding officer make any opening remarks? If so, briefly summarize those remarks.
11. Did the parties present opening statements? If so, briefly summarize those statements.
12. Summarize the testimony of each witness called and describe the other evidence submitted by the parties. Identify which party called the witness and whether the particular statements were adduced on direct examination, cross-examination, redirect examination, or recross-examination.
13. Summarize the legal arguments made by the parties, including any evidence objections raised.
14. Did the parties present closing statements? If so, briefly summarize those statements.
15. Did the presiding officer make closing remarks? If so, briefly summarize those remarks.

III. DECISION AND APPEAL

16. Will the presiding officer issue a decision? Will it be a final, recommended, initial, or other type of decision? Cite and describe the law governing the decision-making process.
17. Cite and describe the law governing administrative appeals.
18. Cite and describe any law providing for judicial review.
19. What is the current status of the case?

8.8 LICENSE CASES

This chapter closes with special mention of license cases. APA §558(c) specifies the procedure that must be followed in license cases.

When an application is made for a license that is required by law, the agency is to complete its proceedings within a reasonable period of time, taking into account the rights and privileges of all interested parties or persons who may be adversely affected. The provision does not alter the other APA provisions concerning hearings. Therefore, no formal adjudication is necessary unless specifically required by statute.

Unless the public safety, health, or interest requires otherwise, the licensee must be given written notice of the facts or conduct supporting the potential adverse action before any action may be taken. Further, the licensee must be given the opportunity to comply with the law before an adverse action is taken. By statute, Congress has provided noncompliant licensees with not only a pretermination hearing, but also an opportunity to correct their errors without suffering loss of license.

Finally, if a licensee has made a timely application for continuation of a license, and the agency does not render the new license before the original expires, the APA provides that the original license will continue in effect until the decision on the renewal is made. This provision is practical because it prevents the due process problems that would result from allowing such licenses to lapse.

8.9 CONCLUSION

Prior to enactment of the APA, agency officials commonly combined investigatory, prosecutorial, and quasi-judicial functions. They would act as police, prosecutor, judge, and jury. Although agencies continue to perform all these functions, in addition to making rules, the APA has erected an internal wall of separation. With the exception of agency heads, agency officials can no longer play the role of police, prosecutor, judge, and jury. The establishment of a system of administrative law judges, with statutory independence from their agencies, has done much for the integrity of agency decision making. Regardless, concerns that ALJs continue to favor agencies over citizens persist. To many people, this concern is aggravated by what they believe to be inadequate judicial review of agency decisions. This is the subject of the next chapter.

LAWLINKS

The adjudication procedural rules of many agencies can be found online in the agency's Web pages. For example, to see the complete set of the Department of Labor's rules, go to www.oalj.dol.gov/public/part18/refrnc/29_18c.htm.

REVIEW **QUESTIONS**

1. How does the APA define *adjudication*?
2. What is required for notice of a hearing to be adequate under the APA?
3. Define *amicus curiae* and explain its importance.
4. What is intervention?
5. What is discovery? Name all the methods of discovery you recall.
6. When must an agency conduct a trial-type hearing under the APA?
7. What are the two aspects of burden of proof? Discuss each.
8. Administrative law judges are not Article III judges under the Constitution of the United States, but Congress has attempted to provide for ALJ independence. Name three methods that Congress has used in this effort.
9. What is required of agencies when issuing decisions following formal and informal adjudications?
10. What is the rule of necessity?

CRITICAL THINKING AND **APPLICATIONS PROBLEMS**

1. State Statute reads as follows:

   If the State Department of Motor Vehicles has cause to believe that a licensed driver has violated some law, ordinance, or regulation that concerns the operation of a motor vehicle, it shall conduct a hearing on the record and determine if the driver's license should be suspended or revoked. The agency shall take appropriate action following the hearing. Appeals of suspensions and revocations under this chapter may be appealed to a state district court.

   Irene receives a document from the State Department of Motor Vehicles entitled "Notice of Hearing: Driver's License Suspension or Revocation." The notice, which she receives on August 25, states that she is to appear at the department's office on September 25 for a hearing to determine if she violated state law and whether her driver's license should be suspended or revoked.

   She appears at the hearing and learns that the issue is whether she operated a vehicle while under the influence of alcohol on August 2. She asks the hearing officer to allow her to call her husband and employer to come to the office to tell the hearing officer that she was in Europe from July 28 to August 10 on vacation. The hearing officer refuses, stating, "You had a month to prepare for this hearing."

   After the hearing concludes, the hearing officer announces his decision orally. He states, "I find that you operated a vehicle while under the influence of alcohol and suspend your license for 90 days. This is my final decision and you may appeal it." Irene appeals the decision to a state district court. The state has adopted an administrative procedure law identical to the federal APA. Identify and discuss all issues you discover in this scenario.

2. What burden of proof do you believe should be applied to agency actions that encroach on civil liberties?

3. The last line of Section 8.8 states that due process problems would result from allowing "such licenses to lapse." Explain.

ENDNOTES

1. *Southern Garment Mfrs. Ass'n v. Fleming*, 122 F.2d 622, 626 (D.C. Cir. 1941).
2. APA § 551(6).
3. *Id.*
4. *Prentis v. Atlantic Coastline Co.*, 211 U.S. 210, 226 (1908).
5. APA § 554(b).
6. *Id.*
7. *David v. Heckler*, 591 F. Supp. 1033, 1043 (E.D.N.Y. 1984).
8. 359 F.2d 994 (D.C. Cir. 1966).
9. Fed. R. Civ. p. 26.
10. Schwartz, *Administrative Procedure* § 6.6 (1991).
11. 18 U.S.C. § 3500.
12. 15 U.S.C. § 45(b).
13. APA § 556(d).
14. 18 U.S.C. § 2510 *et seq.*
15. APA § 556(e).
16. *Id.* § 556(d).
17. *Id.* § 556(c).
18. Burrows, V. (April 13, 2010) *Administrative Law Judges: An Overview.* Congressional Research Service.
19. Association of Administrative Law Judges, opening page of Web site, www.aalj.org, found on April 27, 2013.
20. 5 U.S.C. § 5372.
21. 5 U.S.C. § 7521.
22. 5 U.S.C. § 3105.
23. 273 U.S. 510 (1927).
24. 363 F.2d 757 (6th Cir. 1966).
25. 449 U.S. 200 (1981).
26. APA § 554(d).
27. Jeffrey S. Wolfe & Lisa B. Proszek, *Interaction Dynamics in Federal Administrative Decision Making: The Role of the Inquisitorial Judge and the Adversarial Lawyer*, 33 Tulsa L. J. 293, 293 (1997).
28. *See* Susan Gluck Mezey & Susan M. Olson, *Fee Shifting and Public Policy: The Equal Access to Justice Act*, 77 Judicature 13 (1993).
29. APA § 557(c).
30. *See Southern Garment Mfrs. Ass'n v. Fleming*, 122 F.2d 622 (D.C. Cir. 1941).
31. *Morgan v. United States*, 298 U.S. 468 (1936); *Morgan v. United States*, 304 U.S. 1 (1938); *United States v. Morgan*, 307 U.S. 183 (1939); *United States v. Morgan*, 313 U.S. 409 (1941).
32. APA § 557(c) (1).
33. *Id.* § 557(b).
34. *Id.*
35. APA § 557(c)(A).
36. *Hameetman v. Chicago*, 776 F.2d 636, 645 (7th Cir. 1985).
37. APA § 555(e).
38. 301 U.S. 1 (1937).
39. 430 U.S. 442 (1977).
40. 492 U.S. 33 (1989).
41. The states that do not are Colorado, Louisiana, Utah, and Wyoming. However, these states have statutorily created the right to a jury trial in many civil cases.

chapter **nine**

ACCOUNTABILITY THROUGH REVIEWABILITY

LEARNING OBJECTIVES

After completing this chapter, you should be able to

- List, define, contrast, and apply to a fact scenario the common law and statutory sources of review authority.

- List, define, and apply to a fact scenario the most significant timing and common law limitations upon review authority.

- Determine, from a fact scenario, whether an individual, corporation, or other entity has standing to be heard.

- Identify and apply the appropriate standard of review to fact scenarios.

- Brief a judicial opinion with little outside assistance. You should be successful in identifying the relevant facts. You should also be successful in identifying the legal issue and analyzing the court's rationale in at least 50 percent of your briefs.

Absolute discretion is a ruthless master. It is more destructive of freedom than any of man's other inventions.

JUSTICE DOUGLAS[1]

Justice Douglas, United States v. Wunderlich, 342 U.S. 98 (1951), United States Supreme Court.

9.1 IN GENERAL

You have already read about presidential and congressional control of agencies. This chapter addresses judicial control of agencies. Without judicial review, constitutional, statutory, and other limitations on agency action would be valueless. Generally, there are two types of judicial review. The first involves the direct review of agency action. As examples, plaintiffs file civil actions challenging the denial of licenses, denials of benefits, and agencies' decisions to sell government property. In such cases, the plaintiffs are asking courts to reverse or modify the decisions of agencies. The second type of review is the claim for damages. In some instances, people sue agencies and government officials for damages. This chapter concerns the former. The latter is the subject of Chapter 11.

The availability of judicial review is limited by a number of doctrines, many of which are discussed in this chapter. Some of the doctrines are statutory; others were developed at common law. At the outset, however, two questions must be asked. First, does a court have the authority to review a particular agency action? Second, if so, what is the scope of review? Review authority is addressed first.

9.2 SOURCES OF REVIEW AUTHORITY

Most judicial authority to review agency actions comes from statutes. Constitutional and common law sources may also provide for judicial review.

9.2(a) Statutory

In the federal system, most review authority is derived from statute. The common law system of review has largely been replaced by legislative declarations concerning the availability of review. Congress enjoys great discretion when legislating in this area: It may establish when the review must be sought and where it must be sought, and may set limits on the judiciary's authority in reviewing agency action.

Generally, when a statute provides for review, no other method may be used to establish a court's authority to hear the case, with the possible exception of cases in which a constitutional issue is raised. Hence, in most cases, the statute is the exclusive method to obtain judicial review.

Congress may provide for a time limitation on review. Both 60- and 90-day limits are common although lesser and greater time periods are provided for by some statutes. In at least one instance, a 30-day limitation was upheld.[2]

Time limitations established by Congress are strictly enforced by federal courts. Under nearly all circumstances, an untimely suit will be dismissed. The strength and merits of the case are immaterial because the time limitations are usually found to be jurisdictional—that is, if an appeal is not timely filed, the petitioned court lacks jurisdiction to hear the case.

In addition to setting time limitations, Congress may also prescribe where an action is to be filed. For example, decisions under the Social Security Act (SSA) are appealable to district courts. Once at this level, they may be heard by a U.S. magistrate, who renders a proposed decision, which is then appealable to a U.S. district judge.[3] That decision is then appealable to the appropriate circuit court of appeals.

In many cases, appeals must be brought directly to federal appellate courts. This is so for orders issued by the Federal Trade Commission:

> Any person, partnership, or corporation required by an order of the Commission to cease and desist from using any method of competition or act or practice may obtain a review of such order in the court

of appeals of the United States, within any circuit where the method of competition or the act or practice in question was used or where such person, partnership, or corporation resides or carries on business, by filing in the court, within sixty days from the date of the service of such order, a written petition praying that the order of the Commission be set aside.[4]

Although legislatures enjoy significant discretion in providing for review, this authority is not absolute. Due process must be satisfied by such provisions. If Congress were to require an action to be filed in a location that is preclusive to a plaintiff, or establish a time limitation so short as to preclude review from being obtained, the statute must fail under due process analysis.

Finally, instead of providing for review, Congress may explicitly *preclude* review, by statute. However, courts have been reluctant to read such provisions as excluding all review. For example, in a case involving a deportation, the phrase "deportation orders of the Attorney General shall be final," which appeared in the controlling statute, was interpreted as meaning final administrative orders, not final in the sense that no judicial review is available.[5]

In *Johnson v. Robison*,[6] the Supreme Court strongly implied that Congress may not preclude review of constitutional issues. In that case, the Court decided to construe a statute as not precluding a person from filing a constitutional claim because the contrary interpretation would "raise serious . . . questions concerning the constitutionality" of the statute. In 1988, the issue was again addressed in *Webster v. Doe*.[7] In that case, the CIA terminated an employee's employment after discovering that he was a homosexual. Again, the Court did not expressly state that laws precluding review of constitutional claims are invalid, but it strongly implied as much. It can reasonably be concluded that a statute precluding review of constitutional claims would likely be invalidated.

This does not mean that Congress cannot establish procedures for enforcing constitutional rights. Congress may require that constitutional claims be raised within a certain period of time, filed with a particular court, or raised in a certain manner.

Finally, APA § 702 states in relevant part that "[a] person suffering legal wrong because of agency action, or adversely affected or aggrieved by agency action within the meaning of a relevant statute, is entitled to judicial review thereof." Despite this language, which appears to permit review to all aggrieved persons, the provision has been interpreted as not providing an independent jurisdictional basis for federal courts to review agency actions.[8] It does, however, support the presumption that Congress intends to allow judicial review of agency actions. It also supports the trend toward making judicial review more widely available.

In reality, this reading of § 702 does not limit the availability of judicial review much because another federal statute broadly states that federal courts may hear any claim arising under the Constitution or laws of the United States.[9] This is known as *federal question* jurisdiction. A federal question is broad enough to establish jurisdiction for review in the absence of a contrary statute.

A number of statutes use language similar to, or broader than, that used in the Administrative Procedure Act. The Federal Trade Commission Improvement Act, 15 U.S.C. § 57(e)(1)(A), provides "any interested person may file a petition"; the Occupational Safety and Health Act 29 U.S.C. § 3660 provides "any person who may be adversely affected by a standard issued under this section may . . . file a petition"; and the Surface Mining Control and Reclamation Act, 30 U.S.C.§ 1207(a), states "any person having an interest or who may be adversely affected" may seek review. Specific statutes such as these are controlling within their respective arenas.

LEGAL TERM

Federal Question

One of two means to establish federal court jurisdiction. A claim arising under the Constitution or laws of the United States is a federal question. The other means of acquiring federal jurisdiction is through diversity of the parties.

The APA requires that the form of a lawsuit be as provided for by statute. If not provided for, then the action shall be "brought against the United States, the agency by its official title, or the appropriate officer." The lawsuit may seek any applicable form of legal action, including declaratory judgment, or the common law writs of certiorari, prohibition, mandamus, or habeas corpus.[10]

9.2(b) Nonstatutory

If a statute does not provide for review, nonstatutory review may be available. As discussed in § 9.2(a), there is a strong preference in the courts for review. Similarly, there is a strong presumption that Congress does not intend to preclude review when a statute is silent on the subject.

At common law, courts could issue various writs to agencies and agency officials that were not specifically provided for by statute, such as *certiorari*, *mandamus*, *habeas corpus*, and *prohibition*. The authority of federal courts to issue such writs continues today because Congress has provided for certain of them by statute.[11] However, in the federal system, certiorari is no longer available. It has been replaced by the injunction and declaratory judgment. Similarly, the writ of prohibition is a dead letter in federal administrative law.

The writs of mandamus and habeas corpus are still viable. Under the Federal Rules of Civil Procedure, a mandamus type of remedy exists today; however, it is limited to requiring public officials to perform ministerial acts required of them by law. Mandamus cannot be used to compel a public official to perform a discretionary act.

Finally, habeas corpus is still available. In fact, the right to habeas corpus is assured by Article I, § 9, of the U.S. Constitution. Confinement of aliens by the Immigration and Naturalization Service is an example of when habeas corpus might be used in federal administrative law.

Review is different in every state. Though many, if not all, states have some statutory form of review, some continue to recognize all the common law writs. Other states do not recognize the writs as an alternative to statutory review.

As mentioned previously, review of agency actions that encroach on constitutional rights may be had without the approval of Congress. This theory is premised on concepts of due process and judicial power.

Finally, at common law, agency orders were not self-enforcing. To enforce one of its orders, an agency had to seek the assistance of a court. Under this system, courts reviewed orders for lawfulness. In the federal system today, most orders become final unless appealed within a certain period of time. Failure to comply with an order can result in a fine or penalty.

9.3 AGENCY DISCRETION

Many agency decisions involve findings of fact. Many others require policy and political decisions. Agencies are better equipped to find the facts, in most instances, than are courts. An agency will also be more familiar with the history of a particular case, as well as the facts of the industry involved. Decisions that are inherently political or that involve policy concerns are better left to the agencies because they are better equipped than the courts to deal with such issues.

For this reason, decisions that have been "committed to agency discretion" are not subject to judicial review. Section 701(a)(2) of the APA specifically exempts agency action that is "committed to agency discretion by law" from review.

LEGAL TERMS

Certiorari
Common law writ issued by a superior tribunal to an inferior tribunal requiring the inferior tribunal to produce a record or file so that review may be conducted.

Mandamus
Latin for "we command." Common law writ issued by a superior tribunal to an inferior tribunal or person requiring that some action be taken. Normally, the writ can only compel that ministerial acts be taken.

Habeas Corpus
Latin for "you have the body." Common law writ issued by a court to a custodian of a person to bring the prisoner before the court to determine the lawfulness of the imprisonment.

Prohibition
Common law writ issued by a court to an inferior tribunal or person prohibiting the recipient from taking some act or hearing some case.

If a lawsuit is filed stemming from an action committed to an agency's discretion, it must be dismissed because the reviewing court lacks authority to hear the case. This prevents review of procedural, as well as substantive, issues.

If the decision or action is common in the daily management or operations of an agency or involves issues of national security, it is likely committed to an agency's discretion and thus unreviewable. An example of a decision committed to agency decision at law can be found in the Supreme Court case *Webster v. Doe*.[12] The National Security Act of 1947 provides that the Director of the Central Intelligence Agency "may, in his discretion, terminate the employment of any officer or employee of the Agency whenever he shall deem such termination necessary or advisable in the interests of the United States. . . ."

Doe was an employee who had consistently received excellent employee evaluations, but was terminated after he voluntary disclosed that he was homosexual. Even though Doe passed a CIA polygraph test during which he testified that he had never had sexual relations with foreign nationals or disclosed classified information, the agency terminated him because it found that his homosexuality threatened national security. Doe sued in federal court, alleging that his termination was arbitrary in violation of the APA and also a violation of his constitutionally protected right to privacy. Finding in favor of the CIA, the Supreme Court stressed that deference to executive decisions in matters of national security is particularly important. The Court also found that the language of the act, delegating the power to terminate employees to the director, provides no basis on which a court could review the decision; thus, the act "strongly suggests that its implementation was 'committed to agency discretion by law.'"

Therefore, in *Webster v. Doe* the Court found for the agency for two reasons: the case involved national security, and Congress had not provided any standards to guide the agency official's exercise of discretion. The latter point was the subject of discussion in *Lincoln v. Vigil*.

The question whether a decision was committed to an agency's discretion at law was also at issue in the rather unusual case of *Heckler v. Chaney*.

Heckler v. Chaney

470 U.S. 821 (1985)

This case presents the question of the extent to which a decision of an administrative agency to exercise its "discretion" not to undertake certain enforcement actions is subject to judicial review under the Administrative Procedure Act, 5 U.S.C. § 501 *et seq.* (APA). Respondents are several prison inmates convicted of capital offenses and sentenced to death by lethal injection of drugs. They petitioned the Food and Drug Administration (FDA), alleging that under the circumstances the use of these drugs for capital punishment violated the Federal Food, Drug, and Cosmetic Act (FDCA). . . . The FDA refused their request. We review here a decision of the Court of Appeals for the District of Columbia Circuit, which held the FDA's refusal to take enforcement actions both reviewable and an abuse of discretion, and remanded the case with directions that the agency be required "to fulfill its statutory function."

Respondents have been sentenced to death by lethal injection of drugs under the laws of the States of Oklahoma and Texas. Those States, and several others, have recently adopted this method for carrying out the capital sentence. Respondents first petitioned the FDA, claiming that the drugs used by the States for this purpose, although approved by the FDA for the medical purposes stated on their labels, were not approved for use in human executions. They alleged that the drugs had not been tested

(continued)

for the purpose for which they were to be used, and that, given that the drugs would likely be administered by untrained personnel, it was also likely that the drugs would not induce the quick and painless death intended. They urged that use of these drugs for human execution was the "unapproved use of an approved drug" and constituted a violation of the Act's prohibition against misbranding. They also suggested that the FDCA's requirements for approval of "new drugs" applied, since these drugs were now being used for a new purpose. Accordingly, respondents claimed that the FDA was required to approve the drugs as "safe and effective" for human execution before they could be distributed in interstate commerce. See 21 U.S.C. § 355. They therefore requested the FDA to take various investigatory and enforcement actions to prevent these perceived violations; they requested the FDA to affix warnings to the labels of all the drugs stating that they are unapproved and unsafe for human execution, to send statements to the drug manufacturers and prison administrators stating that the drugs should not be so used, and to adopt procedures for seizing the drugs from state prisons and to recommend the prosecution of all those in the chain of distribution who knowingly distribute or purchase the drugs with intent to use them for human execution.

The FDA Commissioner responded, refusing to take the requested actions. The Commissioner first detailed his disagreement with respondents' understanding of the scope of the FDA jurisdiction over the unapproved use of approved drugs for human execution, concluding that FDA jurisdiction in the area was generally unclear but in any event should not be exercised to interfere with this particular aspect of state criminal justice systems. . . .

That section provides that the chapter on judicial review "applies, according to the provisions thereof, except to the extent that—(1) statutes preclude judicial review; or (2) agency action is committed to agency discretion by law." Petitioner urges that the decision of the FDA to refuse enforcement is an action "committed to agency discretion by law" under § 701(a)(2).

. . . In addition, commentators have pointed out that construction of § (a)(2) is further complicated by the tension between a literal reading of § (a)(2), which exempts from judicial review those decisions committed to agency "discretion," and the primary scope of review prescribed by § 706(2)(A)—whether the agency's action was arbitrary, capricious, or an *abuse of discretion*. How is it, they ask, that an action committed to agency discretion can be unreviewable and yet courts still can review agency actions for abuse of that discretion." . . .

[R]eview is not to be had if the statute is drawn so that a court would have no meaningful standard against which to judge the agency's exercise of discretion. In such a case, the statute ("law") can be taken to have "committed" the decision making to the agency's judgment absolutely. This construction avoids conflict with the "abuse of discretion" standard of review in § 706—if no judicially manageable standards are available for judging how and when an agency should exercise its discretion, then it is impossible to evaluate action for "abuse of discretion." . . .

Respondents nevertheless present three separate authorities that they claim provide the courts with sufficient indicia of an intent to circumscribe enforcement discretion. Two of these may be dealt with summarily. First, we reject respondents' argument that the Act's substantive prohibitions of "misbranding" and the introduction of "new drugs" absent agency approval, see 21 U.S.C. §§ 352(f)(1), 355, supply us with "law to apply." These provisions are simply irrelevant to the agency discretion to refuse to initiate proceedings.

We also find singularly unhelpful the agency "policy statement" on which the Court of Appeals placed great reliance. We would have great difficulty with this statement's vague language even if it were a properly adopted agency rule. Although the statement indicates that the agency considered itself "obligated" to take certain investigative actions, that language did not arise in the course of discussing the agency's discretion to exercise its enforcement power, but rather in the context of describing agency policy with respect to unapproved uses of approved drugs by physicians. . . .

The FDA's decision not to take the enforcement actions requested by respondents is therefore not subject to judicial review under the APA. The general exception to reviewability provided by § 701(a)(2) for action "committed to agency discretion" remains a narrow one . . . but within that exception are included agency refusals to institute investigative or enforcement proceedings, unless Congress has indicated otherwise.

Heckler v. Chaney, 470 U.S. 821 (1985), United States Supreme Court.

Beware: Not all discretionary agency decisions are exempt from review. You will learn later that in some instances courts may review agency actions for "abuse of discretion." How does the abuse of discretion review standard mesh with the no-review rule for actions committed to agency discretion? Courts have interpreted "committed to agency discretion" narrowly, leaving all other discretionary actions to be reviewed under the abuse of discretion standard. The Supreme Court of the United States stated that the "committed to agency discretion" standard is "applicable in those rare instances where statutes are drawn in such broad terms that in a given case there is no law to apply."[13] In determining whether a particular agency action is "committed to agency discretion by law, courts must bear in mind that judicial reviewability of administrative action is the rule, and non-reviewability an exception which must be demonstrated, and which should result only from a showing of 'clear and convincing evidence' of a legislative intent to restrict judicial review."[14]

Lincoln v. Vigil

508 U.S. 182 (1993)

The Indian Health Service, an agency within the Public Health Service of the Department of Health and Human Services, provides health care for some 1.5 million American Indian and Alaska Native people. . . . The Service receives yearly lump-sum appropriations from Congress and expends the funds under authority of the Snyder Act, 42 Stat. 208, as amended, 25 U.S.C. § 13, and the Indian Health Care Improvement Act, 90 Stat. 1400, as amended, 25 U.S.C. § 1601 *et seq*. So far as it concerns us here, the Snyder Act authorizes the Service to "expend such moneys as Congress may from time to time appropriate, for the benefit, care, and assistance of the Indians," for the "relief of distress and conservation of health." 25 U.S.C. § 13. The Improvement Act authorizes expenditures for, inter alia, Indian mental-health care, and specifically for "therapeutic and residential treatment centers. . . ."

This case concerns a collection of related services, commonly known as the Indian Children's Program, that the Service provided from 1978 to 1985. In the words of the Court of Appeals, a "clou[d] [of] bureaucratic haze" obscures the history of the Program, *Vigil v. Rhoades*, 953 F.2d 1225, 1226 [(10th Cir. 1992)], which seems to have grown out of a plan "to establish therapeutic and residential treatment centers for disturbed Indian children." . . . These centers were to be established under a "major cooperative care agreement" between the Service and the Bureau of Indian Affairs . . . and would have provided such children "with intensive care in a residential setting." . . .

Congress never expressly appropriated funds for these centers. In 1978, however, the Service allocated approximately $292,000 from its fiscal year 1978 appropriation to its office in Albuquerque, New Mexico, for the planning and development of a pilot project for handicapped Indian children, which became known as the Indian Children's Program. See 953 F.2d, at 1227. The pilot project apparently convinced

(continued)

the Service that a building was needed, and, in 1979, the Service requested $3.5 million from Congress to construct a diagnostic and treatment center for handicapped Indian children. . . . The appropriation for fiscal year 1980 did not expressly provide the requested funds, however, and legislative reports indicated only that Congress had increased the Service's funding by $300,000 for nationwide expansion and development of the Program in coordination with the Bureau. . . .

Plans for a national program to be managed jointly by the Service and the Bureau were never fulfilled, however, and the Program continued simply as an offering of the Service's Albuquerque office, from which the Program's staff of 11 to 16 employees would make monthly visits to Indian communities in New Mexico and southern Colorado and on the Navajo and Hopi Reservations. . . . The Program's staff provided "diagnostic, evaluation, treatment planning and followup services" for Indian children with emotional, educational, physical, or mental handicaps. "For parents, community groups, school personnel and health care personnel," the staff provided "training in child development, prevention of handicapping conditions, and care of the handicapped child." . . .

Congress never authorized or appropriated moneys expressly for the Program, and the Service continued to pay for its regional activities out of annual lump-sum appropriations from 1980 to 1985, during which period the Service repeatedly apprised Congress of the Program's continuing operation. . . .

Nevertheless, the Service had not abandoned the proposal for a nationwide treatment program, and in June 1985 it notified those who referred patients to the Program that it was "re-evaluating [the Program's] purpose . . . as a national mental health program for Indian children and adolescents." . . . In August 1985, the Service determined that Program staff hitherto assigned to provide direct clinical services should be reassigned as consultants to other nationwide Service programs, 953 F.2d, at 1226, and discontinued the direct clinical services to Indian children in the Southwest. . . .

Respondents, handicapped Indian children eligible to receive services through the Program, subsequently brought this action for declaratory and injunctive relief against petitioners, the Director of the Service and others (collectively, the Service), in the United States District Court for the District of New Mexico. Respondents alleged, inter alia, that the Service's decision to discontinue direct clinical services violated the federal trust responsibility to Indians, the Snyder Act, the Improvement Act, the Administrative Procedure Act, various agency regulations, and the Fifth Amendment's Due Process Clause. . . .

First is the question whether it was error for the Court of Appeals to hold the substance of the Service's decision to terminate the Program reviewable under the APA. The APA provides "[a] person suffering legal wrong because of agency action, or adversely affected or aggrieved by agency action within the meaning of a relevant statute, is entitled to judicial review thereof," 5 U.S.C. § 702, and we have read the APA as embodying a "basic presumption of judicial review. . . ."

Over the years, we have read § 701(a)(2) to preclude judicial review of certain categories of administrative decisions that courts traditionally have regarded as "committed to agency discretion. . . ."

In *Heckler* itself, we held an agency's decision not to institute enforcement proceedings to be presumptively unreviewable under § 701(a)(2). 470 U.S., at 831, 105 S. Ct., at 1655–1656. An agency's "decision not to enforce often involves a complicated balancing of a number of factors which are peculiarly within its expertise," ibid., and for this and other good reasons, we concluded, "such a decision has traditionally been committed to agency discretion. . . ."

Finally, in *Webster*, . . . at 599–601, 108 S. Ct., at 2051–2053, we held that § 701(a)(2) precludes judicial review of a decision by the Director of Central Intelligence to terminate an employee in the interests of national security, an area of executive action "in which courts have long been hesitant to intrude. . . ."

The allocation of funds from a lump-sum appropriation is another administrative decision traditionally regarded as committed to agency discretion. After all, the very point of a lump-sum appropriation is to give an agency the capacity to adapt to changing circumstances and meet its statutory responsibilities in what it sees as the most effective or desirable way. . . .

For this reason, a fundamental principle of appropriations law is that where "Congress merely appropriates lump-sum amounts without statutorily restricting what can be done with those funds, a clear inference arises that it does not intend to impose legally binding restrictions, and indicia in committee reports and other legislative history as to how the funds should or are expected to be spent do not establish any legal requirements on" the agency. . . .

Like the decision against instituting enforcement proceedings, then, an agency's allocation of funds from a lump-sum appropriation requires "a complicated balancing of a number of factors which are peculiarly within its expertise": whether its "resources are best spent" on one program or another; whether it "is likely to succeed" in fulfilling its statutory mandate; whether a particular program "best fits the agency's overall policies"; and, "indeed, whether the agency has enough resources" to fund a program "at all." *Heckler*, 470 U.S., at 831, 105 S. Ct., at 1655. As in *Heckler*, so here, the "agency is far better equipped than the courts to deal with the many variables involved in the proper ordering of its priorities." Of course, an agency is not free simply to disregard statutory responsibilities: Congress may always circumscribe agency discretion to allocate resources by putting restrictions in the operative statutes (though not, as we have seen, just in the legislative history).

. . . And, of course, we hardly need to note that an agency's decision to ignore congressional expectations may expose it to grave political consequences. But as long as the agency allocates funds from a lump-sum appropriation to meet permissible statutory objectives, § 701(a)(2) gives the courts no leave to intrude. "[T]o [that] extent," the decision to allocate funds "is committed to agency discretion by law." § 701(a)(2).

The Service's decision to discontinue the Program is accordingly unreviewable under § 701(a)(2). . . .

Lincoln v. Vigil, 508 U.S. 182 (1993), United States Supreme Court.

Thus, if sufficient standards exist for a court to determine whether an agency has abused its discretion, the action is reviewable under the abuse of discretion standard. If not, the action is unreviewable.

This position has been criticized on two grounds. First, it is inconsistent with democracy to endow a governmental entity with unreviewable authority. Second, if an agency has been provided no standards by which to exercise its discretion, the delegation is unlawfully broad. Regardless, some actions have been determined to be unreviewable. National defense, national security, and foreign affairs are examples of areas committed to agency discretion. Decisions made by agency officials when acting in a managerial capacity are also committed to discretion. For example, the decision of an administrator to transfer a physician is not reviewable.[15] The same would be true for a National Park Service decision establishing the location of an observation station within a park.

9.4 STANDING

The Constitution also plays a part in determining if review is available. The legal system of the United States is adversarial. Article III, § 2, of the Constitution limits the jurisdiction of federal courts to "cases or controversies." This means that an actual dispute must exist before a federal court can exercise jurisdiction. Theoretical and hypothetical disputes may not be decided by a federal court. The purpose of the case or controversy limitation is to prevent the usurpation of executive and legislative power by the judicial branch.

What is the relationship between standing and statutory rights of review? First, if statutory law is silent on the question of who has a right to petition for review, standing principles apply. Second, if statutory law narrows or limits the group that can seek review, the statute applies. Third, if a statute makes review available to those not qualified under standing principles, the statute is likely constitutional. However, this final statement has not been definitively answered by the Supreme Court.

The **standing doctrine** stems from the case or controversy limitation of the Constitution. *Standing* concerns the issue of who may sue. The standing doctrine requires that the person bringing a lawsuit (i.e., plaintiff, petitioner, or complainant) has a personal interest in the case.

Early standing law required that to have standing, a person had to prove that a legally protected interest or right had been violated. Under this test, financial or personal injury alone was not sufficient to establish standing in many instances. This requirement proved unworkable. In many cases, courts had to address the merits of a case simply to decide whether standing existed. It was, therefore, time inefficient. Also, this concept of legally protected interests was dated. As the size of the federal administration grew, so did the need to have a more flexible approach to who should be permitted to sue. A new test was developed, which is the subject of the *Data Processing* case.

LEGAL TERM

Standing Doctrine

Requirement that a person who brings a lawsuit has a personal interest in the case.

Association of Data Processing Service Organizations v. Camp

397 U.S. 150 (1970)

Petitioners sell data processing services to businesses generally. In this suit they seek to challenge a ruling by respondent Comptroller of the Currency that, as an incident to their banking services, national banks, including respondent American National Bank and Trust Company, may make data processing services available to other banks and to bank customers.

Generalizations about standing to sue are largely worthless as such. One generalization is, however, necessary and that is that the question of standing in the federal courts is to be considered in the framework of Article III which restricts judicial power to "cases" and "controversies." As we recently stated in *Flast v. Cohen*, 392 U.S. 83, 101, 88 S. Ct. 1942, 1953, 20 L. Ed. 2d 947, "[I]n terms of Article III limitations on federal court jurisdiction, the question of standing is related only to whether the dispute sought to be adjudicated will be presented in an adversary context and in a form historically viewed as capable of judicial resolution." *Flast* was a taxpayer's suit. The present is a competitor's suit. And while the two have the same Article III starting point, they do not necessarily track one another.

The first question is whether the plaintiff alleges that the challenged action has caused him injury in fact, economic or otherwise. There can be no doubt but that petitioners have satisfied this test. The petitioners not only allege that competition by national banks in the business of providing data processing services might entail some future loss of profits for the petitioners, they also allege that respondent American National Bank and Trust Company was performing or preparing to perform such services for two customers for whom petitioner Data Systems, Inc., had previously agreed or negotiated to perform such services. The Comptroller was alleged to have caused petitioners injury in fact by his 1966 ruling which stated:

> Incidental to its banking services, a national bank may make available its data processing equipment or perform data processing services on such equipment for other banks and bank customers. Comptrollers Manual for National Banks § 3500 (October 15, 1966).

The Court of Appeals viewed the matter differently, stating:

> [A] plaintiff may challenge alleged illegal competition when as complainant it pursues (1) a legal interest by reason of public charter or contract, . . . (2) a legal interest by reason of statutory protection, . . . or (3) a "public interest" in which Congress has recognized the need for review of administrative action and plaintiff is significantly involved to have standing to represent the public . . . 406 F.2d, at 842–843.

> Those tests were based on prior decisions of this Court, such as *Tennessee Electric Co. v. TVA*, 306 U.S. 118, 59 S. Ct. 366, 83 L. Ed. 543, where private power companies sought to enjoin TVA from operating, claiming that the statutory plan under which it was created was unconstitutional. The Court denied the competitors standing, holding that they did not have that status "unless the right invaded is a legal right—one of property, one arising out of contract, one protected against tortious invasion, or one founded on a statute which confers a privilege.". . .

> The "legal interest" test goes to the merits. The question of standing is different. It concerns, apart from the "case" or "controversy" test, the question [of] whether the interest sought to be protected by the complainant is arguably within the zone of interests to be protected or regulated by the statute or constitutional guarantee in question. Thus the Administrative Procedure Act grants standing to a person "aggrieved by agency action within the meaning of a relevant statute." 5 U.S.C. § 702 (1964 ed., Supp. IV). That interest, at times, may reflect "aesthetic, conservational, and recreational" as well as economic values. . . . A person or a family may have a spiritual stake in First Amendment values sufficient to give standing to raise issues concerning the Establishment Clause and the Free Exercise Clause. . . . We mention these noneconomic values to emphasize that standing may stem from them as well as from the economic injury on which petitioners rely here. Certainly he who is "likely to be financially" injured . . . may be a reliable private attorney general to litigate the issues of the public interest in the present case.

Association of Data Processing Service Organizations v. Camp, 397 U.S. 150 (1970), United States Supreme Court.

The new test of standing has three prongs. First, the plaintiff must suffer an "injury in fact." Second, the interests asserted by the plaintiff must be "arguably within the zone of interests to be protected or regulated by the statute or constitutional guarantee in question." Said another way, it must be shown that the plaintiff's injury was caused by the challenged governmental action. Third, it must be shown that it is likely that the injury will be redressed by a favorable decision.

Under this new test, economic and noneconomic injuries are sufficient to establish an injury in fact. Even somewhat abstract injuries, such as aesthetic, conservational, recreational, and environmental injuries, may establish standing under the new test. However, a mere intellectual or metaphysical interest in a problem does not confer standing. One must actually suffer some harm, whether economic or noneconomic. If one suffers an actual economic injury, the case for standing is easily made. For example, a physician has standing to challenge a law that regulates abortions because personal financial injury may be shown. The case for standing is harder to make if one's injuries are noneconomic. In *Summers, et al. v. Earth Island*

Institute, et al., (2009)[16], the Court held that the deprivation of a procedural right to object to a policy is not enough alone to confer standing.

The second part of the test requires a nexus between the injury claimed and the rights asserted. Under the third part of the test, a plaintiff must show that a favorable decision by the court will redress the injuries suffered.

Clapper v. Amnesty International USA provides you with an example of interests that don't satisfy the *Data* Processing test.

Clapper v. Amnesty International USA

568 U.S. ___ (2013)

Alito, J, delivered the opinion of the Court.

[The Court provided background on the Foreign Intelligence Surveillance Act (FISA) and its amendments that are a backdrop to the underlying controversy. Through FISA Congress established the basic rules of foreign surveillance and data collection and created the FISA court and FISA review court. In the wake of the 9/11 attacks, Congress enlarged executive powers to gather intelligence, without FISA Court review in some instances.]

When Congress enacted the FISA Amendments Act of 2008 (FISA Amendments Act), it left much of FISA intact, but it "established a new and independent source of intelligence collection authority, beyond that granted in traditional FISA." As relevant here, §702 of FISA, 50 U. S. C. §1881a (2006 ed., Supp. V), which was enacted as part of the FISA Amendments Act, supplements pre-existing FISA authority by creating a new framework under which the Government may seek the FISC's authorization of certain foreign intelligence surveillance targeting the communications of non-U.S. persons located abroad. Unlike traditional FISA surveillance, §1881a does not require the Government to demonstrate probable cause that the target of the electronic surveillance is a foreign power or agent of a foreign power. And, unlike traditional FISA, §1881a does not require the Government to specify the nature and location of each of the particular facilities or places at which the electronic surveillance will occur. . . .

The present case involves a constitutional challenge to §1881a. Surveillance under §1881a is subject to statutory conditions, judicial authorization, congressional supervision, and compliance with the Fourth Amendment. Section 1881a provides that, upon the issuance of an order from the Foreign Intelligence Surveillance Court, "the Attorney General and the Director of National Intelligence may authorize jointly, for a period of up to 1 year . . . , the targeting of persons reasonably believed to be located outside the United States to acquire foreign intelligence information." §1881a(a). Surveillance under §1881a may not be intentionally targeted at any person known to be in the United States or any U.S. person reasonably believed to be located abroad. . . .

Respondents are attorneys and human rights, labor, legal, and media organizations whose work allegedly requires them to engage in sensitive and sometimes privileged telephone and e-mail communications with colleagues, clients, sources, and other individuals located abroad. Respondents believe that some of the people with whom they exchange foreign intelligence information are likely targets of surveillance under §1881a. Specifically, respondents claim that they communicate by telephone and e-mail with people the Government "believes or believed to be associated with terrorist organizations," "people located in geographic areas that are a special focus" of the Government's counterterrorism or diplomatic efforts, and activists who oppose governments that are supported by the United States Government.

Respondents claim that §1881a compromises their ability to locate witnesses, cultivate sources, obtain information, and communicate confidential information to their clients. Respondents also assert that they "have ceased engaging" in certain telephone and e-mail conversations. According to respondents, the threat of surveillance will compel them to travel abroad in order to have in-person conversations. In addition, respondents declare that they have undertaken "costly and burdensome measures" to protect the confidentiality of sensitive communications. . . .

Article III of the Constitution limits federal courts' jurisdiction to certain "Cases" and "Controversies" . . . .

The law of Article III standing, which is built on separation-of-powers principles, serves to prevent the judicial process from being used to usurp the powers of the political branches. . . .

To establish Article III standing, an injury must be "concrete, particularized, and actual or imminent; fairly traceable to the challenged action; and redressable by a favorable ruling." . . .

[R]espondents' argument rests on their highly speculative fear that: (1) the Government will decide to target the communications of non-U.S. persons with whom they communicate; (2) in doing so, the Government will choose to invoke its authority under §1881a rather than utilizing another method of surveillance; (3) the Article III judges who serve on the Foreign Intelligence Surveillance Court will conclude that the Government's proposed surveillance procedures satisfy §1881a's many safeguards and are consistent with the Fourth Amendment; (4) the Government will succeed in intercepting the communications of respondents' contacts; and (5) respondents will be parties to the particular communications that the Government intercepts. As discussed below, respondents' theory of standing, which relies on a highly attenuated chain of possibilities, does not satisfy the requirement that threatened injury must be certainly impending. Moreover, even if respondents could demonstrate injury in fact, the second link in the above-described chain of contingencies—which amounts to mere speculation about whether surveillance would be under §1881a or some other authority—shows that respondents cannot satisfy the requirement that any injury in fact must be fairly traceable to §1881a.

First, it is speculative whether the Government will imminently target communications to which respondents are parties. . . .

Second, even if respondents could demonstrate that the targeting of their foreign contacts is imminent, respondents can only speculate as to whether the Government will seek to use §1881aauthorized surveillance (rather than other methods) to do so. The Government has numerous other methods of conducting surveillance, none of which is challenged here. Even after the enactment of the FISA Amendments Act, for example, the Government may still conduct electronic surveillance of persons abroad under the older provisions of FISA so long as it satisfies the applicable requirements, including a demonstration of probable cause to believe that the person is a foreign power or agent of a foreign power. . . .

Third, even if respondents could show that the Government will seek the Foreign Intelligence Surveillance Court's authorization to acquire the communications of respondents' foreign contacts under §1881a, respondents can only speculate as to whether that court will authorize such surveillance. . . .

Fourth, even if the Government were to obtain the Foreign Intelligence Surveillance Court's approval to target respondents' foreign contacts under §1881a, it is unclear whether the Government would succeed in acquiring the communications of respondents' foreign contacts. And fifth, even if the Government were to conduct surveillance of respondents' foreign contacts, respondents can only speculate as to whether their own communications with their foreign contacts would be incidentally acquired.

(continued)

> In sum, respondents' speculative chain of possibilities does not establish that injury based on potential future surveillance is certainly impending or is fairly traceable to §1881a.
>
> We hold that respondents lack Article III standing because they cannot demonstrate that the future injury they purportedly fear is certainly impending and because they cannot manufacture standing by incurring costs in anticipation of non-imminent harm. We therefore reverse the judgment of the Second Circuit and remand the case for further proceedings consistent with this opinion.

Clapper v. Amnesty International USA, 568 U.S. (2013), United States Supreme Court.

Let us examine how the new test has been applied to specific subject areas.

9.4(a) Citizen and Taxpayer

A person's status as a citizen does not confer a right to challenge a law or agency action. That is, disagreement with a law or governmental behavior, without any accompanying harm, is not sufficient to confer standing.

Similarly, status as a taxpayer does not give one sufficient interest to challenge the expenditure of public funds in most situations. *Flast v. Cohen*[17] is an exception to this general rule, and opens the door to limited types of taxpayer lawsuits. *Flast* involved a challenge to a statute that provided financing for reading, arithmetic, and other nonreligious courses in religious schools. The plaintiff, a taxpayer, brought an action alleging that the expenditure violated the Establishment Clause of the First Amendment to the U.S. Constitution.

The Court held that taxpayers may have standing if a nexus between the taxpayers' status and the expenditure can be shown *and* it can be shown that the statute exceeds a constitutional limitation. The plaintiff in *Flast* satisfied these requirements because the Court found that the expenditure was significant, that the plaintiff was in the group of taxpayers whose funds were being expended, and that the First Amendment was clearly implicated.

Although *Flast* continues to be the law, the Supreme Court has seriously limited its scope. *Valley Forge Christian College v. Americans for Separation of Church & State, Inc.*,[18] involved a delegation of authority from Congress to the Secretary of Health, Education, and Welfare (now the Secretary of Education). The secretary was authorized to convey surplus property to schools for educational use. The statute further authorized the secretary to discount the price of properties granted. The secretary conveyed surplus property to the Valley Forge Christian College and discounted the price 100 percent. The Court found the grant valid because the grant was not made under Congress's taxing and spending power but under the Property Clause of Article IV of the Constitution.

In addition, the Court held that because the decision to award the grant was made by an administrative agency, rather than Congress, the taxpayer lacked standing. Said another way, a taxpayer has standing only to challenge the actual body responsible for levying a tax or authorizing the expenditure of tax revenues, not the administrative agency or official responsible for collecting the tax or administering the expenditure. You previously learned, however, that Congress may delegate the authority to establish a tax, or other revenue-generating measures, to agencies. When an agency exercises such authority, it is probable that taxpayers could directly challenge the agency because it is the body responsible for levying the tax.

Similarly, an objection to the use of discretionary funds, even if allocated by Congress, by the executive branch may not be challenged under *Flast*. In 2001, President George W. Bush issued an executive order creating the White House Office of Faith Based and Community Initiatives. The purpose of the office is to ensure, "private and charitable community groups, including religious ones . . . have the fullest opportunity permitted by law to compete on a level playing field [for federal funding], so long as they achieve valid public purposes." The E.O. also directed that while faith-based organizations were to be given equal opportunity to compete for federal funds, no federal money could be issued to support inherently religious activities. The objective was to give religious organizations that provide social services, conduct research, or otherwise desire support for nonreligious activities equal access to federal funding. Previously, the administration believed that religious organizations were discriminated against in the award of federal dollars because of the concern that such support amounted to an establishment of religion, as prohibited by the First Amendment.

A nonprofit freedom from religion organization sued the United States, claiming that the expenditure of funds to conduct conferences on the faith-based initiative violated the First Amendment. Relying on *Flast*, the plaintiffs asserted that their status as taxpayers established standing. The Court rejected the standing theory when applied to executive discretionary expenditures in *Hein v. Freedom from Religion Foundation, Inc., et al.*, 551 U.S. 587 (2007). For *Flast* to apply, a citizen must demonstrate a direct Congress-to-expenditure link that violates the Establishment Clause. Otherwise, the Court reasoned, every expenditure by every government official could be challenged, opening a floodgate of litigation.

There is another limitation on taxpayer standing. A taxpayer has standing to sue only when he or she challenges an expenditure that violates a constitutional limitation on that power. Because most financial decisions do not involve such a constitutional limitation, *Flast* represents the exception rather than the rule. Be aware, though, that taxpayer lawsuits are permitted in many states against local government and state government expenditures. One author noted that taxpayer lawsuits are permitted in nearly every state against local action, and three-fourths of the states permit such lawsuits against state actions.[19]

Like citizenship, voter status does not automatically confer standing to challenge governmental action. Like taxpayer status, though, if a voter can demonstrate that agency action interferes with or harms voting rights, standing may exist. This was a disputed issue in *Federal Election Commission v. Akins*.

Federal Election Commission v. Akins

524 U.S. 11 (1998)

The Federal Election Commission (FEC) has determined that the American Israel Public Affairs Committee (AIPAC) is not a "political committee" as defined by the Federal Election Campaign Act of 1971, 86 Stat. 11, as amended, 2 U.S.C. § 431(4) (FECA), and, for that reason, the Commission has refused to require AIPAC to make disclosures regarding its membership, contributions, and expenditures that FECA would otherwise require. We hold that respondents, a group of voters, have standing to challenge the Commission's determination in court, and we remand this case for further proceedings.

. . . As commonly understood, the Federal Election Campaign Act seeks to remedy any actual or perceived corruption of the political process in several

(continued)

important ways. The Act imposes limits upon the amounts that individuals, corporations, "political committees" (including political action committees), and political parties can contribute to a candidate for federal political office. The Act also imposes limits on the amount these individuals or entities can spend in coordination with a candidate. . . .

This case concerns requirements in the Act that extend beyond these better-known contribution and expenditure limitations. In particular the Act imposes extensive recordkeeping and disclosure requirements upon groups that fall within the Act's definition of a "political committee." Those groups must register with the FEC, appoint a treasurer, keep names and addresses of contributors, track the amount and purpose of disbursements, and file complex FEC reports that include lists of donors giving in excess of $200 per year (often, these donors may be the group's members), contributions, expenditures, and any other disbursements irrespective of their purposes. . . .

This case arises out of an effort by respondents, a group of voters with views often opposed to those of AIPAC, to persuade the FEC to treat AIPAC as a "political committee." Respondents filed a complaint with the FEC, stating that AIPAC had made more than $1,000 in qualifying "expenditures" per year, and thereby became a "political committee." . . . They added that AIPAC had violated the FEC provisions requiring "political committee[s]" to register and to make public the information about members, contributions, and expenditures to which we have just referred. Respondents also claimed that AIPAC had violated § 441b of FECA, which prohibits corporate campaign "contribution[s]" and "expenditure[s]." . . . They asked the FEC to find that AIPAC had violated the Act, and, among other things, to order AIPAC to make public the information that FECA demands of a "political committee." . . .

AIPAC asked the FEC to dismiss the complaint. AIPAC described itself as an issue-oriented organization that seeks to maintain friendship and promote goodwill between the United States and Israel. . . . AIPAC conceded that it lobbies elected officials and disseminates information about candidates for public office. . . . But in responding to the § 441b charge, AIPAC denied that it had made the kinds of "expenditures" that matter for FECA purposes. . . .

The FEC nonetheless held that AIPAC was not subject to the disclosure requirements, but for a different reason. In the FEC's view, the Act's definition of "political committee" includes only those organizations that have as a "major purpose" the nomination or election of candidates. . . . AIPAC, it added, was fundamentally an issue-oriented lobbying organization, not a campaign-related organization, and hence AIPAC fell outside the definition of a "political committee" regardless. . . . The FEC consequently dismissed respondents' complaint . . . [and the respondents filed this appeal in a federal district court].

Nor do we agree with the FEC or the dissent that Congress lacks the constitutional power to authorize federal courts to adjudicate this lawsuit. Article III, of course, limits Congress' grant of judicial power to "cases" or "controversies." That limitation means that respondents must show, among other things, an "injury in fact"—a requirement that helps assure that courts will not "pass upon . . . abstract, intellectual problems," but adjudicate "concrete, living contest[s] between adversaries." . . . In our view, respondents here have suffered a genuine "injury in fact." The "injury in fact" that respondents have suffered consists of their inability to obtain information-lists of AIPAC donors (who are, according to AIPAC, its members), and campaign-related contributions and expenditures that, on respondents' view of the law, the statute requires that AIPAC make public. There is no reason to doubt their claim that the information would help them (and others to whom they would communicate it) to evaluate candidates for public office, especially candidates who received assistance from AIPAC, and to evaluate the role that AIPAC's financial assistance might play in a specific election. Respondents' injury consequently seems concrete and particular. Indeed, this Court has previously held that a plaintiff suffers an "injury in fact" when the plaintiff fails to obtain information which must be publicly disclosed pursuant to a statute. . . .

The dissent refers to *United States v. Richardson*, 418 U.S. 166 (1974), a case in which a plaintiff sought information (details of Central Intelligence Agency expenditures) to which, he said, the Constitution's Accounts Clause, Art. I, § 9, cl. 7, entitled him. The Court held that the plaintiff there lacked Article III standing. . . . The dissent says that *Richardson* and this case are "indistinguishable." . . . But as the parties' briefs suggest, for they do not mention *Richardson*, that case does not control the outcome here. *Richardson*'s plaintiff claimed that a statute permitting the CIA to keep its expenditures nonpublic violated the Accounts Clause, which requires that "a regular Statement and Account of the Receipts and Expenditures of all public Money shall be published from time to time." The Court held that the plaintiff lacked standing because there was "no 'logical nexus' between the [plaintiff's] asserted status of taxpayer and the claimed failure of the Congress to require the Executive to supply a more detailed report of the [CIA's] expenditures." (quoting *Flast v. Cohen*, 392 U.S. 83, 102 (1968), for the proposition that in "taxpayer standing" cases, there must be "a logical nexus between the status asserted and the claim sought to be adjudicated").

In this case, however, the "logical nexus" inquiry is not relevant. Here, there is no constitutional provision requiring the demonstration of the "nexus" the Court believed must be shown in *Richardson* and *Flast*. Rather, there is a statute which, as we previously pointed out, . . . does seek to protect individuals such as respondents from the kind of harm they say they have suffered, i.e., failing to receive particular information about campaign-related activities. The fact that the Court in *Richardson* focused upon taxpayer standing, not voter standing, places that case at still a greater distance from the case before us. We are not suggesting, as the dissent implies, that *Richardson* would have come out differently if only the plaintiff had asserted his standing to sue as a voter, rather than as a taxpayer. Faced with such an assertion, the *Richardson* Court would simply have had to consider whether "the Framers . . . ever imagined that general directives [of the Constitution] . . . would be subject to enforcement by an individual citizen." But since that answer (like the answer to whether there was taxpayer standing in *Richardson*) would have rested in significant part upon the Court's view of the Accounts Clause, it still would not control our answer in this case. All this is to say that the legal logic which critically determined *Richardson*'s outcome is beside the point here.

The FEC's strongest argument is its contention that this lawsuit involves only a "generalized grievance." . . . The Solicitor General points out that respondents' asserted harm (their failure to obtain information) is one which is "'shared in substantially equal measure by all or a large class of citizens.'" . . . This Court, he adds, has often said that "generalized grievance[s]" are not the kinds of harms that confer standing. . . . Whether styled as a constitutional or prudential limit on standing, the Court has sometimes determined that where large numbers of Americans suffer alike, the political process, rather than the judicial process, may provide the more appropriate remedy for a widely shared grievance. . . . The kind of judicial language to which the FEC points, however, invariably appears in cases where the harm at issue is not only widely shared, but is also of an abstract and indefinite nature—for example, harm to the "common concern for obedience to law." . . . The abstract nature of the harm—for example, injury to the interest in seeing that the law is obeyed—deprives the case of the concrete specificity that characterized those controversies which were "the traditional concern of the courts at Westminster," *Coleman*, 307 U.S., at 460 (Frankfurter, J., dissenting); and which today prevents a plaintiff from obtaining what would, in effect, amount to an advisory opinion. . . .

Often the fact that an interest is abstract and the fact that it is widely shared go hand in hand. But their association is not invariable, and where a harm is concrete,

(continued)

though widely shared, the Court has found "injury in fact." Thus the fact that a political forum may be more readily available where an injury is widely shared (while counseling against, say, interpreting a statute as conferring standing) does not, by itself, automatically disqualify an interest for Article III purposes. Such an interest, where sufficiently concrete, may count as an "injury in fact." This conclusion seems particularly obvious where (to use a hypothetical example) large numbers of individuals suffer the same common-law injury (say, a widespread mass tort), or where large numbers of voters suffer interference with voting rights conferred by law. We conclude that similarly, the informational injury at issue here, directly related to voting, the most basic of political rights, is sufficiently concrete and specific such that the fact that it is widely shared does not deprive Congress of constitutional power to authorize its vindication in the federal courts.

Respondents have also satisfied the remaining two constitutional standing requirements. The harm asserted is "fairly traceable" to the FEC's decision about which respondents complain. Of course, as the FEC points out, . . . it is possible that even had the FEC agreed with respondents' view of the law, it would still have decided in the exercise of its discretion not to require AIPAC to produce the information. . . . But that fact does not destroy Article III "causation," for we cannot know that the FEC would have exercised its prosecutorial discretion in this way. Agencies often have discretion about whether or not to take a particular action. Yet those adversely affected by a discretionary agency decision generally have standing to complain that the agency based its decision upon an improper legal ground. . . .

Finally, the FEC argues that we should deny respondents standing because this case involves an agency's decision not to undertake an enforcement action—an area generally not subject to judicial review. . . . In *Heckler*, this Court noted that agency enforcement decisions "ha[ve] traditionally been 'committed to agency discretion,'" and concluded that Congress did not intend to alter that tradition in enacting the APA. We deal here with a statute that explicitly indicates the contrary.

In sum, respondents, as voters, have satisfied both prudential and constitutional standing requirements. They may bring this petition for a declaration that the FEC's dismissal of their complaint was unlawful. . . .

Federal Election Commission v. Akins, 524 U.S. 11 (1998), United States Supreme Court.

9.4(b) Qui Tam Actions

Although citizens generally lack standing when there is no concomitant harm, Congress may provide for standing where it otherwise does not exist. The most obvious example is in so-called private attorney general cases. Private individuals may be authorized by Congress to challenge agency action or otherwise act on behalf of the public. "[I]ndividual litigants, acting as private attorneys-general, . . . have standing to represent the public interest, despite their lack of economic or other personal interests, if Congress has appropriately authorized such suits."[20]

A *qui tam* action is such a lawsuit. Qui tam lawsuits are brought by citizens on behalf of the government, not against the government. They are an exception to the basic rule that the government must file its own cases. In qui tam suits, individuals may sue on behalf of the government and recover all or a portion of any judgment awarded. Such suits are used to encourage citizens to assist in protection of the public fisc.

Congress recently amended the federal qui tam statute, the False Claims Act, in an effort to make it more attractive to potential citizen attorneys general. Title 32 U.S.C., § 3729, prohibits making false claims to officials of the United States, as well as other fraudulent acts, which are intended to acquire approval or payment. Title 32 U.S.C., § 3730, contains the qui tam provision, which directs the

LEGAL TERM

Qui Tam

Lawsuit brought by a citizen against one who has defrauded the government. The citizen who brings a qui tam action is entitled to keep a portion of the proceeds of the lawsuit.

Attorney General of the United States to investigate and prosecute cases arising under § 3729.

The statute also permits individuals to bring the same actions as the Attorney General, in the name of the United States. The Attorney General is given the option of intervening and taking over the case or permitting the individual to maintain the prosecution. If the Attorney General decides to proceed with the case filed by an individual (sometimes known as an *informer*), the individual has a right to continue as a party. The complaint is kept under seal for a specific period of time while the Attorney General makes the decision as to whether to become involved. Venue lies in the judicial district in which the offense is alleged to have occurred.

If the Attorney General proceeds, the informer is entitled to 15 to 25 percent of any proceeds recovered. If the informer prosecutes the case, the recovery range is between 25 and 30 percent. The court determines the appropriate amount. Attorney fees and costs may also be recovered from the defendant.

Specifically, the FCA makes it unlawful for a person or corporation to submit a "false record or statement to get a false or fraudulent claim paid or approved by the government . . . and to 'conspire[s] to defraud the government by getting a false or fraudulent claim allowed or paid." In the 2008 case *Allison Engine v. United States*, the Court held that the statute required the false record claim to be presented to the government directly. Because *Allison* involved an alleged false claim by a subcontractor to a contractor, which in turn made its claim for payment to the government, the Court held the FCA didn't apply. In response to this decision, Congress amended the FCA in 2009 to capture such cases.

9.4(c) Environmental Cases

One area in which noneconomic injury has often been recognized is environmental cases. In the *Sierra Club* case, the Supreme Court examined whether harm to a group's aesthetic interests in the beauty of a forest is sufficient to confer standing. Although the plaintiffs lost this specific case, they won on the larger issue: Aesthetic and other environmental interests may confer standing. Six years after *Sierra Club*, the Supreme Court reaffirmed the principle that potential environmental injury may confer standing, in *Duke Power Co. v. Carolina Environmental Study Group*.[21] The Court held that the residents of a community where a nuclear power plant was planned to be constructed could possibly show sufficient environmental injury to confer standing to challenge the law authorizing the construction.

Class actions are common in environmental litigation. *Sierra Club* taught environmental organizations a lesson: At least one individual must suffer harm to confer standing. Because noneconomic interests are adequate to confer standing, conservation organizations usually have little trouble finding a suitable plaintiff.

Sierra Club v. Morton

405 U.S. 727 (1972)

The Mineral King Valley is an area of great natural beauty nestled in the Sierra Nevada Mountains in Tulare County, California, adjacent to Sequoia National Park. It has been part of the Sequoia National Forest since 1926, and is designated as a national game refuge by special Act of Congress. Though once the site of extensive mining activity, Mineral King is now used almost exclusively for recreational purposes. Its relative inaccessibility and lack of development have limited the number of

(continued)

visitors each year, and at the same time have preserved the valley's quality as a quasi-wilderness area largely uncluttered by the products of civilization.

The United States Forest Service, which is entrusted with the maintenance and administration of national forests, began in the late 1940's to give consideration to Mineral King as a potential site for recreational development. Prodded by a rapidly increasing demand for skiing facilities, the Forest Service published a prospectus in 1965, inviting bids from private developers for the construction and operation of a ski resort that would serve as a summer recreation area. The proposal of Walt Disney Enterprises, Inc., was chosen from those of six bidders, and Disney received a three-year permit to conduct surveys and explorations in the valley in connection with its preparation of a complete master plan for the resort.

The final Disney plan, approved by the Forest Service in January 1969, outlines a $35 million complex of motels, restaurants, swimming pools, parking lots, and other structures designed to accommodate 14,000 visitors daily. . . .

Representatives of the Sierra Club, who favor maintaining Mineral King largely in its present state, followed the progress of recreational planning for the valley with close attention and increasing dismay. They unsuccessfully sought a public hearing on the proposed development in 1965, and in subsequent correspondence with officials of the Forest Service and the Department of the Interior, they expressed the Club's objections to Disney's plan as a whole and to particular features included in it. In June 1969 the Club filed the present suit in the United States District for the Northern District of California, seeking a declaratory judgment that various aspects of the proposed development contravene federal laws and regulations governing the preservation of national parks, forests, and game refuges, and also seeking preliminary and permanent injunction restraining federal officials involved from granting their approval or issuing permits. . . .

The first question presented is whether the Sierra Club has alleged facts that entitle it to obtain judicial review of the challenged action. Whether a party has a sufficient stake in an otherwise justiciable controversy to obtain judicial resolution of that controversy is what has traditionally been referred to as the question of standing to sue. Where the party does not rely on any specific statute authorizing invocation of the judicial process, the question of standing depends upon whether the party has alleged such a "personal stake in the outcome of the controversy," . . . as to ensure that "the dispute sought to be adjudicated will be presented in an adversary context and in a form historically viewed as capable of judicial resolution.". . .

The Sierra Club relies upon § 10 of the Administrative Procedure Act (APA), 5 U.S.C. § 702, which provides:

> A person suffering legal wrong because of agency action, or adversely affected or aggrieved by agency action within the meaning of a relevant statute, is entitled to judicial review thereof.

The injury alleged by the Sierra Club will be incurred entirely by reason of the change in the uses to which Mineral King will be put, and the attendant change in the aesthetics and ecology of the area. Thus, in referring to the road to be built through Sequoia National Park, the complaint alleged that the development "would destroy or otherwise adversely affect the scenery, natural and historic objects and wildlife of the park and would impair the enjoyment of the park for future generations.". . .

The trend of cases arising under the APA and other statutes authorizing judicial review of federal agency action has been toward recognizing that injuries other than economic harm are sufficient to bring a person within the meaning of the statutory language, and toward discarding the notion that an injury that is widely shared is *ipso facto* not an injury sufficient to provide the basis for judicial review. We noted this development in [a prior case], in saying that the interest alleged to have been injured "may reflect 'aesthetic, conservational, and recreational' as well as economic values." But broadening the categories of injury that may be alleged in support of standing is a different matter from abandoning the requirement that the party seeking review must himself have suffered an injury.

Some courts have indicated a willingness to take this latter step by conferring standing upon organizations that have demonstrated "an organizational interest in the problem" of environmental or consumer protection. . . . But a mere "interest in a problem," no matter how qualified the organization is in evaluating the problem, is not sufficient by itself to render the organization "adversely affected" or "aggrieved" within the meaning of the APA. The Sierra Club is a large and long-established organization, with a historic commitment to the cause of protecting our Nation's natural heritage from man's depredations. But if a "special interest" in this subject were enough to entitle the Sierra Club to commence this litigation, there would appear to be no objective basis upon which to disallow a suit by any other bona fide "special interest" organization however small or short-lived. And if any group with a bona fide "special interest" could initiate litigation, it is difficult to perceive why any individual citizen with the same bona fide special interest would not also be entitled to do so.

Sierra Club v. Morton, 405 U.S. 727 (1972), United States Supreme Court.

The lesson of *Sierra Club* was not learned by the plaintiffs in *Lujan v. Defenders of Wildlife.*[22] *Lujan* centered around the Endangered Species Act (ESA), a federal statute intended to protect animal species from extinction. The ESA provided that agencies were not to take actions that were likely to jeopardize the continued existence of an endangered species.

Pursuant to the ESA, the Fish and Wildlife Service and National Marine Fisheries Service jointly promulgated regulations stating that the ESA applied to agency actions taken in foreign nations. The agencies later changed their position and promulgated a regulation stating that the ESA had force only in the United States and on the high seas. This action was challenged by the plaintiffs, who sought an order compelling the Secretary of the Interior to promulgate a regulation restoring the ESA's international scope.

The Supreme Court held that the plaintiffs did not have standing. The plaintiff wildlife preservation organizations relied on the affidavits of two members to establish standing; in those affidavits, the members asserted that they had been abroad and intended at some unknown date to return, and that they had an interest in observing endangered species on their return abroad. The Court found this interest inadequate to confer standing. The Court reiterated the principles set out in *Sierra Club v. Morton*—that is, an organization can maintain an action as long as at least one member of that organization satisfies the requisites of standing. An intent to return to a foreign land at some unplanned and unknown date is too conjectural and hypothetical.

It would have been easy to satisfy the standing requirements in *Lujan*. Had a member been a scientist who studied specific endangered species, there would have been standing. Justice Kennedy, in a concurring opinion, asserted that if the members had obtained airline tickets and made plans to visit one of the areas in dispute, there would also have been standing.

Lujan reaffirms prior cases. At least one member of an environmental organization must have a concrete interest in the outcome of a case to satisfy the case and controversy requirement of Article III.

9.4(d) Competitor

Competitor participation was discussed earlier under the topic of interested parties. Recall from that discussion that the problem presented by competitors was that they are not obvious parties. However, the APA does not limit participation in agency proceedings to obvious parties—the test is whether one is an interested party. Under this test, competitors are sometimes permitted to participate in agency proceedings.

The same is true when seeking judicial review. A competitor may have standing to challenge an agency's action because the competitor has an interest in the case. For example, suppose that a change to the regulations concerning commercial aviation resulted in the airlines' being able to offer reduced rates. Competitors, such as bus lines and railroads, would be affected by a reduction in business. Therefore, they would have standing.

9.4(e) Consumer

In some cases, consumers may go unprotected because an agency action meets with the approval of both the regulated parties and their competitors. Recently, courts have recognized that if consumers are not permitted standing, their interests may go unprotected. Therefore, consumers may have the right to participate at the agency level as interested parties and may have standing to seek judicial review of agency actions.

If the price a consumer pays is affected by an agency action, the consumer has adequate interest to obtain judicial review. A consumer may also have standing to challenge agency orders that affect the public interest in other ways, such as reducing the quality of a product. Generally, the fact that an administrative agency is charged with protecting the consumer's interest does not mean that consumers are precluded from bringing consumer lawsuits.

Like environmental cases, many consumer cases are filed as class actions. Consumer groups often bring such actions on behalf of all consumers. Damages are rarely sought; a declaration that an agency action is illegal or injunctive relief are the forms of relief most frequently sought.

9.4(f) Statutory

Congress has some discretion to create rights that will confer standing. In other examples, standing has been found to exist even when the requirements of *Data Processing* and *Lujan* have not been precisely met. In *Massachusetts v. EPA*, 549 U.S. 497 (2007), for example, several states were found to have standing to challenge the EPA's decision not to regulate automobile emissions. In support of the Court's conclusion that the states were suffering harm, the Court penned:

> To ensure the proper adversarial presentation, *Lujan* holds that a litigant must demonstrate that it has suffered a concrete and particularized injury that is either actual or imminent, that the injury is fairly traceable to the defendant, and that it is likely that a favorable decision will redress that injury. See id., at 560–561. However, a litigant to whom Congress has "accorded a procedural right to protect his concrete interests,"— here, the right to challenge agency action unlawfully withheld, § 7607(b)(1)—"can assert that right without meeting all the normal standards for redressability and immediacy," ibid. When a litigant is

vested with a procedural right, that litigant has standing if there is some possibility that the requested relief will prompt the injury-causing party to reconsider the decision that allegedly harmed the litigant. Ibid.; see also *Sugar Cane Growers Cooperative of Fla. v. Veneman*, 289 F. 3d 89, 94–95 (CADC 2002) ("A [litigant] who alleges a deprivation of a procedural protection to which he is entitled never has to prove that if he had received the procedure the substantive result would have been altered. All that is necessary is to show that the procedural step was connected to the substantive result). . . .

Well before the creation of the modern administrative state, we recognized that States are not normal litigants for the purposes of invoking federal jurisdiction. As Justice Holmes explained in *Georgia v. Tennessee Copper Co.*, 206 U.S. 230, 237 (1907), a case in which Georgia sought to protect its citizens from air pollution originating outside its borders:

"The case has been argued largely as if it were one between two private parties; but it is not. The very elements that would be relied upon in a suit between fellow-citizens as a ground for equitable relief are wanting here. The State owns very little of the territory alleged to be affected, and the damage to it capable of estimate in money, possibly, at least, is small. This is a suit by a State for an injury to it in its capacity of quasi-sovereign. In that capacity the State has an interest independent of and behind the titles of its citizens, in all the earth and air within its domain. It has the last word as to whether its mountains shall be stripped of their forests and its inhabitants shall breathe pure air."

Just as Georgia's "independent interest . . . in all the earth and air within its domain" supported federal jurisdiction a century ago, so too does Massachusetts' well-founded desire to preserve its sovereign territory today. Cf. *Alden v. Maine*, 527 U.S. 706, 715 (1999) (observing that in the federal system, the States "are not relegated to the role of mere provinces or political corporations, but retain the dignity, though not the full authority, of sovereignty"). That Massachusetts does in fact own a great deal of the "territory alleged to be affected" only reinforces the conclusion that its stake in the outcome of this case is sufficiently concrete to warrant the exercise of federal judicial power.

When a State enters the Union, it surrenders certain sovereign prerogatives. Massachusetts cannot invade Rhode Island to force reductions in greenhouse gas emissions, it cannot negotiate an emissions treaty with China or India, and in some circumstances the exercise of its police powers to reduce in-state motor-vehicle emissions might well be preempted. See *Alfred L. Snapp & Son, Inc. v. Puerto Rico ex rel. Barez*, 458 U.S. 592, 607 (1982) ("One helpful indication in determining whether an alleged injury to the health and welfare of its citizens suffices to give the State standing to sue parens patriae is whether the injury is one that the State, if it could, would likely attempt to address through its sovereign lawmaking powers").

These sovereign prerogatives are now lodged in the Federal Government, and Congress has ordered EPA to protect Massachusetts (among others) by prescribing standards applicable to the "emission of any air pollutant from any class or classes of new motor vehicle engines, which in [the Administrator's] judgment cause, or contribute to, air pollution, which may reasonably be anticipated to endanger public health or welfare," 42 U. S. C. § 7521(a)(1). Congress has moreover recognized a concomitant procedural right to challenge the rejection of its rulemaking petition as arbitrary and capricious, § 7607(b)(1). Given that procedural right and Massachusetts' stake in protecting its quasi-sovereign interests, the Commonwealth is entitled to special solicitude in our standing analysis.

With that in mind, it is clear that petitioners' submissions as they pertain to Massachusetts have satisfied the most demanding standards of the adversarial process. EPA's steadfast refusal to regulate greenhouse gas emissions presents a risk of harm to Massachusetts that is both "actual" and "imminent." *Lujan*, 504 U.S., at 560 (internal quotation marks omitted). There is, moreover, a "substantial likelihood that the judicial relief requested" will prompt EPA to take steps to reduce that risk, *Duke Power Co. v. Carolina Environmental Study Group*, Inc., 438 U.S. 59, 79.

9.4(g) Constitutional

In some cases, the Constitution may create a right that will confer standing. This is common in criminal cases. An interesting standing question was presented in *Bond v. United States*[23] a 2011 Supreme Court case that involved a jealous and vengeful wife. Bond, the wife, learned that one of her good friends was having an affair with, and became impregnated by, her husband. Bond threatened her husband's lover, stole her mail, and attempted to poison her. Bond was charged with violating federal postal laws and an international treaty that governed the use of chemicals. She challenged the application of the treaty to her as violating the Tenth Amendment. Bond asserted that the treaty regulated a general police power, the crime of injuring another person, and that such powers are reserved to the states under the Tenth Amendment. The federal government responded by asserting that she lacked standing to raise the federalism question, in addition to asserting the legitimacy of the prosecution under the treaty. In a unanimous decision, the Court held that Bond had standing to raise the Tenth Amendment issue. On remand the lower courts determined that the treaty's provisions could be used to prosecute her without violating the Tenth Amendment. She appealed again, the Supreme Court granted certiorari, and the case was pending when this book went to press.

9.5 TIMING OF REVIEW

Various rules govern when review may be sought.

9.5(a) Primary Jurisdiction

LEGAL TERM

Primary Jurisdiction
Requirement that disputes between private parties be raised in an administrative forum before being filed in court if an administrative agency has jurisdiction over the issues in dispute.

Primary jurisdiction applies to cases in which a private party sues another private party about some matter that is under the control of an agency. For example, if a consumer were to sue a retailer for an unlawful business practice, primary jurisdiction might apply if an administrative agency had been given the authority to resolve such disputes.

The doctrine of primary jurisdiction requires that a court refer a case to an agency for an initial decision when the issues involved therein are within the agency's jurisdiction. Primary jurisdiction is intended to protect agency jurisdiction. It does, however, also benefit the courts. If an agency reviews a case over which it has greater expertise than a court, the record to be reviewed by the court will be more complete. The agency decision will give the reviewing court a starting point, a reasoned decision with factual findings made by an informed source. This is good for judicial economy.

Primary jurisdiction doctrine is applied only to closely regulated industries. If an issue is not clearly within an agency's jurisdiction, the court will not make a referral to an agency.

There is also no need for a referral if the issue raised is one of law rather than fact. The purpose of permitting the initial determination to be made by an agency is to preserve its jurisdiction and further judicial economy by allowing the agency to use its expertise and experience when finding the facts and exercising discretion. However, because issues of law are reviewed de novo (with no deference to the agency decision), there is no reason to refer legal issues to an agency.

The unavailability of a desired remedy at the agency level is not material to primary jurisdiction. For example, in *Lichten v. Eastern Air Lines*,[24] a plaintiff sued the defendant airline, alleging that its negligence resulted in the loss of jewelry. The court determined that the Civil Aeronautics Board (CAB) had jurisdiction over the reasonableness of practices relating to claims of this nature; therefore, the case was to be initially decided by the CAB even though it had no authority to award damages. The effect of this decision, which has been criticized, is that a plaintiff must bring two actions: the first in the agency, so that the agency can pass on the issue presented; and the second in a court, to obtain the relief sought.

Although one federal court has found otherwise,[25] *Lichten* remains the general rule. Be aware, however, that many states do not require that a case be presented to an agency for an initial decision if the agency lacks the authority to award the requested relief.

Primary jurisdiction does not preclude judicial review—it merely delays it. If a court determines that referral to an agency is required, it will dismiss the action (or remand it). After the agency has completed its work, review, if otherwise permitted, may proceed.

9.5(b) Exhaustion of Administrative Remedies

Related to the doctrine of primary jurisdiction, the doctrine of exhaustion of administrative remedies is concerned with the timing of a review petition. The exhaustion doctrine provides that all administrative remedies must be pursued and exhausted (completed) before judicial review is available. The administrative process must be given a full and complete opportunity to correct its own errors before judicial intervention occurs.

The doctrine of exhaustion of administrative remedies is the administrative equivalent of the finality rule in judicial settings. That is, only in rare instances is an interlocutory appeal permitted from a trial court. It is equally disruptive and inefficient to allow premature judicial review of an administrative proceeding.

There are a number of reasons why exhaustion of remedies is required. First, exhaustion allows agencies to correct their own mistakes and thereby learn from their errors. Second, it preserves agency autonomy and independence by preventing premature judicial intervention into agency affairs. Third, it promotes judicial economy by allowing a complete record to be made. Fourth, it promotes judicial economy by allowing the agency, rather than the reviewing court, to make findings. Fifth, it encourages cooperation and communication between agencies and parties because judicial intervention is not immediately available.

One must look to statute, regulation, practice, or even contract to determine what remedies are available. As you saw in Figure 8-5, on Social Security claims, a denied claimant must first apply for reconsideration of the decision, followed by an appeal to an administrative law judge, and then appeal to the agency (through a review panel) before review by a federal district court is available. In some instances, a contract may define what administrative process must be exhausted. For example, a government employee's employment contract may contain a provision requiring that grievances or contract disputes be presented to some person or group before judicial review is available. Figure 9-1 shows one agency's appeal form.

OMB NO. 3124-0009
Approval expires 5/31/94

U.S. MERIT SYSTEMS PROTECTION BOARD

APPEAL FORM

INSTRUCTIONS

GENERAL: You do not have to use this form to file an appeal with the Board. However, if you do not, your appeal must still comply with the Board's regulations. 5 C.F.R. Parts 1201 and 1209. Your agency's personnel office will give you access to the regulations, and the Board will expect you to be familiar with them. You also should become familiar with the Board's key case law and controlling court decisions as they may affect your case. **You must tell the Board if you are raising an affirmative defense** (see Part IV), and **you are responsible for proving each defense you raise.**

WHERE TO FILE AN APPEAL: You must file your appeal with the Board's regional office which has responsibility for the geographic area in which you are employed. See 5 C.F.R. Part 1201, Appendix II.

WHEN TO FILE AN APPEAL: Your appeal must be filed during the period beginning with the day after the effective date of the action you are appealing and ending on the 20th day after the effective date. You may not file your appeal before the effective date of the action you are appealing. If you are appealing from a decision which does not set an effective date, you must file within 25 days of the date of the decision you are appealing. If your appeal is late, it may be dismissed as untimely. The date of the filing is the date your appeal is postmarked, the date of the facsimile transmission, or the date of receipt if you personally deliver it to the regional office.

HOW TO FILE AN APPEAL: You may file your appeal by mail, by facsimile, or by personal delivery. You must submit two copies of both your appeal **and** all attachments. You may supplement your response to any question on separate sheets of paper, but if you do, **please put your name and address at the top of each additional page.** All of your submissions must be legible and on 8 1/2" x 11" paper. Your appeal must contain your or your representative's signature in block 6. **If it does not, your appeal will be rejected and returned to you.** If your representative signs block 6, you must sign block 11 or submit a separate written designation of representative.

WHISTLEBLOWING APPEAL/STAY REQUEST: If you believe the action you are appealing was threatened, proposed, taken, or not taken because of whistleblowing activities, **you must complete Part VII of this form. If you are requesting a stay, you must complete Part VIII of this form.**

Privacy Act Statement: *This form requests personal information which is relevant and necessary to reach a decision in your appeal. The U.S. Merit Systems Protection Board collects this information in order to process appeals under its statutory and regulatory authority. Since your appeal is a voluntary action you are not required to provide any personal information in connection with it. However, failure to supply the U.S. Merit Systems Protection Board with all the information essential to reach a decision in your case could result in the rejection of your appeal.*

The U.S. Merit Systems Protection Board is authorized under provisions of Executive Order 9397, dated November 22, 1943, to request your Social Security number, but providing your Social Security number is voluntary and failure to provide it will not result in the rejection of your appeal. Your Social Security number will only be used for identification purposes in the processing of your appeal.

You should know that the decisions of the U.S. Merit Systems Protection Board on appeals are final administrative decisions and, as such, are available to the public under the provisions of the Freedom of Information Act. Additionally, it is possible that information contained in your appeal file may be released as required by the Freedom of Information Act. Some information about your appeal will also be used in depersonalized form as a data base for program statistics.

Public Reporting Burden: *The public reporting burden for this collection of information is estimated to vary from 20 minutes to 1 hour, with an average of 30 minutes per response, including time for reviewing the form, searching existing data sources, gathering the data necessary, and completing and reviewing the collection of information. Send comments regarding the burden estimate or any other aspect of the collection of information, including suggestions for reducing this burden, to the Office of Management Analysis, Merit Systems Protection Board, 1120 Vermont Ave., NW., Washington, DC 20419, and to the Office of Management and Budget, Paperwork Reduction Project (3124-0009), Washington, DC 20503.*

Part I Appellant Identification

1. Name *(last, first, middle initial)*	2. Social Security Number
3. Present address *(number and street, city, state, and ZIP code)* **You must notify the Board of any change of address or telephone number while the appeal is pending with the MSPB.**	4. Home phone *(include area code)* 5. Office phone *(include area code)*
6. I certify that all of the statements made in this appeal are true, complete, and correct to the best of my knowledge and belief.	Signature of appellant or designated representative — Date signed

NSN 7540-01-098-1230
Previous editions obsolete

50283-105

Optional Form 283 (Rev 7/91)
MSPB
5 CFR 1201 and 1209
Page 1

FIGURE 9-1 Appeal form used by the U.S. Merit Systems Protection Board. There are specific instructions on where, when, and how the appeal must be completed.

Part II Designation of Representative

7. You may represent yourself in this appeal, or you may choose someone to represent you. Your representative does not have to be an attorney. You may change your designation of a representative at a later date, if you so desire, but **you must notify the Board promptly of any change**. Where circumstances require, a separate designation of representative may be submitted after the original filing. Include the information requested in blocks 7 through 11.

"I hereby designate _____ to serve as my representative during the course of this appeal. I understand that my representative is authorized to act on my behalf."

8. Representative's address *(number and street, city, state, and ZIP code)*.	9. Representative's employer
	10.a) Representative's telephone number *(include area code)*
	10.b) Representative's facsimile number
	11. Appellant's signature Date

Part III Appealed Action

12. Briefly describe the **agency action** you wish to appeal and attach any relevant documents, including the proposal letter, the decision letter, and the relevant SF 50 or its equivalent.

13. Name and address of the agency that took the action you are appealing *(including bureau or other divisions, as well as street address, city, state and ZIP code)*	14. Your position title and duty station at the time of the action appealed

15. Grade at time of the action appealed	16. Salary at the time of the action appealed $ per	17. Are you a veteran and/or entitled to the employment rights of a veteran? ☐ Yes ☐ No

18. Employment status at the time of the action appealed ☐ Temporary ☐ Applicant ☐ Retired ☐ Permanent ☐ Term ☐ Seasonal	19. If retired, date of retirement *(month, day, year)*	20. Type of service ☐ Competitive ☐ SES ☐ Excepted ☐ Postal Service

21. Length of government service	22. Length of service with acting agency	23. Were you serving a probationary or trial period at the time of the action appealed? ☐ Yes ☐ No

24. Date you received written notice of the proposed action *(month, day, year) (attach a copy)*	25. Date you received the final decision notice *(month, day, year) (attach a copy)*	26. Effective date of the action appealed *(month, day, year)*

Optional Form 283 (Rev 7/91)
MSPB
5 CFR 1201 and 1209
Page 2

FIGURE 9-1 (Continued)   Any deviation from the proper method of completing the appeal form could jeopardize the progress and outcome of the case.

Has an individual exhausted his or her remedies if the complaint is not heard by the agency because the complainant didn't timely file his or her complaint? In most cases, congressional reference to exhaustion requires compliance with the remedial procedures established by the agency. Accordingly, missing an agency's deadline can result in neither the agency nor a reviewing court hearing the case. This is what transpired in *Woodford et al. v. NGO*.

27. Explain briefly why you think the agency was wrong in taking this action.

28. Do you believe the penalty imposed by the agency was too harsh? ☐ *Yes* ☐ *No*	29. What action would you like the Board to take on this case (i.e., what remedy are you asking for)?

Part IV Appellant's Defenses

30.a) Do you believe the agency committed harmful procedural error(s)? ☐ *Yes* ☐ *No*	30.b) If so, what is (are) the error(s)?

30.c) Explain how you were harmed by the error(s).

31.a) Do you believe that the action you are appealing violated the law? ☐ *Yes* ☐ *No*	31.b) If so, what law?

31.c) How was it violated?

32.a) If you believe you were discriminated against by the agency, **in connection with the matter appealed**, because of either your race, color, religion, sex, national origin, marital status, political affiliation, handicapping condition, or age, indicate so and explain why you believe it to be true. You must indicate, by specific examples, how you were discriminated against.

32.b) Have you filed a **formal** discrimination complaint with your agency or any other agency concerning the matter which you are seeking to appeal?   ☐ *Yes* *(attach a copy)*   ☐ *No*

32.c) If yes, place filed *(agency, number and street, city, state, and ZIP code)*	32.d) Date filed *(month, day, year)*
	32.e) Has a decision been issued? ☐ *Yes* *(attach a copy)* ☐ *No*

Optional Form 283 (Rev 7/91)
MSPB
5 CFR 1201 and 1209
Page 3

FIGURE 9-1 (Continued)   In Part IV, discussion of why the agency may have erred is the foundation of the appeal process.

Although the exhaustion doctrine is well established, exceptions exist. First, if there is an unreasonable delay in having an administrative proceeding heard or ruled upon, or if the agency fails to conduct a hearing or make its decision within the time prescribed by statute or rule, judicial review may be had before the agency has completed its work. Second, if an administrative hearing or remedy would be futile, it may be bypassed.

Another exception to the exhaustion requirement is in civil rights cases (i.e., those under 42 U.S.C. § 1983).[26] In 1982, the Supreme Court, in *Patsy v. Board of Regents,*[27] declared that administrative remedies need not be exhausted before a civil rights claim may be filed with a court.

Closely related to the civil rights exception is the exception for constitutional challenges to the law being applied. That is, if a plaintiff alleges that the law being enforced by an agency is unconstitutional, exhaustion on that issue is unnecessary.

33.a) Have you, or anyone in your behalf, filed a formal grievance with your agency concerning this matter, under a negotiated grievance procedure provided by a collective bargaining agreement? ☐ *Yes* *(attach a copy)* ☐ *No*	33.b) Date filed *(month, day, year)*
33.c) If yes, place filed *(agency, number and street, city, state, and ZIP code)*	33.d) Has a decision been issued? ☐ *Yes* *(attach a copy)* ☐ *No*
	33.e) If yes, date issued *(month, day, year)*

Part V Hearing

34. You may have a right to a hearing on this appeal. If you do not want a hearing, the Board will make its decision on the basis of the documents you and the agency submit, after providing you and the agency with an opportunity to submit additional documents. If neither box is checked, the Board will presume you do not want a hearing, and none will be scheduled.

Do you want a hearing? ☐ *Yes* ☐ *No*

If you choose to have a hearing, the Board will notify you where and when it is to be held.

Part VI Reduction In Force

INSTRUCTIONS

Fill out this part only if you are appealing from a Reduction in Force. Your agency's personnel office can furnish you with most of the information requested below.

35. Retention group and sub-group	36. Service computation date	37.a) Has your agency offered you another position rather than separating you? ☐ Yes ☐ No
37.b) Title of position offered	37.c) Grade of position offered	37.d) Salary of position offered $ per
37.e) Location of position offered		37.f) Did you accept this position? ☐ Yes ☐ No

38. Explain why you think you should not have been affected by the Reduction In Force. *(Explanations could include: you were placed in the wrong retention group or sub-group; an error was made in the computation of your service computation date; competitive area was too narrow; improperly reached for separation from competitive level; an exception was made to the regular order of selection; full 30-day notice was not given; you believe you have assignment [bump or retreat] rights; or any other reasons. Please provide as much information as possible regarding each reason.)*

Optional Form 283 (Rev 7/93)
MSPB
5 CFR 1201 and 1209
Page 4

FIGURE 9-1 (Continued)   Question 34 in Part V addresses the right to a hearing or waiver of that right.

It would be futile to present such an issue to an agency because agencies do not have the authority to declare statutes unconstitutional.

Finally, exhaustion is not applicable in criminal cases. Said another way, if an administrative violation is the foundation for a criminal prosecution, the fact that the accused failed to exhaust his or her administrative remedies will not preclude any defense from being heard.

9.5(c) Ripeness

Ripeness is concerned with maturity—that is, whether a case is sufficiently mature to be heard by a court. The APA provides for review of ***final agency action***.[28] With the exception when provided for specifically by statute or when an agency is

LEGAL TERM

Final Agency Action
A judicially reviewable agency action.

Part VII Whistleblowing Activity

INSTRUCTIONS

Complete Parts VII and VIII of this form only if you believe the action you are appealing is based on whistleblowing activities.

39.a) Have you disclosed information that evidences a violation of any law, rule, or regulation; gross mismanagement; a gross waste of funds; an abuse of authority; or a substantial and specific danger to public health or safety? ☐ Yes *(attach a copy or summary of disclosure)* ☐ No	39.b) If yes, provide the name, title, and office address of the person to whom the disclosure was made

39.c) Date the disclosure was made *(month, day, year)*

40. If you believe the action you are appealing was... *(please check appropriate box)*

      ☐ *Threatened*   ☐ *Proposed*

      ☐ *Taken*   ☐ *Not Taken*

...because of a disclosure evidencing a violation of any law, rule, or regulation; gross mismanagement; a gross waste of funds; an abuse of authority; or a substantial and specific danger to public health or safety, provide:

a) a chronology of facts concerning the action appealed; and

b) explain why you believe the action was based on whistleblowing activity and attach a copy of any documentary evidence which supports your statement.

Optional Form 283 (Rev 7/91)
MSPB
5 CFR 1201 and 1209
Page 5

FIGURE 9-1 (Continued)   Part VII is important if the appeal is related to a whistleblowing activity.

clearly violating the law, only final actions may be reviewed by courts. Accordingly, agency investigations, hearings, and rules that are under consideration but not finalized may not be appealed. In 2012, the Supreme Court decided, by unanimous decision, that Environmental Protection Agency "compliance orders" are final and appealable under the APA, even though the EPA had not sought to enforce the agency in court.

There is also a constitutional ripeness doctrine. Recall that Article III of the Constitution requires an actual case or controversy before federal courts have jurisdiction over a dispute. Potential disputes or abstract questions may not be heard.

A common scenario involves the promulgation of a rule that has not yet become effective and that a party believes to be unlawful. Because the new rule has

41.a) Have you sought corrective action from the Office of Special Counsel concerning the action which you are appealing? ☐ *Yes (attach a copy)* ☐ *No*	41.b) If yes, date(s) filed *(month, day, year)*

41.c) Place filed *(location, number and street, city, state, and ZIP code)*

42. Have you received a written notice of your right to file this appeal from the Office of Special Counsel? ☐ *Yes (attach a copy)* ☐ *No*

43.a) Have you already requested a stay from the Board of the action you are seeking to appeal? ☐ *Yes (attach a copy)* ☐ *No*	43.b) If yes, date requested *(month, day, year)*

43.c) Place filed *(location, number and street, city, state, and ZIP code)*	43.d) Has there been a decision? ☐ *Yes (attach a copy)* ☐ *No*

Part VIII Stay Request

INSTRUCTIONS

You may request a stay of a personnel action allegedly based on whistleblowing at any time after you become eligible to file an appeal with the Board under 5 C.F.R. 1209.5, but no later than the time limit set for the close of discovery in the appeal. The stay request may be filed prior to, simultaneous with, or after the filing of an appeal. When you file a stay request with the Board, you must simultaneously serve it upon the agency's local servicing personnel office or the agency's designated representative. 5 C.F.R 1209.8.

If your stay request is being filed prior to filing an appeal with the Board, you must complete Parts I and II and items 41 through 43 above.

44. On separate sheets of paper, please provide the following. Please put your name and address at the top of each page.

a. A chronology of facts, including a description of the disclosure and the action taken by the agency (unless you have already supplied this information in Part VII above).

b. Evidence and/or argument demonstrating that the:

   (1) action threatened, proposed, taken, or not taken is a personnel action, as defined in 5 C.F.R. 1209.4(a); and

   (2) action complained of was based on whistleblowing, as defined in 5 C.F.R. 1209.4(b) (unless you have already supplied this information in Part VII above).

c. Evidence and/or argument demonstrating that there is a

substantial likelihood that you will prevail on the merits of your appeal of the personnel action.

d. Documentary evidence that supports your stay request.

e. Evidence and/or argument addressing how long the stay should remain in effect.

f. Certificate of service specifying how and when the stay request was served on the agency.

g. You **may** provide evidence and/or argument concerning whether a stay would impose extreme hardship on the agency.

Optional Form 283 (Rev 7/91)
MSPB
5 CFR 1201 and 1209
Page 6

FIGURE 9-1 (Continued)   In question number 44, the appellant is instructed to complete a comprehensive chronology of evidence or argument in support of the appeal.

not yet been enforced, no adjudication has taken place. Yet a person who is subject to the rule has two choices: comply, which may involve great expense or encroach upon liberties; or not comply and risk prosecution. This is practically unwise because agencies often regulate large industries for which compliance may be tremendously costly, both to the industry and to its consumers. Later, if the rule is determined unlawful, the costs of returning to precompliance status may also be expensive and disruptive. Therefore, in some cases, preenforcement review may be available.

An important case on ripeness is *Abbott Laboratories v. Gardner*.[29] In *Abbott*, the challenged regulation required that drug manufacturers place certain information on labels. The Food and Drug Administration argued that the

Woodford et al. v. NGO

548 U.S. 81(2006)

Justice Alito delivered the opinion of the Court.

This case presents the question whether a prisoner can satisfy the Prison Litigation Reform Act's exhaustion requirement, 42 U. S. C. § 1997e(a), by filing an untimely or otherwise procedurally defective administrative grievance or appeal. We hold that proper exhaustion of administrative remedies is necessary.

Congress enacted the Prison Litigation Reform Act of 1995 (PLRA), as amended, 42 U.S.C. § 1997e et seq., in 1996 in the wake of a sharp rise in prisoner litigation in the federal courts,. The PLRA contains a variety of provisions designed to bring this litigation under control. See, e.g., § 1997e(c) (requiring district courts to weed out prisoner claims that clearly lack merit); § 1997e(e) (prohibiting claims for emotional injury without prior showing of physical injury); § 1997e(d) (restricting attorney's fees).

A centerpiece of the PLRA's effort "to reduce the quantity . . . of prisoner suits" is an "invigorated" exhaustion provision. Before 1980, prisoners asserting constitutional claims had no obligation to exhaust administrative remedies. . . . In the Civil Rights of Institutionalized Persons Act, § 7, 94 Stat. 349, Congress enacted a weak exhaustion provision, which authorized district courts to stay actions under Rev. Stat. § 1979, 42 U.S.C. § 1983 for a limited time while a prisoner exhausted "such plain, speedy, and effective administrative remedies as are available." "Exhaustion under the 1980 prescription was in large part discretionary; it could be ordered only if the State's prison grievance system met specified federal standards, and even then, only if, in the particular case, the court believed the requirement 'appropriate and in the interests of justice.'" . . . In addition, this provision did not require exhaustion if the prisoner sought only money damages and such relief was not available under the relevant administrative scheme. The PLRA strengthened this exhaustion provision in several ways. Exhaustion is no longer left to the discretion of the district court, but is mandatory. Prisoners must now exhaust all "available" remedies, not just those that meet federal standards. Indeed, as we held in *Booth*, a prisoner must now exhaust administrative remedies even where the relief sought—monetary damages—cannot be granted by the administrative process. Finally, exhaustion of available administrative remedies is required for any suit challenging prison conditions, not just for suits under § 1983.

California has a grievance system for prisoners who seek to challenge their conditions of confinement. To initiate the process, an inmate must fill out a simple form, Dept. of Corrections, Inmate/Parolee Appeal Form, CDC 602 (12/87) (hereinafter Form 602), that is made "readily available to all inmates." The inmate must fill out two parts of the form: part A, which is labeled "Describe Problem," and part B, which is labeled "Action Requested." Then, as explained on Form 602 itself, the prisoner "must first informally seek relief through discussion with the appropriate staff member." The staff member fills in part C of Form 602 under the heading "Staff Response" and then returns the form to the inmate.

If the prisoner is dissatisfied with the result of the informal review, or if informal review is waived by the State, the inmate may pursue a three-step review process. Although California labels this "formal" review (apparently to distinguish this process from the prior step), the three-step process is relatively simple. . . . If the prisoner receives an adverse determination at this first level, or if this level is bypassed, the inmate may proceed to the second level of review conducted by the warden. The inmate does this by filling in part F of Form 602 and submitting the form within 15 working days of the prior decision. Within 10 working days thereafter, the reviewer provides a decision on a letter that is attached to the form. If the prisoner's claim is again denied or the prisoner otherwise is dissatisfied with the result, the prisoner must explain the basis for his or her dissatisfaction on part H of the form and mail the form to the Director of the California Department of Corrections and Rehabilitation within 15 working days. § 3084.5(e)(2). An inmate's appeal may be rejected where "[t]ime limits for submitting the appeal are exceeded and the appellant had the opportunity to file within the prescribed time constraints. . . .

Respondent is a prisoner who was convicted for murder and is serving a life sentence in the California prison system. In October 2000, respondent was placed in administrative segregation for allegedly engaging in "inappropriate activity" in the prison chapel. Two months later, respondent was returned to the general population, but respondent claims that he was prohibited from participating in "special programs," including a variety of religious activities. Approximately six months after that restriction was imposed, respondent filed a grievance with prison officials challenging that action. That grievance was rejected as untimely because it was not filed within 15 working days of the action being challenged. . . .

Respondent appealed that decision internally without success, and subsequently sued petitioners—California correctional officials—under 42 U.S.C. § 1983 in Federal District Court. The District Court granted petitioners' motion to dismiss because respondent had not fully exhausted his administrative remedies as required by § 1997e(a).

The Court of Appeals for the Ninth Circuit reversed and held that respondent had exhausted administrative remedies simply because no such remedies remained available to him. . . .

The PLRA provides as follows:

> "No action shall be brought with respect to prison conditions under section 1983 of this title, or any other Federal law, by a prisoner confined in any jail, prison, or other correctional facility until such administrative remedies as are available are exhausted."

There is no dispute that this language requires a prisoner to "exhaust" administrative remedies, but the parties differ sharply in their understanding of the meaning of this requirement. Petitioners argue that this provision requires proper exhaustion. This means, according to petitioners, that a prisoner must complete the administrative review process in accordance with the applicable procedural rules, including deadlines, as a precondition to bringing suit in federal court. Respondent, on the other hand, argues that this provision demands what he terms "exhaustion simpliciter." In his view, § 1997e(a) simply means that a prisoner may not bring suit in federal court until administrative remedies are no longer available. Under this interpretation, the reason why administrative remedies are no longer available is irrelevant. Bare unavailability suffices even if this results from a prisoner's deliberate strategy of refraining from filing a timely grievance so that the litigation of the prisoner's claim can begin in federal court.

The key for determining which of these interpretations of § 1997e(a) is correct lies in the term of art "exhausted." Exhaustion is an important doctrine in both administrative and habeas law, and we therefore look to those bodies of law for guidance. . . .

"The doctrine of exhaustion of administrative remedies is well established in the jurisprudence of administrative law." *McKart v. United States,* 395 U.S. 185, 193 (1969). "The doctrine provides 'that no one is entitled to judicial relief for a supposed or threatened injury until the prescribed administrative remedy has been exhausted.'" Exhaustion of administrative remedies serves two main purposes. First, exhaustion protects "administrative agency authority." Ibid. Exhaustion gives an agency "an opportunity to correct its own mistakes with respect to the programs it administers before it is haled into federal court," and it discourages "disregard of [the agency's] procedures."

Second, exhaustion promotes efficiency. Claims generally can be resolved much more quickly and economically in proceedings before an agency than in litigation in federal court. In some cases, claims are settled at the administrative level, and

(continued)

in others, the proceedings before the agency convince the losing party not to pursue the matter in federal court. "And even where a controversy survives administrative review, exhaustion of the administrative procedure may produce a useful record for subsequent judicial consideration. . . .

Because exhaustion requirements are designed to deal with parties who do not want to exhaust, administrative law creates an incentive for these parties to do what they would otherwise prefer not to do, namely, to give the agency a fair and full opportunity to adjudicate their claims. Administrative law does this by requiring proper exhaustion of administrative remedies, which "means using all steps that the agency holds out, and doing so properly (so that the agency addresses the issues on the merits)." This Court has described the doctrine as follows: "[A]s a general rule . . . courts should not topple over administrative decisions unless the administrative body not only has erred, but has erred against objection made at the time appropriate under its practice. . . .

The law of habeas corpus has rules that are substantively similar to those described above. . . .

With this background in mind, we are persuaded that the PLRA exhaustion requirement requires proper exhaustion.

A

The text of 42 U.S.C. § 1997e(a) strongly suggests that the PLRA uses the term "exhausted" to mean what the term means in administrative law, where exhaustion means proper exhaustion. Section 1997e(a) refers to "such administrative remedies as are available," and thus points to the doctrine of exhaustion in administrative law. . . .

B

Construing § 1997e(a) to require proper exhaustion also fits with the general scheme of the PLRA, whereas respondent's interpretation would turn that provision into a largely useless appendage. The PLRA attempts to eliminate unwarranted federal-court interference with the administration of prisons, and thus seeks to "affor[d] corrections officials time and opportunity to address complaints internally before allowing the initiation of a federal case." The PLRA also was intended to "reduce the quantity and improve the quality of prisoner suits."

Requiring proper exhaustion serves all of these goals. It gives prisoners an effective incentive to make full use of the prison grievance process and accordingly provides prisons with a fair opportunity to correct their own errors. This is particularly important in relation to state corrections systems because it is "difficult to imagine an activity in which a State has a stronger interest, or one that is more intricately bound up with state laws, regulations, and procedures, than the administration of its prisons."

Proper exhaustion reduces the quantity of prisoner suits because some prisoners are successful in the administrative process, and others are persuaded by the proceedings not to file an action in federal court. Finally, proper exhaustion improves the quality of those prisoner suits that are eventually filed because proper exhaustion often results in the creation of an administrative record that is helpful to the court. When a grievance is filed shortly after the event giving rise to the grievance, witnesses can be identified and questioned while memories are still fresh, and evidence can be gathered and preserved. . . .

Respondent contends that requiring proper exhaustion will lead prison administrators to devise procedural requirements that are designed to trap unwary prisoners and thus to defeat their claims. Respondent does not contend, however, that anything like this occurred in his case, and it is speculative that this will occur in the future. . . . Respondent argues that requiring proper exhaustion is harsh for prisoners, who generally are untrained in the law and are often poorly educated.

This argument overlooks the informality and relative simplicity of prison grievance systems like California's, as well as the fact that prisoners who litigate in federal court generally proceed pro se and are forced to comply with numerous unforgiving deadlines and other procedural requirements.

For these reasons, we reverse the judgment of the Court of Appeals for the Ninth Circuit and remand the case for proceedings consistent with this opinion.

Woodford et al. v. NGO, 548 U.S. 81_(2006),
United States Supreme Court.

Sackett v. EPA

566 U.S. __ (2012)

JUSTICE SCALIA delivered the opinion of the Court.

We consider whether Michael and Chantell Sackett may bring a civil action under the Administrative Procedure Act, 5 U. S. C. § 500 *et seq.*, to challenge the issuance by the Environmental Protection Agency (EPA) of an administrative compliance order under § 309 of the Clean Water Act, 33 U. S. C. § 1319. The order asserts that the Sacketts' property is subject to the Act, and that they have violated its provisions by placing fill material on the property; and on this basis it directs them immediately to restore the property pursuant to an EPA work plan.

The Clean Water Act prohibits, among other things, "the discharge of any pollutant by any person," § 1311, without a permit, into the "navigable waters," § 1344—which the Act defines as "the waters of the United States," § 1362(7). If the EPA determines that any person is in violation of this restriction, the Act directs the agency either to issue a compliance order or to initiate a civil enforcement action. § 1319(a)(3). When the EPA prevails in a civil action, the Act provides for "a civil penalty not to exceed [$37,500] per day for each violation."§ 1319(d). And according to the Government, when the EPA prevails against any person who has been issued a compliance order but has failed to comply, that amount is increased to $75,000—up to $37,500 for the statutory violation and up to an additional $37,500 for violating the compliance order. . . .

The Sacketts are interested parties feeling their way. They own a 2/3-acre residential lot in Bonner County, Idaho. Their property lies just north of Priest Lake, but is separated from the lake by several lots containing permanent structures. In preparation for constructing a house, the Sacketts filled in part of their lot with dirt and [**373]rock. Some months later, they received from the EPA a compliance order. The order contained a number of "Findings and Conclusions," including the following:

"1.4 [The Sacketts' property] contains wetlands within the meaning of 33 C. F. R. § 328.4(8)(b); the wetlands meet the criteria for jurisdictional wetlands in the 1987 'Federal Manual for Identifying and Delineating Jurisdictional Wetlands.'

"1.5 The Site's wetlands are adjacent to Priest Lake within the meaning of 33 C. F. R. § 328.4(8)(c). Priest Lake is a 'navigable water' within the meaning of section 502(7) of the Act, 33 U. S. C. § 1362(7), and 'waters of the United [*1371]States' within the meaning of 40 C. F. R. § 232.2.

"1.6 In April and May, 2007, at times more fully known to [the Sacketts, they] and/or persons acting on their behalf discharged fill material into wetlands at the Site. [They] filled approximately one half acre.

"1.9 By causing such fill material to enter waters of the United States, [the Sacketts] have engaged, and are continuing to engage, in the 'discharge of
(continued)

pollutants' from a point source within the meaning of sections 301 and 502(12) of the Act, 33 U. S. C. §§ 1311 and 1362(12).

"1.11 [The Sacketts'] discharge of pollutants into waters of the United States at the Site without [a] permit constitutes a violation of section 301 of the Act, 33 U. S. C. § 1311." App. 19–20.

On the basis of these findings and conclusions, the order directs the Sacketts, among other things, "immediately [to] undertake activities to restore the Site in accordance with [an EPA-created] Restoration Work Plan" and to "provide and/or obtain access to the Site . . . [and] access to all records and documentation related to the conditions at the Site . . . to EPA employees and/or their designated representatives."

The Sacketts, who do not believe that their property is subject to the Act, asked the EPA for a hearing, but that request was denied. They then brought this action in the United States District Court for the District of Idaho, seeking declaratory and injunctive relief. Their complaint contended that the EPA's issuance of the compliance order was "arbitrary [and] capricious" under the Administrative Procedure Act (APA). . . .

The Sacketts brought suit under Chapter 7 of the APA, which provides for judicial review of "final agency action for which there is no other adequate remedy in a court." 5 U. S. C. § 704. We consider first whether the compliance order is final agency action. . . .

There is no doubt it is agency action, which the APA defines as including even a "failure to act." §§ 551(13), 701(b)(2). But is it *final*? It has all of the hallmarks of APA finality that our opinions establish. Through the order, the EPA "'determined'" "'rights or obligations.'" By reason of the order, the Sacketts have the legal obligation to "restore" their property according to an agency-approved Restoration Work Plan, and must give the EPA access to their property and to "records and documentation related to the conditions at the Site." Also, "'legal consequences . . . flow'" from issuance of the order. For one, according to the Government's current litigating position, the order exposes the Sacketts to double penalties in a future enforcement proceeding. It also severely limits the Sacketts' ability to obtain a permit for their fill from the Army Corps of Engineers, see 33 U. S. C. § 1344. The Corps' regulations provide that, once the EPA has issued a compliance order with respect to certain property, the Corps will not process a permit application for that property unless doing so "is clearly appropriate."

The issuance of the compliance order also marks the "'consummation'" of the agency's decisionmaking process.

As the Sacketts learned when they unsuccessfully sought a hearing, the "Findings and Conclusions" that the compliance order contained were not subject to further agency review. . . .

The APA's judicial review provision also requires that the person seeking APA review of final agency action have "no other adequate remedy in a court," 5 U. S. C. § 704. In Clean Water Act enforcement cases, judicial review ordinarily comes by way of a civil action brought by the EPA under 33 U. S. C. § 1319. But the Sacketts cannot initiate that process, and each day they wait for the agency to drop the hammer, they accrue, by the Government's telling, an additional $75,000 in potential liability. . . .

Nothing in the Clean Water Act *expressly* precludes judicial review under the APA or otherwise. . . .

We conclude that the compliance order in this case is final agency action for which there is no adequate remedy other than APA review, and that the Clean Water Act does not preclude that review. We therefore reverse the judgment of the Court of Appeals and remand the case for further proceedings consistent with this opinion.

Sackett v. EPA, 566 U.S. (2012), United States Supreme Court.

case was not ripe because the rule had not been enforced against any company. The Supreme Court found that the case was ripe because the issues presented were purely legal and the plaintiffs would suffer significant harm if the rule were enforced.

Three factors are considered when determining if a case is ripe. First, are the issues fit for review? Legal issues are more suitable for immediate review than are factual issues. Second, have any administrative remedies been exhausted? The more remedies exhausted, the greater the likelihood that a court will find a case to be ripe. The third factor weighs the harm that will result if preenforcement review is not allowed. The greater the harm, the more likely it is that a court will permit preenforcement review.

Mckart v. United States

395 U.S. 185 (1969)

Petitioner was indicted for willfully and knowingly failing to report for and submit to induction into the Armed Forces of the United States. At trial, petitioner's only defense was that he should have been exempt from military service because he was the "sole surviving son" of a family whose father had been killed in action while serving in the Armed Forces of the United States. The District Court held that he could not raise that defense because he had failed to exhaust the administrative remedies provided in the Selective Services System. Accordingly, petitioner was convicted and sentenced to three years' imprisonment. The Court of Appeals affirmed, with one judge dissenting. . . .

The facts are not in dispute. Petitioner registered with his local Selective Service board shortly after his 18th birthday and thereafter completed his classification questionnaire. . . . Petitioner was ordered to report for a pre-induction physical. He failed to report and was declared a delinquent and ordered to report for induction. He again failed to report and, after further investigation, his criminal prosecution followed. . . .

The Government maintains, however, that petitioner cannot raise the invalidity of his I-A classification and subsequent induction order as a defense to a criminal prosecution for refusal to report for induction. According to the Government, petitioner's failure to appeal his reclassification after the death of his mother constitutes a failure to exhaust available administrative remedies and therefore should bar all judicial review. For the reason set out below, we cannot agree.

The doctrine of exhaustion of administrative remedies is well established in the jurisprudence of administrative law. . . . The doctrine is applied in a number of different situations and is, like most judicial doctrines, subject to numerous exceptions. Application of the doctrine to specific cases requires an understanding of its purposes and of the particular administrative scheme involved. . . .

First of all, it is well to remember that use of the exhaustion doctrine in criminal cases can be exceedingly harsh. The defendant is often stripped of his only defense; he must go to jail without having any judicial review of an assertedly invalid [order]. The deprivation of judicial review occurs not when the affected person is affirmatively asking for assistance from the courts but when the Government is attempting to impose criminal sanctions on him. Such a result should not be tolerated

(continued)

unless the interests underlying the exhaustion rule clearly outweigh the severe burden imposed upon the registrant if he is denied judicial review. The statute as it stood when petitioner was reclassified said nothing which would require registrants to raise all their claims before the appeals boards. We must ask, then, whether there is in this case a governmental interest compelling enough to outweigh the severe burden placed on petitioner. Even if there is no such compelling interest when petitioner's case is viewed in isolation, we must also ask whether allowing all similarly situated registrants to bypass administrative appeal procedures would seriously impair the Selective Service System's ability to perform its functions.

The question of whether petitioner is entitled to exemption as a sole surviving son is, as we have seen, solely one of statutory interpretation. The resolution of that issue does not require any particular expertise on the part of the appeal board; the proper interpretation is certainly not a matter of discretion. In this sense, the issue is different from many Selective Service classification questions which do involve expertise or the exercise of discretion, both by the local boards and the appeal boards. Petitioner's failure to take his claim through all available administrative appeals only deprived the Selective Service System of the opportunity of having its appellate boards resolve a question of statutory interpretation. Since judicial review would not be significantly aided by an additional administrative decision of this sort, we cannot see any compelling reason why petitioner's failure to appeal should bar his only defense to a criminal prosecution.

Mckart v. United States, 395 U.S.185 (1969), United States Supreme Court.

9.6 SCOPE AND STANDARDS OF REVIEW

Once it is determined that review is proper, the next question must be asked: What is the scope of review? In other words, how far will a court delve into the agency's fact findings, conclusions of law, and analyses?

There are two sides to the scope-of-review coin. On one side, review of agency actions is necessary to prevent abuses. Without judicial review, individuals would be at the mercy of administrative agencies. On the other side is the need to defer to an agency's experience and expertise. Judges are not engineers, doctors, or electricians. However, agencies are, in theory, expert in the subjects they regulate. Technical issues, therefore, are better left to be decided by an agency. In addition, there is the need to control courts' caseloads. Deference to agency decisions frees courts from time-consuming fact-finding. The scope of review must, then, provide agencies with some discretion and at the same time prevent abuses of authority.

The degree to which a court defers to an agency's decision is known as a *standard of review*. Some standards offer significant deference; others do not. There are many standards of review, but the three most commonly applied are de novo, substantial evidence, and arbitrary and capricious.

9.6(a) Standard One: De Novo

LEGAL TERM

De Novo Standard
Standard of review that allows the reviewing court to judge a case anew with no deference accorded to the agency's factual findings.

De novo is Latin for "anew." Under the **de novo standard**, courts review agency decisions anew—that is, no deference is given to the agency's factual findings. The reviewing court may substitute its opinion for that of the agency. De novo review comes in two forms. *Pure de novo* permits a reviewing court to start from scratch. A new hearing is conducted by the court, during which the same or new evidence may be presented.

Record de novo permits a court to substitute its opinion for that of the agency although the court is limited to reviewing the record from the agency. No new hearing is conducted nor evidence received. The court is limited to the record as it exists when the agency completes its work. If a court determines that evidence was improperly denied admission by the agency, the case must be remanded with an instruction to admit the evidence and reconsider the decision in light of the new evidence. The court will not admit the evidence and reconsider the decision itself. A remand may also be made, in some cases, with an instruction to an agency to make further findings. For example, if a fact or conclusion is central to a case but was omitted from the agency's decision, a remand may be made requiring the agency to find the fact or make its conclusion. Most de novo review is made of a record.

9.6(b) Standard Two: Substantial Evidence

Under the ***substantial evidence standard***, reviewing courts may examine the facts found and conclusions reached by an agency. A court may not, however, substitute its judgment for that of the agency under the substantial evidence test. Rather, the reviewing court is to affirm the agency's decision if that decision is supported by substantial evidence.

Before enactment of the APA, it was generally held that courts were to uphold an agency decision if, after reviewing the entire record, any evidence was discovered to support the agency decision, regardless of the quantity or quality of contrary evidence. Using this approach, the substantial evidence standard was in reality an "any evidence" standard. The standard, as applied, was ineffective in curbing agency abuses and correcting agency errors. Today, the APA specifically requires that when applying the substantial evidence test, courts are to consider the entire record. A search for a needle in the haystack is no longer necessary because that evidentiary needle would no longer be sufficient to support an agency decision.

Substantial evidence exists if, after reviewing the entire record, a reasonable person could have reached the same conclusion as did the agency. "Substantial evidence is more than a mere scintilla. It means such relevant evidence as a reasonable mind might accept as adequate to support a conclusion. . . . Mere uncorroborated hearsay or rumor does not constitute substantial evidence."[30] In some circumstances, hearsay alone may be adequate to establish substantial evidence. If the probative value of hearsay is so great as to lead a reasonable person to conclude that substantial evidence exists, then hearsay may stand alone.[31] The test recognizes that more than one result may be reasonable. The question is not what a reasonable person would have done; it is whether a reasonable person could have reached the same result as did the agency.

Courts are limited to the administrative record when reviewing agency actions. It is the evidence, findings, decisions, and other information in the record on which review must be conducted; no evidence may be received for the first time by the reviewing court. As is true with record de novo review, remand may be available to the reviewing court to get answers that the record does not provide or to give an agency the opportunity to correct an error.

Rules promulgated through formal rulemaking and decisions resulting from formal adjudications are reviewed under the substantial evidence test.

9.6(c) Standard Three: Arbitrary, Capricious, Abuse of Discretion

For discretionary actions not "committed to agency discretion," judicial review is available under the arbitrary, capricious, ***abuse of discretion standard***. This standard affords agencies significant deference. Generally, agency action is presumed valid and affirmed if founded on a rational basis. There must be a clear error before a court will invalidate an agency decision under the arbitrary, capricious, abuse of discretion standard. Nevertheless, courts are not to rubber-stamp agency decisions. A careful examination of the record must be conducted to ensure that the agency has not abused its discretion.

Federal Communications Commission v. Fox

556 U.S. 502 (2009)

Federal law prohibits the broadcasting of "any . . . indecent . . . language," 18 U. S. C. §1464, which includes expletives referring to sexual or excretory activity or organs, see *FCC v. Pacifica Foundation*, 438 U. S. 726 (1978). This case concerns the adequacy of the Federal Communications Commission's explanation of its decision that this sometimes forbids the broadcasting of indecent expletives even when the offensive words are not repeated.

The Communications Act of 1934 established a system of limited-term broadcast licenses subject to various "conditions" designed "to maintain the control of the United States over all the channels of radio transmission." Twenty-seven years ago we said that "[a] licensed broadcaster is granted the free and exclusive use of a limited and valuable part of the public domain; when he accepts that franchise it is burdened by enforceable public obligations."

One of the burdens that licensees shoulder is the indecency ban—the statutory proscription against "utter[ing] any obscene, indecent, or profane language by means of radio communication," 18 U. S. C. §1464—which Congress has instructed the Commission to enforce between the hours of 6 a.m. and 10 p.m. Public Telecommunications Act of 1992, Congress has given the Commission various means of enforcing the indecency ban, including civil fines, and license revocations or the denial of license renewals.

The Commission first invoked the statutory ban on indecent broadcasts in 1975, declaring a daytime broadcast of George Carlin's "Filthy Words" monologueactionably indecent. At that time, the Commission announced the definition of indecent speech that it uses to this day, prohibiting "language that describes, in terms patently offensive as measured by contemporary community standards for the broadcast medium, sexual or excretory activities or organs, at times of the day when there is a reasonable risk that children may be in the audience."

In *FCC v. Pacifica Foundation, supra*, we upheld the Commission's order against statutory and constitutional challenge. We rejected the broadcasters' argument that the statutory proscription applied only to speech appealing to the prurient interest, noting that "the normal definition of 'indecent' merely refers to nonconformance with accepted standards of morality. And we held that the First Amendment allowed Carlin's monologue to be banned in light of the "uniquely pervasive presence" of the medium and the fact that broadcast programming is "uniquely accessible to children."

In the ensuing years, the Commission took a cautious, but gradually expanding, approach to enforcing the statutory prohibition against indecent broadcasts. . . .

In 2004, the Commission took one step further by declaring for the first time that a nonliteral (expletive) use of the F- and S-Words could be actionably indecent, even when the word is used only once. The first order to this effect dealt with an NBC broadcast of the Golden Globe Awards, in which the performer Bono commented, "'This is really, really, f***ing brilliant.'" Although the Commission had received numerous complaints directed at the broadcast, its enforcement bureau had concluded that the material was not indecent because "Bono did not describe, in context, sexual or excretory organs or activities and . . . the utterance was fleeting and isolated." The full Commission reviewed and reversed the staff ruling.

The Commission first declared that Bono's use of the F-Word fell within its indecency definition, even though the word was used as an intensifier rather than a literal descriptor. "[G]iven the core meaning of the 'F-Word,'" it said, "any use of that word . . . inherently has a sexual connotation. The Commission determined, moreover, that the broadcast was "patently offensive" because the F-Word "is one of the most vulgar, graphic and explicit descriptions of sexual activity in the English language," because "[i]ts use invariably invokes a coarse sexual image," and because Bono's use of the word was entirely "shocking and gratuitous."

The Commission observed that categorically exempting such language from enforcement actions would "likely lead to more widespread use." Commission action was necessary to "safeguard the well-being of the nation's children from the most objectionable, most offensive language." The order noted that technological advances have made it far easier to delete ("bleep out") a "single and gratuitous use of a vulgar expletive," without adulterating the content of a broadcast. . . .

This case concerns utterances in two live broadcasts aired by Fox Television Stations, Inc., and its affiliates prior to the Commission's *Golden Globes Order*. The first occurred during the 2002 Billboard Music Awards, when the singer Cher exclaimed, "I've also had critics for the last 40 years saying that I was on my way out every year. Right. So f***'em." The second involved a segment of the 2003 Billboard Music Awards, during the presentation of an award by Nicole Richie and Paris Hilton, principals in a Fox television series called "The Simple Life." Ms. Hilton began their interchange by reminding Ms. Richie to "watch the bad language," but Ms. Richie proceeded to ask the audience, "Why do they even call it 'The Simple Life?' Have you ever tried to get cow s*** out of a Prada purse? It's not so f***ing simple." Following each of these broadcasts, the Commission received numerous complaints from parents whose children were exposed to the language. . . .

The Administrative Procedure Act, 5 U. S. C. §551 *et seq.*, which sets forth the full extent of judicial authority to review executive agency action for procedural correctness, see *Vermont Yankee Nuclear Power Corp. v. Natural Resources Defense Council, Inc.*, 435 U. S. 519, 545–549 (1978), permits (insofar as relevant here) the setting aside of agency action that is "arbitrary" or "capricious," 5 U. S. C. §706(2)(A). Under what we have called this "narrow" standard of review, we insist that an agency "examine the relevant data and articulate a satisfactory explanation for its action." We have made clear, however, that "a court is not to substitute its judgment for that of the agency," . . .

Judged under the above described standards, the Commission's new enforcement policy and its order finding the broadcasts actionably indecent were neither arbitrary nor capricious. First, the Commission forthrightly acknowledged that its recent actions have broken new ground, taking account of inconsistent "prior Commission and staff action" and explicitly disavowing them as "no longer good law. . . . Moreover, the agency's reasons for expanding the scope of its enforcement activity were entirely rational." It was certainly reasonable to determine that it made no sense to distinguish between literal and nonliteral uses of offensive words, requiring repetitive use to render only the latter indecent. As the Commission said with regard to expletive use of the F-Word, "the word's power to insult and offend derives from its sexual meaning." And the Commission's decision to look at the patent offensiveness of even isolated uses of sexual and excretory words fits with the context-based approach we sanctioned in *Pacifica*, 438 U. S., at 750. Even isolated utterances can be made in "pander[ing,] . . . vulgar and shocking" manners and can constitute harmful "'first blow[s]'"to children. It is surely rational (if not inescapable) to believe that a safe harbor for single words would "likely lead to more widespread use of the offensive language."

(continued)

> The fact that technological advances have made it easier for broadcasters to bleep out offending words further supports the Commission's stepped-up enforcement policy.
>
> [The Court found the rule to not be arbitrary but expressly chose not to review the rule for constitutionality (First Amendment Free Speech) because the courts below did not do so and the Supreme Court is to provide final, not initial, review. However the First Amendment question was subsequently raised, decided at lower levels, and appealed to the Supreme Court. The Court granted certiorari and issued a decision in 2012 where it found that the FCC hadn't given Fox and other broadcasters adequate notice of what it intended to prohibit, violating due process, and again evading the First Amendment question.]

Federal Communications Commission v. Fox, 556 U.S. 502 (2009),
United States Supreme Court.

So when do courts apply these standards? The decision depends on the type of issue appealed. There are appeals of legal conclusions, appeals of fact-finding, and appeals of discretionary decisions. A single appeal can include legal, factual, and discretionary issues, each requiring a different standard of review. The arbitrary and capricious standard applies to all informal agency actions. Therefore, informal rulemaking and informal adjudication are included, as are the multitude of other discretionary acts agencies perform. Although formal rules are reviewed typically (unless Congress specifically says otherwise) under the substantial evidence test, the arbitrary and capricious standard also applies to decisions that are made in the formation of the rule. This includes the decision to not make a rule. For example, the Environmental Protection Agency's decision not to regulate greenhouse gases that may be contributing to climate change was found to be arbitrary and capricious in the 2007 *Massachusetts, et al. v. EPA case.*

Paris Hilton and Nicole Richie at the 2003 Billboard Music Awards.

Massachusetts, et al. v. EPA

549 U.S.497_(2007)

A well-documented rise in global temperatures has coincided with a significant increase in the concentration of carbon dioxide in the atmosphere. Respected scientists believe the two trends are related. For when carbon dioxide is released into the atmosphere, it acts like the ceiling of a greenhouse, trapping solar energy and retarding the escape of reflected heat. It is therefore a species—the most important species—of a "greenhouse gas."

Calling global warming "the most pressing environmental challenge of our time," a group of States, local governments, and private organizations, alleged in a petition for certiorari that the Environmental Protection Agency (EPA) has abdicated its responsibility under the Clean Air Act to regulate the emissions of four greenhouse gases, including carbon dioxide. Specifically, petitioners asked us to answer two questions concerning the meaning of § 202(a)(1) of the Act: whether EPA has the statutory authority to regulate greenhouse gas emissions from new motor vehicles; and if so, whether its stated reasons for refusing to do so are consistent with the statute. . . .

Section 202(a)(1) of the Clean Air Act, as added by Pub. L. 89-272, § 101(8), 79 Stat. 992, and as amended by, inter alia, 84 Stat. 1690 and 91 Stat. 791, 42 U.S.C. § 7521(a)(1), provides:

> "The [EPA] Administrator shall by regulation prescribe (and from time to time revise) in accordance with the provisions of this section, standards applicable to the emission of any air pollutant from any class or classes of new motor vehicles or new motor vehicle engines, which in his judgment cause, or contribute to, air pollution which may reasonably be anticipated to endanger public health or welfare. . . ."

The Act defines "air pollutant" to include "any air pollution agent or combination of such agents, including any physical, chemical, biological, radioactive . . . substance or matter which is emitted into or otherwise enters the ambient air." § 7602(g). "Welfare" is also defined broadly: among other things, it includes "effects on . . . weather . . . and climate." § 7602(h).

When Congress enacted these provisions, the study of climate change was in its infancy. In 1959, shortly after the U.S. Weather Bureau began monitoring atmospheric carbon dioxide levels, an observatory in Mauna Loa, Hawaii, recorded a mean level of 316 parts per million. This was well above the highest carbon dioxide concentration—no more than 300 parts per million—revealed in the 420,000-year-old ice-core record. By the time Congress drafted § 202(a)(1) in 1970, carbon dioxide levels had reached 325 parts per million.

In the late 1970's, the Federal Government began devoting serious attention to the possibility that carbon dioxide emissions associated with human activity could provoke climate change. In 1978, Congress enacted the National Climate Program Act, 92 Stat. 601, which required the President to establish a program to "assist the Nation and the world to understand and respond to natural and man-induced climate processes and their implications," President Carter, in turn, asked the National Research Council, the working arm of the National Academy of Sciences, to investigate the subject. The Council's response was unequivocal: "If carbon dioxide continues to increase, the study group finds no reason to doubt that climate changes will result and no reason to believe that these changes will be negligible. . . . A wait-and-see policy may mean waiting until it is too late."

Congress next addressed the issue in 1987, when it enacted the Global Climate Protection Act, Title XI of Pub. L. 100-204, 101 Stat. 1407, note following 15 U.S.C. § 2901. Finding that "manmade pollution—the release of carbon dioxide,

(continued)

chlorofluorocarbons, methane, and other trace gases into the atmosphere—may be producing a long-term and substantial increase in the average temperature on Earth," § 1102(1), 101 Stat. 1408, Congress directed EPA to propose to Congress a "coordinated national policy on global climate change," § 1103(b), and ordered the Secretary of State to work "through the channels of multilateral diplomacy" and coordinate diplomatic efforts to combat global warming. § 1103(c). Congress emphasized that "ongoing pollution and deforestation may be contributing now to an irreversible process" and that "[n]ecessary actions must be identified and implemented in time to protect the climate." § 1102(4).

Meanwhile, the scientific understanding of climate change progressed. In 1990, the Intergovernmental Panel on Climate Change (IPCC), a multinational scientific body organized under the auspices of the United Nations, published its first comprehensive report on the topic. Drawing on expert opinions from across the globe, the IPCC concluded that "emissions resulting from human activities are substantially increasing the atmospheric concentrations of . . . greenhouse gases [which] will enhance the greenhouse effect, resulting on average in an additional warming of the Earth's surface" . . . .

On October 20, 1999, a group of 19 private organizations filed a rulemaking petition asking EPA to regulate "greenhouse gas emissions from new motor vehicles under § 202 of the Clean Air Act. . . .

Fifteen months after the petition's submission, EPA requested public comment on "all the issues raised in [the] petition," adding a "particular" request for comments on "any scientific, technical, legal, economic or other aspect of these issues that may be relevant to EPA's consideration of this petition." 66 Fed. Reg. 7486, 7487 (2001). EPA received more than 50,000 comments over the next five months. See 68 Fed. Reg. 52924 (2003).

Before the close of the comment period, the White House sought "assistance in identifying the areas in the science of climate change where there are the greatest certainties and uncertainties" from the National Research Council, asking for a response "as soon as possible." The result was a 2001 report titled Climate Change: An Analysis of Some Key Questions (NRC Report), which, drawing heavily on the 1995 IPCC report, concluded that "[g]reenhouse gases are accumulating in Earth's atmosphere as a result of human activities, causing surface air temperatures and subsurface ocean temperatures to rise. Temperatures are, in fact, rising." . . .

On September 8, 2003, EPA entered an order denying the rulemaking petition. . . . [the EPA concluded it lacked the authority under the statute to regulate the subject and it also concluded that the link between human activity and climate change was not unequivocally established.]

EPA has refused to comply with this clear statutory command. Instead, it has offered a laundry list of reasons not to regulate. For example, EPA said that a number of voluntary executive branch programs already provide an effective response to the threat of global warming, 68 Fed. Reg. 52932, that regulating greenhouse gases might impair the President's ability to negotiate with "key developing nations" to reduce emissions, and that curtailing motor-vehicle emissions would reflect "an inefficient, piecemeal approach to address the climate change issue."

Although we have neither the expertise nor the authority to evaluate these policy judgments, it is evident they have nothing to do with whether greenhouse gas emissions contribute to climate change. Still less do they amount to a reasoned justification for declining to form a scientific judgment. In particular, while the President has broad authority in foreign affairs, that authority does not extend to the refusal to execute domestic laws. In the Global Climate Protection Act of 1987, Congress authorized the State Department—not EPA—to formulate United States foreign policy with reference to environmental matters relating to climate. See § 1103(c), 101 Stat. 1409. EPA has made no showing that it issued the ruling in question here after consultation with the State Department. Congress did direct EPA to consult with other agencies in the formulation of its policies and rules, but the State Department is absent from that list. § 1103(b).

Nor can EPA avoid its statutory obligation by noting the uncertainty surrounding various features of climate change and concluding that it would therefore be better not to regulate at this time. See 68 Fed. Reg. 52930–52931. If the scientific uncertainty is so profound that it precludes EPA from making a reasoned judgment as to whether greenhouse gases contribute to global warming, EPA must say so. That EPA would prefer not to regulate greenhouse gases because of some residual uncertainty—which, contrary to Justice Scalia's apparent belief, post, at 5–8, is in fact all that it said, see 68 Fed. Reg. 52929 ("We do not believe . . . that it would be either effective or appropriate for EPA to establish [greenhouse gas] standards for motor vehicles at this time")—is irrelevant. The statutory question is whether sufficient information exists to make an endangerment finding.

In short, EPA has offered no reasoned explanation for its refusal to decide whether greenhouse gases cause or contribute to climate change. Its action was therefore "arbitrary, capricious, . . . or otherwise not in accordance with law." 42 U.S.C. § 7607(d)(9)(A). We need not and do not reach the question whether on remand EPA must make an endangerment finding, or whether policy concerns can inform EPA's actions in the event that it makes such a finding. Cf. *Chevron U. S. A. Inc. v. Natural Resources Defense Council, Inc.*, 467 U.S. 837, 843–844 (1984). We hold only that EPA must ground its reasons for action or inaction in the statute.

Massachusetts, et al. v. EPA, 549 U.S.497 (2007), United States Supreme Court.

9.6(d) Issues of Law

On review, issues of law are separated from those of fact and judgment. Section 706(2) of the APA states that reviewing courts are to "hold unlawful and set aside agency action, findings, and conclusions found to be . . . contrary to constitutional right, power, privilege, or immunity; in excess of statutory jurisdiction, authority, or limitations, or short of statutory right."

Not all legal decisions are reviewed de novo by courts. Courts often give agencies' legal conclusions at least some deference, especially if the agency has particular experience with the statute at issue. The Supreme Court stated in one case, "[w]hen faced with a problem of statutory construction, this Court shows great deference to the interpretation given the statute by the officers or agency charged with its administration."[32]

The most significant case on this point, and one of the most important administrative law cases in history, is *Chevron v. Natural Resources Defense Council.*

Chevron, U.S.A., Inc. v. Natural Resources Defense Council, Inc.

467 U.S. 837 (1984)

In the Clean Air Act Amendments of 1977, Congress enacted certain requirements applicable to states that had not achieved the national air quality standards established by the Environmental Protection Agency (EPA) pursuant to earlier legislation. The amended Clean Air Act required these "nonattainment" states to establish a permit program regulating "new or modified major stationary sources" of air pollution. . . . The EPA regulation promulgated to implement this permit requirement allows a state to adopt a plantwide definition of the term "stationary source." Under this definition, an existing plant that contains several pollution-emitting

(continued)

devices may install or modify one piece of equipment without meeting the permit conditions if the alteration will not increase the total emissions of the plant. The question presented [in this case] is whether EPA's decision to allow States to treat all of the pollution-emitting devices within the same industry grouping as though they were encased within a single "bubble" is based on a reasonable construction of the statutory term "stationary source." . . .

[T]he relevant part of the amended Clean Air Act "does not explicitly define what Congress envisioned as a 'stationary source,' to which the permit program . . . should apply," and further . . . the precise issue was not "squarely addressed in the legislative history." . . .

When a court reviews an agency's construction of the statute which it administers, it is confronted with two questions. First, always, is the question whether Congress has directly spoken to the precise question at issue. If the intent of Congress is clear, that is the end of the matter; for the court as well as the agency must give effect to the unambiguously expressed intent of Congress. If, however, the court determines Congress has not directly addressed the precise question at issue, the court does not simply impose its own construction on the statute, as would be necessary in the absence of an administrative interpretation. Rather, if the statute is silent or ambiguous with respect to the specific issue, the question for the court is whether the agency's answer is based on a permissible construction of the statute.

> The power of an administrative agency to administer a congressionally created . . . program necessarily requires the formulation of policy and the making of rules to fill any gap left, implicitly or explicitly, by Congress.

If Congress has explicitly left a gap for the agency to fill, there is an express delegation of authority to the agency to elucidate a specific provision of the statute by regulation. Such legislative regulations are given controlling weight unless they are arbitrary, capricious, or manifestly contrary to the statute. Sometimes the legislative delegation to an agency on a particular question is implicit rather than explicit. In such a case, a court may not substitute its own construction of a statutory provision for a reasonable interpretation of an agency. . . .

We have long recognized that considerable weight should be accorded to an executive department's construction of a statutory scheme it is entrusted to administer and the principle of deference to administrative interpretations has been consistently followed by this Court whenever decision as to the meaning or reach of a statute has involved reconciling conflicting policies, and a full understanding of the force of the statutory policy in the given situation has depended upon more than ordinary knowledge respecting the matters subjected to agency regulations.

> . . . If this choice represents a reasonable accommodation of conflicting policies that were committed to the agency's care by the statute, we should not disturb it unless it appears from the statute or its legislative history that the accommodation is not one that Congress would have sanctioned. . . .

In light of these well-settled principles, it is clear that the Court of Appeals misconceived the nature of its role in reviewing the regulations at issue. Once it determined, after its own examination of the legislation, that Congress did not actually have an intent regarding the applicability of the bubble concept to the permit program, the question before it was not whether, in its view, the concept is "inappropriate" in the general context of a program designed to improve air quality, but whether the Administrator's view that it is appropriate in the context of this particular program is a reasonable one. Based on the examination of the legislation and its history which follows, we agree with the Court of Appeals that Congress did not have a specific intention on the applicability of the bubble concept in these cases, and conclude that the EPA's use of that concept here is a reasonable policy choice for the agency to make.

The arguments over policy that are advanced in the parties' briefs create the impression that respondents are now waging in a judicial forum a specific policy battle, which they ultimately lost in the agency. . . . Such policy arguments are more properly addressed to legislators or administrators, not to judges. . . .

In these cases, the Administrator's interpretation represents a reasonable accommodation of manifestly competing interests, and is entitled to deference: the regulatory scheme is technical and complex, the agency considered the matter in a detailed and reasoned fashion, and the decision involves reconciling conflicting policies. Congress intended to accommodate both interests, but did not do so itself on the level of specificity presented by these cases. Perhaps that body consciously desired the Administrator to strike the balance at this level, thinking that those with great expertise and charged with responsibility for administering the provision would be in a better position to do so; perhaps it simply did not consider the question at this level; and perhaps Congress was unable to forge a coalition on either side of the question, and those on each side decided to take their chances with the scheme devised by the agency. For judicial purposes, it matters not which of these things occurred.

Judges are not experts in the field, and are not part of either political branch of the Government. Courts must, in some cases, reconcile competing political interests, but not on the basis of the judges' personal policy preferences. In contrast, an agency to which Congress has delegated policymaking responsibilities may, within the limits of that delegation, properly rely upon the incumbent administration's views of wise policy to inform its judgments. While agencies are not directly accountable to the people, the Chief Executive is, and it is entirely appropriate for this political branch of the Government to make such policy choices—resolving the competing interests which Congress itself either inadvertently did not resolve, or intentionally left to be resolved by the agency charged with the administration of the statute in light of everyday realities.

When a challenge to an agency construction of a statutory provision, fairly conceptualized, really centers on the wisdom of the agency's policy, rather than whether it is a reasonable choice within a gap left open by Congress, the challenge must fail. In such a case, federal judges—who have no constituency—have a duty to respect legitimate policy choices made by those who do. The responsibilities for assessing the wisdom of such policy choices and resolving the struggle between competing views of the public interest are not judicial ones: "Our Constitution vests such responsibilities in the political branches."

We hold that the EPA's definition of the term "source" is a permissible construction of the statute which seeks to accommodate progress in reducing air pollution with economic growth.

The Regulations which the Administrator has adopted provide what the agency could allowably view as . . . [an] effective reconciliation of these twofold ends. . . .

[The rule was found to be reasonable.]

Chevron, U.S.A., INC. v. Natural Resources Defense Council, Inc.,
467 U.S. 837 (1984), United States Supreme Court.

Accordingly, the decision as to whether Congress has "directly spoken to the precise question at issue" is reviewed de novo. This is commonly known as a *Chevron Step One* determination. If Congress has not spoken to the question and there is no explicit delegation of authority to an agency to address the question, a court is to reverse the agency decision only if unreasonable. This is commonly known as a *Chevron Step Two* determination. Finally, if a reviewing court determines that Congress has explicitly delegated the authority to develop policy, the agency's policy decisions are reviewed under the arbitrary and capricious standard. Although

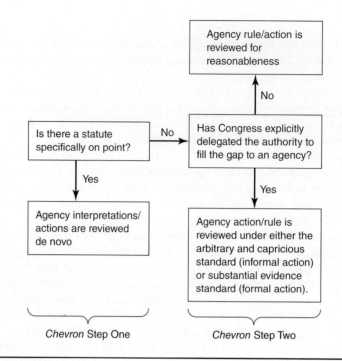

FIGURE 9-2 *Chevron* analysis.

the Court indicated that the arbitrary and capricious standard would apply, this author assumes that the substantial evidence standard would apply to formal actions and the arbitrary and capricious standard would apply to informal actions. See Figure 9-2 for a summary of this process. In *Gonzales v. Oregon*, 546 U.S. 243 (2006), the court extended the *Chevron* rationale to interpretations of validly promulgated administrative regulations. So, if an agency rule has been made pursuant to a congressional delegation of authority, then the agency's interpretation of the rule, when ambiguous, is entitled to substantial deference. If the rule was not specifically authorized, then it receives little deference, or in the words of the Court, deference to the extent that it is persuasive.

An important but unanswered Chevron question is whether an agency is entitled to deference was interpreting its own jurisdiction as delegated from Congress. Deferring to an agency when deciding how Congress intended for it to do its job is quite different from an agency deciding whether Congress intended for it to have the power to do the job. The Supreme Court answered this question in *City of Arlington v. FCC* in 2013.

City of Arlington v. Federal Communications Commission U.S. Supreme Court (2013)

Justice Scalia delivered the opinion of the Court.

We consider whether an agency's interpretation of a statutory ambiguity that concerns the scope of its regulatory authority (that is, its jurisdiction) is entitled to deference under Chevron U.S.A. Inc. v. Natural Resources Defense Council, Inc., 467 U.S. 837 (1984).

Wireless telecommunications networks require towers and antennas; proposed sites for those towers and antennas must be approved by local zoning authorities.

In the Telecommunications Act of 1996, Congress "impose[d] specific limitations on the traditional authority of state and local governments to regulate the location, construction, and modification of such facilities," and incorporated those limitations into the Communications Act of 1934, see 110 Stat. 56, 151. Section 201(b) of that Act empowers the Federal Communications Commission to "prescribe such rules and regulations as may be necessary in the public interest to carry out [its] provisions." Of course, that rulemaking authority extends to the subsequently added portions of the Act.

The Act imposes five substantive limitations, which are codified in 47 U.S.C. §332(c)(7)(B); only one of them, §332(c)(7)(B)(ii), is at issue here. That provision requires state or local governments to act on wireless siting applications "within a reasonable period of time after the request is duly filed." . . .

In theory, §332(c)(7)(B)(ii) requires state and local zoning authorities to take prompt action on siting applications for wireless facilities. But in practice, wireless providers often faced long delays. In July 2008, CTIA—The Wireless Association, which represents wireless service providers, petitioned the FCC to clarify the meaning of §332(c)(7)(B)(ii)'s requirement that zoning authorities act on siting requests "within a reasonable period of time." In November 2009, the Commission, relying on its broad statutory authority to implement the provisions of the Communications Act, issued a declaratory ruling responding to CTIA's petition. . . . A "reasonable period of time" under §332(c)(7)(B)(ii), the Commission determined, is presumptively (but rebuttably) 90 days to process a collocation application (that is, an application to place a new antenna on an existing tower) and 150 days to process all other applications. . . .

As this case turns on the scope of the doctrine enshrined in Chevron, we begin with a description of that case's now-canonical formulation. "When a court reviews an agency's construction of the statute which it administers, it is confronted with two questions." 467 U.S., at 842. First, applying the ordinary tools of statutory construction, the court must determine "whether Congress has directly spoken to the precise question at issue. If the intent of Congress is clear, that is the end of the matter; for the court, as well as the agency, must give effect to the unambiguously expressed intent of Congress." Id., at 842–843. But "if the statute is silent or ambiguous with respect to the specific issue, the question for the court is whether the agency's answer is based on a permissible construction of the statute. . . .

The question here is whether a court must defer under Chevron to an agency's interpretation of a statutory ambiguity that concerns the scope of the agency's statutory authority (that is, its jurisdiction). The argument against deference rests on the premise that there exist two distinct classes of agency interpretations: Some interpretations—the big, important ones, presumably—define the agency's "jurisdiction." Others—humdrum, run-of-the-mill stuff—are simply applications of jurisdiction the agency plainly has. That premise is false, because the distinction between "jurisdictional" and "nonjurisdictional" interpretations is a mirage. No matter how it is framed, the question a court faces when confronted with an agency's interpretation of a statute it administers is always, simply, whether the agency has stayed within the bounds of its statutory authority. . . .

The U.S. Reports are shot through with applications of Chevron to agencies' constructions of the scope of their own jurisdiction. And we have applied Chevron where concerns about agency self-aggrandizement are at their apogee: in cases where an agency's expansive construction of the extent of its own power would have wrought a fundamental change in the regulatory scheme. . . .

Those who assert that applying Chevron to "jurisdictional" interpretations "leaves the fox in charge of the henhouse" overlook the reality that a separate category of "jurisdictional" interpretations does not exist. The fox-in-the-henhouse syndrome is to be avoided not by establishing an arbitrary and undefinable category

(continued)

of agency decisionmaking that is accorded no deference, but by taking seriously, and applying rigorously, in all cases, statutory limits on agencies' authority. Where Congress has established a clear line, the agency cannot go beyond it; and where Congress has established an ambiguous line, the agency can go no further than the ambiguity will fairly allow. But in rigorously applying the latter rule, a court need not pause to puzzle over whether the interpretive question presented is "jurisdictional." If "the agency's answer is based on a permissible construction of the statute," that is the end of the matter.

9.6(e) Issues of Fact

Factual findings are treated differently than legal conclusions. Three standards of review are applied to factual issues: de novo; substantial evidence; and arbitrary, capricious, abuse of discretion. These three standards are recognized by the APA.[33] De novo is applied only when required by law, which is rare. The substantial evidence test is used to review the factual findings of agencies in formal rulemaking and formal adjudication.

Let's examine a scenario in which an agency finds both facts and makes a legal decision. An agency decision whether, or to what degree, a material fact is true is a finding of fact. Do not confuse this with a legal conclusion. For example, assume that a state motor vehicle statute provides that any licensed driver convicted of two or more moving violations within a 12-month period shall have his or her driving privileges suspended for 60 days. I. B. Badriver is sent a letter indicating that he is to appear at a hearing to determine whether his driving privileges should be suspended under this law because the agency's records reflect that he was convicted of a moving violation on February 1 and again on January 3 of the next year.

I. B. asserts two defenses. First, he contends that he was convicted on only one occasion, February 1, and that the second conviction belongs to another person of the same name. His second defense is that he believes that even if he committed both offenses, the 12-month period under the statute should run from January 1 to December 31. The agency, however, concludes that the 12-month period begins at the date of the first conviction. This is a legal conclusion. The determination whether I. B. was the offender convicted in the two cases is a factual conclusion.

9.6(f) Mixed Questions of Law and Fact

In some instances, a question will appear to be one of both fact and law. So-called mixed questions are those that involve the direct application of an interpreted law to a fact issue. For example, the Americans with Disabilities Act requires employers to provide reasonable accommodations for their disabled employees. Whether a particular employer is in compliance is both a question of law (are the employer's accommodations reasonable?) and a question of fact (what accommodations has the employer made?). Because the statute does not further define *reasonable*, the facts of the case blend with the law (reasonability) and a mixed question results: Were the employer's accommodations reasonable?

There is no uniform rule on what standard of review applies to mixed questions. In some cases, courts review these decisions de novo and in others courts apply the substantial evidence test. Generally, the more legal the question, the more likely it is that the de novo test will be applied. The more factual, the more likely it is that the substantial evidence test will be applied.

9.6(g) Issues of Discretion

Recall that decisions committed to agency discretion by law are not reviewable. This is rare, however. In most instances, discretionary decisions are reviewable under the arbitrary, capricious, abuse of discretion standard. The arbitrary and capricious standard applies to informal agency actions, such as informal rulemaking and informal adjudication. Although it does not apply to final decisions from formal rulemaking and formal adjudication, it does apply to many decisions involving the exercise of discretion made during those proceedings. You learned many more examples of discretionary decisions in Chapter 3. These included, *inter alia*, the discretion to determine whether to investigate or prosecute, whether to prosecute, and whether to issue licenses and permits. Table 9-1 summarizes these applications.

9.6(h) Failure to Raise Issues

As a general rule, review is limited to those issues raised at the administrative level. Failure to raise an issue or assert a position at the administrative level bars the party from raising the issue on appeal. An exception to this rule exists for issues of agency jurisdiction. The failure to claim that an agency lacks jurisdiction at the agency level is not fatal. That issue may be raised for the first time before a reviewing court.

TABLE 9-1	Standards of Judicial Review of Agency Actions under the APA

I. Legal Issues:

Action	Standard
Interpretations: Congress's intent is clear	De novo
Interpretations: explicitly delegated authority	Arbitrary and capricious
Interpretations: implicitly delegated authority	Reasonableness
Other legal conclusions	De novo

II. Factual Issues and Discretionary Acts

Action	Standard
Formal rulemaking—The rule	Substantial evidence
Formal rulemaking—Acts taken in the process	Arbitrary and capricious
Informal rulemaking—The rule	Arbitrary and capricious
Informal rulemaking—Acts taken in the process	Arbitrary and capricious
Formal adjudication—The decision	Substantial evidence
Formal adjudication—Acts taken in the process	Arbitrary and capricious
Informal adjudication—The decision	Arbitrary and capricious
Informal adjudication—Acts taken in the process	Arbitrary and capricious
Actions committed to agency discretion by law	No review

Note: The de novo standard is applied to factual issues and discretionary acts only when specifically required by law.

9.6(i) Alternative Rationale

As you have learned, an agency must issue findings and conclusions following formal adjudications. Those must include "findings and conclusions, and the reasons or basis therefor, on all the material issues of fact, law, or discretion presented on the record."[34] What if a court disagrees with an agency's rationale but can find an alternative theory to support the agency's decision? In *Securities & Exchange Commission v. Chenery*,[35] the Supreme Court held that courts are limited to an agency's rationale, even if the court can find an alternative basis for affirming the agency's decision. This holding requires that agencies render thoughtful decisions. It prevents an agency from issuing findings with little analysis or insight into its rationale in hopes that a court will find a means by which it can be affirmed. It is judicially efficient because the burden is not placed on the judge to search for a solid foundation on which to set an agency's findings.

9.7 REVIEW OF RULES

As mentioned earlier, formal rules are reviewed under the substantial evidence test. Informal rules are tested under the less stringent arbitrary and capricious test. Interpretive rules may be tested under a de novo test because they are not actually rulemaking but are an agency statement of what the agency believes a statute to mean, and determining the meaning of law is a responsibility of the judiciary. However, as you previously learned, because of agency expertise and experience, federal courts give deference to agency interpretations of laws that fall within the agency's jurisdiction.

SIDEBAR   *The United States Court of Appeals for the Federal Circuit*

The Supreme Court of the United States hears only a small percentage of the case appealed to it, typically about 4 percent. Therefore the decisions of the United States Courts of Appeals are often the final word on the law. There are 13 courts of appeals in the federal system. Twelve of the courts hear appeals within a defined geographic area, known as a circuit. The 13th, the Federal Circuit, is defined by its subject matter jurisdiction, not by geography. Unlike the other courts of appeals whose decisions are binding only in their respective circuits, it usually exercises national jurisdiction. The Court of Appeals for the Federal Circuit has jurisdiction over intellectual property, international trade, U.S. government liability, and a variety of administrative law appeals. More than half of the cases it hears are appeals from administrative agencies. Because the Supreme Court hears so few cases appealed to it, the Federal Circuit is often the final word in administrative law and accordingly, is the most important federal appellate tribunal in the United States, save the Supreme Court.

9.8 COMMON LAW DOCTRINES

Four common law doctrines—res judicata, collateral estoppel, equitable estoppel, and laches—may be applied by a reviewing court or administrative agency. The foundation of the four doctrines is the same: fairness and economy. All four doctrines were developed by courts in the context of judicial cases. The doctrines, however, are important to administrative law as well.

Res judicata and collateral estoppel are applicable in administrative proceedings. The status of the applicability of equitable estoppel is not clear. In the administrative context, the doctrines may play a dual role, one at the administrative level and another at the judicial review level. Said another way, both administrative agencies and courts may apply the doctrines. This examination begins with res judicata.

9.8(a) Res Judicata

Res judicata is defined as "a matter adjudged; a thing judicially acted upon or decided. A thing or matter settled by judgment. Rule that a final judgment rendered by a court of competent jurisdiction on the merits is conclusive as to the right of the parties and their privies, and as to them, constitutes an absolute bar to a subsequent action involving the same claim, demand, or cause of action."[36]

The doctrine of res judicata, also called *claim preclusion*, prevents the same claim from being filed and litigated more than once. Every person is entitled to his or her *day* in court—not days in court. In the administrative setting, res judicata applies to refiling of claims and applications. For example, if a claim for disability benefits is decided by the Social Security Administration, subsequent claims based on the same facts and law are res judicata. A party alleging that an action is res judicata must prove four elements.

First, there must have been a *previous proceeding*. Within a court system and within a specific agency, prior decisions that satisfy the test of either res judicata or collateral estoppel (see § 9.8[b]) are likely barred. The difficult issue is whether an administrative decision will be treated as barring future claims in courts or different administrative bodies. Some, but not most, administrative decisions will be treated as barring claims in courts. Similarly, some (but not all) administrative agencies treat prior decisions of other administrative agencies as final.

Second, the current case and former case must have an *identity of parties*—that is, the two cases must involve the same parties. Those in privity to a party satisfy this requirement. For example, Shirley files a workers' compensation claim, which is denied. After the decision is made, Shirley dies. Her estate then files a new, but identical, claim. Because the estate is in privity with Shirley, the claim would be res judicata.

Third, the claims of the current and former case must be *identical*. If a new case involves a claim or issue not raised in the first case, res judicata does not apply. Beware: Res judicata applies not only to claims that actually were raised, but also to those that should have been raised in the prior proceeding.[37] A plaintiff has an obligation to assert all claims arising out of the same set of facts in the same action. This prevents defendants from having to defend against multiple suits and courts from having to litigate more than one case when it is possible to have one proceeding fairly resolve all potential claims.

For example, Glen has an automobile collision with Nell, in which Glen's neck and leg are injured. He sues Nell for his personal injuries resulting from the accident. At trial, Glen introduces evidence of his leg injury, but fails to introduce evidence of his neck injury. He prevails and is awarded damages for his leg injury by a jury. He later files a new complaint to recover damages resulting from his neck injury. The second claim is res judicata because there was a previous action that arose out of the same set of facts involving the same parties and resulted in a final decision on the merits.

Fourth, there must have been a *final decision on the merits* in the previous case. Dismissals without prejudice do not satisfy this requirement until the time

---

LEGAL TERM
Res Judicata
Latin for "a matter adjudged." Doctrine that precludes a party from relitigating a final judgment on the merits issued by a competent court or administrative tribunal.

to have them set aside has passed. Summary judgment entered prior to final judgment is not final. Default judgments are not res judicata because they are not on the merits.

Res judicata does not apply to cases involving different facts even if they involve identical parties. Nor does the doctrine apply to appeals, reconsiderations, and rehearings. Res judicata applies only to the judicial (or quasi-judicial) functions of agencies. Executive and legislative functions cannot be res judicata. Therefore, a decision whether to prosecute is not res judicata, nor is rulemaking. The applicability of res judicata against the government in judicial proceedings is discussed further in Section 9.8(c).

9.8(b) Collateral Estoppel

LEGAL TERM
Collateral Estoppel
Doctrine that prevents relitigation of an issue that was decided in a prior case. Collateral estoppel bars relitigation of issues that are part of claims, whereas res judicata bars entire claims.

Collateral estoppel is similar to res judicata. Whereas res judicata prevents the relitigation of claims, collateral estoppel prevents the relitigation of issues. As with res judicata, a person asserting that an issue is estopped bears the burden of proving that collateral estoppel is applicable. The elements of collateral estoppel are slightly different from the elements of res judicata, though.

First, there must have been a previous proceeding. Second, the parties in the current and previous proceedings must be identical. Again, persons in privity with parties satisfy this requirement. Third, there must be an identity of issues—that is, a person must have been given the opportunity to litigate the issue in a prior proceeding before that issue can be estopped. This is not the same as the res judicata identity of claims, which prevents an entire action because it is identical to one previously heard. Collateral estoppel prevents relitigation of identical issues. If collateral estoppel applies, relitigation of an issue may be precluded, but the second case is not necessarily precluded.

SIDEBAR *Synonyms*

> Res judicata is also known as *claim preclusion* and *bar and merger*. Collateral estoppel is also known as *issue preclusion*.

Fourth, the issue must have been decided in the prior proceeding and such decision must have been necessary to the prior verdict, finding, or judgment. If a court rules on an issue that is not central to the outcome of the case, the issue may be reheard in a subsequent proceeding.

Collateral estoppel may or may not apply in an administrative proceeding. This varies from agency to agency.

9.8(c) Application to the Government

Be aware that the Supreme Court has recognized two significant exceptions to the standard res judicata and collateral estoppel rules discussed previously. First, in some instances identity of parties is not required. This is referred to as *nonmutual collateral estoppel*. Second, the Court has eased the common law restriction on who may assert collateral estoppel. At common law, only defendants could assert the doctrine. However, it may now be pled offensively by plaintiffs. These two exceptions are together called *nonmutual offensive collateral estoppel*.

Collateral estoppel and res judicata can be an issue for administrative agencies in judicial proceedings, as well as in administrative proceedings. The applicability of nonmutual offensive collateral estoppel against the government was an issue in *United States v. Mendoza*,[38] in which a Filipino national filed a petition for naturalization, relying on a statute exempting certain aliens who had served in the U.S. armed forces from particular eligibility requirements. Mendoza claimed that the absence of a U.S. representative to accept petitions in the Philippines for part of the period during which petitions were to be submitted denied him due process under the Fifth Amendment.

A similar case, previously filed by another Filipino, was resolved in the Filipino's favor. Mendoza asserted that the agency was estopped from defending the due process issue because that issue had already been decided.

The Court rejected the claim, holding that nonmutual offensive collateral estoppel is inapplicable against the government although it is applicable against private parties. The Court distinguished between the government and private litigants for a variety of reasons. First, the government represents the interests of all people in the United States. Second, many issues the government litigates are of sensitive, strategic, and significant national interest. Third, if the rule were otherwise, the government would be forced to appeal every unfavorable decision because it commonly has multiple suits pending with similar issues. Fourth, it prevents different courts from exploring the same issue and experimenting with remedies.

Hence, nonmutual offensive collateral estoppel is recognized in federal courts but not against the government. The government itself may, however, assert collateral estoppel. Also, if the government is a party to both proceedings and mutuality exists, then collateral estoppel and res judicata can be used against it. For example, if the decision in *Mendoza* had been favorable to the petitioner, the government would have been barred from refiling the case or relitigating the issue in any subsequent case with Mendoza.

9.8(d) Equitable Estoppel

Equitable estoppel prevents parties from raising issues or asserting certain arguments. Generally, if one person makes a representation to another, and that representation is relied upon, the party who made the representation is estopped from arguing the contrary. For example, assume that the Department of Education announces that certain educational grants are available for an upcoming academic year. The notice provides a telephone number to contact for details. Patricia calls the number and is told that the deadline for applications is July 1. She files her application on June 19. However, her application is returned by the Washington, DC, office with a letter explaining that the deadline was June 1. These facts appear to estop the government from asserting the untimeliness of Patricia's application. However, the applicability of the doctrine of equitable estoppel against the government is not clear.

The first major case involving the applicability of equitable estoppel against the government was *Federal Crop Insurance Corp. v. Merrill*.[39] In that case, a farmer relied on the representation of a government agent that his crops were insured. After his crops were destroyed, his claim for proceeds was denied. The government claimed that the type of crops the farmer grew were not insurable. The Supreme Court held that the government was not bound by its agents' representations because it had published a regulation stating what crops were eligible for coverage. The Court concluded that the regulation provided the farmer with adequate notice, despite the representation by the government official.

In 1951, four years after *Merrill*, the High Court issued *Moser v. United States*.[40] In that decision, the Court held that the incorrect advice of a government

LEGAL TERM
Equitable Estoppel
Doctrine that prevents a party from asserting a particular defense or raising a particular issue because it is unfair to allow the party to do so.

agent was binding. This appeared to open the door to application of equitable estoppel against the government. From 1951 to 1981, there was some relaxation of the rule of no estoppel against the government. Then, in 1981, the Court decided *Schweiker v. Hansen.*[41]

Hansen is a step backward in responsible government. The public should be able to rely on its government's representations and guidance. The no-estoppel rule increases the public's distrust of its government. In addition, the no-estoppel rule could encourage carelessness because officials know that the representations they make cannot be used against the government.

The Court has addressed the issue since *Hansen* and has recognized a distinction between cases in which estoppel would result in something contrary to the law and those in which it would not. For example, in *Merrill*, estopping the government from asserting that the farmer was not entitled to compensation could have resulted in the farmer's receiving compensation, contrary to the law. *Moser*, however, involved the granting of a citizenship that was not contrary to law.

This approach is especially useful when the expenditure of public monies is at issue. In *Office of Personnel Management v. Richmond*,[42] the Supreme Court specifically stated that equitable estoppel could never be applied so that a claim or benefit contrary to what Congress authorized is awarded. The Court refused to decide whether estoppel could ever lie against the government.

Whether the Court will ultimately decide that equitable estoppel can never apply against the government, or that its application should be limited to extreme cases in which the result will not be contrary to law, is unknown. Clearly, the doctrine will never be applied against the government to the extent it is against private litigants. Although estoppel against the government should be raised in some cases, it should never be depended on.

One method of making agency advice reliable is the use of declaratory orders. The APA provides for the issuance of declaratory orders to "terminate a controversy or remove uncertainty."[43] This provision allows agencies to issue advance decisions that will be binding so that citizens may seek and rely on an agency's advance decision. There is a limitation on the declaratory order provision: Orders may be issued only in cases for which a trial-type hearing is required.

The APA does not create a citizen right to a declaratory order. The decision on whether to issue a declaratory order is vested in the "sound discretion" of the agency. Conversely, this does not mean that an agency can refuse to issue such an order in every case. Although agencies have significant discretion, that discretion is not unfettered. A refusal to issue a declaratory order that is determined to be an abuse of discretion may be reversed by a reviewing court.

Schweiker v. Hansen

450 U.S. 785 (1981)

On June 12, 1974, respondent met for about 15 minutes with Don Connelly, a field representative of the Social Security Administration (SSA), and orally inquired of him whether she was eligible for "mother's insurance benefits" under § 202(f) of the Social Security Act (Act), 64 Stat. 485, as amended, 42 U.S.C. § 402(g). Connelly erroneously told her that she was not, and she left the SSA office without having filed a written application. By the Act's terms, such benefits are available only to one who, among other qualifications, "has filed application." 20 CFR § 404.601 (1974). The SSA's Claims Manual, and internal Administration handbook, instructs field representatives to advise applicants of the advantages of filing written applications and to recommend to applicants who are uncertain about their eligibility that they file written applications. Connelly, however, did not recommend to respondent that she file a written application, nor did he advise her of the advantages of doing so. The question is whether Connelly's erroneous statement and neglect of the Claims Manual estop petitioner, the Secretary of Health and Human Services, from denying retroactive benefits to respondent for a period in which she was eligible for benefits but had not filed a written application. . . .

. . . If Connelly's minor breach of such a manual suffices to estop petitioner, then the Government is put "at risk that every alleged failure by an agent to follow instructions to the last detail in one of a thousand cases will deprive it of the benefit of the written application requirement which experience has taught to be essential to the honest and effective administration of the Social Security Laws." . . .

In sum, Connelly's errors "fal[l] far short" of conduct which would raise a serious question [as to] whether petitioner is estopped from insisting upon compliance with the valid regulation.

Schweiker v. Hansen, 450 U.S. 785 (1981), United States Supreme Court.

9.8(e) Laches

The last common law doctrine to be discussed is ***laches***. If a party fails to raise an issue or right until such a time as an adverse party has been prejudiced, then laches may be used to estop the first party from asserting the right or claim.

There are three essential elements to laches. First, the party against whom laches is claimed must have been aware of the right or claim that was not raised. Second, there must have been unreasonable delay in raising the right or claim. Third, the delay must cause the adverse party to suffer some prejudice.

Laches may be applied even if statutory deadlines are not violated. For example, if a statute provides three years to raise a claim, laches may estop a person from raising a claim after two years even though the statute is satisfied. However, because laches is not founded on constitutional principles, a legislature may prohibit its application by statute. An administrative agency may not make such a declaration by rule.

LEGAL TERM

Laches
Common law doctrine that prohibits a party from raising a right or claim when the party's delay in asserting the right or claim has prejudiced an adverse party. Paris Hilton and Nicole Richie at the 2003 Billboard Music Awards.

9.9 CONCLUSION

Like Congress and the president, courts play a role in overseeing the American bureaucracy. The degree to which a court will intervene in an agency's decision depends on the function performed and whether the decision was one of law, fact, or discretion. Some legal conclusions are given a hard look by courts; others, such as when an agency is interpreting the statutes it is charged to enforce, are treated with some deference.

Like trial courts, agencies have to find facts in adjudications and in formal rulemaking. For the same reasons appellate courts defer to the fact findings of trial courts, a reviewing court will defer to the findings of an administrative agency, as long as "substantial evidence" can be found in the record to support the agency's decision. The largest number of decisions made by government officials are not formal findings or conclusions of law—they are discretionary. If judicially challenged, discretionary decisions stand unless arbitrary or capricious. Some matters, however, involve matters that are delegated under our Constitution to the political branches of government. Decisions in these matters are committed to agency discretion at law and are not judicially reviewable.

In addition to these standards, there are a number of judicial limitations to obtaining judicial review, such as ripeness and mootness. Taken together, this framework establishes marginal agency accountability. However, some urge greater judicial accountability of agencies especially because the executive and legislative branches of government are often unwilling or unable to control agency behavior.

LAWLINKS

The best computerized legal research services are Westlaw and Lexis. Both are commercial sites. However, many institutions have access to these databases through reduced-fee academic plans. Take advantage of these resources if your institution is a subscriber.

REVIEW **QUESTIONS**

1. At common law, four primary writs were available on review. Name these four and briefly describe them.

2. What is standing?

3. What is a qui tam action?

4. What is the doctrine of exhaustion of administrative remedies? Primary jurisdiction?

5. What standard of review does the APA apply to legal issues? Factual issues?

6. Define *res judicata*, *collateral estoppel*, and *equitable estoppel*.

7. What is federal question jurisdiction?

CRITICAL THINKING AND **APPLICATIONS PROBLEMS**

Congress appropriates $1 million for a scientific grant. The appropriation specifies that the grant money is to be used to study the mating behavior of sea turtles. Congress also enacts legislation requiring businesses that affect sea turtles' migration or habitat to pay a special tax. The revenues are used to help fund the grant. In fact, one-half of the grant money is derived from the general treasury and the other half from the special tax.

1. Kevin believes this expenditure to be wasteful and is outraged that his tax dollars are being spent for useless studies. He files an action in a U.S. district court seeking to block the appropriation. Does Kevin have standing?

2. TransShipping, Inc., has been assessed a $20,000 special tax because its oceanic shipping lines interfere with sea turtle migration. The Shipping Union (SU) is an organization whose membership consists of companies that engage in land, rail, and air shipping. Although the SU members are not engaged in ocean shipping, they believe that this law sets a bad precedent and that similar laws may affect their businesses in the future. At the last SU meeting, its membership voted to hire counsel to oppose the new law. Both TransShipping and Shipping Union have filed separate actions challenging the law. Do they have standing?

ENDNOTES

1. *United States v. Wunderlich*, 342 U.S. 98 (1951).

2. *Yakus v. United States*, 321 U.S. 414 (1944).

3. 42 U.S.C. § 405(g).

4. 15 U.S.C. § 45.

5. *Shaughnessy v. Pedreiro*, 349 U.S. 48 (1955).

6. 415 U.S. 361 (1974).

7. 486 U.S. 592 (1988).

8. *Califano v. Sanders*, 430 U.S. 99 (1977).

9. 28 U.S.C. § 1331.

10. APA § 703.

11. 28 U.S.C. § 361.

12. 486 U.S. 592 (1988).

13. *Citizens to Preserve Overton Park v. Volpe*, 401 U.S. 402, 410 (1971).

14. *Arizona Power Pooling Ass'n v. Morton*, 527 F.2d 721 (9th Cir. 1975), *cert. denied*, 425 U.S. 911 (1976).

15. *Kletchka v. Driver*, 411 F.2d 436 (2d Cir. 1969).

16. 555 U.S. 488 (2009).

17. 392 U.S. 83 (1968).

18. 454 U.S. 464 (1982).

19. Bernard Schwartz, *Administrative Law* § 8.15, at 502 (3d ed. 1989).

20. Harlan, J., dissenting in *Flast v. Cohen*, 392 U.S. 83, 120, 131 (1968).

21. 438 U.S. 59 (1978).

22. 504 U.S. 555 (1992).

23. 564 U.S. ___ (2011).

24. 189 F.2d 939 (2d Cir. 1951).

25. *Klicker v. Northwest Airlines*, 563 F.2d 1310 (9th Cir. 1977).

26. See ch. 10.

27. 457 U.S. 496 (1982).

28. APA § 704.

29. 387 U.S. 136 (1967).

30. *Consolidated Edison Co. v. NLRB*, 305 U.S. 197, 230 (1938).

31. See Lee Modjeska, *Administrative Law* § 6.12, at 212–13 (Lawyers Cooperative, 1982).

32. *Udall v. Tallman*, 380 U.S. 1, 16 (1965), cited in *Johnson v. Robison*, 415 U.S. 367, 369 (1974).

33. APA § 706(2).

34. APA § 557(c)(A).

35. 318 U.S. 80 (1943).

36. *Black's Law Dictionary* (5th ed. 1979).

37. See *Federated Dep't. Stores, Inc. v. Moitie*, 452 U.S. 394, 399 (1947).

38. 464 U.S. 154 (1984).

39. 332 U.S. 380 (1947).

40. 341 U.S. 41 (1951).

41. 450 U.S. 785 (1981).

42. 496 U.S. 414 (1990).

43. APA § 554(e).

chapter **ten**

ACCOUNTABILITY THROUGH ACCESSIBILITY

OUTLINE

LEARNING OBJECTIVES

After completing this chapter, you should be able to

- Describe the basic architecture of the Freedom of Information Act (FOIA), including the three modalities of providing public access to information, listing and describing the major exceptions to the FOIA, and the process for enforcing FOIA rights.

- Describe the basic architecture of the Privacy Act, including the circumstances in which it prohibits or limits public access to information, and apply what you have learned to a fact scenario.

- Compare and contrast the objectives of the FOIA and Privacy Acts, including an explanation of how the two interact; apply what you have learned to a fact scenario.

- Describe the basic architecture of the Government in the Sunshine Act, applying its mandates to a fact scenario.

- Brief a judicial opinion with little outside assistance. You should be successful in identifying the relevant facts. You should also be successful in identifying the legal issue and analyzing the court's rationale in at least 75 percent of your briefs.

No one should be able to pull curtains of secrecy around decisions which can be revealed without injury to the public interest.

PRESIDENT LYNDON B. JOHNSON

Lyndon B Johnson, 1966.

10.1 INTRODUCTION

In previous chapters you learned about the many functions agencies perform, the authorities agencies possess, and how accountability is maintained through oversight by elected and appointed officials. There are other ways to keep government officials accountable. One is to keep government open to public observation. To maintain a free society, citizens should be aware of what their government is doing, plans on doing, and has done.

This chapter examines the public's rights to obtain information from the government and to observe its operations. The discussion begins with the Freedom of Information Act, the primary tool for obtaining information from the United States. Ironically, a discussion of the rights of the public would be incomplete without a discussion of the Privacy Act, a law that prevents governmental disclosure of information in special circumstances. Finally, the chapter closes with an examination of the Government in the Sunshine Act and related laws. Be aware that all states have government in the sunshine laws as well. These laws vary significantly; some require disclosure of nearly all records held by the state and its local governments, whereas others are more restrictive.

10.2 FREEDOM OF INFORMATION ACT

Before 1966, little public right to inspect government records or to observe government hearings existed. This changed with the passage of the ***Freedom of Information Act (FOIA)*** in 1966.[1] Today, the FOIA has been added to the APA section of the United States Code. The FOIA's purpose is to make information held by the government available to the public: "The basic purpose of the FOIA is to ensure an informed citizenry, vital to the functioning of a democratic society, needed to check against corruption and to hold the governors accountable to the governed."[2] See Figure 10-1 for a summary of the FOIA. Although not covered in this text, be aware that each state has its own open government laws. They vary

LEGAL TERMS

Freedom of Information Act (FOIA)
Federal disclosure statute requiring that information held by the government be made available for public review unless one of nine statutory exceptions applies.

Freedom of Information Act 5 U.S.C. § 552	
Purpose	The promotion of democracy by having an informed citizenry to check governmental abuse and corruption. To keep the governors accountable to the governed.
Assumption	All information held by the government is available to the public.
Exemptions	Government may refuse to disclose information only if one of the act's nine exemptions applies: 1. Information concerning national security or foreign policy that has been declared secret by the president 2. Agency personnel rules and practices 3. Information exempted by statute 4. Trade secrets, commercial, and financial information 5. Inter- and intra-agency memoranda 6. Personnel and medical files 7. Law enforcement records 8. Regulation of financial institutions 9. Geological information

FIGURE 10-1   Freedom of Information Act summary.

"Conflicting Values and Laws: Understanding the Paradox of the Privacy Act and the Freedom of Information Act" from 19 Legal Studies Forum 21 by Dean J. Spader. Copyright © 1995 by West Virginia University. Used by permission of West Virginia University.

considerably in what records can be obtained and by whom and what meetings must be public. For example, Florida is a very open state that permits anyone. Virginia on the other hand has more limited access to public records, including limiting access to residents of Virginia.[3]

The volume of requests for information under the FOIA is staggering. In 2011 alone, 644,165 requests were submitted. The Department of Homeland Security received the greater number, 27 percent of the total.[4] The total records provided to persons is much higher because many records are provided in person, through the mail, e-mail, or offered through Web sites without a formal FOIA request.

The statute has a broad reach. It creates a presumption that documents should be available to the public. Only if a document clearly fits into one of the nine exceptions to the FOIA may the government deny a request for disclosure. Before discussing those exceptions, let's look at the statute's disclosure requirements. The FOIA provides for three forms of disclosure: publication, inspection and copying, and production upon request.

10.2(a) Publication Requirement

In some instances, agencies are required to publish specific information in the *Federal Register*. You have already learned two types of information that must be published in the *Federal Register*: notices of proposed rules and final rules. FOIA §552(a)(1) requires that every agency publish the following:

1. A description of its central and field organizations and a statement of from whom, and the method whereby, the public may obtain information or make submittals or requests.
2. A statement of the general course and method by which its functions are channeled and determined, including requirements of formal and informal procedures.
3. Its rules of procedure, descriptions of forms available to the public, where to get those forms, and instructions as to the scope of all papers, reports, or examinations.
4. Its substantive rules and regulations of general applicability, including statements of general policy and interpretations of law.
5. All amendments, revisions, or repeals of any of the above.

The APA specifically provides that personnel and other internal administrative matters need not be published.

Failure to Publish   Parties dealing with an agency are not bound, nor may they be adversely affected, by any information or rule for which the publication requirement was not met unless the party receives actual and timely notice of the information or rule. Thus, if an agency promulgates a procedural rule, but fails to publish it in the *Federal Register*, the procedure cannot be raised by the agency to the detriment of an adverse party. However, if actual and timely notice is given to a party, then the rule may be binding regardless of whether it was published. Of course, due process applies to such procedural notices. For example, assume that the Department of State adopted a rule concerning the process for obtaining a passport. Immediately upon application for her passport, Shirley is given notice of the rules by the agency. Because she has been provided with actual notice, the rules may be used against her, regardless of the lack of publication. Note, however, that some courts may order publication to satisfy the purpose of informing the public while applying the rule against Shirley in her particular case.

10.2(b) Inspection and Copying Requirement

The second form of disclosure entails making information available for public inspection and copying. FOIA §552(a)(1) requires that agencies make the following information available for inspection and copying:

1. All orders and final opinions (including concurring and dissenting) made during adjudication.
2. Those statements of policy and interpretation adopted by the agency but not published in the *Federal Register*.
3. Administrative staff manuals and instructions to staff that affect a member of the public.

This provision is sometimes referred to as the *reading room requirement* because it is satisfied by providing a location for people to inspect and copy documents. As an alternative to providing a reading room, an agency may promptly publish the information and provide copies for sale.

Indexing   In addition to making these documents available to the public, the FOIA requires that all agencies "maintain and make available for public inspection and copying a current index" of materials required to be made available or published. Each agency is required to publish, at least quarterly, and distribute (by sale or otherwise) copies of each index and its supplements. If this is unnecessary or impractical, an agency may issue an order stating that the index and supplements, if any, will not be published or distributed. This order must itself be published in the *Federal Register*. If this is done, the agency must provide the index, upon request, at a cost no greater than the actual cost of duplication.

Failure to Comply   If an agency fails to make information available or fails to index documents, the FOIA provides that such order, opinion, statement of policy, or the like may not be used against a party, unless the party has been given actual and timely notice of the terms thereof.

10.2(c) Production upon Request Requirement

The first two requirements direct agencies to take affirmative steps toward disclosure before any request is made. For information not included in either the publication or inspection and copying requirements, an agency is to make the information promptly available, upon request, if two requirements are met: First, a request for information reasonably describes the records desired; and second, the request complies with the agency's procedures concerning time, place, and fees.

The production-upon-request method is a catch-all, providing people with access to most public records. All documents, other than those specified for publication or inspection and copying, fall into this category. When one files a request for information under the FOIA (see Figure 10-2), it is under this provision—and, indeed, it is well used. Approximately two million requests are filed each year.[5]

Request Procedure   Any person, including a noncitizen, may file a request for disclosure under the third form of disclosure just discussed. Generally, the identity of the person requesting information is immaterial. If the information requested is not exempted from disclosure, it must be provided.

A request must reasonably describe the information desired. A request *reasonably describes* the information sought if an agency employee who is familiar

---

John Q. Citizen
1000 Freedom Way
Anywhere, United States

January 1, 2009

Ms. Government Official
1000 Federal Way
Washington, D.C.

Re: FOIA Request

Dear Ms. Official:

Pursuant to the Freedom of Information Act, 5 U.S.C. § 552, I request the following documents be provided to me:

[insert a reasonable description of the information sought here]

I understand that under the FOIA, I may be charged a fee for these documents. Please be aware that I am [insert information that justifies a lower fee, such as membership in a news organization, academic status, the information is sought for noncommercial purposes, etc.].

Please notify me before completing this request if the total fee will exceed [insert dollar amount here or request a waiver of the fees because the request is noncommercial and disclosure to me is in the public's best interest. Explain why the public will benefit from the waiver and disclosure].

Should you need to contact me concerning this request, please direct your correspondence to the above address [providing telephone number/e-mail address sometimes expedites the process].

Sincerely,

John Q. Citizen

FIGURE 10-2   Sample FOIA request.

---

with the subject matter of the requested records can identify the records sought. Not only must the request reasonably identify the record sought, but it must also permit location of the records without an unreasonable amount of effort. A request for more than 3.5 million records of the Patent Office was determined to be too broad, too costly, and unduly burdensome in one case.[6] In addition, the requester must comply with an agency's requirements for the time and location of filing, as well as paying any required fees.

Once it receives a request, the agency must determine, within 10 days (except Saturdays, Sundays, and legal holidays), whether to comply with the request. Agencies are to establish a telephone or Internet process to track requests and provide the tracking information to the requestor.

If the request has been sent to the wrong division of the agency it has 10 days to route it to the correct office. If the agency plans to not fulfill the request it must immediately notify the requester of its decision, its reasons, and the right to appeal the decision to the head of the agency. The FOIA does not require agencies to deliver documents to requesters; making them available is adequate.

If a decision is appealed, the agency must make its decision within 20 days, except Saturdays, Sundays, and legal holidays. If the decision on appeal affirms the initial decision denying disclosure, the agency shall inform the requester of the right to judicial review.

In "unusual circumstances," the statutory time requirements may be extended by 10 days. The agency must send written notice of such an extension to the requester, explaining why the extension is necessary and the date on which it will issue its decision. The FOIA specifies three situations as "unusual circumstances." First, the need to search for and collect the requested documents from field facilities or other establishments separate from the office that is processing the request qualifies as unusual. Second, it is an unusual circumstance if an agency must search and examine a large number of separate and distinct records. Third, if the agency must consult with another agency that has a substantial interest in the request, an unusual circumstance exists. Also, if within the agency two or more divisions have a substantial interest in the request, an extension for consultation between those divisions is proper. In both instances, however, the consultation must be conducted with all practicable speed.

If a requester exhausts his or her administrative appeals and the agency still has not disclosed the requested information, the requester may bring an appeal to a district court of the United States. The FOIA provides four different choices of forums. The appeal may be filed in the district where the requester resides; where the requester has its principal place of business; where the requested documents are located; or in the U.S. District Court for the District of Columbia. There is no time limitation on the filing of an appeal with the district court.

What Records?   The disclosure requirement of the FOIA applies to "agency records." Other information is not included. Print documents, digital files, and audio and visual materials are all records.

Records in the possession and control of an agency are included, as are records created or obtained by an agency. However, records in the possession of private organizations are not included even if the organization receives public funding or is in another manner associated with the government. If an agency does not have possession of a record, it has no duty to find it to satisfy a FOIA request. Thus, if an agency once had possession of a record, but does no longer, there is no duty to recover it. Similarly, the FOIA does not require agencies to create records.

The FOIA applies only to records in the possession or control of agencies. Access to the sought record from another government source is not the basis for denying a request. For example, the Department of Justice was required to provide copies of court opinions it possessed even though the opinion were available from the courts.[7] In the information age, the number of records held by agencies is staggering and a search for a particular record can be daunting. Agency officials are not expected to search endlessly. Searches must be "reasonably calculated" to find the requested record.

As you learned earlier, government compels people to file documents with agencies in many instances, such as individuals who respond to reporting requirements or persons who apply for employment with government. The records required to be filed may contain confidential information. To avoid a "clearly unwarranted invasion of privacy," the FOIA provides that "an agency may delete identifying details when it" fulfills a request. Such a decision must be justified in writing.

The act does not allow agencies to remove information from all documents. Only opinions, statements of policy, interpretations, and staff manuals are covered by this provision of the FOIA. Other forms of records are not included, and private information may not be withheld under this provision. Figure 10-3 is a one-page document provided to a citizen who made a request concerning an alleged alien spaceship crash at Roswell, New Mexico.

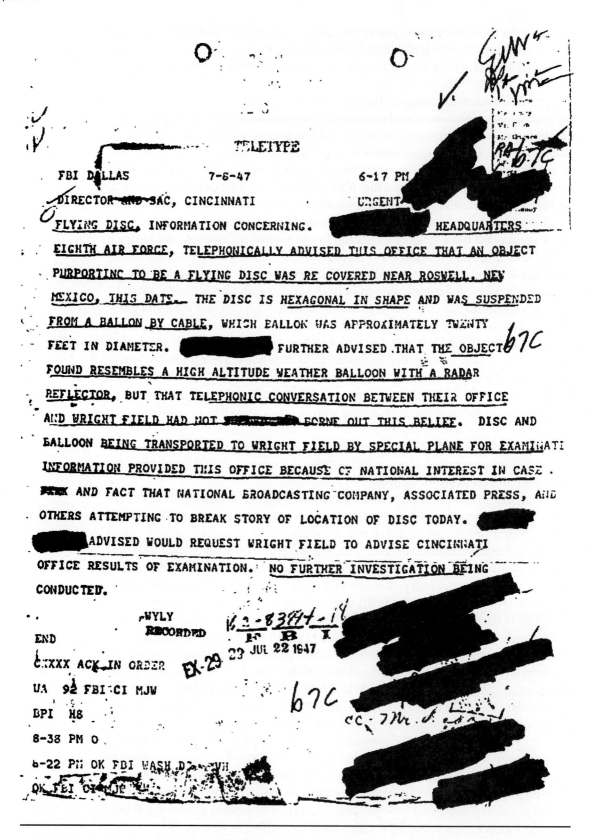

TELETYPE

FBI DALLAS   7-8-47   6-17 PM

DIRECTOR AND SAC, CINCINNATI   URGENT

FLYING DISC, INFORMATION CONCERNING.   HEADQUARTERS

EIGHTH AIR FORCE, TELEPHONICALLY ADVISED THIS OFFICE THAT AN OBJECT

PURPORTING TO BE A FLYING DISC WAS RE COVERED NEAR ROSWELL, NEW

MEXICO, THIS DATE. THE DISC IS HEXAGONAL IN SHAPE AND WAS SUSPENDED

FROM A BALLON BY CABLE, WHICH BALLON WAS APPROXIMATELY TWENTY

FEET IN DIAMETER.   FURTHER ADVISED THAT THE OBJECT

FOUND RESEMBLES A HIGH ALTITUDE WEATHER BALLOON WITH A RADAR

REFLECTOR, BUT THAT TELEPHONIC CONVERSATION BETWEEN THEIR OFFICE

AND WRIGHT FIELD HAD NOT   BORNE OUT THIS BELIEF. DISC AND

BALLOON BEING TRANSPORTED TO WRIGHT FIELD BY SPECIAL PLANE FOR EXAMINATI

INFORMATION PROVIDED THIS OFFICE BECAUSE OF NATIONAL INTEREST IN CASE

AND FACT THAT NATIONAL BROADCASTING COMPANY, ASSOCIATED PRESS, AND

OTHERS ATTEMPTING TO BREAK STORY OF LOCATION OF DISC TODAY.

ADVISED WOULD REQUEST WRIGHT FIELD TO ADVISE CINCINNATI

OFFICE RESULTS OF EXAMINATION. NO FURTHER INVESTIGATION BEING

CONDUCTED.

WYLY

END   RECORDED

CXXXX ACK IN ORDER

UA 92 FBI CI MJW

BPI H8

8-38 PM O

6-22 PM OK FBI WASH D

OK FBI CI

FIGURE 10-3 Government response to Roswell FOIA request. The blackened portions of the document were text redacted by a government official prior to disclosing the document. Information that is exempt from disclosure is commonly removed in this manner. Do you wonder what the government is not revealing about the Roswell crash?

Note that only privacy is protected, not other confidential information such as trade secrets. The Privacy Act, however, may protect individuals from disclosure of such information.

10.2(d) FOIA as Discovery

May the FOIA be used during civil or criminal litigation as a form of discovery? This question was discussed in *North v. Walsh*[8], in which the U.S. Court of Appeals for the District of Columbia Circuit determined that the FOIA may indeed be used as a discovery tool in a criminal proceeding. Not all courts agree with this conclusion. Therefore, the law of a particular jurisdiction must be examined. The cases prohibiting the FOIA from being used as discovery in judicial proceedings appear misguided because the language of the FOIA states that "any person" may make a request, thereby leading to the conclusion that the FOIA may be used during civil or criminal litigation as a discovery tool.

10.2(e) Fees and Waivers

The FOIA allows agencies to charge fees for responding to requests, in some instances.[9] The act has three fee categories. First, when records are requested for commercial use, the requester may be charged for document search, copying, and review expenses incurred by the responding agency. When a request is made by an educational, noncommercial, scientific, or news media organization, only copying fees may be recovered. For all other requests, search and copying expenses may be charged.

No fee can be charged for the first two hours of search time or for the first 100 pages of copying, except for commercial requesters. Finally, a fee may be reduced or waived if disclosure of the documents is in the "public interest because it is likely to contribute significantly to public understanding of the operations or activities of the government" and is not primarily in the commercial interest of the requester.

10.2(f) Exemptions

The FOIA contains nine exemptions. These exemptions are exclusive—that is, none others exist. Furthermore, the nine expressly provided are narrowly construed by the courts. This is consistent with the fundamental policy underlying the FOIA: disclosure in government, not secrecy in government.

The exemption provisions are permissive. An agency does not have to refuse to disclose information just because it falls within one of the FOIA exemptions; the agency has the discretion to decide whether to produce such records. This is true of all information, including that which is private or confidential. The FOIA does not require agencies to protect privacy. However, you will see later that a separate law, the Privacy Act, does prohibit disclosure of some records about individuals in some circumstances (see Section 10.3) in some instances. On appeal, the burden of proving that the document requested falls within an exemption rests with the agency.[10]

Each presidential administration influences the implementation of the FOIA through its interpretation of, and approach to, the exemptions. President Clinton's administration was generally known for favoring disclosure. President George W. Bush's administration, in contrast, favored a more restrictive policy, especially when homeland security and trade secrets were at stake. Attorney

General John Ashcroft, for example, issued a memorandum to all federal officials stating although the administration was committed to complying with the FOIA, it was also committed to safeguarding other values, including national security, business secrets, law enforcement data, and personal privacy. Attorney General Ashcroft advised federal officials to "carefully consider the protection of all such values and interests" when making a decision as to whether disclosure is required under the FOIA.[11]

On his first full day in office, President Barack Obama issued a memorandum to federal employees concerning the FOIA. Heralded as a new day in access to public records, President Obama made it clear that he wanted his administration to be more open than President George W. Bush's. President Obama penned "The Freedom of Information Act should be administered with a clear presumption: In the face of doubt, openness prevails. . . . All agencies should adopt a presumption in favor of disclosure, in order to renew their commitment to the principles embodied in FOIA, and to usher in a new era of open Government. The presumption of disclosure should be applied to all decisions involving FOIA." He directed the attorney general to develop guidelines to implement his policy of increased transparency and accountability. On March 19, 2009, Attorney General Eric Holder issued the guidelines. Whether a new era of openness resulted is disputed. Holder eventually reversed position and issued a directive making it more difficult to obtain some records and some journalists and analysts have complained that FOIA requests are more likely to be denied than in the Bush administration,[12] possibly resulting in an increase in the number of lawsuits filed against the United States to obtain information.[13]

National Defense and Foreign Policy   The FOIA exempts from disclosure records concerning national defense and foreign policy. For this exemption to apply, the president must issue an executive order requiring that the documents sought be kept classified. A lower executive official cannot declare a document classified and thereby avoid disclosure under the FOIA. The documents must actually concern national defense or foreign policy and be properly classified as secret under an applicable executive order. The president need not personally review a document and declare it a secret, however. The president has only to issue an executive order declaring what types of documents are to remain confidential. Thereafter, lower executive officials can determine whether a particular record falls within the scope of the executive order.

Critical Infrastructures   In the wake of the attacks on the United States of September 11, 2001, a new exemption to the FOIA was created. Data voluntarily provided by owners and operators of "critical infrastructures," such as communications, banking, health care, and utilities, about security issues and vulnerabilities in their systems, are exempt from disclosure. The objective of the legislation is to make private parties who plan, construct, or maintain critical infrastructures more comfortable in working with federal government authorities to prevent and respond to attacks on their systems.

Agency Personnel Matters   The second exemption applies to internal agency personnel rules and practices. Rules concerning hiring, vacation leave, and lunch breaks are examples of the rules exempted under this provision.

What qualifies as an agency personnel matter was the subject of the 2011 Supreme Court case *Milner v. Department of Navy.*

Milner v. Department of Navy 562 U.S. ___ (2011)

Justice Kagan delivered the opinion of the Court

The Freedom of Information Act (FOIA), 5 U. S. C. §552, requires federal agencies to make Government records available to the public, subject to nine exemptions for specific categories of material. This case concerns the scope of Exemption 2, which protects from disclosure material that is "related solely to the internal personnel rules and practices of an agency." §552(b)(2). Respondent Department of the Navy (Navy or Government) invoked Exemption 2 to deny a FOIA request for data and maps used to help store explosives at a naval base in Washington State. We hold that Exemption 2 does not stretch so far. . . .

At issue here is Exemption 2, which shields from compelled disclosure documents "related solely to the internal personnel rules and practices of an agency." §552(b)(2). Congress enacted Exemption 2 to replace the APA's exemption for "any matter relating solely to the internal management of an agency," 5 U. S. C. §1002 (1964 ed.). Believing that the "sweep" of the phrase "internal management" had led to excessive withholding, Congress drafted Exemption 2 "to have a narrower reach." . . .

The FOIA request at issue here arises from the Navy's operations at Naval Magazine Indian Island, a base in Puget Sound, Washington. The Navy keeps weapons, ammunition, and explosives on the island. To aid in the storage and transport of these munitions, the Navy uses data known as Explosive Safety Quantity Distance (ESQD) information. ESQD information prescribes "minimum separation distances" for explosives and helps the Navy design and construct storage facilities to prevent chain reactions in case of detonation. The ESQD calculations are often incorporated into specialized maps depicting the effects of hypothetical explosions.

In 2003 and 2004, petitioner Glen Milner, a Puget Sound resident, submitted FOIA requests for all ESQD information relating to Indian Island. The Navy refused to release the data, stating that disclosure would threaten the security of the base and surrounding community. In support of its decision to withhold the records, the Navy invoked Exemption 2. . . .

Our consideration of Exemption 2's scope starts with its text. Judicial decisions since FOIA's enactment have analyzed and reanalyzed the meaning of the exemption. But comparatively little attention has focused on the provision's 12 simple words: "related solely to the internal personnel rules and practices of an agency."

The key word in that dozen—the one that most clearly marks the provision's boundaries—is "personnel." When used as an adjective, as it is here to modify "rules and practices," that term refers to human resources matters. "Personnel," in this common parlance, means "the selection, placement, and training of employees and . . . the formulation of policies, procedures, and relations with [or involving] employees or their representatives." . . .

FOIA itself provides an additional example in Exemption 6. That exemption, just a few short paragraphs down from Exemption 2, protects from disclosure "personnel and medical files and similar files the disclosure of which would constitute a clearly unwarranted invasion of personal privacy." §552(b)(6). Here too, the statute uses the term "personnel" as a modifier meaning "human resources." As we recognized in *Rose*, "the common and congressional meaning of . . . 'personnel file'" is the file "showing, for example, where [an employee] was born, the names of his parents, where he has lived from time to time, his . . . school records, results of examinations, [and] evaluations of his work performance." It is the file typically maintained in the human resources office—otherwise known (to recall an example offered above) as the "personnel department."

(continued)

Exemption 2 uses "personnel" in the exact same way. An agency's "personnel rules and practices" are its rules and practices dealing with employee relations or human resources.

Exemption 2, as we have construed it, does not reach the ESQD information at issue here. These data and maps calculate and visually portray the magnitude of hypothetical detonations. By no stretch of imagination do they relate to "personnel rules and practices," as that term is most naturally understood. They concern the physical rules governing explosives, not the workplace rules governing sailors; they address the handling of dangerous materials, not the treatment of employees. The Navy therefore may not use Exemption 2, interpreted in accord with its plain meaning to cover human resources matters, to prevent disclosure of the requested maps and data. . . .

[T]he Government also offers another construction, which it says we might adopt "on a clean slate," "based on the plain text . . . alone." On this reading, the exemption "encompasses records concerning an agency's internal rules and practices for its personnel to follow in the discharge of their governmental functions." According to the Government, this interpretation makes sense because "the phrase 'personnel rules and practices of an agency' is logically understood to mean an agency's rules and practices *for its personnel*."

But the purported logic in the Government's definition eludes us. We would not say, in ordinary parlance, that a "personnel file" is any file an employee uses, or that a "personnel department" is any department in which an employee serves. No more would we say that a "personnel rule or practice" is any rule or practice that assists an employee in doing her job. The use of the term "personnel" in each of these phrases connotes not that the file or department or practice/rule is *for* personnel, but rather that the file or department or practice/rule is *about* personnel— *i.e.*, that it relates to employee relations or human resources. . . .

And this odd reading would produce a sweeping exemption, posing the risk that FOIA would become less a disclosure than "a withholding statute.". . .

Exemption 2, consistent with the plain meaning of the term "personnel rules and practices," encompasses only records relating to issues of employee relations and human resources. The explosives maps and data requested here do not qualify for withholding under that exemption.

[The Court recognized that disclosure of the ESQD data could threaten the safe storage of munitions. The Court suggested that another FOIA exemption might apply and if not, that the Navy could ask Congress to exempt the information.]

Milner v. Department of Navy, 562 U.S. (2011), United States Supreme Court.

Other Statutes   Many other statutes authorize withholding records from disclosure. The FOIA incorporates these exemptions by reference. Congress may not grant an agency unlimited power to withhold records, though, because the FOIA also requires that the other statute "leave no discretion on the issue" or that it establish "particular criteria for withholding or [refer] to particular types of matters to be withheld." Many statutes independently authorize the withholding of information. For example, the Internal Revenue Code has provisions authorizing nondisclosure of tax information. Census information may not be released or used for any purpose other than compiling statistics.

Trade Secrets and Financial Information   Another exemption permits withholding of trade secrets and other commercial or financial information obtained from a company on a privileged or confidential basis that, if released, could result in competitive harm to the company, impair the government's ability to obtain like information in the future, or to protect government's interest in program effectiveness. As you previously learned, agencies acquire much information from many sources. Even though these records are not created by the government, they are within the scope of the FOIA by virtue of being within the possession or control of the government. Note that there may be an overlap between the trade secret and other statutes' exemptions because both may protect a patented trade secret from disclosure. Although the FOIA does not expressly provide for third-party intervention, courts have recognized, in some circumstances, the right of a submitter of documents to sue to prevent disclosure of records under this exemption.[14]

Reverse FOIA action Lawsuits brought by submitters of records to agencies to prevent the disclosure of information are known as *reverse FOIA actions*.

Reverse FOIA action
Lawsuits brought by submitters of records to agencies to prevent the disclosure of information are known as *reverse FOIA actions*.

Agency Memoranda

The fifth exemption applies to "inter-agency or intra-agency memorandums or letters which would not be available by law to a party other than an agency in litigation with the agency." This language is confusing. As one noted author stated, there are three possibilities if the law of civil discovery were to be applied: The information is always discoverable, never discoverable, and sometimes discoverable. In addition, the exemption does not specify whether the "litigation" is criminal or civil; the rules of discovery are different between the two.[15]

On review, courts have turned to the legislative history of this section to understand Congress's intent. What the courts have determined is that predecisional deliberative information is exempted, but not factual or legal information. This allows employees of agencies to freely discuss and consider ideas without the risk that such information will later be used to attack a decision. What should be attacked is an agency's final decision, not any thoughts it had in reaching the decision. Postdecisional memoranda explaining why an agency took a particular action are not exempted under this provision.

Personnel, Medical, and Similar Files Containing Private Information

An agency may withhold "[p]ersonnel and medical files and similar files the disclosure of which would constitute a clearly unwarranted invasion of privacy." In the course of administering agencies, applications for employment, medical records of employees, and the like are acquired. Similarly, records of nonemployees that contain personal information are acquired.

The exemption includes not only personnel and medical files, but also other similar files. This provision has been interpreted broadly. In one case, disclosure of the results of a study of housing loans was determined to fall within this exemption because names of the loan recipients, marital status, legitimacy of children, welfare payments, and other private information was included. The reviewing court found that the information was protected and ordered that the private information be redacted prior to disclosure.[16]

Exemption 6 permits agencies to withhold such files to avoid a "clearly unwarranted invasion of privacy." A file may be withheld only if disclosure will result in a clearly unwarranted invasion of privacy. When determining whether to disclose information, a balancing of interests takes place. The right of the public to government information must be weighed against the privacy interest of the individual.

Mailing and telephone lists are popular requests today. Companies desiring to market to individuals, for example, may seek lists of telephone numbers and addresses from the government. Insurance companies, for example, may want lists of automobile owners, licensed drivers, and homeowners. Similarly, environmental groups may want lists of people who use government parks, hate groups may want information on the recipients of minority grants and scholarships, and the news media may want to know the names of crime victims. Because of the privacy invasions that attend many requests, §552(b)(6) also permits agencies to refuse disclosure if an unwarranted invasion of privacy would result. This was the issue in *U.S. Department of Defense v. Federal Labor Relations Authority.*

United States Department of Defense v. Federal Labor Relations Authority 510 U.S. 487 (1994)

This case requires us to consider whether disclosure of the home addresses of federal civil service employees by their employing agency pursuant to a request made by the employees' collective-bargaining representative under the Federal Service Labor-Management Relations Statute, *5 U.S.C. §§ 7101–7135* (1988 ed. & Supp. IV), would constitute a "clearly unwarranted invasion" of the employees' personal privacy within the meaning of the Freedom of Information Act, *5 U.S.C. § 552.* Concluding that it would, we reverse the judgment of the Court of Appeals.

The controversy underlying this case arose when two local unions requested the petitioner federal agencies to provide them with the names and home addresses of the agency employees in the bargaining units represented by the unions. The agencies supplied the unions with the employees' names and work stations, but refused to release home addresses. . . .

In response, the unions filed unfair labor practice charges with respondent Federal Labor Relations Authority (Authority), in which they contended that the Federal Service Labor-Management Relations Statute (Labor Statute), *5 U.S.C. §§ 7101–7135* (1988 ed. & Supp. IV), required the agencies to divulge the addresses. The Labor Statute generally provides that agencies must, "to the extent not prohibited by law," furnish unions with data that are necessary for collective-bargaining purposes. *§ 7114(b)(4).* The agencies argued that disclosure of the home addresses was prohibited by the Privacy Act of 1974. . . .

Petitioners contend that the Privacy Act prohibits disclosure. This statute provides in part:

> No agency shall disclose any record which is contained in a system of records by any means of communication to any person, or to another agency, except pursuant to a written request by, or with the prior written consent of, the individual to whom the record pertains, unless disclosure of the record would be . . . (2) required under *section 552* of this title [FOIA]. *5 U.S.C. § 552a(b)(2)* (1988 ed. & Supp. IV).

The employee addresses sought by the unions are "records" covered by the broad terms of the Privacy Act. Therefore, unless FOIA would require release of the addresses, their disclosure is "prohibited by law," and the agencies may not reveal them to the unions. . . .

We turn, then, to FOIA. As we have recognized previously, FOIA reflects "a general philosophy of full agency disclosure unless information is exempted under clearly delineated statutory language. . . ." Thus, while "disclosure, not secrecy, is the dominant objective of [FOIA]," there are a number of exemptions from the statute's broad reach. The exemption potentially applicable to employee addresses is Exemption 6, which provides that FOIA's disclosure requirements do not apply to "personnel and medical files and similar files the disclosure of which would constitute a clearly unwarranted invasion of personal privacy." *5 U.S.C. § 552(b)(6).*

Thus, although this case requires us to follow a somewhat convoluted path of statutory cross-references, its proper resolution depends upon a discrete inquiry: whether disclosure of the home addresses "would constitute a clearly unwarranted invasion of [the] personal privacy" of bargaining unit employees within the meaning of FOIA. . . .

We must weigh the privacy interest of bargaining unit employees in nondisclosure of their addresses against the only relevant public interest in the FOIA balancing analysis—the extent to which disclosure of the information sought would "she[d] light on an agency's performance of its statutory duties" or otherwise let citizens know "what their government is up to." The relevant public interest supporting disclosure in this case is negligible, at best. Disclosure of the addresses might allow the unions to communicate more effectively with employees, but it would not appreciably further "the citizens' right to be informed about what their government is up to." . . . Indeed, such disclosure would reveal little or nothing about the employing agencies or their activities. . . .

Against the virtually nonexistent FOIA-related public interest in disclosure, we weigh the interest of bargaining unit employees in nondisclosure of their home addresses. . . . Because a very slight privacy interest would suffice to outweigh the relevant public interest, we need not be exact in our quantification of the privacy interest. It is enough for present purposes to observe that the employees' interest in nondisclosure is not insubstantial.

It is true that home addresses often are publicly available through sources such as telephone directories and voter registration lists, but "[i]n an organized society, there are few facts that are not at one time or another divulged to another." The privacy interest protected by Exemption 6 "encompass[es] the individual's control of information concerning his or her person." An individual's interest in controlling the dissemination of information regarding personal matters does not dissolve simply because that information may be available to the public in some form. Here, for the most part, the unions seek to obtain the addresses of nonunion employees who have decided not to reveal their addresses to their exclusive representative. Perhaps some of these individuals have failed to join the union that represents them due to lack of familiarity with the union or its services. Others may be opposed to their union or to unionism in general on practical or ideological grounds. Whatever the reason that these employees have chosen not to become members of the union or to provide the union with their addresses, however, it is clear that they have some nontrivial privacy interest in nondisclosure, and in avoiding the influx of union-related mail, and, perhaps, union-related telephone calls or visits, that would follow disclosure.

Many people simply do not want to be disturbed at home by work-related matters. Employees can lessen the chance of such unwanted contacts by not revealing their addresses to their exclusive representative. Even if the direct union/employee communication facilitated by the disclosure of home addresses were limited to mailings, this does not lessen the interest that individuals have in preventing at least some unsolicited, unwanted mail from reaching them at their homes. We are reluctant to disparage the privacy of the home, which is accorded special consideration in our Constitution, laws, and traditions. . . .

Moreover, when we consider that other parties, such as commercial advertisers and solicitors, must have the same access under FOIA as the unions to the employee address lists sought in this case, it is clear that the individual privacy interest that would be protected by nondisclosure is far from insignificant.

Because the privacy interest of bargaining unit employees in nondisclosure of their home addresses substantially outweighs the negligible FOIA-related public interest in disclosure, we conclude that disclosure would constitute a "clearly unwarranted invasion of personal privacy." *5 U.S.C. § 552(b)(6).* FOIA, thus, does not require the agencies to divulge the addresses, and the Privacy Act, therefore, prohibits their release to the unions.

United States Department of Defense v. Federal Labor Relations
Authority, 510 U.S. 487 (1994), United States Supreme Court.

Law Enforcement Records   Law enforcement records may also be withheld, provided that disclosure would:

- interfere with enforcement proceedings
- deprive a person of a right to a fair trial or an impartial adjudication
- constitute an unwarranted invasion of personal privacy
- disclose the identity of a confidential source
- disclose investigative techniques and procedures
- endanger the life or physical safety of law enforcement personnel

This exemption applies to administrative and civil proceedings as well as criminal ones. Investigatory records are not protected forever. Once an enforcement proceeding is completed, the records become available, unless some other exemption applies.

On July 20, 1993, Vincent Foster, White House Deputy Counsel to President William J. Clinton, was found dead in a Washington, DC, park. The U.S. Park Service, the agency with jurisdiction over the park, concluded that Mr. Foster had committed suicide. To many people, however, the circumstances surrounding his death remain mysterious and both the quality and integrity of the investigation remain in question. Allan J. Favish is an individual who continued to be interested in Mr. Foster's death a full decade later. In 2004, the Supreme Court of the United States issued the following decision concerning an FOIA request submitted by Mr. Favish.

National Archives & Records Administration v. Favish 541 U.S. 157 (2004)

This case requires us to interpret the Freedom of Information Act (FOIA), 5 U.S.C. § 552. FOIA does not apply if the requested data fall within one or more exemptions. Exemption 7(C) excuses from disclosure "records or information compiled for law enforcement purposes" if their production "could reasonably be expected to constitute an unwarranted invasion of personal privacy." § 552(b)(7)(C). . . .

Vincent Foster, Jr., deputy counsel to President Clinton, was found dead in Fort Marcy Park, located just outside Washington, D.C. The United States Park Police conducted the initial investigation and took color photographs of the death scene, including 10 pictures of Foster's body. The investigation concluded that Foster committed suicide by shooting himself with a revolver. Subsequent investigations by the Federal Bureau of Investigation, committees of the Senate and the House of Representatives, and independent counsels Robert Fiske and Kenneth Starr reached the same conclusion. Despite the unanimous finding of these five investigations, a citizen interested in the matter, Allan Favish, remained skeptical. Favish is now a respondent in this proceeding. . . . [Mr. Favish sought the release of the photos.]

It is common ground among the parties that the death-scene photographs in OIC's possession are "records or information compiled for law enforcement purposes" as that phrase is used in Exemption 7(C). This leads to the question whether disclosure of the four photographs "could reasonably be expected to constitute an unwarranted invasion of personal privacy." . . .

Favish contends the family has no personal privacy interest covered by Exemption 7(C). His argument rests on the proposition that the information is only about the decedent, not his family. FOIA's right to personal privacy, in his view, means only "the right to control information about oneself." . . .

We disagree. The right to personal privacy is not confined, as Favish argues, to the "right to control information about oneself." . . .

Law enforcement documents obtained by Government investigators often contain information about persons interviewed as witnesses or initial suspects but whose link to the official inquiry may be the result of mere happenstance. There is special reason, therefore, to give protection to this intimate personal data, to which the public does not have a general right of access in the ordinary course. In this class of cases where the subject of the documents "is a private citizen," "the privacy interest . . . is at its apex." . . .

[A] sworn declaration filed with the District Court, Foster's sister, Sheila Foster Anthony, stated that the family had been harassed by, and deluged with requests from, "[p]olitical and commercial opportunists" who sought to profit from Foster's suicide. In particular, she was "horrified and devastated by [a] photograph [already] leaked to the press." "Every time I see it," Sheila Foster Anthony wrote, "I have nightmares and heart-pounding insomnia as I visualize how he must have spent his last few minutes and seconds of his life." She opposed the disclosure of the disputed pictures because "I fear that the release of [additional] photographs certainly would set off another round of intense scrutiny by the media. Undoubtedly, the photographs would be placed on the Internet for world consumption. Once again my family would be the focus of conceivably unsavory and distasteful media coverage." "[R]eleasing any photographs," Sheila Foster Anthony continued, "would constitute a painful unwarranted invasion of my privacy, my mother's privacy, my sister's privacy, and the privacy of Lisa Foster Moody (Vince's widow), her three children, and other members of the Foster family."

As we shall explain below, we think it proper to conclude from Congress' use of the term "personal privacy" that it intended to permit family members to assert their own privacy rights against public intrusions long deemed impermissible under the common law and in our cultural traditions. This does not mean that the family is in the same position as the individual who is the subject of the disclosure. We have little difficulty, however, in finding in our case law and traditions the right of family members to direct and control disposition of the body of the deceased and to limit attempts to exploit pictures of the deceased family member's remains for public purposes.

Burial rites or their counterparts have been respected in almost all civilizations from time immemorial. . . . They are a sign of the respect a society shows for the deceased and for the surviving family members. The power of Sophocles' story in Antigone maintains its hold to this day because of the universal acceptance of the heroine's right to insist on respect for the body of her brother. See Antigone of Sophocles, 8 Harvard Classics: Nine Greek Dramas 255 (C. Eliot ed. 1909). The outrage at seeing the bodies of American soldiers mutilated and dragged through the streets is but a modern instance of the same understanding of the interests decent people have for those whom they have lost. Family members have a personal stake in honoring and mourning their dead and objecting to unwarranted public exploitation that, by intruding upon their own grief, tends to degrade the rites and respect they seek to accord to the deceased person who was once their own.

In addition this well-established cultural tradition acknowledging a family's control over the body and death images of the deceased has long been recognized at common law. . . .

We have observed that the statutory privacy right protected by Exemption 7(C) goes beyond the common law and the Constitution. . . .

For these reasons, we hold that FOIA recognizes surviving family members' right to personal privacy with respect to their close relative's death-scene images. . . .

Our ruling that the personal privacy protected by Exemption 7(C) extends to family members who object to the disclosure of graphic details surrounding their relative's death does not end the case. Although this privacy interest is within the terms of the exemption, the statute directs nondisclosure only where the information "could reasonably be expected to constitute an unwarranted invasion" of the

(continued)

family's personal privacy. The term "unwarranted" requires us to balance the family's privacy interest against the public interest in disclosure. . . .

FOIA is often explained as a means for citizens to know "what the Government is up to." This phrase should not be dismissed as a convenient formalism. It defines a structural necessity in a real democracy. The statement confirms that, as a general rule, when documents are within FOIA's disclosure provisions, citizens should not be required to explain why they seek the information. A person requesting the information needs no preconceived idea of the uses the data might serve. The information belongs to citizens to do with as they choose. Furthermore, as we have noted, the disclosure does not depend on the identity of the requester. As a general rule, if the information is subject to disclosure, it belongs to all. . . .

Where the privacy concerns addressed by Exemption 7(C) are present, the exemption requires the person requesting the information to establish a sufficient reason for the disclosure. First, the citizen must show that the public interest sought to be advanced is a significant one, an interest more specific than having the information for its own sake. Second, the citizen must show the information is likely to advance that interest. Otherwise, the invasion of privacy is unwarranted. . . .

We hold that, where there is a privacy interest protected by Exemption 7(C) and the public interest being asserted is to show that responsible officials acted negligently or otherwise improperly in the performance of their duties, the requester must establish more than a bare suspicion in order to obtain disclosure. Rather, the requester must produce evidence that would warrant a belief by a reasonable person that the alleged Government impropriety might have occurred. . . .

Favish has not produced any evidence that would warrant a belief by a reasonable person that the alleged Government impropriety might have occurred to put the balance into play. [As such, Mr. Favish lost his FOIA action seeking release of four specific photos.]

National archives & Records Administration v. Favish, 541 U.S. 157 (2004),
United States Supreme Court.

The Supreme Court had occasion to interpret the personal privacy provision of the law enforcement exemption again in 2011 in *Federal Communications Commission v. AT&T*.[17] AT&T, working with the FCC, developed a program to provide discounted Internet and communication services to schools and libraries. Subsequently AT&T informed the FCC that it may have overcharged for the services. The FCC conducted an investigation and eventually reached a settlement with AT&T. When a request for all the records resulting from the investigation was made, AT&T invoked the personal privacy exemption and asked that the documents not be made public. In the wake of the Supreme Court's decision that corporations are persons for purposes of the First Amendment in *Citizens United v. Federal Election Commission*[18] in 2010, many observers wondered if AT&T would prevail. But in an unanimous decision (80) the Court held that corporations do not possess personal privacy under the FOIA and therefore the records are to be provided to the requestors.

Financial Institution Information   The eighth exemption applies to records that are "contained in or related to examination, operating, or condition reports prepared by, on behalf of, or for the use of an agency responsible for the regulation or supervision of financial institutions." There is one primary reason for exempting these records from disclosure. It is believed that public access to financial institution information may unnecessarily result in decreasing public confidence in financial institutions or even cause a panic. Weighed against the public's interest in disclosure, Congress decided that nondisclosure was justified.

Geological Information   "Geological and geophysical information, and data, including maps, concerning wells" constitutes the ninth exemption.

10.2(g) Judicial Review and Remedies

The FOIA specifically provides for judicial review. A civil action to enforce a right to disclosure under the act must be brought in a federal district court. A complainant may select one of four districts: where the complainant resides, where the complainant has its principal place of business, where the documents are located, or the District of Columbia.

For a federal court to act, it must be shown that an agency is improperly withholding documents. Exhaustion of administrative remedies is a prerequisite to obtaining a judicial remedy. The primary remedy is an injunction ordering the agency to produce improperly withheld documents.

District courts review FOIA cases de novo. Importantly, the FOIA permits *in camera* examination of records. An in camera inspection is conducted by the presiding judge, usually in chambers outside the presence of the public. An in camera inspection is used to preserve the confidentiality of documents while giving the judge the opportunity to review the records and make an informed decision. If a record contains information that may be withheld and other information that may not be withheld, the FOIA provides that the exempt portion may be deleted and the remainder disclosed.

In Camera
In chambers or in private. A hearing is in camera if conducted outside the presence of the public, such as in the judge's chambers or in a courtroom from which all spectators have been excluded.

Documents are presumed available. Therefore, the burden of proving that a document falls within an exception is upon the agency. A mere claim that information is exempt is insufficient to justify nondisclosure. A court may examine the records in camera, if necessary. The FOIA contains this strongly worded provision:

> [E]xcept as to cases the court considers of greater importance, proceedings before a district court, as authorized by this subsection, and appeals therefrom, take precedence on the docket over all cases and shall be assigned for hearing and trial or for argument at the earliest practicable date and expedited in every way.

Reviewing courts may order agencies to disclose documents deemed improperly withheld. Failure to comply with a court order is punishable as contempt of court. Attorney fees and litigation costs may be awarded by the court against the United States if a complainant "substantially prevails." Pro se litigants, as well as those represented by counsel, may receive attorney fees and costs. There are cases to the contrary, however.

In addition, if an agency employee acts arbitrarily or capriciously with respect to withholding records, the Special Counsel shall promptly initiate a proceeding to determine if the employee should be disciplined. The Special Counsel shall submit a report of findings and recommendations to the employee's employing agency for disciplinary action. The act states that the Special Counsel is to make a "recommendation," but the act states further that the employee's administrative agency *shall* take the corrective action recommended by the Special Counsel.

Note, however, that the FOIA does not create a private right of action for damages.[19] Therefore, injunctive relief (ordering the disclosure of records), with the possibility of compensation for attorney fees and litigation costs, is the primary remedy available to aggrieved persons under the FOIA.

SIDEBAR   *President Kennedy's Assassination and the FOIA*

Public access to information concerning the assassination of President Kennedy has been hotly disputed for more than 20 years. One man, Harold Weisberg, has been involved in more than 10 different suits to compel disclosure of information regarding the assassination under the FOIA.

Mr. Weisberg, as well as other persons and organizations, have been successful in obtaining a plethora of information under the FOIA. In one case alone, the U.S Court of Appeals for the District of Columbia Circuit noted that the Federal Bureau of Investigation had provided Mr. Weisberg with more than 200,000 pages of information in an effort to satisfy his FOIA request.[20] Regardless, much information concerning President Kennedy's assassination has been withheld under the law enforcement and national defense exemptions mentioned in this chapter.

In reaction to strong public opinion favoring disclosure of the records, Congress enacted the President John F. Kennedy Assassination Records Collection Act.[21] Although this act does not create a private right to demand disclosure of information from agencies, it does require agencies possessing such records to organize them and to transmit them to the National Archives, where they will, with few exceptions, be made available to the public.[22]

10.2(h) Congressional Monitoring

In an effort to monitor the administration of the FOIA, Congress requires that each agency submit a yearly report to the Speaker of the House of Representatives and President of the Senate; the report is then referred to the appropriate committees. The agency report must include the following: the number of times the agency refused to produce records and the reasons for those refusals; the number of appeals of agency refusals and the results of these appeals; the name and title of each person denying a request and the number of denials each issued; the results of each disciplinary proceeding against agency employees for noncompliance with the FOIA; a copy of each rule promulgated concerning the FOIA; a copy of each agency's fee schedule and total fees collected; and other information concerning administration of the FOIA. In addition to each agency's report, the Attorney General is directed to report the number of cases arising under the FOIA; the exemptions involved in each case; the disposition of each case; the costs, fees, and penalties imposed; and an explanation of any efforts the Department of Justice has taken to encourage agency compliance with the FOIA.

10.3 PRIVACY ACT

Privacy Act
Federal statute requiring that certain private information held by the government not be disclosed.

The antithesis of the FOIA is the **Privacy Act**.[23] The purpose of the FOIA is to make governmental records available to the public; the purpose of the Privacy Act is to withhold sensitive documents from public disclosure. The Privacy Act is also found in the APA, entitled "Records maintained on individuals." This reflects the act's goal of protecting the privacy of records collected and maintained about individuals, not other governmental records. *Records* are defined as "any item, collection, or grouping of information about an individual that is maintained by an agency, including, but not limited to, his education, financial transactions, medical history, and criminal and employment history and that contains his name, or the identifying number, symbol, or other identifying particular assigned to the individual, such as finger or voice print or a photograph."

The Privacy Act 5 U.S.C. § 522(a)	
Purpose	To safeguard the privacy of individuals by establishing a set of rules governing the collection and dissemination of private information.
Presumptions	1. Only relevant and necessary information about individuals will be collected and maintained. 2. An individual may access information maintained pertaining to him or her. 3. Written consent for disclosure must be obtained before the government may disclose information about an individual.

Exemptions	Information about an individual may be disclosed by the government without obtaining the individual's consent if one of the Act's 11 exemptions applies:
	  1. To agency officials who need the information to perform their duties
	  2. Disclosure is required by FOIA
	  3. Routine use
	  4. To the Bureau of Census
	  5. For statistics and reporting, where individuals will not be identified
	  6. To the National Archives
	  7. To law enforcement officials
	  8. Compelling circumstances when health or safety of a person is at issue
	  9. To Congress or one of its committees
	  10. To the Comptroller General
	  11. Pursuant to a court order

FIGURE 10-4   Privacy Act summary.

The heads of some agencies may promulgate rules exempting certain records from the requirements of the Privacy Act. The agency must include in the rules a statement of reasons for the exemption. Records maintained by the Central Intelligence Agency are specifically exempted, as are records that concern the enforcement of criminal laws,[24] protection of the president and other individuals, the armed services, and other materials.[25] Figure 10-4 summarizes the Privacy Act provisions.

10.3(a) Collection of Information

The Privacy Act does not prohibit agencies from collecting information about people. It does, however, restrict an agency's authority to collect information. The act limits the collection of information about individuals by agencies maintaining a "system of records" to that information "necessary to accomplish a purpose of the agency required to be accomplished by statute or executive order of the President." *Individual* has been interpreted not to include businesses.

The act also requires that, to the greatest extent practicable, personal information be collected directly from the individual if the information might adversely affect the individual. In its request for information, the agency must inform the individual of its authority to make the request, whether disclosure is voluntary or involuntary, for what purpose the information will be used, the routine uses that may be made of the information, and the consequences of not providing the information.

The Privacy Act defines *routine use* as the use of a record for a purpose compatible with the purpose for which it was collected. The term *system of records* means a group of records under the control of an agency from which information may be retrieved by the name of an individual or by some other number or symbol assigned to an individual.

10.3(b) Maintaining Records, Publication, and Rules

An agency must maintain all records that it uses in making any determination about an individual with such accuracy, relevance, timeliness, and completeness as is reasonably necessary to ensure fairness to the individual. Before an individual's records can be disclosed to a requester, the agency must make a reasonable effort to ensure that the records are accurate, complete, timely, and relevant for agency purposes. In addition, the act specifically forbids maintaining a record on how any person exercises his or her rights under the First Amendment to the U.S. Constitution, unless authorized to do so by statute or such information is within the scope of a law enforcement activity.

An agency must make reasonable efforts to inform an individual that his or her records are being made available to another under compulsory legal process, whenever such action will result in the record becoming public.

Agencies are required to establish rules of conduct for persons involved with the design, development, operation, or maintenance of any records. The agency must instruct such persons in the rules and penalties for violating the rules. Agencies must also establish safeguards to protect against threats or hazards to the security of records that could result in harm, embarrassment, inconvenience, or unfairness to an individual. Individuals' names and addresses may not be sold or rented by an agency unless otherwise authorized by Congress. This prevents public records from being sold as mailing lists.

The act also imposes a publication requirement on agencies. At least once a year, each agency must publish in the *Federal Register* notice of its system of records, including the name and location of the system; the categories of individuals included in the system; each routine use of records; its policies and practices regarding the storage, retrievability, access controls, retention, and disposal of records; who is responsible for maintaining the system; the procedures whereby individuals can be provided with copies of their files and contest their contents; and the categories of sources of the records.

Agencies must promulgate rules to carry out the requirements of the Privacy Act. Such rules shall include necessary procedures and fees. The Office of the Federal Register is required to publish all such rules annually.

10.3(c) Disclosure of Records

The Privacy Act prohibits the disclosure of any record, which is part of a system of records, to any person or other agency unless the agency obtains the consent of the individual to whom the information pertains or unless one of the act's 12 (13 including consent of the individual who is the subject of the record) other exemptions applies. Recall that information about individuals comes only within the Privacy Act definition of *record*; therefore, most records are not within the ambit of the Privacy Act. Including consent disclosures, the act contains 12 exceptions to the nondisclosure requirement:

1. The individual to whom the records pertain may consent to disclosure.
2. To agency employees who need the information to perform their duties is permitted.
3. When required by the FOIA. Therefore, unless one of the nine FOIA exceptions applies, the Privacy Act does not prohibit disclosure of records that fall within the FOIA. (The relationship between the FOIA and the Privacy Act is discussed more fully later.)

4. For routine use.
5. To the Bureau of the Census is allowed for purposes of planning or carrying out a census or related activity.
6. To individuals who ensure that the records will be used solely for statistical research or a reporting record, and the agency must first redact any information that identifies individuals.
7. To the National Archives is permitted in some circumstances.
8. To another agency is permitted if the agency head makes a written request explaining a law enforcement activity for which the record is sought.
9. To a person who has made a showing of compelling circumstances, when disclosure will affect the health and safety of an individual.
10. To either body of Congress.
11. To the Comptroller General or his or her representatives as necessary to the performance of their duties.
12. To satisfy court orders.
13. To consumer reporting agencies in accordance with other law.

Agencies are required to keep a record of each disclosure made, including the date, nature, and purpose of each disclosure, and the name and address of the person or agency to whom the disclosure was made. This record shall be kept for five years or the life of the record, whichever is longer. The period begins to run when the disclosure is made. An accounting of these disclosures, except those provided for law enforcement, is to be provided on request to the individual whom the records concern.

10.3(d) Relationship of FOIA and Privacy Act

As mentioned earlier, the Privacy Act specifically exempts records that fall within an FOIA exemption. To say the least, this is confusing. Legal scholar Dean Spader asserts that to understand this complexity, one must understand the conflicting values underlying the two laws. "The Freedom of Information Act (FOIA) and the Privacy Act illustrate the inherent tension between society's need for the free flow of information and the individual's need for personal, intimate, and confidential spheres of privacy." He emphasizes the importance of understanding that both positive values and negative values are connected to both disclosure and nondisclosure of information (see Table 10-1). Mr. Spader identifies those values as follows:[26]

To the list of positive values of publicity, this author adds having a more efficacious government. That is, openness not only prevents governmental abuse and citizen distrust of the government, but also provides the public with the data necessary to help them better understand issues, to support better decision making, and to be better citizens. The FOIA and Privacy Act exist at the two extremes of these different, but not necessarily conflicting, value systems. The two laws, in short, strike a balance between the two value systems. The Supreme Court has reaffirmed the importance of protecting the privacy of individuals through the Privacy and FOIA Acts. In Reporters Committee the Court held that the purpose of the FOIA is to shed light on government and government officials, not individuals. Accordingly, releasing information about individuals that does not inform the public about the operations of their government would not advance the objectives of the FOIA and would undermine the objectives of the Privacy Act.

When analyzing requests for disclosure, the FOIA will almost always apply. The Privacy Act, however, applies in far fewer cases. It applies *only* to data about

TABLE 10-1 Relationship between the FOIA and the Privacy Act	
Privacy: Positive Values	**Publicity: Positive Values**
Preserves individual need for sphere of personal, private, intimate facts: the "individual's right to be" left alone."	Promotes society's need for truth, accountability, communal facts: "public's right to know.
Preserves individuality, trust, autonomy, and the "right to remain silent."	Promotes community of shared knowledge, visibility, and "state's evidence."
Preserves personal facts, control, personal independence, and dignity.	Promotes social facts, social control, social interdependence, and awareness.
Preserves desired silence, confidential relationships, and secluded information.	Promotes desired communication, knowledgeable public, and free flow of information.
Preserves freedom from coercion, excluded facts; encourages trusting communication.	Promotes disclosure, discovery, openness, and efficiency; encourages revelation of facts and accuracy.
Privacy: Negative Values	**Publicity: Negative Values**
Sacrifices the public's need to know for the rights of a few.	Sacrifices the privacy rights of a few for the good of the public.
Allows excessive secrecy, chilling of the truth, and invisible decisions "behind closed doors."	Allows excessive exposure, flagrant notoriety, and loss of control under the "white glare of publicity."
Allows hiding of the truth, deception, and behind-the-scenes actions.	Creates excessive snooping, intrusion, and a glass-house society.
Allows circumvention, connivance, chicanery, sly decisions off the record, and star chamber proceedings.	Creates excessive rumors, leaks, eavesdroppings, scandal mongering, and a dossier society
Allows shameful fraud, and hollow mockery of fact investigations.	Creates premature dissemination, washes dirty linen in public, allows excessive gossip, and creates false light.

Source: Dean J. Spader, *Conflicting Values and Laws: Understanding the Paradox of the Privacy Act and the Freedom of Information Act*, 19 Legal Studies Forum 21, 24–25 (1995).

individuals. So, the plethora of government reports and documents that do not include private, individual information are not covered by the Privacy Act. If the data sought satisfies the definition of a *record* (any item, collection, or grouping of information about an individual that is maintained by an agency, including, but not limited to, his education, financial transactions, medical history, and criminal and employment history and that contains his name, or the identifying number, symbol, or other identifying particular assigned to the individual, such as finger or voice print or a photograph) under the Privacy Act, then both the FOIA and Privacy Act must be co-applied.

As you can see, the practical outcome of the Privacy Act is to convert the discretionary nondisclosures under the FOIA to mandatory nondisclosures. That is, if the record sought is about an individual and one of the FOIA's nine exemptions applies, an agency may not disclose the record. When the same FOIA exemption is applied to a record that does not contain information about an individual, the decision whether to release the record is left with the agency. If the requestor is the subject of the record itself, then disclosure is required in more, but not all,

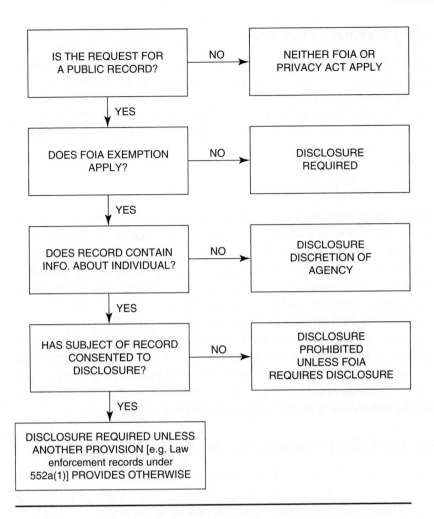

FIGURE 10-5   Anaytical map of request for records under FOIA: Privacy Acts.

circumstances. One of the exceptions is found in 552a(j), which allows agency heads to exempt "systems of records" from disclosure to the individual who is the subject of the record if the record is held by the CIA or for other law enforcement purpose. This prevents spies and wrongdoers from demanding investigative records on themselves or their colleagues in crime. Through this rule, Congress has limited the public's access to private information but assured the individual's right to access records about himself or herself. Hence, the following three scenarios are possible in regard to data about individuals:

1. FOIA requires disclosure (e.g., no FOIA exemption applies). In such cases, the Privacy Act does not apply and disclosure is required.

2. FOIA permits nondisclosure (an FOIA exemption applies) and the requestor is a member of the public. In such cases, the Privacy Act prohibits disclosure (unless one of its exemptions applies).

3. FOIA permits nondisclosure (an FOIA exemption applies) and the requestor is the subject of the record. In such cases, the Privacy Act requires disclosure, unless one of its exemptions applies. An example of a record that may be withheld, even from the person who is the subject of the record, is a record of an ongoing criminal investigation of the individual. Table 10-1 at the beginning of this section highlights the relationship between the FOIA and the Privacy Act.

10.3(e) Individual Access

On request, individuals must be given access to their records or to information about them contained in an agency's records (see Figure 10-6). Individuals must be given the opportunity to review and copy these records. Individuals may bring a person of their own choosing when reviewing the records. Any person may be selected to accompany an individual; a lawyer, family member, or technical expert is commonly chosen.

10.3(f) Amending Records

Individuals are also permitted to request amendment of their records if the records contain inaccurate, irrelevant, untimely, or incomplete information (see Figure 10-7). The agency must, within 10 days (excluding Saturdays, Sundays, and holidays) after receiving a request for amendment, either make a correction or inform the individual that it will not make the correction, stating the reason for the decision and the procedure for appealing the decision to a higher agency official.

Once the individual appeals to the higher agency official (agency head or designee), the agency must issue a final decision promptly. However, this may be extended for good cause for as much as 30 days by the agency head. If the final decision is not favorable to the individual, he or she is permitted to file with the agency a concise statement explaining his or her position. In addition, the agency must notify the individual of the right to judicial review.

10.3(g) Judicial Review and Remedies

The Privacy Act contains both civil and criminal provisions.

Civil Actions   Individuals may file a civil action against an agency if

- a request for amendment of a record is denied;
- an individual is not permitted access to his or her own records;
- the agency fails to maintain a record with the required accuracy, relevance, timeliness, or completeness, and a determination adverse to the individual is made; or
- an agency fails otherwise to comply with the Privacy Act in such a way as to adversely affect the individual.

Venue under the Privacy Act is identical to venue under the FOIA. The lawsuit may be filed in the district where the complainant resides, where the complainant has its principal place of business, where the records are located, or the District of Columbia. The action must be filed within two years after the cause of action arises, or within two years after the date the individual discovers that the agency engaged in willfully misrepresenting material information. Legal guardians are specifically authorized to bring lawsuits under the Privacy Act on behalf of their wards.

The court is to review the agency's action de novo. The reviewing court has the authority to order the amendment of records, the production of records, or that records be withheld. As is true with FOIA actions, the court may conduct an in camera review of the records in question. The burden of proof lies with the agency. In camera review is discussed in the *Ray* case.

REQUEST—FOR ACCESS TO INFORMATION ON
INDIVIDUAL—PRIVACY ACT OF 1974 [5 USCS § 552a(d)(1)]

PRIVACY ACT REQUEST

[Address]
To: _____ [Agency head or Privacy Act Officer]
[Title]
[Name of agency]
Dear _____ *[Name]:*
 Under the provisions of 5 USCS § 552a and _____ CRF § _____, I hereby
request _____ [a copy of *or* access to] the following records: _____ *[describe as
accurately and specifically as possible, and provide all available relevant information].*
 If there are any fees for copying the records I am requesting, please _____ [inform
me before you fill the request *or* supply the records without informing me if the fees do not
exceed $ _____].
 If all or any part of this request is denied, please cite the specific exemption(s) which you
think justifies your refusal to release the information. Also, inform me of your agency's appeal
procedure.
 In order to expedite consideration of my request, I am enclosing a copy of
my _____ *[specify document of identification, such as: current driver's license issued by the
State of _____ or Social Security Card].*
 Thank you for your prompt attention to this matter.
 Dated _____.

               [Signature and address]

FIGURE 10-6 Request for access to information on individual.

REQUEST—FOR AMENDMENT OF RECORD—
PRIVACY ACT OF 1974 [5 USCS § 552a(d)(2)]

PRIVACY ACT AMENDMENT REQUEST

To: _____ *[Agency head or Freedom of Information Officer]*
[Title]
[Name of agency]
[Address]
Dear _____ *[Name]:*
 By letter dated _____, I requested access to the following records: _____.
 In viewing the information forwarded to me, I found that it was _____ *[specify defect,
such as:* inaccurate *or* incomplete *or* outdated *or* not relevant to the purpose of your agency], in
that _____ *[describe errors].*
 Therefore, pursuant to 5 USCS § 552a and ____ CRF § ____ I hereby request that you
amend my record in the following manner: _____ *[specify deletions, corrections, or
additions desired].*
 In accordance with the Privacy Act, I look forward to an acknowledgment of this request
within 10 working days of its receipt.
 Thank you for your assistance in this matter.
 Dated _____.

               [Signature and address]

FIGURE 10-7 Request for amendment of record.

Ray v. Turner 587 F.2d 1187 (D.C. Cir. 1978)

Plaintiffs (appellants) Ellen Ray and William Schaap sent identical letters to the CIA requesting "a copy of any file you may have on me." The CIA replied that while it did not have files on plaintiffs, there were documents in CIA files that referred to plaintiffs. The CIA refused to release those documents, and after administrative appeals were exhausted, plaintiffs brought this action under the FOIA. The CIA subsequently released portions of the withheld documents, and the government then moved for summary judgment, relying principally on affidavits of one Eloise Page. The critical affidavit, set out in the appendix, purports to describe the documents at issue and the grounds for the government's claims of exemption.

The district court granted the government's motion for summary judgment and denied plaintiff's motion for *in camera* inspection. . . . In the case at bar, the district court observed: "With respect to documents withheld under exemption 3, *in camera* inspection is seldom, if ever, necessary or appropriate." The legislative history does not support that conclusion. Congress left the matter of *in camera* inspection to the discretion of the district court, without any indication of the extent of its proper use. The ultimate criterion is simply this: Whether the district judge believes that *in camera* inspection is needed in order to make a responsible de novo determination on claims of exemption.

In camera inspection requires effort and resources and, therefore, a court should not resort to it routinely on the theory that "it can't hurt." When an agency affidavit or other showing is specific, there may be no need for *in camera* inspection.

On the other hand, when the district judge is concerned that he is not prepared to make a responsible de novo determination in the absence of *in camera* inspection, he may proceed *in camera* without anxiety that the law interposes an extraordinary hurdle to such inspection. The government would presumably prefer *in camera* inspection to a ruling that the case stands in doubt or equipoise and hence must be resolved by a ruling that the government has not sustained its burden [of proving that an exemption applies]. . . .

In camera inspection does not depend on a finding or even tentative finding of bad faith. A judge has discretion to order *in camera* inspection on the basis of an uneasiness, on a doubt he wants satisfied before he takes responsibility for a de novo determination. Government officials who would not stoop to misrepresentation may reflect an inherent tendency to resist disclosure, and judges may take this natural inclination into account.

Case, Ray v. Turner, 587 F.2d 1187 (D.C. Cir. 1978),
United States Court of Appeals, District of Columbia Circuit.

Reasonable attorney fees and litigation costs may be assessed against the United States in any case in which the complainant substantially prevails. If a court determines that an agency intentionally or willfully violated the Privacy Act, the United States shall be liable for actual damages resulting from such behavior; however, the recovery shall not be less than $1,000. Delay caused by oversight or incompetence does not amount to a willful violation under the Privacy Act.[27] In addition, reasonable attorney fees and costs are to be awarded when a willful violation is proven.

Common law actions, such as invasion of privacy and infliction of emotional distress, may also be available. A government employee who intentionally discloses private or sensitive information may be sued under one of these theories.

Criminal Penalties   The Privacy Act also provides for criminal penalties. Two provisions apply to governmental employees and one to all people:

1. Any governmental employee who discloses a record that the employee knows is required to be withheld under the Privacy Act is guilty of a misdemeanor and may be fined as much as $5,000.

2. Any governmental employee who willfully maintains records without satisfying the notice requirements of the act is guilty of a misdemeanor and may be fined as much as $5,000.

3. Any person who knowingly and willfully requests or obtains any record concerning an individual under false pretenses is guilty of a misdemeanor and may be fined as much as $5,000.

10.3(h) Congressional Monitoring

The reporting requirements are different for the Privacy Act than for the FOIA. There are two requirements. First, each agency must provide notice to Congress and the Office of Management and Budget of any proposal to establish or alter any system of records.

Second, the president is required to submit annually to the Speaker of the House of Representatives and the President of the Senate a report on all agency systems of records. This report is to include an explanation of exemptions.

10.4 GOVERNMENT IN THE SUNSHINE ACT

A fundamental tenet of democracy is openness of government. The more open and available the government is, the greater the public's confidence and participation in government will be. This is the foundation of the FOIA. It is also the basis of the Government in the Sunshine Act,[28] which generally requires that agency meetings be open to public observation: "[E]very portion of every meeting of an agency shall be open to public observation."

The act applies only to "collegial" agencies—that is, agencies that are headed by more than one person. There is no requirement that a single agency head make his or her deliberations public. On the surface, this appears necessary, but it is rare for an agency head to deliberate alone; other agency employees are likely to be involved in the process. It is debatable whether such deliberations should be public. There is currently no such requirement, and exceptions to the rule that collegial bodies must conduct open meetings exist.

10.4(a) Exemptions

Agencies do not have to conduct open meetings if such meetings will result in the disclosure of specific types of information. The matters exempted are similar to those exempted from the coverage of the FOIA—in fact, many are identical. Unless the public interest requires otherwise, there is no open-meeting requirement if any of the following information is likely to be disclosed:

- Matters of national defense and foreign policy that have been properly classified as secret pursuant to an executive order
- Matters that relate solely to internal personnel rules and practices of an agency
- Matters exempted from disclosure by another statute, provided the statute leaves no discretion on the issue or establishes specific criteria for withholding
- Trade secrets or commercial or financial information obtained from an individual
- An accusation of a crime or formal censure

- Matters of a personal nature, the disclosure of which amounts to a clearly unwarranted invasion of personal privacy
- Investigatory records compiled for law enforcement purposes and related information
- Matters concerning the regulation and supervision of financial institutions
- Information that will endanger the stability of a financial institution or lead to significant speculation in currencies, securities, or commodities
- Matters concerning an agency's issuance of a subpoena, participation in a civil proceeding, participation in a foreign proceeding, an arbitration, and other agency actions

Meetings are presumed to be open and may be closed only if one of the exemptions applies. In some circumstances, the public interest may demand that a meeting remain open even though one of the exemptions applies. If a separate statute requires that a meeting remain open, it may not be closed. The reason for closing a meeting must be certified by the agency, and the decision to close a meeting must be made by majority vote of the agency heads.

Agencies are to keep a complete audio record or transcript of all closed meetings. In some circumstances, such as when a meeting is closed because it concerns the regulation and supervision of financial institutions, a set of minutes may be maintained in the alternative. The record shall be maintained for two years or one year after the conclusion of an agency proceeding, whichever is longer. The agency is to make the minutes, transcript, or audio recording promptly available to the public, except to the extent such information is exempted.

10.4(b) Judicial Review and Remedies

The district courts of the United States are vested with the jurisdiction to review claims brought under the Sunshine Act. Venue lies in the district in which the agency meeting is held, in the district where the agency has its headquarters, or in the District of Columbia.

Declaratory judgment, injunctive relief, and other appropriate relief are expressly made available. The burden is on the agency to justify closure or other violation. Reviewing courts may examine the record in camera and take additional evidence. The Sunshine Act does not create a right to injunctive or declaratory relief for past violations; it is intended only to remedy an existing violation.[29]

Attorney fees and litigation costs may be awarded to plaintiffs who "substantially prevail." That is, costs and fees can be assessed against the United States. Defendants may be awarded fees and costs only if the court determines that the plaintiff filed a frivolous or dilatory lawsuit.

10.4(c) Congressional Monitoring

Every agency must report to Congress annually. A tabulation of the total number of public agencies, the number of closed meetings, the reasons for closing those meetings, and all related litigation must be included in that report.

10.5 FEDERAL ADVISORY COMMITTEE ACT

The Government in the Sunshine Act requires that agency meetings be conducted in public. However, a number of advisory committees in the federal government are not administrative agencies, and therefore, are not included within the coverage of the Sunshine Act. The Federal Advisory Committee Act (FACA) is intended to deal with these entities.[30]

An *advisory committee* is not charged with the administration of law. It has no authority to enforce laws, make rules, conduct investigations for violations of law, or adjudicate cases. Advisory committees are created solely to give advice to administrative agencies. Final decisions must be made by the appropriate agency officials.

Advisory committees may be known as committees, councils, panels, task forces, commissions, or other names. An advisory committee may be created by Congress, the president, or an administrative agency. President Clinton's health reform task force, created in 1993, was an example of such an entity. Hillary Rodham Clinton was appointed to head this group, which included a number of agency officials, such as the heads of the departments of Health and Human Services, Treasury, Commerce, Labor, Defense, Veterans Affairs, and Management and Budget.

The FACA recognizes the importance of these committees, but also establishes rules to govern their behavior and existence. The FACA makes it clear that such committees are to make only recommendations, not final decisions. An advisory committee is to be created only when necessary and is to be disbanded upon completion of its work.

Most important, the FACA requires advisory committees to leave their meetings open to the public, with few exceptions (such as when national security would be jeopardized by a public meeting). Furthermore, notice of public meetings must be published in the *Federal Register*. Interested persons are to be given an opportunity to appear and make a statement or to file a statement with the committee. Detailed minutes of meetings are to be maintained.

10.6 TRADE SECRETS ACT

Finally, another statute, the Trade Secrets Act,[31] prohibits the disclosure of trade secrets and related information by government employees. The act provides that trade secrets possessed by the government are not to be disclosed unless disclosure is required by another law. An unlawful disclosure of information covered by the Trade Secrets Act is a crime punishable by up to one year of imprisonment, a fine, and termination of employment.

10.7 PRIVATIZATION AND THE PUBLIC'S RIGHT TO KNOW

The drafters of the APA and FOIA did not foresee the privatization revolution that would besiege government at the end of the 20th century and continue into the 21st century. Thus, the drafters did not make it clear whether the FOIA is to be applied to the myriad of private parties that provide services to, and receive funding from, the federal government.

Clearly, the accountability objective of the FOIA can be undermined if private parties performing governmental functions are exempt from the FOIA. This is especially troubling when governments contract services that have been traditionally considered core governmental functions, such as operating prisons. However, little public good is served by opening the laboratory records of a lone researcher who receives a small federal research grant and whose research could be threatened by premature public disclosure.

The statute defines *agency* as "any executive department, military department, Government corporation, Government controlled corporation, or other establishment in the executive branch of the Government . . ., or any independent regulatory agency."[32] Although this definition appears to include all federal government agencies, to the exclusion of all private parties, it does not further define when a private party performing governmental functions, receiving governmental monies, or acting under the authority of the government is to be treated as a government-controlled corporation, executive department, or independent regulatory agency. The leading Supreme Court case addressing this issue is *Forsham v. Harris*.

Forsham and subsequent cases indicate that the following factors will be considered by reviewing courts when deciding whether a private party is subject to open government regulations:[33]

- The extent to which the government manages the daily operations of the agency
- The extent to which the government regulates the agency
- The extent to which the government funds the agency
- The amount of authority delegated to the agency by the government (e.g., rulemaking, taxing, and adjudicatory authorities)
- Whether the agency is performing a core government function, especially those involving civil liberties

10.8 CONCLUSION

Public access to information and government meetings is important to governmental accountability. The FOIA requires disclosure except in well-defined circumstances. The Privacy Act, as well as other specific statutes, protects people from overzealous information gathering and from disclosures of sensitive information.

Privatization poses a new problem for the legislative scheme dealing with access to governmental information. The FOIA, for example, was drafted with the assumption that most governmental operations would be performed by agencies that are easily identified as governmental. However, that is no longer true. Today, myriad private parties receive governmental grants, awards, and contracts. Some perform governmental services, others perform public but not necessarily governmental services, and there are those who are engaged in the arts and sciences. If these services can be characterized as a governmental function, or if the private parties or their services are directly operated or supervised by the federal government, open government laws will likely apply. Otherwise, open government laws do not apply.

Forsham v. Harris

445 U.S. 169 (1980)

In 1959, a group of private physicians and scientists specializing in the treatment of diabetes formed the University Group Diabetes Program (UGDP). The UGDP conducted a long-term study of the effectiveness of five diabetes treatment regimens. . . .

The UGDP's participating physicians were located at 12 clinics nationwide and the study was coordinated at the Coordinating Center of the University of Maryland.

The study generated more than 55 million records documenting the treatment of over 1,000 diabetic patients who were monitored for a 5- to 8-year period.

In 1970, the UGDP presented the initial results of its study indicating that the treatment of adult-onset diabetics with tolbutamide increased the risk of death from cardiovascular disease over that present when diabetes was treated by the other methods studied. The UGDP later expanded these findings to report a similarly increased incident of heart disease when patients were treated with phenformin hydrochloride. These findings have in turn generated substantial professional debate.

The Committee on the Care of the Diabetic (CCD), a national association of physicians involved in the treatment of diabetes mellitus patients, have been among those critical of the UGDP study. CCD requested the UGDP to grant it access to the raw data in order to facilitate its review of the UGDP findings, but UGDP has declined to comply with that request. CCD, therefore, sought to obtain the information under the Freedom of Information Act. . . .

The essential facts are not in dispute, and we hereafter set forth those relevant to our decision. The UGDP study has been solely funded by federal grants in the neighborhood of $15 million between 1961 and 1978. These grants were awarded UGDP by the National Institute of Arthritis, Metabolism, and Degenerative Diseases (NIAMDD), a federal agency, pursuant to the Public Health Service Act, *42 U.S.C. § 241(c)*. NIAMDD has not only awarded the federal grants to UGDP, but has exercised a certain amount of supervision over the funded activity. Federal regulations governing supervision of grantees allow for the review of periodic reports submitted by the grantee and on-site visits, and require agency approval of major program or budgetary changes. *45 CFR §§ 74.80–74.85 (1979); 42 CFR § 52.20(b) (1979)*. It is undisputed, however, both that the day-to-day administration of grant-supported activities is in the hands of a grantee, and that NIAMDD's supervision of UGDP conformed to these regulations.

The grantee has also retained control of its records: the patient records and raw data generated by UGDP have at all times remained in the possession of that entity, and neither the NIAMDD grants nor related regulations shift ownership of such data to the Federal Government. NIAMDD does, however, have a right of access to the data in order to insure compliance with the grant. *45 CFR § 74.24(a) (1979)*. And the Government may obtain permanent custody of the documents upon request. *§ 74.21(c)*. But NIAMDD has not exercised its right either to review or to obtain permanent custody of the data.

Although no employees of the NIAMDD have reviewed the UGDP records, the Institute did contract in 1972 with another private grantee, the Biometric Society, for an assessment of the validity of the UGDP study. The Biometric Society was given direct access to the UGDP raw data by the terms of its contract with NIAMDD. The contract with the Biometric Society, however, did not require the Society to seek access to the UGDP raw data, nor did it require that any data actually reviewed be transmitted to the NIAMDD. While the Society did review some UGDP data, it did not submit any raw data reviewed by it to the NIAMDD. The Society issued a report to the Institute in 1974 concluding that the UGDP results were "mixed" but "moderately strong." An additional connection between the Federal Government and the UGDP study has occurred through the activities of the Food and Drug Administration. After the FDA was apprised of the UGDP results, the agency issued a statement recommending that physicians use tolbutamide in the treatment of diabetes only in limited circumstances. After the UGDP reported finding a similarly higher incidence of cardiovascular disease with the administration of phenformin, the FDA proposed changes in the labeling of these oral hypoglycemic drugs to warn patients of cardiovascular hazards. . . . The FDA deferred further action on this labeling proposal, however, until the Biometric Society completed its review of the UGDP study. . . .

We first examine petitioners' claim that the data were at least records of UGDP, and that the federal funding and supervision of UGDP alone provides the close

(continued)

> connection necessary to render its records "agency records" as that term is used in the Freedom of Information Act. Congress did not define "agency record" under the FOIA, but it did define "agency.". . .
>
> Under *5 U.S.C. § 552(e)* an "agency" is defined as "any executive department, military department, Government corporation, Government controlled corporation, or other establishment in the executive branch of the Government . . . , or any independent regulatory agency." The legislative history indicates unequivocally that private organizations receiving federal financial assistance grants are not within the definition of "agency.". . .
>
> This treatment of federal grantees under the FOIA is consistent with congressional treatment of them in other areas of federal law. Grants of federal funds generally do not create a partnership or joint venture with the recipient, nor do they serve to convert the acts of the recipient from private acts to governmental acts absent extensive, detailed, and virtually day-to-day supervision. . . .
>
> Congress could have provided that the records generated by a federally funded grantee were federal property even though the grantee has not been adopted as a federal entity. But Congress has not done so, reflecting the same regard for the autonomy of the grantee's records as for the grantee itself. . . .
>
> We think the foregoing reasons dispose of all petitioners' arguments. We, therefore, conclude that the data petitioners seek are not "agency records" within the meaning of the FOIA. UGDP is not a "federal agency" as that term is defined in the FOIA, and the data petitioners seek have not been created or obtained by a federal agency. Having failed to establish this threshold requirement, petitioners' FOIA claim must fail, and the judgment of the Court of Appeals is accordingly Affirmed.

Forsham v. Harris, 445 U.S. 169 (1980), United States Supreme Court.

LAWLINKS

Nearly all government agencies have their rules and other information concerning FOIA requests on their Web sites. The Federal Bureau of Investigation has an interesting site that contains that agency's responses to requests for information on famous people, famous events, and unusual occurrences. This information can be obtained at www.fbi.gov by clicking on the Famous Cases link in the index found on the home page.

Many nongovernment sites have information on how best to use the FOIA. The American Civil Liberties Union, for example, has a guide where sample forms and suggestions for using the FOIA can be found. Go to *www.aclu.org* for this information.

REVIEW **QUESTIONS**

1. What is the Freedom of Information Act? What is its purpose?
2. List the nine exemptions to the FOIA.
3. What is the Privacy Act? What is its purpose?
4. List the exemptions to the Privacy Act.
5. What is the Government in the Sunshine Act? What is its purpose?

CRITICAL THINKING AND **APPLICATIONS PROBLEMS**

1. Grace Yang requests the Federal Bureau of Investigation (FBI) to provide all records maintained on Kenneth, an applicant for employment with her company. This request is denied. Grace believes the decision was incorrect. Unbeknownst to her, Kenneth is currently being investigated by the FBI. Stacey has a friend, Eva Ping, who works at the Department of Health and Human Services. Eva checks her office's records and discovers an application for benefits filed by Kenneth. In that application Kenneth states that he is receiving psychological counseling and has attempted suicide. Eva provides this information to Grace.

   a. Was Grace's request properly denied? If not, what remedies are available to her?

   b. Kenneth discovers Eva's disclosure. Was the disclosure proper? If not, what remedies are available to him?

2. After working for the Internal Revenue Service (IRS) as an auditor and investigator for 10 years, Grace resigns. She then applies for employment at the New Enterprise Company (NEC), a private business that conducts background checks. Eva works for NEC and her position includes the responsibility of interviewing and hiring all new employees. After reviewing Grace's application and interviewing Grace, Eva denies her application for employment. Curious about the reasons for her denial, Grace files a FOIA request with the IRS and learns that Eva had also filed a FOIA request for any information about Grace that the IRS holds. In response to her request, the IRS informed Grace that they gave Eva the following documents and information:

   - Grace's former *home addresses*;
   - Grace's college *transcripts* that she provided the IRS at the time of application for her prior job;
   - a *letter* from Grace's supervisor that recommended against hiring her for a position involving sensitive data;
   - a copy of the written *decision* of an administrative law judge (ALJ) in a case filed by Grace against the IRS in which she challenged the results of an audit

done by the IRS on *her own tax return*. Grace appealed the initial decision in the audit to an ALJ. In the official decision, the ALJ ruled in favor of the IRS and ordered Grace to pay back taxes and interest penalties.

   - The *report* of the internal investigation of Grace by the IRS concerning allegations involving two audits that Grace conducted for two taxpayers whom she appeared to know personally. The allegations suggested that the taxpayers and Grace stayed at the same hotel in the Bahamas, and flew to and from the Bahamas on the same flight (and were assigned three seats together on both flights), all of which occurred prior to the audit. Grace claimed that she did not know or remember the two taxpayers from the flights and thus did not recuse herself or turn their audits over to another auditor within the IRS. The investigation found insufficient evidence to cite her for a violation of internal, operational rules of the IRS. However, the report concluded as follows: "Although we uncovered no unreported income of the two taxpayers, nor any undue influence on Grace as an auditor, we believe that she violated the spirit of the rules by not reporting her relationships prior to or in her final report of the audit."

   Grace comes to you, her attorney, and asks you to write her a memo explaining the FOIA, the Privacy Act, and whether she has any rights under either act that have been violated.

   Explain the conflicting values and limitations of each act, and how the two acts interrelate to offset the negative values of the other. Then, starting with the FOIA, explain the major provisions of each act, citing and applying any specific rules or exceptions in the FOIA that may pertain to Grace's case. Next, explain the Privacy Act and its major provisions, citing and applying any specific rules or exceptions that may pertain to Grace's case. Finally, if you find that any of Grace's rights under either act have been violated, state the remedies available to her under the act. End with your prediction of whether Grace will prevail.

ENDNOTES

1. 5 U.S.C. §552.
2. *NLRB v. Robbins Tire & Rubber Co.*, 437 U.S. 214, 242 (1978).
3. See *Mv. v. Young*, 568 U.S. ___ (2013).
4. The FOIA Project, found at http://trac.syr.edu/foiaproject/foia_requests.shtml.
5. *Id.*
6. *Irons v. Schuyler*, 465 F.2d 608 (D.C. Cir. 1972).
7. *United States Department of Justice v. Tax Analysts*, 492 U.S. 136 (1989).
8. *North v. Walsh*, 881 F. 2d 1088 (D.C. Cir. 1989)
9. 5 U.S.C. § 552(a)(4)(A).

10. *Antonelli v. Drug Enforcement Admin.*, 739 F.2d 302 (7th Cir. 1984).

11. Attorney Gen. John Ashcroft, memorandum dated October 12, 2001.

12. Gillum, J. and Bridis, T., FOIA Requests Being Denied Due to Security Reasons More than in Any Time Since Obama Took Office, March 11, 2013, *Huffington Post*; Timm, T., Under Obama, the Freedom of Information Act is Still in Shackles, *Electronic Frontier Foundation*, January 26, 2012. Found at http://www.eff.org/deeplinks/2012/01/under-obama-administration-freedom-information-act-still-shackles

13. FOIA Lawsuits Increase During Obama Administration, The FOIA Project. December 20, 2012. Found at http://foiaproject.org/2012/12/20/increase-in-foia-lawsuits-during-obama-administration/

14. *Chrysler Corp. v. Brown*, 441 U.S. 294 (1979).

15. L. K. Davis, *Administrative Law* (2nd ed. 1978).

16. *Rural Hous. Alliance v. U.S. Dep't of Agric.*, 498 F.2d 73 (D.C. Cir. 1974).

17. 562 U.S. ___ (2011).

18. 558 U.S. 310 (2010).

19. *Gale v. U.S. Dep't of Justice Fed. Bureau of Prisons*, 628 F.2d 224 (D.C. Cir. 1980).

20. *See Weisberg v. Webster*, 749 F.2d 864 (D.C. Cir. 1984).

21. Pub. L. No. 102926, 106 Stat. 3443 (1992).

22. *See Assassination Archives & Research Center v. U.S. Department of Justice*, 1993 U.S. Dist. LEXIS 5569 (1993).

23. APA § 552(a).

24. *Doe v. FBI*, 936 F.2d 1346 (D.C. Cir. 1991).

25. APA § 552a(k).

26. Dean J. Spader, *Conflicting Values and Laws: Understanding the Paradox of the Privacy Act and the Freedom of Information Act*, 19 Legal Studies Forum 21, 24–25 (1995).

27. *Perry v. Block*, 684 F.2d 121 (D.C. Cir. 1982).

28. APA § 552b.

29. *Hastings v. Judicial Conference*, 770 F.2d 1093 (D.C. Cir. 1985).

30. 5 U.S.C. app. 1.

31. 18 U.S.C. § 1905.

32. This does not include the president or vice president, who is subject to a presidential records law. It also does not apply to special committees and task forces created by the president to render him advice so long as such groups do not possess "substantial independent authority." *Meyer v. Bush*, 981 F.2d 1288 (D.C. Cir. 1993).

33. See Craig Feiser, *Privatization and the Freedom of Information Act: An Analysis of Public Access to Private Entities under Federal Law*, 52 Fed. Comms. L.J. 125 (1999).

chapter eleven

ACCOUNTABILITY THROUGH LIABILITY

LEARNING OBJECTIVES

After completing this chapter, you should be able to

- Identify and describe the historic source of governmental immunity.

- Describe the arguments both in favor of and in opposition to immunity for governments and government officers.

- Describe the various common law immunities that applied to official government actors and governments

- Identify and describe the various forms of federal and state governmental liability and apply those to given fact scenarios

- Describe the architecture (who may sue and be sued, the elements, and basic process) of the Federal Tort Claims Act, including its purpose, the basic rule, and its exceptions. You should be able to do the same for constitutional claims, common law claims, and Tucker Act claims against governments.

- Describe the architecture (who may sue and be sued, the elements, and basic process) of Section 1983 actions, the degree to which immunities limit §1983 actions against governments and government officials, and the remedies available under § 1983.

- Apply the law of governmental liability and immunities to private actors when they are performing governmental functions.

- Explain the circumstances that can lead to private parties being treated like government officials for purposes of the liabilities covered in this chapter

- Apply the liabilities described in this chapter to cases involving free speech and takings

- Brief a judicial opinion with little outside assistance. You should be successful in identifying the relevant facts. You should also be successful in identifying the legal issue and analyzing the court's rationale in at least 75 percent of your briefs. Describe the history and current state of the Sovereign Immunity Doctrine in the United States

A sovereign is exempt from suit, not because of any formal conception or obsolete theory, but on the logical and practical ground that there can be no legal right as against the authority that makes the law on which the right depends.

JUSTICE HOLMES[1]

The strongest support for sovereign immunity is provided by that four-horse team that often seems so powerful— historical accident, habit, a natural tendency to favor the familiar, and inertia.

KENNETH CULP DAVIS[2]

11.1 INTRODUCTION

Governments are responsible for providing a multitude of public services, many of which are critical to the health, welfare, and safety of the public. Many also involve significant risks and expenditures. Government provides its services without a profit incentive, and its revenues are derived from the people. Liability can jeopardize government objectives, but lack of government liability leaves those with valid claims against the government uncompensated. The extent to which the public fisc should be subject to attack for government error is controversial. Few agree with the Holmes quotation that opened this chapter, but many agree that some limitation on government liability must exist.

This chapter examines the law of government liability, including both public (agency) liability and the liability of those who act under the authority of a government. This is different from the issues you already examined when studying judicial review. The remedies discussed in the chapter on judicial review were limited to reversing, modifying, and compelling agency action. The APA does not govern money damages claims. This chapter is concerned with damages and injunctive relief.

Having a system in which governments and their employees can be liable to pay for the injuries they cause is surely a tool for controlling discretion and preventing abuse. This is not, however, the only purpose served by determining culpability for the misdeeds of government. Providing compensation to harmed citizens is another equally important objective of government liability.

Nevertheless, government liability is more limited than is personal liability. There are several doctrines and immunities, many developed from the old common law, that bar recovery from the government even if negligence or otherwise legally wrong behavior can be proved. This discussion will begin with the long-standing doctrine of sovereign immunity.

11.2 SOVEREIGN IMMUNITY

In old England, the crown could do no wrong; the king or queen could not be held accountable to the people for his or her actions. This theory is the historical sources of the doctrine of ***sovereign immunity***, which holds that the government is immune from suit.

LEGAL TERM

Sovereign Immunity
Doctrine holding that the government is immune or free from liability.

The doctrine of sovereign immunity was accepted and adopted by states early in American history, albeit not without criticism. In England, the crown was sovereign. However, in the United States, the people are sovereign. One court stated: "In preserving the sovereign immunity theory, courts have overlooked the fact that the Revolutionary War was fought to abolish that 'divine right of the kings' on which the theory was based."[3] For this reason, many contend the doctrine has no place in a democracy. Contemporary proponents of the doctrine focus on its financial aspect. Whether the government would be truly threatened by greater liability is beyond the scope of this text. Be aware, though, that there is a substantial body of authority criticizing sovereign immunity.

Regardless of the controversy, it is generally held that the government must consent to be sued. This is true of both the federal government and state governments because all are constitutionally sovereign. In a few states, sovereign immunity has been abolished or limited by judicial decision. In most instances, however, a citizen's right to sue the government is derived from the legislature. This is true of the federal government; the United States is liable only to the extent it has authorized suit or when liability is constitutionally imposed.

This chapter examines government liability with special attention to the United States. Before your attention is turned to liability of the federal government and its employees, a few basic principles about state liability should be mentioned. Like the federal government, the state by their individual constitutions, enjoys sovereign immunity. However, most, if not all, have in some form and to varying degrees, waived their sovereign immunity.

The Eleventh Amendment also immunizes states from liability in federal court. However, there are exceptions. Although a state and its employees may not be sued for damages, a plaintiff may sue a state, through its officers, in federal court for a prospective order requiring the official to comply with federal law. This is known as the Ex Parte Young Doctrine, named for the case (*Ex Parte Young*, 209 U.S. 123 [1908]) where the U.S. Supreme Court announced the exception to the Eleventh Amendment. The federal government also conditions the receipt of certain federal monies on the state's waiver of immunity from federal laws. For example, states must waive immunity for violations of the Individuals with Disabilities Education Act in order to qualify for funds to support special education programs. Additionally, the Eleventh Amendment does not immunize political subdivisions of the states, such as counties and cities. The U.S. Supreme Court has held this includes political subdivisions that do not act as an "arm of the State."[4] 547 U.S. 189 (2006). (The County was not entitled to immunity because it failed to demonstrate that it was acting as arm of the State when operating a drawbridge.)

With these basic principles of state liability presented, let's now turn to the liability of the federal government, including the liability of government employees, officials, and officers when performing their official duties. The liability of the government officials is discussed because plaintiffs often choose to sue a government employee rather than (or in addition to) the government itself. This may be done because although the government itself may not be sued in some instances, its officers may be liable. Also, a plaintiff may believe that the officer is at fault and should be held personally liable, or a statute may require the officer to be named.

In any event, officers may be sued in either an *individual capacity* or an *official capacity*. A lawsuit against an officer in his or her individual capacity is the same as suing the officer personally. A lawsuit against an officer in his or her official capacity is the same as suing the government[5]. However, a suit against an official in an official capacity that seeks injunctive relief, as opposed to monetary damages, is a suit against the individual, not the government[6].

Although a governmental entity does not have respondeat superior liability[7] for all conduct of its employees, because a lawsuit against an officer in his or her official capacity is the same as suing the government, judgments against an officer in their official capacity are paid by the governmental employer. By statute, 28 U.S.C.S. § 2679 requires judgments against officers sued in their individual capacity to likewise be paid by the governmental employer. However, if an officer's conduct is so outrageous as to be deemed outside his or her scope of employment, it abrogates the governmental employer's obligation to indemnify him or her. [8] For the purposes of 28 U.S.C.S. § 2679, "scope of employment" is defined by the respondeat superior law of the state where the incident occurred. See *Sandoval v. Martinez-Barnish*, 435 F. App'x 775, 778 (10th Cir. 2011). For example, if the incident at issue in the federal lawsuit occurred in Ohio, the federal court would apply the respondeat superior law of Ohio. Under Ohio law, if a police officer's misconduct rises to the level of "willful or wanton," his or her governmental employer is not obligated to indemnify judgments obtained against the officer in his or her individual capacity.

By suing an administrative agency, a plaintiff is likewise suing the governmental entity itself. Therefore, the rules discussed in this chapter that apply to government liability apply to actions naming the government itself (e.g., state of Florida) and those naming an agency of the government (e.g., Department of Justice of the United States) as defendant.

11.3 FEDERAL TORT CLAIMS ACT AND ITS EXCEPTIONS

In 1946, the Federal Tort Claims Act (FTCA) was enacted by Congress to give private parties the right to sue the United States in federal court for certain torts committed by persons acting on behalf of the United States.[9] Through this statute, the United States has partially waived immunity from suit for a number of specific torts. The law is found in several sections of Title 28 in the United States Code. The basic waiver of 28 U.S.C. § 1346 provides that federal courts shall have

> Exclusive jurisdiction of civil actions on claims against the United States, for money damages . . . for injury or loss of property, or personal injury or death caused by the negligent or wrongful act or omission of any employee of the Government while acting within the scope of his office or employment, under circumstances where the United States, if a private person, would be liable to the claimant in accordance with the law of the place where the act or omission occurred.[10]

This creates the general rule of liability of the United States for torts. There is no federal tort common law, nor any federal statutory law other than is provided for by the FTCA. Despite the rather broad scope of the waiver initially set forth in §1346, the FTCA contains a number of exceptions which function to then place limitations on the federal government's liability,[11] three of which are discussed here.

The number of claims brought under the Federal Torts Claims Act against the United States is continually increasing. More than 3,000 FTCA suits are pending at any one time and involve more than $5 billion in claims. About 1,500 new FTCA suits are filed each year.

11.3(a) Executive Functions

The first FTCA exception is for specific administrative functions and for claims arising in foreign nations. The "foreign nation" exception bars all claims against the federal government based on any injury suffered in a foreign country, regardless of where the tortious act or omission giving rise to that injury occurred.[12] (Prohibiting a lawsuit under the FTCA for an arbitrary arrest that was planned in the United States but carried out in a foreign country). These exceptions are built on separation of powers principles and are premised on the theory that internal administrative matters and foreign affairs are particularly executive in nature and typically outside the purview of courts.

11.3(b) Intentional Torts

The second FTCA exception is an exclusion of liability for "any claim arising out of assault, battery, false imprisonment, false arrest, malicious prosecution, abuse of process, libel, slander, misrepresentation, deceit, or interference with contractual rights."[13] However, this provision was amended in 1974 to allow liability for assault, battery, false imprisonment, false arrest, abuse of process, or malicious prosecution committed by law enforcement officers. Libel, slander, misrepresentation, deceit, and interference with a contractual right—even by law enforcement officers—continue to be protected by immunity.

The FTCA's detailed listing of specific intentional torts suggests that only the torts mentioned are to be excluded. Courts have held this exception does not apply to actions that fall outside the scope of the general waiver of the FTCA, including claims of sexual harassment, invasion of privacy, and wrongful death.[14]

11.3(c) Discretionary Function Doctrine

The third FTCA exception shields the federal government from liability for "discretionary"—as opposed to "ministerial"—acts of government employees, officers, and officials. This exception applies even if an agency abuses its discretion. Its purpose is to prevent the judicial branch from second guessing legislative and administrative decisions grounded in social, economic, and political policy.[15]

The distinction between what is a "discretionary" and what is a "ministerial" function is not always clear. An act is *discretionary* if it involves making a choice from a variety of options. Discretionary acts involve judgment, planning, and policy decisions. The greater the policy considerations, the more likely the decision will enjoy immunity.

Conversely, if the law requires the performance of a specific act or applies specific standards to the performance of an act, then the act is likely *ministerial*, or, as some courts characterize it, *operational*. Similarly, once a discretionary decision to act is made, the remaining acts employed to carry out the decision are usually deemed ministerial.

For example, the decision whether to fight a fire is discretionary, whereas fighting the fire is ministerial. The same is true of rescues, treating patients, installing safety devices, constructing government facilities, or conducting inspections. Specific examples of federal cases distinguishing between ministerial and discretionary acts include *LeGrande v. United States*, 687 F.3d 800, 808 (7th Cir. 2012) (Federal Aviation Administration's determination as to which weather products are useful to pilots is a discretionary function), and *Kohl v. United States*, 699 F.3d 935 (6th Cir. 2012) (Department of Energy's decisions about how to extract evidence from the site of an explosion, and what types of equipment to use to do so, were discretionary and thus shielded from liability).

The *Bowers* case further illustrates the distinction between discretionary and ministerial functions. Although it is a state case rather than a case arising under the FTCA, it provides a good illustration of the distinction between ministerial and discretionary functions.

Bowers v. City of Chattanooga

826 S.W.2d 427 (Tenn. 1992)

In this personal injury action, brought under the Tennessee Governmental Tort Liability Act, we granted Plaintiff's application for permission to appeal in order to determine the sole issue of whether [Tenn. Code Ann.] § 29-20-205 (1) (1980) protects the defendant City of Chattanooga from a suit alleging negligence on the part of a public school bus driver. The minor plaintiff Danny Leon Bowers, his mother, and his father, brought suit to recover for injuries sustained when he was struck by an automobile shortly after departing from a Chattanooga Public School bus. . . .

Six-year-old Danny Bowers, who was in the first grade of the Chattanooga Public School System, was injured on September 9, 1986, when he was struck by an automobile as he attempted to cross Dodds Avenue shortly after disembarking from a school bus owned and operated by the Chattanooga Public School System. The automobile that struck Danny Bowers was driven by Brett A. Newmyer and owned by John Newmyer. The Newmyers were originally named as defendants in this case; they and the Plaintiffs have entered into a settlement agreement.

Dodds Avenue is a congested four-lane street in central Chattanooga that runs north to south. Pro Re Bona Day Care Center is located in the northwest quadrant of the intersection of Dodds Avenue and 18th Street; 18th is a stop street which crosses Dodds in an east-west direction. There are no traffic controls for Dodds Avenue traffic at 18th. The entrance to Pro Re Bona is located on the 18th Street side of the building. In 1980 or 1981, the Transportation Division of the Chattanooga Public School system established a school bus stop at the day care center.

Danny lived with his mother and grandmother on the east side of Dodds Avenue, across the street from the day care center. Throughout his 1985-86 kindergarten school year, and for approximately the first four weeks of school of the 1986-87 school year, Danny Bowers rode a public school bus, getting on and off at the Pro Re Bona stop.

Every school day prior to the day of the accident, Danny Bowers was accompanied to and from the bus stop by his mother or grandmother. They would walk him across Dodds Avenue in the morning, meeting him in the afternoon, and accompany him back. . . .

The bus route, established by the Chattanooga School System Transportation Division, did not designate precisely where the bus was to stop, only that its stop was the "Pro Re Bona Nursery.". . .

On the day of the accident, September 8, 1986, a change was made in the bus schedule. Because of overcrowded conditions, the School System's Transportation Department decided that the children who normally disembarked at the Pro Re Bona bus stop would ride a different bus with a different driver. Under this new schedule, the bus carrying Danny arrived at the day care center approximately ten minutes earlier than under the old schedule.

On September 9, the bus did not stop on Dodds Avenue, but only at the 18th entrance to the day care center. Danny got off the bus there and began walking east towards Dodds Avenue. Because of the bus's earlier arrival (of which Danny's mother had no prior notice), his mother did not meet him on the west side of Dodds. She had just arrived at the east side of Dodds Avenue when Danny began crossing Dodds with other students. She unsuccessfully tried to tell him to wait, but Danny attempted to cross Dodds and was hit by the car driven by Brett Newmyer. . . .

I

With respect to the threshold issue of immunity, section 29-20-205 of the Tennessee Tort Liability Act (the "Act") provides in part:

> Immunity from suit of all governmental entities is removed for injury proximately caused by a negligent act or omission of any employee within the scope of his employment except if the injury: (1) arises out of the exercise or performance or failure to exercise or perform a discretionary function, whether or not the discretion is abused.

While the Act does not define "discretionary function," this Court has repeatedly applied the following common law definition:

> Where the duty is absolute, certain and imperative, and is simply ministerial, the officer is liable in damages to any one specially injured, either by his omitting to perform the task or by performing it negligently or unskillfully. On the other hand, where his powers are discretionary, and to be exerted or withheld according to his own judgment, he is not liable to any private person for a neglect to exercise those powers, nor for the consequences of a willful exercise of them, where no corruption or malice can be imputed to him, and he keeps within the scope of his authority.

We find that time has come to provide more guidance with respect to which activities are within the grasp of the "discretionary function" exception. . . . Today we approve of the analysis that determines which acts are entitled to immunity by distinguishing those performed at the "planning" level from those performed at the "operational" level. As Chief Justice Shepard of Indiana said in *Pearl v. Board of Commissioners*, 528 N.E.2d 40, 45 (Ind. 1988):

> The distinction between planning and operational functions is a standard, rather than a precise rule. The focus must remain on the policy underlying governmental immunity. If the act is one committed to coordinate branches of government involving policy decisions not reviewable under traditional tort standards of reasonableness, the government is immune from liability even if the act was performed negligently.

Under the "planning-operational" test, decisions that rise to the level of planning or policy-making are considered discretionary acts which do not give rise to tort liability, while decisions that are merely operational are not considered discretionary acts and, therefore, do not give rise to immunity. The distinction between planning and operational depends on the type of decision rather than merely the identity of the decision maker. . . .

(continued)

Under the planning-operational test, discretionary function immunity does not automatically attach to all acts involving choice or judgment. Such an analysis recognizes that, to some extent, every act involves discretion. . . .

A consideration of the decision-making process, as well as the factors influencing a particular decision, will often reveal whether that decision is to be viewed as planning or operational. If a particular course of conduct is determined after consideration or debate by an individual or group charged with the formulation of plans or policies, it strongly suggests the result is a planning decision. These decisions often result from assessing priorities; allocating resources; developing policies; or establishing plans, specifications, or schedules.

On the other hand, a decision resulting from a determination based on preexisting laws, regulations, policies, or standards, usually indicates that its maker is performing an operational act. . . . Another factor bearing on whether an act should be considered planning or operational is whether the decision is the type properly reviewable by the courts. The discretionary function exception "recognizes that courts are ill-equipped to investigate and balance numerous factors that go into an executive or legislative decision" and, therefore, allows the government to operate without undue interferences by the courts. . . .

The decision by the City to change the bus route for children utilizing the Pro Re Bona stop was a planning/policy decision of the type intended to be immune from judicial challenge. Scheduling is a prime example of an act which involves a balancing of factors, an assessing of priorities, and an allocation of available resources. . . .

There being a clear plan and policy of the State of Tennessee and City of Chattanooga to provide safe passage across an immediate street towards a child's destination, we find that a decision left to a school bus driver on where to stop at a particular intersection is an operational act not within the discretionary function exception to governmental immunity.

Bowers v. City of Chattanooga, 826 S.W.2d 427 (Tenn. 1992), Supreme Court of Tennessee.

There is no bright line between discretionary and ministerial functions. In reality, most decisions and actions have both discretionary and ministerial functions. The best way to distinguish between the two is to read all the cases from your jurisdiction in which courts have addressed the ministerial/discretionary issue, paying particular attention to the facts of each.

11.3(d) Scope of Employment

Finally, the government is liable only for acts of its employees, officers, officials, or other agents who are acting within the scope of their employment. If an officer performs some act outside the scope of employment that injures another, the government is not liable. This is true even if the injury occurred during working hours or was caused by government property, such as a vehicle.

To determine whether an employee is acting within the scope of his employment for the purposes of the FTCA, courts look at the law of the state where the alleged tortious acts took place.[16] For example, South Dakota courts consider factors such as: "(1) whether the act is commonly done in the course of business; (2) the time, place, and purpose of the act; (3) whether the act is within the enterprise of the master; the similarity of the act done to the act authorized; (4) whether the means of doing harm has been furnished by the master; and (5) the extent of departure from the normal method of accomplishing an authorized result."[17] Similarly, in Texas, courts look to whether the alleged tortious acts were "(1) within the general authority given [the employee]; (2) in furtherance of the employer's business; and (3) for the accomplishment of the object for which the employee was employed."[18]

11.3(e) Public Duty Doctrine

A cousin to both sovereign immunity and the discretionary function doctrine, the public duty doctrine immunizes both governments and their officials for acts that are owed to the public generally and no specific duty is owed to an individual. In short, this doctrine holds that a duty to all translates as a duty to no one. The public duty doctrine is founded on a separation of powers theory. Public agencies provide a public service, and, accordingly, owe the public at large a duty. The performance of a public duty is checked by political processes. Government officials who are not adequately serving the public are subject to removal by the voters at election or by other elected officials. The public duty doctrine keeps courts from meddling in the affairs of the other two branches of government.

However, the courts have also held that it is possible for public officials to cross the line and convert their duty to an individual one. For example, police officers owe a general public duty to prevent crime. No duty to an individual exists unless a special relationship exists or the police increase the danger of victimization to an individual. Thus, everyday victims of crime may not sue the police under the theory that more could have been done to prevent the crime.

In *Marin v. United States*, a case similar to *Kirk v. City of Shawnee*, 27 Kan. App. 2d 946, 10 P.3d 27 (2000) (discussed in detail next), a court of a different jurisdiction held that federal officials did have a duty to protect a woman against the attack of a stalker. However, the difference in the two outcomes is explained by examining the differences in the facts of each case. The plaintiffs in *Marin* were the three surviving children of a woman who was murdered. The murderer, Quintil Lopez-Fuentes, was a federal prisoner who was released at the request of the Immigration and Naturalization Service to work undercover for the agency. Immediately after his release, Lopez-Fuentes absconded. Records indicate that the United States was aware that Lopez-Fuentes was infatuated with the victim; had a history of harassing her; had assaulted her, had a record of rape, theft, and intimidating witnesses; and had threatened the victim's life. In spite of this, the United States did not notify Marin that Lopez-Fuentes had escaped. The court found that because the United States was responsible for securing Lopez-Fuentes's release, failed to adequately supervise him once released, and was aware of the danger he posed to the victim, the duty to prevent the crime was personal to Marin.

Kirk v. City of Shawnee

---

27 Kan. App. 2d 946, 10 P. 3d 27 (2000)

Appellants James S. Kirk, as heir at law, and Darlene Mullin, as executrix of the estate of Kathryn Stewart Morse, deceased, sued the City of Shawnee (City) for the police department's failure to protect Morse from her estranged husband. Appellants appeal from the entry of summary judgment in favor of the City.

Kathryn Stewart Morse and Roland James Morse were married. In September 1997, Kathryn filed for divorce in Johnson County District Court. On September 15, 1997, she filed a petition for protection from abuse (PFA). At this time, the court issued a temporary PFA order, prohibiting Roland from contacting Kathryn or entering their house in Shawnee. Roland also was ordered to turn over a handgun to the sheriff.

On September 16, 1997, Kathryn completed a "house watch" form and delivered it to the Shawnee Police Department. The form indicated that she had a PFA order against Roland, that he had threatened her life, and that he possessed a gun.

(continued)

On September 17, 1997, Kathryn called the Shawnee Police Department to report that Roland had violated the PFA order. The police dispatcher confirmed a PFA order had been entered and dispatched an officer to Kathryn's residence to take a report. However, Kathryn was not at home when she made the call, but was in the police station. By the time the dispatcher determined the source of the call, Kathryn had left. On the same day, Shawnee police were notified that Roland had removed a gun from the house prior to being served with court papers and that Roland was extremely upset.

On September 18, 1997, Kathryn obtained a long-term PFA order—valid for 5 months—which prohibited Roland from entering or approaching their residence. The order contained the statutory language stating: "Law enforcement officers are directed to grant any assistance necessary to protect the plaintiff . . . from abuse by the defendant, and to provide any assistance necessary to enforce these orders."

In addition, the PFA order allowed Roland access to the residence the evening of September 18 and all day September 19 to remove personal belongings and business records. During the hearing, Kathryn's attorney commented they wanted a third person in the house while Roland was there, and the court agreed it was a good idea. During this hearing, Roland advised the court he had taken the revolver he was ordered to deliver to the sheriff and had delivered it to his son for safekeeping.

Kathryn talked to a police dispatcher in the mid-afternoon of September 18. This conversation was recorded. During the conversation with the dispatcher, Kathryn advised the dispatcher that Roland had changed his arrival time and they were "shooting for" 7:30 p.m. Kathryn told the dispatcher "I will let you know as soon as I know."

Minutes later, Kathryn talked with Sergeant Rob Moser. Kathryn advised Moser her husband had threatened her in the past and had a gun. When she asked for police presence at the home while Roland was there, Sergeant Moser advised Kathryn they could not keep an officer at her home for extended periods of time. He suggested she call a private security company or talk to another officer about police officers who might be willing to provide security while off-duty. Sergeant Moser offered to send two officers to her home, if they were available, for a short period of time when Roland arrived. Sergeant Moser specifically advised Kathryn to call back shortly before or when Roland arrived and they would send officers over to the home for a few minutes. Sergeant Moser also advised Kathryn to stay near the phone and to call 911 if matters deteriorated.

That same day, Kathryn's aunt, Geraldine (Gerry) Stewart, called and requested an officer to come out and protect Kathryn. Stewart wanted an officer to come out to stay with them while Roland was in the house. There was no indication Roland was at the house or what time this call took place. Again, the dispatcher advised they could not send out a police officer simply to sit there while Roland was there for an extended period of time.

The next day, Roland shot and killed Kathryn at their home and then killed himself. At the time, Tommy Smith (a friend of a friend) was at Kathryn's house to provide her some protection. According to Smith, Roland arrived that morning, went down to the basement, and began taking boxes out of his truck. Smith, Kathryn, and Stewart were eating in the kitchen when Roland reentered the home with a shotgun. Roland used the gun to force Smith out the door of the house. The shootings then occurred.

Under policies of the Shawnee Police Department at the time, certain standards were established for enforcing PFA orders, including completing reports on all violations of a PFA order. The standards provided that the department's policy was the "vigorous enforcement of laws relating to domestic violence." Dispatchers were required to give domestic violence calls the same priority as any other life-threatening call. The department also had a policy for assisting in civil matters (a "civil standby") in order to preserve the peace in situations involving evictions, transfer of custody of children, and other civil matters.

In 1998, appellants James S. Kirk, Kathryn's son, and Darlene Mullin, the executrix of Kathryn's estate, filed a wrongful death and survivor action against the City and Roland's estate. The appellants claimed the City had breached a specific duty owed to Kathryn and had been negligent in failing to protect her from Roland. In answering the petition, the City asserted it was immune under the Kansas Tort Claims Act (KTCA), K.S.A. 75-6101

et seq. . . .

THE PUBLIC DUTY DOCTRINE

When a negligence claim is asserted against a governmental agency, the court must consider the so-called "public duty doctrine." That doctrine establishes the general principle that a governmental agency owes duties to the public at large rather than to individuals. *Fudge v. City of Kansas City*, 239 Kan. 369, 372, 720 P. 2d 1093 (1986). Under this doctrine, the fact the governmental entity owes a legal duty to the public at large does not establish a basis for an individual to claim the agency owed a legal duty to him or her personally.*Jarboe v. Board of Sedgwick County Comm'rs*, 262 Kan. 615, 631, 938 P. 2d 1293 (1997). No duty exists unless the plaintiff establishes that the agency owed a special duty to the injured party. *Fudge*, 239 Kan. at 372, 720 P. 2d 1093.

Situations where a "special duty" have been found vary greatly. However, the cases generally fall into two categories. One is where a special relationship existed between the governmental agency and the wrongdoers (i.e., the State has custody of the wrongdoer). See, e.g., *Cansler v. State*, 234 Kan. 554, 564-65, 675 P. 2d 57 (1984) (State correctional officials owe a special duty to nearby residents to exercise reasonable care in maintaining prison security and issuing warnings when dangerous inmates escape); *Washington v. State*, 17 Kan. App. 2d 518, 523, 839 P. 2d 555, rev. denied. 252 Kan. 1095 (1992) (prison officials owe duty of reasonable care to safeguard a prisoner in their custody or control from attack by other prisoners). The second category involves cases where a special relationship existed between the agency and the injured person. See, e.g., *C.J.W. v. State*, 253 Kan. 1, 12, 853 P. 2d 4 (1993) (State had duty to warn of a detained child's propensity toward violence and to protect other children in custody from the violent child); *Nero*, 253 Kan. at 584-85, 861 P. 2d 768 (state university, as landlord of dormitory students, had duty to protect students from reasonably foreseeable dangers, including other students known to be dangerous).

On the other hand, tort claims against a governmental entity have been dismissed on a number of occasions because no special duty was owed to the plaintiff. In *P.W. v. Kansas Dep't of SRS*, 255 Kan. 827, 877 P. 2d 430 (1994), for example, the Kansas Supreme Court held that state regulatory agencies did not owe a special duty to children in state-licensed daycare centers to protect them from abuse. 255 Kan. at 833-34, 877 P. 2d 430. Likewise, SRS and its agents also owed no special duty to allegedly abused children or alleged child abusers to avoid negligence in investigation of allegations of child abuse. See *Burney v. Kansas Dep't of SRS*, 23 Kan. App. 2d at 398, 931 P. 2d 26 (no special duty owed to man accused of child abuse); *Beebe v. Fraktman*, 22 Kan. App. 2d 493, 496, 921 P. 2d 216 (1996) (no special duty owed to allegedly abused child to protect him from the alleged abuser).

Similarly, the public duty doctrine applies to policing functions as well. For example, in *Robertson v. City of Topeka*, 231 Kan. 358, 363, 644 P. 2d 458 (1982), the court held that a law enforcement officer owed no special duty to a homeowner when the officer refused to remove a trespasser from the premises.

In this case, appellants seem to be arguing [that] the PFA order imposed a specific duty on the City to protect Kathryn from her husband. Appellants cite the

(continued)

language of the order requiring law enforcement to provide assistance, as well as the police department's policies, to support his contention.

While the existence of the PFA order indicates there were problems of violence between Kathryn and Roland, the order clearly does not put either of them within the control of the police department sufficient to create an individualized duty of care. Absent a special relationship, there is no duty to control the conduct of a third party to prevent harm to others. *Schmidt v. HTG, Inc.*, 265 Kan. 372, Syl. ¶ 4, 961 P. 2d 677, *cert. denied*, 525 U.S. 964, 119 S. Ct. 409, 142 L. Ed. 2d 332 (1998).

In this case, the facts do not fall within any of the cases discussed above that recognize special relationships creating a duty. Moreover, in light of the *Schmidt* case, finding such a special relationship under the present facts is unjustified. In *Schmidt*, the Supreme Court held a special relationship did not exist between a parolee and his parole officer to create a duty on the parole officer to warn others about the parolee's status or propensities. 265 Kan. at 387-90, 961 P. 2d 677. If a special relationship did not exist in *Schmit*, it clearly could not exist in this case.

[8] A special duty to an individual also can be created when the governmental entity performs an affirmative act that causes injury or where it made a specific promise or representation that under the circumstances creates a justifiable reliance on the part of the person injured. *P.W. v. Kansas Dep't of SRS*, 255 Kan. at 835-37, 877 P. 2d 430. Appellants contend Kathryn relied on the government's affirmative acts promising protection.

Appellants' contentions are not supported by the facts or the law. The only citation to the record to support Kathryn's alleged reliance is the deposition testimony of Stewart, who testified that Kathryn understood after the PFA hearing that a police officer would be present when Roland came to the house. Nothing in the transcript from that hearing indicates that any governmental official (and certainly not an agent of the City) told Kathryn that police would be present during the periods her husband was allowed to be in the house. Likewise, there is no evidence that Kathryn was aware of, or relied upon, any of the police department policies regarding domestic abuse cases or civil standbys. Moreover, even if a promise was made at the courthouse at the time of the PFA hearing, the record shows Kathryn was advised that afternoon, by both a police dispatcher and a police sergeant, that police officers could not be provided for any extended period when Roland was allowed, by court order, to be in the house. The only "promise" made was that the department would send over a couple of officers, if they were available, to Kathryn's home if she called them right before or when Roland arrived; she was told these officers would stay for a brief period, presumably to make a point to Roland that the police were concerned. There was no evidence that Kathryn called the department when Roland arrived on the evening of September 18 or the next day, when the shootings occurred.

Finally, appellants rely on the PFA order's language which required all "[l]aw enforcement officers" to "grant any assistance necessary to protect the plaintiff . . . from abuse by the defendant." While the Shawnee Police Department knew of the order, the order did not (and should not be read to) require the department to provide police protection 24 hours a day, 7 days a week, nor to be guarantors of Kathryn's safety. The court specifically allowed Roland to be in the house on September 18 or 19, but made no specific order requiring police to be present. From the transcript of the PFA hearing, while it is clear that the court believed it would be a good idea if a third person were present, the order did not expressly or impliedly require the City to provide constant police presence during this period.

For these reasons, the trial court correctly found the City did not owe an individualized duty to Kathryn under the facts of this case. The PFA order did not create the type of obligation appellants seek to impose on the City in this case. Moreover, there is no evidence the City made any promise of constant protection on which Kathryn relied. Finally, there is no special relationship between the City and either Roland or Kathryn other than the same duty police owe to members of the public in general. Absent a basis for an individualized duty to Kathryn, the appellants' claim fails as a matter of law.

[The court further held that the city was also shielded from liability under the discretionary function doctrine.]

Kirk v. City of Shawnee, 27 Kan. App. 2d 946, 10 P. 3d 27 (2000), Kansas Judicial Branch.

Just as distinguishing between discretionary and ministerial functions is not always easy, neither is drawing the line between public and individual duties. An otherwise public duty may be converted into a personal one if any of these questions are answered in the affirmative:

1. Did government officials create the risk that caused the plaintiff's injuries?
2. Did government officials increase the risk of injury to the plaintiff?
3. Did government officials aggravate an existing injury of the plaintiff's?
4. Did government officials have custody of or in some other way control the plaintiff?
5. Did government officials have a legal duty to this person by ordinance, custom, policy, contract, statute, or other law?

The public duty doctrine is not specifically mentioned in the FTCA, but because the FTCA requires the application of state law, the doctrine applies in those states that recognize the public duty doctrine. Furthermore, because the discretionary function doctrine is expressly provided for in the FTCA, the discretionary function doctrine applies to all claims against the United States.

In addition to these limitations on liability, there is also a significant limitation on the damages that can be obtained from the United States.

11.3(f) Damages and Other Limitations

Congress has decided that the "United States shall be liable, respecting . . . tort claims, in the same manner and to the same extent as a private individual under like circumstances, but shall not be liable for interest prior to judgment or for punitive damages."[19] This means that the damages law of the state where the FTCA action is filed is applied even though the case is against the United States and is heard by a federal court. Today many states have passed legislation to limit damages that may be awarded and/or collected. For example, California limits awards greater than $250,000 for noneconomic damages. Florida provides that judgment amounts up to $200,000 are to be paid, but amounts greater than $200,000 are to be reported to the legislature for determination whether to award the balance. For example, in *Colburn v. United States*, 45 F. Supp. 2d 787, 793 (S.D. Cal. 1998) (limiting recovery of noneconomic damages under the FTCA to $250,000 pursuant to California damages limitations. Otherwise, there is no federal dollar limit on judgments against the United States. Note also that although a similar state law case may be heard by a jury, there is no jury right for FTCA actions. The FTCA employees a strict exhaustion of administrative remedies requirement. If a federal agency has jurisdiction to hear a claim, FTCA actions may not be entertained until the agency has exhausted its processes.

11.4 FEDERAL EMPLOYEE REFORM AND TORT COMPENSATION ACT

The Federal Employee Reform and Tort Compensation Act of 1988, also known as the Westfall Act, protects federal employees from liability for all acts taken in the course of their official duties. If sued in state court, the Attorney General of the United States can certify the case for removal to federal court. Once certified, removal is mandatory and the employee is dismissed from the suit, with the federal government replacing him or her as the defendant. Then, the Federal Tort Claims Act, or other applicable law, governs.

11.5 SECTION 1983 ACTIONS

A large number of cases are filed every year alleging a violation of civil rights. There is a large body of law governing civil rights claims. Two important sources of remedies for civil rights violations by the government and its officials are discussed in this chapter: the Civil Rights Act of 1871 and the Constitution of the United States.

An important law in the protection of civil rights is the Civil Rights Act of 1871. This act has been amended a number of times since 1871, and it is now codified as 42 U.S.C. § 1983. For this reason, claims brought under the statute are known as *§ 1983 actions.*

The Civil Rights Act of 1871 was enacted to enforce the Fourteenth Amendment. That amendment provides, in part, that states shall not "make or enforce any law which shall abridge the privileges or immunities of citizens of the United States; nor shall any State deprive any person of life, liberty, or property, without due process of law; nor deny any person within its jurisdiction equal protection of the laws." The Fourteenth Amendment resulted from the Civil War. The Civil Rights Act resulted from the need to enforce the Fourteenth Amendment. The statute's goal is to prevent states from violating the Fourteenth Amendment and to provide plaintiffs with compensation for violations of civil rights.

Today, the statute encompasses more than Fourteenth Amendment violations. Any violation of a constitutionally protected right may give rise to a § 1983 action and remedy. Also, if a state violates a person's right protected by federal statute, as opposed to the Constitution, a § 1983 action may be maintained to seek compensation.

There is an enormous body of case law interpreting § 1983 actions. The statute itself is easy to read, but its application is sometimes confusing, so this section discusses the fundamentals of § 1983. Section 1983 reads:

> Every person who, under color of any statute, ordinance, regulation, custom, or usage, of any State or Territory or the District of Columbia, subjects, or causes to be subjected, any citizen of the United States or other person within the jurisdiction thereof to the deprivation of any rights, privileges, or immunities secured by the Constitution and laws, shall be liable to the party injured in any action at law, suit in equity, or other proper proceeding for redress. For the purposes of this section, any Act of Congress applicable exclusively to the District of Columbia shall be considered to be a statute of the District of Columbia.

You may wish to refer back to this quote during the following discussion.

11.5(a) Plaintiffs and Defendants

The statute provides that "citizens" and other "persons" may maintain a suit under § 1983. Although "citizens" has been interpreted to mean only natural persons, and while business entities (such as corporations and labor unions) are not natural persons, *person* has been interpreted to be broader than *citizens*. Because businesses are considered persons in constitutional jurisprudence, both natural persons and corporations may seek redress under § 1983.

Be aware, however, that the underlying law that is being sued under in a § 1983 suit may limit recovery to citizens. For example, the Privileges and Immunities Clause of the Fourteenth Amendment refers to "citizens." Therefore, although a corporation generally may sue as a person under § 1983, it may not sue for a violation of the Privileges and Immunities Clause under § 1983 because corporations are outside the scope of the protections offered by that specific provision.

State and local forms of government (e.g., cities and counties) may not sue under § 1983. The one exception is when the state sues on behalf of a person who has standing to sue under § 1983, under a **parens patriae** theory. Section 1983 claims may be brought as class actions, and the government may represent a class.

The statute provides that persons who violate another's rights may be sued under § 1983. States are not persons under § 1983; hence, suits for redress against a state under § 1983 may not be maintained. This is true not only because states are not within the definition of *person*, but also because the Eleventh Amendment shields states from liability in federal courts under § 1983. While a § 1983 action may not be maintained against one of the fifty states, suits under § 1983 may be maintained against local forms of government (e.g., cities and counties).

For example, in *Monell v. Department of Social Services*, the Supreme Court overruled *Monroe v. Pape*, 365 U.S. 167 (1961) and held that municipalities are persons who could be sued under 42 U.S.C. § 1983. *Monell v. Dept. of Soc. Servs.*, 436 U.S. 658 (1978). In so ruling, the *Monell* Court upheld the rule that respondeat superior was not a basis for rendering municipalities liable under 42 U.S.C. § 1983 for constitutional torts of employees. Rather, for a local government to be liable under § 1983, there must be a policy statement, ordinance, regulation, custom or decision of the locality that caused the plaintiff's injuries. *See also Los Angeles Cnty. v. Humphries*, 131 S. Ct. 447 (2010); *Connick v. Thompson*, 131 S. Ct. 1350 (2011). Thus, if an officer's action which violates a person's rights is not consistent with government policy or custom, there is no government liability. Rather, the government custom or policy itself must actually cause the violation of the person's constitutional rights. The custom aspect is important because if a local government has a practice that is violative of a right, the fact that the custom has not been formally adopted does not preclude a § 1983 action.

Furthermore, understanding the difference between government officers sued in their individual and official capacities is important. Government officers may be sued in both their individual and official capacities. Individual liability is imposed for the personal actions of the individual taken under color of state law. Meanwhile, official liability is the equivalent of suing the government entity because in order to prevail the plaintiff must show that a government policy or custom caused the constitutional violation. Therefore, state officers may be sued in their individual capacities, but an action against a state officer in his or her official capacity is usually invalid because such actions are actually against the state which, as discussed earlier, is not permitted as a matter of law. However, in some instances a plaintiff may seek injunctive relief against government officials in their official capacities. Conversely, and as noted earlier, under *Monell*, a plaintiff may

LEGAL TERM
Parens Patriae
Latin term meaning "parent of his country." Used when a government acts on behalf of an individual.

§ 1983: Liability of Governments	
National government	No liability; scope of § 1983 is limited to actions under color of state law.
State government	No liability, for two reasons. First, § 1983 provides that "persons" may be liable and states are not persons. Second, the Eleventh Amendment shields states from liability.
Local forms of government	Liability if action is taken pursuant to law, policy, or custom.

FIGURE 11-1   Summary of governmental liability.

seek actual damages, declaratory relief, and injunctive relief against local governments (e.g., cities and counties), but not punitive damages.

As is true of states, the federal government may not be sued under § 1983. The status of territories varies. For example, the territory of Guam is not a person and is not suable. However, the Commonwealth of the Northern Mariana Islands is a person for § 1983 purposes. The District of Columbia may be sued under § 1983. Figure 11-1 summarizes these various immunities; Figure 11-2 provides an analytical tool for tracking damages liability.

Monell v. Department of Social Services

436 U.S. 658 (1978)

Petitioners, a class of female employees of the Department of Social Services and of the Board of Education of the city of New York, commenced this action under 42 U.S.C. § 1983 in July 1971. The gravamen of the complaint was that the Board and the Department had as a matter of official policy compelled pregnant employees to take unpaid leaves of absence before such leaves were required for medical reasons. The suit sought injunctive relief and back pay for periods of unlawful forced leave. Named as defendants in the action were the Department and its Commissioner, the Board and its Chancellor, and the city of New York and its Mayor. In each case, the individual defendants were sued solely in their official capacities. . . .

We granted certiorari in this case, 429 U.S. 1071, 97 S. Ct. 807, 50 L. Ed. 2d 789, to consider "Whether local governmental officials and/or local independent school boards are 'persons' within the meaning of 42 U.S.C. § 1983 when equitable relief in the nature of back pay is sought against them in their official capacities?". . .

. . . [W]e now overrule *Monroe v. Pape, supra*, insofar as it holds that local governments are wholly immune from suit under § 1983. . . .

Our analysis of the legislative history of the Civil Rights Act of 1871 compels the conclusion that Congress did not intend municipalities and other local government units to be included among those persons to whom § 1983 applies. Local governing bodies, therefore, can be sued directly under § 1983 for monetary, declaratory, or injunctive relief where, as here, the action that is alleged to be unconstitutional implements or executes a policy statement, ordinance, regulation, or decision officially adopted and promulgated by that body's officers. Moreover, although the touchstone of the § 1983 action against a government body is an allegation that official policy is responsible for a deprivation of rights protected by the Constitution, local governments, like every other § 1983 "person," by the very terms of the statute, may be sued for constitutional deprivations visited pursuant to governmental "custom" even though such a custom has not received formal approval through the body's official decision making channels. . . .

On the other hand, the language of § 1983, read against the background of the same legislative history, compels the conclusion that Congress did not intend municipalities to be held liable unless action pursuant to official policy of some nature caused a constitutional tort. In particular, we conclude that a municipality cannot be held liable solely because it employs a tortfeasor—or, in other words, a municipality cannot be held liable under § 1983 on a respondeat superior theory. . . .

We conclude, therefore, that a local government may not be sued under § 1983 for an injury inflicted solely by its employees or agents. Instead, it is when execution of a government's policy or custom, whether made by its lawmakers or by those whose edicts or acts may fairly be said to represent official policy, inflicts the injury that the government as an entity is responsible under § 1983. Because this case unquestionably involves official policy as the moving force of the constitutional violation found by the District Court . . . we must reverse the [Court of Appeals which followed *Monroe*].

Monell v. Department of Social Services, 436 U.S. 658 (1978), United States Supreme Court.

11.5(b) Deprivation and Color of Law

To prove a § 1983 claim, a plaintiff must establish (1) that the defendant, while acting under "color of law," (2) caused (3) the plaintiff to be deprived of a right protected by the Constitution of laws of the United States. *Am. Mfr.'s Mut. Ins. Co. v. Sullivan*, 526 U.S. 40, 49-50 (1999).

Let us first examine the "color of law" requirement. Section 1983 states that "[e]very person who, under color of any statute, ordinance, regulation, custom, or usage, of any State or Territory or the District of Columbia, subjects, or causes to be subjected" another person to a deprivation of certain rights shall be subject to a proceeding for redress.

What is *color of law*? Generally, it means that the action that caused the deprivation must have been taken under the authority of the state. "Color of law" under § 1983 is defined similarly to "state action" under the Fourteenth Amendment. Color of law does not mean legal, authorized, or required by the law. It refers to actions taken pursuant to the authority of the law. For example, an intrusive inspection by a health officer who intends to harass a store owner is taken under color of law because the law creates the inspection authority. This is true even if the inspection is not authorized by the inspector's supervisor. The color-of-law requirement is broader than the scope of employment test used in other legal contexts. Thus, a local officer and police department can be found liable for the off-duty behavior of a police officer if the officer is in uniform or identifies herself as a law enforcement officer.

Clearly, if an officer acts as required or permitted under state law, the color-of-law requirement is satisfied. In some circumstances, the color-of-state law requirement is satisfied when the officer acts in a manner not authorized by law. In even fewer situations, a nongovernmental actor may be liable if the action can fairly be attributed to the government.

In addition to the color-of-law requirement, there must be a deprivation of a constitutional or other right established by law for § 1983 to be violated. Any right secured by the Constitution or laws of the United States can be the basis of § 1983 claims. Initially, the act was intended to apply to violations

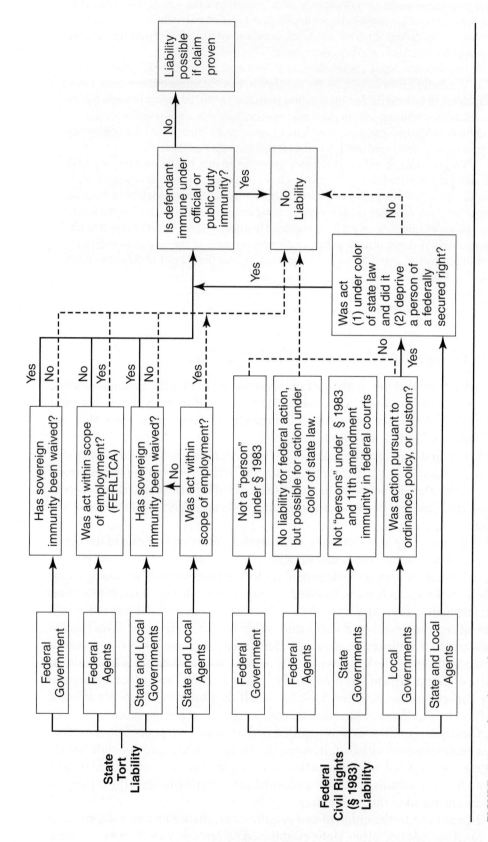

FIGURE 11-2 Analytical map of governmental damages liability.

of the Fourteenth Amendment. Today, § 1983 actions may be brought for violations of any constitutional provision, as well as for violations of other federal laws. The following are examples of § 1983 actions:

- A claim based on the Fourth Amendment, for unreasonable search and seizure.
- A claim, based on the Fourth Amendment's reasonableness requirement, of excessive use of force during arrest.
- A violation of the attorney–client privilege of confidential communication under the Sixth Amendment.
- A claim of cruel and unusual punishment under the Eighth Amendment.
- A claim of deprivation of due process under the Fourteenth Amendment (this last category includes any deprivation of due process or violation of equal protection).

Rights expressly provided for in the Constitution are within the ambit of § 1983, as are those that are implicitly protected. For example, a violation of a person's right to privacy, such as interfering with a woman's right to elect abortion in some circumstances, is actionable under § 1983 claim, although there are some early cases to the contrary.

Section 1983 actions apply not only to constitutional deprivations, but also to deprivations of other rights recognized by federal law. However, this provision has been narrowly construed. Section 1983 was not intended to become a general federal tort statute, and the purpose of the underlying constitutional protection must be advanced by a § 1983 claim. For example, the Court rejected a § 1983 claim in *Collins v. Harker Heights*, 503 U.S. 115 (1992). The plaintiff in this case sued the city of Harker Heights after her husband, a city employee, was killed in a work-related accident. She alleged that the city violated her husband's right to life under the Fourteenth Amendment's Due Process Clause because it demonstrated deliberate indifference to the safety of its employees by not adequately training them. The Court found no arbitrary or shocking behavior on behalf of the city and concluded that the case should be dismissed, even if negligence could be proven, because the purpose of the Fourteenth Amendment was to protect people from arbitrary government action. This was an issue in a case over a high-speed police chase, *County of Sacramento v. Lewis*.

County of Sacramento v. Lewis

523 U.S. 833 (1998)

The issue in this case is whether a police officer violates the Fourteenth Amendment's guarantee of substantive due process by causing death through deliberate or reckless indifference to life in a high-speed automobile chase aimed at apprehending a suspected offender. We answer no, and hold that in such circumstances only a purpose to cause harm unrelated to the legitimate object of arrest will satisfy the element of arbitrary conduct shocking to the conscience, necessary for a due process violation.

The first question is whether a substantive due process claim was a proper cause of action in the context of the high-speed chase and apprehension of a suspect that ultimately resulted in the death of the non-suspect passenger on the fleeing motorcycle. As set forth in more detail below, when a constitutional claim is covered by a specific constitutional provision like the Fourth Amendment, then the claim must be analyzed under the standard appropriate to that specific provision

(continued)

(e.g., the objectively reasonable standard of the Fourth Amendment), not under the substantive due process standard of shocking the conscience. *Graham v. Connor*, 490 U.S. 386, 395 (1989); *United States v. Lanier*, 520 U.S. 259, 272, n. 7 (1997).

On May 22, 1990, at approximately 8:30 p.m., petitioner James Everett Smith, a Sacramento County sheriff's deputy, along with another officer, Murray Stapp, responded to a call to break up a fight. Upon returning to his patrol car, Stapp saw a motorcycle approaching at high speed. It was operated by 18-year-old Brian Willard and carried Philip Lewis, respondents' 16-year-old-decedent, as a passenger. Neither boy had anything to do with the fight that prompted the call to the police.

Stapp turned on his overhead rotating lights, yelled to the boys to stop, and pulled his patrol car closer to Smith's attempting to pen the motorcycle in. Instead of pulling over in response to Stapp's warning lights and commands, Willard slowly maneuvered the cycle between the two police cars and sped off. Smith immediately switched on his own emergency lights and siren, made a quick turn, and began pursuit at high speed. For 75 seconds over a course of 1.3 miles in a residential neighborhood, the motorcycle wove in and out of oncoming traffic, forcing two cars and a bicycle to swerve off of the road. The motorcycle and patrol car reached speeds up to 100 miles an hour, with Smith following at a distance as short as 100 feet; at that speed, his car would have required 650 feet to stop.

The chase ended after the motorcycle tipped over as Willard tried a sharp left turn. By the time Smith slammed on his brakes, Willard was out of the way, but Lewis was not. The patrol car skidded into him at 40 miles an hour, propelling him some 70 feet down the road and inflicting massive injuries. Lewis was pronounced dead at the scene.

Respondents, Philip Lewis's parents and the representatives of his estate, brought this action under Rev. Stat. § 1979, 42 U.S.C. § 1983 against petitioners Sacramento County, the Sacramento County Sheriff's Department and Deputy Smith, alleging a deprivation of Philip Lewis's Fourteenth Amendment substantive due process right to life. . . .

Because we have "always been reluctant to expand the concept of substantive due process," *Collins v. Harker Heights, supra,* at 125, we held in *Graham v. Connor* that "[w]here a particular amendment provides an explicit textual source of constitutional protection against a particular sort of government behavior, that Amendment, not the more generalized notion of substantive due process, must be the guide for analyzing these claims." *Albright v. Oliver*, 510 U.S. 266, 273 (1994) (plurality opinion of Rehnquist, C.J.) (quoting *Graham v. Connor*, 490 U.S. 386, 395 [1989]) (internal quotation marks omitted). Given the rule in *Graham*, we were presented at oral argument with the threshold issue raised in several amicus briefs, whether facts involving a police chase aimed at apprehending suspects can ever support a due process claim. The argument runs that in chasing the motorcycle, Smith was attempting to make a seizure within the meaning of the Fourth Amendment, and, perhaps, even that he succeeded when Lewis was stopped by the fatal collision. Hence, any liability must turn on an application of the reasonableness standard governing searches and seizures, not the due process standard of liability for constitutionally arbitrary executive action.

However, the "more-specific-provision" rule of *Graham v. Connor*, 490 U.S. 386, 395, 104 L. Ed. 2d 443, 109 S. Ct. 1865, is not applicable because the officer did not terminate Lewis' freedom of movement through means intentionally applied, and therefore the Fourth Amendment requiring an intentional seizure did not bar the respondents' suit under the Fourteenth Amendment's guarantee of substantive due process.

Since the time of our early explanations of due process, we have understood the core of the concept to be protection against arbitrary action:

> The principal and true meaning of the phrase has never been more tersely or accurately stated than by Mr. Justice Johnson, in *Bank of*

> *Columbia v. Okely*, 17 U.S. 235,4 Wheat. 235-244 [(1819)]: "As to the words from Magna Charta, incorporated into the Constitution of Maryland, after volumes spoken and written with a view to their exposition, the good sense of mankind has at last settled down to this: that they were intended to secure the individual from the arbitrary exercise of the powers of government, unrestrained by the established principles of private right and distributive justice." *Hurtado v. California*, 110 U.S. 516, 527 (1884). We have emphasized time and again that "[t]he touchstone of the due process is protection of the individual against arbitrary action of government. . . .
>
> Our cases dealing with abusive executive action have repeatedly emphasized that only the most egregious official conduct can be said to be "arbitrary in the constitutional sense. . . ."
>
> To this end, for half a century now we have spoken of the cognizable level of executive abuse of power as that which shocks the conscience. . . .
>
> The fault claimed on Smith's part in this case accordingly fails to meet the shocks-the-conscience test. . . .
>
> Smith was faced with a course of lawless behavior for which the police were not to blame. They had done nothing to cause Willard's high-speed driving in the first place, nothing to excuse his flouting of the commonly understood law enforcement authority to control traffic, and nothing (beyond a refusal to call off the chase) to encourage him to race through traffic at breakneck speed forcing other drivers out of their travel lanes. Willard's outrageous behavior was practically instantaneous, and so was Smith's instinctive response. While prudence would have repressed the reaction, the officer's instinct was to do his job as a law enforcement officer, not to induce Willard's lawlessness, or to terrorize, cause harm, or kill. Prudence, that is, was subject to countervailing enforcement considerations, and while Smith exaggerated their demands, there is no reason to believe that they were tainted by an improper or malicious motive on his part.
>
> Regardless whether Smith's behavior offended the reasonableness held up by tort law or the balance struck in law enforcement's own codes of sound practice, it does not shock the conscience, and petitioners are not called upon to answer for it under § 1983.

County of Sacramento v. Lewis, 523 U.S. 833 (1998), United States Supreme Court.

Finally, once a plaintiff has jumped the color-of-law and deprivation hurdles, it must be proved that the defendant was the cause-in-fact of the plaintiff's injuries. If this is done, the plaintiff's case is proved. The issue then turns to remedies.

11.5(c) Remedies, Fees, and Costs

Section 1983 states that defendants "shall be liable to the party injured in an action at law, suit in equity, or other proper proceeding for redress." Therefore, damages, injunctions, and declaratory relief may be awarded.

The courts have held that nominal, actual, and punitive damages may all be awarded. *Nominal damages* (i.e., one dollar or some other small amount) are awarded when there has been a violation, but no actual damages have been proven. *Actual* or compensatory damages are intended to compensate plaintiffs for their injuries. Actual damages are of two types. *Special damages* may be awarded for medical expenses, damage to property, loss of income, and other similar injuries. Most out-of-pocket expenses are recoverable as compensatory damages. *General damages* may be awarded for pain and suffering, emotional distress, humiliation, and other similar injuries.

LEGAL TERMS

Nominal Damages
A monetary award, typically small, intended to recognize a legal wrong. Nominal damages do not compensate for actual injuries or losses.

Actual Damages (also called *compensatory damages*)
A monetary award intended to make a plaintiff whole, to compensate for actual monetary losses and injuries.

Special Damages
Form of compensatory damages; reimburses plaintiffs for actual out-of-pocket injuries, such as medical expenses.

General Damages
Form of compensatory damages; intended to compensate plaintiffs for pain and suffering, humiliation, and other related injuries.

Punitive Damages
A monetary award intended to punish or deter future misconduct. The amount is not compensation for, but may be determined or limited by, actual monetary losses or injuries.

Declaratory Judgment
Declaration by a court of the rights, obligations, and legal relations between parties.

Injunction
Form of equitable relief; an order of a court requiring someone either to take some action or to refrain from acting.

As with most torts, the plaintiff must show that the defendant was the case of the claimed damages. Common law doctrines, such as *mitigation*, which requires plaintiffs to attempt to minimize their damages, apply to § 1983 actions.

Punitive damages may also be awarded. Punitive damages are not intended to compensate the plaintiff and bear no relation to actual damages. Punitive damages are awarded in extreme cases when it is determined that a defendant should be punished or there is a need to deter that defendant or others from engaging in similar future conduct. Be aware, however, that punitive damages may not be awarded against local governments, but only against individuals. In *Smith v. Wade*, 461 U.S. 30 (1983), the Court rejected the defendant's assertion that punitive damages should be available only when actual malice is proven. Hence, in § 1983 actions, punitive damages may be awarded when a defendant's actions are reckless or malicious.

Declaratory judgments may also be awarded in § 1983 actions. A declaratory judgment is a declaration by a court of the rights, obligations, and legal relations of parties. Case or controversy concerns are applicable to requests for declaratory relief; therefore, standing, mootness, ripeness, similar issues must be dealt with.

Injunctions may also be issued. This includes temporary restraining orders, which are viable for 10 days (and may be extended for an additional 10 days); preliminary injunctions; and so-called permanent injunctions.

There are a number of limitations on the availability of these remedies, in particular § 1983 actions, but a discussion of these limitations is beyond the scope of this text.

Finally, attorney fees and costs may be awarded to "prevailing parties." Said another way, the party that wins or prevails may have its attorney fees paid by the losing party. Fees and costs are normally awarded to prevailing plaintiffs. However, prevailing defendants may recover fees when a plaintiff's action is frivolous or malicious. Included in attorney fees is the reasonable compensation not only for the attorney's time and expertise, but also for the expenses of researchers and other employees of the attorney. Costs include, but are not limited to, filing fees, service fees, court reporter and transcript expenses, photocopying expenses, and witness fees. The award of attorneys' fees is a significant concern for defendants because even if the jury awards only nominal or low compensatory damages, the defendant is responsible for paying plaintiffs' reasonable attorneys' fees in addition to what nominal or compensatory damages were already awarded by the bench or jury. By the time a case is actually tried, these fees can be quite large.

11.5(d) Procedure

Jurisdiction over § 1983 action is conferred by 28 U.S.C. §§ 1331 and 1343(a)(3). Under § 1331, federal courts have jurisdiction to hear cases "arising under" the Constitution and laws of the United States. Unlike diversity cases, there is no requirement of a minimum amount of controversy under § 1331.

Jurisdiction over § 1983 actions is also acquired through § 1343(a)(3). This section gives district courts jurisdiction over lawsuits that seek to redress deprivations of Constitutional and statutory rights. As with § 1331, there is no amount-in-controversy requirement.

Section § 1343(a)(3) is limited to constitutional and equal protection claims, whereas § 1331 is not. Therefore, a claim concerning deprivation of a statutory right, which is not an equal protection right, must be brought under § 1331.

Congress has also permitted § 1983 actions to be brought in state courts as well as federal courts, thereby providing state courts concurrent jurisdiction over § 1983 claims.

Smith v. Wade

461 U.S. 30 (1983)

The petitioner, William H. Smith, is a guard at Algoa Reformatory, a unit of the Missouri Division of Corrections for youthful first offenders. The respondent, Daniel R. Wade, was assigned to Algoa as an inmate in 1976. In the summer of 1976 Wade voluntarily checked into Algoa's protective custody unit. Because of disciplinary violations during his stay in protective custody, Wade was given a short term in punitive segregation and then transferred to administrative segregation. On the evening of Wade's first day in administrative segregation, he was placed in a cell with another inmate. Later, when Smith came on duty in Wade's dormitory, he placed a third inmate in Wade's cell. According to Wade's testimony, his cellmates harassed, beat, and sexually assaulted him.

Wade brought suit under 42 U.S.C. § 1983 against Smith and four other guards and correctional officials, alleging that his Eighth Amendment rights had been violated. At trial his evidence showed that he had placed himself in protective custody because of prior incidents of violence against him by the other inmates. The third prisoner whom Smith added to the cell had been placed in administrative segregation for fighting. Smith had made no effort to find out whether another cell was available; in fact there was another cell in the same dormitory with only one occupant. Further, only a few weeks earlier, another inmate had been beaten to death in the same dormitory during the same shift while Smith had been on duty. Wade asserted that Smith and the other defendants knew or should have known that an assault against him was likely under the circumstances. . . .

The jury returned verdicts for two of the three remaining defendants. It found Smith liable, however, and awarded $25,000 in compensatory damages and $5,000 in punitive damages. The District Court entered judgment on the verdict, and the Court of Appeals affirmed.

In this Court, Smith attacks only the award of punitive damages. . . .

We hold that a jury may be permitted to assess punitive damages in an action under § 1983 when the defendant's conduct is shown to be motivated by evil motive or intent, or when it involves reckless to callous indifference to the federally protected rights of others. We further hold that this threshold applies even when the underlying standard of liability for compensatory damages is one of recklessness. Because the jury instructions in this case are in accord with this rule, the judgment of the Court of Appeals is affirmed.

Smith v. Wade, 461 U.S. 30 (1983), United States Supreme Court.

Section 1983 actions are filed in the district where the defendant resides; in the district where a substantial part of the events or omissions took place; where a substantial part of the property that is the subject of the litigation is located; or where the defendant can be found if the case cannot be filed elsewhere.

In the alternative, § 1983 actions may be filed in state courts, which have the responsibility to adjudicate such federal claims. State courts must apply substantive federal law when adjudicating 1983 actions. Defendants nevertheless have a right to have § 1983 actions initially filed in state court **removed** to federal court.

Pendent jurisdiction may be exercised over state claims that arise out of the same set of facts as a valid § 1983 claim. Pendent jurisdiction is an exception to the rule that federal courts may not hear state cases. Federal courts apply substantive state law to pendent claims. Since 1990, federal courts are required

LEGAL TERMS

Removed
Tranferred from a state court to a federal court. The process of so transferring a case is known as *removal*. Any civil action over which district courts have original jurisdiction and that is founded on a claim or right arising under the Constitution, treaties, or laws of the United States may be removed

Pendent Jurisdiction
Power of a federal court to hear state law claims that are related to an underlying federal law claim. Pendent jurisdiction is an exception to the rule that prohibits federal courts from hearing state cases.

to accept pendent jurisdiction over "claims that are so related to claims in the action within the original jurisdiction that they form part of the same case or controversy," even if this means joining additional parties. There are four exceptions to this mandate to exercise pendent jurisdiction: if a claim involves a novel issue of state law, if the state claim predominates over the federal claim, if the federal court dismisses all the state claims, or if there are other compelling reasons.

The doctrine of exhaustion of remedies does not apply to § 1983 actions. Neither administrative nor state judicial remedies must be exhausted before a plaintiff may file a § 1983 action.

Section 1983 does not contain a specific statute of limitation. *Owens v. Okure*, 488 U.S. 235 (1989). Title 42 U.S.C. § 1988, provides that state law is to be referred to as long as the state statute of limitation is consistent with the purposes underlying federal civil rights actions. In most cases, the appropriate analogous statute of limitation will be the limitation applicable to personal injury actions; periods of two and three years are common.

11.5(e) Immunities

A number of immunities developed at common law. For a person in government, to be immune means to be free from liability. The Supreme Court has decided that Congress did not intend to abrogate those immunities by enacting § 1983. Therefore, immunities that existed when § 1983 was enacted continue to be recognized, but Congress retains the authority to grant, alter, and eliminate the immunities discussed in this section (see Figure 11-3).

The immunities discussed here are personal. The government is not protected by these immunities. However, recall that the federal government and the states are not persons under § 1983. Therefore, they are free from liability. Similarly, the Eleventh Amendment shields states from liabilities in many instances. Thus, when a government official is sued in both an official and personal capacity, the government official is protected by immunity in his or individual capacity, but not in his official capacity because a claim against an individual in his official capacity in the context of a § 1983 action is the equivalent of a claim against the governmental entity which is afforded no immunity.

Absolute and Qualified   Two forms of personal immunity, absolute and qualified, have been recognized. The most important difference is that if a person is entitled to absolute immunity, it is more likely the case may be disposed of with a motion to dismiss for failure to state a claim under Fed. R. Civ. P. 12(b)(6) or its equivalent. If a person is shielded by only qualified immunity, the case is often not ripe for a dispositive motion until the summary judgment stage.

This is because discovery is often necessary to fully develop the underlying facts necessary to resolve the question of whether qualified immunity applies. See *Harlow v. Fitzgerald*, 457 U.S. 800 (1982) (discussed in sidebar). Indeed, the doctrine of qualified immunity protects government officials from liability for civil damages insofar as their conduct does not violate clearly established statutory or constitutional rights of which a reasonable person would have known." *Pearson v. Callahan*, 555 U.S. 223 (2009). To overcome qualified immunity in § 1983 cases, a plaintiff must show that a "clearly established" right was violated. The Supreme

Court has created a two-tiered test to determine whether or not defendants are entitled to qualified immunity. *Saucier v. Katz*, 533 U.S. 194 (2001). The first question a court must answer is whether the facts alleged show the defendants' conduct violated any of plaintiff's constitutional rights. If that question is answered affirmatively, the court must then resolve whether the right alleged was clearly established when the violation was alleged to have occurred. *Saucier*, 533 U.S. 194. While the sequence for answering those questions was recently relaxed by the Supreme Court, the essential questions related to qualified immunity remain unchanged. *Pearson*, 555 U.S. 223.

An objective test is used—that is, the defendant's actual state of mind is not dispositive. Allegations of bad faith or improper motive are not sufficient. Objectively, it must be determined that the officer should have known that his or her act would violate a clearly established right.

For example, the Supreme Court held that a "reasonable police officer" could have believed that the Fourth Amendment permitted him to enter a residence without a warrant, if he had a reasonable basis for concluding there was an imminent threat of violence. *Ryburn v. Huff*, 132 S. Ct. 987 (2012). In *Ryburn*, officers observed unusual behavior by a child's mother when the mother: (1) did not immediately answer the door or telephone; (2) upon answering the door, she expressed no concern over the investigation of her son; and (3) upon being asked if there were guns in the house, she ran back into the house while being questioned. The officers had also learned at the school that the son was a victim of bullying, was absent from school for two days, and had threatened to "shoot up" the school. Based on the circumstances, the officers reasonably believed that there could have been weapons inside the house and that family members or the officers were in danger. Judged from the proper perspective of a reasonable officer forced to make a split-second decision in response to a rapidly unfolding chain of events that culminated with the mother turning and running into the house after refusing to answer a question about guns, the officers' belief that entry was necessary to avoid injury to themselves or others was reasonable.

Denials of motions for dismissal and summary judgment that assert immunity can be final and immediately appealable. This is contrary to the general rule that denials of dismissals and summary judgment motions are not immediately appealable because they are not final orders.

Functional Approach   A person is not entitled to immunity by virtue of the position he or she holds. Rather, the function being performed that is alleged to have violated a plaintiff's rights is dispositive. Immunity is justified and defined by the functions it protects and serves, not by the person to whom it attaches. Figure 11-3 charts the various functions and immunities.

For example, you will learn that there is a judicial immunity, but the fact that a person is a judge does not automatically create judicial immunity. The question is whether the judge is being sued for undertaking a judicial act. If the act is judicial in nature, then the judge is entitled to immunity. Alternatively, if the judge was performing a nonjudicial function like disciplining an employee, then judicial immunity does not shield the judge from liability. Because the immunity attaches to the function performed and not the title of the person performing the function, there are instances when laypersons are entitled to an immunity. For example, witnesses who testify at judicial proceedings are protected by witness immunity.

§ 1983 ACTIONS AND IMMUNITY: FUNCTIONS AND IMMUNITY		
Position	**Entitled to Absolute Immunity When Performing the Following:**	**Entitled to Qualified Immunity When Performing the Following:**
Judges, including ALJs	Judicial acts, such as conducting hearings and trials, issuing orders and warrants, and making statements during judicial or administrative proceedings	Administrative acts Personnel actions
Prosecutors	Quasi-judicial acts, such as appearing in court and complying with court orders	Investigations Counseling law enforcement officers Administrative acts Personnel actions
Law enforcement officers	Enforcing court orders Testifying in court	Investigations Warrantless searches and arrests Administrative acts Personnel actions
Witnesses	Testifying in court and administrative tribunals	
Legislators and administrative officials responsible for promulgating regulations	Statements and writings resulting from legislative sessions or committee meetings and smaller administrative actions Voting Promulgating a rule	Administrative acts Personnel actions
Public defenders (criminal cases)	No immunity	No immunity

FIGURE 11-3   Summary of absolute and qualified immunities.

Harlow v. Fitzgerald

457 U.S. 800 (1982)

In this suit for civil damages petitioners Bryce Harlow and Alexander Butterfield are alleged to have participated in a conspiracy to violate the constitutional and statutory rights of the respondent A. Ernest Fitzgerald. Respondent avers that petitioners entered the conspiracy in their capacities as senior White House aides to former President Richard M. Nixon. . . .

Consistently with the balance at which we aimed in [a prior case], we conclude today that bare allegations of malice should not suffice to subject government officials either to the costs of trial or to the burdens of broad-reaching discovery. We therefore hold that government officials performing discretionary functions generally are shielded from liability for civil damages insofar as their conduct does not violate clearly established statutory or constitutional rights of which a reasonable person would have known. . . .

Reliance on the objective reasonableness of an official's conduct, as measured by reference to clearly established law, should avoid excessive disruption of government and permit the resolution of many insubstantial claims on summary judgment. On summary judgment, the judge appropriately may determine, not only the currently applicable law, but whether the law was clearly established at the time an action occurred. If the law at that time was not clearly established, an official could not reasonably be expected to anticipate subsequent legal developments, nor could he fairly be said to "know" that the law forbade conduct not previously identified as unlawful. Until this threshold immunity question is resolved, discovery should not be allowed. If the law was clearly established, the immunity defense ordinarily should fail, since a reasonably competent public official should know the law governing his conduct. Nevertheless, if the official pleading the defense claims extraordinary circumstances and can prove that he neither knew nor should have known of the relevant legal standard, the defense should be sustained. But again, the defense would turn primarily on objective factors.

Harlow v. Fitzgerald, 457 U.S. 800 (1982), United States Supreme Court.

Judges   Judges are absolutely immune for judicial acts. All acts that are part of the judicial function even if wrongly taken, are within the reach of judicial immunity.

Nevertheless, if a judge acts in the clear absence of jurisdiction, there may be no immunity. A mere error in determining that jurisdiction to act exists is not a clear absence of jurisdiction. A judge must act outrageously or in a nonjudicial manner before immunity no longer applies. For example, a judge who had a merchant arrested and brought to appear before the court in handcuffs for selling "putrid"-tasting coffee was not shielded by immunity.

A judge's state of mind is not important to the inquiry. A judge is immune from liability even if acting with malice, so long as the function performed is judicial. For example, a judge would be entitled to absolute immunity for the issuance of an arrest warrant even if the warrant issuance were motivated by hostile or malicious feelings toward the arrestee.

Judges are not absolutely immune for acts that are administrative rather than judicial in nature. For example, judges are not protected by qualified immunity, not absolute immunity, for personnel decisions.

Judicial immunity extends to all who perform judicial functions. Trial and appellate judges, justices of the peace, municipal referees, and police court judges all perform judicial functions and, as such, are immune for their judicial acts. All others who perform judicial acts are also absolutely immune even though they do not hold judicial titles. Law enforcement officers are absolutely immune was enforcing court orders. Probation officer and other court personnel are immune when performing judicial functions, such as when court clerks issue warrants. Prison and parole officials are absolutely immune when conducting hearings. Administrative officers are absolutely immune for court appearances in connection with enforcement of an agency's mandate. Administrative law judges are immune when fulfilling quasi judicial functions.

Finally, although judges are immune from damages while acting in their judicial capacities, there is no immunity from prospective injunctive relief. That is, judges can be enjoined from engaging in behavior that violates § 1983. This extends to all aspects of judicial immunity.

Prosecutors   Prosecutors are absolutely immune in some circumstances and have qualified immunity in others. Prosecutors are absolutely immune when engaging in activities that are "intimately associated with the judicial phase of the criminal process." This is known as quasi-judicial immunity. The Supreme Court said, in defense of judicial and prosecutorial immunity, that

> [t]he common law immunity of a prosecutor is based upon the same considerations that underlie the common law immunities of judges and grand jurors acting within the scope of their duties. These include concern that harassment by unfounded litigation would cause a deflection of the prosecutor's energies from his public duties, and the possibility that he would shape his decisions instead of exercising the independence of judgment required by his public trust.

Imbler v. Pachtman, 424 U.S. 409, 423 (1976).

Case, Imbler v. Pachtman, 424 U.S. 409, 423 (1976), United States Supreme Court.

It is recognized that affording immunity leaves some plaintiffs who would have been damaged with no legal recourse. However, it is better to leave unredressed the wrongs of a few bad officials than to subject those who try to do their duty faithfully to constant retaliation.

It has been determined that, as an extension of judicial immunity, prosecutors are absolutely immune when acting in an advocacy role. This includes appearing in court and before grand juries, and initiating prosecutions. Prosecutors are protected by only qualified immunity when performing investigative, law enforcement, and administrative functions. Also, prosecutors have only qualified immunity when rendering advice to law enforcement officers or performing a law enforcement function, such as assisting in a search or arrest. As is true of judges, prosecutors are not immune from prospective injunctive relief or violations of 1983.

Law Enforcement Officers   Law enforcement are entitled to qualified immunity when acting in an investigative or law enforcement capacity. For example, officers are protected with qualified immunity when executing a warrant, even if it is later determined that probable cause didn't exist to support the warrant so long as the officer acted in good faith and the judge's decision was reasonable, even though wrong[20]

Law enforcement officers can also be entitled to absolute immunity when performing quasi-judicial acts. For example, the service of writs is protected by absolute immunity. Officers also have the protection of absolute immunity when testifying as witnesses. This is true even if the officer commits perjury. However, perjury is a crime and there is no immunity from criminal prosecution.

When acting outside the law enforcement function, officers are not protected by any immunity whatsoever.

Witnesses and Jurors   Witnesses at trials and hearings are absolutely immune for their testimony even if they commit perjury. However, perjury is a crime and there is no immunity from criminal prosecution. The protection of witness absolute immunity extends to trials, hearings, grand jury sessions, and administrative proceedings. Similarly, jurors, both petit and grand, are absolutely immune from suit.

Public Defenders   In most instances, public defenders do not act under color of state law. For this reason, it is rare to reach the issue of immunity. However, if a public defender is accused of conspiring with state officials to deprive someone of his or her rights, then the color-of-law requirement can be met.

Unlike prosecutors, there is no immunity for public defenders. At the time 1983 was adopted, and throughout history, public defenders were not afforded immunity. Because only the immunities that existed when § 1983 was enacted continue to be recognized, public defenders have no immunity, either absolute or qualified.

Legislators Legislators are shielded by absolute immunity when performing legislative functions. Such functions include speaking on the floor of the legislative body, conducting hearings, compelling attendance at committee hearings, interrogating witnesses at investigative hearings, and trying persons for legislative contempt. Unlike judges and prosecutors, legislators are immune from both damages and injunctive relief.

Recall that it is the function served, not the individual's status, that determine if an immunity applies. Therefore, anyone who performs a legislative function is entitled to legislative immunity. For example, the Supreme Court held that courts are entitled to legislative immunity for the promulgation of rules governing professional conduct and ethics of attorneys. By analogy, this immunity should include agency officials responsible for the promulgation of regulations.

Agents Private individuals are entitled to the same immunities as government employees when working for the government, as found in *Filarsky v. Delia*.

Filarsky v. Delia

566 U.S. ___ (2012)

Chief Justice Roberts delivered the opinion of the Court.

Section 1983 provides a cause of action against state actors who violate an individual's rights under federal law. 42 U.S.C. § 1983. At common law, those who carried out the work of government enjoyed various protections from liability when doing so, in order to allow them to serve the government without undue fear of personal exposure. Our decisions have looked to these common law protections in affording either absolute or qualified immunity to individuals sued under § 1983. The question in this case is whether an individual hired by the government to do its work is prohibited from seeking such immunity, solely because he works for the government on something other than a permanent or full-time basis.

Nicholas Delia, a firefighter employed by the City of Rialto, California, became ill while responding to a toxic spill in August 2006. Under a doctor's orders, Delia missed three weeks of work. The City became suspicious of Delia's extended absence, and hired a private investigation firm to conduct surveillance on him. The private investigators observed Delia purchasing building supplies—including several rolls of fiberglass insulation—from a home improvement store. The City surmised that Delia was missing work to do construction on his home rather than because of illness, and it initiated a formal internal affairs investigation of him.

Delia was ordered to appear for an administrative investigation interview. The City hired Steve Filarsky to conduct the interview. Filarsky was an experienced employment lawyer who had previously represented the City in several investigations. Delia and his attorney attended the interview, along with Filarsky and two fire department officials, Mike Peel and Frank Bekker. During the interview, Filarsky questioned Delia about the building supplies. Delia acknowledged that he had purchased the supplies, but claimed that he had not yet done the work on his home.

During a break, Filarsky met with Peel, Bekker, and Fire Chief Stephen Wells. Filarsky proposed resolving the investigation by verifying Delia's claim that he had not done any work on his home. To do so, Filarsky recommended asking Delia to produce the building materials. Chief Wells approved the plan.

When the meeting resumed, Filarsky requested permission for Peel to enter Delia's home to view the materials. On the advice of counsel, Delia refused. Filarsky then asked Delia if he would be willing to bring the materials out onto his lawn, so that Peel could observe them without entering his home. Delia again refused to

(continued)

consent. Unable to obtain Delia's cooperation, Filarsky ordered him to produce the materials for inspection.

Delia's counsel objected to the order, asserting that it would violate the Fourth Amendment. When that objection proved unavailing, Delia's counsel threatened to sue the City. He went on to tell Filarsky that "[w]e might quite possibly find a way to figure if we can name you Mr. Filarsky. . . . If you want to take that chance, you go right ahead." The threat was repeated over and over: "[E]verybody is going to get named, and they are going to sweat it out as to whether or not they have individual liability. . . ." "[Y]ou order him and you will be named and that is not an idle threat." "Whoever issues that order is going to be named in the lawsuit." "[W]e will seek any and all damages including individual liability. . . . [W]e are coming if you order this." "[M]ake sure the spelling is clear [in the order] so we know who to sue." Despite these threats, Filarsky prepared an order directing Delia to produce the materials, which Chief Wells signed.

As soon as the interview concluded, Peel and Bekker followed Delia to his home. Once there, Delia, his attorney, and a union representative went into Delia's house, brought out the four rolls of insulation, and placed them on Delia's lawn. Peel and Bekker, who remained in their car during this process, thanked Delia for showing them the insulation and drove off.

Delia brought an action under 42 U.S.C. § 1983 against the City, its Fire Department, Chief Wells, Peel, Bekker, Filarsky, and ten unidentified individuals, alleging that the order to produce the building materials violated his rights under the Fourth and Fourteenth Amendments. The District Court granted summary judgment to all the individual defendants, concluding that they were protected by qualified immunity. The court held that Delia had "not demonstrated a violation of a clearly established constitutional right," because "Delia was not threatened with insubordination or termination if he did not comply with any order given and none of these defendants entered [his] house."

The Court of Appeals for the Ninth Circuit affirmed with respect to all defendants except Filarsky. The Court of Appeals concluded that the order violated the Fourth Amendment, but agreed with the District Court that Delia "ha[d] not demonstrated that a constitutional right was clearly established as of the date of Chief Wells's order, such that defendants would have known that their actions were unlawful." As to Filarsky, however, the court concluded that because he was a private attorney and not a City employee, he was not entitled to seek the protection of qualified immunity.

Section 1983 provides a cause of action against any person who deprives an individual of federally guaranteed rights "under color" of state law. 42 U.S.C. § 1983. Anyone whose conduct is "fairly attributable to the state" can be sued as a state actor under § 1983. At common law, government actors were afforded certain protections from liability, based on the reasoning that "the public good can best be secured by allowing officers charged with the duty of deciding upon the rights of others, to act upon their own free, unbiased convictions, uninfluenced by any apprehensions." Our decisions have recognized similar immunities under § 1983, reasoning that common law protections " 'well grounded in history and reason' had not been abrogated 'by covert inclusion in the general language' of § 1983."

In this case, there is no dispute that qualified immunity is available for the sort of investigative activities at issue. The Court of Appeals granted this protection to Chief Wells, Peel, and Bekker, but denied it to Filarsky, because he was not a public employee but was instead a private individual "retained by the City to participate in internal affairs investigations." In determining whether this distinction is valid, we look to the "general principles of tort immunities and defenses" applicable at common law, and the reasons we have afforded protection from suit under § 1983.

Under our precedent, the inquiry begins with the common law as it existed when Congress passed § 1983 in 1871. . . .

As one commentator has observed, there was at that time "no very clear conception of a professional office, that is, an office the incumbent of which devotes his entire time to the discharge of public functions, who has no other occupation, and who receives a sufficiently large compensation to enable him to live without resorting to other means." Instead, to a significant extent, government was "administered by members of society who temporarily or occasionally discharge[d] public functions." Whether government relied primarily upon professionals or occasional workers obviously varied across the country and across different government functions. But even at the turn of the twentieth century, a public servant was often one who "does not devote his entire time to his public duties, but is, at the same time that he is holding public office, permitted to carry on some other regular business, and as a matter of fact finds his main means of support in such business or in his private means since he receives from his office a compensation insufficient to support him."

Private citizens were actively involved in government work, especially where the work most directly touched the lives of the people. It was not unusual, for example, to see the owner of the local general store step behind a window in his shop to don his postman's hat. Nor would it have been a surprise to find, on a trip to the docks, the local ferryman collecting harbor fees as public wharfmaster.

Even such a core government activity as criminal prosecution was often carried out by a mixture of public employees and private individuals temporarily serving the public. At the time § 1983 was enacted, private lawyers were regularly engaged to conduct criminal prosecutions on behalf of the State. Abraham Lincoln himself accepted several such appointments. In addition, private lawyers often assisted public prosecutors in significant cases. And public prosecutors themselves continued to represent private clients while in office—sometimes creating odd conflicts of interest.

This mixture of public responsibility and private pursuits extended even to the highest levels of government. Until the position became full-time in 1853, for example, the Attorney General of the United States was expected to and did maintain an active private law practice. . . .

Given all this, it should come as no surprise that the common law did not draw a distinction between public servants and private individuals engaged in public service in according protection to those carrying out government responsibilities. . . .

The common law also extended certain protections to individuals engaged in law enforcement activities, such as sheriffs and constables. At the time § 1983 was enacted, however, "[t]he line between public and private policing was frequently hazy. Private detectives and privately employed patrol personnel often were publicly appointed as special policemen, and the means and objects of detective work, in particular, made it difficult to distinguish between those on the public payroll and private detectives." . . .

Sheriffs executing a warrant were empowered by the common law to enlist the aid of the able-bodied men of the community in doing so. . . .

Indeed, examples of individuals receiving immunity for actions taken while engaged in public service on a temporary or occasional basis are as varied as the reach of government itself. . . .

Affording immunity not only to public employees but also to others acting on behalf of the government similarly serves to " 'ensure that talented candidates [are] not deterred by the threat of damages suits from entering public service. . . .

In light of the foregoing, the judgment of the Court of Appeals denying qualified immunity to Filarsky is reversed.

Filarsky v. Delia, 566 U.S (2012), United States Supreme Court.

Procedure and Immunity Claims   Claims of immunity are commonly raised through pretrial disposition motions, such as a motion to dismiss for failure to state a claim for which relief can be granted (under Fed. R. Civ. P. 12[b][6]) and a motion for summary judgment (under Fed. R. Civ. P. 56).

Claims of absolute immunity are commonly resolved through a motion for dismissal made pursuant to Federal Rule of Civil Procedure 12(b)(6). A motion for dismissal may be filed early in a lawsuit. The rules of civil procedure provide that a motion for dismissal may be filed in lieu of answering a complaint although a motion for judgment on the pleadings may also follow the defendant's answer.

For the purposes of a Rule 12 motion, a reviewing court assumes that all the information in the complaint is true and gives the plaintiff the benefit of all reasonable inferences. Facts may not be contested through a Rule 12 motion. While the Court must accept all well-pleaded factual allegations as true, however, the Court need not accept as true a legal conclusion couched as a factual allegation. *Bell Atl. Corp. v. Twombly*, 550 U.S. 544, 570 (2007) (quoting *Papasan v. Allain*, 478 U.S. 265, 286 [1986]). A complaint must provide more that an unadorned, the-defendant-unlawfully-harmed-me accusation.*Ashcroft v. Iqbal*, 556 U.S. 662, 678 (2009) (citing *Twombly*, 550 U.S. at 555). A Rule 12 motion may be appropriate in both absolute and qualified immunity cases; however, it is more likely to be successful for defendants who are entitled to absolute immunity.

Under Fed. R. Civ. P. 56, summary judgment may be granted where no genuine issue of material fact exists and a party is entitled to a judgment as a matter of law. Facts may be examined through a Rule 56 motion only to the extent necessary to determine if a genuine issue of material facts exists. If contested material factual issues arise, the case must proceed beyond summary judgment. Issues of qualified immunity are commonly resolved through motions for summary judgment.

Defendants who claim qualified immunity may attempt to limit the scope of discovery to only those facts necessary to resolve the question of whether qualified immunity is applicable. This can save the defendant from being forced to engage in other time-consuming, expensive, and needless discovery. Note that a poorly drafted complaint may lead to dismissal of a claim even if the defendant is entitled to only qualified immunity. For example, if a defendant is entitled to immunity unless malice is shown, and malice is not alleged in the complaint, dismissal is appropriate.

Although a court will examine some of the facts of the case when reviewing a motion for summary judgment, the summary judgment proceeding is not to be transformed into a substitute for trial. Summary judgment is to be granted only when there is no genuine issue of material fact in the lawsuit and the moving party is entitled to judgment as a matter of law. As is true of dismissal motions, the non-moving party is to receive the benefit of all reasonable inferences.

A mere denial of a fact is not sufficient to survive summary judgment. However, if a party can point to any evidence in the record contradicting an opposing party's motion for summary judgment, the case should proceed to trial, where it is proper to compare, evaluate, and weigh the evidence in the case.

Normal appellate rules govern appeals in § 1983 actions. However, although denials of dismissal motions and summary judgment motions are not ordinarily final and appealable, denial of a response that asserts immunity is immediately appealable. This exception was carved out to save public officials from the expense and time of needless discovery and other pretrial matters. All other dismissal and summary judgment denials are nonfinal and nonappealable.

sound, light manipulation, threats of indefinite detention, denial of food, denial of water, denial of needed medical care, yelling, prolonged solitary confinement, *incommunicado* detention, falsified allegations and other psychologically-disruptive and injurious techniques." . . .

The Detainee Status Board eventually concluded that both Vance and Ertel were innocent of the allegations that had been made against them. Neither was charged with a crime.

In December 2006 Vance and Ertel filed this suit against persons who conducted or approved their detention and interrogation, and many others who had supervisory authority over those persons. The defendants included Secretary of Defense Donald Rumsfeld. . . .

The political branches have not been indifferent to detainees' interests. To the contrary, the treatment of military detainees has occasioned extended debate and led to a series of statutes. . . . These statutes have one thing in common: *none* provides for damages against military personnel or their civilian superiors. Some, such as the Detainee Treatment Act, expressly block damages liability. Others provide compensation to victims of military errors or misconduct, but the compensation comes from the public fisc rather than private pockets. . . .

The Detainee Treatment Act can be—and has been—enforced by criminal prosecutions. . . . But Congress has not authorized awards of damages against soldiers and their superiors, and creating a right of action in common-law fashion would intrude inappropriately into the military command structure.

Vance v. Rumsfeld , 701 F.3d 193 (7th Cir. 2012) (en banc), United States
Court of Appeals for the Seventh Circuit.

SIDEBAR   *Bivens Actions*

Cases claiming constitutional violations, which are brought directly under the Constitution against government officers, are commonly known as "*Bivens* actions," named for the landmark case *Bivens v. Six Unknown Agents*, 403 U.S. 388 (1971).

11.7 COMMON LAW TORTS AND OFFICIAL IMMUNITY

In addition to statutory and constitutional claims, there are common law torts. Intentional infliction of emotional distress, defamation of character, and invasion of privacy are examples of common law torts recognized in many states. Federal government officials are protected by **official immunity** from common law torts, as discussed in the *Strothman* case. *Official immunity* is absolute immunity from common law tort actions. It may be asserted by any public official for those acts taken in furtherance of an official duty that is discretionary in nature.

Official immunity does not apply to ministerial acts. The discretionary/ministerial distinction is the same as that under the Federal Tort Claims Act (see Section 11.3). If an act requires judgment, decision making, or policy, it is likely discretionary. An act that is required by law or follows a discretionary decision is likely ministerial.

Do not confuse statutory, constitutional, and common law immunities. For claims arising under the Constitution and laws of the United States, individuals may be immune under judicial, prosecutorial, or legislative immunity. This immunity may be either absolute or qualified. When a public official is sued for a common law tort, absolute immunity applies if the act sued for involved the exercise of a discretionary function.

LEGAL TERM
Official Immunity
Doctrine holding that public officials are absolutely immune from common law tort actions for the performance of discretionary functions

Strothman v. Gefreh

739 F.2d 515 (10th Cir. 1984)

The only question presented by this appeal is whether defendants, seven of the eight Administrative Law Judges (ALJs) in the Denver Office of Hearings and Appeals of the Social Security Administration, are entitled to absolute immunity from tort claims asserted against them by plaintiff, the remaining ALJ, and arising out of their respective positions as ALJs. The district court found that although defendants might be entitled to qualified privilege, absolute immunity was unwarranted. The court therefore denied defendants' motion for summary judgment. We reverse in part and remand for further proceedings.

Frederick Strothman was at the time of the events giving rise to this lawsuit Administrative Law Judge in Charge (ALJIC) of the Denver Hearing Office. In this capacity, Strothman was responsible for the overall management and effectiveness of the office, in addition to his duties as a judge. He had managerial and administrative authority over all personnel, including defendants. In October 1981, Strothman was relieved of his duties as ALJIC. He filed this suit in Colorado state court shortly thereafter, asserting claims of defamation against defendants Harmatz, Paynter, Bunten, and Panzarella and claims of conspiracy, and extreme and outrageous conduct against all defendants. Strothman alleges that defendants conspired to induce his termination by accusing him of being incompetent, lodging unfounded complaints against him, and harassing him in a variety of ways.

The case was removed to federal district court pursuant to 28 U.S.C. §§ 1441(a) and 1442(a)(1) (1982). Defendants filed a motion to dismiss or in the alternative for summary judgment, contending inter alia that they were absolutely immune from liability. In denying the motion, the district court concluded that defendants were unprotected by absolute immunity because they were not functioning in a judicial capacity when they engaged in the conduct here at issue. On appeal, defendants do not contest the district court's finding as to the applicability of judicial immunity. They argue instead that under the doctrine of "official immunity" set forth in *Barr v. Mateo*, 360 U.S. 564, 79 S. Ct. 1335, 3 L. Ed. 2d 1434 (1959), and its progeny, they are absolutely immune for the common law tort claims Strothman has asserted.

In *Barr*, the Acting Director of the Office of Rent Stabilization was sued for libel after he issued a press release stating the reasons why he intended to suspend two officers of the agency. In determining whether the defendant's conduct was absolutely privileged, the Court was called upon to balance:

> on the one hand, the protection of the individual citizen against pecuniary damages caused by oppressive or malicious action on the part of officials of the Federal Government; and on the other, the protection of the public interest by shielding responsible governmental officers against the harassment and inevitable hazards of vindictive or ill-founded damage suits brought on account of action taken in the exercise of their official responsibilities.

Id. at 565.

Tracing the history and purpose of the judicially created official immunity doctrine, the Court emphasized the necessity of freeing government officials from the fear of damage suits based on action taken in the course of their duties—"suits which would consume time and energies which would otherwise be devoted to governmental service and the threat of which might appreciably inhibit the fearless, vigorous, and effective administration of policies of government.". . . Numerous cases since *Barr* have applied the doctrine of official immunity, and this court has long recognized the general rule that federal officials are absolutely immune from liability for "alleged torts which result from acts done within the framework or scope of their duties which necessarily involve the exercise of discretion which public policy requires be made without fear of personal liability." . . .

Under [a prior Tenth Circuit case] and subsequent cases in this circuit, our inquiry is essentially threefold: (1) Whether the defendant was acting within the scope of his official duties; (2) whether the act complained of involved the exercise of discretion; and (3) whether a grant of absolute immunity under the circumstances of the case would further the policies underlying the official immunity doctrine. . . .

The first question then is whether defendants were acting within the scope of their employment when they committed the acts about which plaintiff complains. . . . With respect to the defamation claims, Strothman alleges that defendants Harmatz, Paynter, Bunten, and Panzarella made certain false and malicious statements about him in writings that were read by the Regional Chief Administrative Law Judge, the ALJs' immediate superior. In affidavits filed in support of their motion for summary judgment on the immunity issue, defendants did not dispute that the statements were made. Rather, defendants attached the writings, showing that they were directed to Strothman himself or to the Regional Chief ALJ and were related to an ongoing dispute about Strothman's management of the Denver office. The district court found that defendants wrote the letters

> in response to either memos from ALJ Strothman and his superior, Carney, or earlier meetings and personal conferences on related subjects. In none of the writings complained of . . . did the ALJ in question initiate the correspondence. In each instance the letters involved managerial duties and performance evaluations of personnel in the Denver Hearing Office. The issue arose because of dissension between the ALJ Strothman and the other ALJs and their support staff, concerning Strothman's expectations, and the manner in which he handled his administrative and supervisory duties.

In light of these facts, the court found it "abundantly clear" that defendants were acting within the scope of their employment. We agree that in "responding to criticisms and questions relating to morale and productivity," defendants were acting well within the "outer perimeter of [their] line of duty." . . .

Strothman v. Gefreh , 739 F .2d 515 (10th Cir. 1984), United States
Court of Appeals, Tenth Circuit.

11.8 TUCKER ACT

Other actions may be maintained against the United States through the Tucker Act.[21] The Tucker Act gives the U.S. Claims Court jurisdiction over any claim for damages against the United States that is founded on the Constitution, statutes, or regulations of the United States. However, the court has no jurisdiction over tort cases. Tort actions must be filed under the Federal Tort Claims Act or other law.

An example of an action founded on the Constitution that may be heard by the Claims Court is one concerning a taking of personal property by the government for public use. The Fifth Amendment requires that such takings satisfy due process and that the government compensate the property owner for the loss. Nearly all claims against the government concerning takings under the Fifth Amendment may be heard by the Claims Court.

The Tucker Act also gives the Claims Court jurisdiction to hear contract claims, both express and implied, brought against the United States.

The Tucker Act sets out other actions over which the Claims Court has jurisdiction. Certain patent and copyright cases, claims of unjust conviction and imprisonment, and petitions by agency officials to be relieved of responsibility for losing, in the line of duty, government funds, vouchers, records, or papers are just a few examples.

In what is known as the Indian Tucker Act, the United States has waived its immunity for certain classes of cases filed by Native American tribes. By 2009, the Navajo Nation had been in dispute with the United States over a coal lease for 15 years. In 2003, the Supreme Court ruled against the Navajo Nation (Navajo I). It did so again on sovereign immunity grounds in the following case.

United States v. Navajo Nation

556 U.S. 287 (2009)

Introduction:

Federal law permits the Secretary of Interior to issue leases to coal mining companies to mine Native American reservation lands in exchange for a royalty payment to the tribe. The law further provides that the royalty rate may be changed by the Secretary every ten years after the first twenty year lease period. After the requisite period, the Navajo Nation requested an increase in its royalties. The Secretary didn't approve the increase and administrative processes ensued. Eventually, the Navajo Nation sued the United States, seeking $600 million in damages. It asserted the Indian Tucker Act to bypass sovereign immunity.

The Court began its opinion by noting the relevant law:

The Federal Government cannot be sued without its consent. Limited consent has been granted through a variety of statutes, including one colloquially referred to as the Indian Tucker Act:

"The United States Court of Federal Claims shall have jurisdiction of any claim against the United States accruing after August 13, 1946, in favor of any tribe . . . whenever such claim is one arising under the Constitution, laws or treaties of the United States, or Executive orders of the President, or is one which otherwise would be cognizable in the Court of Federal Claims if the claimant were not an Indian tribe, band or group."

The last clause refers to the (ordinary) Tucker Act, which waives immunity with respect to any claim "founded either upon the Constitution, or any Act of Congress or any regulation of an executive department, or upon any express or implied contract with the United States, or for liquidated or unliquidated damages in cases not sounding in tort.

Neither the Tucker Act nor the Indian Tucker Act creates substantive rights; they are simply jurisdictional provisions that operate to waive sovereign immunity for claims premised on other sources of law. . .

As we explained in *Navajo I*, there are thus two hurdles that must be cleared before a tribe can invoke jurisdiction under the Indian Tucker Act. First, the tribe "must identify a substantive source of law that establishes specific fiduciary or other duties, and allege that the Government has failed faithfully to perform those duties." . . . "If that threshold is passed, the court must then determine whether the relevant source of substantive law 'can fairly be interpreted as mandating compensation for damages sustained as a result of a breach of the duties [the governing law] impose[s].' (alteration in original). At the second stage, principles of trust law might be relevant "in drawing the inference that Congress intended damages to remedy a breach. . . ."

United States v. Navajo, 556 U.S. 287,289-91 (2009) (internal citations omitted).

Summary of the Court's Analysis:

The Court then analyzed three statutes that the Navajo Nation asserted as creating a fiduciary duty by the Secretary of Interior to approve the

> requested royalty increase. The Court found none of them meritorious, stating "[n]one of the sources of law cited by the Federal Circuit and relied upon by the Tribe provides any more sound a basis for its breach-of-trust lawsuit against the Federal Government than those we analyzed in *Navajo* 1. This case is at an end. The judgment of the Court of Appeals is reversed, and the case is remanded with instructions to affirm the Court of Federal Claims' dismissal of the Tribe's complaint." *Id.* at 302.

Conversely, in *United States v. White Mountain Apache Tribe*, 537 U.S. 465 (2003), the Supreme Court concluded that the Indian Tucker Act did provide the court with jurisdiction over the Indian tribe's claim. In that case, the Indian tribe sought money damages against the United States for its alleged breach of fiduciary duty to manage land it held in trust for the tribe and which the United States occupied. The United States argued the court lacked subject matter jurisdiction over the claim because no statute or regulation imposed a legal duty on the United States to maintain the trust property, and thus the Indian Tucker Act did not give the court jurisdiction. The Government argued that, while the Indian Tucker Act provided jurisdiction as to certain claims, the waiver of immunity operated only when the underlying substantive law could be fairly interpreted as giving rise to a particular duty, the breach of which would be compensable in money damages.

The Supreme Court disagreed with the Government and ruled the Indian Tucker Act *did* provide jurisdiction to the Court of Federal Claims over the Indian tribe's claim because the Act of 1960, which provided that the land at issue would be held in trust by the United States, provided a fair inference that the United States was subject to duties as a trustee of the land and liable for damages for such breach, especially considering that the United States occupied the trust land as the trustee.

Finally, the "Little Tucker Act"[22] provides that federal district courts have concurrent jurisdiction with the Claims Court over these types of cases if the amount in controversy in the case does not exceed $10,000.

11.9 ETHICAL EXPECTATIONS AND LIABILITY

Several statutes, regulations, and executive orders impose ethical requirements on employees of the federal government. A few of the most prominent are reviewed in this section.

The Ethics in Government Act of 1978 (5 U.S.C. §§ 101 et. seq.), as amended by the Ethics Reform Act of 1989 and other laws, is a landmark piece of legislation that was enacted following the Watergate affair. It requires the president, vice president, candidates for political offices, all high-ranking executive branch officers, judges and most of their employees, and members of Congress and their employees to file financial statements detailing their income, the sources of income, assets, debts, positions held in corporations and not-for-profits, and other personal and professional information. Failure to file the report, or willfully falsifying the report, can lead to a fine and employment discipline.

The act also prohibits certain employees from working or consulting for, or lending a name to, or investing in enterprises with whom the employee will have a fiduciary relationship. So, this means that a government employee may not be a partner in a law firm, for example. Even more, these employees are forbidden from receiving compensation for any work that involves a fiduciary relationship. This excludes law practice all together. There are also detailed rules concerning the amount of income that certain government employees may earn in outside employment. Outside employment may not interfere with an employee's professional judgment in his or her federal position and the employee may not be hired because of his or her federal position. The Office of Government Ethics was established under the act to oversee the administration, and enforcement, of its provisions.

Federal law also addresses potential conflicts of interest at 18 U.S.C. § 201 et seq. This law provides for civil, criminal, and administrative punishments for violators. Bribery is prohibited, as is representing any person or agency against the United States in a controversy. Employees are also prohibited from participating in matters involving parties with whom the employee dealt as an employee. The ban is for life. Senior officers are also prohibited from representing parties before the agencies where they were employed, regardless of connection to the represented party. Cabinet officers are further restricted from representing parties before any agency.

Concerned that governmental employees could be coerced into supporting candidates and issues by high-ranking or elected officers, Congress enacted the Hatch Act (5 U.S.C. § 1501, et. seq. and § 7321 et seq.) The purpose of the act was expressed by Congress in the act itself:

> It is the policy of Congress that employees should be encouraged to exercise fully, freely, and without fear of penalty or reprisal, and to the extent not expressly prohibited by law, their right to participate or to refrain from participating in the political processes of the Nation.

Pursuant to the Hatch Act, employees may not hold, or be candidates for, a partisan elected office. Employees violate the statute only if their activities are active. Specifically, they may not raise funds, identify themselves as government employees while expressing support for a partisan candidate or issue, use governmental facilities, or support a partisan candidate or issue while at work. Employees are, however, entitled to vote and express their opinions about partisan candidates and issues. The act applies to federal government employees and state and local government employees who work for agencies that benefit from federal monies. Many exceptions and exclusions exist in the statute. Violation of the Hatch Act may be punished with removal from office.

What has been covered in this section represents only a small fraction of the law governing government employee ethics. Today, compliance with ethics rules by government employees is complex and has become a cottage industry for attorneys who specialize in the subject.

11.10 PRIVATE PARTIES AS GOVERNMENT ACTORS

As discussed in an earlier chapter, in recent years there has been a significant increase in the privatization of what were previously governmental services. Privatization raises many difficult legal questions. This is a relatively new area of law and thus there are many unanswered questions.[23] Here are examples of the types of questions raised by privatization:

> What happens to the jobs and employment benefits of public employees, who may be protected by civil service or a collective bargaining agreement, after the transfer from public control to private control occurs?

> Are private parties who are providing public services subject to government in the sunshine laws, such as freedom of information for public records and open meetings requirements?
>
> Do people who interact with privatized agencies enjoy the same constitutional and other legally protected rights they enjoy when they interact with government agencies?
>
> Are private parties who are providing public services liable for torts and civil rights violations in the same manner as government actors?

There are no easy answers to any of these questions. This discussion is limited to an overview of the answer to the fourth question, concerning liability of private parties who are providing what were previously publicly provided services.

Generally, there are two forms of privatization. The first involves the jettisoning of a service by a governmental body or agency. In such cases, whether the service will be provided, and at what cost if provided, is left to the private market. Generally, governments are not required to provide services; hence, decisions not to provide services are usually legitimate. However, a few core government functions must be either provided or, at the least, if provided, must be provided by government authorities. (See Chapter 5 for a more thorough discussion of this topic.)

The second and most common form of privatization occurs when a government delegates the administration of a specific program or project to a private party. Historically, it has been common for governments to hire contractors for one-time or rarely occurring needs that require expertise not possessed by the agency. In recent years, though, governments have begun delegating much more than the occasional specialized service. Federal, state, and local governments have begun delegating the administration of entire programs to private parties, including social services (e.g., welfare), corrections, education, transportation, waste collection, tax collection, emergency medical and fire services, and recreation.

Let's first examine liability under state law. Generally, the states are split on the issue of whether private parties who have contracted with them are protected by the immunities that protect state officers when performing the same functions. Federal contractors enjoy an immunity against state tort claims if the contractor can demonstrate that it designed the product pursuant to federal guidelines and that it made the federal government aware of any known risks. The remainder of this discussion will focus on § 1983 liability.

As you learned earlier, one is subject to § 1983 only if acting under color of state law. Generally, one who acts as a contractor for a government does not necessarily act under color of law. Accordingly, contractors that build roads or buildings, for example, are not acting under color of law for purposes of § 1983. Similarly, a private, but closely regulated, business is not operating as a state actor simply because much of its decision making is directed, or limited, by state law. There is a point, however, at which the agency and contractor become so connected that the contractor can fairly be characterized as a state actor. Courts have used different tests to determine if an individual is a state actor. These include the public function test, the compulsion test, and the symbiosis test, sometimes also referred to as the *nexus test*. See Figure 11-5 for a summary of these tests.

Test	Description	Affirmative Example	Negative Example
Public Function	If the function performed has historically been exclusively public, the likelihood of applying § 1983 is high.	Maintaining and owning sidewalk intended for the public in a commercial district is a public function even though owned and maintained by private party. *Marsh v. Alabama,* 326 U.S. 501 (1945), limited by *Lloyd v. Tanner,* 407 U.S. 551 (1972). See also *Terry v.Adams,* 345 U.S. 461 (1953) (concluding that the state violated the Fifteenth Amendment by permitting such circumvention within its borders, which produced the equivalent of a prohibited election) A physician who worked part-time for a state correctional institution treating inmates was found to be performing a state function; as such, he was a state actor that could be sued under § 1983. *West v. Atkins,* 487 U.S. 42 (1988). *See also Fitzgerald v. Barnstable Sch.Comm.,* 555 U.S. 246, 257 (2009) (concluding that §1983 equal protection actions could be brought against individuals and municipal and other state entities)	Landlord's storage and sale of evicted tenant's items was not a traditional state function. *Flagg Bros., Inc. v. Brooks,* 436 U.S. 149 (1978). *See also Am. Mfrs. Mut. Ins. Co. v. Sullivan,* 526 U.S. 40, 50 (1999) (concluding that workers' compensation insurers were not state actors)
Symbiosis	The nature and extent of the relationship between the government and the private party are examined. As the interconnectedness of the two increases, so does the possibility of applying § 1983.	State action found when restaurant located in a publicly owned parking garage was sued for not permitting African-Americans to dine. In that case, the municipality rented space to the restaurant and received a portion of its profits. This financial relationship created a symbiotic relationship. *Burton v. Wilmington Parking Authority,* 365 U.S. 715 (1961). *See also Jackson v Metro* Amendment right of free speech because there was no state action)	A private school received nearly all of its revenues from government sources, was subject to substantial regulation, and was providing a governmental service (secondary education); however, no state action was found between Massachusetts and the school because the state did not benefit from the relationship. *Rendell-Baker v. Kohn,* 457 U.S. 830 (1982). *See also Gonazalez-Maldonado v. MMM Healthcare, Inc.,* 693 F. 3d 244, 248 (1st Cir.. 2012) (concluding that HMO's are not state actors). No state action between Nevada and NCAA when the NCAA conducted an investigation and recommended suspension of coach, but university was a voluntary member of the NCAA and retained the authority over the final decision. *NCAA v. Tarkanian,* 488 U.S. 179 (1988).

| Compulsion | If a private party is acting under the direction of or pursuant to law, § 1983 will likely apply. | Federal law strongly encouraging drug testing of railway employees by private employers, which preempted state law in the area, by prohibited companies from bargaining away testing authority, and establishing mechanism to report violations to federal agency, amounted to compulsion. *Skinner v. Railway Labor Executive Ass'n*, 489 U.S. 602 (1989). See also *Lugar v. Edmondson Oil Co.*, 457 U.S. 922 (1982) (reversing and remanding concluding that petitioner debtor did state a claim for relief in a civil rights action against respondent creditor because respondent acted under color of state law in joint participation with the state to deprive petitioner of his property through the execution of a state writ of attachment). | The existence of a statute that authorized landlords to store and sell items of evicted tenants did not make landlord state actor because state did not direct action, but merely authorized it. *Flagg Bros., Inc. v. Brooks*, 436 U.S. 149 (1978). |

FIGURE 11-5   State action tests.

Interestingly, even if a private party is determined to be subject to liability under § 1983, it is not entitled to the immunities that protect government employees in § 1983 actions.[24]

Even if § 1983 does not apply, in some cases, private contractors may be sued under traditional tort and contract theories and the government, subject to immunities and other defenses, may be sued directly. Establishing § 1983 liability has benefits other than collecting money damages. Injunctive relief may be obtained. For example, establishing that the Constitution applies in prisons empowers inmates to enforce Fourteenth Amendment due process rights and the Eighth Amendment prohibition of cruel and unusual punishments against private prison officials.

As privatization expands and takes on new forms in the years ahead, difficult questions concerning substantive rights and procedures, transparency of operation, and liability will have to be resolved.

In certain instances, rather than governmental functions being privatized, the government performs functions that are typically performed by private entities. One example of this is Ohio workers' compensation system. In the state of Ohio, workers' compensation is provided by the State of Ohio, rather than private insurance companies. However, the State is still bound by the rules and laws implemented to regulate the provision of insurance, and when such laws are violated, the State is liable for the penalties. See *San Allen, Inc. v. Buehrer*, No. CV-07-644950 (Cuyahoga County C.P. 2012) (concluding that the Bureau of Workers' Compensation had overcharged a class of companies who had been unable to participate in group-rating by potentially billions of dollars in violation of R.C. 4123.29 and 4123.34(C), and ordering the repayment of the overcharges).

11.11 OTHER CONSTITUTIONAL ISSUES: TAKINGS AND FREE SPEECH

Takings

In addition to the constitutional violations involving excessive force or false arrest that have already been discussed in this chapter, constitutional violations can also arise from governmental regulation of property use. When the government institutes regulations that prohibit a property owner from using his or her property as he or she intended, the property owner can argue that the government action constitutes a regulatory taking. In these instances, the property owner must demonstrate that the regulation denies the property owner "all economically viable use of his land." If successful, the property owner would have established a regulatory taking of his or her property in violation of the Fifth and Fourteenth Amendments, which would require the government to pay just compensation for the land. See *Lucas v. S.C. Coastal Council*, 505 U.S. 1003 (1992) (recognizing that a regulatory scheme that prohibited a landowner from constructing homes on residential lots might constitute a regulatory taking if it removed all economically viable use of the land).

Free Speech

There is also a line of cases that address liability for violations of the right to free speech. For example, while the First Amendment guarantees individuals the right to say anything they want about their employers, private employers are generally permitted to discipline or terminate them for their statements. However, when the government is the employer, the ability of the employer to respond to employee statements is limited by the First Amendment, which prohibits the government from abridging free speech. In determining whether speech by a public employee is protected, the question is whether the employee spoke as a citizen on a matter of public concern. If the answer is no, the government has broader discretion to restrict the speech, similar to a private employer. If the individual spoke as a citizen on an issue of public concern, the government can restrict speech only to the extent necessary to ensure the efficient and effective operation of the employer. *See Garcetti v. Ceballos*, 547 U.S. 410 (2006) (concluding that a district attorney's memorandum outlining his concerns with a search warrant did not constitute protected speech, and thus his termination was not an abridgement of free speech, because the memorandum was written in the course of his official job responsibilities). Whether speech is on matters of public concern is also relevant for determining whether public speech is protected under the First Amendment. See also *Snyder v. Phelps*, 131 S. Ct. 1207 (2011) (determining that protesters picketing outside of a marine soldier's funeral were engaged in protected free speech because they were on public property and were speaking on issues of public concern). In 2012, the Supreme Court decided *Reichle v. Howards*[25] wherein it was decided that suing for a wrongful arrest in violation of the Fourth Amendment because of a person's speech that was protected under the First Amendment was not clearly established and accordingly, the secret service agent who made the arrest was shielded from liability by qualified immunity.

11.12 CONCLUSION

Section 1983, federal and state tort claims acts, *Bivens* actions, and other statutes provide a means through which injured people may seek compensation from the government. Even though sovereign immunity has been waived in many instances, other immunities, such as the discretionary function and public duty doctrines, limit the liability of the government even if negligence or bad behavior by government officials can be proven. In addition, the government gives itself advantages by specifying and limiting the procedures and types of damages that may be obtained.

In spite of these limitations, it is likely that fear of litigation and liability control the exercise of discretion, at least marginally. You are left to decide whether the many structural, organizational, political, and legal limits on agency authority that you have learned about in this book keep agencies adequately accountable to the people.

LAWLINKS

Data on litigation in the United States can be found at both the Bureau of Justice Statistics (BJS) and National Institute of Justice (NIJ) Web sites. Both the BJS and NIJ are federal government agencies. The sites contain much additional information, focusing especially on crime and criminal justice.

- http://bjs.ojp.usdoj.gov/
- http://www.ojp.usdoj.gov/nij/

REVIEW **QUESTIONS**

1. What is sovereign immunity? What is the status of sovereign immunity today in most jurisdictions?
2. Distinguish a lawsuit against a government official in an official capacity from one against a government official in an individual capacity.
3. Generally, what must be proven to establish a § 1983 violation?
4. May the United States, its various states, or local governments be sued under § 1983? May officials of the United States, states, or local governments be sued individually under § 1983?
5. Distinguish absolute from qualified immunity.
6. Are judges entitled to absolute or qualified immunity? Are agency prosecutors?
7. What is a *Bivens* action?
8. What is official immunity?

CRITICAL THINKING AND **APPLICATIONS PROBLEMS**

Chuck and Dwayne have been enemies since Dwayne's wife, Pam, left him and began living with Chuck. Dwayne is a county deputy sheriff. One evening when Dwayne was on patrol, he noticed Chuck driving down a deserted road. Overcome with anger, Dwayne stopped Chuck. When Chuck inquired what he had done wrong, Dwayne responded, "I'll find something." He detained Chuck for more than 30 minutes. During that time, he inspected Chuck's vehicle and eventually arrested Chuck for operating his vehicle with underinflated tires. At the probable cause hearing, Dwayne testified that he had pulled Chuck over for driving dangerously and having underinflated tires.

Chuck files a civil rights action under § 1983 against Dwayne, seeking an injunction prohibiting Dwayne from harassing him further, and also seeking both general and punitive damages. He alleges that Dwayne's behavior when he stopped and arrested Chuck and at the hearing violated Chuck's rights secured by the Constitution. Chuck also sues the county and state. Based on these facts, answer the following.

1. Dwayne files a motion for dismissal of the entire action under Fed. R. Civ. P. 12, claiming immunity. Should he prevail?
2. Assuming that Chuck can prove his constitutional claims, can general damages be awarded? Punitive damages? Injunctive relief?
3. Can Chuck prevail against the county? Against the state?
4. What must be proven to be successful against the county or the state?

ENDNOTES

1. *Kawananakoa v. Polyblank*, 205 U.S. 349, 353 (1907).

2. K. Davis, *Administrative Law*§ 27.02, at 499 (3rd ed. 1972).

3. *Molitor v. Kaneland Cmty. Unit Dist.*, 163 N.E.2d 89, 94 (Ill. 1959), superceded by statute 745 ILCS 10/1-101 et seq. (West 1998).

4. *N. Ins. Co. of N.Y. v. Chatham Cnty., Ga.*,

5. *Will v. Michigan Dep't of State Police*, 491 U.S. 58, 71 (1989)

6. *Kentucky v. Graham*, 473 U.S. 159 (1985)

7. *Respondeat superior* is the doctrine holding an employer or principal liable for the employee's or agent's wrongful acts committed within the scope of the employment or agency.

8. See *Ohio Rev. Code Ann.* §§2743.01 et seq.

9. 28 U.S.C. §§1291, 1346, 1402, 1504, 2110, 24012402, 24112412, 26712678, 2680.

10. 28 U.S.C. § 1346.

11. 28 U.S.C. § 2680.

12. *Sosa v. Alvarez-Machain*, 542 U.S. 692 (2004)

13. 28 U.S.C. § 2680.

14. *Ritchie v. United States*, 210 F. SupP. 2d 1120 (N.D. Cal. 2002); *Vu v. Meese*, 755 F. SupP. 1375 (E.D. La. 1991).

15. *Four v. U.S. ex rel. Bureau of Indian Affairs*, 431 F. SupP. 2nd 985 (D.N.D. 2006).

16. *Johnson v. United States*, 534 F.3d 958, 963 (8th Cir. 2008).

17. *Id.*

18. *Counts v. Guevara*, 328 F.3d 212, 214 (5th Cir. 2003).

19. 28 U.S.C. § 2674. *See Git v. Dep't of the Treasury*, No. 951899, 1996 U.S. App. LEXIS 86, *56 (8th Cir. Jan. 4, 1996).

20. *Messerschmidt v. Millender*, 565 U.S. ____ (2012).

21. 28 U.S.C. § 1346.

22. 28 U.S.C. § 1346(a)(2).

23. For further discussion, see Jody Freeman, "Extending Public Law Norms through Privatization," 116 *Harvard L. Rev.* 1285 (2003); Nicole B. Casarez, *Furthering the Accountability Principle in Privatized Federal Corrections: The Need/or Access to Private Prison Records*, 28 U. Mich. 1. L. Reform 249 (1995).

24. *Wyatt v. Cole*, 504 U.S. 158 (1992); *Richardson v. McKnight*, 521 U.S. 399 (1997). See also *Toussie v. Powell*, 323 F.3d 178, 183 (2nd Cir. 2003) (concluding that a private defendant facing 1983 liability for conspiring with state officials . . . are not protected by qualified immunity).

25. 566 U.S. ___ (2012)

Appendix **A**

CONSTITUTION OF THE UNITED STATES OF AMERICA

We the People of the United States, in Order to form a more perfect Union, establish Justice, insure domestic Tranquility, provide for the common defense, promote the general Welfare, and secure the Blessings of Liberty to ourselves and our Posterity, do ordain and establish this Constitution for the United States of America.

ARTICLE I
Section 1

All legislative Powers herein granted shall be vested in a Congress of the United States, which shall consist of a Senate and House of Representatives.

Section 2

The House of Representatives shall be composed of Members chosen every second Year by the People of the several States, and the Electors in each State shall have the Qualifications requisite for Electors of the most numerous Branch of the State Legislature.

No Person shall be a Representative who shall not have attained to the Age of twenty five Years, and been seven Years a Citizen of the United States, and who shall not, when elected, be an Inhabitant of that State in which he shall be chosen.

Representatives and direct Taxes shall be apportioned among the several States, which may be included within this Union, according to their respective Numbers, which shall be determined by adding to the whole Number of free Persons, including those bound to Service for a Term of Years, and excluding Indians not taxed, three fifths of all other Persons. The actual Enumeration shall be made within three Years after the first Meeting of the Congress of the United States, and within every subsequent Term of ten Years, in such Manner as they shall by Law direct. The Number of Representatives shall not exceed one for every thirty Thousand, but each State shall have at Least one Representative; and until such enumeration shall be made, the State of New Hampshire shall be entitled to chuse three, Massachusetts eight, Rhode-Island and Providence Plantations one, Connecticut five, New-York six, New Jersey four, Pennsylvania eight, Delaware one, Maryland six, Virginia ten, North Carolina five, South Carolina five, and Georgia three.

When vacancies happen in the Representation from any State, the Executive Authority thereof shall issue Writs of Election to fill such Vacancies.

The House of Representatives shall chuse their Speaker and other Officers; and shall have the sole Power of Impeachment.

Section 3

The Senate of the United States shall be composed of two Senators from each State, *chosen by the Legislature thereof* for six Years; and each Senator shall have one Vote.

Immediately after they shall be assembled in Consequence of the first Election, they shall be divided as equally as may be into three Classes. The Seats of the Senators of the first Class shall be vacated at the Expiration of the second Year, of the second Class at the Expiration of the fourth Year, and of the third Class at the Expiration of the sixth Year, so that one third may be chosen every second Year; *and if Vacancies happen by Resignation, or otherwise, during the Recess of the Legislature of any State, the Executive thereof may make temporary Appointments until the next Meeting of the Legislature, which shall then fill such Vacancies.*

No Person shall be a Senator who shall not have attained to the Age of thirty Years, and been nine Years a Citizen of the United States, and who shall not, when elected, be an Inhabitant of that State for which he shall be chosen.

The Vice President of the United States shall be President of the Senate, but shall have no Vote, unless they be equally divided.

The Senate shall chuse their other Officers, and also a President pro tempore, in the Absence of the Vice President, or when he shall exercise the Office of President of the United States.

The Senate shall have the sole Power to try all Impeachments. When sitting for that Purpose, they shall be on Oath or Affirmation. When the President of the United States is tried, the Chief Justice shall preside: And no Person shall be convicted without the Concurrence of two thirds of the Members present.

Judgment in Cases of Impeachment shall not extend further than to removal from Office, and disqualification to hold and enjoy any Office of honor, Trust or Profit under the United States: but the Party convicted shall nevertheless be liable and subject to Indictment, Trial, Judgment and Punishment, according to Law.

Section 4

The Times, Places and Manner of holding Elections for Senators and Representatives, shall be prescribed in each State by the Legislature thereof; but the Congress may at any time by Law make or alter such Regulations, except as to the Places of chusing Senators.

The Congress shall assemble at least once in every Year, and such Meeting shall be on the *first Monday in December,* unless they shall by Law appoint a different Day.

Section 5

Each House shall be the Judge of the Elections, Returns and Qualifications of its own Members, and a Majority of each shall constitute a Quorum to do Business; but a smaller Number may adjourn from day to day, and may be authorized to compel the Attendance of absent Members, in such Manner, and under such Penalties as each House may provide.

Each House may determine the Rules of its Proceedings, punish its Members for disorderly Behaviour, and, with the Concurrence of two thirds, expel a Member.

Each House shall keep a Journal of its Proceedings, and from time to time publish the same, excepting such Parts as may in their Judgment require Secrecy; and the Yeas and Nays of the Members of either House on any question shall, at the Desire of one fifth of those Present, be entered on the Journal.

Neither House, during the Session of Congress, shall, without the Consent of the other, adjourn for more than three days, nor to any other Place than that in which the two Houses shall be sitting.

Section 6

The Senators and Representatives shall receive a Compensation for their Services, to be ascertained by Law, and paid out of the Treasury of the United States. They shall in all Cases, except Treason, Felony and Breach of the Peace, be privileged from Arrest during their Attendance at the Session of their respective Houses, and in going to and returning from the same; and for any Speech or Debate in either House, they shall not be questioned in any other Place.

No Senator or Representative shall, during the Time for which he was elected, be appointed to any civil Office under the Authority of the United States, which shall have been created, or the Emoluments whereof shall have been encreased during such time; and no Person holding any Office under the United States, shall be a Member of either House during his Continuance in Office.

Section 7

All Bills for raising Revenue shall originate in the House of Representatives; but the Senate may propose or concur with Amendments as on other Bills.

Every Bill, which shall have passed the House of Representatives and the Senate, shall, before it become a Law, be presented to the President of the United States: If he approve he shall sign it, but if not he shall return it, with his Objections to that House in which it shall have originated, who shall enter the Objections at large on their Journal, and proceed to reconsider it. If after such Reconsideration two thirds of that House shall agree to pass the Bill, it shall be sent, together with the Objections, to the other House, by which it shall likewise be reconsidered, and if approved by two thirds of that House, it shall become a Law. But in all such Cases the Votes of both Houses shall be determined by Yeas and Nays, and the Names of the Persons voting for and against the Bill shall be entered on the Journal of each House respectively. If any Bill shall not be returned by the President within ten Days (Sundays excepted) after it shall have been presented to him, the Same shall be a Law, in like Manner as if he had signed it, unless the Congress by their Adjournment prevent its Return, in which Case it shall not be a Law.

Every Order, Resolution, or Vote to which the Concurrence of the Senate and House of Representatives may be necessary (except on a question of Adjournment) shall be presented to the President of the United States; and before the Same shall take Effect, shall be approved by him, or being disapproved by him, shall be repassed by two thirds of the Senate and House of Representatives, according to the Rules and Limitations prescribed in the Case of a Bill.

Section 8

The Congress shall have Power to lay and collect Taxes, Duties, Imposts and Excises, to pay the Debts and provide for the common Defence and general Welfare of the United States; but all Duties, Imposts and Excises shall be uniform throughout the United States;

To borrow Money on the credit of the United States;

To regulate Commerce with foreign Nations, and among the several States, and with the Indian Tribes;

To establish an uniform Rule of Naturalization, and uniform Laws on the subject of Bankruptcies throughout the United States;

To coin Money, regulate the Value thereof, and of foreign Coin, and fix the Standard of Weights and Measures;

To provide for the Punishment of counterfeiting the Securities and current Coin of the United States;

To establish Post Offices and post Roads;

To promote the Progress of Science and useful Arts, by securing for limited Times to Authors and Inventors the exclusive Right to their respective Writings and Discoveries;

To constitute Tribunals inferior to the supreme Court;

To define and punish Piracies and Felonies committed on the high Seas, and Offences against the Law of Nations;

To declare War, grant Letters of Marque and Reprisal, and make Rules concerning Captures on Land and Water;

To raise and support Armies, but no Appropriation of Money to that Use shall be for a longer Term than two Years;

To provide and maintain a Navy;

To make Rules for the Government and Regulation of the land and naval Forces;

To provide for calling forth the Militia to execute the Laws of the Union, suppress Insurrections and repel Invasions;

To provide for organizing, arming, and disciplining the Militia, and for governing such Part of them as may be employed in the Service of the United States, reserving to the States respectively, the Appointment of the Officers, and the Authority of training the Militia according to the discipline prescribed by Congress;

To exercise exclusive Legislation in all Cases whatsoever, over such District (not exceeding ten Miles square) as may, by Cession of particular States, and the Acceptance of Congress, become the Seat of the Government of the United States, and to exercise like Authority over all Places purchased by the Consent of the Legislature of the State in which the Same shall be, for the Erection of Forts, Magazines, Arsenals, dock-Yards, and other needful Buildings;—And

To make all Laws, which shall be necessary and proper for carrying into Execution the foregoing Powers, and all other Powers vested by this Constitution in the Government of the United States, or in any Department or Officer thereof.

Section 9

The Migration or Importation of such Persons as any of the States now existing shall think proper to admit, shall not be prohibited by the Congress prior to the Year one thousand eight hundred and eight, but a Tax or duty may be imposed on such Importation, not exceeding ten dollars for each Person.

The Privilege of the Writ of Habeas Corpus shall not be suspended, unless when in Cases of Rebellion or Invasion the public Safety may require it.

No Bill of Attainder or ex post facto Law shall be passed.

No Capitation, or other direct, Tax shall be laid, *unless in Proportion to the Census or enumeration herein before directed to be taken.*

No Tax or Duty shall be laid on Articles exported from any State.

No Preference shall be given by any Regulation of Commerce or Revenue to the Ports of one State over those of another; nor shall Vessels bound to, or from, one State, be obliged to enter, clear, or pay Duties in another.

No Money shall be drawn from the Treasury, but in Consequence of Appropriations made by Law; and a regular Statement and Account of the Receipts and Expenditures of all public Money shall be published from time to time.

No Title of Nobility shall be granted by the United States: And no Person holding any Office of Profit or Trust under them, shall, without the Consent of the Congress, accept of any present, Emolument, Office, or Title, of any kind whatever, from any King, Prince, or foreign State.

Section 10

No State shall enter into any Treaty, Alliance, or Confederation; grant Letters of Marque and Reprisal; coin Money; emit Bills of Credit; make any Thing but gold and silver Coin a Tender in Payment of Debts; pass any Bill of Attainder, ex post facto Law, or Law impairing the Obligation of Contracts, or grant any Title of Nobility.

No State shall, without the Consent of the Congress, lay any Imposts or Duties on Imports or Exports, except what may be absolutely necessary for executing its inspection Laws: and the net Produce of all Duties and Imposts, laid by any State on Imports or Exports, shall be for the Use of the Treasury of the United States; and all such Laws shall be subject to the Revision and Controul of the Congress.

No State shall, without the Consent of Congress, lay any Duty of Tonnage, keep Troops, or Ships of War in time of Peace, enter into any Agreement or Compact with another State, or with a foreign Power, or engage in War, unless actually invaded, or in such imminent Danger as will not admit of delay.

ARTICLE II
Section 1

The executive Power shall be vested in a President of the United States of America. He shall hold his Office during the Term of four Years, and, together with the Vice President, chosen for the same Term, be elected, as follows:

Each State shall appoint, in such Manner as the Legislature thereof may direct, a Number of Electors, equal to the whole Number of Senators and Representatives to which the State may be entitled in the Congress: but no Senator or Representative, or Person holding an Office of Trust or Profit under the United States, shall be appointed an Elector.

The Electors shall meet in their respective States, and vote by Ballot for two Persons, of whom one at least shall not be an Inhabitant of the same State with themselves. And they shall make a List of all the Persons voted for, and of the Number of Votes for each; which List they shall sign and certify, and trans-mit sealed to the Seat of the Government of the United States, directed to the President of the Senate. The President of the Senate shall, in the Presence of the Senate and House of Representatives, open all the Certificates, and the Votes shall then be counted. The Person having the greatest Number of Votes shall be the President, if such Number be a Majority of the whole Number of Electors appointed; and if there be more than one who have such Majority, and have an equal Number of Votes, then the House of Representatives shall immediately chuse by Ballot one of them for President; and if no Person have a Majority, then from the five highest on the List the said House shall in like Manner chuse the President. But in chusing the President, the Votes shall be taken by States, the Representation from each State hav-ing one Vote; A quorum for this purpose shall consist of a Member or Members from two thirds of the States, and a Majority of all the States shall be necessary to a Choice. In every Case, after the Choice of the President, the Person having the greatest Number of Votes of the Electors shall be the Vice President. But if there should remain two or more who have equal Votes, the Senate shall chuse from them by Bal-lot the Vice President.

The Congress may determine the Time of chusing the Electors, and the Day on which they shall give their Votes; which Day shall be the same throughout the United States.

No Person except a natural born Citizen, or a Citizen of the United States, at the time of the Adoption of this Constitution, shall be eligible to the Office of President; neither shall any Person be eligible to that Office who shall not have attained to the Age of thirty five Years, and been fourteen Years a Resident within the United States.

In Case of the Removal of the President from Office, or of his Death, Resignation, or Inability to dis-charge the Powers and Duties of the said Office, the Same shall devolve on the Vice President, and the Congress may by Law provide for the Case of Removal, Death, Resignation or Inability, both of the President and Vice President, declaring what Officer shall then act as President, and such Officer shall act accordingly, until the Disability be removed, or a President shall be elected.

The President shall, at stated Times, receive for his Services, a Compensation, which shall neither be increased nor diminished during the Period for which he shall have been elected, and he shall not receive within that Period any other Emolument from the United States, or any of them.

Before he enter on the Execution of his Office, he shall take the following Oath or Affirmation:— "I do solemnly swear (or affirm) that I will faithfully execute the Office of President of the United States, and will to the best of my Ability, preserve, protect and defend the Constitution of the United States."

Section 2

The President shall be Commander in Chief of the Army and Navy of the United States, and of the Militia of the several States, when called into the actual Service of the United States; he may require the Opinion, in writing, of the principal Officer in each of the executive Departments, upon any Sub-ject relating to the Duties of their respective Offices, and he shall have Power to grant Reprieves and Pardons for Offences against the United States, except in Cases of Impeachment.

He shall have Power, by and with the Advice and Consent of the Senate, to make Treaties, provided two thirds of the Senators present concur; and he shall nominate, and by and with the Advice and Consent of the Senate, shall appoint Ambassadors, other public Ministers and Consuls, Judges of the supreme Court, and all other Officers of the United States, whose Appointments are not herein otherwise provided for, and which shall be established by Law: but the Congress may by Law vest the Appointment of such inferior Officers, as they think proper, in the President alone, in the Courts of Law, or in the Heads of Departments.

The President shall have Power to fill up all Vacancies that may happen during the Recess of the Senate, by granting Commissions, which shall expire at the End of their next Session.

Section 3

He shall from time to time give to the Congress Information of the State of the Union, and recommend to their Consideration such Measures as he shall judge necessary and expedient; he may, on extraordinary Occasions, convene both Houses, or either of them, and in Case of Disagreement between them, with Respect to the Time of Adjournment, he may adjourn them to such Time as he shall think proper; he shall receive Ambassadors and other public Ministers; he shall take Care that the Laws be faithfully executed, and shall Commission all the Officers of the United States.

Section 4

The President, Vice President and all civil Officers of the United States, shall be removed from Office on Impeachment for, and Conviction of, Treason, Bribery, or other high Crimes and Misdemeanors.

ARTICLE III
Section 1

The judicial Power of the United States shall be vested in one supreme Court, and in such inferior Courts as the Congress may from time to time ordain and establish. The Judges, both of the supreme and inferior Courts, shall hold their Offices during good Behaviour, and shall, at stated Times, receive for their Services a Compensation, which shall not be diminished during their Continuance in Office.

Section 2

The judicial Power shall extend to all Cases, in Law and Equity, arising under this Constitution, the Laws of the United States, and Treaties made, or which shall be made, under their Authority;—to all Cases affecting Ambassadors, other public Ministers and Consuls;—to all Cases of admiralty and maritime Jurisdiction;—to Controversies to which the United States shall be a Party;—to Controversies between two or more States;—*between a State and Citizens of another State;*—between Citizens of different States;—between Citizens of the same State claiming Lands under Grants of different States, and between a State, or the Citizens thereof, and foreign States, Citizens or Subjects.

In all Cases affecting Ambassadors, other public Ministers and Consuls, and those in which a State shall be Party, the supreme Court shall have original Jurisdiction. In all the other Cases before mentioned, the supreme Court shall have appellate Jurisdiction, both as to Law and Fact, with such Exceptions, and under such Regulations as the Congress shall make.

The Trial of all Crimes, except in Cases of Impeachment, shall be by Jury; and such Trial shall be held in the State where the said Crimes shall have been committed; but when not committed within any State, the Trial shall be at such Place or Places as the Congress may by Law have directed.

Section 3

Treason against the United States, shall consist only in levying War against them, or in adhering to their Enemies, giving them Aid and Comfort. No Person shall be convicted of Treason unless on the Testimony of two Witnesses to the same overt Act, or on Confession in open Court.

The Congress shall have Power to declare the Punishment of Treason, but no Attainder of Treason shall work Corruption of Blood, or Forfeiture except during the Life of the Person attainted.

ARTICLE IV
Section 1

Full Faith and Credit shall be given in each State to the public Acts, Records, and judicial Proceedings of every other State. And the Congress may by general Laws prescribe the Manner in which such Acts, Records and Proceedings shall be proved, and the Effect thereof.

Section 2

The Citizens of each State shall be entitled to all Privileges and Immunities of Citizens in the several States.

A Person charged in any State with Treason, Felony, or other Crime, who shall flee from Justice, and be found in another State, shall on Demand of the executive Authority of the State from which he fled, be delivered up, to be removed to the State having Jurisdiction of the Crime.

No Person held to Service or Labour in one State, under the Laws thereof, escaping into another, shall, in Consequence of any Law or Regulation therein, be discharged from such Service or Labour, but shall be delivered up on Claim of the Party to whom such Service or Labour may be due.

Section 3

New States may be admitted by the Congress into this Union; but no new State shall be formed or erected within the Jurisdiction of any other State; nor any State be formed by the Junction of two or more States, or Parts of States, without the Consent of the Legislatures of the States concerned as well as of the Congress.

The Congress shall have Power to dispose of and make all needful Rules and Regulations respecting the Territory or other Property belonging to the United States; and nothing in this Constitution shall be so construed as to Prejudice any Claims of the United States, or of any particular State.

Section 4

The United States shall guarantee to every State in this Union a Republican Form of Government, and shall protect each of them against Invasion; and on Application of the Legislature, or of the Executive (when the Legislature cannot be convened), against domestic Violence.

ARTICLE V

The Congress, whenever two thirds of both Houses shall deem it necessary, shall propose Amendments to this Constitution, or, on the Application of the Legislatures of two thirds of the several States, shall call a Convention for proposing Amendments, which, in either Case, shall be valid to all Intents and Purposes, as Part of this Constitution, when ratified by the Legislatures of three fourths of the several States, or by Conventions in three fourths thereof, as the one or the other Mode of Ratification may be proposed by the Congress; Provided that no Amendment which may be made prior to the Year One thousand eight hundred and eight shall in any Manner affect the first and fourth Clauses in the Ninth Section of the first Article; and that no State, without its Consent, shall be deprived of its equal Suffrage in the Senate.

ARTICLE VI

All Debts contracted and Engagements entered into, before the Adoption of this Constitution, shall be as valid against the United States under this Constitution, as under the Confederation.

This Constitution, and the Laws of the United States which shall be made in Pursuance thereof; and all Treaties made, or which shall be made, under the Authority of the United States, shall be the supreme Law of the Land; and the Judges in every State shall be bound thereby, any Thing in the Constitution or Laws of any State to the Contrary notwithstanding.

The Senators and Representatives before mentioned, and the Members of the several State Legislatures, and all executive and judicial Officers, both of the United States and of the several States, shall be bound by Oath or Affirmation, to support this Constitution; but no religious Test shall ever be required as a Qualification to any Office or public Trust under the United States.

ARTICLE VII

The Ratification of the Conventions of nine States, shall be sufficient for the Establishment of this Constitution between the States so ratifying the Same.

The Word, "the," being interlined between the seventh and eighth Lines of the first Page, the Word "Thirty" being partly written on an Erazure in the fifteenth Line of the first Page, the Words "is tried" being interlined between the thirty second and thirty third Lines of the first Page and the Word "the" being interlined between the forty third and forty fourth Lines of the second Page.

Attest William Jackson Secretary

Done in Convention by the Unanimous Consent of the States present the Seventeenth Day of September in the Year of our Lord one thousand seven hundred and Eighty seven and of the Independence of the United States of America the Twelfth In witness whereof We have hereunto subscribed our Names,

G°. Washington
Presidt and deputy from Virginia
Delaware
Geo: Read
Gunning Bedford jun
John Dickinson
Richard Bassett
Jaco: Broom
Maryland
James McHenry
Dan of St Thos. Jenifer
Danl. Carroll
Virginia
John Blair
James Madison Jr.
North Carolina
Wm. Blount
Richd. Dobbs Spaight
Hu Williamson
South Carolina
J. Rutledge
Charles Cotesworth Pinckney
Charles Pinckney
Pierce Butler
Georgia
William Few
Abr Baldwin
New Hampshire
John Langdon
Nicholas Gilman
Massachusetts
Nathaniel Gorham
Rufus King
Connecticut
Wm. Saml. Johnson
Roger Sherman
New York
Alexander Hamilton
New Jersey

Wil: Livingston
David Brearley
Wm. Paterson
Jona: Dayton
Pennsylvania
B Franklin
Thomas Mifflin
Robt. Morris
Geo. Clymer
Thos. FitzSimons
Jared Ingersoll
James Wilson
Gouv Morris

AMENDMENT I (1791)

Congress shall make no law respecting an establishment of religion, or prohibiting the free exercise thereof; or abridging the freedom of speech, or of the press; or the right of the people peaceably to assemble, and to petition the Government for a redress of grievances.

AMENDMENT II (1791)

A well regulated Militia being necessary to the security of a free state, the right of the people to keep and bear Arms, shall not be infringed.

AMENDMENT III (1791)

No Soldier shall, in time of peace be quartered in any House, without the consent of the Owner, nor in time of war, but in a manner to be prescribed by law.

AMENDMENT IV (1791)

The right of the people to be secure in their persons, houses, papers, and effects, against unreasonable searches and seizures, shall not be violated, and no Warrants shall issue, but upon probable cause, supported by Oath or affirmation, and particularly describing the place to be searched, and the persons or things to be seized.

AMENDMENT V (1791)

No person shall be held to answer for a capital, or otherwise infamous crime, unless on a presentment or indictment of a Grand Jury, except in cases arising in the land or naval forces, or in the Militia, when in actual service in time of War or public danger; nor shall any person be subject for the same offence to be twice put in jeopardy of life or limb; nor shall be compelled in any criminal case to be a witness against himself, nor be deprived of life, liberty, or property, without due process of law; nor shall private property be taken for public use, without just compensation.

AMENDMENT VI (1791)

In all criminal prosecutions, the accused shall enjoy the right to a speedy and public trial, by an impartial jury of the State and district wherein the crime shall have been committed, which district shall have been previously ascertained by law, and to be informed of the nature and cause of the accusation; to be confronted with the witnesses against him; to have compulsory process for obtaining witnesses in his favor; and to have the Assistance of Counsel for his defence.

AMENDMENT VII (1791)

In Suits at common law, where the value in controversy shall exceed twenty dollars, the right of trial by jury shall be preserved, and no fact tried by a jury, shall be otherwise re-examined in any Court of the United States, than according to the rules of the common law.

AMENDMENT VIII (1791)

Excessive bail shall not be required, nor excessive fines imposed, nor cruel and unusual punishments inflicted.

AMENDMENT IX (1791)

The enumeration in the Constitution, of certain rights, shall not be construed to deny or disparage others retained by the people.

AMENDMENT X (1791)

The powers not delegated to the United States by the Constitution, nor prohibited by it to the States, are reserved to the States respectively, or to the people.

AMENDMENT XI (1798)

The Judicial power of the United States shall not be construed to extend to any suit in law or equity, commenced or prosecuted against one of the United States by Citizens of another State, or by Citizens or Subjects of any Foreign State.

AMENDMENT XII (1804)

The Electors shall meet in their respective states and vote by ballot for President and Vice-President, one of whom, at least, shall not be an inhabitant of the same state with themselves; they shall name in their ballots the person voted for as President, and in distinct ballots the person voted for as Vice-President, and they shall make distinct lists of all persons voted for as President, and of all persons voted for as Vice-President, and of the number of votes for each, which lists they shall sign and certify, and transmit sealed to the seat of the Government of the United States, directed to the President of the Senate;—The President of the Senate shall, in the presence of the Senate and House of Representatives, open all the certificates and the votes shall then be counted;—The person having the greatest number of votes for President, shall be the President, if such number be a majority of the whole number of Electors appointed; and if no person have such majority, then from the persons having the highest numbers not exceeding three on the list of those voted for as President, the House of Representatives shall choose immediately, by ballot, the President. But in choosing the President, the votes shall be taken by states, the representation from each state having one vote; a quorum for this purpose shall consist of a member or members from two-thirds of the states, and a majority of all the states shall be necessary to a choice. And if the House of Representatives shall not choose a President whenever the right of choice shall devolve upon them, before the fourth day of March next following, then the Vice-President shall act as President, as in the case of the death or other constitutional disability of the President—The person having the greatest number of votes as Vice-President, shall be the Vice-President, if such number be a majority of the whole number of Electors appointed, and if no person have a majority, then from the two highest numbers on the list, the Senate shall choose the Vice-President; A quorum for the purpose shall consist of two-thirds of the whole number of Senators, and a majority of the whole number shall be necessary to a choice. But no person constitutionally ineligible to the office of President shall be eligible to that of Vice-President of the United States.

AMENDMENT XIII (1865)
Section 1

Neither slavery nor involuntary servitude, except as a punishment for crime whereof the party shall have been duly convicted, shall exist within the United States, or any place subject to their jurisdiction.

Section 2

Congress shall have power to enforce this article by appropriate legislation.

AMENDMENT XIV (1868)
Section 1

All persons born or naturalized in the United States and subject to the jurisdiction thereof, are citizens of the United States and of the State wherein they reside. No State shall make or enforce any law, which shall abridge the privileges or immunities of citizens of the United States; nor shall any State deprive any person of life, liberty, or property, without due process of law; nor deny to any person within its jurisdiction the equal protection of the laws.

Section 2

Representatives shall be apportioned among the several States according to their respective numbers, counting the whole number of persons in each State, excluding Indians not taxed. But when the right to vote at any election for the choice of electors for President and Vice-President of the United States, Representatives in Congress, the Executive and Judicial officers of a State, or the members of the Legislature thereof, is denied to any of the male inhabitants of such State, being twenty-one years of age, and citizens of the United States, or in any way abridged, except for participation in rebellion, or other crime, the basis of representation therein shall be reduced in the proportion which the number of such male citizens shall bear to the whole number of male citizens twenty-one years of age in such State.

Section 3

No person shall be a Senator or Representative in Congress, or elector of President and Vice-President, or hold any office, civil or military, under the United States, or under any State, who, having previously taken an oath, as a member of Congress, or as an officer of the United States, or as a member of any State legislature, or as an executive or judicial officer of any State, to support the Constitution of the United States, shall have engaged in insurrection or rebellion against the same, or given aid or comfort to the enemies thereof. But Congress may by a vote of two-thirds of each House, remove such disability.

Section 4

The validity of the public debt of the United States, authorized by law, including debts incurred for payment of pensions and bounties for services in suppressing insurrection or rebellion, shall not be questioned. But neither the United States nor any State shall assume or pay any debt or obligation incurred in aid of insurrection or rebellion against the United States, or any claim for the loss or emancipation of any slave; but all such debts, obligations and claims shall be held illegal and void.

Section 5

The Congress shall have power to enforce, by appropriate legislation, the provisions of this article.

AMENDMENT XV (1870)
Section 1

The right of citizens of the United States to vote shall not be denied or abridged by the United States or by any State on account of race, color, or previous condition of servitude.

Section 2

The Congress shall have power to enforce this article by appropriate legislation.

AMENDMENT XVI (1913)

The Congress shall have power to lay and collect taxes on incomes, from whatever source derived, without apportionment among the several States, and without regard to any census or enumeration.

AMENDMENT XVII (1913)

The Senate of the United States shall be composed of two Senators from each State, elected by the people thereof, for six years; and each Senator shall have one vote. The electors in each State shall have the qualifications requisite for electors of the most numerous branch of the State legislatures.

When vacancies happen in the representation of any State in the Senate, the executive authority of such State shall issue writs of election to fill such vacancies: *Provided,* That the legislature of any State may empower the executive thereof to make temporary appointments until the people fill the vacancies by election as the legislature may direct.

This amendment shall not be so construed as to affect the election or term of any Senator chosen before it becomes valid as part of the Constitution.

AMENDMENT XVIII (1919)
Section 1

After one year from the ratification of this article the manufacture, sale, or transportation of intoxicating liquors within, the importation thereof into, or the exportation thereof from the United States and all territory subject to the jurisdiction thereof for beverage purposes is hereby prohibited.

Section 2

The Congress and the several States shall have concurrent power to enforce this article by appropriate legislation.

Section 3

This article shall be inoperative unless it shall have been ratified as an amendment to the Constitution by the legislatures of the several States, as provided in the Constitution, within seven years from the date of the submission hereof to the States by the Congress.

AMENDMENT XIX (1920)

The right of citizens of the United States to vote shall not be denied or abridged by the United States or by any State on account of sex.

Congress shall have power to enforce this article by appropriate legislation.

AMENDMENT XX (1933)
Section 1

The terms of the President and Vice President shall end at noon on the 20th day of January, and the terms of Senators and Representatives at noon on the 3rd day of January, of the years in which such terms would have ended if this article had not been ratified; and the terms of their successors shall then begin.

Section 2

The Congress shall assemble at least once in every year, and such meeting shall begin at noon on the 3rd day of January, unless they shall by law appoint a different day.

Section 3

If, at the time fixed for the beginning of the term of the President, the president elect shall have died, the Vice President elect shall become President. If a President shall not have been chosen before the time fixed for the beginning of his term, or if the President elect shall have failed to qualify, then the

Vice President elect shall act as President until a President shall have qualified; and the Congress may by law provide for the case wherein neither a President elect nor a Vice President elect shall have qualified, declaring who shall then act as President, or the manner in which one who is to act shall be selected, and such person shall act accordingly until a President or Vice President shall have qualified.

Section 4

The Congress may by law provide for the case of the death of any of the persons from whom the House of Representatives may choose a President whenever the right of choice shall have devolved upon them, and for the case of the death of any of the persons from whom the Senate may choose a Vice President whenever the right of choice shall have devolved upon them.

Section 5

Sections 1 and 2 shall take effect on the 15th day of October following the ratification of this article.

Section 6

This article shall be inoperative unless it shall have been ratified as an amendment to the Constitution by the legislatures of three-fourths of the several States within seven years from the date of its submission.

AMENDMENT XXI (1933)

Section 1

The eighteenth article of amendment to the Constitution of the United States is hereby repealed.

Section 2

The transportation or importation into any State, Territory or possession of the United States for delivery or use therein of intoxicating liquors, in violation of the laws thereof, is hereby prohibited.

Section 3

This article shall be inoperative unless it shall have been ratified as an amendment to the Constitution by conventions in the several States, as provided in the Constitution, within seven years from the date of the submission hereof to the States by the Congress.

AMENDMENT XXII (1951)
Section 1

No person shall be elected to the office of the President more than twice, and no person who has held the office of President, or acted as President, for more than two years of a term to which some other person was elected President shall be elected to the office of the President more than once. But this Article shall not apply to any person holding the office of President when this Article was proposed by the Congress, and shall not prevent any person who may be holding the office of President, or acting as President, during the term within which this Article becomes operative from holding the office of President or acting as President during the remainder of such term.

Section 2

This Article shall be inoperative unless it shall have been ratified as an amendment to the Constitution by the legislatures of three-fourths of the several States within seven years from the date of its submission to the States by the Congress.

AMENDMENT XXIII (1961)
Section 1

The District constituting the seat of Government of the United States shall appoint in such manner as the Congress may direct:

A number of electors of President and Vice President equal to the whole number of Senators and Representatives in Congress to which the District would be entitled if it were a State, but in no event more than the least populous State; they shall be in addition to those appointed by the States, but they shall be considered, for the purposes of the election of President and Vice President, to be electors appointed by a State; and they shall meet in the District and perform such duties as provided by the twelfth article of amendment.

Section 2

The Congress shall have power to enforce this article by appropriate legislation.

AMENDMENT XXIV (1964)
Section 1

The right of citizens of the United States to vote in any primary or other election for President or Vice President, for electors for President or Vice President, or for Senator or Representative in Congress, shall not be denied or abridged by the United States or any State by reason of failure to pay any poll tax or other tax.

Section 2

The Congress shall have power to enforce this article by appropriate legislation.

AMENDMENT XXV (1967)
Section 1

In case of the removal of the President from office or of his death or resignation, the Vice President shall become President.

Section 2

Whenever there is a vacancy in the office of the Vice President, the President shall nominate a Vice President who shall take office upon confirmation by a majority vote of both Houses of Congress.

Section 3

Whenever the President transmits to the President pro tempore of the Senate and the Speaker of the House of Representatives his written declaration that he is unable to discharge the powers and duties of his office, and until he transmits to them a written declaration to the contrary, such powers and duties shall be discharged by the Vice President as Acting President.

Section 4

Whenever the Vice President and a majority of either the principal officers of the executive departments or of such other body as Congress may by law provide, transmit to the President pro tempore of the Senate and the Speaker of the House of Representatives their written declaration that the President is unable to discharge the powers and duties of his office, the Vice President shall immediately assume the powers and duties of the office as Acting President.

Thereafter, when the President transmits to the President pro tempore of the Senate and the Speaker of the House of Representatives his written declaration that no inability exists, he shall resume the powers and duties of his office unless the Vice President and a majority of either the principal officers of the executive department or of such other body as Congress may by law provide, transmit within four days to the President pro tempore of the Senate and the Speaker of the House of Representatives their written declaration that the President is unable to discharge the powers and duties of his office. Thereupon Congress shall decide the issue, assembling within forty-eight hours for that purpose if not in session. If the Congress, within twenty-one days after receipt of the latter written declaration, or, if Congress is not in session, within twenty-one days after Congress is required to assemble, determines by two-thirds vote of both Houses that the President is unable to discharge the powers and duties of his office, the Vice President shall continue to discharge the same as Acting President; otherwise, the President shall resume the powers and duties of his office.

AMENDMENT XXVI (1971)

Section 1

The right of citizens of the United States, who are eighteen years of age or older, to vote shall not be denied or abridged by the United States or by any State on account of age.

Section 2

The Congress shall have power to enforce this article by appropriate legislation.

AMENDMENT XXVII (1992)

No law varying the compensation for the services of the senators and representatives shall take effect, until an election of representatives shall have intervened.

Constitution of the United States of America

Appendix **B**

ADMINISTRATIVE PROCEDURE ACT (5 U.S.C. § 551 *ET SEQ.*) EXCERPTS

Title 5—Government Organization and Employees

Chapter 5—Administrative Procedure

Subchapter II—Administrative Procedure

§ 551. Definitions   For the purpose of this subchapter—

(1) "agency" means each authority of the Government of the United States, whether or not it is within or subject to review by another agency, but does not include—
   (A) the Congress;
   (B) the courts of the United States;
   (C) the governments of the territories or possessions of the United States;
   (D) the government of the District of Columbia; or except as to the requirements of section 552 of this title—
   (E) agencies composed of representatives of the parties or of representatives of organizations of the parties to the disputes determined by them;
   (F) courts martial and military commissions;

    (G) military authority exercised in the field in time of war or in occupied territory; or

    (H) functions conferred by sections 1738, 1739, 1743, and 1744 of title 12; Chapter 2 of title 41; or sections 1622, 1884, 1891–1902, and former section 1641(b)(2), of title 50, appendix;

(2) "person" includes an individual, partnership, corporation, association, or public or private organization other than an agency;

(3) "party" includes a person or agency named or admitted as a party, or properly seeking and entitled as of right to be admitted as a party, in an agency proceeding, and a person or agency admitted by an agency as a party for limited purposes;

(4) "rule" means the whole or a part of an agency statement of general or particular applicability and future effect designed to implement, interpret, or prescribe law or policy or escribing the organization, procedure, or practice requirements of an agency and includes the approval or prescription for the future of rates, wages, corporate or financial structures or reorganization thereof, prices, facilities, appliances, services or allowances thereof, or of valuations, costs, or accounting, or practices bearing on any of the foregoing;

(5) "rule making" means agency process for formulating, amending, or repealing a rule;

(6) "order" means the whole or a part of a final disposition, whether affirmative, negative, injunctive, or declaratory in form, of an agency in a matter other than rule making but including licensing;

(7) "adjudication" means agency process for the formulation of an order;

(8) "license" includes the whole or a part of an agency permit, certificate, approval, registration, charter, membership, statutory exemption or other form of permission;

(9) "licensing" includes agency process respecting the grant, renewal, denial, revocation, suspension, annulment, withdrawal, limitation, amendment, modification, or conditioning of a license;

(10) "sanction" includes the whole or a part of an agency—

    (A) prohibition, requirement, limitation, or other condition affecting the freedom of a person;

    (B) withholding of relief;

    (C) imposition of penalty or fine;

    (D) destruction, taking, seizure, or withholding of property;

    (E) assessment of damages, reimbursement, restitution, compensation, costs, charges, or fees;

    (F) requirement, revocation, or suspension of a license; or

    (G) taking other compulsory or restrictive action;

(11) "relief" includes the whole or a part of an agency—

    (A) grant of money, assistance, license, authority, exemption, exception, privilege, or remedy;

    (B) recognition of a claim, right, immunity, privilege, exemption, or exception; or

    (C) taking of other action on the application or petition of, and beneficial to, a person;

(12) "agency proceeding" means an agency process as defined by paragraphs (5), (7), and (9) of this section; and

(13) "agency action" includes the whole or a part of an agency rule, order, license, sanction, relief, or the equivalent or denial thereof, or failure to act.

(14) "Ex parte communication" means an oral or written communication not on the public record with respect to which reasonable prior notice to all parties is not given, but it shall not include requests for status reports on any matter or proceeding covered by this subchapter.

§ 552. Public information; agency rules, opinions, orders, records, and proceedings

(a) Each agency shall make available to the public information as follows:

    (1) Each agency shall separately state and currently publish in the Federal Register for the guidance of the public—

        (A) descriptions of its central and field organization and the established places at which, the employees (and in the case of a uniformed service, the members) from whom, and the methods whereby, the public may obtain information, make submittals or requests, or obtain decisions;

        (B) statements of the general course and method by which its functions are channeled and determined, including the nature and requirements of all formal and informal procedures available;

        (C) rules of procedure, descriptions of forms available or the places at which forms may be obtained, and instructions as to the scope and contents of all papers, reports, or examinations;

(D)   substantive rules of general applicability adopted as authorized by law, and statements of general policy or interpretations of general applicability formulated and adopted by the agency; and

(E)   each amendment, revision, or repeal of the foregoing.

Except to the extent that a person has actual and timely notice of the terms thereof, a person may not in any manner be required to resort to, or be adversely affected by, a matter required to be published in the Federal Register and not so published. For the purpose of this paragraph, matter reasonably available to the class of persons affected thereby is deemed published in the Federal Register when incorporated by reference therein with the approval of the Director of the Federal Register.

(2)   Each agency, in accordance with published rules, shall make available for public inspection and copying—

(A)   final opinions, including concurring and dissenting opinions, as well as orders, made in the adjudication of cases;

(B)   those statements of policy and interpretations, which have been adopted by the agency and are not published in the Federal Register; and

(C)   administrative staff manuals and instructions to staff that affect a member of the public;

unless the materials are promptly published and copies offered for sale. To the extent required to prevent a clearly unwarranted invasion of personal privacy, an agency may delete identifying details when it makes available or publishes an opinion, statement of policy, interpretation, or staff manual or instruction. However, in each case the justification for the deletion shall be explained fully in writing. Each agency also shall maintain and make available for public inspection and copying a current index providing identifying information for the public as to any matter issued, adopted, or promulgated after July 4, 1967, and required by this paragraph to be made available or published. Each agency shall promptly publish, quarterly or more frequently, and distribute (by sale or otherwise) copies of each index or supplements thereto unless it determines by order published in the Federal Register that the publication would be unnecessary and impracticable, in which case the agency shall nonetheless provide copies of such index on request at a cost not to exceed the direct cost of duplication. A final order, opinion, statement of policy, interpretation, or staff manual or instruction that affects a member of the public may be relied on, used, or cited as precedent by an agency against a party other than an agency only if—

(i)   it has been indexed and either made available or published as provided by this paragraph; or

(ii) the party has actual and timely notice of the terms thereof.

(3)   Except with respect to the records made available under paragraphs (1) and (2) of this subsection, each agency, upon any request for records, which (A) reasonably describes such records and (B) is made in accordance with published rules stating the time, place, fees (if any), and procedures to be followed, shall make the records promptly available to any person.

(4)   (A)   In order to carry out the provisions of this section, each agency shall promulgate regulations, pursuant to notice and receipt of public comment, specifying a uniform schedule of fees applicable to all constituent units of such agency. Such fees shall be limited to reasonable standard charges for document search and duplication and provide for recovery of only the direct costs of such search and duplication. Documents shall be furnished without charge or at a reduced charge where the agency determines that waiver or reduction of the fee is in the public interest because furnishing the information can be considered as primarily benefiting the general public.

(B)   On complaint, the district court of the United States in the district in which the complainant resides, or has his principal place of business, or in which the agency records are situated, or in the District of Columbia, has jurisdiction to enjoin the agency from withholding agency records and to order the production of any agency records improperly withheld from the complainant. In such a case the court shall determine the matter de novo, and may examine the contents of such agency records in camera to determine whether such records or any part thereof shall be withheld under any of the exemptions set forth in subsection (b) of this section, and the burden is on the agency to sustain its action.

(C)   Notwithstanding any other provision of law, the defendant shall serve an answer or otherwise plead to any complaint made under this subsection within thirty days after service upon the defendant of the pleading in which such complaint is made, unless the court otherwise directs for good cause shown.

(D) [Repealed.]

(E) The court may assess against the United States reasonable attorney fees and other litigation costs reasonably incurred in any case under this section in which the complainant has substantially prevailed.

(F) Whenever the court orders the production of any agency records improperly withheld from the complainant and assesses against the United States reasonable attorney fees and other litigation costs, and the court additionally issues a written finding that the circumstances surrounding the withholding raise questions whether agency personnel acted arbitrarily or capriciously with respect to the withholding, the Special Counsel shall promptly initiate a proceeding to determine whether disciplinary action is warranted against the officer or employee who was primarily responsible for the withholding. The Special Counsel, after investigation and consideration of the evidence submitted, shall submit its findings and recommendations to the administrative authority of the agency concerned and shall send copies of the findings and recommendations to the officer or employee, or his representative. The administrative authority shall take the corrective action that the Special Counsel recommends.

(G) In the event of noncompliance with the order of the court, the district court may punish for contempt the responsible employee, and in the case of a uniformed service, the responsible member.

(5) Each agency having more than one member shall maintain and make available for public inspection a record of the final votes of each member in every agency proceeding.

(6) (A) Each agency, upon any request for records made under paragraph (1), (2), or (3) of this subsection, shall—

(i) determine within ten days (excepting Saturdays, Sundays, and legal public holidays) after the receipt of any such request whether to comply with such request and shall immediately notify the person making such request of such determination and the reasons therefor, and of the right of such person to appeal to the head of the agency any adverse determination; and

(ii) make a determination with respect to any appeal within twenty days (excepting Saturdays, Sundays, and legal public holidays) after the receipt of such appeal. If on appeal the denial of the request for records is in whole or in part upheld, the agency shall notify the person making such request of the provisions for judicial review of that determination under paragraph (4) of this subsection.

(B) In unusual circumstances as specified in this subparagraph, the time limits prescribed in either clause (i) or clause (ii) of subparagraph (A) may be extended by written notice to the person making such request setting forth the reasons for such extension and the date on which a determination is expected to be dispatched. No such notice shall specify a date that would result in an extension for more than ten working days. As used in this subparagraph, "unusual circumstances" means, but only to the extent reasonably necessary to the proper processing of the particular request—

(i) the need to search for and collect the requested records from field facilities or other establishments that are separate from the office processing the request;

(ii) the need to search for, collect, and appropriately examine a voluminous amount of separate and distinct records, which are demanded in a single request; or

(iii) the need for consultation, which shall be conducted with all practicable speed, with another agency having a substantial interest in the determination of the request or among two or more components of the agency having substantial subject-matter interest therein.

(C) Any person making a request to any agency for records under paragraph (1), (2), or (3) of this subsection shall be deemed to have exhausted his administrative remedies with respect to such request if the agency fails to comply with the applicable time limit provisions of this paragraph. If the Government can show exceptional circumstances exist and that the agency is exercising due diligence in responding to the request, the court may retain jurisdiction and allow the agency additional time to complete its review of the records. Upon any determination by an agency to comply with a request for records, the records shall be made promptly available to such person making such request. Any notification of denial of any request for records under this subsection shall set forth the names and titles or positions of each person responsible for the denial of such request.

(b) This section does not apply to matters that are—
  (1) (A) specifically authorized under criteria established by an Executive order to be kept secret in the interest of national defense or foreign policy and (B) are in fact properly classified pursuant to such Executive order;
  (2) related solely to the internal personnel rules and practices of an agency;
  (3) specifically exempted from disclosure by statute (other than section 552b of this title), provided that such statute (A) requires that the matters be withheld from the public in such a manner as to leave no discretion on the issue, or (B) establishes particular criteria for withholding or refers to particular types of matters to be withheld;
  (4) trade secrets and commercial or financial information obtained from a person and privileged or confidential;
  (5) inter-agency or intra-agency memorandums or letters, which would not be available by law to a party other than an agency in litigation with the agency;
  (6) personnel and medical files and similar files the disclosure of which would constitute a clearly unwarranted invasion of personal privacy;
  (7) investigatory records compiled for law enforcement purposes, but only to the extent that the production of such records would (A) interfere with enforcement proceedings, (B) deprive a person of a right to a fair trial or an impartial adjudication, (C) constitute an unwarranted invasion of personal privacy, (D) disclose the identity of a confidential source and, in the case of a record compiled by a criminal law enforcement authority in the course of a criminal investigation, or by an agency conducting a lawful national security intelligence investigation, confidential information furnished only by the confidential source, (E) disclose investigative techniques and procedures, or (F) endanger the life or physical safety of law enforcement personnel;
  (8) contained in or related to examination, operating, or condition reports prepared by, on behalf of, or for the use of an agency responsible for the regulation or supervision of financial institutions; or
  (9) geological and geophysical information and data, including maps, concerning wells.

  Any reasonably segregable portion of a record shall be provided to any person requesting such record after deletion of the portions, which are exempt under this subsection.

(c) This section does not authorize withholding of information or limit the availability of records to the public, except as specifically stated in this section. This section is not authority to withhold information from Congress.

(d) On or before March 1 of each calendar year, each agency shall submit a report covering the preceding calendar year to the Speaker of the House of Representatives and President of the Senate for referral to the appropriate committees of the Congress. The report shall include—
  (1) the number of determinations made by such agency not to comply with requests for records made to such agency under subsection (a) and the reasons for each such determination;
  (2) the number of appeals made by persons under subsection (a)(6), the result of such appeals, and the reason for the action upon each appeal that results in a denial of information;
  (3) the names and titles or positions of each person responsible for the denial of records requested under this section, and the number of instances of participation for each;
  (4) the results of each proceeding conducted pursuant to subsection (a)(4)(F), including a report of the disciplinary action taken against the officer or employee who was primarily responsible for improperly withholding records or an explanation of why disciplinary action was not taken;
  (5) a copy of every rule made by such agency regarding this section;
  (6) a copy of the fee schedule and the total amount of fees collected by the agency for making records available under this section; and
  (7) such other information as indicates efforts to administer fully this section. The Attorney General shall submit an annual report on or before March 1 of each calendar year, which shall include for the prior calendar year a listing of the number of cases arising under this section, the exemption involved in each case, the disposition of such case, and the cost, fees, and penalties assessed under subsections (a)(4)(E), (F), and (G). Such report shall also include a description of the efforts undertaken by the Department of Justice to encourage agency compliance with this section.

(e) For purposes of this section, the term "agency" as defined in section 551(1) of this title includes any executive department, military department, Government corporation, Government controlled corporation, or other establishment in the executive branch of the Government (including the Executive Office of the President), or any independent regulatory agency.

§ 552a. Records maintained on individuals

(a) Definitions. For purposes of this section—

    (1) the term "agency" means agency as defined in section 552(e) of this title [5 USCS § 552(e)];

    (2) the term "individual" means a citizen of the United States or an alien lawfully admitted for permanent residence;

    (3) the term "maintain" includes maintain, collect, use, or disseminate;

    (4) the term "record" means any item, collection, or grouping of information about an individual that is maintained by an agency, including, but not limited to, his education, financial transactions, medical history, and criminal or employment history and that contains his name, or the identifying number, symbol, or other identifying particular assigned to the individual, such as a finger or voice print or a photograph;

    (5) the term "system of records" means a group of any records under the control of any agency from which information is retrieved by the name of the individual or by some identifying number, symbol, or other identifying particular assigned to the individual;

    (6) the term "statistical record" means a record in a system of records maintained for statistical research or reporting purposes only and not used in whole or in part in making any determination about an identifiable individual, except as provided by section 8 of title 13;

    (7) the term "routine use" means, with respect to the disclosure of a record, the use of such record for a purpose, which is compatible with the purpose for which it was collected; and

    (8) the term "matching program"—

        (A) means any computerized comparison of—

            (i) two or more automated systems of records or a system of records with non-Federal records for the purpose of—

                (I) establishing or verifying the eligibility of, or continuing compliance with statutory and regulatory requirements by, applicants for, recipients or beneficiaries of, participants in, or providers of services with respect to, cash or in-kind assistance or payments under Federal benefit programs, or

                (II) recouping payments or delinquent debts under such Federal benefit programs, or

            (ii) two or more automated Federal personnel or payroll systems of records or a system of Federal personnel or payroll records with non-Federal records,

        (B) but does not include—

            (i) matches performed to produce aggregate statistical data without any personal identifiers;

            (ii) matches performed to support any research or statistical project, the specific data of which may not be used to make decisions concerning the rights, benefits, or privileges of specific individuals;

            (iii) matches performed by an agency (or component thereof) which performs as its principal function any activity pertaining to the enforcement of criminal laws, subsequent to the initiation of a specific criminal or civil law enforcement investigation of a named person or persons for the purpose of gathering evidence against such person or persons;

            (iv) matches of tax information (I) pursuant to section 6103(d) of the Internal Revenue Code of 1986 [26 USCS § 6103(d)], (II) for purposes of tax administration as defined in section 6103(b)(4) of such Code [26 USCS § 6103(b)(4)], (III) for the purpose of intercepting a tax refund due an individual under authority granted by section 464 or 1137 of the Social Security Act [42 USCS § 664 or 1320b-7]; or (IV) for the purpose of intercepting a tax refund due an individual under any other tax refund intercept program authorized by statute, which has been determined by the Director of the Office of Management and Budget to contain verification, notice, and hearing requirements that are substantially similar to the procedures in section 1137 of the Social Security Act [42 USCS § 1320b-7];

            (v) matches—

                (I) using records predominantly relating to Federal personnel, that are performed for routing administrative purposes (subject to guidance provided by the Director of the Office of Management and Budget pursuant to subsection (v)); or

(II) conducted by an agency using only records from systems of records maintained by that agency; if the purpose of the match is not to take any adverse financial, personnel, disciplinary, or other adverse action against Federal personnel; or

(vi) matches performed for foreign counterintelligence purposes or to produce background checks for security clearances of Federal personnel or Federal contractor personnel;

(9) the term "recipient agency" means any agency, or contractor thereof, receiving records contained in a system of records from a source agency for use in a matching program;

(10) the term "non-Federal agency" means any State or local government, or agency thereof, which receives records contained in a system of records from a source agency for use in a matching program;

(11) the term "source agency" means any agency, which discloses records contained in a system of records to be used in a matching program, or any State or local government, or agency thereof, which discloses records to be used in a matching program;

(12) the term "Federal benefit program" means any program administered or funded by the Federal Government, or by any agent or State on behalf of the Federal Government, providing cash or in-kind assistance in the form of payments, grants, loans, or loan guarantees to individuals; and

(13) the term "Federal personnel" means officers and employees of the Government of the United States, members of the uniformed services (including members of the Reserve Components), individuals entitled to receive immediate or deferred retirement benefits under any retirement program of the Government of the United States (including survivor benefits).

(b) Conditions of Disclosure. No agency shall disclose any record, which is contained in a system of records by any means of communication to any person, or to another agency, except pursuant to a written request by, or with the prior written consent of, the individual to whom the record pertains, unless disclosure of the record would be—

(1) to those officers and employees of the agency, which maintains the record who have a need for the record in the performance of their duties;

(2) required under section 552 of this title [5 USCS § 552];

(3) for a routine use as defined in subsection (a)(7) of this section and described under subsection (e)(4)(D) of this section;

(4) to the Bureau of the Census for purposes of planning or carrying out a census or survey or related activity pursuant to the provisions of title 13 [13 USCS § 1 *et seq.*];

(5) to a recipient who has provided the agency with advance adequate written assurance that the record will be used solely as a statistical research or reporting record, and the record is to be transferred in a form that is not individually identifiable;

(6) to the National Archives and Records Administration as a record which has sufficient historical or other value to warrant its continued preservation by the United States Government, or for evaluation by the Archivist of the United States or the designee of the Archivist to determine whether the record has such value;

(7) to another agency or to an instrumentality of any governmental jurisdiction within or under the control of the United States for a civil or criminal law enforcement activity if the activity is authorized by law, and if the head of the agency or instrumentality has made a written request to the agency, which maintains the record specifying the particular portion desired and the law enforcement activity for which the record is sought;

(8) to a person pursuant to a showing of compelling circumstances affecting the health or safety of an individual if upon such disclosure notification is transmitted to the last known address of such individual;

(9) to either House of Congress, or, to the extent of matter within its jurisdiction, any committee or subcommittee thereof, any joint committee of Congress or subcommittee of any such joint committee;

(10) to the Comptroller General, or any of his authorized representatives, in the course of the performance of the duties of the General Accounting Office;

(11) pursuant to the order of a court of competent jurisdiction; or

(12) to a consumer reporting agency in accordance with section 3711(f) of title 31 [31 USCS § 3711(f)].

(c) Accounting of Certain Disclosures. Each agency, with respect to each system of records under its control, shall—

    (1) except for disclosures made under subsections (b)(1) or (b)(2) of this section, keep an accurate accounting of—

        (A) the date, nature, and purpose of each disclosure of a record to any person or to another agency made under subsection (b) of this section; and

        (B) the name and address of the person or agency to whom the disclosure is made;

    (2) retain the accounting made under paragraph (1) of this subsection for at least five years or the life of the record, whichever is longer, after the disclosure for which the accounting is made;

    (3) except for disclosures made under subsection (b)(7) of this section, make the accounting made under paragraph (1) of this subsection available to the individual named in the record at his request; and

    (4) inform any person or other agency about any correction or notation of dispute made by the agency in accordance with subsection (d) of this section of any record that has been disclosed to the person or agency if an accounting of the disclosure was made.

(d) Access to Records. Each agency that maintains a system of records shall—

    (1) upon request by any individual to gain access to his record or to any information pertaining to him which is contained in the system, permit him and upon his request, a person of his own choosing to accompany him, to review the record and have a copy made of all or any portion thereof in a form comprehensible to him, except that the agency may require the individual to furnish a written statement authorizing discussion of that individual's record in the accompanying person's presence;

    (2) permit the individual to request amendment of a record pertaining to him and—

        (A) not later than 10 days (excluding Saturdays, Sundays, and legal public holidays) after the date of receipt of such request, acknowledge in writing such receipt; and

        (B) promptly, either—

            (i) make any correction of any portion thereof which the individual believes is not accurate, relevant, timely, or complete; or

            (ii) inform the individual of its refusal to amend the record in accordance with his request, the reason for the refusal, the procedures established by the agency for the individual to request a review of that refusal by the head of the agency or an officer designated by the head of the agency, and the name and business address of that official;

    (3) permit the individual who disagrees with the refusal of the agency to amend his record to request a review of such refusal, and not later than 30 days (excluding Saturdays, Sundays, and legal public holidays) from the date on which the individual requests such review, complete such review and make a final determination unless, for good cause shown, the head of the agency extends such 30-day period; and if, after his review, the reviewing official also refuses to amend the record in accordance with the request, permit the individual to file with the agency a concise statement setting forth the reasons for his disagreement with the refusal of the agency, and notify the individual of the provisions for judicial review of the reviewing official's determination under subsection (g)(1)(A) of this section;

    (4) in any disclosure, containing information about which the individual has filed a statement of disagreement, occurring after the filing of the statement under paragraph (3) of this subsection, clearly note any portion of the record, which is disputed and provide copies of the statement and, if the agency deems it appropriate, copies of a concise statement of the reasons of the agency for not making the amendments requested, to persons or other agencies to whom the disputed record has been disclosed; and

    (5) nothing in this section shall allow an individual access to any information compiled in reasonable anticipation of a civil action or proceeding.

(e) Agency Requirements. Each agency that maintains a system of records shall—

    (1) maintain in its records only such information about an individual as is relevant and necessary to accomplish a purpose of the agency required to be accomplished by statute or by executive order of the President;

    (2) collect information to the greatest extent practicable directly from the subject individual when the information may result in adverse determinations about an individual's rights, benefits, and privileges under Federal programs;

(3)   inform each individual whom it asks to supply information, on the form, which it uses to collect the information or on a separate form that can be retained by the individual—

   (A)   the authority (whether granted by statute, or by executive order of the President) which authorizes the solicitation of the information and whether disclosure of such information is mandatory or voluntary;

   (B)   the principal purpose or purposes for which the information is intended to be used;

   (C)   the routine uses, which may be made of the information, as published pursuant to paragraph (4)(D) of this subsection; and

   (D)   the effects on him, if any, of not providing all or any part of the requested information;

(4)   subject to the provisions of paragraph (11) of this subsection, publish in the Federal Register upon establishment or revision a notice of the existence and character of the system of records, which notice shall include—

   (A)   the name and location of the system;

   (B)   the categories of individuals on whom records are maintained in the system;

   (C)   the categories of records maintained in the system;

   (D)   each routine use of the records contained in the system, including the categories of users and the purpose of such use;

   (E)   the policies and practices of the agency regarding storage, retrievability, access controls, retention, and disposal of the records;

   (F)   the title and business address of the agency official who is responsible for the system of records;

   (G)   the agency procedures whereby an individual can be notified at his request if the system of records contains a record pertaining to him;

   (H)   the agency procedures whereby an individual can be notified at his request how he can gain access to any record pertaining to him contained in the system of records, and how he can contest its content; and

   (I)   the categories of sources or records in the system;

(5)   maintain all records, which are used by the agency in making any determination about any individual with such accuracy, relevance, timeliness, and completeness as is reasonably necessary to assure fairness to the individual in the determination;

(6)   prior to disseminating any record about an individual to any person other than an agency, unless the dissemination is made pursuant to subsection (b)(2) of this section, make reasonable efforts to assure that such records are accurate, complete, timely, and relevant for agency purposes;

(7)   maintain no record describing how any individual exercises rights guaranteed by the First Amendment unless expressly authorized by statute or by the individual about whom the record is maintained or unless pertinent to and within the scope of an authorized law enforcement activity;

(8)   make reasonable efforts to serve notice on an individual when any record on such individual is made available to any person under compulsory legal process when such process becomes a matter of public record;

(9)   establish rules of conduct for persons involved in the design, development, operation, or maintenance of any system of records, or in maintaining any record, and instruct each such person with respect to such rules and the requirements of this section, including any other rules and procedures adopted pursuant to this section and the penalties for noncompliance;

(10) establish appropriate administrative, technical, and physical safeguards to insure the security and confidentiality of records and to protect against any anticipated threats or hazards to their security or integrity, which could result in substantial harm, embarrassment, inconvenience, or unfairness to any individual on whom information is maintained;

(11) at least 30 days prior to publication of information under paragraph (4)(D) of this subsection, publish in the Federal Register notice of any new use or intended use of the information in the system, and provide an opportunity for interested persons to submit written data, views, or arguments to the agency; and

(12) if such agency is a recipient agency or a source agency in a matching program with a non-Federal agency, with respect to any establishment or revision of a matching program, at least 30 days prior to conducting such program, publish in the Federal Register notice of such establishment or revision.

(f) Agency Rules. In order to carry out the provisions of this section, each agency that maintains a system of records shall promulgate rules, in accordance with the requirements (including general notice) of section 553 of this title [5 USCS § 553], which shall—

    (1) establish procedures whereby an individual can be notified in response to his request if any system of records named by the individual contains a record pertaining to him;

    (2) define reasonable times, places, and requirements for identifying an individual who requests his record or information pertaining to him before the agency shall make the record or information available to the individual;

    (3) establish procedures for the disclosure to an individual upon his request of his record or information pertaining to him, including special procedure, if deemed necessary, for the disclosure to an individual of medical records, including psychological records, pertaining to him;

    (4) establish procedures for reviewing a request from an individual concerning the amendment of any record or information pertaining to the individual, for making a determination on the request, for an appeal within the agency of an initial adverse agency determination, and for whatever additional means may be necessary for each individual to be able to exercise fully his rights under this section; and

    (5) establish fees to be charged, if any, to any individual for making copies of his record, excluding the cost of any search for and review of the record.

The Office of the Federal Register shall biennially compile and publish the rules promulgated under this subsection and agency notices published under subsection (e)(4) of this section in a form available to the public at low cost.

(g) (1) Civil Remedies. Whenever any agency—

    (A) makes a determination under subsection (d)(3) of this section not to amend an individual's record in accordance with his request, or fails to make such review in conformity with that subsection;

    (B) refuses to comply with an individual request under subsection (d)(1) of this section;

    (C) fails to maintain any record concerning any individual with such accuracy, relevance, timeliness, and completeness as is necessary to assure fairness in any determination relating to the qualifications, character, rights, or opportunities of, or benefits to the individual that may be made on the basis of such record, and consequently a determination is made which is adverse to the individual; or

    (D) fails to comply with any other provision of this section, or any rule promulgated thereunder, in such a way as to have an adverse effect on an individual, the individual may bring a civil action against the agency, and the district courts of the United States shall have jurisdiction in the matters under the provisions of this subsection.

  (2) (A) In any suit brought under the provisions of subsection (g)(1)(A) of this section, the court may order the agency to amend the individual's record in accordance with his request or in such other way as the court may direct. In such a case the court shall determine the matter de novo.

    (B) The court may assess against the United States reasonable attorney fees and other litigation costs reasonably incurred in any case under this paragraph in which the complainant has substantially prevailed.

  (3) (A) In any suit brought under the provisions of subsection (g)(1)(B) of this section, the court may enjoin the agency from withholding the records and order the production to the complainant of any agency records improperly withheld from him. In such a case the court shall determine the matter de novo, and may examine the contents of any agency records in camera to determine whether the records or any portion thereof may be withheld under any of the exemptions set forth in subsection (k) of this section, and the burden is on the agency to sustain its action.

    (B) The court may assess against the United States reasonable attorney fees and other litigation costs reasonably incurred in any case under this paragraph in which the complainant has substantially prevailed.

  (4) In any suit brought under the provisions of subsection (g)(1)(C) or (D) of this section in which the court determines that the agency acted in a manner which was intentional or willful, the United States shall be liable to the individual in an amount equal to the sum of—

    (A) actual damages sustained by the individual as a result of the refusal or failure, but in no case shall a person entitled to recovery receive less than the sum of $1,000; and

    (B) the costs of the action together with reasonable attorney fees as determined by the court.

(5) An action to enforce any liability created under this section may be brought in the district court of the United States in the district in which the complainant resides, or has his principal place of business, or in which the agency records are situated, or in the District of Columbia, without regard to the amount in controversy, within two years from the date on which the cause of action arises, except that where an agency has materially and willfully misrepresented any information required under this section to be disclosed to an individual and the information so misrepresented is material to establishment of the liability of the agency to the individual under this section, the action may be brought at any time within two years after discovery by the individual of the misrepresentation. Nothing in this section shall be construed to authorize any civil action by reason of any injury sustained as the result of a disclosure of a record prior to September 27, 1975.

(h) Rights of Legal Guardians. For the purposes of this section, the parent of any minor, or the legal guardian of any individual who has been declared to be incompetent due to physical or mental incapacity or age by a court of competent jurisdiction, may act on behalf of the individual.

(i) (1) Criminal Penalties. Any officer or employee of an agency, who by virtue of his employment or official position, has possession of, or access to, agency records, which contain individually identifiable information the disclosure of which is prohibited by this section or by rules or regulations established thereunder, and who knowing that disclosure of the specific material is so prohibited, willfully discloses the material in any manner to any person or agency not entitled to receive it, shall be guilty of a misdemeanor and fined not more than $5,000.

(2) Any officer or employee of any agency who willfully maintains a system of records without meeting the notice requirements of subsection (e)(4) of this section shall be guilty of a misdemeanor and fined not more than $5,000.

(3) Any person who knowingly and willfully requests or obtains any record concerning an individual from an agency under false pretenses shall be guilty of a misdemeanor and fined not more than $5,000.

(j) General Exemptions. The head of any agency may promulgate rules, in accordance with the requirements (including general notice) of sections 553(b)(1), (2), and (3), (c), and (e) of this title [5 USCS §§ 553(b)(1)–(3), (c), and (e)], to exempt any system of records within the agency from any part of this section except subsections (b), (c)(1) and (2), (e)(4)(A) through (F), (e)(6), (7), (9), (10), and (11), and (i) if the system of records is—

(1) maintained by the Central Intelligence Agency; or

(2) maintained by an agency or component thereof which performs as its principal function any activity pertaining to the enforcement of criminal laws, including police efforts to prevent, control, or reduce crime or to apprehend criminals, and the activities of prosecutors, courts, correctional, probation, pardon, or parole authorities, and which consists of (A) information compiled for the purpose of identifying individual criminal offenders and alleged offenders and consisting only of identifying data and notations of arrests, the nature and disposition of criminal charges, sentencing, confinement, release, and parole and probation status; (B) information compiled for the purpose of a criminal investigation, including reports of informants and investigators, and associated with an identifiable individual; or (C) reports identifiable to an individual compiled at any stage of the process of enforcement of the criminal laws from arrest or indictment through release from supervision.

At the time rules are adopted under this subsection, the agency shall include in the statement required under section 553(c) of this title [5 USCS § 553(c)], the reasons why the system of records is to be exempted from a provision of this section.

(k) Specific Exemptions. The head of any agency may promulgate rules, in accordance with the requirements (including general notice) of sections 553(b)(1), (2), and (3), (c), and (e) of this title [5 USCS § 553(b)(1), (2), (3), (c), and (e)], to exempt any system of records within the agency from subsections (c)(3), (d), (e)(1), (e)(4)(G), (H), and (1) and (f) of this section if the system of records is—

(1) subject to the provisions of section 552(b)(1) of this title [5 USCS § 552(b)(1)];

(2) investigatory material compiled for law enforcement purposes, other than material within the scope of subsection (j)(2) of this section: Provided, however, that if any individual is denied any right, privilege, or benefit that he would otherwise be entitled by Federal law, or for which he would otherwise be eligible, as a result of the maintenance of such material, such material shall be provided to such individual, except to the extent that the disclosure of such material would reveal the identity of a source who furnished information to the

Government under an express promise that the identity of the source would be held in confidence, or, prior to the effective date of this section, under an implied promise that the identity of the source would be held in confidence;

(3) maintained in connection with providing protective services to the President of the United States or other individuals pursuant to section 3056 of title 18 [18 USCS § 3056];

(4) required by statute to be maintained and used solely as statistical records;

(5) investigatory material compiled solely for the purpose of determining suitability, eligibility, or qualifications for Federal civilian employment, military service, Federal contracts, or access to classified information, but only to the extent that the disclosure of such material would reveal the identity of a source who furnished information to the Government under an express promise that the identity of the source would be held in confidence, or, prior to the effective date of this section, under an implied promise that the identity of the source would be held in confidence;

(6) testing or examination material used solely to determine individual qualifications for appointment or promotion in the Federal service the disclosure of which would compromise the objectivity or fairness of the testing or examination process; or

(7) evaluation material used to determine potential for promotion in the armed services, but only to the extent that the disclosure of such material would reveal the identity of a source who furnished information to the Government under an express promise that the identity of the source would be held in confidence, or, prior to the effective date of this section, under an implied promise that the identity of the source would be held in confidence.

At the time rules are adopted under this subsection, the agency shall include in the statement required under section 553(c) of this title [5 USCS § 553(c)], the reasons why the system of records is to be exempted from a provision of this section.

(l) (1) Archival Records. Each agency record, which is accepted by the Archivist of the United States for storage, processing, and servicing in accordance with section 3103 of title 44 [44 USCS § 3103] shall, for the purposes of this section, be considered to be maintained by the agency, which deposited the record and shall be subject to the provisions of this section. The Archivist of the United States shall not disclose the record except to the agency, which maintains the record, or under rules established by that agency which are not inconsistent with the provisions of this section.

(2) Each agency record pertaining to an identifiable individual, which was transferred to the National Archives of the United States as a record which has sufficient historical or other value to warrant its continued preservation by the United States Government, prior to the effective date of this section, shall, for the purposes of this section, be considered to be maintained by the National Archives and shall not be subject to the provisions of this section, except that a statement generally describing such records (modeled after the requirements relating to records subject to subsections (e)(4)(A) through (G) of this section) shall be published in the Federal Register.

(3) Each agency record pertaining to an identifiable individual, which is transferred to the National Archives of the United States as a record which has sufficient historical or other value to warrant its continued preservation by the United States Government, on or after the effective date of this section [effective 270 days following Dec. 31, 1974], shall, for the purposes of this section, be considered to be maintained by the National Archives and shall be exempt from the requirements of this section except subsections (e)(4)(A) through (G) and (e)(9) of this section.

(m) Government Contractors. When an agency provides by a contract for the operation by or on behalf of the agency of a system of records to accomplish an agency function, the agency shall, consistent with its authority, cause the requirements of this section to be applied to such system. For purposes of subsection (i) of this section any such contractor and any employee of such contractor, if such contract is agreed to on or after the effective date of this section, shall be considered to be an employee of an agency. A consumer reporting agency to which a record is disclosed under section 3711(f) of title 31 [31 USCS § 3711(f)] shall not be considered a contractor for the purposes of this section.

(n) Mailing Lists. An individual's name and address may not be sold or rented by an agency unless such action is specifically authorized by law. This provision shall not be construed to require the withholding of names and addresses otherwise permitted to be made public.

(o) Matching agreements. (1) No record which is contained in a system of records may be disclosed to a recipient agency or non-Federal agency for use in a computer matching program except pursuant to a written agreement between the source agency and the recipient agency or non-Federal agency specifying—

    (A) the purpose and legal authority for conducting the program;

    (B) the justification for the program and the anticipated results, including a specific estimate of any savings;

    (C) a description of the records that will be matched, including each data element that will be used, the approximate number of records that will be matched, and the projected starting and completion dates of the matching program;

    (D) procedures for providing individualized notice at the time of application, and notice periodically thereafter as directed by the Data Integrity Board of such agency (subject to guidance provided by the Director of the Office of Management and Budget pursuant to subsection [v]), to—

        (i) applicants for and recipients of financial assistance or payments under Federal benefit programs; and

        (ii) applicants for and holders of positions as Federal personnel, that any information provided by such applicants, recipients, holders and individuals may be subject to verification through matching programs;

    (E) procedures for verifying information produced in such matching program as required by subsection (p);

    (F) procedures for the retention and timely destruction of identifiable records created by a recipient agency or non-Federal agency in such matching program;

    (G) procedures for ensuring the administrative, technical, and physical security of the records matched and the results of such programs;

    (H) prohibitions on duplication and redisclosure of records provided by the source agency within or outside the recipient agency or the non-Federal agency, except where required by law or essential to the conduct of the matching program;

    (I) procedures governing the use by a recipient agency or non-Federal agency of records provided in a matching program by a source agency, including procedures governing return of the records to the source agency or destruction of records used in such program;

    (J) information on assessments that have been made on the accuracy of the records that will be used in such matching program; and

    (K) that the Comptroller General may have access to all records of a recipient agency or a non-Federal agency that the Comptroller General deems necessary in order to monitor or verify compliance with the agreement.

  (2) (A) A copy of each agreement entered into pursuant to paragraph (1) shall—

        (i) be transmitted to the Committee on Governmental Affairs of the Senate and the Committee on Government Operations of the House of Representatives; and

        (ii) be available upon request to the public.

    (B) No such agreement shall be effective until 30 days after the date on which such a copy is transmitted pursuant to subparagraph (A)(i).

    (C) Such an agreement shall remain in effect only for such period, not to exceed 18 months, as the Data Integrity Board of the agency determines is appropriate in light of the purposes, and length of time necessary for the conduct, of the matching program.

    (D) Within 3 months prior to the expiration of such an agreement pursuant to subparagraph (C), the Data Integrity Board of the agency may, without additional review, renew the matching agreement for a current, ongoing matching program for not more than one additional year if—

        (i) such program will be conducted without any change and

        (ii) each party to the agreement certifies to the Board in writing that the program has been conducted in compliance with the agreement.

(p) Verification and opportunity to contest findings.

  (1) In order to protect any individual whose records are used in a matching program, no recipient agency, non-Federal agency, or source agency may suspend, terminate, reduce, or make a final denial of any financial assistance or payment under a Federal benefit program to such individual, or take other adverse action against such individual as a result of information produced by such matching programs, until—

    (A) (i) the agency has independently verified the information; or

        (ii) the Data Integrity Board if the agency, or in the case of a non-Federal agency the Data Integrity Agency of the source agency, determines in accordance with guidance issued by the Director of the Office of Management and Budget that—

    (I)   the information is limited to identification and amount of benefits paid by the source agency under a Federal benefit program; and

    (II) there is a high degree of confidence that the information provided to the recipient agency is accurate;

  (B) the individual receives a notice from the agency containing a statement of its findings and informing the individual of the opportunity to contest such findings; and

  (C)   (i) the expiration of any time period established for the program by statute or regulation for the individual to respond to that notice; or

     (ii) in the case of a program for which no such period is established, the end of the 30-day period beginning on the date on which notice under subparagraph (b) is mailed or otherwise provided to the individual.

(2) Independent verification referred to in paragraph (1) requires investigation and confirmation of specific information relating to an individual that is used as a basis for an adverse action against the individual including, where applicable investigation and confirmation of—

  (A) the amount of the asset or income involved;

  (B) whether such individual actually has or had access to such asset or income for such individual's own use; and

  (C) the period or periods when the individual actually had such asset or income.

(3) Notwithstanding paragraph (1), an agency may take any appropriate action otherwise prohibited by such paragraph if the agency determines that the public health or public safety may be adversely affected or significantly threatened during any notice period required by such paragraph, (A) unless such individual has received notice from such agency containing a statement of its findings and informing the individual of the opportunity to contest such findings, and (B) until the subsequent expiration of any notice period provided by the program's law or regulations, or 30 days, whichever is later. Such opportunity to contest may be satisfied by notice, hearing, and appeal rights governing such Federal benefit program. The exercise of any such rights shall not affect any rights available under this section.

(4) Notwithstanding paragraph (3), an agency may take any appropriate action otherwise prohibited by such paragraph if the agency determines that the public health or public safety may be adversely affected or significantly threatened during the notice period required by such paragraph.

(q) Sanctions.

  (1) Notwithstanding any other provision of law, no source agency may disclose any record which is contained in a system of records to a recipient agency or non-Federal agency for a matching program if such source agency has reason to believe that the requirements of subsection (p), or any matching agreement entered into pursuant to subsection (o), or both, are not being met by such recipient agency.

  (2) No source agency may renew a matching agreement unless—

    (A) the recipient agency or non-Federal agency has certified that it has complied with the provisions of that agreement; and

    (B) the source agency has no reason to believe that the certification is inaccurate.

(r) Report on new systems and matching programs. Each agency that proposes to establish or make a significant change in a system of records or a matching program shall provide adequate advance notice of any such proposal (in duplicate) to the Committee on Government Operations of the House of Representatives, the Committee on Government Affairs of the Senate, and the Office of Management and Budget in order to permit an evaluation of the probable or potential effect of such proposal on the privacy or other rights of individuals.

(s) Biennial report. The President shall biennially submit to the Speaker of the House of Representatives and the President pro tempore of the Senate a report—

  (1) describing the actions of the Director of the Office of Management and Budget pursuant to section 6 of the Privacy Act of 1974 during the preceding 2 years;

  (2) describing the exercise of individual rights of access and amendment under this section during such years;

  (3) identifying changes in or additions to systems of records;

  (4) containing such other information concerning administration of this section as may be necessary or useful to the Congress in reviewing the effectiveness of this section in carrying out the purposes of the Privacy Act of 1974 [note to this section].

(t)

    (1) Effect of other laws. No agency shall rely on any exemption contained in section 552 of this title to withhold from an individual any record which is otherwise accessible to such individual under the provisions of this section.

    (2) No agency shall rely on any exemption in this section to withhold from an individual any record which is otherwise accessible to such individual under the provisions of section 552 of this title.

(u) Data Integrity Boards.

    (1) Every agency conducting or participating in a matching program shall establish a Data Integrity Board to oversee and coordinate among the various components of such agency the agency's implementation of this section.

    (2) Each Data Integrity Board shall consist of senior officials designated by the head of the agency, and shall include any senior official designated by the head of the agency as responsible for implementation of this section, and the inspector general of the agency, if any. The inspector general shall not serve as chairman of the Data Integrity Board.

    (3) Each Data Integrity Board—

        (A) shall review, approve, and maintain all written agreements for receipt or disclosure of agency records for matching programs to ensure compliance with subsection (o), and all relevant statutes, regulations, and guidelines;

        (B) shall review all matching programs in which the agency has participated during the year, either as a source agency or recipient agency, determine compliance with applicable laws, regulations, guidelines, and agency agreements, and assess the costs and benefits of such programs;

        (C) shall review all recurring matching programs in which the agency has participated during the year, either as a source agency or recipient agency, for continued justification for such disclosures;

        (D) shall compile an annual report, which shall be submitted to the head of the agency and the Office of Management and Budget and made available to the public on request, describing the matching activities of the agency, including—

            (i) matching programs in which the agency has participated as a source agency or recipient agency;

            (ii) matching agreements proposed under subsection (o) that were disapproved by the Board;

            (iii) any changes in membership or structure of the Board in the preceding year;

            (iv) the reasons for any waiver of the requirement in paragraph (4) of this section for completion and submission of a cost-benefit analysis prior to the approval of a matching program;

            (v) any violations of matching agreements that have been alleged or identified and any corrective action taken; and

            (vi) any other information required by the Director of the Office of Management and Budget to be included in such report;

        (E) shall serve as a clearinghouse for receiving and providing information on the accuracy, completeness, and reliability of records used in matching programs;

        (F) shall provide interpretation and guidance to agency components and personnel on the requirements of this section for matching programs;

        (G) shall review agency recordkeeping and disposal policies and practices for matching programs to assure compliance with this section; and

        (H) may review and report on any agency matching activities that are not matching programs.

    (4) (A) Except as provided in subparagraphs (B) and (C), a Data Integrity Board shall not approve any written agreement for a matching program unless the agency has completed and submitted to such Board a cost-benefit analysis of the proposed program and such analysis demonstrates that the program is likely to be cost effective.

        (B) The Board may waive the requirements of subparagraph (A) of this paragraph if it determines in writing, in accordance with guidelines prescribed by the Director of the Office of Management and Budget, that a cost-benefit analysis is not required.

        (C) A cost-benefit analysis shall not be required under subparagraph (A) prior to the initial approval of a written agreement for a matching program that is specifically required by statute. Any subsequent written agreement for such a program shall not be approved by the Data Integrity Board unless the agency has submitted a cost-benefit analysis of the program as conducted under the preceding approval of such agreement.

(5) (A) If a matching agreement is disapproved by a Data Integrity Board, any party to such agreement may appeal the disapproval to the Director of the Office of Management and Budget. Timely notice of the filing of such an appeal shall be provided by the Director of the Office of Management and Budget to the Committee on Governmental Affairs of the Senate and the Committee on Government Operations of the House of Representatives.

(B) The Director of the Office of Management and Budget may approve a matching agreement notwithstanding the disapproval of a Data Integrity Board of the Director determines that—

(i) the matching program will be consistent with all applicable legal, regulatory, and policy requirements;

(ii) there is adequate evidence that the matching agreement will be cost-effective; and

(iii) the matching program is in the public interest.

(C) The decision of the Director to approve a matching agreement shall not take effect until 30 days after it is reported to [the] committees described in subparagraph (A).

(D) If the Data Integrity Board and the Director of the Office of Management and Budget disapprove a matching program proposed by the inspector general of an agency, the inspector general may report the disapproval to the head of the agency and to the Congress.

(6) The Director of the Office of Management and Budget shall, annually during the first 3 years after the date of enactment of this subsection [enacted Oct. 18, 1988] and biennially thereafter, consolidate in a report to the Congress the information contained in the reports from the various Data Integrity Boards under paragraph (3)(D). Such report shall include detailed information about costs and benefits of matching programs that are conducted during the period covered by such consolidated report, and shall identify each waiver granted by a Data Integrity Board of the requirement for completion and submission of a cost-benefit analysis and the reasons for granting the waiver.

(7) In the reports required by paragraphs (3)(D) and (6), agency matching activities that are not matching programs may be reported on an aggregate basis, if and to the extent necessary to protect ongoing law enforcement or counterintelligence investigations.

(v) Office of Management and Budget Responsibilities. The Director of the Office of Management and Budget shall—

(1) develop and, after notice and opportunity for public comment, prescribe guidelines and regulations for the use of agencies in implementing the provisions of this section; and

(2) provide continuing assistance to and oversight of the implementation of this section by agencies.

§ 552b. Open meetings

(a) For purposes of this section—

(1) the term "agency" means any agency, as defined in section 552(e) of this title, headed by a collegial body composed of two or more individual members, a majority of whom are appointed to such position by the President with the advice and consent of the Senate, and any subdivision thereof authorized to act on behalf of the agency;

(2) the term "meeting" means the deliberations of at least the number of individual agency members required to take action on behalf of the agency where such deliberations determine or result in the joint conduct or disposition of official agency business, but does not include deliberations required or permitted by subsection (d) or (e); and

(3) the term "member" means an individual who belongs to a collegial body heading an agency.

(b) Members shall not jointly conduct or dispose of agency business other than in accordance with this section. Except as provided in subsection (c), every portion of every meeting of an agency shall be open to public observation.

(c) Except in a case where the agency finds that the public interest requires otherwise, the second sentence of subsection (b) shall not apply to any portion of an agency meeting, and the requirements of subsections (d) and (e) shall not apply to any information pertaining to such meeting otherwise required by this section to be disclosed to the public, where the agency properly determines that such portion or portions of its meeting or the disclosure of such information is likely to—

(1) disclose matters that are (A) specifically authorized under criteria established by an Executive order to be kept secret in the interests of national defense or foreign policy and (B) in fact properly classified pursuant to such Executive order;

(2) relate solely to the internal personnel rules and practices of an agency;

(3) disclose matters specifically exempted from disclosure by statute (other than section 552 of this title), provided that such statute (A) requires that the matters be withheld from the public in such a manner as to leave no discretion on the issue, or (B) establishes particular criteria for withholding or refers to particular types of matters to be withheld;

(4) disclose trade secrets and commercial or financial information obtained from a person and privileged or confidential;

(5) involve accusing any person of a crime, or formally censuring any person;

(6) disclose information of a personal nature where disclosure would constitute a clearly unwarranted invasion of personal privacy;

(7) disclose investigatory records compiled for law enforcement purposes, or information, which, if written would be contained in such records, but only to the extent that the production of such records or information would (A) interfere with enforcement proceedings, (B) deprive a person of a right to a fair trial or an impartial adjudication, (C) constitute an unwarranted invasion of personal privacy, (D) disclose the identity of a confidential source and, in the case of a record compiled by a criminal law enforcement authority in the course of a criminal investigation, or by an agency conducting a lawful national security intelligence investigation, confidential information furnished only by the confidential source, (E) disclose investigative techniques and procedures, or (F) endanger the life or physical safety of law enforcement personnel;

(8) disclose information contained in or related to examination, operating, or condition reports prepared by, on behalf of, or for the use of an agency responsible for the regulation or supervision of financial institutions;

(9) disclose information the premature disclosure of which would—

(A) in the case of an agency, which regulates currencies, securities, commodities, or financial institutions, be likely to (i) lead to significant financial speculation in currencies, securities, or commodities, or (ii) significantly endanger the stability of any financial institution; or

(B) in the case of any agency, be likely to significantly frustrate implementation of a proposed agency action,

except that subparagraph (B) shall not apply in any instance where the agency has already disclosed to the public the content or nature of its proposed action, or where the agency is required by law to make such disclosure on its own initiative prior to taking final agency action on such proposal; or

(10) specifically concern the agency's issuance of a subpoena, or the agency's participation in a civil action or proceeding, an action in a foreign court or international tribunal, or an arbitration, or the initiation, conduct, or disposition by the agency of a particular case of formal agency adjudication pursuant to the procedures in section 554 of this title or otherwise involving a determination on the record after opportunity for a hearing.

(d) (1) Action under subsection (c) shall be taken only when a majority of the entire membership of the agency (as defined in subsection (a)(1)) votes to take such action. A separate vote of the agency members shall be taken with respect to each agency meeting a portion or portions of which are proposed to be closed to the public pursuant to subsection (c), or with respect to any information, which is proposed to be withheld under subsection (c). A single vote may be taken with respect to a series of meetings, a portion or portions of which are proposed to be closed to the public, or with respect to any information concerning such series of meetings, so long as each meeting in such series involves the same particular matters and is scheduled to be held no more than thirty days after the initial meeting in such series. The vote of each agency member participating in such vote shall be recorded and no proxies shall be allowed.

(2) Whenever any person whose interests may be directly affected by a portion of a meeting requests that the agency close such portion to the public for any of the reasons referred to in paragraph (5), (6), or (7) of subsection (c), the agency, upon request of any one of its members, shall vote by recorded vote whether to close such meeting.

(3) Within one day of any vote taken pursuant to paragraph (1) or (2), the agency shall make publicly available a written copy of such vote reflecting the vote of each member on the question. If a portion of a meeting is to be closed to the public, the agency shall, within one day of the vote taken pursuant to paragraph (1) or (2) of this subsection, make publicly available a full written explanation of its action closing the portion together with a list of all persons expected to attend the meeting and their affiliation. . . .

(e) (1) In the case of each meeting, the agency shall make public announcement, at least one week before the meeting, of the time, place, and subject matter of the meeting, whether it is to be open or closed to the public, and the name and phone number of the official designated by the agency to respond to requests for information about the meeting. Such announcement shall be made unless a majority of the members of the agency determines by a recorded vote that agency business requires that such meeting be called at an earlier date, in which case the agency shall make public announcement of the time, place, and subject matter of such meeting, and whether open or closed to the public, at the earliest practicable time.

(2) The time or place of a meeting may be changed following the public announcement required by paragraph (1) only if the agency publicly announces such change at the earliest practicable time. The subject matter of a meeting, or the determination of the agency to open or close a meeting, or portion of a meeting, to the public, may be changed following the public announcement required by this subsection only if (A) a majority of the entire membership of the agency determines by a recorded vote that agency business so requires and that no earlier announcement of the change was possible, and (B) the agency publicly announces such change and the vote of each member upon such change at the earliest practicable time. . . .

(f) (1) For every meeting closed pursuant to paragraphs (1) through (10) of subsection (c), the General Counsel or chief legal officer of the agency shall publicly certify that, in his or her opinion, the meeting may be closed to the public and shall state each relevant exemptive provision. A copy of such certification, together with a statement from the presiding officer of the meeting setting forth the time and place of the meeting, and the persons present, shall be retained by the agency. The agency shall maintain a complete transcript or electronic recording adequate to record fully the proceedings of each meeting, or portion of a meeting, closed to the public, except that in the case of a meeting, or portion of a meeting, closed to the public pursuant to paragraph (8), (9)(A), or (10) of subsection (c), the agency shall maintain either such a transcript or recording, or a set of minutes. Such minutes shall fully and clearly describe all matters discussed and shall provide a full and accurate summary of any actions taken, and the reasons therefor, including a description of each of the views expressed on any item and the record of any rollcall vote (reflecting the vote of each member on the question). All documents considered in connection with any action shall be identified in such minutes.

(2) The agency shall make promptly available to the public, in a place easily accessible to the public, the transcript, electronic recording, or minutes (as required by paragraph (1)) of the discussion of any item on the agenda, or of any item of the testimony of any witness received at the meeting, except for such item or items of such discussion or testimony as the agency determines to contain information which may be withheld under subsection (c)....

(g) (1) The district courts of the United States shall have jurisdiction to enforce the requirements of subsections (b) through (f) of this section by declaratory judgment, injunctive relief, or other relief as may be appropriate. Such actions may be brought by any person against an agency prior to, or within sixty days after, the meeting out of which the violation of this section arises, except that if public announcement of such meeting is not initially provided by the agency in accordance with the requirements of this section, such action may be instituted pursuant to this section at any time prior to sixty days after any public announcement of such meeting. Such actions may be brought in the district court of the United States for the district in which the agency meeting is held or in which the agency in question has its headquarters, or in the District Court for the District of Columbia. In such actions a defendant shall serve his answer within thirty days after the service of the complaint. The burden is on the defendant to sustain his action. In deciding such cases the court may examine in camera any portion of the transcript, electronic recording, or minutes of a meeting closed to the public, and may take such additional evidence as it deems necessary. The court, having due regard for orderly administration and the public interest, as well as the interests of the parties, may grant such equitable relief as it deems appropriate, including granting an injunction against future violations of this section or ordering the agency to make available to the public such portion of the transcript, recording, or minutes of a meeting as is not authorized to be withheld under subsection (c) of this section.

(2) Any Federal court otherwise authorized by law to review agency action may, at the application of any person properly participating in the proceeding pursuant to other applicable law, inquire into violations by the agency of the requirements of this section and afford such relief as it deems appropriate. Nothing in this section authorizes any Federal court having jurisdiction solely on the basis of paragraph (1) to set aside, enjoin, or invalidate any agency action (other than an action to close a meeting or to withhold information under this section) taken or discussed at any agency meeting out of which the violation of this section arose.

(h) The court may assess against any party reasonable attorney fees and other litigation costs reasonably incurred by any other party who substantially prevails in any action brought in accordance with the provisions of subsection (g) or (h) of this section, except that costs may be assessed against the plaintiff only where the court finds that the suit was initiated by the plaintiff primarily for frivolous or dilatory purposes. In the case of assessment of costs against an agency, the costs may be assessed by the court against the United States.

(i) Each agency subject to the requirements of this section shall annually report to Congress regarding its compliance with such requirements. . . .

(j) This section does not constitute authority to withhold any information from Congress, and does not authorize the closing of any agency meeting or portion thereof required by any other provision of law to be open. . . .

§ 553. Rule making

(a) This section applies, accordingly to the provisions thereof, except to the extent that there is involved—
   (1) a military or foreign affairs function of the United States; or
   (2) a matter relating to agency management or personnel or to public property, loans, grants, benefits, or contracts.

(b) General notice of proposed rule making shall be published in the Federal Register, unless persons subject thereto are named and either personally served or otherwise have actual notice thereof in accordance with law. The notice shall include—
   (1) a statement of the time, place, and nature of public rule making proceedings;
   (2) reference to the legal authority under which the rule is proposed; and
   (3) either the terms or substance of the proposed rule or a description of the subjects and issues involved.
   Except when notice or hearing is required by statute, this subsection does not apply—
   (A) to interpretative rules, general statements of policy, or rules of agency organization, procedure, or practice; or
   (B) when the agency for good cause finds (and incorporates the finding and a brief statement of reasons thereof in the rules issued) that notice and public procedure thereon are impracticable, unnecessary, or contrary to the public interest.

(c) After notice required by this section, the agency shall give interested persons an opportunity to participate in the rule making through submission of written data, views, or arguments with or without opportunity for oral presentation. After consideration of the relevant matter presented, the agency shall incorporate in the rules adopted a concise general statement of their basis and purpose. When rules are required by statute to be made on the record after opportunity for an agency hearing, sections 556 and 557 of this title apply instead of this subsection.

(d) The required publication or service of a substantive rule shall be made not less than 30 days before its effective date, except—
   (1) a substantive rule which grants or recognizes an exemption or relieves a restriction;
   (2) interpretative rules and statements of policy; or
   (3) as otherwise provided by the agency for good cause found and published with the rule.

(e) Each agency shall give an interested person the right to petition for the issuance, amendment, or repeal of a rule.

§ 554. Adjudications

(a) This section applies, according to the provisions thereof, in every case of adjudication required by statute to be determined on the record after opportunity for an agency hearing, except to the extent that there is involved—

    (1) a matter subject to a subsequent trial of the law and the facts de novo in a court;

    (2) the selection or tenure of an employee, except an administrative law judge appointed under section 3105 of this title;

    (3) proceedings in which decisions rest solely on inspections, tests, or elections;

    (4) the conduct of military or foreign affairs functions;

    (5) cases in which an agency is acting as an agent for a court; or

    (6) the certification of worker representatives.

(b) Persons entitled to notice of an agency hearing shall be timely informed of—

    (1) the time, place, and nature of the hearing;

    (2) the legal authority and jurisdiction under which the hearing is to be held; and

    (3) the matters of fact and law asserted.

When private persons are the moving parties, other parties to the proceeding shall give prompt notice of issues controverted in fact or law, and in other instances agencies may by rule require responsive pleading. In fixing the time and place for hearings, due regard shall be had for the convenience and necessity of the parties or their representatives.

(c) The agency shall give all interested parties opportunity for—

    (1) the submission and consideration of facts, arguments, offers of settlement, or proposals of adjustment when time, the nature of the proceeding, and the public interest permit; and

    (2) to the extent that the parties are unable so to determine a controversy by consent, hearing and decision on notice and in accordance with sections 556 and 557 of this title.

(d) The employee who presides at the reception of evidence pursuant to section 556 of this title shall make the recommended decision or initial decision required by section 557 of this title, unless he becomes unavailable to the agency. Except to the extent required for the disposition of ex parte matters as authorized by law, such an employee may not—

    (1) consult a person or party on a fact in issue, unless on notice and opportunity for all parties to participate; or

    (2) be responsible to or subject to the supervision or direction of an employee or agent engaged in the performance of investigative or prosecuting functions for an agency.

An employee or agent engaged in the performance of investigative or prosecuting functions for an agency in a case may not, in that or a factually related case, participate or advise in the decision, recommended decision or agency review pursuant to section 557 of this title, except as witness or counsel in public proceedings. This subsection does not apply—

    (A) in determining applications for initial licenses;

    (B) to proceedings involving the validity or application of rates, facilities, or practices of public utilities or carriers; or

    (C) to the agency or a member or members of the body comprising the agency.

(e) The agency, with like effect as in the case of other orders, and in its sound discretion, may issue a declaratory order to terminate a controversy or remove uncertainty.

§ 555. Ancillary matters

(a) This section applies, according to the provisions thereof, except as otherwise provided by this subchapter.

(b) A person compelled to appear in person before an agency or representative thereof is entitled to be accompanied, represented, and advised by counsel or, if permitted by the agency, by other qualified representative. A party is entitled to appear in person or by or with counsel or other duly qualified representative in an agency proceeding. So far as the orderly conduct of public business permits, an interested person may appear before an agency or its responsible employees for the presentation, adjustment, or determination of an issue, request, or controversy in a proceeding, whether interlocutory, summary, or otherwise, or in connection with an agency function. With due regard for the convenience and necessity of the parties or their representatives and within a reasonable time, each agency shall proceed to conclude a matter presented to it. This subsection does not grant or deny a person who is not a lawyer the right to appear for or represent others before an agency or in an agency proceeding.

(c) Process, requirement of a report, inspection, or other investigative act or demand may not be issued, made, or enforced except as authorized by law. A person compelled to submit data or evidence is entitled to retain or, on payment of lawfully prescribed costs, procure a copy or transcript thereof, except that in a nonpublic investigatory proceeding the witness may for good cause be limited to inspection of the official transcript of his testimony.

(d) Agency subpoenas authorized by law shall be issued to a party on request and, when required by rules of procedure, on a statement or showing of general relevance and reasonable scope of the evidence sought. On contest, the court shall sustain the subpoena or similar process or demand to the extent that it is found to be in accordance with law. In a proceeding for enforcement, the court shall issue an order requiring the appearance of the witness or the production of the evidence or data within a reasonable time under penalty of punishment for contempt in case of contumacious failure to comply.

(e) Prompt notice shall be given of the denial in whole or in part of a written application, petition, or other request of an interested person made in connection with any agency proceeding. Except in affirming a prior denial or when the denial is self-explanatory, the notice shall be accompanied by a brief statement of the grounds for denial.

§ 556. Hearings; presiding employees; powers and duties; burden of proof; evidence; record as basis of decision

(a) This section applies, according to the provisions thereof, to hearings required by section 553 or 554 of this title to be conducted in accordance with this section.

(b) There shall preside at the taking of evidence—
   (1) the agency;
   (2) one or more members of the body which comprises the agency; or
   (3) one or more administrative law judges appointed under section 3105 of this title.

This subchapter does not supersede the conduct of specified classes of proceedings, in whole or in part, by or before boards or other employees specially provided for by or designated under statute. The functions of presiding employees and of employees participating in decisions in accordance with section 557 of this title shall be conducted in an impartial manner. A presiding or participating employee may at any time disqualify himself. On the filing in good faith of a timely and sufficient affidavit of personal bias or other disqualification of a presiding or participating employee, the agency shall determine the matters as a part of the record and decision in the case.

(c) Subject to published rules of the agency and within its powers, employees presiding at hearings may—
   (1) administer oaths and affirmations;
   (2) issue subpoenas authorized by law;
   (3) rule on offers of proof and receive relevant evidence;
   (4) take depositions or have depositions taken when the ends of justice would be served;
   (5) regulate the course of the hearing;
   (6) hold conferences for the settlement or simplification of the issues by consent of the parties or by the use of alternative means of dispute resolution as provided in subchapter IV of this chapter [5 USCS § 581 *et seq.*];
   (7) inform the parties as to the availability of one or more alternative means of dispute resolution, and encourage use of such methods;
   (8) require the attendance at any conference held pursuant to paragraph (6) of at least one representative of each party who has authority to negotiate concerning resolution of issues in controversy;
   (9) dispose of procedural requests or similar matters;
   (10) make or recommend decisions in accordance with section 557 of this title; and
   (11) take other action authorized by agency rule consistent with this subchapter.

(d) Except as otherwise provided by statute, the proponent of a rule or order has the burden of proof. Any oral or documentary evidence may be received, but the agency as a matter of policy shall provide for the exclusion of irrelevant, immaterial, or unduly repetitious evidence. A sanction may not be imposed or rule or order issued except on consideration of the whole record or those parts thereof cited by a party and supported by and in accordance with the reliable, probative, and substantial evidence. The agency may, to the extent consistent with the interests of justice and the policy of the underlying statutes administered by the agency, consider a violation of section 557(d) of this title sufficient grounds for a decision adverse to a party who has knowingly committed such violation or knowingly caused such violation to occur. A party is entitled to present his case or defense by oral or documentary evidence, to submit rebuttal evidence, and to conduct such cross-examination as may be required for a full and true disclosure of the facts. In rule making or determining claims for money or benefits or applications for initial licenses an agency may, when a party will not be prejudiced thereby, adopt procedures for the submission of all or part of the evidence in written form.

(e) The transcript of testimony and exhibits, together with all papers and requests filed in the proceeding, constitutes the exclusive record for decision in accordance with section 557 of this title and, on payment of lawfully prescribed costs, shall be made available to the parties. When an agency decision rests on official notice of a material fact not appearing in the evidence in the record, a party is entitled, on timely request, to an opportunity to show the contrary.

§ 557. Initial decisions; conclusiveness; review by agency; submissions by parties; contents of decisions; record

(a) This section applies, according to the provisions thereof, when a hearing is required to be conducted in accordance with section 556 of this title.

(b) When the agency did not preside at the reception of the evidence, the presiding employee or, in cases not subject to section 554(d) of this title, an employee qualified to preside at hearings pursuant to section 556 of this title, shall initially decide the case unless the agency requires, either in specific cases or by general rule, the entire record to be certified to it for decision. When the presiding employee makes an initial decision, that decision then becomes the decision of the agency without further proceedings unless there is an appeal to, or review on motion of, the agency within time provided by rule. On appeal from or review of the initial decision, the agency has all the powers, which it would have in making the initial decision except as it may limit the issues on notice or by rule. When the agency makes the decision without having presided at the reception of the evidence, the presiding employee or an employee qualified to preside at hearings pursuant to section 556 of this title shall first recommend a decision, except that in rule making or determining application for initial licenses—

(1) instead thereof the agency may issue a tentative decision or one of its responsible employees may recommend a decision; or

(2) this procedure may be omitted in a case in which the agency finds on the record that due and timely execution of its functions imperatively and unavoidably so requires.

(c) Before a recommended, initial, or tentative decision, or a decision on agency review of the decision of subordinate employees, the parties are entitled to a reasonable opportunity to submit for the consideration of the employees participating in the decisions—

(1) proposed findings and conclusions; or

(2) exceptions to the decisions or recommended decisions of subordinate employees or to tentative agency decisions; and

(3) supporting reasons for the exceptions or proposed findings or conclusions.

The record shall show the ruling on each finding, conclusion, or exception presented. All decisions, including initial, recommended, and tentative decisions, are a part of the record and shall include a statement of—

(A) findings and conclusions, and the reasons or basis therefor, on all the material issues of fact, law, or discretion presented on the record; and

(B) the appropriate rule, order, sanction, relief, or denial thereof.

(d)(1) In any agency proceeding which is subject to subsection (a) of this section, except to the extent required for the disposition of ex parte matters as authorized by law—

(A) no interested person outside the agency shall make or knowingly cause to be made to any member of the body comprising the agency, administrative law judge, or other employee who is or may reasonably be expected to be involved in the decisional process of the proceeding, an ex parte communication relevant to the merits of the proceeding;

(B) no member of the body comprising the agency, administrative law judge, or other employee who is or may reasonably be expected to be involved in the decisional process of the proceeding, shall make or knowingly cause to be made to any interested person outside the agency an ex parte communication relevant to the merits of the proceeding;

(C) a member of the body comprising the agency, administrative law judge, or other employee who is or may reasonably be expected to be involved in the decisional process of such proceeding who receives, or who makes or knowingly causes to be made, a communication prohibited by this subsection shall place on the public record of the proceeding:

    (i) all such written communications;

    (ii) memoranda stating the substance of all such oral communications; and

    (iii) all written responses, and memoranda stating the substance of all oral responses, to the materials described in clauses (i) and (ii) of this subparagraph;

(D) upon receipt of a communication knowingly made or knowingly caused to be made by a party in violation of this subsection, the agency, administrative law judge, or other employee presiding at the hearing may, to the extent consistent with the interests of justice and the policy of the underlying statutes, require the party to show cause why his claim or interest in the proceeding should not be dismissed, denied, disregarded, or otherwise adversely affected on account of such violation; and

(E) the prohibitions of this subsection shall apply beginning at such time as the agency may designate, but in no case shall they begin to apply later than the time at which a proceeding is noticed for hearing unless the person responsible for the communication has knowledge that it will be noticed, in which case the prohibitions shall apply beginning at the time of his acquisition of such knowledge.

(2) This subsection does not constitute authority to withhold information from Congress.

§ 558. Imposition of sanctions; determination of applications for licenses; suspension, revocation, and expiration of licenses

(a) This section applies, according to the provisions thereof, to the exercise of a power or authority.

(b) A sanction may not be imposed or a substantive rule or order issued except within jurisdiction delegated to the agency and as authorized by law.

(c) When application is made for a license required by law, the agency, with due regard for the rights and privileges of all the interested parties or adversely affected persons and within a reasonable time, shall set and complete proceedings required to be conducted in accordance with sections 556 and 557 of this title or other proceedings required by law and shall make its decision. Except in cases of willfulness or those in which public health, interest, or safety requires otherwise, the withdrawal, suspension, revocation, or annulment of a license is lawful only if, before the institution of agency proceedings therefor, the licensee has been given—

(1) notice by the agency in writing of the facts or conduct, which may warrant the action; and

(2) opportunity to demonstrate or achieve compliance with all lawful requirements. When the licensee has made timely and sufficient application for a renewal or a new license in accordance with agency rules, a license with reference to an activity of a continuing nature does not expire until the application has been finally determined by the agency.

§ 559. Effect on other laws; effect of subsequent statute

This subchapter, Chapter 7, and sections 1305, 3105, 3344, 4301(2)(E), 5362, and 7521, and the provisions of section 5335(a)(B) of this title that relate to administrative law judges, do not limit or repeal additional requirements imposed by statute or otherwise recognized by law. Except as otherwise required by law, requirements or privileges relating to evidence or procedure apply equally to agencies and persons. Each agency is granted the authority necessary to comply with the requirements of this subchapter through the issuance of rules or otherwise. Subsequent statute may not be held to supersede or modify this subchapter, Chapter 7, sections 1305, 3105, 3344, 4301(2)(E), 5362, or 7521, or the provisions of section 5335(a)(B) of this title that relate to administrative law judges, except to the extent that it does so expressly. . . .

Chapter 7—Judicial Review

Sec.

§ 701. Application; definitions

(a) This chapter applies, according to the provisions thereof, except to the extent that—
    (1) statutes preclude judicial review; or
    (2) agency action is committed to agency discretion by law.

(b) (1) ["agency" is defined precisely as in § 551(1)(A) through (H), above];
    (2) "person," "rule," "order," "license," "sanction," "relief," and "agency action" have the meanings given them by section 551 of this title.

§ 702. Right of review

A person suffering legal wrong because of agency action, or adversely affected or aggrieved by agency action within the meaning of a relevant statute, is entitled to judicial review thereof. An action in a court of the United States seeking relief other than money damages and stating a claim that an agency or an officer or employee thereof acted or failed to act in an official capacity or under color of legal authority shall not be dismissed nor relief therein be denied on the ground that it is against the United States or that the United States is an indispensable party. The United States may be named as a defendant in any such action, and a judgment or decree may be entered against the United States: Provided, That any mandatory or injunctive decree shall specify the Federal officer or officers (by name or by title), and their successors in office, personally responsible for compliance. Nothing herein (1) affects other limitations on judicial review or the power or duty of the court to dismiss any action or deny relief on any other appropriate legal or equitable ground; or (2) confers authority to grant relief if any other statute that grants consent to suit expressly or impliedly forbids the relief, which is sought.

§ 703. Form and venue of proceeding

The form of proceeding for judicial review is the special statutory review proceeding relevant to the subject matter in a court specified by statute or, in the absence or inadequacy thereof, any applicable form of legal action, including actions for declaratory judgments or writs of prohibitory or mandatory injunction or habeas corpus, in a court of competent jurisdiction. If no special statutory review proceeding is applicable, the action for judicial review may be brought against the United States, the agency by its official title, or the appropriate officer. Except to the extent that prior, adequate, and exclusive opportunity for judicial review is provided by law, agency action is subject to judicial review in civil or criminal proceedings for judicial enforcement.

§ 704. Actions reviewable

Agency action made reviewable by statute and final agency action for which there is no other adequate remedy in a court are subject to judicial review. A preliminary, procedural, or intermediate agency action or ruling not directly reviewable is subject to review on the review of the final agency action. Except as otherwise expressly required by statute, agency action otherwise final is final for the purposes of this section whether or not there has been presented or determined an application for a declaratory order, for any form of reconsideration, or, unless the agency otherwise requires by rule and provides that the action meanwhile is inoperative, for an appeal to superior agency authority.

§ 705. Relief pending review

When an agency finds that justice so requires, it may postpone the effective date of action taken by it, pending judicial review. On such conditions as may be required and to the extent necessary to prevent irreparable injury, the reviewing court, including the court to which a case may be taken on appeal from or on application for certiorari or other writ to a reviewing court, may issue all necessary and appropriate process to postpone the effective date of an agency action or to preserve status or rights pending conclusion of the review proceedings.

§ 706. Scope of review

To the extent necessary to decision and when presented, the reviewing court shall decide all relevant questions of law, interpret constitutional and statutory provisions, and determine the meaning or applicability of the terms of an agency action. The reviewing court shall—

(1) compel agency action unlawfully withheld or unreasonably delayed; and

(2) hold unlawful and set aside agency action, findings, and conclusions found to be—
    (A) arbitrary, capricious, an abuse of discretion, or otherwise not in accordance with law;
    (B) contrary to constitutional right, power, privilege, or immunity;
    (C) in excess of statutory jurisdiction, authority, or limitations, or short of statutory right;
    (D) without observance of procedure required by law;
    (E) unsupported by substantial evidence in a case subject to section 556 and 557 of this title or otherwise reviewed on the record of an agency hearing provided by statute; or
    (F) unwarranted by the facts to the extent that the facts are subject to trial de novo by the reviewing court.

In making the foregoing determinations, the court shall review the whole record or those parts of it cited by a party, and due account shall be taken of the rule of prejudicial error. . . .

§ 1305. Administrative law judges

For the purpose of sections 3105, 3344, 4301(2)(D), and 5372 of this title 7521 and the provisions of section 5335(a)(B) of this title that relate to administrative law judges, the Office of Personnel Management may, and for the purpose of section 7521 of this title, the Merit Systems Protection Board may investigate, require reports by agencies, issue reports, including an annual report to Congress, prescribe regulations, appoint advisory committees as necessary, recommend legislation, subpoena witnesses and records, and pay witness fees as established for the courts of the United States.

§ 3105. Appointment of administrative law judges

Each agency shall appoint as many administrative law judges as are necessary for proceedings required to be conducted in accordance with sections 556 and 557 of this title. Administrative law judges shall be assigned to cases in rotation so far as practicable, and may not perform duties inconsistent with their duties and responsibilities as administrative law judges.

§ 3344. Details; administrative law judges

An agency as defined by section 551 of this title, which occasionally or temporarily is insufficiently staffed with administrative law judges appointed under section 3105 of this title may use administrative law judges selected by the Office of Personnel Management from and with the consent of other agencies.

§ 5372. Administrative law judges

Administrative law judges appointed under section 3105 of this title are entitled to pay prescribed by the Office of Personnel Management independently of agency recommendations or ratings and in accordance with subchapter III of this chapter and Chapter 51 of this title.

§ 7521. Actions against administrative law judges

(a) An action may be taken against an administrative law judge appointed under section 3105 of this title by the agency in which the administrative law judge is employed only for good cause established and determined by the Merit Systems Protection Board on the record after opportunity for hearing before the Board.

(b) The actions covered by this section are—

(1) a removal;
(2) a suspension;
(3) a reduction in grade;
(4) a reduction in pay; and
(5) a furlough of 30 days or less; but do not include—

    (A) a suspension or removal [in the interest of national security];
    (B) a reduction-in-force action. . .; or
    (C) any action initiated [by the Special Counsel of the Board].

Appendix **C**

SELECTED EXECUTIVE ORDERS

Executive Order 9066 (President Franklin D. Roosevelt 1942)

Authorizing the Secretary of War to Prescribe Military Areas

Whereas the successful prosecution of the war requires every possible protection against espionage and against sabotage to national-defense material, national-defense premises, and national-defense utilities as defined in Section 4, Act of April 20, 1918, 40 Stat. 533, as amended by the Act of November 30, 1940, 54 Stat. 1220, and the Act of August 21, 1941, 55 Stat. 655 (U.S.C., Title 50, Sec. 104);

Now, therefore, by virtue of the authority vested in me as President of the United States, and Commander in Chief of the Army and Navy, I hereby authorize and direct the Secretary of War, and the Military Commanders whom he may from time to time designate, whenever he or any designated Commander deems such action necessary or desirable, to prescribe military areas in such places and of such extent as he or the appropriate Military Commander may determine, from which any or all persons may be excluded, and with respect to which, the right of any person to enter, remain in, or leave shall be subject to whatever restrictions the Secretary of War or the appropriate Military Commander may impose in his discretion. The Secretary of War is hereby authorized to provide for residents of any such area who are excluded therefrom, such transportation, food, shelter, and other accommodations as may be necessary, in the judgment of the Secretary of War or the said Military Commander, and until other arrangements are made, to accomplish the purpose of this order. The designation of military areas in any region or locality shall supersede designations of prohibited and restricted areas by the Attorney General under the Proclamations of December 7 and 8, 1941, and shall supersede the responsibility and authority of the Attorney General under the said Proclamations in respect of such prohibited and restricted areas.

I hereby further authorize and direct the Secretary of War and the said Military Commanders to take such other steps as he or the appropriate Military Commander may deem advisable to enforce compliance with the restrictions applicable to each Military area hereinabove authorized to be designated, including the use of Federal troops and other Federal Agencies, with authority to accept assistance of state and local agencies.

I hereby further authorize and direct all Executive Departments, independent establishments and other Federal Agencies, to assist the Secretary of War or the said Military Commanders in carrying out this Executive Order, including the furnishing of medical aid, hospitalization, food, clothing, transportation, use of land, shelter, and other supplies, equipment, utilities, facilities, and services.

This order shall not be construed as modifying or limiting in any way the authority heretofore granted under Executive Order No. 8972, dated December 12, 1941, nor shall it be construed as limiting or modifying the duty and responsibility of the Federal Bureau of Investigation, with respect to the investigation of alleged acts of sabotage or the duty and responsibility of the Attorney General and the Department of Justice under the Proclamations of December 7 and 8, 1941, prescribing regulations for the conduct and control of alien enemies, except as such duty and responsibility is superseded by the designation of military areas hereunder.

Executive Order 9066 was followed by this executive order:

Executive order 9102 (President Franklin D. Roosevelt 1942)

War Relocation Authority   By virtue of the authority vested in me by the Constitution and statutes of the United States, as President of the United States and Commander in Chief of the Army and Navy, and in order to provide for the removal from designated areas of persons whose removal is necessary in the interests of national security, it is ordered as follows:

1. There is established in the Office for Emergency Management of the Executive Office of the President the War Relocation Authority, at the head of which shall be a Director appointed by and responsible to the President.

2. The Director of the War Relocation Authority is authorized and directed to formulate and effectuate a program for the removal, from the areas designated from time to time by the Secretary of War or appropriate military commander under the authority of Executive Order No. 9066 of February 19, 1942, of the persons or classes of persons designated under such Executive Order, and for their relocation, maintenance, and supervision.

3. In effectuating such program the Director shall have authority to
    (a) —Accomplish all necessary evacuation not undertaken by the Secretary of War or appropriate military commander, provide for the relocation of such persons in appropriate places, provide for their needs in such manner as may be appropriate, and supervise their activities.
    (b) Provide, insofar as feasible and desirable, for the employment of such persons at useful work in industry, commerce, agriculture, or public projects, prescribe the terms and conditions of such public employment, and safeguard the public interest in the private employment of such persons.
    (c) Secure the cooperation, assistance, or services of any governmental agency.
    (d) Prescribe regulations necessary or desirable to promote effective execution of such program, and, as a means of coordinating evacuation and relocation activities, consult with the Secretary of War with respect to regulations issued and measures taken by him.
    (e) Make such delegations of authority as he may deem necessary.
    (f) Employ necessary personnel, and make such expenditures, including the making of loans and grants and the purchase of real property, as may be necessary, within the limits of such funds as may be made available to the Authority.

4. The Director shall consult with the United States Employment Service and other agencies on employment and other problems incident to activities under this Order.

5. The Director shall cooperate with the Alien Property Custodian appointed pursuant to Executive Order No. 9095 of March 11, 1942, in formulating policies to govern the custody, management, and disposal by the Alien Property Custodian of property belonging to foreign nationals removed under this Order or under Executive Order No. 9066 of February 19, 1942; and may assist all other persons removed under either of such Executive Orders in the management and disposal of their property.

6. Departments and agencies of the United States are directed to cooperate with and assist the Director in his activities hereunder. The Departments of War and Justice, under the direction of the Secretary of War and the Attorney General, respectively, shall insofar as consistent with the national interest provide such protective, police, and investigational services as the Director shall find necessary in connection with activities under this Order.

7. There is established within the War Relocation Authority the War Relocation Work Corps. The Director shall provide, by general regulations, for the enlistment in such Corps, for the duration of the present war, of persons removed under this Order or under Executive Order No. 9066 of February 19, 1942, and shall prescribe the terms and conditions of the work to be performed by such Corps, and the compensation to be paid.

8. There is established within the War Relocation Authority a Liaison Committee on War Relocation, which shall consist of the Secretary of War, the Secretary of the Treasury, the Attorney General, the Secretary of Agriculture, the Secretary of Labor, the Federal Security Administrator, the Director of Civilian Defense, and the Alien Property Custodian, or their deputies, and such other persons or agencies as the Director may designate. The Liaison Committee shall meet at the call of the Director and shall assist him in his duties.

9. The Director shall keep the President informed with regard to the progress made in carrying out this Order, and perform such related duties as the President may from time to time assign to him.

10. In order to avoid duplication of evacuation activities under this Order and Executive Order No. 9066 of February 19, 1942, the Director shall not undertake any evacuation activities within military areas designated under said Executive Order No. 9066, without the prior approval of the Secretary of War or the appropriate military commander.

11. This Order does not limit the authority granted in Executive Order No. 8972 of December 12, 1941; Executive Order No. 9066 of February 19, 1942; Executive Order No. 9095 of March 11, 1942; Executive Proclamation No. 2525 of December 7, 1941; Executive Proclamation No. 2526 of December 8, 1941; Executive Proclamation No. 2527 of December 8, 1941; Executive Proclamation No. 2533 of December 19, 1941; or Executive Proclamation No. 2537 of January 14, 1942; nor does it limit the functions of the Federal Bureau of Investigation.

[Although E.O. 9066 is somewhat innocuous, if not cryptic, it was understood to be used to relocate residents of the west coast of Japanese descent. The order was a consequence of the fear of espionage following Japan's attack on Pearl Harbor and the belief that the west coast was vulnerable to attack. It is also believed that the historical context of racism toward Japanese on the west coast contributed to the relocation decision. Congress quickly enacted 18 U.S.C. sec. 97a (1942), which made it a crime to disobey the military commander or Secretary of War in their relocation efforts. Over 100,000 people, many citizens of the United States, were relocated and interned. President Roosevelt rescinded E.O. 9066 in 1944 and the interned individuals (most people of Japanese ethnicity but also individuals of German and Italian ancestry) were released. In 1988 Congress, with the support of President Reagan, formally apologized to the internees. Subsequently all internees were paid $20,000 in reparations by the United States.]

Executive Order 12291 (President Ronald Reagan 1981)

Federal Regulation   By the authority vested in me as President by the Constitution and laws of the United States of America, and in order to reduce the burdens of existing and future regulations, increase agency accountability for regulatory actions, provide for presidential oversight of the regulatory process, minimize duplication and conflict of regulations, and insure well-reasoned regulations, it is hereby ordered as follows:

Sec. 1.   *Definitions. For the purposes of this Order:*

(a) "Regulation" or "rule" means an agency statement of general applicability and future effect designed to implement, interpret, or prescribe law or policy or describing the procedure or practice requirements of an agency, but does not include:
   (1) Administrative actions governed by the provisions of Sections 556 and 557 of Title 5 of the United States Code;
   (2) Regulations issued with respect to a military or foreign affairs function of the United States; or
   (3) Regulations related to agency organization, management, or personnel.

(b) "Major rule" means any regulation that is likely to result in:
   (1) An annual effect on the economy of $100 million or more;
   (2) A major increase in costs or prices for consumers, individual industries, Federal, State, or local government agencies, or geographic regions; or
   (3) Significant adverse effects on competition, employment, investment, productivity, innovation, or on the ability of United States-based enterprises to compete with foreign-based enterprises in domestic or export markets.

(c) "Director" means the Director of the Office of Management and Budget.

(d) "Agency" means any authority of the United States that is an "agency" under 44 U.S.C. 3502 (1), excluding those agencies specified in 44 U.S.C. 3502(10).

(e) "Task Force" means the Presidential Task Force on Regulatory Relief.

Sec. 2.   *General Requirements.*

In promulgating new regulations, reviewing existing regulations, and developing legislative proposals concerning regulation, all agencies, to the extent permitted by law, shall adhere to the following requirements:

(a) Administrative decisions shall be based on adequate information concerning the need for and consequences of proposed government action;

(b) Regulatory action shall not be undertaken unless the potential benefits to society for the regulation outweigh the potential costs to society;

(c) Regulatory objectives shall be chosen to maximize the net benefits to society;

(d) Among alternative approaches to any given regulatory objective, the alternative involving the least net cost to society shall be chosen; and

(e) Agencies shall set regulatory priorities with the aim of maximizing the aggregate net benefits to society, taking into account the condition of the particular industries affected by regulations, the condition of the national economy, and other regulatory actions contemplated for the future.

Sec. 3. *Regulatory Impact Analysis and Review.*

(a) In order to implement Section 2 of this Order, each agency shall, in connection with every major rule, prepare, and to the extent permitted by law consider, a Regulatory Impact Analysis. Such Analysis may be combined with any Regulatory Flexibility Analyses performed under 5 U.S.C. 603 and 604.

(b) Each agency shall initially determine whether a rule it intends to propose or to issue is a major rule, provided that, the Director, subject to the direction of the Task Force, shall have authority, in accordance with Sections 1(b) and 2 of this Order, to prescribe criteria for making such determinations, to order a rule to be treated as a major rule, and to require any set of related rules to be considered together as a major rule.

(c) Except as provided in Section 8 of this Order, agencies shall prepare Regulatory Impact Analyses of major rules and transmit them, along with all notices of proposed rule-making and all final rules, to the Director as follows:

    (1) If no notice of proposed rulemaking is to be published for a proposed major rule that is not an emergency rule, the agency shall prepare only a final Regulatory Impact Analysis, which shall be transmitted, along with the proposed rule, to the Director at least 60 days prior to the publication of the major rule as a final rule;

    (2) With respect to all other major rules, the agency shall prepare a preliminary Regulatory Impact Analysis, which shall be transmitted, along with a notice of proposed rulemaking, to the Director at least 60 days prior to the publication of a notice of proposed rulemaking, and a final Regulatory Impact Analysis, which shall be transmitted along with the final rule at least 30 days prior to the publication of the major rule as a final rule;

    (3) For all rules other than major rules, agencies shall submit to the Director, at least 10 days prior to publication, every notice of proposed rulemaking and final rule.

(d) To permit each proposed major rule to be analyzed in light of the requirements stated in Section 2 of this Order, each preliminary and final Regulatory Impact Analysis shall contain the following information:

    (1) A description of the potential benefits of the rule, including any beneficial effects that cannot be quantified in monetary terms, and the identification of those likely to receive the benefits;

    (2) A description of the potential costs of the rule, including any adverse effects that cannot be quantified in monetary terms, and the identification of those likely to bear the costs;

    (3) A determination of the potential net benefits of the rule, including an evaluation of effects that cannot be quantified in monetary terms;

    (4) A description of alternative approaches that could substantially achieve the same regulatory goal at lower cost, together with an analysis of this potential benefit and costs and a brief explanation of the legal reasons why such alternatives, if proposed, could not be adopted; and

    (5) Unless covered by the description required under paragraph (4) of this subsection, an explanation of any legal reasons why the rule cannot be based on the requirements set forth in Section 2 of this Order.

(e) (1) The Director, subject to the direction of the Task Force, which shall resolve any issues raised under this Order or ensure that they are presented to the President, is authorized to review any preliminary or final Regulatory Impact Analysis, notice of proposed rulemaking, or final rule based on the requirements of this Order.

(2) The Director shall be deemed to have concluded review unless the Director advises an agency to the contrary under subsection (f) of this Section:

    (A) Within 60 days of a submission under subsection (c)(1) or a submission of a preliminary Regulatory Impact Analysis or notice of proposed rule making under subsection (c)(2);

    (B) Within 30 days of the submission of a final Regulatory Impact Analysis and a final rule under subsection (c)(2); and

    (C) Within 10 days of the submission of a notice of proposed rulemaking or final rule under subsection (c)(3).

(f) (1) Upon the request of the Director, an agency shall consult with the Director concerning the review of a preliminary Regulatory Impact Analysis or notice of proposed rulemaking under this Order, and shall, subject to Section 8(a)(2) of this Order, refrain from publishing its preliminary Regulatory Impact Analysis or notice of proposed rulemaking until such review is concluded.

    (2) Upon receiving notice that the Director intends to submit views with respect to any final Regulatory Impact Analysis or final rule, the agency shall, subject to Section 8(a)(2) of this Order, refrain from publishing its final Regulatory Impact Analysis or final rule until the agency has responded to the Director's views, and incorporated those views and the agency's response in the rulemaking file.

    (3) Nothing in this subsection shall be construed as displacing the agencies' responsibilities delegated by law.

(g) For every rule for which an agency publishes a notice of proposed rulemaking, the agency shall include in its notice:

    (1) A brief statement setting forth the agency's initial determination whether the proposed rule is a major rule, together with the reasons underlying that determination; and

    (2) For each proposed major rule, a brief summary of the agency's preliminary Regulatory Impact Analysis.

(h) Agencies shall make their preliminary and final Regulatory Impact Analyses available to the public.

(i) Agencies shall initiate reviews of currently effective rules in accordance with the purposes of this Order, and perform Regulatory Impact Analyses of currently effective major rules. The Director, subject to the direction of the Task Force, may designate currently effective rules for review in accordance with this Order, and establish schedules for reviews and Analyses under this Order.

Sec. 4. *Regulatory Review. Before approving any final major rule, such agency shall:*

(a) Make a determination that the regulation is clearly within the authority delegated by law and consistent with congressional intent, and include in the Federal Register at the time of promulgation a memorandum of law supporting that determination.

(b) Make a determination that the factual conclusions upon which the rule is based have substantial support in the agency record, viewed as a whole, with full attention to public comments in general and the comments of persons directly affected by the rule in particular.

Sec. 5. *Regulatory Agendas.*

(a) Each agency shall publish, in October and April of each year, an agenda of proposed regulations that the agency has issued or expects to issue, and currently effective rules that are under agency review pursuant to this Order. These agendas may be incorporated with the agendas published under 5 U.S.C. 602, and must contain at the minimum:

    (1) A summary of the nature of each major rule being considered, the objectives and legal basis for the issuance of the rule, and an approximate § *13196* schedule for completing action on any major rule for which the agency has issued a notice of proposed rulemaking;

    (2) The name and telephone number of a knowledgeable agency official for each item on the agenda; and

    (3) A list of existing regulations to be reviewed under the terms of this Order, and a brief discussion of each such regulation.

(b) The Director, subject to the direction of the Task Force, may, to the extent permitted by law:

    (1) Require agencies to provide additional information in an agenda; and

    (2) Require publication of the agenda in any form.

Sec. 6.   *The Task Force and Office of Management and Budget.*

(a) To the extent permitted by law, the Director shall have authority, subject to the direction of the Task Force, to:

  (1) Designate any proposed or existing rule as a major rule in accordance with Section 1(b) of this Order;

  (2) Prepare and promulgate uniform standards for the identification of major rules and the development of Regulatory Impact Analyses;

  (3) Require an agency to obtain and evaluate, in connection with a regulation, any additional relevant data from any appropriate source;

  (4) Waive the requirements of Sections 3, 4, or 7 of this Order with respect to any proposed or existing major rule;

  (5) Identify duplicative, overlapping and conflicting rules, existing or proposed, and existing or proposed rules that are inconsistent with the policies underlying statutes governing agencies other than the issuing agency or with the purposes of this Order, and, in each such case, require appropriate interagency consultation to minimize or eliminate such duplication, overlap, or conflict;

  (6) Develop procedures for estimating the annual benefits and costs of agency regulations, on both an aggregate and economic or industrial sector basis, for purposes of compiling a regulatory budget;

  (7) In consultation with interested agencies, prepare for consideration by the President recommendations for changes in the agencies' statutes; and

  (8) Monitor agency compliance with the requirements of this Order and advise the President with respect to such compliance.

(b) The Director, subject to the direction of the Task Force, is authorized to establish procedures for the performance of all functions vested in the Director by this Order. The Director shall take appropriate steps to coordinate the implementation of the analysis, transmittal, review, and clearance provisions of this Order with the authorities and requirements provided for or imposed upon the Director and agencies under the Regulatory Flexibility Act, 5 U.S.C. 601 *et seq.*, and the Paperwork Reduction Plan Act of 1980, 44 U.S.C. 3501 *et seq.*

Sec. 7.   *Pending Regulations.*

(a) To the extent necessary to permit reconsideration in accordance with this Order, agencies shall, except as provided in Section 8 of this Order, suspend or postpone the effective dates of all major rules that they have promulgated in final form as of the date of this Order, but that have not yet become effective, excluding:

  (1) Major rules that cannot legally be postponed or suspended;

  (2) Major rules that, for good cause, ought to become effective as final rules without reconsideration. Agencies shall prepare, in accordance with Section 3 of this Order, a final Regulatory Impact Analysis for each major rule that they suspend or postpone.

(b) Agencies shall report to the Director no later than 15 days prior to the effective date of any rule that the agency has promulgated in final form as of the date of this Order, and that has not yet become effective, and that will not be reconsidered under subsection (a) of this Section:

  (1) That the rule is excepted from reconsideration under subsection (a), including a brief statement of the legal or other reasons for that determination; or

  (2) That the rule is not a major rule.

(c) The Director, subject to the direction of the Task Force, is authorized, to the extent permitted by law, to:

  (1) Require reconsideration, in accordance with this Order, of any major rule that an agency has issued in final form as of the date of this Order and that has not become effective; and

  (2) Designate a rule that an agency has issued in final form as of the date of this Order and that has not yet become effective as a major rule in accordance with Section 1(b) of this Order.

(d) Agencies may, in accordance with the Administrative Procedure Act and other applicable statutes, permit major rules that they have issued in final form as of the date of this Order, and that have not yet become effective, to take effect as interim rules while they are being reconsidered in accordance with this Order, provided that, agencies shall report to the Director, no later than 15 days before any such rule is proposed to take effect as an interim rule, that the rule should appropriately take effect as an interim rule while the rule is under reconsideration.

(e) Except as provided in Section 8 of this Order, agencies shall, to the extent permitted by law, refrain from promulgating as a final rule any proposed major rule that has been published or issued as of the date of this Order until a final Regulatory Impact Analysis, in accordance with Section 3 of this Order, has been prepared for the proposed major rule.

(f) Agencies shall report to the Director, no later than 30 days prior to promulgating as a final rule any proposed rule that the agency has published or issued as of the date of this Order and that has not been considered under the terms of this Order:

(1) That the rule cannot legally be considered in accordance with the Order, together with a brief explanation of the legal reasons barring such consideration; or

(2) That the rule is not a major rule, in which case the agency shall submit to the Director a copy of the proposed rule.

(g) The Director, subject to the direction of the Task Force, is authorized, to the extent permitted by law, to:

(1) Require consideration, in accordance with this Order, of any proposed major rule that the agency has published or issued as of the date of this Order; and

(2) Designate a proposed rule that an agency has published or issued as of the date of this Order, as a major rule in accordance with Section 1(b) of this Order.

(h) The Director shall be deemed to have determined that an agency's report to the Director under subsections (b), (d), or (f) of this Section is consistent with the purposes of this Order, unless the Director advises the agency to the contrary:

(1) Within 15 days of its report, in the case of any report under subsections (b) or (d); or

(2) Within 30 days of its report, in the case of any report under subsection (f).

(i) This Section does not supersede the President's Memorandum of January 29, 1981, entitled "Postponement of Pending Regulations," which shall remain in effect until March 30, 1981.

(j) In complying with this Section, agencies shall comply with all applicable provisions of the Administrative Procedure Act, and with any other procedural requirements made applicable to the agencies by other statutes.

Sec. 8. *Exemptions.*

(a) The procedures prescribed by this Order shall not apply to:

(1) Any regulation that responds to an emergency situation, provided that, any such regulation shall be reported to the Director as soon as is practicable, the agency shall publish in the Federal Register a statement of the reasons why it is impracticable for the agency to follow the procedures of this Order with respect to such a rule, and the agency shall prepare and transmit as soon as is practicable a Regulatory Impact Analysis of any such major rule; and

(2) Any regulation for which consideration or reconsideration under the terms of this Order would conflict with deadlines imposed by statute or by judicial order, provided that, any such regulation shall be reported to the Director together with a brief explanation of the conflict, the agency shall publish in the Federal Register a statement of the reasons why it is impracticable for the agency to follow the procedures of this Order with respect to such a rule, and the agency, in consultation with the Director, shall adhere to the requirements of this Order to the extent permitted by statutory or judicial deadlines.

(b) The Director, subject to the direction of the Task Force, may, in accordance with the purposes of this Order, exempt any class or category of regulations from any or all requirements of this Order.

Sec. 9. *Judicial Review.*

(a) This Order is intended only to improve the internal management of the Federal government, and is not intended to create any right or benefit, substantive or procedural, enforceable at law by a party against the United States, its agencies, its officers or any person. The determinations made by agencies under Section 4 of this Order, and any Regulatory Impact Analyses for any rule, shall be made part of the whole record of agency action in connection with the rule.

Sec. 10. *Revocations. Executive Orders No. 12044, as amended, and No. 12174 are revoked.*

Executive Order 12866 (President Clinton 1993)

Regulatory Planning and Review   The American people deserve a regulatory system that works for them, not against them: a regulatory system that protects and improves their health, safety, environment, and well-being and improves the performance of the economy without imposing unacceptable or unreasonable costs on society; regulatory policies that recognize that the private sector and private markets are the best engine for economic growth; regulatory approaches that respect the role of State, local, and tribal governments; and regulations that are effective, consistent, sensible, and understandable. We do not have such a regulatory system today.

With this Executive order, the Federal Government begins a program to reform and make more efficient the regulatory process. The objectives of this Executive order are to enhance planning and coordination with respect to both new and existing regulations; to reaffirm the primacy of Federal agencies in the regulatory decision-making process; to restore the integrity and legitimacy of regulatory review and oversight; and to make the process more accessible and open to the public. In pursuing these objectives, the regulatory process shall be conducted so as to meet applicable statutory requirements and with due regard to the discretion that has been entrusted to the Federal agencies.

Accordingly, by the authority vested in me as President by the Constitution and the laws of the United States of America, it is hereby ordered as follows:

Sec. 1.   *Statement of Regulatory Philosophy and Principles.*

(a) *The Regulatory Philosophy.* Federal agencies should promulgate only such regulations as are required by law, are necessary to interpret the law, or are made necessary by compelling public need, such as material failures of private markets to protect or improve the health and safety of the public, the environment, or the well-being of the American people. In deciding whether and how to regulate, agencies should assess all costs and benefits of available regulatory alternatives, including the alternative of not regulating. Costs and benefits shall be understood to include both quantifiable measures (to the fullest extent that these can be usefully estimated) and qualitative measures of costs and benefits that are difficult to quantify, but nevertheless essential to consider. Further, in choosing among alternative regulatory approaches, agencies should select those approaches that maximize net benefits (including potential economic, environmental, public health and safety, and other advantages; distributive impacts; and equity), unless a statute requires another regulatory approach.

(b) *The Principles of Regulation.* To ensure that the agencies' regulatory programs are consistent with the philosophy set forth above, agencies should adhere to the following principles, to the extent permitted by law and where applicable:

(1) Each agency shall identify the problem that it intends to address (including, where applicable, the failures of private markets or public institutions that warrant new agency action) as well as assess the significance of that problem.

(2) Each agency shall examine whether existing regulations (or other law) have created, or contributed to, the problem that a new regulation is intended to correct and whether those regulations (or other law) should be modified to achieve the intended goal of regulation more effectively.

(3) Each agency shall identify and assess available alternatives to direct regulation, including providing economic incentives to encourage the desired behavior, such as user fees or marketable permits, or providing information upon which choices can be made by the public.

(4) In setting regulatory priorities, each agency shall consider, to the extent reasonable, the degree and nature of the risks posed by various substances or activities within its jurisdiction.

(5) When an agency determines that a regulation is the best available method of achieving the regulatory objective, it shall design its regulations in the most cost-effective manner to achieve the regulatory objective. In doing so, each agency shall consider incentives for innovation, consistency, predictability, the costs of enforcement and compliance (to the government, regulated entities, and the public), flexibility, distributive impacts, and equity.

(6) Each agency shall assess both the costs and the benefits of the intended regulation and, recognizing that some costs and benefits are difficult to quantify, propose or adopt a regulation only upon a reasoned determination that the benefits of the intended regulation justify its costs.

(7) Each agency shall base its decisions on the best reasonably obtainable scientific, technical, economic, and other information concerning the need for, and consequences of, the intended regulation.

(8) Each agency shall identify and assess alternative forms of regulation and shall, to the extent feasible, specify performance objectives, rather than specifying the behavior or manner of compliance that regulated entities must adopt.

(9) Wherever feasible, agencies shall seek views of appropriate State, local, and tribal officials before imposing regulatory requirements that might significantly or uniquely affect those governmental entities. Each agency shall assess the effects of Federal regulations on State, local, and tribal governments, including specifically the availability of resources to carry out those mandates, and seek to minimize those burdens that uniquely or significantly affect such governmental entities, consistent with achieving regulatory objectives. In addition, as appropriate, agencies shall seek to harmonize Federal regulatory actions with related State, local, and tribal regulatory and other governmental functions.

(10) Each agency shall avoid regulations that are inconsistent, incompatible, or duplicative with its other regulations or those of other Federal agencies.

(11) Each agency shall tailor its regulations to impose the least burden on society, including individuals, businesses of differing sizes, and other entities (including small communities and governmental entities), consistent with obtaining the regulatory objectives, taking into account, among other things, and to the extent practicable, the costs of cumulative regulations.

(12) Each agency shall draft its regulations to be simple and easy to understand, with the goal of minimizing the potential for uncertainty and litigation arising from such uncertainty.

Sec. 2. *Organization.*

An efficient regulatory planning and review process is vital to ensure that the Federal Government's regulatory system best serves the American people.

(a) *The Agencies.* Because Federal agencies are the repositories of significant substantive expertise and experience, they are responsible for developing regulations and assuring that the regulations are consistent with applicable law, the President's priorities, and the principles set forth in this Executive order.

(b) *The Office of Management and Budget.* Coordinated review of agency rulemaking is necessary to ensure that regulations are consistent with applicable law, the President's priorities, and the principles set forth in this Executive order, and that decisions made by one agency do not conflict with the policies or actions taken or planned by another agency. The Office of Management and Budget (OMB) shall carry out that review function. Within OMB, the Office of Information and Regulatory Affairs (OIRA) is the repository of expertise concerning regulatory issues, including methodologies and procedures that affect more than one agency, this Executive order, and the President's regulatory policies. To the extent permitted by law, OMB shall provide guidance to agencies and assist the President, the Vice President, and other regulatory policy advisors to the President in regulatory planning and shall be the entity that reviews individual regulations, as provided by this Executive order.

(c) *The Vice President.* The Vice President is the principal advisor to the President on, and shall coordinate the development and presentation of recommendations concerning, regulatory policy, planning, and review, as set forth in this Executive order. In fulfilling their responsibilities under this Executive order, the President and the Vice President shall be assisted by the regulatory policy advisors within the Executive Office of the President and by such agency officials and personnel as the President and the Vice President may, from time to time, consult.

Sec. 3. *Definitions. For purposes of this Executive order:*

(a) "Advisors" refers to such regulatory policy advisors to the President as the President and Vice President may from time to time consult, including, among others:
  (1) the Director of OMB;
  (2) the Chair (or another member) of the Council of Economic Advisers;
  (3) the Assistant to the President for Economic Policy;
  (4) the Assistant to the President for Domestic Policy;
  (5) the Assistant to the President for National Security Affairs;
  (6) the Assistant to the President for Science and Technology;
  (7) the Assistant to the President for Intergovernmental Affairs;
  (8) the Assistant to the President and Staff Secretary;
  (9) the Assistant to the President and Chief of Staff to the Vice President;
  (10) the Assistant to the President and Counsel to the President;
  (11) the Deputy Assistant to the President and Director of the White House Office on Environmental Policy; and

(12) the Administrator of OIRA, who also shall coordinate communications relating to this Executive order among the agencies, OMB, the other Advisors, and the Office of the Vice President.

(b) "Agency," unless otherwise indicated, means any authority of the United States that is an "agency" under 44 U.S.C. 3502(1), other than those considered to be independent regulatory agencies, as defined in 44 U.S.C. 3502(10).

(c) "Director" means the Director of OMB.

(d) "Regulation" or "rule" means an agency statement of general applicability and future effect, which the agency intends to have the force and effect of law, that is designed to implement, interpret, or prescribe law or policy or to describe the procedure or practice requirements of an agency. It does not, however, include:
   (1) Regulations or rules issued in accordance with the formal rulemaking provisions of 5 U.S.C. 556, 557;
   (2) Regulations or rules that pertain to a military or foreign affairs function of the United States, other than procurement regulations and regulations involving the import or export of non-defense articles and services;
   (3) Regulations or rules that are limited to agency organization, management, or personnel matters; or
   (4) Any other category of regulations exempted by the Administrator of OIRA.

(e) "Regulatory action" means any substantive action by an agency (normally published in the **Federal Register**) that promulgates or is expected to lead to the promulgation of a final rule or regulation, including notices of inquiry, advance notices of proposed rulemaking, and notices of proposed rulemaking.

(f) "Significant regulatory action" means any regulatory action that is likely to result in a rule that may:

   (1) Have an annual effect on the economy of $100 million or more or adversely affect in a material way the economy, a sector of the economy, productivity, competition, jobs, the environment, public health or safety, or State, local, or tribal governments or communities;
   (2) Create a serious inconsistency or otherwise interfere with an action taken or planned by another agency;
   (3) Materially alter the budgetary impact of entitlements, grants, user fees, or loan programs or the rights and obligations of recipients thereof; or
   (4) Raise novel legal or policy issues arising out of legal mandates, the President's priorities, or the principles set forth in this Executive order.

Sec. 4. *Planning Mechanism.*

In order to have an effective regulatory program, to provide for coordination of regulations, to maximize consultation and the resolution of potential conflicts at an early stage, to involve the public and its State, local, and tribal officials in regulatory planning, and to ensure that new or revised regulations promote the President's priorities and the principles set forth in this Executive order, these procedures shall be followed, to the extent permitted by law:

(a) *Agencies' Policy Meeting.* Early in each year's planning cycle, the Vice President shall convene a meeting of the Advisors and the heads of agencies to seek a common understanding of priorities and to coordinate regulatory efforts to be accomplished in the upcoming year.

(b) *Unified Regulatory Agenda.* For purposes of this subsection, the term "agency" or "agencies" shall also include those considered to be independent regulatory agencies, as defined in 44 U.S.C. 3502(10). Each agency shall prepare an agenda of all regulations under development or review, at a time and in a manner specified by the Administrator of OIRA. The description of each regulatory action shall contain, at a minimum, a regulation identifier number, a brief summary of the action, the legal authority for the action, any legal deadline for the action, and the name and telephone number of a knowledgeable agency official. Agencies may incorporate the information required under 5 U.S.C. 602 and 41 U.S.C. 402 into these agendas.

(c) The Regulatory Plan. For purposes of this subsection, the term "agency" or "agencies" shall also include those considered to be independent regulatory agencies, as defined in 44 U.S.C. 3502(10).
   (1) As part of the Unified Regulatory Agenda, beginning in 1994, each agency shall prepare a Regulatory Plan (Plan) of the most important significant regulatory actions that the

agency reasonably expects to issue in proposed or final form in that fiscal year or thereafter. The Plan shall be approved personally by the agency head and shall contain at a minimum:

   (a)   A statement of the agency's regulatory objectives and priorities and how they relate to the President's priorities;

   (b)   A summary of each planned significant regulatory action including, to the extent possible, alternatives to be considered and preliminary estimates of the anticipated costs and benefits;

   (c)   A summary of the legal basis for each such action, including whether any aspect of the action is required by statute or court order;

   (d)   A statement of the need for each such action and, if applicable, how the action will reduce risks to public health, safety, or the environment, as well as how the magnitude of the risk addressed by the action relates to other risks within the jurisdiction of the agency;

   (e)   The agency's schedule for action, including a statement of any applicable statutory or judicial deadlines; and

   (f)   The name, address, and telephone number of a person the public may contact for additional information about the planned regulatory action.

(2) Each agency shall forward its Plan to OIRA by June 1st of each year.

(3) Within 10 calendar days after OIRA has received an agency's Plan, OIRA shall circulate it to other affected agencies, the Advisors, and the Vice President.

(4) An agency head who believes that a planned regulatory action of another agency may conflict with its own policy or action taken or planned shall promptly notify, in writing, the Administrator of OIRA, who shall forward that communication to the issuing agency, the Advisors, and the Vice President.

(5) If the Administrator of OIRA believes that a planned regulatory action of an agency may be inconsistent with the President's priorities or the principles set forth in this Executive order or may be in conflict with any policy or action taken or planned by another agency, the Administrator of OIRA shall promptly notify, in writing, the affected agencies, the Advisors, and the Vice President.

(6) The Vice President, with the Advisors' assistance, may consult with the heads of agencies with respect to their Plans and, in appropriate instances, request further consideration or interagency coordination.

(7) The Plans developed by the issuing agency shall be published annually in the October publication of the Unified Regulatory Agenda. This publication shall be made available to the Congress; State, local, and tribal governments; and the public. Any views on any aspect of any agency Plan, including whether any planned regulatory action might conflict with any other planned or existing regulation, impose any unintended consequences on the public, or confer any unclaimed benefits on the public, should be directed to the issuing agency, with a copy to OIRA.

(d) *Regulatory Working Group.* Within 30 days of the date of this Executive order, the Administrator of OIRA shall convene a Regulatory Working Group ("Working Group"), which shall consist of representatives of the heads of each agency that the Administrator determines to have significant domestic regulatory responsibility, the Advisors, and the Vice President. The Administrator of OIRA shall chair the Working Group and shall periodically advise the Vice President on the activities of the Working Group. The Working Group shall serve as a forum to assist agencies in identifying and analyzing important regulatory issues (including, among others (1) the development of innovative regulatory techniques, (2) the methods, efficacy, and utility of comparative risk assessment in regulatory decision-making, and (3) the development of short forms and other streamlined regulatory approaches for small businesses and other entities). The Working Group shall meet at least quarterly and may meet as a whole or in subgroups of agencies with an interest in particular issues or subject areas. To inform its discussions, the Working Group may commission analytical studies and reports by OIRA, the Administrative Conference of the United States, or any other agency.

(e) *Conferences.* The Administrator of OIRA shall meet quarterly with representatives of State, local, and tribal governments to identify both existing and proposed regulations that may uniquely or significantly affect those governmental entities. The Administrator of OIRA shall also convene, from time to time, conferences with representatives of businesses, nongovernmental organizations, and the public to discuss regulatory issues of common concern.

Sec. 5. *Existing Regulations.*

In order to reduce the regulatory burden on the American people, their families, their communities, their State, local, and tribal governments, and their industries; to determine whether regulations promulgated by the executive branch of the Federal Government have become unjustified or unnecessary as a result of changed circumstances; to confirm that regulations are both compatible with each other and not duplicative or inappropriately burdensome in the aggregate; to ensure that all regulations are consistent with the President's priorities and the principles set forth in this Executive order, within applicable law; and to otherwise improve the effectiveness of existing regulations:

(a) Within 90 days of the date of this Executive order, each agency shall submit to OIRA a program, consistent with its resources and regulatory priorities, under which the agency will periodically review its existing significant regulations to determine whether any such regulations should be modified or eliminated so as to make the agency's regulatory program more effective in achieving the regulatory objectives, less burdensome, or in greater alignment with the President's priorities and the principles set forth in this Executive order. Any significant regulations selected for review shall be included in the agency's annual Plan. The agency shall also identify any legislative mandates that require the agency to promulgate or continue to impose regulations that the agency believes are unnecessary or outdated by reason of changed circumstances.

(b) The Administrator of OIRA shall work with the Regulatory Working Group and other interested entities to pursue the objectives of this section. State, local, and tribal governments are specifically encouraged to assist in the identification of regulations that impose significant or unique burdens on those governmental entities and that appear to have outlived their justification or be otherwise inconsistent with the public interest.

(c) The Vice President, in consultation with the Advisors, may identify for review by the appropriate agency or agencies other existing regulations of an agency or groups of regulations of more than one agency that affect a particular group, industry, or sector of the economy, or may identify legislative mandates that may be appropriate for reconsideration by the Congress.

Sec. 6. *Centralized Review of Regulations.*

The guidelines set forth below shall apply to all regulatory actions, for both new and existing regulations, by agencies other than those agencies specifically exempted by the Administrator of OIRA:

(a) Agency Responsibilities.

(1) Each agency shall (consistent with its own rules, regulations, or procedures) provide the public with meaningful participation in the regulatory process. In particular, before issuing a notice of proposed rulemaking, each agency should, where appropriate, seek the involvement of those who are intended to benefit from and those expected to be burdened by any regulation (including, specifically, State, local, and tribal officials). In addition, each agency should afford the public a meaningful opportunity to comment on any proposed regulation, which in most cases should include a comment period of not less than 60 days. Each agency also is directed to explore and, where appropriate, use consensual mechanisms for developing regulations, including negotiated rulemaking.

(2) Within 60 days of the date of this Executive order, each agency head shall designate a Regulatory Policy Officer who shall report to the agency head. The Regulatory Policy Officer shall be involved at each stage of the regulatory process to foster the development of effective, innovative, and least burdensome regulations and to further the principles set forth in this Executive order.

(3) In addition to adhering to its own rules and procedures and to the requirements of the Administrative Procedure Act, the Regulatory Flexibility Act, the Paperwork Reduction Act, and other applicable law, each agency shall develop its regulatory actions in a timely fashion and adhere to the following procedures with respect to a regulatory action:

(A) Each agency shall provide OIRA, at such times and in the manner specified by the Administrator of OIRA, with a list of its planned regulatory actions, indicating those which the agency believes are significant regulatory actions within the meaning of this Executive order. Absent a material change in the development of the planned regulatory action, those not designated as significant will not be subject to review under this section unless, within 10 working days of receipt of the list, the Administrator of OIRA notifies the agency that OIRA has determined that a planned regulation is a significant regulatory action within the meaning of this Executive order. The Administrator of OIRA may waive review of any planned regulatory action designated by the agency as significant, in which case the agency need not further comply with subsection (a)(3)(B) or subsection (a)(3)(C) of this section.

(B) For each matter identified as, or determined by the Administrator of OIRA to be, a significant regulatory action, the issuing agency shall provide to OIRA:

   (i) The text of the draft regulatory action, together with a reasonably detailed description of the need for the regulatory action and an explanation of how the regulatory action will meet that need; and

   (ii) An assessment of the potential costs and benefits of the regulatory action, including an explanation of the manner in which the regulatory action is consistent with a statutory mandate and, to the extent permitted by law, promotes the President's priorities and avoids undue interference with State, local, and tribal governments in the exercise of their governmental functions.

(C) For those matters identified as, or determined by the Administrator of OIRA to be, a significant regulatory action within the scope of section 3(f)(1), the agency shall also provide to OIRA the following additional information developed as part of the agency's decision-making process (unless prohibited by law):

   (i) An assessment, including the underlying analysis, of benefits anticipated from the regulatory action (such as, but not limited to, the promotion of the efficient functioning of the economy and private markets, the enhancement of health and safety, the protection of the natural environment, and the elimination or reduction of discrimination or bias) together with, to the extent feasible, a quantification of those benefits;

   (ii) An assessment, including the underlying analysis, of costs anticipated from the regulatory action (such as, but not limited to, the direct cost both to the government in administering the regulation and to businesses and others in complying with the regulation, and any adverse effects on the efficient functioning of the economy, private markets (including productivity, employment, and competitiveness), health, safety, and the natural environment), together with, to the extent feasible, a quantification of those costs; and

   (iii) An assessment, including the underlying analysis, of costs and benefits of potentially effective and reasonably feasible alternatives to the planned regulation, identified by the agencies or the public (including improving the current regulation and reasonably viable nonregulatory actions), and an explanation why the planned regulatory action is preferable to the identified potential alternatives.

(D) In emergency situations or when an agency is obligated by law to act more quickly than normal review procedures allow, the agency shall notify OIRA as soon as possible and, to the extent practicable, comply with subsections (a)(3)(B) and (C) of this section. For those regulatory actions that are governed by a statutory or court-imposed deadline, the agency shall, to the extent practicable, schedule rulemaking proceedings so as to permit sufficient time for OIRA to conduct its review, as set forth below in subsection (b)(2) through (4) of this section.

(E) After the regulatory action has been published in the **Federal Register** or otherwise issued to the public, the agency shall:

   (i) Make available to the public the information set forth in subsections (a)(3)(B) and (C);

   (ii) Identify for the public, in a complete, clear, and simple manner, the substantive changes between the draft submitted to OIRA for review and the action subsequently announced; and

   (iii) Identify for the public those changes in the regulatory action that were made at the suggestion or recommendation of OIRA.

(F) All information provided to the public by the agency shall be in plain, understandable language.

(b) *OIRA Responsibilities.* The Administrator of OIRA shall provide meaningful guidance and oversight so that each agency's regulatory actions are consistent with applicable law, the President's priorities, and the principles set forth in this Executive order and do not conflict with the policies or actions of another agency. OIRA shall, to the extent permitted by law, adhere to the following guidelines:

(1) OIRA may review only actions identified by the agency or by OIRA as significant regulatory actions under subsection (a)(3)(A) of this section.

(2) OIRA shall waive review or notify the agency in writing of the results of its review within the following time periods:

   (A) For any notices of inquiry, advance notices of proposed rulemaking, or other preliminary regulatory actions prior to a Notice of Proposed Rulemaking, within 10 working days after the date of submission of the draft action to OIRA;

   (B) For all other regulatory actions, within 90 calendar days after the date of submission of the information set forth in subsections (a)(3)(B) and (C) of this section, unless OIRA has previously reviewed this information and, since that review, there has been no material change in the facts and circumstances upon which the regulatory action is based, in which case, OIRA shall complete its review within 45 days; and

   (C) The review process may be extended (1) once by no more than 30 calendar days upon the written approval of the Director and (2) at the request of the agency head.

(3) For each regulatory action that the Administrator of OIRA returns to an agency for further consideration of some or all of its provisions, the Administrator of OIRA shall provide the issuing agency a written explanation for such return, setting forth the pertinent provision of this Executive order on which OIRA is relying. If the agency head disagrees with some or all of the bases for the return, the agency head shall so inform the Administrator of OIRA in writing.

(4) Except as otherwise provided by law or required by a Court, in order to ensure greater openness, accessibility, and accountability in the regulatory review process, OIRA shall be governed by the following disclosure requirements:

   (A) Only the Administrator of OIRA (or a particular designee) shall receive oral communications initiated by persons not employed by the executive branch of the Federal Government regarding the substance of a regulatory action under OIRA review;

   (B) All substantive communications between OIRA personnel and persons not employed by the executive branch of the Federal Government regarding a regulatory action under review shall be governed by the following guidelines:

      (i) A representative from the issuing agency shall be invited to any meeting between OIRA personnel and such person(s);

      (ii) OIRA shall forward to the issuing agency, within 10 working days of receipt of the communication(s), all written communications, regardless of format, between OIRA personnel and any person who is not employed by the executive branch of the Federal Government, and the dates and names of individuals involved in all substantive oral communications (including meetings to which an agency representative was invited, but did not attend, and telephone conversations between OIRA personnel and any such persons); and

      (iii) OIRA shall publicly disclose relevant information about such communication(s), as set forth below in subsection (b)(4)(C) of this section.

   (C) OIRA shall maintain a publicly available log that shall contain, at a minimum, the following information pertinent to regulatory actions under review:

      (i) The status of all regulatory actions, including if (and if so, when and by whom) Vice Presidential and Presidential consideration was requested;

      (ii) A notation of all written communications forwarded to an issuing agency under subsection (b)(4)(B)(ii) of this section; and

      (iii) The dates and names of individuals involved in all substantive oral communications, including meetings and telephone conversations, between OIRA personnel and any person not employed by the executive branch of the Federal Government, and the subject matter discussed during such communications.

   (D) After the regulatory action has been published in the **Federal Register** or otherwise issued to the public, or after the agency has announced its decision not to publish or issue the regulatory action, OIRA shall make available to the public all documents exchanged between OIRA and the agency during the review by OIRA under this section.

(5) All information provided to the public by OIRA shall be in plain, understandable language.

Sec. 7.   *Resolution of Conflicts.*

To the extent permitted by law, disagreements or conflicts between or among agency heads or between OMB and any agency that cannot be resolved by the Administrator of OIRA shall be resolved by the President, or by the Vice President acting at the request of the President, with the relevant agency head (and, as appropriate, other interested government officials). Vice Presidential and Presidential consideration of such disagreements may be initiated only by the Director, by the head of the issuing agency, or by the head of an agency that has a significant interest in the regulatory action at issue. Such review will not be undertaken at the request of other persons, entities, or their agents.

Resolution of such conflicts shall be informed by recommendations developed by the Vice President, after consultation with the Advisors (and other executive branch officials or personnel whose responsibilities to the President include the subject matter at issue). The development of these recommendations shall be concluded within 60 days after review has been requested.

During the Vice Presidential and Presidential review period, communications with any person not employed by the Federal Government relating to the substance of the regulatory action under review and directed to the Advisors or their staffs or to the staff of the Vice President shall be in writing and shall be forwarded by the recipient to the affected agency(ies) for inclusion in the public docket(s). When the communication is not in writing, such Advisors or staff members shall inform the outside party that the matter is under review and that any comments should be submitted in writing.

At the end of this review process, the President, or the Vice President acting at the request of the President, shall notify the affected agency and the Administrator of OIRA of the President's decision with respect to the matter.

Sec. 8.   *Publication.*

Except to the extent required by law, an agency shall not publish in the **Federal Register** or otherwise issue to the public any regulatory action that is subject to review under section 6 of this Executive order until

(1)   the Administrator of OIRA notifies the agency that OIRA has waived its review of the action or has completed its review without any requests for further consideration, or

(2)   the applicable time period in section 6(b)(2) expires without OIRA having notified the agency that it is returning the regulatory action for further consideration under section 6(b)(3), whichever occurs first. If the terms of the preceding sentence have not been satisfied and an agency wants to publish or otherwise issue a regulatory action, the head of that agency may request Presidential consideration through the Vice President, as provided under section 7 of this order. Upon receipt of this request, the Vice President shall notify OIRA and the Advisors. The guidelines and time period set forth in section 7 shall apply to the publication of regulatory actions for which Presidential consideration has been sought.

Sec. 9.   *Agency Authority.*

Nothing in this order shall be construed as displacing the agencies' authority or responsibilities, as authorized by law.

Sec. 10.   *Judicial Review.*

Nothing in this Executive order shall affect any otherwise available judicial review of agency action. This Executive order is intended only to improve the internal management of the Federal Government and does not create any right or benefit, substantive or procedural, enforceable at law or equity by a party against the United States, its agencies or instrumentalities, its officers or employees, or any other person.

Sec. 11.   *Revocations.*

Executive Orders Nos. 12291 and 12498; all amendments to those Executive orders; all guidelines issued under those orders; and any exemptions from those orders heretofore granted for any category of rule are revoked.

Executive Order 13132 (President William J. Clinton 1999)

Federalism   By the authority vested in me as President by the Constitution and the laws of the United States of America, and in order to guarantee the division of governmental responsibilities between the national government and the States that was intended by the Framers of the Constitution, to ensure that the principles of federalism established by the Framers guide the executive departments and agencies in the formulation and implementation of policies, and to further the policies of the Unfunded Mandates Reform Act, it is hereby ordered as follows:

Sec. 1.   *Definitions. For purposes of this order:*

(a) "Policies that have federalism implications" refers to regulations, legislative comments or proposed legislation, and other policy statements or actions that have substantial direct effects on the States, on the relationship between the national government and the States, or on the distribution of power and responsibilities among the various levels of government.

(b) "State" or "States" refer to the States of the United States of America, individually or collectively, and, where relevant, to State governments, including units of local government and other political subdivisions established by the States.

(c) "Agency" means any authority of the United States that is an "agency" under 44 U.S.C. 3502(1), other than those considered to be independent regulatory agencies, as defined in 44 U.S.C. 3502(5).

(d) "State and local officials" means elected officials of State and local governments or their representative national organizations.

Sec. 2.   *Fundamental Federalism Principles. In formulating and implementing policies that have federalism implications, agencies shall be guided by the following fundamental federalism principles:*

(a) Federalism is rooted in the belief that issues that are not national in scope or significance are most appropriately addressed by the level of government closest to the people.

(b) The people of the States created the national government and delegated to it enumerated governmental powers. All other sovereign powers, save those expressly prohibited the States by the Constitution, are reserved to the States or to the people.

(c) The constitutional relationship among sovereign governments, State and national, is inherent in the very structure of the Constitution and is formalized in and protected by the Tenth Amendment to the Constitution.

(d) The people of the States are free, subject only to restrictions in the Constitution itself or in constitutionally authorized Acts of Congress, to define the moral, political, and legal character of their lives.

(e) The Framers recognized that the States possess unique authorities, qualities, and abilities to meet the needs of the people and should function as laboratories of democracy.

(f) The nature of our constitutional system encourages a healthy diversity in the public policies adopted by the people of the several States according to their own conditions, needs, and desires. In the search for enlightened public policy, individual States and communities are free to experiment with a variety of approaches to public issues. One-size-fits-all approaches to public policy problems can inhibit the creation of effective solutions to those problems.

(g) Acts of the national government—whether legislative, executive, or judicial in nature—that exceed the enumerated powers of that government under the Constitution violate the principle of federalism established by the Framers.

(h) Policies of the national government should recognize the responsibility of—and should encourage opportunities for—individuals, families, neighborhoods, local governments, and private associations to achieve their personal, social, and economic objectives through cooperative effort.

(i) The national government should be deferential to the States when taking action that affects the policymaking discretion of the States and should act only with the greatest caution where State or local governments have identified uncertainties regarding the constitutional or statutory authority of the national government.

Sec. 3. *Federalism Policymaking Criteria. In addition to adhering to the fundamental federalism principles set forth in section 2, agencies shall adhere, to the extent permitted by law, to the following criteria when formulating and implementing policies that have federalism implications:*

(a) There shall be strict adherence to constitutional principles. Agencies shall closely examine the constitutional and statutory authority supporting any action that would limit the policymaking discretion of the States and shall carefully assess the necessity for such action. To the extent practicable, State and local officials shall be consulted before any such action is implemented. Executive Order 12372 of July 14, 1982 ("Intergovernmental Review of Federal Programs") remains in effect for the programs and activities to which it is applicable.

(b) National action limiting the policymaking discretion of the States shall be taken only where there is constitutional and statutory authority for the action and the national activity is appropriate in light of the presence of a problem of national significance. Where there are significant uncertainties as to whether national action is authorized or appropriate, agencies shall consult with appropriate State and local officials to determine whether Federal objectives can be attained by other means.

(c) With respect to Federal statutes and regulations administered by the States, the national government shall grant the States the maximum administrative discretion possible. Intrusive Federal oversight of State administration is neither necessary nor desirable.

(d) When undertaking to formulate and implement policies that have federalism implications, agencies shall:

   (1) encourage States to develop their own policies to achieve program objectives and to work with appropriate officials in other States;

   (2) where possible, defer to the States to establish standards;

   (3) in determining whether to establish uniform national standards, consult with appropriate State and local officials as to the need for national standards and any alternatives that would limit the scope of national standards or otherwise preserve State prerogatives and authority; and

   (4) where national standards are required by Federal statutes, consult with appropriate State and local officials in developing those standards.

Sec. 4. *Special Requirements for Preemption. Agencies, in taking action that preempts State law, shall act in strict accordance with governing law.*

(a) Agencies shall construe, in regulations and otherwise, a Federal statute to preempt State law only where the statute contains an express preemption provision or there is some other clear evidence that the Congress intended preemption of State law, or where the exercise of State authority conflicts with the exercise of Federal authority under the Federal statute.

(b) Where a Federal statute does not preempt State law (as addressed in subsection (a) of this section), agencies shall construe any authorization in the statute for the issuance of regulations as authorizing preemption of State law by rulemaking only when the exercise of State authority directly conflicts with the exercise of Federal authority under the Federal statute or there is clear evidence to conclude that the Congress intended the agency to have the authority to preempt State law.

(c) Any regulatory preemption of State law shall be restricted to the minimum level necessary to achieve the objectives of the statute pursuant to which the regulations are promulgated.

(d) When an agency foresees the possibility of a conflict between State law and Federally protected interests within its area of regulatory responsibility, the agency shall consult, to the extent practicable, with appropriate State and local officials in an effort to avoid such a conflict.

(e) When an agency proposes to act through adjudication or rulemaking to preempt State law, the agency shall provide all affected State and local officials notice and an opportunity for appropriate participation in the proceedings.

Sec. 5. *Special Requirements for Legislative Proposals. Agencies shall not submit to the Congress legislation that would:*

(a) directly regulate the States in ways that would either interfere with functions essential to the States' separate and independent existence or be inconsistent with the fundamental federalism principles in section 2;

(b) attach to Federal grants conditions that are not reasonably related to the purpose of the grant; or

(c) preempt State law, unless preemption is consistent with the fundamental federalism principles set forth in section 2, and unless a clearly legitimate national purpose, consistent with the federalism policymaking criteria set forth in section 3, cannot otherwise be met.

Sec. 6. *Consultation.*

(a) Each agency shall have an accountable process to ensure meaningful and timely input by State and local officials in the development of regulatory policies that have federalism implications. Within 90 days after the effective date of this order, the head of each agency shall designate an official with principal responsibility for the agency's implementation of this order and that designated official shall submit to the Office of Management and Budget a description of the agency's consultation process.

(b) To the extent practicable and permitted by law, no agency shall promulgate any regulation that has federalism implications, that imposes substantial direct compliance costs on State and local governments, and that is not required by statute, unless:

    (1) funds necessary to pay the direct costs incurred by the State and local governments in complying with the regulation are provided by the Federal Government; or

    (2) the agency, prior to the formal promulgation of the regulation,

        (A) consulted with State and local officials early in the process of developing the proposed regulation;

        (B) in a separately identified portion of the preamble to the regulation as it is to be issued in the Federal Register, provides to the Director of the Office of Management and Budget a federalism summary impact statement, which consists of a description of the extent of the agency's prior consultation with State and local officials, a summary of the nature of their concerns and the agency's position supporting the need to issue the regulation, and a statement of the extent to which the concerns of State and local officials have been met; and

        (C) makes available to the Director of the Office of Management and Budget any written communications submitted to the agency by State and local officials.

(c) To the extent practicable and permitted by law, no agency shall promulgate any regulation that has federalism implications and that preempts State law, unless the agency, prior to the formal promulgation of the regulation,

    (1) consulted with State and local officials early in the process of developing the proposed regulation;

    (2) in a separately identified portion of the preamble to the regulation as it is to be issued in the Federal Register, provides to the Director of the Office of Management and Budget a federalism summary impact statement, which consists of a description of the extent of the agency's prior consultation with State and local officials, a summary of the nature of their concerns and the agency's position supporting the need to issue the regulation, and a statement of the extent to which the concerns of State and local officials have been met; and

    (3) makes available to the Director of the Office of Management and Budget any written communications submitted to the agency by State and local officials.

Sec. 7. *Increasing Flexibility for State and Local Waivers.*

(a) Agencies shall review the processes under which State and local governments apply for waivers of statutory and regulatory requirements and take appropriate steps to streamline those processes.

(b) Each agency shall, to the extent practicable and permitted by law, consider any application by a State for a waiver of statutory or regulatory requirements in connection with any program administered by that agency with a general view toward increasing opportunities for utilizing flexible policy approaches at the State or local level in cases in which the proposed waiver is consistent with applicable Federal policy objectives and is otherwise appropriate.

(c) Each agency shall, to the extent practicable and permitted by law, render a decision upon a complete application for a waiver within 120 days of receipt of such application by the agency. If the application for a waiver is not granted, the agency shall provide the applicant with timely written notice of the decision and the reasons therefor.

(d) This section applies only to statutory or regulatory requirements that are discretionary and subject to waiver by the agency.

Sec. 8. *Accountability.*

(a) In transmitting any draft final regulation that has federalism implications to the Office of Management and Budget pursuant to Executive Order 12866 of September 30, 1993, each agency shall include a certification from the official designated to ensure compliance with this order stating that the requirements of this order have been met in a meaningful and timely manner.

(b) In transmitting proposed legislation that has federalism implications to the Office of Management and Budget, each agency shall include a certification from the official designated to ensure compliance with this order that all relevant requirements of this order have been met.

(c) Within 180 days after the effective date of this order, the Director of the Office of Management and Budget and the Assistant to the President for Intergovernmental Affairs shall confer with State and local officials to ensure that this order is being properly and effectively implemented.

Sec. 9. *Independent Agencies. Independent regulatory agencies are encouraged to comply with the provisions of this order.*

Sec. 10. *General Provisions.*

(a) This order shall supplement but not supersede the requirements contained in Executive Order 12372 ("Intergovernmental Review of Federal Programs"), Executive Order 12866 ("Regulatory Planning and Review"), Executive Order 12988 ("Civil Justice Reform"), and OMB Circular A-19.

(b) Executive Order 12612 ("Federalism"), Executive Order 12875 ("Enhancing the Intergovernmental Partnership"), Executive Order 13083 ("Federalism"), and Executive Order 13095 ("Suspension of Executive Order 13083") are revoked.

(c) This order shall be effective 90 days after the date of this order.

Sec. 11. *Judicial Review. This order is intended only to improve the internal management of the executive branch, and is not intended to create any right or benefit, substantive or procedural, enforceable at law by a party against the United States, its agencies, its officers, or any person.*

Executive Order 13228 (President George W. Bush 2001)

Establishing the Office of Homeland Security and the Homeland Security Council

(1) By the authority vested in me as President by the Constitution and the laws of the United States of America, it is hereby ordered as follows:

Sec. 1. *Establishment. I hereby establish within the Executive Office of the President an Office of Homeland Security (the "Office") to be headed by the Assistant to the President for Homeland Security.*

Sec. 2. *Mission. The mission of the Office shall be to develop and coordinate the implementation of a comprehensive national strategy to secure the United States from terrorist threats or attacks. The Office shall perform the functions necessary to carry out this mission, including the functions specified in Section 3 of this order.*

Sec. 3. *Functions. The functions of the Office shall be to coordinate the executive branch's efforts to detect, prepare for, prevent, protect against, respond to, and recover from terrorist attacks within the United States.*

(a) National Strategy. The Office shall work with executive departments and agencies, State and local governments, and private entities to ensure the adequacy of the national strategy for detecting, preparing for, preventing, protecting against, responding to, and recovering from terrorist threats or attacks within the United States and shall periodically review and coordinate revisions to that strategy as necessary.

(b) Detection. The Office shall identify priorities and coordinate efforts for collection and analysis of information within the United States regarding threats of terrorism against the United States and activities of terrorists or terrorist groups within the United States. The Office also shall identify, in coordination with the Assistant to the President for National Security Affairs, priorities for collection of intelligence outside the United States regarding threats of terrorism within the United States.

   (i) In performing these functions, the Office shall work with Federal, State, and local agencies, as appropriate, to:

     (A) facilitate collection from State and local governments and private entities of information pertaining to terrorist threats or activities within the United States;

     (B) coordinate and prioritize the requirements for foreign intelligence relating to terrorism within the United States of executive departments and agencies responsible for homeland security and provide these requirements and priorities to the Director of Central Intelligence and other agencies responsible for collection of foreign intelligence;

     (C) coordinate efforts to ensure that all executive departments and agencies that have intelligence collection responsibilities have sufficient technological capabilities and resources to collect intelligence and data relating to terrorist activities or possible terrorist acts within the United States, working with the Assistant to the President for National Security Affairs, as appropriate;

     (D) coordinate development of monitoring protocols and equipment for use in detecting the release of biological, chemical, and radiological hazards; and

     (E) ensure that, to the extent permitted by law, all appropriate and necessary intelligence and law enforcement information relating to homeland security is disseminated to and exchanged among appropriate executive departments and agencies responsible for homeland security and, where appropriate for reasons of homeland security, promote exchange of such information with and among State and local governments and private entities.

   (ii) Executive departments and agencies shall, to the extent permitted by law, make available to the Office all information relating to terrorist threats and activities within the United States.

(c) Preparedness. The Office of Homeland Security shall coordinate national efforts to prepare for and mitigate the consequences of terrorist threats or attacks within the United States. In performing this function, the Office shall work with Federal, State, and local agencies, and private entities, as appropriate, to:

   (i) review and assess the adequacy of the portions of all Federal emergency response plans that pertain to terrorist threats or attacks within the United States;

   (ii) coordinate domestic exercises and simulations designed to assess and practice systems that would be called upon to respond to a terrorist threat or attack within the United States and coordinate programs and activities for training Federal, State, and local employees who would be called upon to respond to such a threat or attack;

   (iii) coordinate national efforts to ensure public health preparedness for a terrorist attack, including reviewing vaccination policies and reviewing the adequacy of and, if necessary, increasing vaccine and pharmaceutical stockpiles and hospital capacity;

   (iv) coordinate Federal assistance to State and local authorities and nongovernmental organizations to prepare for and respond to terrorist threats or attacks within the United States;

   (v) ensure that national preparedness programs and activities for terrorist threats or attacks are developed and are regularly evaluated under appropriate standards and that resources are allocated to improving and sustaining preparedness based on such evaluations; and

   (vi) ensure the readiness and coordinated deployment of Federal response teams to respond to terrorist threats or attacks, working with the Assistant to the President for National Security Affairs, when appropriate.

(d) Prevention. The Office shall coordinate efforts to prevent terrorist attacks within the United States. In performing this function, the Office shall work with Federal, State, and local agencies, and private entities, as appropriate, to:

   (i) facilitate the exchange of information among such agencies relating to immigration and visa matters and shipments of cargo; and, working with the Assistant to the President for National Security Affairs, ensure coordination among such agencies to prevent the entry of terrorists and terrorist materials and supplies into the United States and facilitate removal of such terrorists from the United States, when appropriate;

   (ii) coordinate efforts to investigate terrorist threats and attacks within the United States; and

   (iii) coordinate efforts to improve the security of United States borders, territorial waters, and airspace in order to prevent acts of terrorism within the United States, working with the Assistant to the President for National Security Affairs, when appropriate.

(e) Protection. The Office shall coordinate efforts to protect the United States and its critical infrastructure from the consequences of terrorist attacks. In performing this function, the Office shall work with Federal, State, and local agencies, and private entities, as appropriate, to:

   (i) strengthen measures for protecting energy production, transmission, and distribution services and critical facilities; other utilities; telecommunications; facilities that produce, use, store, or dispose of nuclear material; and other critical infrastructure services and critical facilities within the United States from terrorist attack;

   (ii) coordinate efforts to protect critical public and privately owned information systems within the United States from terrorist attack;

   (iii) develop criteria for reviewing whether appropriate security measures are in place at major public and privately owned facilities within the United States;

   (iv) coordinate domestic efforts to ensure that special events determined by appropriate senior officials to have national significance are protected from terrorist attack;

   (v) coordinate efforts to protect transportation systems within the United States, including railways, highways, shipping, ports and waterways, and airports and civilian aircraft, from terrorist attack;

   (vi) coordinate efforts to protect United States livestock, agriculture, and systems for the provision of water and food for human use and consumption from terrorist attack; and

   (vii) coordinate efforts to prevent unauthorized access to, development of, and unlawful importation into the United States of, chemical, biological, radiological, nuclear, explosive, or other related materials that have the potential to be used in terrorist attacks.

(f) Response and Recovery. The Office shall coordinate efforts to respond to and promote recovery from terrorist threats or attacks within the United States. In performing this function, the Office shall work with Federal, State, and local agencies, and private entities, as appropriate, to:

   (i) coordinate efforts to ensure rapid restoration of transportation systems, energy production, transmission, and distribution systems; telecommunications; other utilities; and other critical infrastructure facilities after disruption by a terrorist threat or attack;

   (ii) coordinate efforts to ensure rapid restoration of public and private critical information systems after disruption by a terrorist threat or attack;

   (iii) work with the National Economic Council to coordinate efforts to stabilize United States financial markets after a terrorist threat or attack and manage the immediate economic and financial consequences of the incident;

   (iv) coordinate Federal plans and programs to provide medical, financial, and other assistance to victims of terrorist attacks and their families; and

   (v) coordinate containment and removal of biological, chemical, radiological, explosive, or other hazardous materials in the event of a terrorist threat or attack involving such hazards and coordinate efforts to mitigate the effects of such an attack.

(g) Incident Management. The Assistant to the President for Homeland Security shall be the individual primarily responsible for coordinating the domestic response efforts of all departments and agencies in the event of an imminent terrorist threat and during and in the immediate aftermath of a terrorist attack within the United States and shall be the principal point of contact for and to the President with respect to coordination of such efforts. The Assistant to the President for Homeland Security shall coordinate with the Assistant to the President for National Security Affairs, as appropriate.

(h) Continuity of Government. The Assistant to the President for Homeland Security, in coordination with the Assistant to the President for National Security Affairs, shall review plans and preparations for ensuring the continuity of the Federal Government in the event of a terrorist attack that threatens the safety and security of the United States Government or its leadership.

(i) Public Affairs. The Office, subject to the direction of the White House Office of Communications, shall coordinate the strategy of the executive branch for communicating with the public in the event of a terrorist threat or attack within the United States. The Office also shall coordinate the development of programs for educating the public about the nature of terrorist threats and appropriate precautions and responses.

(j) Cooperation with State and Local Governments and Private Entities. The Office shall encourage and invite the participation of State and local governments and private entities, as appropriate, in carrying out the Office's functions.

(k) Review of Legal Authorities and Development of Legislative Proposals. The Office shall coordinate a periodic review and assessment of the legal authorities available to executive departments and agencies to permit them to perform the functions described in this order. When the Office determines that such legal authorities are inadequate, the Office shall develop, in consultation with executive departments and agencies, proposals for presidential action and legislative proposals for submission to the Office of Management and Budget to enhance the ability of executive departments and agencies to perform those functions. The Office shall work with State and local governments in assessing the adequacy of their legal authorities to permit them to detect, prepare for, prevent, protect against, and recover from terrorist threats and attacks.

(l) Budget Review. The Assistant to the President for Homeland Security, in consultation with the Director of the Office of Management and Budget (the "Director") and the heads of executive departments and agencies, shall identify programs that contribute to the Administration's strategy for homeland security and, in the development of the President's annual budget submission, shall review and provide advice to the heads of departments and agencies for such programs. The Assistant to the President for Homeland Security shall provide advice to the Director on the level and use of funding in departments and agencies for homeland security-related activities and, prior to the Director's forwarding of the proposed annual budget submission to the President for transmittal to the Congress, shall certify to the Director the funding levels that the Assistant to the President for Homeland Security believes are necessary and appropriate for the homeland security-related activities of the executive branch.

Sec. 4. *Administration.*

(a) The Office of Homeland Security shall be directed by the Assistant to the President for Homeland Security.

(b) The Office of Administration within the Executive Office of the President shall provide the Office of Homeland Security with such personnel, funding, and administrative support, to the extent permitted by law and subject to the availability of appropriations, as directed by the Chief of Staff to carry out the provisions of this order.

(c) Heads of executive departments and agencies are authorized, to the extent permitted by law, to detail or assign personnel of such departments and agencies to the Office of Homeland Security upon request of the Assistant to the President for Homeland Security, subject to the approval of the Chief of Staff.

Sec. 5. *Establishment of Homeland Security Council.*

(a) I hereby establish a Homeland Security Council (the "Council"), which shall be responsible for advising and assisting the President with respect to all aspects of homeland security. The Council shall serve as the mechanism for ensuring coordination of homeland security-related activities of executive departments and agencies and effective development and implementation of homeland security policies.

(b) The Council shall have as its members the President, the Vice President, the Secretary of the Treasury, the Secretary of Defense, the Attorney General, the Secretary of Health and Human Services, the Secretary of Transportation, the Director of the Federal Emergency Management Agency, the Director of the Federal Bureau of Investigation, the Director of Central Intelligence, the Assistant to the President for Homeland Security, and such other officers of the executive branch as the President may from time to time designate. The Chief of Staff, the Chief of Staff to the Vice President, the Assistant to the President for National Security Affairs, the Counsel to the President, and the Director of the Office of Management and Budget also are invited to attend any Council meeting. The Secretary of State, the Secretary of Agriculture, the Secretary of the Interior, the Secretary of Energy, the Secretary of Labor, the Secretary of Commerce, the Secretary of Veterans Affairs, the Administrator of the Environmental Protection Agency, the Assistant to the President for Economic Policy, and the Assistant to the President for Domestic Policy shall be invited to attend meetings pertaining to their responsibilities. The heads of other executive departments and agencies and other senior officials shall be invited to attend Council meetings when appropriate.

(c) The Council shall meet at the President's direction. When the President is absent from a meeting of the Council, at the President's direction the Vice President may preside. The Assistant to the President for Homeland Security shall be responsible, at the President's direction, for determining the agenda, ensuring that necessary papers are prepared, and recording Council actions and Presidential decisions.

Sec. 6. *Original Classification Authority. I hereby delegate the authority to classify information originally as Top Secret, in accordance with Executive Order 12958 or any successor Executive Order, to the Assistant to the President for Homeland Security.*

Sec. 7. *Continuing Authorities. This order does not alter the existing authorities of United States Government departments and agencies. All executive departments and agencies are directed to assist the Council and the Assistant to the President for Homeland Security in carrying out the purposes of this order.*

Sec. 8. *General Provisions.*

(a) This order does not create any right or benefit, substantive or procedural, enforceable at law or equity by a party against the United States, its departments, agencies or instrumentalities, its officers or employees, or any other person.

(b) References in this order to State and local governments shall be construed to include tribal governments and United States territories and other possessions.

(c) References to the "United States" shall be construed to include United States territories and possessions.

Sec. 9. *Amendments to Executive Order 12656. Executive Order 12656 of November 18, 1988, as amended, is hereby further amended as follows:*

(a) Section 101(a) is amended by adding at the end of the fourth sentence: "except that the Homeland Security Council shall be responsible for administering such policy with respect to terrorist threats and attacks within the United States."

(b) Section 104(a) is amended by adding at the end: "except that the Homeland Security Council is the principal forum for consideration of policy relating to terrorist threats and attacks within the United States."

(c) Section 104(b) is amended by inserting the words "and the Homeland Security Council" after the words "National Security Council."

(d) The first sentence of section 104(c) is amended by inserting the words "and the Homeland Security Council" after the words "National Security Council."

(e) The second sentence of section 104(c) is replaced with the following two sentences: "Pursuant to such procedures for the organization and management of the National Security Council and Homeland Security Council processes as the President may establish, the Director of the Federal Emergency Management Agency also shall assist in the implementation of and management of those processes as the President may establish. The Director of the Federal Emergency Management Agency also shall assist in the implementation of national security emergency preparedness policy by coordinating with the other Federal departments and agencies and with State and local governments, and by providing periodic reports to the National Security Council and the Homeland Security Council on implementation of national security emergency preparedness policy."

(f) Section 201(7) is amended by inserting the words "and the Homeland Security Council" after the words "National Security Council."

(g) Section 206 is amended by inserting the words "and the Homeland Security Council" after the words "National Security Council."

(h) Section 208 is amended by inserting the words "or the Homeland Security Council" after the words "National Security Council."

Military Order 1 (President George W. Bush 2001)

Detention, Treatment, and Trial of Certain Non-Citizens in the War Against Terrorism

By the authority vested in me as President and as Commander in Chief of the Armed Forces of the United States by the Constitution and the laws of the United States of America, including the Authorization for Use of Military Force Joint Resolution (Public Law 107-40, 115 Stat. 224) and sections 821 and 836 of title 10, United States Code, it is hereby ordered as follows:

Sec. 1. *Findings.*

(a) International terrorists, including members of al Qaida, have carried out attacks on United States diplomatic and military personnel and facilities abroad and on citizens and property within the United States on a scale that has created a state of armed conflict that requires the use of the United States Armed Forces.

(b) In light of grave acts of terrorism and threats of terrorism, including the terrorist attacks on September 11, 2001, on the headquarters of the United States Department of Defense in the national capital region, on the World Trade Center in New York, and on civilian aircraft such as in Pennsylvania, I proclaimed a national emergency on September 14, 2001 (Proc. 7463, Declaration of National Emergency by Reason of Certain Terrorist Attacks).

(c) Individuals acting alone and in concert involved in international terrorism possess both the capability and the intention to undertake further terrorist attacks against the United States that, if not detected and prevented, will cause mass deaths, mass injuries, and massive destruction of property, and may place at risk the continuity of the operations of the United States Government.

(d) The ability of the United States to protect the United States and its citizens, and to help its allies and other cooperating nations protect their nations and their citizens, from such further terrorist attacks depends in significant part upon using the United States Armed Forces to identify terrorists and those who support them, to disrupt their activities, and to eliminate their ability to conduct or support such attacks.

(e) To protect the United States and its citizens, and for the effective conduct of military operations and prevention of terrorist attacks, it is necessary for individuals subject to this order pursuant to Section 2 hereof to be detained, and, when tried, to be tried for violations of the laws of war and other applicable laws by military tribunals.

(f) Given the danger to the safety of the United States and the nature of international terrorism, and to the extent provided by and under this order, I find consistent with Section 836 of title 10, United States Code, that it is not practicable to apply in military commissions under this order the principles of law and the rules of evidence generally recognized in the trial of criminal cases in the United States district courts.

(g) Having fully considered the magnitude of the potential deaths, injuries, and property destruction that would result from potential acts of terrorism against the United States, and the probability that such acts will occur, I have determined that an extraordinary emergency exists for national defense purposes, that this emergency constitutes an urgent and compelling government interest, and that issuance of this order is necessary to meet the emergency.

Sec. 2. *Definition and Policy.*

(a) The term "individual subject to this order" shall mean any individual who is not a United States citizen with respect to whom I determine from time to time in writing that:
  (1) there is reason to believe that such individual, at the relevant times,
     (i) is or was a member of the organization known as al Qaida;
     (ii) has engaged in, aided or abetted, or conspired to commit, acts of international terrorism, or acts in preparation therefore, that have caused, threaten to cause, or have as their aim to cause, injury to or adverse effects on the United States, its citizens, national security, foreign policy, or economy; or
     (iii) has knowingly harbored one or more individuals described in subpara-graphs (i) or (ii) of subsection 2(a)(1) of this order; and
  (2) it is in the interest of the United States that such individual be subject to this order.

(b) It is the policy of the United States that the Secretary of Defense shall take all necessary measures to ensure that any individual subject to this order is detained in accordance with Section 3, and, if the individual is to be tried, that such individual is tried only in accordance with Section 4.

(c) It is further the policy of the United States that any individual subject to this order who is not already under the control of the Secretary of Defense but who is under the control of any other officer or agent of the United States or any State shall, upon delivery of a copy of such written determination to such officer or agent, forthwith be placed under the control of the Secretary of Defense.

Sec. 3. *Detention Authority of the Secretary of Defense. Any individual subject to this order shall be—*

(a) detained at an appropriate location designated by the Secretary of Defense outside or within the United States;

(b) treated humanely, without any adverse distinction based on race, color, religion, gender, birth, wealth, or any similar criteria;

(c) afforded adequate food, drinking water, shelter, clothing, and medical treatment;

(d) allowed the free exercise of religion consistent with the requirements of such detention; and

(e) detained in accordance with such other conditions as the Secretary of Defense may prescribe.

Sec. 4. *Authority of the Secretary of Defense Regarding Trials of Individuals Subject to this Order.*

(a) Any individual subject to this order shall, when tried, be tried by military commission for any and all offenses triable by military commission that such individual is alleged to have committed, and may be punished in accordance with the penalties provided under applicable law, including life imprisonment or death.

(b) As a military function and in light of the findings in Section 1, including subsection (f) thereof, the Secretary of Defense shall issue such orders and regulations, including orders for the appointment of one or more military commissions, as may be necessary to carry out subsection (a) of this section.

(c) Orders and regulations issued under subsection (b) of this section shall include, but not be limited to, rules for the conduct of the proceedings of military commissions, including pretrial, trial, and post-trial procedures, modes of proof, issuance of process, and qualifications of attorneys, which shall at a minimum provide for—

(1) military commissions to sit at any time and any place, consistent with such guidance regarding time and place as the Secretary of Defense may provide;

(2) a full and fair trial, with the military commission sitting as the triers of both fact and law;

(3) admission of such evidence as would, in the opinion of the presiding officer of the military commission (or instead, if any other member of the commission so requests at the time the presiding officer renders that opinion, the opinion of the commission rendered at that time by a majority of the commission), have probative value to a reasonable person;

(4) in a manner consistent with the protection of information classified or classifiable under Executive Order 12958 of April 17, 1995, as amended, or any successor Executive Order, protected by statute or rule from unauthorized disclosure, or otherwise protected by law, (A) the handling of, admission into evidence of, and access to materials and information, and (B) the conduct, closure of, and access to proceedings;

(5) conduct of the prosecution by one or more attorneys designated by the Secretary of Defense and conduct of the defense by attorneys for the individual subject to this order;

(6) conviction only upon the concurrence of two-thirds of the members of the commission present at the time of the vote, a majority being present;

(7) sentencing only upon the concurrence of two-thirds of the members of the commission present at the time of the vote, a majority being present; and

(8) submission of the record of the trial, including any conviction or sentence, for review and final decision by me or by the Secretary of Defense if so designated by me for that purpose.

Sec. 5. *Obligation of Other Agencies to Assist the Secretary of Defense.*

(a) Departments, agencies, entities, and officers of the United States shall, to the maximum extent permitted by law, provide to the Secretary of Defense such assistance as he may request to implement this order.

Sec. 6. *Additional Authorities of the Secretary of Defense.*

(a) As a military function and in light of the findings in section 1, the Secretary of Defense shall issue such orders and regulations as may be necessary to carry out any of the provisions of this order.

(b) The Secretary of Defense may perform any of his functions or duties, and may exercise any of the powers provided to him under this order (other than under section 4(c)(8) hereof) in accordance with section 113(d) of title 10, United States Code.

Sec. 7. *Relationship to Other Law and Forums.*

(a) Nothing in this order shall be construed to—

(1) authorize the disclosure of state secrets to any person not otherwise authorized to have access to them;

(2) limit the authority of the President as Commander in Chief of the Armed Forces or the power of the President to grant reprieves and pardons; or

(3) limit the lawful authority of the Secretary of Defense, any military commander, or any other officer or agent of the United States or of any State to detain or try any person who is not an individual subject to this order.

(b) With respect to any individual subject to this order—

(1) military tribunals shall have exclusive jurisdiction with respect to offenses by the individual; and

(2) the individual shall not be privileged to seek any remedy or maintain any proceeding, directly or indirectly, or to have any such remedy or proceeding sought on the individual's behalf, in (i) any court of the United States, or any State thereof, (ii) any court of any foreign nation, or (iii) any international tribunal.

(c) This order is not intended to and does not create any right, benefit, or privilege, substantive or procedural, enforceable at law or equity by any party, against the United States, its departments, agencies, or other entities, its officers or employees, or any other person.

(d) For purposes of this order, the term "State" includes any State, district, territory, or possession of the United States.

(e) I reserve the authority to direct the Secretary of Defense, at any time hereafter, to transfer to a governmental authority control of any individual subject to this order. Nothing in this order shall be construed to limit the authority of any such governmental authority to prosecute any individual for whom control is transferred.

Sec. 8. *Publication.*

(1) This order shall be published in the Federal Register.

Presidential Documents

Executive Order 13422 (President George W. Bush 2007)

Further Amendment to Executive Order 12866 on Regulatory Planning and Review
By the authority vested in me as President by the Constitution and laws of the United States of America, it is hereby ordered that Executive Order 12866 of September 30, 1993, as amended, is further amended as follows:

Sec. 1. *Section 1 is amended as follows:*

(a) Section 1(b)(1) is amended to read as follows:

"(1) Each agency shall identify in writing the specific market failure (such as externalities, market power, lack of information) or other specific problem that it intends to address (including, where applicable, the failures of public institutions) that warrant new agency action, as well as assess the significance of that problem, to enable assessment of whether any new regulation is warranted."

(b) by inserting in section 1(b)(7) after "regulation" the words "or guidance document."

(c) by inserting in section 1(b)(10) in both places after "regulations" the words "and guidance documents."

(d) by inserting in section 1(b)(11) after "its regulations" the words "and guidance documents."

(e) by inserting in section 1(b)(12) after "regulations" the words "and guidance documents."

Sec. 2. *Section 2 is amended as follows:*

(a) by inserting in section 2(a) in both places after "regulations" the words "and guidance documents."

(b) by inserting in section 2(b) in both places after "regulations" the words "and guidance documents."

Sec. 3. *Section 3 is amended as follows:*

(a) by striking in section 3(d) "or 'rule'" after "'Regulation'";

(b) by striking in section 3(d)(1) "or rules" after "Regulations";

(c) by striking in section 3(d)(2) "or rules" after "Regulations";

(d) by striking in section 3(d)(3) "or rules" after "Regulations";

(e) by striking in section 3(e) "rule or" from "final rule or regulation";

(f) by striking in section 3(f) "rule or" from "rule or regulation";

(g) by inserting after section 3(f) the following:

"(g) "Guidance document" means an agency statement of general applicability and future effect, other than a regulatory action, that sets forth a policy on a statutory, regulatory, or technical issue or an interpretation of a statutory or regulatory issue.

(h) "Significant guidance document"—

(1) Means a guidance document disseminated to regulated entities or the general public that, for purposes of this order, may reasonably be anticipated to:
  (A) Lead to an annual effect of $100 million or more or adversely affect in a material way the economy, a sector of the economy, productivity, competition, jobs, the environment, public health or safety, or State, local, or tribal governments or communities;
  (B) Create a serious inconsistency or otherwise interfere with an action taken or planned by another agency;
  (C) Materially alter the budgetary impact of entitlements, grants, user fees, or loan programs or the rights or obligations of recipients thereof; or
  (D) Raise novel legal or policy issues arising out of legal mandates, the President's priorities, or the principles set forth in this Executive order; and

(2) Does not include:
  (A) Guidance documents on regulations issued in accordance with the formal rulemaking provisions of 5 U.S.C. 556, 557;
  (B) Guidance documents that pertain to a military or foreign affairs function of the United States, other than procurement regulations and regulations involving the import or export of non-defense articles and services;
  (C) Guidance documents on regulations that are limited to agency organization, management, or personnel matters; or
  (D) Any other category of guidance documents exempted by the Administrator of OIRA."

Sec. 4. *Section 4 is amended as follows:*

(a) Section 4(a) is amended to read as follows: "The Director may convene a meeting of agency heads and other government personnel as appropriate to seek a common understanding of priorities and to coordinate regulatory efforts to be accomplished in the upcoming year."

(b) The last sentence of section 4(c)(1) is amended to read as follows: "Unless specifically authorized by the head of the agency, no rulemaking shall commence nor be included on the Plan without the approval of the agency's Regulatory Policy Office, and the Plan shall contain at a minimum."

(c) Section 4(c)(1)(B) is amended by inserting "of each rule as well as the agency's best estimate of the combined aggregate costs and benefits of all its regulations planned for that calendar year to assist with the identification of priorities" after "of the anticipated costs and benefits."

(d) Section 4(c)(1)(C) is amended by inserting "and specific citation to such statute, order, or other legal authority" after "court order."

Sec. 5. *Section 6 is amended as follows:*

(a) by inserting in section 6(a)(1) "In consultation with OIRA, each agency may also consider whether to utilize formal rulemaking procedures under 5 U.S.C. 556 and 557 for the resolution of complex determinations" after "comment period of not less than 60 days."

(b) by amending the first sentence of section 6(a)(2) to read as follows: "Within 60 days of the date of this Executive order, each agency head shall designate one of the agency's Presidential Appointees to be its Regulatory Policy Officer, advise OMB of such designation, and annually update OMB on the status of this designation."

Sec. 6. *Sections 9–11 are redesignated respectively as sections 10–12.*

Sec. 7.   *After section 8, a new section 9 is inserted as follows:*

"**Sec. 9.** Significant Guidance Documents. Each agency shall provide OIRA, at such times and in the manner specified by the Administrator of OIRA, with advance notification of any significant guidance documents. Each agency shall take such steps as are necessary for its Regulatory Policy Officer to ensure the agency's compliance with the requirements of this section. Upon the request of the Administrator, for each matter identified as, or determined by the Administrator to be, a significant guidance document, the issuing agency shall provide to OIRA the content of the draft guidance document, together with a brief explanation of the need for the guidance document and how it will meet that need. The OIRA Administrator shall notify the agency when additional consultation will be required before the issuance of the significant guidance document."

Sec. 8.   *Newly designated section 10 is amended to read as follows:*

"**Sec. 10.** Preservation of Agency Authority. Nothing in this order shall be construed to impair or otherwise affect the authority vested by law in an agency or the head thereof, including the authority of the Attorney General relating to litigation."

Memorandum for the Heads of Executive Departments and Agencies (President Barack Obama, May 20, 2009)

SUBJECT: Preemption

From our Nation's founding, the American constitutional order has been a Federal system, ensuring a strong role for both the national Government and the States. The Federal Government's role in promoting the general welfare and guarding individual liberties is critical, but State law and national law often operate concurrently to provide independent safeguards for the public. Throughout our history, State and local governments have frequently protected health, safety, and the environment more aggressively than has the national Government.

An understanding of the important role of State governments in our Federal system is reflected in longstanding practices by executive departments and agencies, which have shown respect for the traditional prerogatives of the States. In recent years, however, notwithstanding Executive Order 13132 of August 4, 1999 (Federalism), executive departments and agencies have sometimes announced that their regulations preempt State law, including State common law, without explicit preemption by the Congress or an otherwise sufficient basis under applicable legal principles.

The purpose of this memorandum is to state the general policy of my Administration that preemption of State law by executive departments and agencies should be undertaken only with full consideration of the legitimate prerogatives of the States and with a sufficient legal basis for preemption. Executive departments and agencies should be mindful that in our Federal system, the citizens of the several States have distinctive circumstances and values, and that in many instances it is appropriate for them to apply to themselves rules and principles that reflect these circumstances and values. As Justice Brandeis explained more than 70 years ago, "[i]t is one of the happy incidents of the federal system that a single courageous state may, if its citizens choose, serve as a laboratory; and try novel social and economic experiments without risk to the rest of the country."

To ensure that executive departments and agencies include statements of preemption in regulations only when such statements have a sufficient legal basis:

1. Heads of departments and agencies should not include in regulatory preambles statements that the department or agency intends to preempt State law through the regulation except where preemption provisions are also included in the codified regulation.
2. Heads of departments and agencies should not include preemption provisions in codified regulations except where such provisions would be justified under legal principles governing preemption, including the principles outlined in Executive Order 13132.
3. Heads of departments and agencies should review regulations issued within the past 10 years that contain statements in regulatory preambles or codified provisions intended by the department or agency to preempt State law, in order to decide whether such statements or provisions are justified under applicable legal principles governing preemption. Where the head of a department or agency determines that a regulatory statement of preemption or codified regulatory provision cannot be so justified, the head of that department or agency should initiate appropriate action, which may include amendment of the relevant regulation.

Executive departments and agencies shall carry out the provisions of this memorandum to the extent permitted by law and consistent with their statutory authorities. Heads of departments and agencies should consult as necessary with the Attorney General and the Office of Management and Budget's Office of Information and Regulatory Affairs to determine how the requirements of this memorandum apply to particular situations.

This memorandum is not intended to, and does not, create any right or benefit, substantive or procedural, enforceable at law or in equity by any party against the United States, its departments, agencies, or entities, its officers, employees, or agents, or any other person.

The Director of the Office of Management and Budget is authorized and directed to publish this memorandum in the Federal Register.

BARACK OBAMA

Executive Order

Closing of Executive Departments and Agencies of the Federal Government on Monday, December 24, 2012

By the authority vested in me as President by the Constitution and the laws of the United States of America, it is hereby ordered as follows:

Sec. 1. All executive branch departments and agencies of the Federal Government shall be closed and their employees excused from duty on Monday, December 24, 2012, the day before Christmas Day, except as provided in section 2 of this order.

Sec. 2. The heads of executive branch departments and agencies may determine that certain offices and installations of their organizations, or parts thereof, must remain open and that certain employees must report for duty on December 24, 2012, for reasons of national security, defense, or other public need.

Sec. 3. Monday, December 24, 2012, shall be considered as falling within the scope of Executive Order 11582 of February 11, 1971, and of 5 U.S.C. 5546 and 6103(b) and other similar statutes insofar as they relate to the pay and leave of employees of the United States.

Sec. 4. The Director of the Office of Personnel Management shall take such actions as may be necessary to implement this order.

Sec. 5. General Provisions. (a) This order shall be implemented consistent with applicable law and subject to the availability of appropriations.

(b) Nothing in this order shall be construed to impair or otherwise affect:
  (i)   the authority granted by law to an executive department or agency, or the head thereof; or
  (ii) the functions of the Director of the Office of Management and Budget relating to budgetary, administrative, or legislative proposals.

(c) This order is not intended to, and does not, create any right or benefit, substantive or procedural, enforceable at law or in equity by any party against the United States, its departments, agencies, or entities, its officers, employees, or agents, or any other person.

BARACK OBAMA

Index